HUMAN RIGHTS AND IN

Mapping the Global Interface

This book analyzes the interface between intellectual property and human rights law and policy. The relationship between these two fields has captured the attention of governments, policymakers, and activist communities in a diverse array of international and domestic venues. These actors often raise human rights arguments as counterweights to the expansion of intellectual property in areas including freedom of expression, public health, education, privacy, agriculture, and the rights of indigenous peoples. At the same time, creators and owners of intellectual property are asserting a human rights justification for the expansion of legal protections.

This book explores the legal, institutional, and political implications of these competing claims in three ways: (1) by offering a framework for exploring the connections and divergences between these subjects; (2) by identifying the pathways along which jurisprudence, policy, and political discourse are likely to evolve; and (3) by serving as a teaching and learning resource for scholars, activists, and students.

Laurence R. Helfer is the Harry R. Chadwick, Sr., Professor of Law at Duke University School of Law, where he codirects the Center for International and Comparative Law and is a member of the faculty steering committee of the Duke Center on Human Rights. He has authored more than 50 publications and has lectured widely on his diverse research interests, which include interdisciplinary analysis of international law and institutions, human rights, and international intellectual property law and policy. He is the coauthor of *Human Rights* (2d ed., 2009) and the author of *Intellectual Property Rights in Plant Varieties: International Legal Regimes and Policy Options for National Governments* (2004).

Graeme W. Austin is a Professor of Law at Melbourne University and Victoria University of Wellington. Until 2010, he was the J. Byron McCormick Professor of Law at the University of Arizona. He has lectured on intellectual property law in a variety of settings and is an elected member of the American Law Institute. He has published widely on the topic of intellectual property, including in the *Law Quarterly Review* and the *International Review of Intellectual Property and Competition Law*. He is coauthor of *International Intellectual Property: Law and Policy* (2008).

Human Rights and Intellectual Property

Mapping the Global Interface

LAURENCE R. HELFER

Harry R. Chadwick, Sr., Professor of Law

Duke University School of Law

GRAEME W. AUSTIN

Professor of Law

Melbourne University

and Victoria University of Wellington

CAMBRIDGE UNIVERSITY PRESS
Cambridge, New York, Melbourne, Madrid, Cape Town,
Singapore, São Paulo, Delhi, Mexico City

Cambridge University Press
32 Avenue of the Americas, New York, NY 10013-2473, USA

www.cambridge.org
Information on this title: www.cambridge.org/9780521711528

First published 2011
Reprinted 2012

A catalog record for this publication is available from the British Library.

Library of Congress Cataloging in Publication Data

Austin, Graeme.
Human rights and intellectual property : mapping the global interface / Graeme
W. Austin, Laurence R. Helfer.
    p. cm.
Includes bibliographical references and index.
ISBN 978-0-521-88437-2 (hardback) – ISBN 978-0-521-71125-8 (pbk.)
1. Intellectual property. 2. Intellectual property (International law) 3. Human
rights. I. Helfer, Laurence R. II. Title.
K1401.A98 2011
346.04′8–dc22   2010031359

ISBN 978-0-521-88437-2 Hardback
ISBN 978-0-521-71125-8 Paperback

Contents

Preface

The key terms in this book's subtitle – "mapping," "global," and "interface" – reflect our approach to analyzing the relationship between human rights and intellectual property.

Consider first the cartographical trope, "mapping." It is possible to envision intellectual property law and human rights law as the product of the gradual accretion and spread of international and domestic laws and institutions. The terrain of international intellectual property law was the first to emerge. Initially the subject of discrete bilateral agreements between sovereign nations, its modern form came to be established with the two great multilateral intellectual property treaties from the end of the 19th century: the Paris Convention on industrial property (1883) and the Berne Convention on literary and artistic works (1886). The international human rights regime emerged more recently, with the founding of the United Nations after World War II, and, in particular, the adoption of the Universal Declaration of Human Rights (1948).

From these beginnings, the terrain occupied by both issue areas has expanded significantly in substantive reach, in prescriptive detail, and in geographic scope. In the intellectual property context, the international law relating to patents illustrates this point. At the end of the 19th century, the desirability of domestic – let alone international – patent protection was a matter of sharp debate, even among industrialized nations. For this reason, the Paris Convention contains few substantive rules – although its national treatment and international priority rules for patent registrations were important achievements – and (like the Berne Convention) it has no effective enforcement mechanisms.

Today, in contrast, international intellectual property law imposes a significant and detailed array of substantive and enforcement obligations. The Agreement on Trade Related Aspects of Intellectual Property (TRIPS), which came into force in 1995, obliges member states to recognize patents

in all fields of technology (subject to transitional arrangements for developing nations). TRIPS also dictates the standard by which domestic law deviations from international patent rules are to be tested, and it sets forth detailed
requirements in areas such as domestic enforcement procedures. Perhaps
most significantly, noncompliance with TRIPS can trigger meaningful sanctions, as a result of the treaty's integration into the international trade regime
now administered by the World Trade Organization. That body, through its
dispute settlement system, also contributes to the development of international intellectual property norms, along with a number of other key agencies,
most notably the World Intellectual Property Organization (WIPO). The
expansion of international patent law did not stop with TRIPS. International
norms continue to emerge and develop as a result of multilateral, regional,
and bilateral agreements. A potentially important new initiative, the Anti-
Counterfeiting Trade Agreement (ACTA), is currently being negotiated.
If adopted, ACTA will shape international intellectual property rules and
enforcement mechanisms in a range of different contexts.

The space occupied by the international human rights regime has also
grown significantly since its inauguration in the middle of the 20th century.
The Universal Declaration gave birth to two foundational treaties that entered
into force in 1976 – the International Covenant on Civil and Political Rights
and the International Covenant on Economic, Social, and Cultural Rights. The
Covenants, together with the general comments, case law, and recommendations of their respective treaty bodies, and the decisions of regional human
rights courts and commissions, have significantly bolstered the prescriptive
force of human rights law. A particularly noteworthy development has been
the widening acceptance of social, economic, and cultural rights that, until
the 1990s, remained mostly underdeveloped, particularly in the West. New
recognition of the human rights of groups has also emerged – commitments
that are especially important to the world's indigenous peoples.

In terms of enforcement, the most important activities are occurring at the
regional and domestic levels, especially in Europe but also in the Americas
and other regions. National courts increasingly adjudicate human rights
treaties directly or draw upon international norms when construing national
constitutions and statutes. At all levels, multiple review mechanisms and judicial bodies shape human rights law through their investigative and interpretive activities. Indeed, one critique of the international human rights regime
is that it suffers from a surfeit of rules, institutions, and decision makers that
risks weakening the system as a whole.

As a result of these and related developments, the respective terrains of
both the human rights and intellectual property regimes have grown significantly and the intersections between them have expanded. There now exists a

broad range of legal, social, political, practical, and philosophical issues that straddle both fields. These intersections are evolving rapidly, requiring a new conceptual cartography to help map the changing landscape.

We explore a number of these intersections in this book. To continue with the patent example introduced earlier, consider the human right to the highest attainable standard of health in the light of the protection of pharmaceutical patents. Many nations once denied patents for new drugs on public health grounds; today, TRIPS obliges member nations to recognize and enforce patents in all fields of technology, including medicines. As a result of these countervailing legal commitments, government agencies, international organizations, and civil society groups must engage with the disciplines of both human rights and intellectual property to develop effective, just, and enduring responses to public health crises and to identify new mechanisms for harnessing private innovation to serve the wider social good. This is already occurring as a growing number of actors typically concerned with human rights issues are becoming engaged in intellectual property issues and (although perhaps to a lesser extent) vice versa.

This discussion also underscores the salience of the term "global" in the book's subtitle. State and private actors in legal regimes have long recognized the inadequacy of purely domestic responses. In the human rights context, the atrocities of the Second World War engendered a commitment to the idea that sovereign nations cannot be the sole arbiter of the fundamental human entitlements. The founders of the United Nations and the drafters of the Universal Declaration recognized that human rights must be bolstered by international institutions and international legal obligations. In the intellectual property context, both private firms and governments have long recognized that effective responses to piracy and counterfeiting, and, more recently, the protection of genetic resources and indigenous knowledge, cannot be adequately addressed at the domestic level. In addition, there now exist important feedback mechanisms in intellectual property lawmaking, whereby norms developed at the international and domestic levels mutually influence each other.

As we discuss in Chapter 1, the existence of *any* meaningful engagement between the two areas of law is a relatively recent phenomenon. Scholars and policymakers in each regime are only beginning to recognize areas of mutual concern. Because law is shaped by human agency, the way in which human rights and intellectual property intersect is not an inevitable or predetermined process. The actors who engage with the legal and social policy issues to which both regimes are relevant have a large measure of discretion in determining the character of this interaction. Will there be a seismic clash, a rupturing of tectonic plates, as the two areas move ever closer together and finally collide? Or will the engagement be carefully considered, nuanced, and accommodating? Our preference is for the latter kind of engagement, and one of the aims of this book is to provide the substantive materials and original analytical content to help others to explore the intersections between the two regimes in a productive and coherent fashion.

These considerations also explain the use of the term "interface" in our subtitle. The most familiar use of the term is in the computing context. It denotes mechanisms for conjoining distinct or contrasting elements and systems: software and hardware, or interfaces between operating systems. Human rights and intellectual property exhibit distinctive systemic characteristics. For the most part they have evolved independently – although, as we discuss in Chapter 3, there is an often-overlooked set of human rights obligations that recognize the rights of creators in their artistic and scientific works – and have been shaped by different sets of actors in distinct institutional contexts and informed by divergent analytical traditions. A key aim of the book, suggested by our use of the term "interface," is to provide a structure for dialog and engagement between these two – hitherto largely separate – systems.

To that end, Chapter 1 offers a conceptual overview of the relationship between human rights and intellectual property, as well as a brief summary of each area of law. The latter will be useful for readers less familiar with the traditions and substance of one or both areas. Chapter 1 also explores different ways that the relationship between human rights and intellectual property has been understood by scholars and in different legal and policy contexts. The chapters that follow develop the latter theme and present "case studies" of several distinct controversies. Chapter 2 considers the right to health and patented pharmaceuticals; Chapter 3 addresses the human rights associated with certain types of creative activity; Chapter 4 examines the rights of freedom of expression and cultural participation and the right to benefit from scientific progress; Chapter 5 explores the right to education and the potential tensions with copyright protection in learning materials; Chapter 6 examines the human right to food in the context of intellectual property protections in plant genetic materials; Chapter 7 considers the claims that have emerged in the context of indigenous peoples' struggles for recognition of their rights in respect of traditional knowledge and other forms of cultural production. In a final chapter, we offer a fuller exposition of our own framework for conceptualizing the most productive connections between the human rights and intellectual property regimes.

The decision to defer the exposition of our conceptual framework until the Conclusion in part reflects the genesis of this book. Several years ago, one of us developed a law school course entitled Human Rights and Intellectual

Property. Partly because of the novelty of the topic, no teaching materials existed, a gap that endures today. Teaching the course was a very fulfilling experience. The course brought together students from an array of different backgrounds and with a range of different interests – not only intellectual property and human rights, but also international trade and indigenous peoples' law and policy issues. The course invited these groups to engage with each other across the intellectual, heuristic, and, sometimes, cultural divides that had informed their thinking about the various issues to which human rights and intellectual property are relevant – issues that we consider at greater length in the case studies in each chapter of this book. The aims of the course included introducing students to the substantive laws, policies, and institutional frameworks of both human rights and intellectual property. But a more ambitious aim was to invite students to develop their own conceptions of how the two areas might interact. Although we have our own views on how the contours of the interface might be mapped, as a pedagogical matter we believe that readers' engagement with this topic will be richer if they are also encouraged to form their own views as to how this might be achieved. Hence our decision on the placement of the final chapter.

These concerns also reflect the thinking behind our use of the term "map*ping*" – the present participle form of the verb. Engagement between the two areas of law is a dynamic and evolving process, one to which we hope this book will contribute. But we labor under no pretension that this work is by any measure complete. We look forward to engaging with the responses – including, we imagine, rigorous critiques – that this text might invite.

Our aspirations for the book also extend beyond the classroom context. We hope that it will contribute to the emerging scholarship in the field and to the policy debates that are beginning to occur in both regimes. Here we offer a personal anecdote. When we first entered law teaching in the 1990s, human rights and intellectual property were separate components of our respective research agendas. Our decision to focus our scholarly efforts in these two discrete areas was highly unusual. In fact, a senior colleague counseled one of us to choose one field and abandon the other, warning that there was little benefit – and potentially much risk – in attempting to develop expertise in two such different and unrelated fields. The response offered by the recipient of this well-meaning advice was to acknowledge the lack of substantive connections between the two legal regimes, but to counter that there was much to be learned by interacting with different communities of scholars, government officials, and civil society groups, who rarely, if ever, interacted directly with each other.

More than a decade later, much has changed. When we now explain to colleagues and students that our research explores the intersections between intellectual property and human rights, the usual response is a gleam of recognition and a question or two – most often about patented medicines and HIV-AIDS, but increasingly about freedom of expression and online technologies or the moral rights of artists. We are hardly alone in exploring these issues. As we indicated earlier, growing numbers of civil society organizations now include both human rights and intellectual property in their mandates, often specializing in subissues such as patents and the right to health, access to knowledge, or the intersection of human rights, intellectual property, and development. And the global network of commentators and journalists who write about the interface of the two fields is expanding, as revealed by the numerous and diverse entries in this book's extensive References.

For law students, as well as students in cognate disciplines, such as political theory and international relations, much of the value of the book may lie in the extensive Notes and Questions that follow the analysis of each substantive topic. These sections invite the kind of deep engagement and interrogation of substantive issues and conceptual frameworks that characterize university-level instruction, at both undergraduate and graduate levels. We also hope that this book will be useful in other contexts and for other actors, including government officials, international organizations, activists, and civil society groups. To that end, discussions of substantive topics often are followed by Issues in Focus. These sections perform a number of functions, including summarizing recent developments and highlighting emerging issues. By deploying a range of different analytical techniques and materials, we hope that the book can be used by, and will be useful for, a wider range of constituencies.

Finally, we would like to acknowledge the many scholars who have contributed to the writing of this book with comments and criticisms. They include Barbara Atwood, Molly Beutz, Jamie Boyle, Audrey Chapman, Graeme Dinwoodie, Maureen Garmon, Toni Massaro, Ruth Okediji, and Peter Yu. We are also grateful for the help of several research assistants, including Laura Duncan, Eric Larson, Lisa Lindemenn, María Méndoza, Casey Mock, Pedro Paranagua, Meryl Thomas, and Amy Zavidow. Erin Daniel provided invaluable assistance in obtaining permissions to reproduce copyrighted materials. Last, but by no means least, are the unswerving dedication and patience of our respective partners, David Boyd and Bryan Patchett, the acknowledgment of whose manifold contributions is itself a reflection of hard-fought human rights struggles.

Laurence R. Helfer   Graeme W. Austin
Durham, North Carolina, USA   Wellington, New Zealand
December 2010

Chapter 1

Mapping the Interface of Human Rights
and Intellectual Property

1.1. Thematic Overview and Introduction

This book explores the relationship between human rights and intellectual property. Long ignored by both the human rights and intellectual property communities, the relationship between these two fields has now captured the attention of government officials, judges, activist communities, and scholars in domestic legal systems and in international venues such as the World Intellectual Property Organization, the United Nations Human Rights Council, the Committee on Economic, Social and Cultural Rights, the World Trade Organization, the World Health Organization, and the Food and Agriculture Organization.

Widespread recognition of the relationship between human rights and intellectual property has a relatively recent vintage. Little more than a decade ago, few observers acknowledged the existence of such a relationship or viewed it as more than marginally relevant to the important issues and debates in each field. For participants in the human rights movement, the 1990s was a heady and hopeful period. In rapid succession, the world experienced the end of the Cold War, the birth of new democracies, the widespread ratification of human rights treaties, and the use of U.N.-sanctioned military force in response to widespread atrocities. These events, coming in quick succession after decades of political conflict, seemed to herald an "age of rights"[1] and an "era of humanitarian intervention."[2] For the international intellectual property system, the 1990s was a time of rapidly expanding rules and institutions. In terms of norm creation, the shift of intellectual property

---

[1] LOUIS HENKIN, THE AGE OF RIGHTS (1990).
[2] Michael Ignatieff, Editorial, *Is the Human Rights Era Ending?* N.Y. TIMES, Feb. 5, 2002, at A25.

lawmaking from the World Intellectual Property Organization (WIPO) to the General Agreement on Tariffs and Trade (GATT) to the Agreement on Trade-Related Aspects of Intellectual Property Rights (TRIPS)[3] made patents, copyrights, trademarks, and trade secrets central, if controversial, components of the global trading system.[4] In the private sector, the emergence of new industries such as biotechnology and new modes of distribution such as the Internet increased the salience of new forms of intellectual property protection and new ways for intellectual property owners to enforce their economic interests.[5]

The first decade of the twenty-first century, by contrast, has seen increasingly high-profile and contentious debates over legal and political issues that arise at the interface of human rights and intellectual property. These debates are attempting to map the boundaries of this new policy space and to define the appropriate relationships between the two fields. Some governments, courts, public interest NGOs, and commentators view intellectual property protection as implicating potential violations of the rights to life, health, food, privacy, freedom of expression, and enjoyment of the benefits of scientific progress. At the same time, corporations and other business entities are invoking human rights law in an effort to strengthen intellectual property protection rules.

The increasing number of social, economic, and legal contexts in which both intellectual property and human rights are relevant are creating new, and as yet unresolved, tensions between the two regimes. Both international human rights agreements and the growing network of multilateral, regional, and bilateral trade and intellectual property treaties impose international law obligations on nation states. Consider a few examples:

- Most countries must protect pharmaceutical patents; yet they are also required to protect the rights to life and health.
- Plant breeders' rights limit what farmers can do on their land, such as whether they can save and exchange seed; yet human rights law also provides for a right to adequate food.
- Certain types of intellectual property protection impose limitations on traditional agrarian practices that are themselves recognized in international human rights instruments.

---

[3] Agreement on Trade-Related Aspects of Intellectual Property Rights, Apr. 15, 1994, 1869 U.N.T.S. 299 [TRIPS Agreement].

[4] FRIEDRICH-KARL BEIER & GERHARD SCHRICKER (EDS.), FROM GATT TO TRIPS: THE AGREEMENT ON TRADE-RELATED ASPECTS OF INTELLECTUAL PROPERTY RIGHTS, STUDIES IN INDUSTRIAL PROPERTY AND COPYRIGHT LAW (1996).

[5] See, e.g., Laurence R. Helfer & Graeme B. Dinwoodie, *Designing Non-National Systems: The Case of the Uniform Domain Name Dispute Resolution Policy*, 43 WM. & MARY L. REV. 141 (2001).

- Some indigenous communities invoke intellectual property rights as vehicles for preserving their ways of life and protecting their cultural and economic heritage – a subject also regulated by international human rights instruments.
- Copyright laws have the potential to implicate rights to freedom of expression and education, and even the right to associate with others.
- Trademarks, as a 2005 decision of the Constitutional Court of South Africa confirms, have the potential to impede expressive freedoms.[6]

This chapter introduces these developments and provides a conceptual framework for analyzing the competing arguments of government officials, courts, civil society groups, and scholars. We explore the major fault lines along which the intersection of human rights and intellectual property currently runs, fault lines whose specific geographical features we explore in subsequent chapters of this book. To lay the groundwork for this more in-depth analysis, we first provide an introduction to the international human rights system and the international intellectual property system, including their substantive legal rules and domestic and international institutions. Readers familiar with either or both of these topics may consider skimming or passing over these sections. The next chapter analyzes the events that caused the two formerly distinct regimes to intersect in increasingly complex ways. We conclude with an evaluation of alternative approaches for analyzing the relationship between the two fields.

1.2. The International Human Rights System: A Substantive and Institutional Overview

The idea that individuals can turn to international law to protect their fundamental liberties is a fairly recent development. While there are antecedents to the modern human rights movement, such as the law of state responsibility for injuries to aliens and prohibitions on slavery, only in the last six decades have national governments devoted significant attention to establishing international legal rules and institutions to protect the rights of all human beings. The horrors of the Nazi Holocaust provided the impetus for these developments. Confronted with unambiguous evidence of atrocities on a massive scale, the victors of the Second World War resolved to overturn international law's prevailing presumption that abuses committed by a nation state against its citizens and within its borders were the concern of that state alone.

---

[6] *Laugh It Off Promotions CC v. S. Afr. Breweries Int'l (Finance) BV* 2005 (8) BCLR 743 (CC) (S. Afr.). A discussion of this decision appears in Chapter 4.

During the ensuing decades, the international human rights system broadened and deepened by focusing on two principal tasks: (1) articulating and refining a catalog of "rights" and "freedoms" that merited international protection, and (2) establishing international institutions and monitoring mechanisms to ensure that governments actually respected those rights and freedoms.

Governments achieved the first objective by drafting nonbinding declarations and, later, legally binding covenants, conventions, treaties, and other international agreements to protect individual rights and, in a few cases, group rights. The freedoms and liberties contained in these documents included a broad spectrum of civil, political, economic, social, and cultural rights. Over time, many of the rights articulated in these declarations and international agreements became embedded in national constitutions, legislation, administrative regulations, and judicial decisions.

This penetration of international law into domestic law had two important consequences. First, it helped to buttress claims that human rights were protected as customary international law – the general practice of states that is accepted as law.[7] Second, national incorporation made it possible to protect individual rights, and to seek redress for their violation, within domestic legal orders – at least in those states in which open political systems and independent judiciaries provided meaningful opportunities to challenge government action.

The possibility that individuals could receive domestic remedies for international human rights violations was a major conceptual shift in international law. But human rights advocates understood that governments would often be unwilling or unable to police their own conduct. As a result, a second objective of the human rights movement was to establish international institutions to ensure that governments were in fact respecting the rights that they had pledged to protect in treaties and in customary law.

Not surprisingly, many governments were reluctant to submit their conduct to the scrutiny of new and untested international institutions, and they resisted proposals to create a single international court or monitoring

---

[7] Customary international law "results from a general and consistent practice of states followed by them from a sense of legal obligation." RESTATEMENT (THIRD) OF FOREIGN RELATIONS LAW OF THE UNITED STATES § 102.2 (1987). International lawyers draw upon numerous sources to prove consistent state practice that is followed out of a sense of legal obligation (*opinion juris*). Many of these sources are international, such as diplomatic exchanges, treaties in consistent form, and the resolutions of intergovernmental organizations. However, international lawyers also rely on domestic sources, such as national constitutions, laws, and high court decisions, as important evidence of custom.

mechanism to review all allegations of human rights violations. As a result, human rights institutions evolved in a decentralized, piecemeal fashion as new treaties were adopted. The result, sixty years later, is a dizzying array of international courts, tribunals, commissions, committees, working groups, and special rapporteurs, each of which reviews only a subset of the entire corpus of international human rights law.

A comprehensive discussion of these diverse international institutions would require an entire book in itself. However, for purposes of analyzing the intersection of human rights and intellectual property, it is important to understand the basic functions of two distinct parts of the international human rights system, both of which operate under the umbrella of the United Nations: (1) the Universal Declaration on Human Rights, the two International Covenants that grew out of the Declaration, and the "treaty bodies" that monitor the behavior of the governments who have ratified one or both of the Covenants; and (2) the mechanisms and procedures established under the authority of the United Nations Charter and falling principally within the jurisdiction of the U.N. Human Rights Council.

A. The U.N. Human Rights Treaty System
The two articles excerpted below describe the evolution of human rights within the United Nations and explore the content and structure of the U.N. human rights treaty system.

Thomas Buergenthal, *International Human Rights Law and Institutions: Accomplishments and Prospects*, 63 WASH. L. REV. 1, 2–3, 5–6 (1988)

II. The United Nations Charter

A. Birth of Fundamental Principles
The international law of human rights as we know it today is a post–World War II phenomenon.... The need for international legal norms and institutions addressing human rights violations became apparent in the 1930's and 1940's. As early as 1941, President Franklin D. Roosevelt called, in his famous "Four Freedoms" speech, for "a world founded upon four essential human freedoms," namely, "freedom of speech and expression," "freedom of every person to worship God in his own way," "freedom from want," and "freedom from fear." Roosevelt's vision became the clarion call of the nations that fought the Axis in the Second World War and that founded the United Nations....

B. Human Rights Principles of the United Nations Charter

The United Nations Charter is both the constitution of the Organization and a legally binding multilateral treaty. Article 1, paragraph 3 of the Charter declares that one of the purposes of the United Nations is "to achieve international cooperation ... in promoting and encouraging respect for human rights and for fundamental freedoms for all without distinction as to race, sex, language, or religion." The obligation of the Organization for achieving these purposes is set out in Article 55:

> With a view to the creation of conditions of stability and well-being which are necessary for peaceful and friendly relations among nations based on respect for the principle of equal rights and self-determination of peoples, the United Nations shall promote:
>
> ...
>
> (c) universal respect for, and observance of, human rights and fundamental freedoms for all without distinction as to race, sex, language, or religion.

In Article 56 the Member States "pledge themselves to take joint and separate action in cooperation with the Organization for the achievement of the purposes set forth in Article 55."

Although these Charter provisions created only weak and vague obligations, they were very important from a legal point of view: they transformed human rights, once only a matter of domestic concern, into the subject of international treaty obligations. As such, human rights could conceptually no longer be considered exclusively within the domestic jurisdiction of the Member States of the United Nations....

III. The International Bill of Human Rights

When the United Nations Charter was being drafted in San Francisco in 1945, various smaller countries attempted to append a bill of human rights. This effort failed, but its proponents extracted a promise that the drafting of such an instrument become the first order of business of the United Nations. The promise was kept. But it was soon recognized that there was no agreement on what should be included in a bill of rights.... [T]he Member States decided to proceed in stages.

The first stage of this drafting process proved relatively easy; by 1948 the United Nations had proclaimed the Universal Declaration of Human Rights. The second set of documents – the International Covenants on Human Rights – took eighteen years to draft. They entered into force ten years later in 1976....

A. The Universal Declaration

The United Nations Charter internationalized human rights; but the Universal Declaration of Human Rights has become the centerpiece of the international human rights revolution. The Declaration is the first comprehensive statement enumerating the basic rights of the individual to be promulgated by a universal international organization. As such, it ranks with the Magna Carta, the French Declaration of the Rights of Man, and the American Declaration of Independence as a milestone in mankind's struggle for freedom and human dignity. Its debt to these great historic documents is unmistakable. "All human beings are born free and equal in dignity and rights," proclaims Article 1 of the Universal Declaration, and Article 28 adds "everyone is entitled to a social and international order in which the rights and freedoms set forth in this Declaration can be fully realized...."

The Declaration's list of civil and political rights includes the right to life, liberty, and security of person; the prohibition of slavery, torture, and cruel, inhuman, or degrading treatment; the right not to be subjected to arbitrary arrest, detention, or exile; the right to a fair trial in both civil and criminal matters; the presumption of innocence and the prohibition against the application of ex post facto laws and penalties. The Declaration recognizes the right to privacy and the right to own property. It proclaims freedom of speech, religion, and assembly. The Declaration acknowledges the right to freedom of movement and provides in Article 13 that everyone has the right to leave any country, including his own, and to return to his country. Important political rights are proclaimed in Article 21 of the Declaration, including the right to take part in the government of one's country, directly or through freely chosen representatives.

The economic, social, and cultural rights proclaimed in the Declaration have their starting point in the proposition, expressed in Article 22, that "[e]veryone, as a member of society ... is entitled to realization, through national effort and international co-operation and in accordance with the organization and resources of each State, of the economic, social and cultural rights indispensable for his dignity and the free development of his personality." The Declaration accordingly proclaims the individual's right to social security, to work, and to "protection against unemployment." The right to education is dealt with in Article 26 of the Declaration, which provides, among other things, that education shall be free "at least in the elementary and fundamental stages." It established a "prior right" of parents "to choose the kind of education that shall be given to their children." Article 27 of the Declaration deals with cultural rights and proclaims that every human being has "the right freely to participate in the cultural life of the community, to enjoy the arts and to share in scientific advancement and its benefits."

The Declaration recognizes that the rights it proclaims are not absolute. It permits a state to enact laws limiting the exercise of these rights solely for the purpose of securing "due recognition and respect for the rights and freedoms of others and of meeting the just requirements of morality, public order and the general welfare in a democratic society." A government's authority to impose such restrictions is further limited by the stipulation that "nothing in this Declaration may be interpreted as implying for any State, group or person any right to engage in any activity or to perform any act aimed at the destruction of any of the rights and freedoms set forth herein."

The Universal Declaration is not a treaty. It was adopted by the United Nations General Assembly in the form of a resolution that has no force of law, and it was not intended by the Assembly to create binding legal obligations. Contrary to popular myth, it was not signed, nor is it an instrument intended to be signed. The Declaration was designed, as its preamble indicates, to provide "a common understanding" of the human rights and fundamental freedoms referred to in the United Nations Charter, and to serve "as a common standard for achievement for all peoples and all nations...."

Time, however, transformed the normative status of the Universal Declaration. Today few international lawyers would deny that the Universal Declaration imposes some international legal obligations. There is dispute, however, about whether all the rights it proclaims are binding and under what circumstances, and about whether its obligatory character derives from its status as an authoritative interpretation of the human rights obligation contained in the United Nations Charter, or its status as customary international law.

B. The Covenants

The International Covenants on Human Rights consist of three separate treaties – the International Covenant on Civil and Political Rights, the Optional Protocol to the International Covenant on Civil and Political Rights, and the International Covenant on Economic, Social and Cultural Rights. These treaties were adopted by the United Nations General Assembly in 1966. Another decade passed before thirty-five states – the number required to bring the two Covenants into force – ratified them....

The Covenants were designed to transform the general principles proclaimed in the Universal Declaration into binding treaty obligations. This meant that the lofty rhetoric of the Declaration had to give way to precise statutory language, and that exceptions, limitations, and restrictions on the exercise of various rights had to be spelled out in considerable detail. The Covenants also sought to establish an international machinery to ensure governmental compliance....

The Covenants have a number of common substantive provisions. Two of these deal with what might be described as "group" or "collective" rights. Article 1, paragraph 1 of both Covenants proclaims that "all peoples have the right of self-determination." Article 1, paragraph 2 of both instruments also recognizes that "all peoples" have the right to freely dispose of their natural resources and that "in no case may a people be deprived of its own means of subsistence." Both Covenants also bar discrimination based on race, color, sex, language, religion, political or other opinion, national or social origin, property, or birth.

The catalog of civil and political rights spelled out in the Covenant on Civil and Political Rights is formulated with greater juridical precision and is somewhat longer than the list of comparable rights proclaimed in the Universal Declaration. An important addition is the provision which bars states from denying members of ethnic, religious, or linguistic minorities the right, "in community with other members of their group, to enjoy their own culture, to profess and practice their own religion, or to use their own language." Some rights that the Universal Declaration proclaims are not guaranteed by the Covenant on Civil and Political Rights. Among these is the right to own property. This right was not included in the Covenant because the different ideological blocs represented in the United Nations were unable to agree on its scope and definition.

The Covenant on Economic, Social and Cultural Rights contains a longer and more comprehensive list of economic, social, and cultural rights than does the Universal Declaration. This Covenant recognizes the right to work; the right to enjoy just and favorable conditions of work and to form and join trade unions; the right to social security, the protection of the family, and an adequate standard of living; the right to enjoy the highest attainable standard of physical and mental health; and the right to education and to take part in cultural life.

The decision to have two separate treaties, one for civil and political rights and another for economic, social, and cultural rights, was dictated in part by the consideration that these two broad categories of rights require very different methods of implementation. In general, all a government has to do to respect civil and political rights is to adopt and enforce appropriate laws on the subject. This approach will in most cases not work with regard to economic, social, and cultural rights. Their implementation usually necessitates economic and technical resources, training, and time.

Consequently, most governments cannot assume the same legal obligations for both categories of rights.

A State Party to the Covenant on Civil and Political Rights is under an immediate legal obligation to comply with its provisions. This is not the case under the Covenant on Economic, Social and Cultural Rights. The latter Covenant requires progressive, as distinguished from immediate, implementation, and merely obligates each State Party "to take steps ... to the maximum of its available resources, with a view to achieving progressively the full realization of the rights recognized in the present Covenant by all appropriate means, including particularly the adoption of legislative measures." Had this "progressive" or "promotional" approach not been adopted, few governments, if any, could in good faith have agreed to be bound by this Covenant.

Each Covenant has its own international machinery to encourage and to supervise compliance by the parties to these treaties.

Laurence R. Helfer & Anne-Marie Slaughter, *Toward A Theory of Effective Supranational Adjudication*, 107 YALE L.J. 273 (1997)

[This article discusses the activities of the U.N. Human Rights Committee, a body of eighteen human rights experts elected in their individual capacities to monitor the behavior of the now more than 160 countries that have ratified the International Covenant on Civil and Political Rights (ICCPR). The functions that the Human Rights Committee performs are similar to those performed by the Committee on Economic, Social and Cultural Rights, which supervises the implementation of the International Covenant on Economic, Social and Cultural Rights and which has given considerable attention to the intersection of intellectual property and human rights. The Committee's functions are also similar to the activities of other "treaty bodies" that monitor government adherence to subject-specific U.N. human rights agreements, including treaties on racial discrimination, torture, women's rights, and children's rights.]

1. The Reporting Process

Article 40 of the ICCPR requires all states parties to file reports with the Committee "on the measures they have adopted which give effect to the rights recognized herein and on the progress made in the enjoyment of those rights." Initial reports are due within one year of the treaty's entry into force with the subsequent reports due at five year intervals thereafter.... Once a state party files its report, the Committee reviews its submission in a public session in New York or Geneva. Government representatives are invited to attend, make brief oral presentations, and respond to the Committee's substantive questions about the report. The scope of the Committee's inquiry is not limited by a state's submission and it is free to use any information available, including documents provided by nongovernmental organizations. After the public hearing, the Committee drafts written comments on the report and on the state party's responses to its questions; these comments are published in its annual report to the General Assembly....

2. General Comments

Instead of directly critiquing each report, the Committee addresses common problems collectively by issuing "general comments" to states parties.... The general comments provide a crucial opportunity for the Committee to articulate its understanding of the treaty's protected rights and freedoms. Although the first two comments concerned procedural aspects of the reporting process, the remainder have addressed the Committee's understanding of the substantive rights enshrined in the treaty. Most of these comments have analyzed individual articles of the ICCPR, such as the right to life protected in Article 6 or the prohibition of torture in Article 7. But the Committee has also adopted issue-oriented comments, [for example] on the position of aliens and on the rights of detainees.

In developing its analysis, the Committee has relied on the expertise of individual members, information submitted by states parties in their reports, and cases decided under the Optional Protocol [described in the next paragraph]. Although adoption of the general comments has "serve[d] rapidly to develop the jurisprudence of the [Committee] under the Covenant," the statements issued are not scholarly studies. Moreover, "since they are couched in general terms their interpretation may easily create problems of application to specific cases...."

3. The Petition System

The Committee's other major jurisprudential function is the consideration of written "communications" from individuals under the First Optional Protocol to the ICCPR. The Committee has taken on quasi-judicial functions in interpreting the treaty in these cases. Specifically, it acts as an arbiter of contentious disputes between individuals and states, provides victims of human rights violations with an international forum for relief where domestic remedies are unavailable or insufficient, and generates a "specific problem-centred jurisprudence...." The Committee cannot perform these functions for all of the states party to the Covenant, however, since it is only authorized to consider complaints against states that have ratified the Optional Protocol.

Even once a state has ratified the Optional Protocol, the ability to file a petition with the Committee is subject to several [procedural] restrictions.... Assuming an individual overcomes these hurdles, the Committee declares the communication admissible and then receives written submissions by both the aggrieved individual and the state party.... The Committee then authors an opinion ... which "follow[s] a judicial pattern and are effectively decisions on the merits...." [T]he decisions contain a statement of "the view of the [Committee] on the 'obligation' of the State party in light of [its] findings."

Note on the Relationship between Civil and Political Rights and Economic, Social, and Cultural Rights
The Universal Declaration on Human Rights (UDHR) encompasses both civil and political rights (sometimes described as "first generation" human rights) as well as economic, social, and cultural rights (sometimes referred to as "second generation" human rights). When state representatives considered how to incorporate the UDHR's statement of principles into binding international law, they divided the two generations of rights and assigned each to a different treaty – the International Covenant on Civil and Political Rights (ICCPR) and the International Covenant on Economic, Social and Cultural Rights (ICESCR).

As a formal matter, this separation does not imply any hierarchical ordering. To the contrary, United Nations bodies have repeatedly insisted that economic, social, and cultural rights are equal in status to civil and political rights. The closely equivalent number of states parties to the ICESCR and the ICCPR appears to support these assertions,[8] as does the Vienna Declaration and Programme of Action, adopted by the World Conference on Human Rights in 1993:

> All human rights are universal, indivisible and interdependent and interrelated. The international community must treat human rights globally in a fair and

---

[8] As of May 1, 2010, 165 states had ratified the ICCPR and 160 had ratified the ICESCR. The United States has not joined the trend toward dual ratification of the two covenants. President Jimmy Carter signed both the ICESCR and the ICCPR in the late 1970s. The United States ratified the latter covenant in 1992. But it has never ratified the former, and, as of 2010, there is no indication that the U.S. Senate will consent to ratification, in part because of anticipated domestic opposition to recognizing economic and social benefits as "rights." *See* LOUIS HENKIN ET AL., HUMAN RIGHTS 148 (2d ed. 2009).

equal manner, on the same footing, and with the same emphasis.... [I]t is the duty of States, regardless of their political, economic and cultural systems, to promote and protect all human rights and fundamental freedoms.[9]

As a practical matter, however, the formal equality of the two generations of rights masks a deeper debate over competing conceptions of state responsibility to satisfy basic human needs. The drafters of the ICESCR and the ICCPR intended both treaties to be acceptable to socialist states, developing nations, and industrialized free-market countries. But the substantive and institutional differences between the two Covenants are often characterized as reflecting political and ideological divisions between these groups of countries. In addition, some wealthy nations have resisted what many poorer states demanded: commitments by the former to provide economic assistance to the latter to help satisfy the economic and social needs of their inhabitants.[10] And only relatively recently have longstanding human rights NGOs, such as Amnesty International, added economic and social rights to their mandates.[11]

Some government officials, civil society groups, and commentators, especially in developing nations, have challenged the propensity of certain industrialized countries and human rights NGOs to emphasize civil and political rights over economic, social, and cultural rights. Other critics of civil and political rights primacy have "look[ed] askance at the starkly individualistic ethos of the West in which authority tends to be seen as oppressive and rights are an individual's 'trump' over the state," preferring instead "a situation in which distinctions between the individual, society, and state are less clear-cut, or at least less adversarial."[12]

Proponents of giving greater attention to second generation rights have also responded to skeptics who question whether economic and social benefits should be treated as human rights. First, they have challenged as misleading the claim that civil and political rights are "negative liberties" that governments can satisfy merely by abstention, that is, by leaving individuals alone.[13] Second, in response to the contention that second generation rights

---

[9] Vienna Declaration and Programme of Action, adopted by the United Nations World Conference on Human Rights, para. 5, June 25, 1993, U.N. Doc. A/CONF.157/24 (Part I) at 20–46 (1993); *reprinted in* 32 I.L.M. 1661 (1993).

[10] *See* HENKIN ET AL., *supra* note 8, at 219.

[11] *See* Daniel A. Bell & Joseph H. Carens, *The Ethical Dilemmas of International Human Rights and Humanitarian NGOs: Reflections on a Dialogue between Practitioners and Theorists*, 26 HUM. RTS. Q. 300 (2004) (discussing the 2001 decision by Amnesty International to incorporate social and economic rights into its mandate).

[12] Bilahari Kausikan, *Asia's Different Standard*, 92 FOREIGN POL. 24, 36 (1993).

[13] As Jeremy Waldron has explained: "The correlation of first- and second-generation rights with the distinction between negative and positive rights simply will not stand up. Many

lack meaningful normative content because they are achieved progressively and are dependent upon available resources,[14] proponents point to *General Comments* adopted by the Committee on Economic Social and Cultural Rights[15] and to the growing number of judicial decisions, including by courts in Brazil, Colombia, India, and South Africa, that provide comprehensive analyses of states' legal obligations to satisfy the economic, social, and cultural entitlements of individuals and groups.[16]

The interface between human rights and intellectual property both accentuates and challenges the tensions between first and second generation rights. For example, the rights of creators and the right to enjoy the benefits of scientific progress and its applications, analyzed in Chapter 3, long remained normatively undeveloped even in comparison to other social and economic rights. The recent expansion of intellectual property protection rules acted as a catalyst for international experts and commentators to rediscover these rights and, in doing so, to consider how they relate to civil and political rights. Different tensions arise with respect to the right to education and copyright in learning materials, the subject of Chapter 5. In this context, the interaction of the two fields highlights the ways in which legal entitlements to education straddle first and second generation rights. We highlight other examples and illustrations elsewhere in this book.

B. Mechanisms for Protecting Human Rights under the U.N. Charter

Several institutions established under the authority of the United Nations Charter exercise important functions to further the organization's goals of

first-generation rights (for example, the right to vote) require the positive establishment and maintenance of certain frameworks, and all of them make costly claims on scarce police and forensic resources. The right to vote is not a matter of the negative freedom to mark a cross against the name of one's favorite politician, and it is not secured by the individual simply being left alone to do this as and when he pleases. The vote must be counted and given effect in a political system in which the exercise of that power is rendered effective along with its similar exercise by millions of other individuals." JEREMY WALDRON, LIBERAL RIGHTS: COLLECTED PAPERS 1981–1991, at 24–25 (1993).

[14] ICESCR, art. 2(1) (requiring each state party to "take steps ... to the maximum of its available resources, with a view to achieving progressively the full realization of the rights recognized in the present Covenant").

[15] As of May 2010, the ICESCR Committee had issued 21 *General Comments* interpreting a wide variety of rights protected in the Covenant, including the right to health, the right to education, the right to adequate food and water, creators' rights, and the right to take part in cultural life. *See* Committee on Economic, Social and Cultural Rights – General Comments, *available at* http://www2.ohchr.org/english/bodies/cescr/comments.htm.

[16] *See* HENKIN ET AL., *supra* note 8, at 1406–1514 (analyzing *General Comments* and national court decisions).

promoting and protecting human rights. These institutions include, most notably, the Human Rights Council, an elected body of forty-seven U.N. member states. The Council's functions include the normative development of human rights standards, the appointment of independent experts to conduct studies and fact-finding missions to specific states or on specific topics, and the review of allegations of human rights violations in public and private meetings. In response to these allegations and to the experts' reports, the Council may issue resolutions or take other actions to promote and protect human rights.

Prior to 2006, the Human Rights Council's activities were entrusted to the U.N. Commission on Human Rights (not to be confused with the similarly named Human Rights Committee, discussed earlier). Established at the time of the United Nations' founding in the mid-1940s, the Commission's first major task was to draft the Universal Declaration on Human Rights.

Much of the Commission's work was carried out by the Sub-Commission on the Promotion and Protection of Human Rights.[17] The Sub-Commission was composed of twenty-six experts who were appointed by the Commission to serve in their individual capacities. The Sub-Commission developed its own agenda regarding human rights issues and, as we discuss in Section 1.5 of this chapter, was among the first U.N. bodies to address the intersection of human rights and intellectual property. In 2006, the Sub-Commission was replaced by a new Advisory Committee of eighteen independent experts that performs the same functions as its predecessor and that reports to the Human Rights Council.

A third human rights mechanism created under the auspices of the U.N. Charter is the Office of the U.N. High Commissioner for Human Rights (OHCHR). The High Commissioner is appointed by the U.N. Secretary-General with the approval of the General Assembly for a four-year term, with the possibility of one four-year renewal. Established in 1993, the OHCHR has a capacious mandate that includes promoting respect for human rights and deterring violations worldwide. The Office provides research and expertise to the Human Rights Council and the Advisory Committee and also drafts its own reports and studies. It has requested observer status with other intergovernmental organizations, such as the World Trade Organization, to monitor their activities and urge them to take human rights into account when carrying out their activities.

---

[17] From 1946 to 1999, this body was known as the Sub-Commission on the Prevention of Discrimination and Protection of Minorities.

1.3. The International Intellectual Property System:
A Substantive and Institutional Overview

This section provides general background about the international intellectual property system. Following a brief description of the major forms of intellectual property protection, we introduce the international law of intellectual property and the institutions that administer it.

A. Types of Intellectual Property

As defined in the 1967 Convention Establishing the World Intellectual Property Organization, intellectual property includes "rights relating to: literary, artistic and scientific works; performances of performing artists, phonograms and broadcasts; inventions in all fields of human endeavour; scientific discoveries; industrial designs; trademarks, service marks and commercial names and designations; protection against unfair competition; and all other rights resulting from intellectual activity in the industrial, scientific, literary or artistic fields."

Copyrights protect original works of authorship, including literary, dramatic, musical, artistic, and certain other intellectual works, including computer programs. (In civil law systems, the term "authors' rights" or "*droit d'auteur*" is more typically used. In subsequent chapters, we indicate where this distinction might be relevant to the relationship between intellectual property and human rights.) Copyright protection is available for both published and unpublished works. Unlike a patent, which is granted by governmental authorities, a copyright exists as soon as an original work is expressed in a tangible form. Originally, a copyright provided its owner with the exclusive right to prevent others from reproducing the work. Now, however, an owner's rights are much broader. Typically, a copyright confers the right to prepare derivative works (which includes the preparation of translations); the right to distribute copies of the work to the public by sale or other transfer of ownership, and, in some cases, by rental, lease, or lending; the right to perform the work publicly, in the case of literary, musical, dramatic, and choreographic works, pantomimes, and motion pictures and other audiovisual works; and, for some types of works, the right to display the work publicly. Copyright systems can include more specific rights, such as the right to perform sound recordings by way of a digital audio transmission. At both domestic and international law levels, copyright also encompasses a right to make a work "available" (e.g., for others to download) in the on-line context. In addition to these economic rights, a copyright also protects the creator's "moral" rights, including the right to be named as the author and to be able to object to derogatory treatment of his or her works. Moral rights have their genesis in "authors' rights" systems, which emphasize authors' personal or natural rights rather more than is the case in common law jurisdictions. More specific protection for authors' moral rights is required by Article 6*bis* of the Berne Convention, the first truly multinational copyright treaty, which came into force at the end of the nineteenth century.

The Berne Convention requires copyright protection for most classes of works to last for fifty years after the death of the author, but a number of countries have increased the copyright term to life of the author plus seventy years. Many national copyright systems include limitations on the rights of authors for specific purposes, such as certain uses by archives and libraries, provision of Braille copies, and certain uses in educational contexts. In addition, some copyright systems provide for fair dealing and fair use defenses, perhaps the broadest of which is the fair use defense in the U.S. Copyright Act.

Patents are exclusive rights awarded to inventors to prevent others from making, using, offering for sale, or selling their inventions. Patent systems also typically provide patentees the right to prohibit "importing" the invention. Like copyrights, patent rights last for a limited period. The minimum period specified in the TRIPS Agreement is twenty years. In return for granting patent rights, a patent applicant must disclose the invention in a manner that enables others to put it into practice. This increases the body of knowledge available for further research. Other prerequisites for patentability include novelty (new characteristics that are not "prior art"), nonobviousness (an inventive step not obvious to one skilled in the field), and "utility" or "industrial applicability." The details can vary substantially between countries. The U.S. Patent Act, for example, recognizes three types of patents: utility patents, which may be granted to anyone who invents any new and useful process, machine, article of manufacture, or composition of matter, or any new and useful improvement; design patents, which may be granted to anyone who invents a new, original, and ornamental design for an article of manufacture; and plant patents, which may be granted to anyone who invents and asexually reproduces any distinct and new variety of plant. Some nations have enacted laws to provide *sui generis* protections for plant varieties, usually known as plant breeders' rights, or plant variety protection.

Industrial designs protect the aesthetic aspects (such as shape, texture, pattern, color) of an object, rather than its technical features. In some nations, such as the United States, these features are protected by "design patents." Other nations have *sui generis* designs statutes. Intellectual property rights in designs protect against the unauthorized use of the design for a limited period. TRIPS requires a minimum of ten years of protection.

Trademarks provide exclusive rights to use distinctive signs, such as symbols, letters, shapes, names, and (in some jurisdictions) colors. Trademarks are used to identify the source of products and services, and to distinguish one firm's products and services from those of other firms. The main purpose of a trademark is to prevent customers from being misled or deceived. Some economists argue that by providing consumers with accurate information about the source of products and services, trademarks reduce consumer search costs. Trademarks also encourage firms to maintain and enhance the goodwill associated with the goods and services they produce and market. Consumers pay for this information through higher prices often charged for goods and services that are marketed under reliable trademarks. A trademark can be renewed indefinitely. Exclusive rights in a mark generally persist so long as the mark continues to distinguish goods and services. Unfair competition laws can supplement trademark rights by prohibiting misrepresentations as to the origin of goods and services.

Geographical Indications: Rights in geographical indications (GIs) protect another form of designation of source – not a specific firm, as in the case of trademarks, but a particular geographical region, which may have the associated qualities, reputation, or other characteristics that consumers find relevant. The owners of GIs can prevent unauthorized parties from using a protected indication for products not from that region or from misleading the public as to the true origin of the product.

B. Rationales for Intellectual Property

The following extract from the 2002 Report by the U.K. Governmental Commission on Intellectual Property examines various rationales for patents and copyrights. It then traces some of the history of intellectual property rights in more detail, provides an international context for that history, and explores reasons why different nations might have had different approaches to intellectual property protection. As will be discussed in more detail later in this chapter, one important feature of the modern international intellectual property regime is the "upward harmonization" agenda, which seeks to achieve stronger intellectual property rights and more uniform intellectual property laws across nations with different histories and different levels of technological and economic development. A second feature of that regime concerns the tension between intellectual property laws and the efforts of indigenous communities to achieve recognition of and control over their culture and traditional knowledge in areas such as biodiversity, medicines, and agriculture. We defer discussion of those issues until Chapter 7.

Final Report of the Commission on Intellectual Property: *Integrating Intellectual Property Rights and Development Policy,* **report prepared by the U.K. Commission on Intellectual Property Rights (2002)**

Introduction

Intellectual property is a form of knowledge which societies have decided can be assigned specific property rights. They have some resemblance to ownership rights over physical property or land. But knowledge is much more than intellectual property. Knowledge is embodied in people, in institutions and in new technologies in ways that have long been seen as a major engine of economic growth.... With recent scientific and technical advances, particularly in biotechnology and information and communications technologies, knowledge has become to an even greater degree than before the principal source of competitive advantage for both companies and countries. Trade in high technology goods and services which are knowledge-intensive, and where IP protection is most common, tends to be among the fastest-growing in international trade.

In developed countries, there is good evidence that intellectual property is, and has been, important for the promotion of invention in some industrial sectors, although the evidence as to exactly how important it is in different sectors is mixed. For example, evidence from the 1980s indicates that the pharmaceutical, chemical and petroleum industries were predominant in recognising that the patent system was essential to innovation. Today, one would need to add biotechnology and some components of information technology. Copyright has also proven essential for the music, film and publishing industries.

For developing countries, like the developed countries before them, the development of indigenous technological capacity has proved to be a key determinant of economic growth and poverty reduction. This capacity determines the extent to which these countries can assimilate and apply foreign technology. Many studies have concluded the most distinctive single factor determining the success of technology transfer is the early emergence of an indigenous technological capacity. But developing countries vary widely in the quality and capacity of their scientific and technical infrastructures.... The crucial question is whether or not the extension of IP regimes assists developing countries in obtaining access to such technologies, and whether and how intellectual property right protection might help developing countries to achieve economic and social development and to reduce poverty.

The Rationale for IP Protection

Intellectual property creates a legal means to appropriate knowledge. A characteristic of knowledge is that one person's use does not diminish another's (for example, reading this report). Moreover the extra cost of extending use to another person is often very low or nil (for example, lending a book or copying an electronic file). From the point of view of society, the more people who use knowledge the better because each user gains something from it at low or no cost, and society is in some sense better off. Economists therefore say that knowledge has the character of a *non-rival public good*.

The other aspect of knowledge, or products embodying knowledge, is the difficulty – often intrinsic – of preventing others from using or copying it. Many products, incorporating new knowledge, can be easily copied. Probably most products, with sufficient effort, can be copied at a fraction (albeit not necessarily small) of the cost it took to invent and market them. Economists refer to this latter characteristic as contributing to *market failure*. If a product takes considerable effort, ingenuity and research, but can be copied easily, there is unlikely to be a sufficient financial incentive from society's point of view to devote resources to invention.

Patents: Patents are one way of addressing this market failure. By conferring temporary market exclusivities, patents allow producers to recoup the costs of investment in R&D [research and development] and reap a profit, in return for making publicly available the knowledge on which the invention is based. However, someone else can only put that knowledge to potential commercial use with the authorisation of the patentee. The costs of investment in R&D and the return on that investment are met by charging the consumer a price based on the ability to exclude competition. Protection is therefore a bargain struck by society on the premise that, in its absence, there would be insufficient invention and innovation. The assumption is that in the longer run, consumers will be better off, in spite of the higher costs conferred by monopoly pricing, because the short term losses to consumers are more than offset by the value to them of the new inventions created through additional R&D. Economists take the view that the patent system improves dynamic efficiency (by stimulating technical progress) at the cost of static efficiency (arising from the costs associated with monopoly).

This rationale for patent protection is relatively straightforward, but it is dependent on a number of simplifying assumptions that may not be borne out in practice. For instance, the optimal degree of patent protection cannot be accurately defined. If protection is too weak, then the development of technology may be inhibited through insufficient incentives for R&D. If too much protection is conferred, consumers may not benefit, even in the long run, and patentees may generate profits far in excess of the overall costs of R&D. Moreover, further innovation based on the protected technology may be stifled because, for instance, the length of the patent term is too long or the scope of the protection granted is too broad.

The length of the monopoly granted is one determinant of the strength of patent protection. Another is the scope of the patent. A broad patent is one that allows a right that goes considerably beyond the claimed invention itself. For example, a patent which claims a gene might only specify one use of that gene. But, under certain approaches to the scope of protection, the patentee will also have the rights to uses of the genetic information other than those disclosed in the patent, including those discovered later by someone else. Broad patents can tend to discourage subsequent innovation by other researchers in the general area of the patent. In contrast, narrow claims will encourage others to "work around" the patent, offering less restriction on related research by others. They may also tend to create stronger rights which are less vulnerable to challenge in the courts. The licensing policy pursued by the patentee will also have an important effect on the dissemination of new technologies, and the extent to which further research is affected by the granted rights.

The optimal degree of protection (where the social benefits are judged to exceed the social costs) will also vary widely by product and sector and will be linked to variations in demand, market structures, R&D costs and the nature of the innovative process. In practice IPR [intellectual property rights] regimes cannot be tailored so precisely and therefore the level of protection afforded in practice is necessarily a compromise. Striking the wrong compromise – whether too much or too little – may be costly to society, especially in the longer term.

One underlying assumption is that there is a latent supply of innovative capacity in the private sector waiting to be unleashed by the grant of the protection that the IP system provides. That may be so in countries where there is substantial research capacity. But in most developing countries local innovation systems (at least of the kind established in developed countries) are weak. Even where such systems are stronger, there is often more capacity in the public than the private sectors. Thus, in such contexts, the dynamic benefit from IP protection is uncertain. The patent system may provide an incentive but there may be limited local capacity to make use of it. Even when technologies are developed, firms in developing countries can seldom bear the costs of acquisition and maintenance of rights and, above all, of litigation if disputes arise.

Economists are also now very aware of what they call *transactions costs*. Establishing the infrastructure of an IPR regime, and mechanisms for the enforcement of IP rights, is costly both to governments, and private stakeholders. In developing countries, where human and financial resources are scarce, and legal systems not well developed, the opportunity costs of operating the system effectively are high. Those costs include the costs of scrutinising the validity of claims to patent rights (both at the application stage and in the courts) and adjudicating upon actions for infringement. Considerable costs are generated by the inherent uncertainties of litigation. These costs too need to be weighed against the benefits arising from the IP system.

Thus the value of the patent system needs to be assessed in a balanced way, acknowledging that it has both costs and benefits, and that the balance of costs and benefits is likely to differ markedly in diverse circumstances.

Amongst academics, notably economists, IPRs have generally been viewed critically. Such rights necessarily involve restrictions on competition which may be to the detriment of consumers and the freedom of trade, and the question is whether these costs are outweighed by the incentives for research and invention.... This ambivalence has tended to strengthen as the IP system has embraced new technologies.

Copyright: The rationale for copyright protection is not dissimilar to that of patents, although historically greater weight has been given to the inherent rights of creative artists to receive fair remuneration for their works than to the incentive effects. Copyright protects the form in which ideas are expressed, not the ideas themselves. Copyright was and remains the basis for making the publishing of literary and artistic works an economic proposition by preventing copying. Unlike patents, copyright protection does not require registration or other formalities (although this was not always the case).

As with patents, the trade-off for society is between the incentive offered to creators of literary and artistic works and the restrictions this places on the free flow of protected works. But, unlike patents, copyright in principle protects the expression of ideas, and not the ideas as such, which may be used by others. And it only prevents the copying of that expression, not independent derivation. The central issue for developing countries concerns the cost of access to physical or digital embodiments of the protected works, and the approach taken to enforcement of copyright protection. [There] are normally exceptions in law where the rights of owners are moderated in the wider public interest, known in some countries as "fair use" provisions (for example in the US), as "fair dealing" in the UK tradition, and exceptions to the reproduction right in the European tradition. It is the issue concerning the cost of access, and the interpretation of "fair use," that is particularly critical for developing countries, made more so by the extension of copyright to electronic material, and to software.

Copyright protects works for much longer than patents but does not protect against independent derivation of the work in question. Under TRIPS copyright allows a minimum of fifty years after the death of the author, but most developed countries and several developing countries have increased this to 70 years or more. While the main reason for the extension of copyright has been pressure from the copyright industries (notably the film industry in the US), there is no clear economic rationale for copyright protection being so much longer than that for patents. Indeed, the rate of technical change has led in several industries to a shorter effective product life (for example, successive editions of software programmes) which point to longer copyright protection being redundant....

As with patents, a key issue for developing countries is whether the gains to be elicited from the incentives provided by copyright outweigh the increased costs associated with the restrictions on use that flow from copyright. Although there are exceptions, such as India's film or software industry, most developing countries are net importers of copyrighted material, just as they are net importers of technologies. Since copyright does not need registration or other formalities, once a country has copyright laws in place, the impact of copyright is more ubiquitous than in the case of patents. Software, textbooks, and academic journals are key items where copyright is a determining factor in pricing and access, and which are also essential ingredients in education and other spheres crucial to the development process. For instance, a reasonable selection of academic journals is far beyond the purchasing budgets of university libraries in most developing countries, and increasingly in developed countries as well.

The interaction of the Internet and copyright is an issue of particular and growing importance for developing countries. With printed media, there are provisions for "fair use" under copyright law, and the nature of the medium lends itself to multiple use either formally through libraries or informally through borrowing and browsing (as may be done in a bookshop before deciding to purchase). With material accessed through the Internet, the technology allows encryption and other means to exclude potential users even from browsing, unless they have paid the relevant charge. While the "philosophy" of the Internet has hitherto been about free access, increasingly sites with material of value are moving towards charging for use, or limiting access in other ways. Further, the DMCA [Digital Millennium Copyright Act] in the US and Europe's Database Directive have provisions that go well beyond what is required under TRIPS, and are held by many users to have shifted the balance of protection too far in favour of investors and originators of collections of data.

Thus, as with patents, there is a need for balance. Too much protection by copyright, by other forms of IP protection, or by technology, may restrict the free flow of ideas on which the further progress of ideas and technology depends. For developing countries, affordable access to works essential for development such as educational materials and scientific and technical knowledge may be affected by unduly strong copyright rules.

———————

C. The International Institutional Framework

The following article examines the internationalization of intellectual property and introduces some of the important institutional players and enforcement mechanisms in the international intellectual property regime. Until recently, compliance with the leading nineteenth-century intellectual property treaties (the Paris Convention,[18] which concerns industrial property rights, such as patents and trademarks, and the Berne Convention,[19] which concerns copyright, or, more formally, property rights in "literary and artistic works") was largely a matter of politics, rather than legal enforceability. Today, however, adherence to multilateral intellectual property protection standards as embodied in TRIPS is a requirement for membership of the World Trade Organization (WTO). A violation of TRIPS can trigger the filing of a complaint to the WTO dispute settlement body, which may authorize the imposition of trade sanctions as a remedy for transgressions of the treaty.

Marney L. Cheek, *The Limits of Informal Regulatory Cooperation in International Affairs: A Review of the Global Intellectual Property Regime*, 33 Geo. Wash. Int'l L. Rev. 277, 284–86, 289–99 (2001)

. . .

The Internationalization of Intellectual Property: A Brief History

International agreements in the intellectual property field are not a new phenomenon. The quintessential treaties protecting copyrighted works and

---

[18] Paris Convention for the Protection of Industrial Property, Mar. 20, 1883, 21 U.S.T. 1583, 828 U.N.T.S. 305 (last revised at Stockholm, July 14, 1967) [Paris Convention].

[19] Berne Convention for the Protection of Literary and Artistic Works, Sept. 9, 1886, 1161 U.N.T.S. 31 (last revised at Paris, July 24, 1971) [Berne Convention].

industrial property were signed in the 1880s. Even though these international treaties governed relations among states for over a hundred years, for most of the twentieth century intellectual property was neither a highly political nor controversial international concern....

Despite existing international treaties on industrial property and copyright, intellectual property laws around the world were far from uniform in the 1980s. Most international agreements focused on procedural coordination and national treatment, leaving substantive protection to individual states. The "national treatment" obligation precluded discrimination against foreign creators of intellectual property, so long as certain other requirements are met – such as first publication of a copyright-protected work in a member state. Even when treaties called for national treatment, however, the weakness of some countries' intellectual property regimes meant that national treatment clauses amounted to very little protection. For example, many countries offered limited patent protection for chemicals and pharmaceuticals and/or had compulsory licensing schemes for certain technologies. As a result, intellectual property owners were not granted the same proprietary rights in some nations, typically developing countries, as they were assured in industrialized countries.

Differing levels of protection between industrialized and developing countries more often than not reflected deep ideological divisions about the proper role of intellectual property rights in a growing economy. Under certain circumstances, developing countries required compulsory licensing schemes or refused to provide protection unless the patented technology benefited their citizens. India and Brazil, for example, emphasized throughout international negotiations in the 1980s and 1990s that in sectors such as health, nutrition, and agriculture, public policy reasons mandated compulsory licensing of technology and/or restrictions on patent rights in order to benefit consumers as a whole.

For these developing countries and others, intellectual property was a key component of their economic and development strategy. Intellectual property rights regimes in these countries were designed to promote technology transfer and the dissemination of technology, not to protect the inventions of industrialized countries from piracy. In a 1988 study of Argentina, Brazil, India, Mexico, South Korea, Singapore, and Taiwan (all countries with large piracy industries), not a single country was found to have the same protections for intellectual property as those found in industrialized countries. Argentina, Brazil, India, and Mexico had the weakest protections, coupled with poor enforcement and large piracy industries. These states became some of the industrialized countries' biggest foes in the debate over intellectual property standards within the Uruguay Round of the General Agreement on Tariffs and Trade (GATT).

. . .

Traditional Types of International Dialogue

[T]he desire for international consensus on intellectual property rights is not a new phenomenon. The Paris Convention for the Protection of Industrial Property and the Berne Convention for the Protection of Literary and Artistic Works codified international intellectual property norms in 1883 and 1886, respectively. While the Paris and Berne Conventions do contain some substantive standards, these treaties focus on national treatment and the harmonization of procedural law. The Paris Convention, for example, stipulates that the filing date for a patent application in one country can serve as the filing date in all member countries. Such procedures are not without significance; the patent filing date determines the priority of claimants on a given invention in most countries, and the filing date may also determine the length of protection received under domestic law. While such international procedural coordination benefits inventors by facilitating attempts to receive patent protection in several different countries, the Paris Convention does not mandate any particular level of protection.

The Paris and Berne Conventions remained the cornerstones of international intellectual property law throughout most of the twentieth century. Both treaties have been revised from time to time to account for developments in intellectual property law and the changing needs of member countries. Eventually, WIPO was founded to govern the Berne and Paris Conventions, and serve as a forum for international discourse on intellectual property. WIPO sponsors treaty negotiations to revise existing agreements, and sponsors conferences to discuss new international treaties....

WIPO remained the primary forum for international discussion in the 1970s and early 1980s, but substantive coordination efforts proceeded at a slow pace. Many developing countries balked at the thought of establishing substantive international standards because they viewed intellectual property "less as a body of fundamental rights than as a subset of their general economic policies, to be managed for their contribution to economic growth and industrial development." These countries felt that intellectual property should remain a domestic concern.

As global trade flourished in the 1980s, it became clear that inconsistent levels of protection in different markets translated into real economic costs for intellectual property owners. The flourishing piracy industry was

particularly troublesome for rights holders from industrialized countries....
Pirated goods are successful in the marketplace because, without outlay for
research and development costs, pirates can sell their goods for a fraction of
the cost of the original. Pharmaceuticals are one example where millions of
dollars in research may be necessary to develop a drug; however a pirated
version can be created and sold for one-tenth to one-fifth the cost of the original product.

The United States began to pursue an aggressive unilateral trade policy
in the late 1980s in an attempt to stem piracy and recapture some of the
significant economic losses accruing to U.S. computer, pharmaceutical and
entertainment companies. The U.S. government also decided to pursue
multilateral talks on minimum protections for intellectual property. WIPO
was disfavored by multinational corporations and industrialized countries
because its voting structure paralleled the power blocs found in the U.N.,
including the Group of 77 developing countries who tended to block indus-
trialized-country substantive harmonization initiatives. Thus, the United
States and other industrialized countries introduced intellectual property
issues into the trade negotiations underway in the GATT.

...

The inclusion of intellectual property rights in the GATT framework effectively shifted the focus of international discussion from procedural uniformity found in prior WIPO treaties to minimum standards of substantive
protection. The TRIPS Agreement ... established these minimum standards
and mandated mutual recognition of intellectual property rights. As part of
the newly established WTO, a dispute settlement system was established to
enforce WTO agreements. Thus, for the first time, a mechanism for the global
enforcement of intellectual property rights came into existence....

Intergovernmental Organizations

The World Trade Organization

The TRIPS Agreement: The Uruguay Round of the GATT ... ended in April
1994 with the signing of a historical agreement establishing the WTO. The
treaty ending the Uruguay Round also achieved significant reductions in tar-
iff and non-tariff barriers among more than one hundred trading partners. In
addition to traditional trade accords on dumping, subsidies, countervailing
measures and product standards, intellectual property rights were addressed
in a multilateral trade forum for the first time. The TRIPS Agreement, which
emerged from the prolonged negotiation process, obligates WTO-member

countries to (1) provide minimum intellectual property rights protection through domestic laws; (2) provide effective enforcement of those rights; and (3) agree to submit disputes to the WTO dispute settlement system. The TRIPS Agreement goes beyond the voluntary alignment of domestic laws and mandates the mutual recognition of domestic laws that provide minimum levels of substantive intellectual property protection. At the same time, the TRIPS Agreement "is not intended to be a harmonization agreement," meaning that countries are not required to create identical regimes. Countries are free to determine their own methods of compliance with TRIPS Agreement obligations, and they may provide more extensive protections than those mandated in the treaty. Under a most-favored nation regime, however, any protections extended to one country's citizens must be extended to all.

The TRIPS Agreement requires WTO members to adhere to the Berne and Paris Conventions. The TRIPS Agreement also goes beyond existing treaty obligations to establish a number of rights previously subject to disparate treatment. Most commentators agree that these additional obligations bring the level of intellectual property rights protection up to the standards already found in most industrialized countries.... The TRIPS Agreement also includes provisions on industrial designs, integrated circuits and trade secrets.

The TRIPS Agreement obligates WTO members to "provide procedures and remedies under their domestic law to ensure that intellectual property rights can be effectively enforced, by foreign-right holders as well as by their own nationals." This enforcement provision is one of the main innovations of the TRIPS Agreement. Countries must not only enact legislation to be in compliance with TRIPS, but must implement domestic enforcement mechanisms to ensure that intellectual property rights are upheld. Furthermore, WTO members are responsible for implementing broader measures to prevent the export of infringing goods. The TRIPS Agreement is the first multinational intellectual property treaty to contain such an enforcement provision. Under the TRIPS Agreement, countries must also ensure that criminal sanctions provide for "the seizure, forfeiture, and destruction of the infringing goods and of any materials and [instruments used] in the commission of the offence."

With the TRIPS Agreement in place, many WTO members found themselves committed to significant domestic reform. Even the United States had to enact domestic legislation to comply with some of the TRIPS Agreement requirements....

The TRIPS requirements have had the most transformative effect in developing countries. One reason for this is that several developing countries are not signatories to the Paris and/or Berne Conventions. By signing the TRIPS Agreement, these countries have committed themselves to passing significant new substantive laws and to establishing the domestic enforcement mechanisms required by the treaty.

When the TRIPS Agreement was signed in 1994, many WTO members did not have pre-existing intellectual property regimes in place. To address this lack of capacity, a staggered system of accession was established to provide developing countries with a transition period in which to implement reform. While TRIPS obligations had to be implemented by all industrialized countries by January 1, 1996, developing countries had until January 1, 2000 and least developed countries have until January 1, 2006 to reform their laws. Some developing countries, such as India and Pakistan, were given extensions beyond the 2000 deadline to reform their patent systems. However, in order to take advantage of this extension these countries had to create "mailbox" provisions allowing patent applications filed from January 1, 1995 to have priority once the new patent system is in place. [We discuss additional flexibilities and extensions of deadlines in Chapter 2.-Eds.]

The TRIPS Agreement also established the TRIPS Council, responsible for overseeing the implementation of obligations and serving as a forum for continued discussion of intellectual property issues. The TRIPS Council first reviewed all industrialized country laws in 1996 to ensure compliance with TRIPS obligations. The Council also monitors technical assistance to developing countries. Under Article 67 of the TRIPS Agreement, industrialized countries are obligated to provide both technical and financial support to developing and least-developed countries who are reforming their domestic intellectual property regimes in order to fulfill their obligations under the TRIPS Agreement.

WTO Mechanisms to Ensure Treaty Compliance: Under Article 64, the TRIPS Agreement subjects disputes to the WTO's dispute settlement procedure. Prior to the TRIPS Agreement, international disputes in this area were not regularly submitted to a formal dispute resolution process. The dispute resolution procedure provides a real threat to those countries that might consider shirking their obligations under the TRIPS Agreement. Under the dispute settlement procedure of the WTO, an aggrieved member may retaliate by withdrawing trade concessions. This retaliation provision is intended to be a last resort, but it lends credibility to the adjudicatory procedures. While the United States plans to use the dispute settlement procedure to make sure that countries adhere to their TRIPS obligations, the rest of the world hopes that the dispute resolution provision will rein in U.S. unilateral aggression by forcing the United States to bring its disputes before an international tribunal.

...

The World Intellectual Property Organization

WIPO Treaties: The World Intellectual Property Organization (WIPO) was founded in 1967 and became a specialized agency of the United Nations in 1974. WIPO administers several international intellectual property treaties, including the Paris and Berne Conventions, and "promote[s] the protection of intellectual property throughout the world through cooperation among States and, where appropriate, in collaboration with any other international organization."[20] As of 1998 WIPO had 171 members.[21] WIPO has been responsible for the creation and/or the administration of twenty treaties in the intellectual property area. These treaties cover copyright and neighboring rights, patent, trademark and industrial design....

WIPO has a General Assembly in which each member country has one vote [although in practice most decisions are adopted by consensus rather than by a vote]. The International Bureau is WIPO's Secretariat, providing technical assistance and training to developing countries and sponsoring Experts Meetings and Information Meetings to discuss revisions of old treaties and the creation of new treaties. Until recently, the International Bureau tightly controlled the treaty process, drafting initial treaty language and convening meetings where the International Bureau's proposals would be discussed by WIPO members.

In the last several years, WIPO has sponsored five to ten meetings per year on a variety of intellectual property issues. However, the treaty process has

---

[20] Convention Establishing the World Intellectual Property Organization, art. 3(i), July 14, 1967, 21 U.S.T. 1749, 828 U.N.T.S. 3 (as amended Sept. 28, 1979) [WIPO Convention]. Although the convention speaks of promoting intellectual property protection on a global basis, there is authority for interpreting the WIPO's mandate much more capaciously. In 1974 WIPO entered into an agreement designating it as a specialized agency of the United Nations. Agreement between the United Nations and the World Intellectual Property Organization, art. 1, Dec. 17, 1974, *available at* http://www.wipo.int/treaties/en/agreement/pdf/un_wipo_agreement.pdf. The agreement states that WIPO is responsible for "promoting creative intellectual activity and facilitating the transfer of technology ... to developing countries in order to accelerate economic, social and cultural development." *Id.* art. 1. Section 1.5 explains how, in 2004, advocates of a "Development Agenda" seized upon this long-forgotten treaty language to articulate a revised mission for WIPO. – Eds.

[21] As of September 2009, the number of WIPO member states had increased to 184. WIPO, About WIPO: Member States, *available at* http://www.wipo.int/members/en/–Eds.

been a notoriously slow one. In some cases, experts have met up to fifteen times over a period of several years before a draft treaty has been presented to the General Assembly at a Diplomatic Conference. Despite the TRIPS Agreement and the re-definition of intellectual property as a trade issue, WIPO remains committed to international consensus-building in the intellectual property field. Significantly, in December 1995 WIPO and the WTO signed an agreement designed to further cooperation between the two entities. WIPO agreed to respond to requests from developing countries for legal and technical assistance relating specifically to TRIPS obligations.

WIPO has also continued to sponsor discussions on international policy coordination efforts, despite the fact that it does not administer the TRIPS Agreement. In December 1996 WIPO sponsored a Diplomatic Conference focusing on copyright protection for digital works and databases. While the database treaty was tabled for further discussion, the WIPO Copyright Treaty and the WIPO Performances and Phonograms Treaty were adopted. Both database protection and copyright protection for digital works are at the forefront of the current intellectual property debate. As technological developments and the Internet raise new challenges for the current international intellectual property regime, WIPO may be able to provide a more targeted response than its WTO counterpart.

The Role of Other Intergovernmental Organizations: The Organization for Economic Cooperation and Development (OECD), the Group of Seven (G-7) industrialized countries, the Asian-Pacific Economic Cooperation (APEC) forum, and numerous other intergovernmental organizations are engaged in varying levels of discussion about intellectual property law. Some of these discussions are trade-oriented; both the North American Free Trade Agreement (NAFTA) and APEC mention intellectual property as one of several areas for policy coordination. Other intergovernmental organizations, such as OECD and the G-7, are interested in creating an intellectual property framework that can regulate the Internet and electronic commerce, issues of particular relevance to industrialized countries.

1.4. Historical Isolation of the Human Rights and Intellectual Property Regimes

It is perhaps curious that the relationship between human rights and intellectual property has only recently become a subject of interest for government officials, international organizations, public interest NGOs, and scholars. No less august statement of foundational principles than the UDHR provides that "everyone has the right to the protection of the moral and material interests resulting from any scientific, literary or artistic production of which he [or she] is the author."[22] Support for these rights also finds expression in nearly identical language in the ICESCR, which has now been ratified by more than 150 nations.[23] The drafting history of these international instruments makes clear that the protection of creators' rights was no accident, even if the drafters' precise intentions remain elusive.[24] For decades, however, creators' rights and intellectual property more generally remained a normative backwater in the human rights regime, neglected by tribunals, treaty bodies, governments, and commentators while other human rights emerged from the jurisprudential shadows.

The human rights system's nominal interest in the connection between these regimes has not, however, been reciprocated by governments and private parties active in the international intellectual property system. No references to human rights appear in the Paris,[25] Berne,[26] and Rome Conventions,[27] or in

---

[22] Universal Declaration of Human Rights, G.A. Res. 217A, art. 27, U.N. GAOR, 3d Sess., 1st plen. mtg., U.N. Doc. A/810 (Dec. 12, 1948).

[23] International Covenant on Economic, Social and Cultural Rights, art. 15(1)(b)–(c), *adopted* Dec. 16, 1966, S. Exec. Doc. D, 95–2 (1977), 993 U.N.T.S. 3 (entered into force Jan. 3, 1976) [ICESCR] (recognizing the right "to benefit from the protection of the moral and material interests resulting from any scientific, literary or artistic production of which he is the author" and "to enjoy the benefits of scientific progress and its applications"); *see also* ECOSOC, Comm. on Econ., Soc. and Cultural Rights, *Drafting History of the Article 15(1)(c) of the International Covenant on Economic, Social and Cultural Rights*, E/C.12/2000/15 (Oct. 9, 2000) (*prepared by* Maria Green). As of March 31, 2010, 160 states were parties to the ICESCR.

[24] JOHANNES MORSINK, THE UNIVERSAL DECLARATION OF HUMAN RIGHTS: ORIGINS, DRAFTING AND INTENT 220–221 (1999). As one scholar has observed, although the motivations of governments who favored inclusion of Article 27 in the UDHR are somewhat obscure, the proponents appear to be divided into two camps: "What we know is that the initial strong criticism that intellectual property was not properly speaking a Human Right or that is already attracted sufficient protection under the regime of protection afforded to property rights in general was eventually defeated by a coalition of those who primarily voted in favour because they felt that the moral rights deserved and needed protection and met the Human Rights standard and those who felt the ongoing internationalization of copyright needed a boost and that this could be a tool in this respect." Paul Torremans, *Copyright as a Human Right*, in PAUL L. C. TORREMANS (ED.), COPYRIGHT AND HUMAN RIGHTS: FREEDOM OF EXPRESSION – INTELLECTUAL PROPERTY – PRIVACY 1, 6 (2004). For additional thoughtful analysis of the drafting history and its implications, *see* Peter K. Yu, *Reconceptualizing Intellectual Property Interests in a Human Rights Framework*, 40 U.C. DAVIS L. REV. 1039, 1070–75 (2007) [Yu, *Human Rights Framework*].

[25] Paris Convention, *supra* note 18.

[26] Berne Convention, *supra* note 19.

[27] International Convention for the Protection of Performers, Producers of Phonograms and Broadcasting Organizations, *adopted at Rome, Italy*, Oct. 26, 1961, 496 U.N.T.S. 43 [Rome Convention].

the more recently adopted TRIPS Agreement.[28] These treaties do refer to the protections granted to authors and inventors as "rights."[29] But the principal justification for such rights lies not in deontological claims about the inalienable liberties of human beings, but rather in the economic and instrumental benefits that flow from the protection of intellectual property across national borders.[30]

What explains the longstanding jurisprudential separation of the two legal regimes? During the decades following the Second World War, the most pressing concerns for the human rights movement were elaborating and codifying legal norms, enhancing international monitoring mechanisms, and implementing fundamental rights protections in national legal systems.[31] This evolutionary process resulted in a de facto separation of human rights into categories, including a core set of peremptory norms for the most egregious forms of misconduct; civil and political rights; and economic, social, and cultural rights.[32] Among these categories, economic, social, and cultural rights – the group that includes creators' rights – were the least well developed and the least prescriptive.[33]

For advocates of intellectual property protection, by contrast, the central focus of international lawmaking in the postwar era was twofold: first, the gradual expansion of subject matters and rights through periodic revisions to the Berne, Paris, and other multilateral conventions, and later, the creation of a link between intellectual property and trade.[34] Human rights law added little to these enterprises. It offered neither a necessary nor a sufficient

---

[28] TRIPS Agreement, *supra* note 3.

[29] *Id.* at pmbl. ("recognizing that intellectual property rights are private rights").

[30] For a more detailed discussion, see Laurence R. Helfer, *Adjudicating Copyright Claims under the TRIPS Agreement, The Case for a European Human Rights Analogy*, 39 HARV. INT'L L.J. 357, 397–99 (1998).

[31] *See* Laurence R. Helfer, *Forum Shopping for Human Rights*, 148 U. PA. L. REV. 285, 296–301 (1999) (discussing evolution of UN human rights system and its monitoring mechanisms).

[32] *See* Theodor Meron, *Norm Making and Supervision in International Human Rights: Reflections on Institutional Order*, 76 AM. J. INT'L L. 754 (1982).

[33] *See* Audrey R. Chapman, *A Human Rights Perspective on Intellectual Property, Scientific Progress, and Access to the Benefits of Science* 127–68, in INTELLECTUAL PROPERTY AND HUMAN RIGHTS (World Intellectual Property Organization 1999) (characterizing ICESCR Article 15 as "the most neglected set of the provisions within an international human rights instrument whose norms are not well developed").

[34] The most prominent examples are the TRIPS Agreement and the intellectual property provisions of the North American Free Trade Agreement (NAFTA). For early and influential analyses, see J. H. Reichman, *Universal Minimum Standards of Intellectual Property Protection under the TRIPS Component of the WTO Agreement*, 29 INT'L LAW. 345 (1995); James A. R. Nafziger, *NAFTA's Regime for Intellectual Property: In the Mainstream of Public International Law*, 19 HOUS. J. INT'L L. 807 (1997).

justification for state-granted monopolies in intangible knowledge goods; nor, conversely, did it serve to check the expansion of intellectual property protection standards.

In sum, the longstanding isolation of human rights and intellectual property can be attributed to the fact that each legal regime was preoccupied with its own distinct concerns and neither saw the other as either aiding or threatening its sphere of influence or opportunities for expansion. Moreover, as a pragmatic matter, until recently there was relatively little overlap among the actors involved in the development of each area, or in the kinds of legal expertise considered relevant to each regime.

1.5. Catalysts for the Expanding Intersection of the Human Rights and Intellectual Property Regimes

Several catalysts – some in intellectual property, others in human rights – ended this historical isolation and triggered fresh controversies over the intersection of the two legal regimes. The first group of developments relates to efforts by industrialized nations and their knowledge industries to strengthen intellectual property protection standards and enforcement mechanisms in developing countries by incorporating intellectual property into the global trading system. These efforts, which began in earnest in the 1980s and early 1990s, led to the inclusion of intellectual property protection rules in the TRIPS Agreement of the WTO and in the subsequent negotiation of regional and bilateral trade treaties containing IP protection rules that exceed TRIPS standards. The pressures to adopt these rules eventually precipitated a backlash whose most prominent manifestations are the Doha Declaration on TRIPs and Public Health, adopted by the WTO membership in 2001, and the WIPO Development Agenda, launched by a consortium of developing countries and civil society groups in 2004.

The second cluster of events centers on changes in human rights law. It includes a focus on the cultural rights of indigenous peoples, including traditional knowledge; increased attention in the U.N. human rights system to the adverse consequences of TRIPS for economic, social, and cultural rights; efforts to develop human rights obligations for multinational corporations; and claims of violations of the right of property by corporate intellectual property owners.

A. International Intellectual Property Protection Standards and Enforcement Mechanisms: Reactions and Counterreactions

Three related developments contributed to a marked expansion of intellectual property protection standards and enforcement mechanisms beginning in the mid-1990s: (1) intensive lobbying by corporate intellectual property owners to induce the United States and the European Union to pressure developing countries to protect foreign intellectual property rights; (2) the successful effort by the United States and European Union to move intellectual property negotiations from the WIPO to the GATT, leading to the adoption of the TRIPS Agreement; and (3) pressure from these same states and nonstate actors for intellectual property protection standards that exceed those found in TRIPS. These expansions later triggered counterreactions in the WTO and WIPO, dramatically slowing the pace of international IP treaty making and increasing pressure from developing countries to clarify and expand exceptions and limitations and to recognize nonproprietary methods for encouraging creativity and innovation.

1. Pressure by U.S. Intellectual Property Industries to Expand Intellectual Property Protection Standards and Enforcement Mechanisms

The 1980s witnessed a growing awareness in the United States, and in other industrialized countries, of the strategic role of technology and the protection of intangible knowledge-based goods for economic growth and international trade. This awareness led U.S.-based multinational corporations whose business models and profit margins depended on intellectual property protection to lobby the U.S. government to bolster the intellectual property laws and enforcement mechanisms in developing nations. Pursuant to the "Special 301" procedure,[35] for example, the U.S. Trade Representative (USTR) investigated these countries and recommended retaliatory trade measures if their governments refused to increase IP protection and enforcement measures. As Carolyn Deere has concisely explained:

> In the United States, over 25 per cent of exports in the 1980s contained a high IP component (chemicals, books, movies, records, electrical equipment, and computers) compared to 10 per cent in the post-war period. While rapid advances in information and communication technologies had increased opportunities for international trade in knowledge-based goods, they also multiplied the possibilities for imitation, copying, and authorized use of technologies. Together, these factors altered the economic dynamics of the so-called content and R&D- [research and development] based industries. U.S. corporations drew attention to a range of challenges posed by weak protection of IP within and beyond national borders, claiming that stronger rights were central to their business model both at home and abroad.…
>
> Facing cuts to their profit margins, foreign export markets, and also domestic market shares, U.S. industries complained that competitors were "free-riding"

---

[35] Trade Act of 1974 § 301, 19 U.S.C. § 2242(a)(1)(A) (2006).

on their R&D investments. They called on the U.S. government to help halt imitation and reverse engineering abroad. Like-minded leaders of major U.S. corporations then mobilized to consolidate a U.S. agenda for a trade-based conception of intellectual property rights and to integrate IP into international trade policies.... Their push to link trade and intellectual property was facilitated by reforms to U.S. trade law and USTR, which gave U.S. corporations even greater access to, and influence on, the U.S. trade policymaking process....

A core concern of developed country multinationals was that intellectual property laws and practices in developing countries favoured domestic intellectual property holders over foreigners and offered little effective protection to non-national intellectual property holders. Pharmaceutical companies facing competitive threats from cheaper generic versions of medicines complained about the narrow scope and short term of patent protection in many developing countries, lack of transparency in the patent-granting process, and limited legal security in respect of the enforcement of patent rights. Together, representatives of companies from many different sectors alleged that developing countries lacked vigilance in preventing the production of counterfeit goods and the unauthorized use of trademarks. Companies in the entertainment industry charged that developing countries were too tolerant of piracy of sound recordings and video, citing losses of billions of dollars per year.[36]

The preceding passage reveals that the intellectual property industries had leveled three distinct criticisms of the international intellectual property regime as it existed in the 1980s – first, that laws "on the books" were insufficiently protective of innovations, creative works, distinctive signs, and other forms of intellectual property; second, that even where those laws adequately protected intellectual property in theory, the practical ability of states and private parties to enforce those laws was deficient; and third, that the penalties for violating the applicable legal rules were too weak to deter future violations. Each of these three concerns informed debates over whether – and if so, how – to modify the international intellectual property regime to provide stronger protection of intellectual property.

2. The Shift from WIPO to GATT to TRIPS

The proponents of stronger intellectual property protection standards, enforcement mechanisms, and sanctions rules now faced an important strategic question: in which forum should they pursue this agenda? A logical

---

[36] CAROLYN DEERE, THE IMPLEMENTATION GAME: THE TRIPS AGREEMENT AND THE GLOBAL POLITICS OF INTELLECTUAL PROPERTY REFORM IN DEVELOPING COUNTRIES 46–47 (2009). For an earlier authoritative analysis, see SUSAN K. SELL, PRIVATE POWER, PUBLIC LAW: THE GLOBALIZATION OF INTELLECTUAL PROPERTY RIGHTS 75–120 (2003) (analyzing the activities and influence of 12 U.S.-based transnational corporations who formed the Intellectual Property Committee to advocate the incorporation of intellectual property into the international trade regime).

choice was the World Intellectual Property Organization (WIPO), a specialized international organization created in the late 1960s with a mandate to "promote the protection of intellectual property throughout the world."[37] WIPO's Secretariat sought to achieve this goal by hosting diplomatic conferences at which states negotiated new multilateral intellectual property treaties, administering existing intellectual property agreements, and offering technical assistance and advice to national intellectual property offices, especially in developing countries.[38]

Notwithstanding the functional salience of WIPO's mandate and its subject matter expertise, industrialized countries viewed the organization as an inhospitable venue. Instead, they chose to relocate their efforts to remake the international intellectual property regime to GATT. There were two principal reasons that industrialized countries adopted this "regime shifting" strategy.[39] The first concerns the result of patent treaty negotiations that WIPO hosted in the 1980s. The second relates to institutional features of GATT that facilitated the adoption of more expansive intellectual property protection rules, enforcement mechanisms, and sanctions opportunities.[40]

The dissatisfaction with WIPO dated to a diplomatic conference in the early 1980s at which developing nations demanded a revision of the Paris Convention to grant them preferential treatment. The United States and other industrialized countries strongly opposed this initiative and fought developing countries to a standstill.[41] Although successful in fending off efforts to weaken international patent rules, the United States interpreted the failed diplomatic conference as a signal that it would be futile to seek expanded

---

[37] WIPO Convention, *supra* note 20. WIPO's mandate was later broadened considerably as a result of the agreement designating it as a specialized agency of the United Nations. *See infra* text accompanying notes 67–70.

[38] *See* WIPO, Summary of WIPO Technical Assistance for the Least Developed Countries, *available at* http://www.wipo.int/ldcs/en/ip/tech_assistance.html. WIPO's technical and legal assistance activities have been criticized by some public interest NGOs. "There are two main concerns. The first is that the [organization] has tended to over-emphasise the benefits of intellectual property while giving very little attention to its costs. Other critics have accused the International Bureau of being partisan and not giving developing countries the best advice." Sisule F. Musungu & Graham Dutfield, *Multilateral Agreements and a TRIPS-Plus World: The World Intellectual Property Organisation (WIPO)* 16 (TRIPS Issues Papers No. 3, 2003), *available at* http://www.quno.org/geneva/pdf/economic/Issues/Multilateral-Agreements-in-TRIPS-plus-English.pdf.

[39] Laurence R. Helfer, *Regime Shifting: The TRIPS Agreement and New Dynamics of International Intellectual Property Lawmaking*, 29 YALE INT'L L.J. 1 (2004) [Helfer, *Regime Shifting*].

[40] *Id.* at 19–23.

[41] For a detailed analysis of the Paris Convention diplomatic conference, see SUSAN K. SELL, POWER AND IDEAS: NORTH-SOUTH POLITICS OF INTELLECTUAL PROPERTY AND ANTITRUST 107–30 (1998).

intellectual property protection standards at WIPO.[42] The United States had, however, achieved that goal by including intellectual property in a series of unilateral trade measures and bilateral trade consultations with developing countries. Buoyed by the success of that linkage strategy, the United States (later joined by Canada, Japan, and the EU member countries) shifted to a multilateral approach, adding intellectual property to the negotiating mandate for the Uruguay Round of GATT negotiations leading to the creation of the WTO.[43]

Three institutional features of GATT/WTO made it a superior venue in which to negotiate stronger intellectual property protection standards and enforcement mechanisms. First, as the region and the nation with the largest domestic markets, the EC and the United States enjoyed greater negotiating leverage in GATT/WTO than in WIPO. Second, the ability to link intellectual property to trade rules expanded the zone of agreement among states with divergent interests. According to some accounts of the negotiations, developing countries accepted a grand bargain: greater access to the markets of industrialized states for agricultural products, textiles, and other goods in exchange for including intellectual property protection rules and enforcement mechanisms in the global trading system.[44] Third, the GATT dispute settlement system was far more effective than the moribund international adjudication mechanisms associated with the WIPO conventions.[45] In addition, the Uruguay Round negotiators enhanced the legalized aspects of

---

[42] *See* Bal Gopal Das, Intellectual Property Dispute, *GATT, WIPO: Of Playing by the Game Rules and Rules of the Game*, 35 IDEA: J.L. & TECH. 149, 158 n.45 (1994) ("Dissatisfaction with WIPO's ineffectiveness as a forum to end the impasse which ensued after the failed Paris Revision Conference, aggravated by the continued intransigence of Developing countries, motivated the movement away from WIPO to GATT as the negotiating forum.")

[43] *See* SELL, POWER AND IDEAS, *supra* note 36, at 132–36.

[44] *See* Ernst-Ulrich Petersmann, *Constitutionalism and International Organizations*, 17 Nw. J. INT'L L. & BUS. 398, 442 (1996–97) (characterizing agreements relating to services and intellectual property as part of "global package deals" negotiated within the GATT/WTO). *But see* Peter Drahos, *Developing Countries and International Intellectual Property Standard-Setting*, 5 J. WORLD INTELL. PROP. 765, 769–70 (2002) (arguing that TRIPS' negotiating history undermines the claim that the treaty was the "result of bargaining amongst sovereign and equal States ... which agreed to TRIPS as part of a larger package of trade-offs that contained gains for all").

[45] The Berne and Paris Conventions each contain a clause allowing states parties to resolve their treaty-based disputes before the International Court of Justice. No country has ever filed such a suit, however, leading commentators to describe the Conventions' dispute settlement provisions as "effectively worthless." Frank Emmert, *Intellectual Property in the Uruguay Round – Negotiating Strategies of the Western Industrialized Countries*, 11 MICH. J. INT'L L. 1317, 1343 (1989); *see also* Monique L. Cordray, *GATT v. WIPO*, 76 J. PAT. & TRADEMARK OFF. SOC'Y 121, 131–32 (1994) (critiquing dispute settlement provisions of intellectual property conventions).

GATT dispute settlement by providing for binding panel rulings, a standing Appellate Body, and resort to retaliatory sanctions to promote compliance with global trade rules.

3. The Impact of TRIPS and the Rise of TRIPS Plus Treaties

By the spring of 1994, the United States and its industrialized country allies had achieved their core objective – an Agreement on Trade-Related Aspects of Intellectual Property Rights (TRIPS). TRIPS effectuated nothing short of a revolution in intellectual property law. It enhanced the substantive standards of intellectual property conventions negotiated within WIPO and incorporated them into a single comprehensive agreement. And its obligations extended to the entire WTO membership, including many developing countries whose commitment to strong intellectual property protection rules was tenuous or equivocal.

In addition, and in contrast to earlier intellectual property treaties, compliance with TRIPS could not be shirked through reliance on partial implementation or weak dispute settlement procedures. For private intellectual property owners, TRIPS promised meaningful enforcement in national laws, a promise that required WTO members to undertake extensive revisions of their domestic judicial and administrative systems. For states dissatisfied with the weak intellectual property laws of their fellow WTO members, TRIPS promised high levels of compliance through two new institutions: (1) a TRIPS Council, which reviews national implementation measures and highlights potential areas of noncompliance; and (2) a Dispute Settlement Body with the power to adjudicate complaints and, if necessary, penalize treaty violators. Faced with the prospect of robust international review and enforcement of TRIPS, WTO members devoted significant time and resources to implementing the treaty's provisions in their national legal systems.[46]

TRIPS' negotiators recognized that the overhaul of domestic intellectual property protection and enforcement rules would be controversial and time-consuming. They thus provided transition periods for least developed nations, developing states, and countries with economies in transition to comply fully with the treaty. More importantly, the negotiators also included provisions – such as compulsory licenses, exceptions to exclusive rights, and parallel importation rules – that allow all WTO members a modicum of flexibility to balance intellectual property protection against other social and economic concerns.[47]

---

[46] *See* Helfer, *Regime Shifting, supra* note 39, at 23.

[47] *See, e.g.,* WIPO, Advice on Flexibilities under the TRIPS Agreement, *available at* http://www.wipo.int/ip-development/en/legislative_assistance/advice_trips.html.

These transition clauses and flexibility provisions softened TRIPS' hard edges. But those edges were quickly sharpened again by the bilateral and regional trade pacts that the United States and European Union negotiated with many developing countries. Commentators refer to these agreements as "TRIPS Plus" treaties because they (1) contain intellectual property protection standards more stringent than those found in TRIPS; (2) oblige developing countries to implement TRIPS fully before the end of its specified transition periods; or (3) require such countries to accede to or conform to the requirements of other multilateral intellectual property agreements.[48] By negotiating with developing nations on a one-on-one basis or in small groups, the United States and European Union sought to "push[] harmonization forward at a pace that is greater than is apparently possible within the framework of the WTO."[49] The result was what some commentators derisively labeled as a "one size ('extra large') fits all" approach to intellectual property protection.[50]

In addition to strengthening intellectual property protection standards and enforcement mechanisms, both TRIPS and TRIPS Plus treaties had another important although less well-known effect: they increased tensions between the international intellectual property regime and other international regimes, including human rights. These tensions had both substantive and procedural dimensions. Substantively, TRIPS and its bilateral and regional offspring required treaty parties to grant intellectual property rights in items such as seeds, plant varieties, and pharmaceuticals that in other international regimes had been placed outside private ownership on moral, cultural, or public health grounds.[51] Procedurally, tensions were engendered

---

[48] Genetic Resources Action International [GRAIN], *"TRIPs-plus" through the Back Door: How Bilateral Treaties Impose Much Stronger Rules for IPRs on Life Than the WTO*, available at http://www.grain.org/docs/trips-plus-en.pdf (July 2001); ORGANIZATION FOR ECONOMIC CO-OPERATION AND DEVELOPMENT, REGIONALISM AND THE MULTILATERAL TRADING SYSTEM 111–22 (2003) [OECD Regionalism Report].

[49] OECD Regionalism Report, *supra* note 48, at 112; *see also* Peter Drahos, *BITs and BIPs*, 4 J. WORLD INTELL. PROP. 791, 792–807 (2001).

[50] James Boyle, *A Manifesto on WIPO and the Future of Intellectual Property*, 2004 DUKE L. & TECH. REV. 9, 3. *But see* Jean-Frédéric Morin, *Multilateralizing TRIPS-Plus Agreements: Is the US Strategy a Failure?*, 12 J. WORLD INTELL. PROP. 175, 177 (2009).

[51] *See, e.g.*, COMM'N ON INTELLECTUAL PROP. RIGHTS, INTEGRATING INTELLECTUAL PROPERTY RIGHTS AND DEVELOPMENT POLICY 59 (2002) (reviewing objections "to the patenting of life forms on ethical grounds" based on the belief that "private ownership of substances created by nature is wrong, and inimical to cultural values in different parts of the world"); CARLOS M. CORREA, TRADE-RELATED ASPECTS OF INTELLECTUAL PROPERTY RIGHTS: A COMMENTARY ON THE TRIPS AGREEMENT 271 (2007) (stating that, prior to 1994, approximately 50 countries did not recognize intellectual property protection for medicines); Sean

by the intellectual property treaties' more stringent enforcement mechanisms as compared to those of treaties outside the WTO – including human rights agreements.[52] These enforcement disparities created an imbalance whereby compliance with the latter set of treaties could be subordinated to compliance with TRIPS and TRIPS Plus treaties in areas where the two international regimes overlapped.

Industrialized countries and their intellectual property industries exacerbated fears of such subordination by filing complaints in the WTO and in national courts that ignored countervailing social and public policies in favor of maximalist conceptions of intellectual property protection. The most infamous examples were (1) a WTO complaint filed by United States alleging that Brazil had violated TRIPS by requiring foreign patent owners to "work" their inventions in Brazil or be subject to compulsory licenses – a provision that the country had adopted to increase access to a new generation of patented drugs used to treat HIV/AIDS; and (2) litigation filed in South Africa by the pharmaceutical industry challenging the Medicines and Related Substances Control Amendment Act, which empowered South Africa's Minister of Health to issue compulsory licenses in response to public health emergencies such as HIV/AIDS.[53]

Both complaints were later withdrawn after sustained public pressure from a broad consortium of civil society groups advocating for access to essential medicines.[54] These public interest NGOs used a diverse array of tools

---

D. Murphy, *Biotechnology and International Law*, 42 HARV. INT'L L.J. 47, 65 (2001) (noting some developing states' "ethical or moral belief" that life-forms "were considered special and different and not reducible to property rights that might be possessed by some and denied to others"); Thammasat Resolution (Dec. 5, 1997), *available at* http://web.greens. org/s-r/16/16–13.html (nonbinding resolution of 45 representatives of indigenous, nongovernmental, academic, and governmental organizations from 19 countries opposing TRIPS' privatization of biodiversity, life-forms, and traditional knowledge).

[52] *See, e.g.*, Oona A. Hathaway, *Do Human Rights Treaties Make a Difference?*, 111 YALE L.J. 1935, 1938, 2008 (2002) (stating that "the major engines of compliance that exist in other areas of international law are for the most part absent in the area of human rights," and describing human rights monitoring systems as "woefully inadequate"); Laurence R. Helfer, *Overlegalizing Human Rights: International Relations Theory and the Commonwealth Caribbean Backlash against Human Rights Regimes*, 102 COLUM. L. REV. 1832, 1856 (2002) (stating that "outside of Europe, [human rights] treaty review procedures are generally weak and only limited opportunities exist to impose direct or indirect sanctions for noncompliance").

[53] We discuss these developments in greater detail in Chapter 2.

[54] *See, e.g.*, Naomi Bass, *Implication of the TRIPS Agreement for Developing Countries: Pharmaceutical Patent Law in Brazil and South Africa in the 21st Century*, 34 GEO. WASH. INT'L L. REV. 191 (2002); Heinz Klug, *Law, Politics and Access to Essential Medicines in*

and strategies to advance their respective interests, including "conferences, high-profile campaigns, appeals to the international media, and outreach through email list services."[55] The NGOs also formed strategic alliances with developing country governments to advance the shared goal of reforming the global intellectual property system. The most well known result of these efforts was the Declaration on the TRIPS Agreement and Public Health,[56] adopted in 2001 as part of the launch of a new round of WTO trade talks in Doha, Qatar. The Declaration asserts that TRIPS "can and should be interpreted and implemented in a manner supportive of WTO Members' right to protect public health and, in particular, to promote access to medicines for all." It reaffirms "the right of WTO Members to use, to the full, the provisions in the TRIPS Agreement, which provide flexibility for this purpose." And it acknowledges the need for incremental adjustments to TRIPS to facilitate exports to countries with insufficient domestic pharmaceutical manufacturing capacity.[57]

In Chapter 2, which concerns patents and the human right to health, we discuss whether the Public Health Declaration has been effective in promoting access to medicines. For purposes of this chapter, the Declaration highlights the fact that a global consensus in favor of strong intellectual property protection rules did not materialize in the decade following the adoption of the TRIPS Agreement. To the contrary, the treaty's merger of trade and intellectual property fostered a growing belief – shared by many developing country governments, civil society groups, and commentators – that TRIPS and its bilateral and regional progeny should be resisted rather than embraced.[58] That resistance was not limited to the issue of patented medicines for pandemic diseases but instead represented a more expansive challenge to the law and politics of international intellectual property, a subject to which we now turn.

Developing Countries, 36 Pol. & Soc. 207 (2008); Susan K. Sell, *TRIPS and the Access to Medicines Campaign*, 20 Wisc. Int'l L.J. 481 (2002).

55 Deere, *supra* note 36, at 131. The civil society groups active in these campaigns included ActionAid, the Consumer Project on Technology (CPTech), the Center for International Environmental Law (CIEL), Health Action International (HAI), the Institute for Agriculture and Trade Policy (IATP), the International Centre for Trade and Sustainable Development (ICTSD), Médecins sans Frontières (MSF), Oxfam International, the Quaker United Nations Office (QUNO), and the Third World Network (TWN). *See id.*

56 WTO, Ministerial Declaration on the TRIPs Agreement and Public Health, WT/MIN(01)/DEC/W/2 (Nov. 14, 2001) [Public Health Declaration].

57 *Id.* paras. 4, 6.

58 Helfer, *Regime Shifting, supra* note 39, at 24 & n.101; Donald P. Harris, *Carrying a Good Joke Too Far: TRIPS and Treaties of Adhesion*, 27 U. Pa. J. Int'l Econ. L. 681 (2006).

4. Access to Knowledge and the New Politics of Intellectual Property

Over the last several years, developing countries and civil society groups have launched a range of new initiatives that seek to realign fundamentally the intellectual property protection rules embodied in TRIPS and TRIPS Plus treaties. These initiatives have been labeled as a "new politics of intellectual property."[59] They include work by "grassroots" political organizations, such as the self-described "Free Culture" movement, whose activities are aimed, in part, at ensuring that assertions of copyrights do not restrict discussion of critical political questions.[60] The emerging right of access to knowledge is a key organizing principle for many of these endeavors.

The rise of the "Creative Commons" licensing project in 2001, for example, can be understood as a response to intellectual property's perceived impact on expressive freedoms and the availability of knowledge and information more generally.[61] Creative Commons offers content producers a range of licenses that accompany dissemination of their works while providing consumers with a greater number of options for using the works than would typically be afforded under the "default" copyright laws. A typical Creative Commons license enables the creator of a work to allow users to make their own derivative works[62] without negotiating a license.[63] This should lower the costs of follow-on creativity.

---

[59] Amy Kapczynski, *The Access to Knowledge Mobilization and the New Politics of Intellectual Property*, 117 YALE L.J. 804 (2008).

[60] The "Free Culture" movement was initially advanced by two college students who founded a group that met regularly to discuss issues of the "intellectual commons." An early controversy involved the posting to an e-mail archive of internal memoranda discussing technical flaws in voting machines produced by Diebold, Inc. (Problems with the machines were also discussed in *American Association of People with Disabilities v. Shelley*, 324 F. Supp. 2d 1120, 1128 [C.D. Cal. 2004] [upholding the decision of the Secretary of State of California to decertify and withdraw approval of some Diebold electronic voting machines on the ground that the machines were not yet "stable, reliable and secure enough to use in the absence of an accessible; voter-verified, paper audit trail"]). To prevent further viewing of the e-mail archive, Diebold sent cease-and-desist letters asserting that the online posting was a breach of its copyright in the memoranda. Eventually, the students litigated and a U.S. District Court held that the firm had knowingly misrepresented its copyright interest. *Online Policy Group v. Diebold, Inc.*, 337 F. Supp. 2d 1195 (N.D. Cal. 2004). *See generally* FreeCulture. org, Free Culture Manifesto, *available at* http://wiki.freeculture.org/wiki.phtml?title=Free_ Culture_Manifesto (last visited Mar. 31, 2010).

[61] *See* Christopher M. Kelty, *Punt to Culture*, 77 ANTHROPOLOGICAL Q. 547, 549 (2004).

[62] For an argument that for U.S. copyright law to be consistent with the First Amendment, copyright owners should be precluded from requiring a license in a wide range of circumstances, see Jed Rubenfeld, *Freedom of Imagination: Copyright's Constitutionality*, 112 YALE L.J. 1 (2002).

[63] *See* Creative Commons, Licenses: Creative Commons Licenses, *available at* http://creative-commons.org/about/licenses/meet-the-licenses (last visited Mar. 31, 2010).

As Amy Kapcynzki recounts, "bottom up" initiatives such as Creative Commons have been accompanied by advocacy for "top down" legal change[64] to prevent further expansion of intellectual property rights, and, in some instances, to roll back existing standards. An important recent initiative along these lines is the "Geneva Declaration on the Future of the World Intellectual Property Organization,"[65] which arose from a 2004 meeting of a variety of advocacy groups, including Creative Commons and other public interest NGOs involved in various "access to knowledge" initiatives. The Geneva Declaration occurred in conjunction with an initiative spearheaded by Argentina and Brazil to have WIPO adopt a "Development Agenda" focused on the concerns of developing countries and urging WIPO to give greater attention to nonproprietary models of innovation.[66]

The Geneva Declaration is a striking illustration of how to employ core institutional principles to foment comprehensive institutional reform. Although the convention establishing WIPO speaks of promoting intellectual property protection on a global basis,[67] there is precedent for interpreting the organization's mandate far more capaciously. In 1974 WIPO entered into an agreement designating it as a specialized agency of the United Nations.[68] Adopted during a period when pressure by newly independent developing countries for a New International Economic Order was at its zenith,[69] the agreement states that WIPO is responsible for "promoting creative intellectual activity and facilitating the transfer of technology ... to developing countries in order to accelerate economic, social and cultural development."[70]

---

[64] Kapczynski, *supra* note 59, at 831.

[65] *See Geneva Declaration on the Future of the World Intellectual Property Organization*, available *at* http://www.cptech.org/ip/wipo/futureofwipodeclaration.pdf [Geneva Declaration].

[66] WIPO General Assembly, *Report of the Twenty-First (15th Extraordinary) Session*, para. 218, WO/GA/31/15 (Oct. 5, 2004), *available at* http://www.cptech.org/ip/wipo/wipo10042004. html. For additional discussion, see Pedro De Paranaguá Moniz, *The Development Agenda for WIPO: Another Stillbirth? A Battle between Access to Knowledge and Enclosure* (2005), *available at* http://papers.ssrn.com/sol3/papers.cfm?abstract_id=844366.

[67] WIPO Convention, *supra* note 20, art. 3(i).

[68] Agreement between the United Nations and the World Intellectual Property Organization art. 1, Dec. 17, 1974, *available at* http://www.wipo.int/treaties/en/agreement/pdf/un_wipo_ agreement.pdf [UN-WIPO Agreement].

[69] As Peter Yu has stated, "The New International Economic Order sought to bring about fundamental changes in the international economic system by redistributing power, wealth, and resources from the developed North to the less developed South." Peter K. Yu, *Currents and Crosscurrents in the International Intellectual Property Regime*, 38 Loy. L.A. L. REV. 323, 409 n.392 (2004) (citing Declaration on the Establishment of a New International Economic Order, G.A. Res. 3201, at 527, U.N. GAOR, 6th Special Sess., Supp. No. 1, U.N. Doc. A/9559 [May 1, 1974]).

[70] UN-WIPO Agreement, *supra* note 68, art. 1.

The Geneva Declaration seizes upon this long-forgotten treaty language to articulate a revised mission for WIPO. It announces that "humanity faces a global crisis in the governance of knowledge, technology and culture," that is manifest in a variety of ways:

- Without access to essential medicines, millions suffer and die;
- Morally repugnant inequality of access to education, knowledge and technology undermines development and social cohesion;
- Anticompetitive practices in the knowledge economy impose enormous costs on consumers and retard innovation;
- Authors, artists and inventors face mounting barriers to follow-on innovation;
- Concentrated ownership and control of knowledge, technology, biological resources, and culture harm development, diversity and democratic institutions;
- Technological measures designed to enforce intellectual property rights in digital environments threaten core exceptions in copyright laws for disabled persons, libraries, educators, authors and consumers and undermine privacy and freedom;
- Key mechanisms to compensate and support creative individuals and communities are unfair to both creative persons and consumers;
- Private interests misappropriate social and public goods and lock up the public domain.[71]

At the same time, the Declaration notes:

There are astoundingly promising innovations in information, medical and other essential technologies, as well as in social movements and business models. We are witnessing highly successful campaigns for access to drugs for AIDS, scientific journals, genomic information and other databases, and hundreds of innovative collaborative efforts to create public goods, including the Internet, the World Wide Web, Wikipedia, the Creative Commons, GNU Linux and other free and open software projects, as well as distance education tools and medical research tools. Technologies such as Google now provide tens of millions with powerful tools to find information. Alternative compensation systems have been proposed to expand access and interest in cultural works, while providing both artists and consumers with efficient and fair systems for compensation. There is renewed interest in compensatory liability rules, innovation prizes, or competitive intermediators, as models for economic incentives for science and technology that can facilitate sequential follow-on innovation and avoid monopolist abuses.[72]

[71] Geneva Declaration, *supra* note 65, at 1.
[72] *Id.*

The document then asks:

> Will we evaluate, learn and profit from the best of these new ideas and oppor-
> tunities, or will we respond to the most unimaginative pleas to suppress all of
> this in favor of intellectually weak, ideologically rigid, and sometimes brutally
> unfair and inefficient policies?[73]

The Geneva Declaration calls for WIPO to revisit the need for uniform domestic intellectual property laws, asserting that a "one size fits all" approach to
intellectual property can lead to unjust and burdensome outcomes for countries "that are struggling to meet the most basic needs of their citizens." The
Declaration also advocates for a moratorium on new treaties and harmonization of intellectual property standards and calls for greater attention to
be given to alternative methods of encouraging and producing innovation.
Supporting WIPO's increasing openness to public interest NGOs, the document also demands that the organization be more responsive to the needs of
developing countries and to "substantive concerns" that include the protection of consumer and human rights.[74]

The Geneva Declaration has engendered several concrete proposals. Among
these is a draft Treaty on Access to Knowledge and Technology (A2K treaty), a
document that has circulated for several years in various institutional and civil
society fora.[75] The draft A2K treaty is a proposal for an interstate agreement.
It is thus "top down" in form, and possibly in aspiration, and it has recently
received the backing of influential developing countries such as Brazil and
India. Even so, the origins of the A2K treaty are firmly rooted in civil society.
Its text is the product of work by a diverse group of public interest NGOs,
whose members include medical researchers, educators, archivists, disabled
people, and librarians from industrialized and developing nations.

The current draft treaty does not specifically invoke the UDHR or other
international human rights instruments. But the draft is partly motivated
by a commitment to the view that "access to knowledge is a basic human
right, and that restrictions on access ought to be the exception, not the other
way around." The objectives of the A2K treaty thus include "protect[ing] and
enhanc[ing] access to knowledge, and ... facilitat[ing] the transfer of technology to developing countries."[76]

---

[73] *Id.*
[74] *Id.* at 2.
[75] *See* Treaty on Access to Knowledge, Draft, May 9, 2005, *available at* http://www.cptech.org/
a2k/a2k_treaty_may9.pdf [A2K].
[76] A2K art. 1(1). For a more detailed discussion of the commonalities between the human
rights and A2K movements, see Molly Beutz Land, *Protecting Rights Online*, 34 Yale J. Int'l
L. 1 (2009).

The document specifically proscribes overriding the treaty's public policy goals by private contract.[77] Its preamble lists those goals as: "enhanc[ing] participation in cultural, civic and educational affairs and sharing the benefits of scientific advancement"; "creat[ing] the broadest opportunities to participate in the development of knowledge resources"; preventing "private misappropriation of social and public knowledge resources"; "protect[ing], preserv[ing] and enhanc[ing] the public domain, which is essential for creativity and sustainable innovation"; and addressing the "concer[n] [that] technological measures that restrict access to knowledge goods will harm authors, libraries, education institutions, archives, and persons with disabilities."[78]

In addition to the draft A2K treaty, WIPO member states have submitted more than 100 proposals to advance one or more of the Geneva Declaration's goals. These proposals have engendered divisions over the scope and pace of the organization's development-related activities. After more than three years of deliberation and debate, the WIPO General Assembly formally adopted a Development Agenda in October 2007.[79] The agenda includes forty-five recommendations organized into six groups or clusters: (1) "technical assistance and capacity building"; (2) "normsetting, flexibilities, public policy and public domain"; (3) "technology transfer, information and communication technologies and access to knowledge"; (4) "assessment, evaluation and impact studies"; (5) "institutional matters including mandate and governance"; and (6) "other issues."[80] The Assembly also created a new Committee on Development and Intellectual Property to be the principal venue for addressing these recommendations, which Peter Yu has described as "cover[ing] reforms that go in two directions."

> One set of recommendations seeks to enhance the development dimension of WIPO and reform the institution itself. Such reform is particularly important in light of the institution's heavy reliance on filing fees from the Patent Cooperation Treaty, the narrow definition of its mandate, and the development of training programs that serve this narrow mandate....
>
> The second set of recommendations focuses on restoring balance in the international intellectual property system. They "call[] into question whether economic development and wealth creation are the sole metrics for measuring development ... [and] put an end to WIPO's monolithic 'IP as power tool of development' approach." Taking advantage of the technical expertise and institutional

---

[77] A2K art. 1(3).
[78] A2K preamble.
[79] Press release, WIPO, Member States Adopt a Development Agenda for WIPO (Oct. 1, 2007), *available at* http://www.wipo.int/pressroom/en/articles/2007/article_0071.html.
[80] WIPO, The 45 Adopted Recommendations under the WIPO Development Agenda, para. 7, *available at* http://www.wipo.int/ip-development/en/agenda/recommendations.html.

legitimacy of WIPO, these recommendations seek to address development-related problems created by the high intellectual property standards of the TRIPs Agreement and the continued push for even higher standards through the TRIPs-plus bilateral and plurilateral trade agreements. The recommendations also underscore the growing interest among less developed countries in obtaining protection for traditional knowledge and cultural expressions.[81]

Yu further notes that "it remains to be seen how effective the agenda will be," in particular whether the recommendations will translate into concrete action.[82] In his October 2009 speech to the General Assembly, WIPO Director General Francis Gurry stressed the need to be "ambitious" in transforming the agenda's core objectives "into an operational reality."[83] One recent example of forward movement is the compromise allowing "negotiations to advance on a possible international agreement on the protection of genetic resources, traditional knowledge, and folklore."[84] Another is the proposal for a treaty on access to copyrighted works for the visually impaired, discussed in Chapter 4.

B. New Developments in Human Rights
While international intellectual property protection rules and enforcement mechanisms were expanding, international human rights law was itself undergoing important transformations. These changes included (1) increased

---

[81] Peter K. Yu, *A Tale of Two Development Agendas*, 35 Ohio N.U. L. Rev. 465, 519–20 (2009) (quoting Neil Weinstock Netanel, *Introduction: The WIPO Development Agenda and Its Development Policy Context*, in Neil Weinstock Netanel (Ed.), The Development Agenda: Global Intellectual Property and Developing Countries 4, 14 (2009) [Development Agenda]).

[82] *Id.* at 521. For two comprehensive recent assessments of the Development Agenda, *see* Jeremy De Beer (Ed.), Implementing WIPO's Development Agenda (2009); Development Agenda, *supra* note 81. In 2007, the Human Rights Commission created a high-level task force on the implementation of the right to development. In 2009, the task force assessed the Development Agenda's contribution to the realization of the right to development. It concluded that the agenda "has enormous potential for advancing the right to development," but that much depends "on implementation which is still in the early stages." Human Rights Council, *Technical mission in order to review the WIPO Development Agenda from the perspective of its contribution to the realization of the right to development*, A/HRC/15/WG.2/TF/CRP.1 (Nov. 19, 2009).

[83] Francis Gurry, Director General, WIPO, *Report of the Director General to the Assemblies of the Member States of WIPO*, September 22 to October 1, 2009, *available at* http://www.wipo.int/meetings/en/2009/a_47/a47_dg_speech.html.

[84] Daniel Pruzin, *WIPO Advances on Global Legal Instrument to Protect Traditional Knowledge, Folklore*, WTO Rptr. (BNA) No. 151 (Aug. 10, 2010). The African Group of WIPO member states referenced human rights instruments in support of its call for a legally binding treaty on these issues. Daniel Pruzin, *WIPO Members Endorse Compromise on Protection of Traditional Knowledge*, WTO Rptr. (BNA) No. 190 (Oct. 5, 2009).

attention to the neglected cultural rights of indigenous communities; (2) efforts to identify the adverse consequences of TRIPS and TRIPS Plus treaties for the realization of economic, social, and cultural rights; (3) a growing recognition of the human rights responsibilities of multinational corporations; and (4) attempts by those same corporations to invoke the human right of property as an alternative legal basis for protecting intellectual property. These four developments, each in its own way, exposed serious normative deficiencies of expansive intellectual property protection rules from a human rights perspective. And they prompted fresh attention to intellectual property issues within the human rights system that increased the points of intersection between the two regimes.

1. The Rights of Indigenous Peoples and Traditional Knowledge

Beginning in the early 1990s, political bodies in the U.N. human rights system[85] began to devote significant attention to the rights of indigenous communities.[86] Among the many claims made by these communities was the right to recognition of and control over their culture, including "traditional knowledge" relating to biodiversity, medicines, and agriculture.[87] TRIPS and national intellectual property laws viewed such knowledge as part of the public domain, either because it did not meet established subject matter criteria or because indigenous communities eschewed its private ownership.[88] By categorizing traditional knowledge as effectively unowned, however, intellectual property rules made it freely available to third parties as upstream inputs for later downstream innovations that were themselves privatized through patents, copyrights, and plant breeders' rights.[89] Adding insult to injury, the financial and technological benefits of downstream innovations were rarely shared with indigenous communities.[90]

---

[85] For a description of these bodies and their functions, see *supra* Part 1.2.

[86] *See* Erica-Irene Daes, *Intellectual Property and Indigenous Peoples*, 95 Am. Soc'y Int'l L. Proc. 143, 147 (2001).

[87] *See, e.g.*, Graham Dutfield, *TRIPS-Related Aspects of Traditional Knowledge*, 33 Case W. Res. J. Int'l L. 233, 234–39 (2001); Srividhya Ragavan, *Protection of Traditional Knowledge*, 2 Minn. Intell. Prop. Rev. 1, 4 (2001); Madhavi Sunder, *The Invention of Traditional Knowledge*, 69 Law & Contemp. Probs. 97, 100–01 (2007).

[88] *See, e.g.*, Dutfield, *supra* note 87, at 238 (stating that "TK [traditional knowledge] is often (and conveniently) assumed to be in the public domain," an assumption that encourages the view "that nobody is harmed and no rules are broken when research institutions and corporations use it freely").

[89] *See* Laurence R. Helfer, Food and Agric. Org. of the U.N., Intellectual Property Rights in Plant Varieties: International Legal Regimes and Policy Options for National Governments 2–3 (2004).

[90] *See* ECOSOC, Sub-Comm'n on Human Rights, *Written Statements Submitted by International Indian Treaty Council* 3, U.N. Doc. E/CN/4/2003/NGO/127 (Mar. 12, 2003). In theory,

U.N. human rights bodies sought to mend this hole in the fabric of intellectual property law by establishing a working group and a special rapporteur to develop a Draft Declaration on the Rights of Indigenous Peoples[91] and Principles and Guidelines for the Protection of the Heritage of Indigenous People.[92] These documents urge states to protect traditional knowledge using legal mechanisms that fit comfortably within existing intellectual property paradigms, such as allowing indigenous communities to seek injunctions and damages for unauthorized uses.[93] But they also define protectable subject matter more broadly than existing intellectual property laws, and they urge states to deny patents, copyrights, and other exclusive rights over "any element of indigenous peoples' heritage" that do not provide for "sharing of ownership, control, use and benefits" with those peoples.[94]

The United Nations Declaration on the Rights of Indigenous Peoples, adopted in September 2007,[95] further expands the interface between the two regimes. Among its thirty-seven articles ranging across the length and breadth of human rights law and beyond,[96] the Declaration includes two

bioprospecting agreements between indigenous groups and private entities in industrialized countries provide a mechanism for benefit sharing. *See* Charles R. McManis, *Intellectual Property, Genetic Resources and Traditional Knowledge Protection: Thinking Globally, Acting Locally* (Univ. of Washington Occasional Papers No. 1, 2003). In practice, however, there are significant impediments to negotiating such agreements. *See* Sabrina Safrin, *Hyperownership in a Time of Biotechnology Promises: The International Conflict to Control the Building Blocks of Life*, 98 Am. J. Int'l L. 641, 657 (2004).

[91] ESOSOC, Sub-Comm'n on Prevention of Discrimination & Prot. of Minorities, *Draft Declaration on the Rights of Indigenous Peoples*, U.N. Doc. E/CN.4/Sub.2/1994/2/Add.1 (Apr. 20, 1994).

[92] *See* ESOSOC, Sub-Comm'n on Prevention of Discrimination & Prot. of Minorities, *Draft Principles and Guidelines for the Protection of the Heritage of Indigenous People, Final Report of the Special Rapporteur*, U.N. Doc. E/CN.4/Sub.2/1995/26, Annex 1 (June 21, 1995) (initial text draft of Principles and Guidelines); ESOSOC, Sub-Comm'n on Prevention of Discrimination & Prot. of Minorities, *Human Rights of Indigenous Peoples: Report of the Seminar on the Draft Principles and Guidelines for the Protection of the Heritage of Indigenous People*, U.N. Doc. E/CN.4/Sub.2/2000/26 (June 19, 2000) (revised text of draft Principles and Guidelines).

[93] ESOSOC, Sub-Comm'n on Promotion & Prot. of Human Rights, *Revised Draft Principles and Guidelines*, § 23(b) (providing that national laws to protect indigenous peoples' heritage should provide means for indigenous peoples to prevent and obtain damages for "the acquisition, documentation or use of their heritage without proper authorization of the traditional owners").

[94] *Id.* § 23(c).

[95] United Nations Declaration on the Rights of Indigenous Peoples, G.A. Res. 61/295, U.N. Doc. A/RES/61/295 (Sept. 13, 2007) [2007 Indigenous Peoples Declaration]; *see* Stefania Errico, *The UN Declaration on the Rights of Indigenous Peoples Is Adopted: An Overview*, 7 Hum. Rts. L. Rev. 756 (2007).

[96] As we discuss more fully in Chapter 7, some of the provisions of the Declaration extend beyond the existing contours of international human rights law. In particular, the Declaration

provisions relating to intellectual property. The first of these, Article 31, contains a capacious description of protectable subject matter and of the rights that the Declaration's beneficiaries enjoy with respect to that subject matter.

> Indigenous peoples have the right to maintain, control, protect and develop their cultural heritage, traditional knowledge and traditional cultural expressions, as well as the manifestations of their sciences, technologies and cultures, including human and genetic resources, seeds, medicines, knowledge of the properties of fauna and flora, oral traditions, literatures, designs, sports and traditional games and visual and performing arts. They also have the right to maintain, control, protect and develop their intellectual property over such cultural heritage, traditional knowledge, and traditional cultural expressions.[97]

The second paragraph of Article 31 directs states, "in conjunction with indigenous peoples," to "take effective measures to recognize and protect the exercise of these rights."[98] In similar fashion, Article 11 of the Declaration directs states to "provide redress through effective mechanisms ... with respect to [indigenous peoples'] intellectual ... property taken without their free, prior and informed consent or in violation of their laws, traditions and customs."[99]

It remains to be seen what effects, if any, these provisions will have. The vote to adopt the Declaration in the General Assembly reveals one source of uncertainty. Although a large majority of U.N. member states voted in favor of the Declaration, Australia, Canada, New Zealand, and the United States – all countries with prominent indigenous communities – voted against the document, and eleven other states abstained. Representatives of Australia, Canada, and New Zealand indicated that concerns about the Declaration's intellectual property provisions were among the reasons that they opposed the document's adoption.[100]

---

may be interpreted as providing a set of guarantees relating to property – including intellectual property – that facilitate the economic development of indigenous communities.

[97] 2007 Indigenous Peoples Declaration, *supra* note 95, art. 31(1).

[98] *Id.* art. 31(2).

[99] *Id.* art. 11(2). In Chapter 7, we analyze the relationship between the enforcement obligations of the Declaration and those of TRIPS.

[100] U.N. GAOR, 61st Sess., 107th plen. mtg. at 11, U.N. Doc. A/61/PV.107 (Sept. 13, 2007), *available at* http://www.un.org/News/Press/docs//2007/ga10612.doc.htm (statement of Ambassador Robert Hill, Permanent Representative of Australia) (stating that Australia "did not support the inclusion of intellectual property rights for indigenous peoples" and that "in seeking to give indigenous people exclusive rights over property, both intellectual, real and cultural, the Declaration did not acknowledge the rights of third parties ... under national law"); *id.* at 12–13 (statement of Ambassador John McNee, Permanent Representative of Canada) (describing Canada's "significant concerns with the wording of the current text, including provisions on ... prior and informed consent when used as a veto [and on] intellectual property"); Rosemary Banks, New Zealand Permanent Representative

A second source of uncertainty relates to the legal status of the Declaration. All observers agree that the Declaration does not itself create legally binding obligations. What remains contested, however, is whether certain parts of the document are declarative of customary international law and, if they are not, whether the document will or should influence the development of such rules through future state practice and *opinio juris.*[101] As we explain in the next section, similar anxieties about the relationship between soft and hard law pervade analyses of whether TRIPS has adverse consequences for the realization of economic, social, and cultural rights.

2. Conflicts between TRIPS and Economic, Social, and Cultural Rights
The U.N. human rights system first turned its attention to TRIPS in 2000. In July of that year, the Sub-Commission on the Promotion and Protection of Human Rights received a statement from a consortium of public interest NGOs that forcefully challenged the treaty's compatibility with international human rights law.[102] The consortium's views colored the debate on the topic in the Sub-Commission, a debate that later resulted in the unanimous adoption of a resolution on "Intellectual Property Rights and Human Rights."[103] The resolution is highly critical of TRIPS. It states that "actual or potential conflicts exist between the implementation of" the treaty "and the realization of economic, social and cultural rights."[104] These conflicts cut across an exceptionally wide swath of legal terrain, including:

to the United Nations, Explanation of Vote on Declaration of the Rights of Indigenous Peoples (Sept. 13, 2007), *available at* http://www.mfat.govt.nz/Media-and-publications/Media/MFAT-speeches/2007/0–13-September-2007.php (stating that "we also have concerns about Article 31 concerning intellectual property").

[101] *See* Christopher J. Fromherz, Comment, *Indigenous Peoples' Courts: Egalitarian Juridical Pluralism, Self-Determination, and the United Nations Declaration on the Rights of Indigenous Peoples*, 156 U. Pa. L. Rev. 1341, 1343 (2008). Rules that states implicitly accept as legally binding may develop into customary international law. For further discussion, see *supra* note 7.

[102] ECOSOC, Comm'n on Human Rights, Statement of Lutheran World Fed'n, Habitat Int'l Coalition, & the Int'l NGO Comm. on Human Rights in Trade and Investment, *The Realization of Economic, Social and Cultural Rights*, U.N. Doc. E/CN.4/Sub.2/2000/NGO/14 (July 28, 2002) (urging the Sub-Commission to "reassert the primacy of human rights obligations over the commercial and profit-driven motives upon which agreements such as TRIPS are based"). For a more detailed discussion, see David Weissbrodt & Kell Schoff, *A Human Rights Approach to Intellectual Property Protection: The Genesis and Application of Sub-Commission Resolution 2000/7*, 5 Minn. Intell. Prop. Rev. 1, 26–27 (2003).

[103] ESOSOC, Sub-Comm'n on Promotion & Prot. of Human Rights, *Intellectual Property Rights and Human Rights*, Res. 2000/7, U.N. Doc. E/CN.4/Sub.2/RES/2000/7 (Aug. 17, 2000) [Resolution 2000/7].

[104] *Id.* at pmbl. para. 11.

impediments to the transfer of technology to developing countries, the consequences for the enjoyment of the right to food of plant variety rights and the
patenting of genetically modified organisms, "bio-piracy"[105] and the reduction
of communities' (especially indigenous communities') control over their own
genetic and natural resources and cultural values, and restrictions on access to
patented pharmaceuticals and the implications for the enjoyment of the right
to health.[106]

To resolve these conflicts, the Sub-Commission urged states, intergovernmental organizations, and NGOs to recognize that human rights have
"primacy ... over economic policies and agreements."[107] This assertion of
preeminence had no immediate legal consequences, however, because the
Sub-Commission's resolutions are, by their own terms, nonbinding. Nor did
the Sub-Commission attempt to parse treaty texts to identify the specific
(and legally binding) human rights obligations that TRIPS violates. The resolution's principal objective was instead to launch an ambitious new agenda
for the review of intellectual property issues within the U.N. human rights
system, an agenda animated by the principle of human rights primacy.

In the decade since the resolution's adoption, the response to the
Sub-Commission's invitation has been nothing short of overwhelming.
U.N. human rights bodies have produced numerous resolutions, reports,
comments, and statements, and taken a variety of other actions relating
to TRIPS and to intellectual property protection rules more generally. We
analyze in detail many of these documents and actions in later chapters.
Here, we simply list the most significant documents and events and briefly
describe their contents to give readers a flavor of the breadth and depth of the
responses engendered by the Sub-Commission's initial foray into intellectual
property issues:

- Resolutions by the Commission on Human Rights urging states to
  ensure "Access to Medication in the Context of Pandemics such as HIV/
  AIDS, Tuberculosis and Malaria;"[108]

---

[105] The term "biopiracy" has been used to describe any act by which a commercial entity obtains
intellectual property rights over biological resources that are seen as "belonging" to developing states or indigenous communities. CEAS Consultants (Wye) Ltd, Ctr. for European
Agric. Studies, *Final Report for DG TRADE Eur. Comm.: Study on the Relationship between
the Agreement on TRIPS and Biodiversity Related Issues* 78 (2000).

[106] Resolution 2000/7, *supra* note 103, pmbl. para. 11; *see also id.* para. 2 (identifying conflicts
between TRIPS and "the right of everyone to enjoy the benefits of scientific progress and its
applications, the right to health, the right to food and the right to self-determination").

[107] *Id.* para. 3.

[108] *See* Comm'n on Human Rights, Res. 2003/29, U.N. Doc. E/CN.4/RES/2003/29 (Apr. 22,
2003); Comm'n on Human Rights, Res. 2001/33, U.N. Doc. E/CN.4/RES/2001/33 (Apr.

- A detailed analysis of TRIPS by the U.N. High Commissioner for Human Rights, which asserts that intellectual property laws must promote access to knowledge and innovations, opposes TRIPS Plus treaties, and emphasizes states' obligations to provide access to essential medicines to treat HIV/AIDS;[109]
- A report by two Special Rapporteurs on Globalization, which asserts that intellectual property protection undermines human rights objectives;[110]
- A resolution by the Sub-Commission that identifies a widening set of conflicts between TRIPS and human rights, including "the rights to self-determination, food, housing, work, health and education, and ... transfers of technology to developing countries;"[111]
- An effort (thus far unsuccessful) by the U.N. High Commissioner for Human Rights to seek observer status with the WTO to participate in reviews of TRIPS;[112]
- A report by the U.N. Secretary General on intellectual property and human rights based on information submitted by states, intergovernmental organizations, and public interest NGOs;[113]

23, 2001); Comm'n on Human Rights, Res. 2002/32, U.N. Doc. E/CN.4/RES/2002/32 (Apr. 22, 2002); *see also* Human Rights Council, Res. 12/24, U.N. Doc. A/HRC/RES/12/24 (Oct. 2, 2009), para. 2 (emphasizing "the responsibility of States to ensure access to all, without discrimination, of medicines, in particular essential medicines, that are affordable, safe, effective and of good quality"); *Human Rights Commission Calls on States to Use TRIPS Flexibilities*, BRIDGES WKLY. TRADE NEWS DIG. (Switz.), Apr. 20, 2005, at 5. The first resolution, sponsored by Brazil in 2001, mandates that states, in implementing the right to the highest attainable standard of health, "adopt legislation or other measures, in accordance with applicable international law" to "safeguard access" to such medications "from any limitations by third parties." Comm'n on Human Rights, Res. 2001/33, para. 3(b).

[109] Comm'n on Human Rights, *Report of the High Commissioner on the Impact of the Agreement on Trade-Related Aspects of Intellectual Property Rights on Human Rights*, paras. 10–15, 27–58, U.N. Doc. E/CN.4/Sub.2/2001/13 (June 27, 2001) [*High Commissioner Report*].

[110] ECOSOC, Sub-Comm'n on the Promotion and Prot. of Human Rights, *Globalization and Its Impact on the Full Enjoyment of Human Rights*, paras. 19–34, U.N. Doc. E/CN.4/Sub.2/2001/10 (Aug. 2, 2001) (prepared by J. Oloka-Onyango & Deepika Udagama) [*Globalization Report*].

[111] ECOSOC, Sub-Comm'n on the Promotion and Prot. of Human Rights, *Intellectual Property and Human Rights*, Res. 2001/21, U.N. Doc. E/CN.4/Sub.2/RES/2001/21 (Aug. 16, 2001) (identifying "actual or potential conflicts" between human rights obligations and TRIPS, and asserting "need to clarify the scope and meaning of several provisions of the TRIPS Agreement").

[112] *See High Commissioner Report*, *supra* note 109, para. 68; *see also* WTO, International Intergovernmental Organizations Granted Observer Status to WTO Bodies, *available at* http://www.wto.org/english/thewto_e/igo_obs_e.htm (last visited Mar. 31, 2010).

[113] The Secretary-General, *Report of the Secretary-General on Economic, Social and Cultural Rights, Intellectual Property Rights and Human Rights*, U.N. Doc. E/CN.4/Sub.2/2001/12 (June 14, 2001).

- A "Statement on Human Rights and Intellectual Property" adopted by the Committee on Economic, Social and Cultural Rights (CESCR Committee), which asserts that intellectual property rights "must be balanced with the right to take part in cultural life and to enjoy the benefits of scientific progress and its applications," and that "national and international intellectual property regimes must be consistent with" the obligation of states parties set forth in the ICESCR;[114]
- A CESCR Committee *General Comment* interpreting ICESCR Article 15.1(c) – "the right of everyone to benefit from the protection of the moral and material interests resulting from any scientific, literary or artistic production of which he is the author;"[115]
- The publication of Human Rights Guidelines for Pharmaceutical Companies in Relation to Access to Medicines, which asserts that such companies "have human rights responsibilities in relation to access to medicines" and urges them to "make and respect a public commitment not to lobby for more demanding protection of intellectual property interests than those required by TRIPS;"[116]
- Reports by Special Rapporteurs on the Right to Food that criticize the use of patents to control the quality, supply, and price of plant materials, including genetically modified seeds;[117] and

---

[114] ECOSOC, Comm. on Econ., Soc. & Cultural Rights, *Substantive Issues Arising in the Implementation of the International Covenant on Economic, Social and Cultural Rights*, U.N. Doc. E/C12/2001/15 (Dec. 14, 2001) [*Statement on Human Rights and Intellectual Property*].

[115] Comm. Econ., Soc. & Cultural Rights, *General Comment No. 17: The Right of Everyone to Benefit from the Protection of the Moral and Material Interests Resulting from Any Scientific, Literary or Artistic Production of Which He Is the Author*, art. 15(1)(c), U.N. Doc. E/C.12/GC/17 (Jan. 12, 2006) [*General Comment No. 17*]. In May 2008, the CESCR Committee held a day of discussion devoted to Article 15(1)(a) of the Covenant, which protects the right to take part in cultural life. Several of the background papers and submissions from experts referenced intellectual property. *See* Comm. on Econ., Soc. & Cultural Rights, *Day of General Discussion on "The right to take part in cultural life"* (May 9, 2008), available at http://www2.ohchr.org/english/bodies/cescr/discussion 090508.htm.

[116] U.N. Special Rapporteur on the Right of Everyone to the Enjoyment of the Highest Attainable Standard of Physical and Mental Health, *Human Rights Guidelines for Pharmaceutical Companies in Relation to Access to Medicines*, UN Doc. A/63/263, pmbl. para. i & Guideline 26 (Aug. 11, 2008) (prepared by Paul Hunt) [*Pharmaceutical Company Guidelines*].

[117] *See, e.g.,* U.N. Special Rapporteur on the Right to Food, Report to U.N. General Assembly, U.N. Doc. A/64/170 (July 23, 2009) (prepared by Olivier De Schutter); U.N. Special Rapporteur of the Commission on Human Rights on the Right to Food, *Report to Commission on Human Rights*, U.N. Doc. E/CN.4/2004/10, para. 39 (Feb. 9, 2004) (prepared by Jean Ziegler).

- Concluding observations and recommendations by U.N. human rights treaty bodies concerning the compatibility of national intellectual property laws and policies with states parties' human rights treaty obligations.[118]

Several of these resolutions, reports, and studies contain trenchant critiques of TRIPS, of TRIPS Plus treaties, and of expansive intellectual property protection rules more generally. Others contain detailed textual analyses of human rights treaty provisions. And still other documents assess the empirical effects of intellectual property protection on specific human rights, with special emphasis on the right to health in the context of global pandemics such as HIV/AIDS.[119] Without exception, however, none of these documents is legally binding.

Why would U.N. expert and political bodies devote such extensive efforts to generating a surfeit of nonbinding norms? Efforts to counter the expansion of intellectual property protection rules in TRIPS and TRIPS Plus treaties provide one plausible answer. Actors seeking to contest or roll back this expansion must identify with precision the competing rules that conflict or are at least in tension with these treaties. One way to create such oppositional rules is by drafting new international agreements. But treaties often require protracted and time-consuming negotiations, and even when such negotiations occur they often produce legal rules that are ambiguous or articulated at a high level of generality. For this reason, states, public interest NGOs, and independent experts have turned to the faster, more fluid (and, some would argue, less accountable) mechanisms of soft lawmaking to bolster claims that expansive intellectual property protection rules are inconsistent with human rights.[120]

---

[118] *See, e.g.,* 3D – Trade Human Rights Equitable Economy, *UN Human Rights Treaty Monitoring Bodies Review of State Implementation of International Conventions (ICESCR, ICCPR and CRC): References to Intellectual Property and Human Rights, available at* http://www.3dthree.org/pdf_3D/TreatyBodyIPrefs_en.pdf.

[119] *See, e.g., High Commissioner Report, supra* note 109, para. 15 (stressing need for TRIPS to "be assessed empirically to determine the effects of the Agreement on human rights in practice"); *General Comment No. 17, supra* note 115, paras. 6–46 (setting forth comprehensive analysis of ICESCR Article 15.1(c)); *Globalization Report, supra* note 110, paras. 19–34 (critiquing TRIPS and international trade rules generally).

[120] The development of nonbinding human rights norms relating to intellectual property is a specific example of a broader phenomenon in the international human rights regime. According to Professor Dinah Shelton, the expanding universe of "soft" human rights norms can be divided into two categories – primary and secondary. Primary soft law encompasses "those normative texts not adopted in treaty form that are addressed to the international community as a whole or to the entire membership of the adopting institution or

The incentive to generate soft law is especially acute for human rights treaties such as the ICESCR that contain many open-textured and vague provisions. Viewed solely at the level of treaty text, it would be difficult to find any clear incompatibility between the Covenant, on the one hand, and TRIPS or its bilateral progeny, on the other. Yet treaty text alone does not exhaust the potential for such conflicts. Human rights treaties establish other mechanisms – such as *General Comments* and individual complaint mechanisms – that lead to the development of more precise and exacting legal norms over time. These treaty-based processes are supplemented by myriad political and expert human rights mechanisms established under the auspices of the U.N. Charter. When acting in concert, these treaty and Charter-based mechanisms can rapidly develop a body of interpretive norms that create widely shared expectations as to the meaning of particular human rights. As a formal matter, the norms that generate these expectations occupy a "twilight zone of normativity" that falls short of legally binding obligations.[121] But as the number, density, and specificity of the norms increase, it becomes progressively more difficult for states, nonstate actors, and international organizations to contest their validity.

3. The Human Rights Obligations of Transnational Corporations

The growing number of resolutions, recommendations, reports, and other nonbinding analyses of intellectual property issues in the U.N. human rights system can be traced to another source – attempts to extend human rights standards to transnational corporations and other business entities. Since its inception at the end of the Second World War, international human rights law has been principally concerned with the activities of states, governments, and public officials. But the increasingly pervasive activities of multinational corporations, together with the inadequacies of traditional public

---

organization. Such an instrument may declare new norms, often as an intended precursor to adoption of a later treaty, or it may reaffirm or further elaborate norms previously set forth in binding or non-binding texts." Dinah Shelton, *Commentary and Conclusions*, in DINAH SHELTON (ED.), COMMITMENT AND COMPLIANCE: THE ROLE OF NON–BINDING NORMS IN THE INTERNATIONAL LEGAL SYSTEM 449, 449–50 (2000). Professor Shelton describes secondary soft law as including "the recommendations and general comments of international human rights supervisory organs, the jurisprudence of courts and commissions, decisions of special rapporteurs and other ad hoc bodies, and the resolutions of political organs of international organizations applying primary norms. Most of this secondary soft law is pronounced by institutions whose existence and jurisdiction are derived from a treaty and who apply norms contained in the same treaty." *Id.* at 452.

[121] Peter Drahos, *Intellectual Property and Human Rights*, 3 INTELL. PROP. Q. 349, 361 (1999).

law regulation of those activities, have generated several initiatives focusing on private actors. These initiatives have special significance for intellectual property rights, whose substantive scope and enforcement in national legal systems are heavily influenced by lobbying and litigation by private firms in the innovation, entertainment, and content industries.

Efforts to subject the activities of these businesses to human rights scrutiny have proceeded along two distinct axes: first, interpreting the treaty-based obligations of states to include a duty to prevent and remedy violations by private actors subject to the state's jurisdiction; and second, developing principles to hold corporations and other business entities directly responsible for violating certain human rights.

The *General Comments* of the CESCR Committee illustrate the first of these developments. In an attempt to elaborate Covenant rights with greater precision, the Committee has developed a tripartite framework of duties for all states parties – the obligation to "respect," the obligation to "protect," and the obligation to "fulfill."[122] Whereas the obligations to respect and fulfill target government actors, the obligation to protect requires states to prevent nonstate actors from interfering with economic, social, and cultural rights. In its 2000 *General Comment on the Right to the Highest Attainable Standard of Health*,[123] the Committee offered a detailed exegesis of the obligation to protect as applied to this right:

> Violations of the obligation to protect follow from the failure of a State to take all necessary measures to safeguard persons within their jurisdiction from infringements of the right to health by third parties. This category includes such omissions as the failure to regulate the activities of individuals, groups or corporations so as to prevent them from violating the right to health of others; [and] the failure to protect consumers ... from practices detrimental to health, e.g. by ... manufacturers of medicines.[124]

Inasmuch as "only States are parties to the Covenant and thus ultimately accountable for compliance with it," the *General Comment* did not address whether businesses and other private actors have independent human rights duties. The Committee merely asserted in passing that "all members of society – [including] the private business sector – have responsibilities regarding the realization of the right to health."[125]

---

[122] Michael J. Dennis & David P. Stewart, *Justiciability of Economic, Social, and Cultural Rights: Should There Be an International Complaints Mechanism to Adjudicate the Rights to Food, Water, Housing, and Health?*, 98 Am. J. Int'l L. 462, 491 (2004).

[123] Comm. on Econ., Soc., & Cultural Rights, *General Comment No. 14 – the Right to the Highest Attainable Standard of Health*, para. 43, U.N. Doc. E/C.12/2000/4 (Aug. 11, 2000).

[124] *Id.* para. 51.

[125] *Id.* para. 42.

Since the *General Comment*'s adoption, NGOs, shareholders, consumers, and some governments have increasingly pressured U.N. bodies to address this issue. In 2003, the Sub-Commission issued the Draft Norms on the Responsibilities of Transnational Corporations and Other Business Enterprises with Regard to Human Rights.[126] The Draft Norms were expressly nonbinding. But they attempted to articulate a comprehensive and authoritative statement of the human rights obligations of corporations within their "spheres of activity and influence."[127]

The Draft Norms did not expressly address intellectual property issues. But the commentary that accompanied them did, providing that businesses "shall respect, protect and apply intellectual property rights in a manner that contributes to the promotion of technological innovation and to the transfer and dissemination of technology, to the mutual advantage of producers and users of technological knowledge, in a manner conducive to social and economic welfare, such as the protection of public health, and to a balance of rights and obligations."[128] This provision closely tracks the language of TRIPS Article 7.[129]

Although the Draft Norms generated considerable public and scholarly commentary, the U.N. Human Rights Commission declined to adopt them, in part because of opposition from business interests.[130] Instead, in 2005 the Commission requested that the U.N. Secretary General appoint a special representative to examine the international legal responsibilities of corporations and the concept of corporate "spheres of influence."[131] After extensive

---

[126] ECOSOC, Sub-Comm'n on Promotion and Prot. of Human Rights, *Draft Norms on the Responsibilities of Transnational Corporations and Other Business Enterprises with Regard to Human Rights*, U.N. Doc. E/CN.4/Sub.2/2003/12/Rev.2 (Aug. 26, 2003).

[127] *Id.* para. 1 (stating that "within their respective spheres of activity and influence, transnational corporations and other business enterprises have the obligation to promote, secure the fulfillment of, respect, ensure respect of, and protect human rights recognized in international as well as national law").

[128] ECOSOC, Sub-Comm'n on Promotion and Prot. of Human Rights, *Commentary on the Norms on the Responsibilities of Transnational Corporations and Other Business Enterprises with Regard to Human Rights*, para. 10 cmt. d, U.N. Doc. E/CN.4/Sub.2/2003/38/Rev.2 (Aug. 26, 2003).

[129] TRIPS Agreement, *supra* note 3, art. 7 ("The protection and enforcement of intellectual property rights should contribute to the promotion of technological innovation and to the transfer and dissemination of technology, to the mutual advantage of producers and users of technological knowledge and in a manner conducive to social and economic welfare, and to a balance of rights and obligations.").

[130] *See* David Kinley & Rachel Chambers, *The UN Human Rights Norms for Corporations: The Private Implications of Public International Law*, 6 HUM. RTS. L. REV. 447, 462–78 (2006) (discussing responses to the draft norms).

[131] Comm'n on Human Rights Res. 2005/69, U.N. Doc. E/CN.4/RES/2005/69 (Apr. 20, 2005). The secretary-general appointed John Ruggie, a professor at Harvard University's John F. Kennedy School of Government, to serve as the special representative.

consultations with interested stakeholders, the special representative published a report in April 2008 setting forth

> a conceptual and policy framework to anchor the business and human rights debate, and to help guide all relevant actors. The framework comprises three core principles: [1] the State duty to protect against human rights abuses by third parties, including business; [2] the corporate responsibility to respect human rights; and [3] the need for more effective access to remedies.[132]

In June 2008 the Human Rights Council (the successor to the Human Rights Commission) endorsed this tripartite framework and renewed the special representative's mandate for an additional three years. The Council has asked the special representative, *inter alia*, to recommend "ways to strengthen the fulfillment of the duty of the State to protect all human rights from abuses by transnational corporations and other business enterprises" and "elaborate further on the scope and content of the corporate responsibility to respect all human rights" by providing "concrete guidance to business and other stakeholders."[133]

Other actors in the U.N. human rights system quickly built upon the foundation laid by the special representative. In August 2008, the Special Rapporteur on the Right to Health published Human Rights Guidelines for Pharmaceutical Companies in relation to Access to Medicines.[134] In addition to explaining why such firms "have human rights responsibilities in relation to access to medicines," the Guidelines seek to "provide practical, constructive and specific guidance to pharmaceutical companies and other interested parties, including those who wish to monitor companies and hold them to account."[135] Although the Special Rapporteur sought input from all interested parties in formulating the Guidelines, most drug companies characterized the effort as "misguided," impractical, and "an undue burden on companies."[136]

---

[132] Special Representative of the Secretary-General on the Issue of Human Rights and Transnational Corporations and Other Business Enterprises (John Ruggie), *Protect, Respect and Remedy: A Framework for Business and Human Rights*, summary, U.N. Doc. A/HRC/8/5 (Apr. 7, 2008).

[133] Human Rights Council Res. A/HRC/8/L.8 (June 12, 2008).

[134] *Pharmaceutical Company Guidelines, supra* note 116.

[135] *Id.* at 15, 11.

[136] Letter from Jeffrey Sturchio, Merck & Co., to U.N. Special Rapporteur on the Right to Health (Feb. 29, 2008) (concerning UN draft guidelines for pharmaceutical companies on access to medicines), *available at* http://www.reports-and-materials.org/Merck-response-to-UN-Special-Rapporteur-Hunt-29-Feb-2008.pdf; *see also Pharmaceutical Company Guidelines, supra* note 116, at 8–10 (describing refusal of most pharmaceutical companies to participate in the development or drafting of the guidelines).

One basis for the companies' objection was that the Guidelines "could have the unintended consequence of supporting arguments for weakening intellectual property protection."[137] Seven of the Guideline's forty-seven articles address "patents and licensing." A few provisions urge drug companies to respect the right of states to protect public health and to utilize TRIPS flexibility provisions to promote access to medicines. These recommendations seek to apply to the pharmaceutical industry the consensus views of WTO members set forth in the Doha Declaration on TRIPS and Public Health.[138] Other intellectual property-related clauses in the Guidelines are more novel. They include recommendations that drug companies "make and respect a public commitment not to lobby for more demanding protection of intellectual property interests than those required by TRIPS"; not pressure least-developed nations "to grant or enforce patents"; waive test data exclusivity in such countries; issue "non-exclusive voluntary licenses" to increase access to medicines in low-income and middle-income countries; and refrain from "apply[ing] for patents for insignificant or trivial modifications of existing medicines" in such countries.[139] If adopted, these recommendations would negate many of the additional intellectual property protections that drug companies lobbied industrialized nations to secure by means of TRIPS Plus treaties.

4. The Human Right of Property and Corporate Intellectual Property Interests

The fourth contribution to the expanding interface of human rights and intellectual property involves claims by corporations that invoke the right of property – a right included in the UDHR and in several regional human rights conventions but not in the two U.N. Covenants.[140] This development differs from the three analyzed earlier in at least two respects. First, corporations and other business entities – not natural persons or groups of such persons – are the alleged victims. These corporate entities claim that restrictions on vested intellectual property interests should be analyzed in the same way as expropriations of real or tangible property. Second, all of the three previously described developments share a focus on remedying the adverse consequences of expansive intellectual property protection.

---

[137] Letter from Jeffrey Sturchio, *supra* note 136, at 2.
[138] Public Health Declaration, *supra* note 56.
[139] *Pharmaceutical Company Guidelines, supra* note 116, at 21–22 (Guidelines 26 through 32).
[140] The right of property is protected, in various forms, in the following treaties: Article 17 of the UDHR; Article 5(d)(v) of the International Convention on the Elimination of All Forms of Racial Discrimination; Article 1 of Protocol No. 1 to the European Convention on Human Rights; Article 21 of the American Convention on Human Rights; and Article 4 of the African Charter on Human and Peoples' Rights.

Claims involving corporate property violations, by contrast, allege that human rights law requires *more extensive* protection of inventions, trademarks, and creative works. As we discuss in extensive detail in Chapter 3, corporations do not, according to the emerging jurisprudence, possess the right to benefit from the moral and material interests of creators, a right that is recognized in both the UDHR and the ICESCR. This exclusion makes the right of property especially salient in the context of corporate ownership of intellectual property.

Protecting the intellectual property of corporations under the rubric of fundamental rights may strike many observers as fundamentally misguided. But the text and drafting history of several human rights treaties reveal a desire to protect the possessory interests of both business entities and natural persons.[141] In particular, the treaties' drafters understood that the rule of law in general and the stability and predictability of property rights in particular would be undermined if governments could arbitrarily deprive any class of owners of their possessions, although they also recognized that states should have considerable leeway to adopt and modify economic and social policies that adversely affect private property interests.[142]

Building upon these arguments, the human right of property has been invoked in a variety of venues to support the protection of intellectual property. These venues include treaties,[143] EU directives,[144] judgments of the European

---

[141] *See, e.g.,* European Convention for the Protection of Human Rights and Fundamental Freedoms, Protocol No. 1, art. 1, Nov. 4, 1950, 213 U.N.T.S. 221 [Protocol No. 1] ("Every natural *or legal person* is entitled to the peaceful enjoyment of his possessions") (emphasis added); ALI RIZA ÇOBAN, PROTECTION OF PROPERTY RIGHTS WITHIN THE EUROPEAN CONVENTION ON HUMAN RIGHTS 35–77 (2004) (reviewing justifications for including the right of property in international human rights agreements).

[142] *See* MARIUS EMBERLAND, THE HUMAN RIGHTS OF COMPANIES: EXPLORING THE STRUCTURE OF ECHR PROTECTION 44 (2006) ("The rule of law also helps explain why corporate persons enjoy ECHR protection."); Laurence R. Helfer, *The New Innovation Frontier? Intellectual Property and the European Court of Human Rights,* 49 HARV. INT'L L.J. 1, 7–8, 36–37 (2008) (analyzing different rationales for protecting property interests of corporations and other business entities in the European human rights system).

[143] *See* Charter of Fundamental Rights of the European Union art. 17, 2000 O.J. (C 364) 1 ("Everyone has the right to own, use, dispose of and bequeath his or her lawfully acquired possessions.... Intellectual property shall be protected."), *available at* http://www.europarl. europa.eu/charter/pdf/text_en.pdf. For a critical analysis, see Christophe Geiger, *Intellectual Property Shall be Protected!? – Article 17 (2) of the Charter of Fundamental Rights of the European Union: A Mysterious Provision with an Unclear Scope,* 31 EUR. INTELL. PROP. REV. 113, 115 (2009) (arguing that the intellectual property provision of the Charter "is ambiguous and can consequently easily lead to abusive interpretation").

[144] *See, e.g.,* Council Directive 2004/48, 2004 O.J. (L. 157) 45, recital 32 ("this Directive seeks to ensure full respect for intellectual property, in accordance with Article 17 (2) of th[e] Charter [of Fundamental Rights of the European Union]").

Court of Human Rights,[145] national court rulings in Europe[146] and the United States,[147] international negotiations,[148] and academic commentary.[149]

Some scholars fear that these arguments will enable corporate intellectual property owners to secure greater legal protection for inventions, trademarks, and creative works than they could obtain from the existing intellectual property regime. In particular, these commentators warn that "the embrace of [IP] by human rights advocates and entities ... is likely to further entrench some dangerous ideas about property: in particular, that property rights as human rights ought to be inviolable and ought to receive extremely solicitous attention from the international community."[150] Other scholars disagree,

[145] *See, e.g., Anheuser-Busch Inc. v. Portugal,* No. 73049/01 (Eur. Ct. H.R. Grand Chamber Jan. 11, 2007) (holding that the right to "peaceful enjoyment of ... possessions" in Article 1 of Protocol No. 1 to the European Convention on Human Rights includes trademarks and trademark applications), *available at* http://cmiskp.echr.coe.int/tkp197/view.asp?item=1&portal=hbkm&action=html&highlight=73049/01&sessionid=50183840&skin=hudoc-en.

[146] *See, e.g.,* Joseph Straus, *Design Protection for Spare Parts Gone in Europe? Proposed Changes to the EC Directive: The Commission's Mandate and Its Doubtful Execution,* 27 EUR. INTELL. PROP. REV. 391, 398 (2005) (discussing 2000 decision of the Federal Constitutional Court holding that patents constitute property under the German Constitution); Thomas Crampton, *Apple Gets French Support in Music Compatibility Case,* N.Y. TIMES, July 29, 2006, at C9 (discussing a ruling of the French Constitutional Council, the country's highest judicial body, which "declared major aspects of the so-called iPod law unconstitutional" and "made frequent reference to the 1789 Declaration on Human Rights and concluded that the law violated the constitutional protections of property").

[147] *See, e.g., Zoltek Corp. v. United States,* 442 F.3d 1345 (Fed. Cir. 2006) (rejecting a claim that the federal government's uncompensated use of a patent amounts to a taking of private property in violation of the U.S. Constitution), *reh'g denied,* 464 F.3d 1335 (Fed. Cir. 2006).

[148] *See, e.g.,* Third World Network, Statement at the Third Intersessional Intergovernmental Meeting (July 22, 2005), *available at* http://lists.essential.org/pipermail/a2k/2005-July/000539.html (challenging the claim by a pro-IP business NGO that "IP rights have been recognized as human rights" as "a misreading of the existing international conventions").

[149] *See, e.g.,* Hoe Lim, *Trade and Human Rights: What's at Issue?* (Working Paper submitted to Comm. on Econ., Soc. and Cultural Rights), U.N. Doc. No. E/C.12/2001/WP.2 (Apr. 10, 2001), *available at* http://www.unhchr.ch/tbs/doc.nsf/0/907f88e4d28e4cb9c1256a63003069fd?Opendocument (asserting that ICESCR Article 15(1)(c) protects "the human right to intellectual property protection"); Adam Mossoff, *Exclusion and Exclusive Use in Patent Law,* 22 HARV. J. L. & TECH. 321 (2009); Robert L. Ostergard Jr., *Intellectual Property: A Universal Human Right?,* 21 HUM. RTS. Q. 156, 175 (1999) ("The basis for such a claim without doubt lies in the Western conception of property rights."); Mary W. S. Wong, *Toward an Alternative Normative Framework for Copyright: From Private Property to Human Rights,* 26 CARDOZO ARTS & ENT. L.J. 775, 810 (2009) (identifying one argument for treating intellectual property as a human right as follows: "insofar as property ownership is a fundamental human right, since intellectual property is property and IPRs are property rights, it follows that IPRs are also human rights").

[150] Kal Raustiala, *Density and Conflict in International Intellectual Property Law,* 40 U.C. DAVIS L. REV. 1021, 1032 (2007); *see also* Ruth Okediji, *Securing Intellectual Property*

reasoning that the human right of property, as applied to intellectual property, does not "protect the unqualified property-based interests in intellectual creations," but rather is limited to ensuring "the narrow interest of just remuneration for intellectual labor."[151]

The empirical record does not yet provide sufficient evidence to evaluate decisively these contending views. What is certain, however, is that state and nonstate actors will continue to raise human rights arguments to support and oppose particular intellectual property protection rules and enforcement mechanisms. The analysis of these competing claims is the subject of the next section.

1.6. Competing Conceptual Frameworks for Mapping the Interface of Human Rights and Intellectual Property

Over the last several years, commentators in law and political science have noted the rapid expansion of the intellectual property and human rights regimes analyzed in previous sections of this chapter. These expansions have increased the complexity of both regimes and the challenges that states and nonstate actors face in navigating the growing number of international and domestic venues within which relevant rules and policies are created. These developments have created increasingly "dense 'policy spaces' in which formerly unrelated sets of principles, norms, and rules increasingly overlap in incoherent and inconsistent ways."[152]

In this section, we describe and assess several alternative frameworks for analyzing these expansions and the complexities they have engendered. Our analysis encompasses legal rules and the methods for reconciling them, the governments and civil society groups that influence the evolution of these rules and the political and judicial institutions within which these actors vie

---

Objectives: New Approaches to Human Rights Considerations, in Margot E. Salomon et al. (Eds.), Casting the Net Wider: Human Rights, Development and New Duty-Bearers 211, 223 (2007) (stating that "a reading of the UDHR and the ICESCR that indentifies intellectual property as part of the property rubric cuts in favour of the strongest version of intellectual property protection, directly contradicting the goal of involving human rights as a limitation on this subject matter").

[151] Yu, *Human Rights Framework, supra* note 24, at 1129.

[152] Laurence R. Helfer, *Toward a Human Rights Framework for Intellectual Property*, 40 U.C. Davis L. Rev. 971, 980 (2007) (quoting Robert O. Keohane & Joseph S. Nye, Jr., *The Club Model of Multilateral Cooperation and Problems of Democratic Legitimacy*, in Roger B. Porter et al. (Eds.), Efficiency, Equity, and Legitimacy: The Multilateral Trading System at the Millennium 264, 266 [2001]); *see also* Laurence R. Helfer, *Regime Shifting in the International Intellectual Property System*, 7 Persp. on Pol. 39 (2009).

for dominance. The frameworks we identify are further developed in subsequent chapters, which analyze specific subjects that straddle the interface of human rights and intellectual property.

A. Conflict

One way to reconcile the relationship of human rights and intellectual property is to frame the two sets of legal rules as fundamentally in conflict.[153] In the U.N. human rights system, endorsements of this approach appear in the 2000 resolution of the Sub-Commission, which asserts that "actual or potential conflicts exist between the implementation of the TRIPS Agreement and the realization of economic, social and cultural rights,"[154] and in the 2001 Statement of the CESCR Committee, which concludes that "any intellectual property regime that makes it more difficult for a State party to comply with its core obligations in relation to health, food, education, especially, or any other right set out in the Covenant, is inconsistent with the legally binding obligations of the State party."[155] To resolve these conflicts, U.N. human rights bodies have urged states to recognize "the primacy of human rights obligations over economic policies and agreements."[156] As Paul Torremans has written, "this solution imposes itself in the view of its proponents because in normative terms human rights are fundamental and of higher importance than intellectual property rights."[157]

Although the conflicts approach appears conceptually straightforward, in fact it masks a number of embedded assumptions and ambiguities. Among the most important of these are (1) identifying the nature of the conflict that must exist before a state's human rights obligations supersede its intellectual property commitments, and (2) analyzing the legal justification for giving primacy to human rights over other international rules.

As to the first issue, public international law scholars have identified multiple ways to conceptualize conflicts between overlapping legal obligations.[158] Framed narrowly, a conflict arises only where two legal rules are

---

[153] Laurence R. Helfer, *Human Rights and Intellectual Property: Conflict or Coexistence?*, 5 Minn. Intell. Prop. Rev. 47, 48 (2003) [Helfer, *Conflict or Coexistence*].

[154] Resolution 2000/7, *supra* note 103, pmbl. para. 11.

[155] Statement on Human Rights and Intellectual Property, *supra* note 114, para. 12.

[156] Resolution 2000/7, *supra* note 103, para. 3.

[157] Paul L. C. Torremans, *Copyright (and Other Intellectual Property Rights) as a Human Right*, in Paul L. C. Torremans (Ed.), Intellectual Property and Human Rights 195, 196 (2008).

[158] *See* Nele Matz-Lück, *Treaties, Conflicts Between*, in Rudolf Bernhardt & Peter Macalister-Smith (Eds.), Max Planck Encyclopedia of Public International

mutually inconsistent, in the sense that a state's compliance with one rule necessarily compels it to violate the other. If this is the type of inconsistency required by the conflicts approach, the principle of human rights primacy would have little if any bite. Some human rights – such as the prohibitions on genocide, slavery, and torture – are bright line, categorical rules whose *jus cogens* status gives them undisputed primacy over other international laws. But those human rights that intersect with intellectual property – such as the rights to health, food, culture, education, and freedom of expression – are vague and open-textured or permit states to restrict rights to achieve other socially salutary objectives. Seen from this perspective, it is difficult to conceive of conduct that an intellectual property treaty categorically mandates but that a human rights agreement simultaneously prohibits, or vice versa.[159]

The conflicts approach has greater traction if one adopts a broader notion of inconsistency, such as exists when an earlier treaty authorizes or even encourages (but does not compel) a state to act in a certain way and a later agreement prohibits the very same conduct. To be sure, one could argue that no inconsistency exists in this circumstance, first because the state voluntarily renounced the authority granted to it by the earlier treaty when it ratified the later agreement, and second because the state can act in a way that avoids violating both commitments. These formalistic responses fail to appreciate, however, that nations often join multiple treaties that regulate the same or related subjects, and that a rule that restricts a state's freedom of action can be just as constraining of its legal and policy discretion as a rule that mandates incompatible behavior.[160]

LAW (2010), *available at* http://www.mpepil.com/; JOOST PAUWELYN, CONFLICT OF NORMS IN PUBLIC INTERNATIONAL LAW: HOW WTO LAW RELATES TO OTHER RULES OF INTERNATIONAL LAW (2003).

[159] *See* Estelle Derclaye, *Intellectual Property Rights and Human Rights: Coinciding and Cooperating*, in INTELLECTUAL PROPERTY AND HUMAN RIGHTS, *supra* note 157, at 133, 140 ("No conflicts have been identified at the level of treaty obligations. Thus countries which have adhered to both human rights and intellectual property treaties do not have conflicting international obligations."); *see also* Gabrielle Marceau, *WTO Dispute Settlement and Human Rights*, 13 EUR. J. INT'L L. 753, 792 (2002) ("For a conflict to exist between a WTO provision and a provision of a human rights treaty, evidence must be put forward that the WTO mandates or prohibits an action that a human rights treaty conversely prohibits or mandates. Such situations would be rare.").

[160] *See* Study Group of the International Law Commission, *Fragmentation of International Law: Difficulties Arising from the Diversification and Expansion of International Law* (Analytical Study), paras. 25–26, U.N. Doc. A/CN.4/L.682 (Apr. 13, 2006) (explaining that one treaty "may sometimes frustrate the goals of another treaty without there being any strict incompatibility between their provisions" and endorsing a "wide notion of conflict as a situation where two rules or principles suggest different ways of dealing with a problem");

This more capacious (and more realistic) understanding of rule conflicts suffers from other shortcomings, however. It does not determine the type or degree of constraint required before the primacy principle becomes operative. Nor, more fundamentally, does a broader approach take into account the values or policies that opposing rules embody. Rather than seeking to identify conflicts between rules, decision makers might increase the welfare of all affected actors were they instead to interpret those rules in a manner that harmonizes, or at least reconciles, the values and policies that underlie them.[161] It is for this reason that public international law maxims of treaty interpretation presume that two agreements relating to the same subject matter are compatible and seek to bolster that compatibility by interpreting the relevant provisions in light of other treaties, state practice, and the parties' tacit political understandings.[162] A focus on foundational principles and context might help to engender a conflicts approach in which human rights serve as "corrective[s] when [intellectual property] rights are used excessively and contrary to their functions."[163]

The second embedded assumption of a conflicts framework concerns the legal rationales for giving primacy to human rights over intellectual property when instances of conflict arise. The following excerpt from a report prepared on behalf of two health-related NGOs provides the most extensive analysis of these rationales.[164]

Matz-Lück, *supra* note 158, para. 6 ("A strict approach to the definition of conflicts between treaties ... is too limited to take account of the varying degree of contradictions between treaty provisions and their effect on the coherence of international law.").

[161] *See* Matz-Lück, *supra* note 158, para. 6 (stating that "the need for interpretation may also offer a tool for harmonization, once a potential contradiction has been discovered").

[162] *See* John H. Knox, *The Judicial Resolution of Conflicts between Trade and the Environment*, 28 HARV. ENVT'L L. REV. 1 (2004); *see also* Matz-Lück, *supra* note 158, para. 20 (stating noting the preference in international law for "harmonizing interpretation that attempts to settle the conflict while giving the widest possible degree of application to both colliding provisions").

[163] Christophe Geiger, *Fundamental Rights, a Safeguard for the Coherence of Intellectual Property Law?*, 35 INT'L REV. INTELL. PROP. & COMPETITION L. 268, 278 (2004); *see also* Derclaye, *supra* note 159, at 141 (stating that conflicts can arise from "unbalanced IPR legislation, often itself an unfortunate consequence of heavy lobbying on the part of IPR holders," and arguing that in such cases "courts must interpret IPR restrictively to restore their intrinsic balance and ... to fulfil their [countries'] obligations concerning human rights").

[164] For a similar analysis, see Robert Howse & Makau Mutua, *Protecting Human Rights in a Global Economy: Challenges for the World Trade Organization* (Int'l Centre for Human Rights & Democratic Dev., Policy Paper, 2000) ("Human rights, to the extent they are obligations erga omnes, or have the status of custom, or of general principles, will normally prevail over specific, conflicting provisions of treaties such as trade agreements."), *available at* http://www.ichrdd.ca/english/commdoc/publications/globalization/wtoRights Glob.html.

Richard Elliott, *TRIPS and Rights: International Human Rights Law, Access to Medicines, and the Interpretation of the WTO Agreement on Trade-Related Aspects of Intellectual Property Rights* 2, 27–32 (Canadian HIV/AIDS Legal Network & AIDS Law Project, South Africa, 2001)

The goal of this document is to set out the basis, in international law, for the following conclusions:

    (a) States' binding legal obligations to realize human rights have primacy in international law;

    (b) therefore, the TRIPS Agreement must be interpreted in a fashion consistent with States' superseding obligations under international law to respect, protect and fulfill human rights; and

    (c) where this is not possible, States' obligations under the TRIPS Agreement must be recognized as not binding to the extent there is a conflict with their human rights obligations under international law.

. . .

This section sets out the legal basis for the claim that human rights claims (and the corresponding obligations on States) enjoy primacy in international law, such that in the event of a conflict with some other international legal norm, a State's obligations to respect, protect and fulfill human rights supersede any conflicting obligation. The foundation for such a claim is to be found in Article 103 of the UN Charter, which has been confirmed by the International Court of Justice. Furthermore, this section looks at a few selected examples of state practice affirming the primacy of UN Charter obligations in international law. The Universal Declaration of Human Rights is the authoritative elaboration of States' human rights obligations under the UN Charter, and States have recognized the primacy of human rights in international law through such instruments as the 1993 Vienna Declaration from the World Conference on Human Rights....

1. Charter of the United Nations

... Articles 55 and 56 of the UN Charter create binding legal obligations ... on member States "to take joint and separate action" to achieve: higher standards of living and conditions of economic and social progress and development; solutions of international health problems; and universal respect for, and observance of, human rights.[165]

---

[165] Article 1(3) of the U.N. Charter declares that the "purposes of the United Nations" include "promoting and encouraging respect for human rights and for fundamental freedoms for

But what is the standing of these legal obligations in international law? Again, the UN Charter explicitly and unambiguously addresses this question:

> Article 103
> In the event of a conflict between the obligations of the Members of the United Nations under the present Charter and their obligations under any other international agreement, their obligations under the present Charter shall prevail.

. . .

The International Court of Justice has also confirmed that, pursuant to Article 103 of the UN Charter, a State's obligations under the Charter supersede any conflicting obligation under any other international agreement. In the *Aerial Incident over Lockerbie Case*,[166] the State of Libya claimed that, under the Montreal Convention for the Suppression of Unlawful Acts against the Safety of Civil Aviation, it was entitled to choose domestic prosecution over extradition of those accused of the airplane bombing in question. However, the International Court of Justice ruled that the UN Charter (Article 25) requires UN member states to carry out the decisions of the Security Council, and this Charter obligation prevailed over the provisions of the Montreal Convention. As a result, Libya was legally required to comply with the UN Security Council's resolution requiring extradition of the accused.

. . .

States themselves have subsequently confirmed the precedence of the Charter in international law. For example, the *Vienna Convention on the Law of Treaties* recognizes that the determination of States' rights and obligations pursuant to their treaties are "subject to Article 103 of the Charter of the United Nations." On numerous occasions, the UN General Assembly has reiterated the primacy of the UN Charter....

2. The Relationship between Human Rights and Trade Agreements

What are the implications of the UN Charter for States' human rights obligations? More specifically, what is the relationship in international law between States' human rights obligations and their obligations under trade treaties?

---

all without distinction as to race, sex, language, or religion." Article 55(c) directs the United Nations to promote "universal respect for, and observance of, human rights and fundamental freedoms for all without distinction as to race, sex, language, or religion." – Eds.

[166] Order of April 14, 1992 (regarding Request for Indication of Provisional Measures), [1992] ICJ Reports 3 at para. 42.

2.1. The UDHR as Authoritative Elaboration of UN Charter Obligations

The International Court of Justice has ruled that State action "which constitute[s] a denial of fundamental human rights is a flagrant violation of the purposes and principles of the Charter."[167] And as has been pointed out, "the Charter's preamble is clear about the principal mission that the international community has agreed to uphold. This mission is explicitly based on the respect of the dignity and value of the individual and on the equality of people and nations. The protection, promotion and fulfilment of human rights and the rights of peoples constitute the primary means of reaching this objective."[168]

Therefore, as two leading jurists in this field have noted, in the light of Article 103, "there can be no doubt that the U.N. Charter takes precedence over other international agreements.... The emergence of the Universal Declaration of Human Rights as the authoritative elaboration of human rights obligations contained in the UN Charter means that any international agreement conflicting with the Declaration is to be subordinated to that document through the operation of Article 103. International agreement, in this context, would clearly include international trade and investment treaties, including the WTO."[169]

2.2. State Recognition of the Primacy of Human Rights

The States of the United Nations have expressly recognized the primacy of their human rights obligations in international law. As has already been noted, at the 1993 World Conference on Human Rights, 171 States of the United Nations reiterated in the Vienna Declaration that the protection and promotion of human rights "is the first responsibility of Governments."[170] But both before and after this declaration, the UN member countries have on numerous occasions reiterated the paramountcy of States' obligations to

---

[167] *Namibia Opinion* [Legal Consequences for States of the Continued Presence of South Africa in Namibia (South West Africa) Notwithstanding Security Council Resolution 276 (1970), Advisory Opinion, 1971 I.C.J. 16] at 57 (para. 131).

[168] Diana Bronson & Lucie Lamarche, "*A human rights framework for trade in the Americas*" 4 (March 2001) Rights & Democracy (International Centre for Human Rights and Democratic Development), in partnership with International Federation of Human Rights, International NGO Committee on Human Rights in Trade and Investment, and Inter-American Platform for Human Rights, Democracy and Development (www.ichrdd.ca).

[169] Rights & Democracy – International Centre for Human Rights and Democratic Development. "*Trading in human rights: The need for human rights sensitivity at the World Trade Organization.*" Brief to the House of Commons Standing Committee on Foreign Affairs & International Trade, Parliament of Canada, March 24, 1999.

[170] *Vienna Declaration and Programme of Action, supra* note 9, at Part I, Article 1.

respect and realize human rights. A few examples provide evidence of their recognition of this obligation.

Adopted as a resolution in 1975 by an overwhelming majority of the UN General Assembly, the Charter of Economic Rights and Duties of States[171] declares that:

> Economic as well as political and other relations among States shall be governed, inter alia, by the following principles: ... (e) mutual and equitable benefit; ... (j) fulfilment in good faith of international obligations; ... *(k) respect for human rights and fundamental freedoms*; ... (m) promotion of international social justice; [and] (n) international co-operation for development.

Furthermore, the General Assembly declared that each State "has the right ... to regulate and supervise the activities of transnational corporations within its national jurisdiction and take measures to ensure that such activities comply with its laws, rules and regulations and conform with its economic and social policies.... Every State should, with full regard for its sovereign rights, co-operate with other States in the exercise of the right set forth in this subparagraph."

The Charter of Economic Rights and Duties is not, strictly speaking, a legally binding document. It is, however, strong evidence of State practice in recognizing that their economic relations must be consistent with their human rights obligations.

Notes and Questions

1. Review the broad and narrow understandings, described in the previous materials, of when a conflict exists between two overlapping international rules. Have U.N. human rights bodies endorsed either of these definitions expressly or implicitly? If not, which definition should they endorse and why?

2. Does the *TRIPS and Rights* report achieve each of the three goals listed at the beginning of the report? What strengths and weaknesses can you identify in the report's analysis of the legal basis for the principle of human rights primacy?

3. Assume for purposes of argument that there is only a weak legal basis for the human rights primacy principle. Are there other reasons why U.N.

---

[171] U.N. General Assembly, Resolution 3281 (XXIX), U.N. Doc. A/RES/3281 (XXIX), at (1975) 14 ILM 251, adopted by a vote of 120 in favor to 6 against, with 10 abstentions (emphasis added).

human rights bodies and public interest NGOs might nevertheless endorse the principle? Are there any risks associated with such endorsements?

4. The intended audiences of the *TRIPS and Rights* report are "heads of state, trade ministers and other government policy-makers, and human rights advocates," whom the report's drafters hope to convince "that international treaties, including international trade agreements, must be interpreted in a fashion that is consistent with States' legal obligations under international law to respect, promote and fulfil human rights." After reading the portion of the report excerpted previously, what actions, if any, would you take if you were (a) a trade ministry official or (b) an activist affiliated with a human rights NGO?

5. The *TRIPS and Rights* report concludes with several recommendations "regarding what should be done in the international legal arena to ensure that the WTO's TRIPS Agreement is correctly interpreted and applied." The recommendations include the following:

> WTO Ministerial Conference should adopt a Ministerial Declaration stating that ... in the event of a conflict between States' obligations under current or future WTO agreements and their obligations under the international law of human rights, the latter obligation(s) shall take precedence; ...

> When interpreting the TRIPS Agreement ..., the Dispute Settlement Body (including Panels and the Appellate Body) must prefer any reasonable interpretation of the agreement that is consistent with States' obligations under international human rights ... over any alternative interpretation that is inconsistent with those obligations.

> The TRIPS Agreement should be amended to include express reference to States' obligations under international human rights law, and to include a clause which recognizes the non-binding status of their obligations under the Agreement when these require States to act (or refrain from acting) in breach of their obligations under international human rights law.[172]

Do these recommendations reinforce or weaken the report's analysis of the primacy principle in international law? What are the costs and benefits of each recommendation? Would you favor or oppose the recommendations if you were the head of your country's (a) trade ministry, (b) intellectual property agency, (c) health ministry, (d) national human rights institution?

---

[172] Richard Elliott, *TRIPS and Rights: International Human Rights Law, Access to Medicines, and the Interpretation of the WTO Agreement on Trade-Related Aspects of Intellectual Property Rights* 52 (Canadian HIV/AIDS Legal Network & AIDS Law Project, South Africa, 2001).

B. Coexistence

A second conceptual framework for analyzing the intersection of human rights and intellectual property views both legal regimes as asking the same fundamental question – how to define the scope of private monopoly power to give authors and inventors sufficient incentives to create and innovate, while providing the consuming public with adequate access to the fruits of their intellectual efforts. This approach sees human rights law and intellectual property law as essentially compatible but as in tension over where to strike the balance between incentives on the one hand and access on the other.[173]

In the U.N. human rights system, statements acknowledging the common objectives of the two regimes appear in numerous documents. These include the High Commissioner's report on TRIPS Agreement,[174] a statement submitted by the WTO to the CESCR Committee analyzing the relationship between human rights and TRIPS,[175] and *General Comment No. 17* on creators' rights.[176] In addition, numerous commentators have analyzed areas of coexistence between human rights and intellectual property from a variety of different perspectives.[177]

A key question that the coexistence approach raises is precisely how existing intellectual property protection rules should be modified in light of human rights concerns. The following two analyses proceed from a common

---

[173] Helfer, *Conflict or Coexistence, supra* note 153, at 48–49.

[174] *High Commissioner Report, supra* note 109, paras. 11–12 (stating that "the balance between public and private interests found under article 15 [of the ICESCR] – and article 27 of the Universal Declaration – is one familiar to intellectual property law" but asserting that the key question "is where to strike the right balance").

[175] World Trade Organization, *Protection of Intellectual Property under the TRIPS Agreement*, para. 13, U.N. Doc. E/C.12/2000/18 (Nov. 27, 2002) ("The tensions inherent between subparagraphs (a) and (b), on the one hand, and subparagraph (c) of article 15.1 of the ICESCR, on the other hand, are those that underlie also the considerations of balance in intellectual property systems.").

[176] *General Comment No. 17, supra* note 115, para. 35 (concluding that "states parties are … obliged to strike an adequate balance between their obligations under article 15, paragraph 1 (c), on one hand, and under the other provisions of the Covenant, on the other hand, with a view to promoting and protecting the full range of rights guaranteed in the Covenant").

[177] *See, e.g.*, Robert D. Anderson & Hannu Wager, *Human Rights, Development, and the WTO: The Cases of Intellectual Property and Competition Policy*, 9 J. INT'L ECON. L. 707 (2006); Abbe E. L. Brown, *Socially Responsible Intellectual Property: A Solution?*, 2 SCRIPT-ED 485 (2005); Philippe Cullet, *Human Rights and Intellectual Property in the TRIPS Era*, 29 HUM. RTS. Q. 403 (2007); Hans Morten Haugen, *Human Rights and TRIPS Exclusion and Exception Provisions*, 11 J. WORLD INTELL. PROP. 345 (2008); E. S. Nwauche, *Human Rights – Relevant Considerations in Respect of Intellectual Property and Competition Law*, 2 SCRIPT-ED 467 (2005).

premise – that intellectual property systems' balance between innovation incentives and public access must give greater weight to promoting social and economic welfare. However, they develop the implications of that premise in significantly different ways.

Human Rights Commission, *Report of the High Commissioner on the Impact of the Agreement on Trade-Related Aspects of Intellectual Property Rights on Human Rights,* **U.N. Doc. E/CN.4/Sub.2/2001/13 (June 27, 2001)**

. . .

59. What then are the obligations on States? On the one hand, the TRIPS Agreement encourages States to implement intellectual property systems that promote economic and social development taking into account the need to balance rights with responsibilities. The Agreement allows members to take measures to protect the public interest, including the promotion of public health. Article 15 of [the] ICESCR requires States to balance public and private interests in the design of IP protection....

60. Out of the 141 members of [the] WTO that have undertaken to implement the minimum standards of IP protection in the TRIPS Agreement, 111 have ratified [the] ICESCR. Members should therefore implement the minimum standards of the TRIPS Agreement bearing in mind both their human rights obligations as well as the flexibility inherent in the TRIPS Agreement, and recognizing that "human rights are the first responsibility of Governments." In light of this, the High Commissioner believes that implementation of the TRIPS Agreement should be characterized by the following objectives.

61. The promotion of article 15 of [the] ICESCR. States, in implementing systems for intellectual property protection, are encouraged to consider the most appropriate mechanisms that will promote, on the one hand, the right of everyone to take part in cultural life and to enjoy the benefits of scientific progress and its applications and, on the other hand, the right of everyone to benefit from the protection of the moral and material interests resulting from any scientific, literary or artistic production of which he or she is the author. In this sense, the High Commissioner encourages States to monitor the implementation of the TRIPS Agreement to ensure that its minimum standards are achieving this balance between the interests of the general public and those of the authors....

62. The promotion of the right of all to enjoy the benefits of scientific progress and its applications. The design of IP systems should take into account

the fact that the grant of overly broad patents can be used to block future medical research. The design of IP systems should, in calculating the difficult trade-off between public and private interests, take into consideration that the increasing tendency to grant patents for "me-too" drugs may run counter to the primary objective of IP systems to promote innovation, and focus too heavily on promoting private commercial interests. The requirements under the TRIPS Agreement for the grant of patents – novelty, inventive step and industrial applicability – are open to interpretation under national legislation and each country can decide according to local conditions. Consequently, the High Commissioner encourages interpretations of these requirements that do not lose sight of the public interest in the wide dissemination of knowledge under article 15.

63. The promotion of the right to health. The High Commissioner supports WHO's call that "(w)hen establishing standards of patentability for pharmaceuticals, countries should consider the implications for health of those standards."

...

65. The protection of the cultural rights of indigenous peoples and local communities. The TRIPS Agreement does not refer specifically to the protection of the innovations of local and indigenous communities – a fact which indicates the Agreement is tipped in favour of the protection of modern technology but not of other forms.... The High Commissioner encourages the adaptation of IP systems so that they fully take into account cultural and other rights of indigenous and local communities.

66. The promotion of access to affordable essential drugs. Several provisions in the TRIPS Agreement offer flexibility that could be useful in promoting access to affordable essential drugs. Importantly, article 31 allows States to grant compulsory licenses for patents so long as certain conditions are fulfilled. Article 31 holds significant potential for the protection of the public interest in areas such as the promotion of the right to health.... The High Commissioner encourages member States to implement these provisions in national legislation as safeguards to protect access to essential drugs as a component of the right to health as well as other human rights.

67. The promotion of international cooperation in the implementation of the TRIPS Agreement. International cooperation is an important ingredient in the promotion and protection of human rights.... Article 66 (2) of the TRIPS Agreement, obliges developed country members to provide incentives to enterprises and institutions in their territories to promote technology

transfer to least developed countries – a provision which could be used beneficially to promote access to affordable drugs for least developed countries. The High Commissioner encourages developed countries to establish clear incentives to promote technology transfer and the supply of affordable drugs to developing countries.

68. The promotion and protection of all human rights. An important aspect of the human rights approach to IP protection is the express linkage of human rights in relevant legislation. Express reference to the promotion and protection of human rights in the TRIPS Agreement would clearly link States' obligations under international trade law and human rights law.... This would assist States to implement the "permitted exceptions" in the TRIPS Agreement in line with their obligations under ICESCR. To this end, the High Commissioner intends to seek observer status at the TRIPS Council....

69. IP legislation that maintains flexibility and a balance of rights with responsibilities. The High Commissioner joins WHO in recommending that developing countries be cautious about enacting "TRIPS plus" legislation that is more stringent than present requirements under the TRIPS Agreement without first understanding the impact of such legislation on the protection of human rights.

Audrey R. Chapman, *Approaching Intellectual Property as a Human Right (obligations related to Article 15(1)(c))*, 35 COPYRIGHT BULL. 4, 14–17, 28–29, 30 (2001)

...

A human-rights approach takes the implicit balance between the rights of inventors and creators and the interest of the wider society within intellectual property paradigms and make[s] it more explicit and exacting. A human-rights orientation is predicated on the centrality of protecting and nurturing human dignity and the common good. By extension, the right of the creator or the author are conditional on contributing to the common good and welfare of society....

A human-rights approach also establishes a different and often more exacting standard for evaluating the appropriateness of granting intellectual property protection to a specific artistic work, invention or set of knowledge than those specified under intellectual property law....

A human-rights approach must be particularly sensitive to the interconnections between intellectual property and the rights "to take part in cultural life" and "to enjoy the benefits of scientific progress and its applications". To be consistent with the full provisions of Article 15, the type and level of protection afforded under any intellectual property regime must facilitate and promote cultural participation and scientific progress and do so in a manner that will broadly benefit members of society both on an individual and collective level. These considerations go well beyond a simple economic calculus often governing intellectual property law.

A human-rights approach further establishes a requirement for the State to protect its citizens from the negative effects of intellectual property. To do so, governments need to undertake a very rigorous and disaggregated analysis of the likely impact of specific innovations, as well as an evaluation of proposed changes in intellectual property paradigms, and to utilize these data to assure nondiscrimination in the end result. When making choices and decisions, it calls for particular sensitivity to the effect on those groups whose welfare tends to be absent from the calculus of decision-making about intellectual property: the poor, the disadvantaged, racial, ethnic and linguistic minorities, women, rural residents.

. . .

Proposed obligations of States parties

Minimum Core Obligation
... To be consistent with human rights norms, [intellectual property systems] must meet the following criteria:

- Intellectual property law should incorporate explicit human rights and ethical provisions as criteria for the evaluation of applications for patents and trademarks and develop an institutional mechanism capable of making these determinations. In most cases patent and trademark offices are not competent to undertake such a review and are inclined to subordinate human-rights considerations to an economic calculus. Therefore a meaningful human-rights input requires ... the establishment of a body competent to review patent and trademark decisions on human-rights grounds and/or the ability to appeal decisions to a court or tribunal able to make a determination of the human rights implications. This body should have the jurisdiction to invalidate an existing or pending patent by virtue of a ruling that it would infringe on human rights or be inconsistent with ethical principles or the cultural norms of major groups in the society.

- The nature of the intellectual property regimes adopted must reflect the country's development requirements and be consistent with the cultural orientations of major groups. Even the TRIPS Agreement offers some flexibility to countries bound by its provisions....

- To promote realization of the right to cultural participation, States parties should develop intellectual property regimes that are consistent with the practice and revitalization of cultural traditions within their country....

- At present, traditional and indigenous knowledge and artistic works rarely qualify for intellectual property protection and for that reason are vulnerable to expropriation and inappropriate utilization by persons outside the group....

- The development of appropriate protections therefore requires adapting existing intellectual property instruments and/or developing new types of intellectual property rights....

- Intellectual property rights related to science should promote scientific progress and broad access to its benefits. To do so, these protections must respect the freedom indispensable for scientific research and creative activity.

. . .

Violations

As noted above, the absence of international human-rights standards in the intellectual property field makes it difficult to utilize violations language. Nevertheless, the following clearly constitute violations.

Failure to Develop Intellectual Property Regimes That Reflect Ethical and Human Rights Considerations

Even when legally mandated to do so under existing law, patent offices rarely consider the ethical dimensions of patenting. On those occasions that patent offices consider ethical concerns, they tend to construe moral criteria so narrowly that few, if any, tests are likely to exclude patent applications. The European Patent Office, for example, interprets Article 53 (a) of the European Patent Convention, which prohibits the grant of patents that would be contrary to "*ordre public* or morality", as only excluding patents whose exploitation would be "abhorrent to the overwhelming majority of the public" or a contravention of the "totality of accepted norms"....

Uncompensated Expropriation of Traditional Knowledge
It has been estimated that in 1995 the market value of pharmaceutical
derivatives from indigenous peoples' traditional knowledge amounted to
$43 billion.... In [many instances], individual prospectors and corporate
developers have expropriated the knowledge through filing patents in their
own name without any form of remuneration....

Interference in the Intellectual Property Policies of Other Countries
To further its foreign policy interests of promoting strict intellectual property
regimes, the United States Government has exercised considerable diplomatic
pressure and threatened trade sanctions on a number of occasions. In 1997,
for example, the United States Government unilaterally imposed import
duties on $260 million of Argentine exports in retaliation for Argentina's
refusal to revise its patent legislation to conform with US standards.... The
United States has also attempted to influence the development of patent laws
and policies to suit its interests in other countries, including Ecuador, India,
Pakistan, South Africa, and Brazil.

Notes and Questions

1. Review the proposals to modify intellectual property protection rules
set forth in the excerpts of the High Commissioner's report and the article
by Audrey Chapman. Which of these proposals, if any, would you favor
adopting and why? Choose one of the proposals and identify the arguments that you would raise to convince your government to adopt the
proposal.

2. Consider the information in paragraph 60 of the High Commissioner's
report listing the number of WTO members that have also ratified the
ICESCR (141 and 111 states, respectively, as of 2001). Why does the High
Commissioner cite these statistics? What are the implications for countries,
such as the United States, that have not ratified the ICESCR?

3. The excerpt from *Approaching Intellectual Property as a Human Right*,
reproduced earlier, includes one section on "proposed obligations of States
parties" and another on "violations." Why does Chapman bifurcate her analysis in this way? Do these categories represent legal distinctions? Political
distinctions? Moral ones? Do you agree that the conduct that Chapman
labels as "proposed obligations" and as "violations" are properly included in
those categories?

4. Chapman states that a "human rights approach establishes a different and often more exacting standard for evaluating the appropriateness of granting intellectual property protection to a specific artistic work, invention or set of knowledge than those specified under intellectual property law." What substantive or procedural elements should this standard contain, and who should determine whether a particular work meets the standard?

5. Consider Chapman's proposal to "eliminate inventions that are inconsistent with protecting human dignity." Which inventions should be precluded on this basis? Recall that TRIPS Article 27.2 permits WTO members to deny patent to inventions if "necessary to protect *ordre public* or morality, including to protect human, animal or plant life or health or to avoid serious prejudice to the environment." Does Chapman suggest the need for broader subject matter exclusions? If so, what might those exclusions be, and what are their costs and benefits? *General Comment No. 17* of the CESCR Committee, which we analyze in detail in Chapter 3, recommends that states parties to the ICESCR "consider to what extent the patenting of the human body and its parts would affect their obligations under the Covenant or under other relevant international human rights instruments," citing Article 4 of the UNESCO Universal Declaration on the Human Genome and Human Rights.

6. Geiger has written that fundamental rights should serve both as "corrective[s] when [intellectual property] rights are used excessively and contrary to their functions,"[178] and as "guidelines for reorganizing intellectual property law."[179] Using human rights for these purposes, he argues, would promote a "fair and balanced intellectual property system" that includes the following elements:

[D]ecisions that on principle favour the right-holder, like the principle of the restrictive interpretation of exceptions, would not be justified under a system based on fundamental rights.

. . .

A certain number of creations could be excluded from protection because of their importance for society by a positive definition of the public domain.

. . .

Limitations to intellectual property rights, which are based on fundamental rights and thereby represent basic democratic values within IP law, are rights of the users (and not mere interests to be taken into account), which are of

---

[178] Geiger, *Fundamental Rights, supra* note 163, at 278.
[179] Christophe Geiger, *The Constitutional Dimension of Intellectual Property, in* INTELLECTUAL PROPERTY AND HUMAN RIGHTS, *supra* note 157, at 101, 121.

equal value as the exclusive right. The consequence of this is that they should be considered mandatory (which means the user's exercise of statutory limitations cannot be restricted by contract) and should prevail over technical measures [that restrict access to works in electronic format].

. . .

Different rules should apply to different works: A work in which no elements of the personality of the creator can be found, cannot enjoy the same protection as those with such elements because the justification of personality protection is lacking. That means the extent of protection of creations with a low level of creativity ... must be smaller than that of classical works (a short term of protection, no "droit moral," the employer can be the holder of the rights, registration, and so on). Creativity or innovation must clearly be differentiated from investment. This would lead to the establishment of a graduated intellectual property system.[180]

How do Geiger's proposals for revising intellectual property protection rules compare to those advanced by the High Commissioner for Human Rights and by Chapman? Do Geiger's recommendations respond to the same human rights concerns as those identified by Chapman? If not, what differences can you identify?

C. Beyond Conflict and Coexistence

In recent writings, several commentators have developed frameworks for analyzing the interface of human rights and intellectual property that move beyond the conflicts and coexistence approaches analyzed previously. The publications excerpted in the following pages articulate three such frameworks.

Peter K. Yu, *Reconceptualizing Intellectual Property Interests in a Human Rights Framework*, 40 U.C. DAVIS L. REV. 1039, 1077–78, 1096, 1108–09, 1113, 1114 (2007)

. . .

While [the conflict and coexistence] approaches have their benefits and disadvantages, they ignore the fact that some attributes of intellectual property rights are protected in international or regional human rights instruments, while other attributes do not have any human rights basis at all. By encouraging a focus on specific situations and problems, the use of these approaches has made it difficult for one to engage in a more general discussion of the rights involved and the relationship of the two related fields. While the inclusion of

---

[180]   *Id.* at 121–22, 123, 125–26.

the right to the protection of interests in intellectual creations in the UDHR and the ICESCR was controversial, the two provisions now expressly protect this right. Thus, it is misleading to inquire whether human rights and intellectual property rights coexist or conflict with each other. Because of the overlapping human rights attributes, these two sets of rights both coexist and conflict with each other. A better, and more important, question is how we can alleviate the tension and resolve the conflict between human rights and the non-human-rights aspects of intellectual property protection.

To answer this question, this Part separates the conflicts between human rights and intellectual property rights into two sets of conflicts: external conflicts and internal conflicts. With respect to external conflicts, the key resolution technique is to separate the human rights aspects of intellectual property protection from others that have no human rights basis. To do so, section A explores the scope and normative content of article 27(2) of the UDHR and article 15(1)(c) of the ICESCR. This section then explains how the principle of human right primacy can be used to resolve the external conflict once the human rights attributes of intellectual property have been identified. With respect to internal conflicts, however, this Part points out that the above resolution technique would not work. Because all of the conflicting rights have human rights bases, the principle of human rights primacy does not apply. In lack of an overarching principle, section B identifies three approaches that have been advanced by policymakers, judges, and scholars: (1) the just remuneration approach, (2) the core minimum approach, and (3) the progressive realization approach....

. . .

Under the just remuneration approach, individuals are free to use creative works in the enjoyment or exercise of their human rights. Authors and inventors cannot prevent them from doing so, but they can seek economic compensation for any injury to the moral and material interests in their creations. The key lesson about this approach is that human rights grant to the individual a compulsory license, as compared to a free license, and to the right holder a right to remuneration, rather than exclusive control.

. . .

Th[e] core minimum approach is important to authors and inventors. When it is used in relation to the right to the protection of interests in intellectual creations, it provides them with the minimum essential levels of protection even in situations where states need resources to realize other human rights. Meanwhile, it also benefits future authors and users as well as individuals in less developed countries, poorer neighborhoods, and traditional communities. When such an approach is used in relation to other human rights, such as the right to food, the right to health, the right to education, and the right to self-determination, it creates the maximum limits of intellectual property protection that are needed but are often omitted in international treaties. Such limits, in turn, will facilitate greater access to protected materials and will thereby promote creativity, innovation, and cultural participation and development.

· · ·

The progressive realization approach ... was specially designed to address the increased allocation of resources to the realization of economic, social, and cultural rights as these resources become available. Unlike the core minimum approach, which seeks to identify the minimum obligations of each party, the progressive realization approach focuses on how each party can use additional resources to improve its human rights protection. Under this approach, states will undertake their best efforts based on the availability of resources to comply with all of their obligations under human rights instruments.... They not only agree to refrain from taking retrogressive measures, but strive to improve on the protection of human rights until they have fully discharged their obligations.

· · ·

What is attractive about [proposals adopting the progressive realization approach] is that they not only ask what should be protected, but also how it can be protected in a way that would allow for the progressive, or even full, realization of other human rights....

Laurence R. Helfer, *Toward a Human Rights Framework for Intellectual Property*, 40 U.C. Davis L. Rev. 971, 1018–20 (2007)

· · ·

[Helfer first describes two plausible future human rights frameworks for intellectual property – "Using Human Rights to Expand Intellectual Property" and "Using Human Rights to Impose External Limits on Intellectual Property." He argues that these two frameworks "share a common strategy. They each take the existing baseline of intellectual property protection as a given and then invoke human rights law to bolster arguments for moving that baseline in one direction or the other." Helfer then turns to a third framework, which he describes as follows.]

Achieving Human Rights Ends through Intellectual Property Means

A third human rights framework for intellectual property proceeds from a very different premise. It first specifies the minimum outcomes – in terms of health, poverty, education, and so forth – that human rights law requires of states. The framework next works backwards to identify different mechanisms available to states to achieve those outcomes. Intellectual property plays only a secondary role in this version of the framework. Where intellectual property laws help to achieve human rights outcomes, governments should embrace it. Where it hinders those outcomes, its rules should be modified (but not necessarily restricted, as I indicate below). But the focus remains on the minimum levels of human well-being that states must provide, using either appropriate intellectual property rules or other means.

A 2001 report by the UN High Commissioner for Human Rights analyzing the impact of the TRIPs Agreement on the right to health exemplifies this outcome-focused, inductive approach.[181] The report reviews the components of the right to health protected by Article 12 of the ICESCR. According to a *General Comment* issued by the CESCR Committee, the right to health includes an obligation for states to promote medical research and to provide access to affordable treatments, including essential drugs.

The High Commissioner's report analyzes how intellectual property affects these two obligations. It acknowledges that patents help governments promote medical research by providing an incentive to invent new medical technologies, including new drugs. But the report also asserts that pharmaceutical companies' "commercial motivation ... means that research is directed, first and foremost, towards 'profitable' disease. Diseases that predominantly affect people in poorer countries ... remain relatively under-researched." One way to remedy this market imperfection is to create incentives for innovation outside of the patent system.

A similar perspective informs the High Commissioner's discussion of access to essential medicines. The report states that patent protection decreases the affordability of drugs. But affordability also depends on factors unrelated to intellectual property, "such as the level of import duties, taxes, and local market approval costs." In light of these dual impediments, governments can improve access to patented pharmaceuticals in two ways. First,

---

[181]   *High Commissioner Report, supra* note 109.

they can exploit the flexibilities already embedded in the TRIPs Agreement, such as issuing compulsory licenses to manufacture generic drugs and importing cheaper drugs from other countries. Second, they can adopt affordability-enhancing mechanisms outside of the intellectual property system, for example through differential pricing, "the exchange of price information, price competition and price negotiation with public procurement and insurance schemes...." Strikingly, the efficacy of these mechanisms may require augmenting existing intellectual property protection rules, such as negotiating "drug licensing agreements with geographical restrictions[,] ... so that cheaper drugs do not leak back to wealthier markets."

Ruth Okediji, *Securing Intellectual Property Objectives: New Approaches to Human Rights Considerations*, in Casting the Net Wider: Human Rights, Development and New Duty-Bearers **211, 211–12, 213–14, 227–29, 234 (Margot E. Salomon et al. eds., 2007)**

The current global discourse on the relationship between human rights and intellectual property reflects a significant level of incertitude about the relevance or efficacy of human rights for addressing development challenges that are only partially attributable to the mandatory imposition of global rules for intellectual property protection pursuant to the ... TRIPS Agreement. Much of the literature begins with two standard assumptions. The first is that the two systems are in conflict or, at best, in an uneasy alliance. The second assumption then naturally follows, namely that the two systems should be reconciled, with tentative proposals for such a resolution. The ostensible goal of this strong call for a détente between the two disciplines is unarguably the expectation that the intellectual property rules and policy will benefit from human rights norms, although there is hardly consensus on what mechanisms *within* the human rights scheme might occasion this outcome or any consideration that human rights might have a different, undesirable effect on intellectual property entirely.

...

... I highlight the important aspirations of human right norms and the particularized vision of intellectual property rights as a critical means of achieving those aspirations using tools *internal* to the intellectual property scheme that dictate specific objectives for national and international intellectual property regulation.... In my view, accounting for development at the human rights/intellectual property interface requires primarily a challenge to multilateral obligations that distort the welfare balance that has characterised intellectual property regulation for well over a century. In this context, human rights should be viewed as a means of preserving the objectives of intellectual property using existing intellectual property tools....

...

Using Human Rights to Promote Intellectual Property Objectives

... It is important that the current regime of intellectual property rights reflects the pervasiveness of human rights goals. But it is also important for human rights to advance the goals of intellectual property and, certainly there is nothing inherent in the UDHR directed at a particular scheme of intellectual property rights. This point is well taken but does not extend far enough to evaluate the network of interlocking rights between the two disciplines. The dominant focus on the first paragraph of Article 27(2) overshadows the fact that there are a number of human rights enshrined in the UDHR that are reflected in the normative design of contemporary intellectual property law. Of those rights recognized by the UDHR, the rights to liberty and security of person, privacy, freedom of thought, conscience and religion, freedom of opinion and expression, freedom of association, just and favourable conditions of work, education, participation in cultural life, and property all reflect aspects of intellectual property regulation. The possible relationships between these rights and intellectual property subject matter are illustrated below:

IP Policy Mechanisms and Fundamental HR Goals: Relationship Overview

Human Right[182]	Intellectual Property Subject Matter	Doctrinal Mechanisms for Full or Partial Realisation/ Implementation	Direct or Indirect Effect on HR Goal[183]
Freedom of expression	Copyright	Fair use; idea/expression dichotomy	Direct effect
Privacy	Copyright	Fair use	Indirect effect
Education	Copyright	Explicit provisions for use of materials in the course of face-to-face instructions; fair use	Direct effect

[182] Limited to rights included in the UDHR.
[183] In other words, is the effect on the identified human right deliberately built into the doctrine at issue?

Participation in cultural life	Copyright	Fair use	Direct effect
Freedom of thought, conscience and religion	Copyright	Fair use	Direct and indirect effect
Work	Patents, copyright	Authorship recognized as basis for ownership; bundle of exclusive proprietary rights provided by statute	Direct effect
Property	Patents, copyright	Bundle of exclusive proprietary rights	Direct effect
Just and favourable conditions of work	Copyright and patents	Work for hire doctrine; for patents, requirement that the individual inventor always be named on the patent application	Indirect effect

The correlation between intellectual property and human rights goals is clearly strongest in the area of copyright and not, ironically, with respect to patents, where nevertheless the greatest advances have been made as regards curbing the rights of patent owners with respect to access to medicines. This fact alone suggests the importance of external mechanisms in ensuring that the effects of intellectual property protection are consistent with the internal obligations of the discipline. Identifying how intellectual property rights may affect human rights obligations also serves to show that intellectual property can be justified by reference to human rights. But this is *not* the same as saying that intellectual property is a human right, that human rights justify or require the particular type, scope and design of contemporary intellectual property rights, or that there are no other means by which these human rights goals might be attained.

...

I have argued that human rights have a role to play in the pursuit of intellectual property objectives as reflected in national constitutions and multilateral treaties. At the very least, human rights justify the objectives of intellectual property and could be used to impose an internal constraint within the intellectual property system so that those objectives remain critical to the legitimacy of the system.

Notes and Questions

1. Review the critiques of the conflict and coexistence approaches described by Yu, Helfer, and Okediji. What are the strengths and weaknesses of the frameworks that the three commentators propose as alternatives? Are the proposed frameworks complementary, or would adopting one framework preclude the adoption of the others?

2. What are the benefits and costs of limiting intellectual property using legal doctrines and policy levers *internal* to the intellectual property regime (such as subject matter exclusions, limits on terms of protection, and exceptions to exclusive rights), as compared to *external* doctrines and policy tools found in international human rights law (such as a "core minimum" approach to realizing economic, social, and cultural rights)? What are the views of the three commentators as to whether internal or external limits are more desirable? Are internal or external mechanisms more likely to promote legal certainty? To address the utilitarian and welfare arguments relevant to intellectual property law and policy? To contribute to social welfare?[184]

3. Okediji argues that commentators have failed to consider "that human rights might have a different, undesirable effect on intellectual property entirely." What negative consequences does Okediji envision? What other undesirable effects, if any, are reasonably foreseeable?

4. Review the table "IP Policy Mechanisms and Fundamental HR Goals" contained in the Okediji reading excerpted earlier. Do you agree with her conclusion that the table reveals that "the correlation between intellectual property and human rights goals is clearly strongest in the area of copyright" as compared to patents or other types of intellectual property?

5. Estelle Derclaye has criticized Helfer's claim that it is possible to achieve human rights ends through intellectual property means. She argues that his proposal "fails to more clearly state that human rights and intellectual property rights have the same goal. In fact, as intellectual property rights are a type of human right obviously, their goal is the same as all human rights, human

---

[184] *Compare* Rochelle Cooper Dreyfuss, *Patents and Human Rights: Where Is the Paradox?*, in WILLEM GROSHEIDE (ED.), INTELLECTUAL PROPERTY AND HUMAN RIGHTS: A PARADOX 72 (2010) (critiquing human rights approaches to intellectual property as ignoring utilitarian concerns) *with* Christophe Geiger, *"Constitutionalising" Intellectual Property Law? The Influence of Fundamental Rights on Intellectual Property in the European Union*, 37 INT'L REV. INTELL. PROP. & COMPETITION L. 371, 388 (2006) (arguing that human rights "are effective tools to guarantee a balanced development and understanding of intellectual property rights and a remedy for the overprotective tendencies of lobby-driven legislation").

welfare."[185] Are you persuaded by this critique? Based on the excerpted readings, how would Yu and Okediji respond to Derclaye's argument?

6. After reviewing the materials in this chapter, how would you characterize the relationship between the TRIPS Agreement and the ICESCR? Are the two treaties complementary, or do you agree with the concerns expressed by some U.N. human rights bodies that TRIPS makes it more difficult for governments to respect, protect, and fulfill economic, social, and cultural rights?

---

[185] Derclaye, *supra* note 159, at 138 n.19.

Chapter 2

The Human Right to Health, Access
to Patented Medicines, and the Restructuring
of Global Innovation Policy

2.1. Introduction

No other issue so clearly epitomizes the clash between human rights and intellectual property as access to patented medicines. And with good reason. The idea of withholding livesaving drugs from individuals suffering from fatal or debilitating diseases when the means exist to distribute those drugs cheaply and effectively is anathema to all notions of morality.[1] Yet medical treatments such as new pharmaceuticals do not fall from the sky. They are the product of years or even decades of painstaking research, much of which yields little if any therapeutic benefit. If providing widespread access to new medicines were to choke off this research, the results would be less medical innovation and fewer treatments for future diseases – results surely incompatible with the spirit if not the letter of the international human rights regime.[2]

The compatibility of patent protection with access to lifesaving drugs is thus inextricably linked to how societies allocate resources to medical innovation. Governments can provide such resources directly, for example through government-funded research or grants from the public fisc. They can also provide indirect incentives for research through a system of patent protection. In the latter case, private actors – most notably pharmaceutical companies – recoup their research costs and earn a profit through what in

---

[1] See, e.g., Thomas Pogge, *Access to Medicines*, 1 Pub. Health Ethics 73 (2008) (special issue on access to medicines, justice, and alternative innovation mechanisms).

[2] See, e.g., Comm'n on Intell. Prop. Rights, Integrating Intellectual Property Rights and Development Policy 29 (2002), *available at* http://www.iprcommission.org/graphic/documents/final_report.htm ("without the incentive of patents it is doubtful the private sector would have invested so much in the discovery or development of medicines, many of which are currently in use both in developed and developing countries").

most countries is a twenty-year monopoly over the sale, licensing, and distribution of medical inventions. In addition to these private gains, intellectual property-based systems of medical innovation provide numerous social benefits. They incentivize the search for new medical knowledge, they mandate public disclosure of medical processes and products and thereby stimulate future innovation, and, after patent protection expires, they enable companies to manufacture and distribute generic drugs at marginal cost prices. These benefits are no doubt considerable. But they offer cold comfort to anyone suffering from a life-threatening illness who cannot afford lifesaving medicines protected by patents.

The question that naturally arises is whether it is possible to revise existing legal rules and institutions to maximize *both* medical innovation *and* access to medicines. The answer to that question has been the subject of protracted studies and heated debates by national governments, international organizations, academics and expert bodies, industry officials, and public interest NGOs. This chapter analyzes several alternative proposals advanced by these actors and considers how these proposals would restructure global innovation policy and expand access to essential medicines. To lay the foundation for this analysis, we first provide a theoretical and conceptual assessment of (1) the human right to health and the emerging right of access to medicines, (2) international and national patent protection rules, and (3) the tools that each regime contains for accommodating the concerns of the other.

Throughout the chapter, we focus on the example of access to medicines for treating HIV/AIDS. We highlight this topic for several reasons. First, HIV/AIDS is a genuinely global problem that afflicts millions of individuals and every country on the planet. The pandemic thus directly implicates international laws both protecting human rights and intellectual property. Second, the discovery in the mid-1990s of antiretroviral drugs transformed HIV/AIDS from a life-threatening illness into a treatable chronic condition. A daily regimen that combines several of these drugs reduces viral loads, diminishes the virus' ability to replicate, and lowers the risk of transmission. Third, however, nearly all of the new drugs that produce these striking health benefits qualify for patent protection under TRIPS and national patent laws. Efforts by pharmaceutical companies to enforce these patents and demand high prices for antiretrovirals – effectively making the drugs unaffordable for millions infected with HIV – provoked an international battle that pitted developing states (especially Brazil and South Africa) and human rights and health care activists (including Médicins sans Frontières and Oxfam) against some of the world's largest pharmaceutical firms (such as Merck and GlaxoSmithKline) and the industrialized nations in which they are based (in particular the United States and European countries).

The controversies over patents and antiretroviral drugs for HIV/AIDS thus map across fault lines that separate rich states from poor nations, and intellectual property industries from civil society groups opposed to patents that restrict access to medicines. We emphasize, however, that HIV/AIDS is illustrative of more pervasive tensions between the tools available to incentivize medical innovation and the rights claims of individuals seeking to access the fruits of that innovation. These tensions have particular force with regard to efforts to combat the "global drug gap," a phrase coined to emphasize the fact that most new drugs remain beyond the financial reach of most of the world's population, and that private research and development largely ignore the many diseases (such as tuberculosis, malaria, and Dengue fever) prevalent in poor developing countries.

Section 2.2 of this chapter begins with some basic facts and information about the global HIV/AIDS crisis. Section 2.3 turns to the human right to health. We first assess the justifications for and critiques of the right and then analyze legally binding rules and aspirational norms that protect the emerging right of access to medicines. Section 2.4 reviews the major international intellectual property protection rules relating to patented medicines and the mechanisms and flexibilities available to accommodate public health concerns. The section includes a discussion of recent efforts by member countries of the World Trade Organization (WTO) to facilitate transborder compulsory licensing of patented medicines. Section 2.5 considers several alternative approaches that governments and courts have adopted to enhance access to medicines. It also reviews a diverse array of proposals that seek to restructure medical innovation to focus on neglected diseases, especially diseases prevalent in the developing world.

2.2. Background on the HIV/AIDS Pandemic and Access to Antiretroviral Drugs

The following is an excerpt from a 2008 report prepared by Joint United Nations Programme on HIV/AIDS (UNAIDS), an interorganizational effort to combat HIV/AIDS sponsored by ten United Nations specialized agencies. The report describes the scope of the pandemic, recent gains in improving access to medicines, and future challenges to prevention and treatment of the disease.

UNAIDS, 2008 Report on the Global AIDS Epidemic 13, 15–16, 131–32, 134–38 (2008)

The HIV Epidemic Has Changed Our World

In the countries most heavily affected, HIV has reduced life expectancy by more than 20 years, slowed economic growth, and deepened household poverty. In sub-Saharan Africa alone, the epidemic has orphaned nearly 12 million children aged under 18 years. The natural age distribution in many national populations in sub-Saharan Africa has been dramatically skewed by HIV, with potentially perilous consequences for the transfer of knowledge and values from one generation to the next. In Asia, where infection rates are much lower than in Africa, HIV causes a greater loss of productivity than any other disease, and is likely to push an additional 6 million households into poverty by 2015 unless national responses are strengthened. According to the United Nations Development Programme (UNDP), HIV has inflicted the "single greatest reversal in human development" in modern history.

At the same time, the epidemic has heightened global consciousness of health disparities, and catalysed unprecedented action to confront some of the world's most serious development challenges. No disease in history has prompted a comparable mobilization of political, financial, and human resources, and no development challenge has led to such a strong level of leadership and ownership by the communities and countries most heavily affected. In large part due to the impact of HIV, people throughout the world have become less willing to tolerate inequities in global health and economic status that have long gone unaddressed.

...

Promising Progress, but Enduring Challenges

The 6-fold increase in financing for HIV activities in low- and middle-income countries during this decade is beginning to yield results. For the first time since what we now know as AIDS was recognized 27 years ago, signs of major progress in the HIV response have become apparent. The annual number of AIDS deaths [with confidence intervals in brackets] has declined in the past two years from 2.2 million [1.9 million–2.6 million] in 2005 to 2.0 million [1.8 million–2.3 million] in 2007, in part as a result of the substantial increase in access to HIV treatment in recent years. In a number of heavily affected countries – such as Kenya, Rwanda, Uganda, and Zimbabwe – dramatic changes in sexual behaviour have been accompanied by declines in the number of new HIV infections, contributing to a global stabilization, beginning in the late 1990s, in the percentage of people aged 15–49 who are infected with HIV.

But these gains have not been consistent within and between regions, and favourable epidemiological and behavioural trends have not been sustained in some countries. Infections are on the rise in a number of countries including China, Germany, Indonesia, Mozambique, Papua New Guinea, the Russian Federation, Ukraine, the United Kingdom, and Viet Nam. In other countries – such as Lesotho, Namibia, South Africa and Swaziland – HIV prevalence appears to have stabilized at extraordinarily high levels. Although the number of people on antiretroviral drugs in low- and middle-income countries has risen, most of those who need such therapies are not currently receiving them. Moreover, the epidemic is outpacing the rate at which these drugs are being delivered. In 2007, the estimated number of new HIV infections was 2.5 times higher than the increase in the number of people on antiretroviral drugs in that year, underscoring the need for substantially greater success in preventing new HIV infections.

The recent stabilization of the global epidemic cannot obscure its most important aspect – its profound human toll. Since the beginning of the epidemic, 25 million people have died of HIV-related causes. Collectively, these deaths represent an incalculable loss of human potential. Individually, each is associated with enduring trauma in households and communities.

There is also a risk that the important progress achieved in recent years might lull some into complacency. Indications that the annual global number of new HIV infections may have peaked around the beginning of the century have generated speculation in the popular media that the epidemic may have entered a long-term decline. Yet the history of infectious disease suggests that epidemics are often cyclical, characterized by waves of infection that make it difficult to predict the epidemic's future course. Indeed, the HIV epidemic has repeatedly defied predictions derived from epidemiological modelling....

Above all, the dimensions of the epidemic remain staggering. In 2007 alone, 33 million [30 million–36 million] people were living with HIV, 2.7 million [2.2 million–3.2 million] people became infected with the virus, and 2 million [1.8 million–2.3 million] people died of HIV-related causes.

...

Treatment and Care: Unprecedented Progress, Remaining Challenges

The decision of the global community to push towards universal access to HIV prevention, treatment, care, and support represents a moral commitment of historic proportions.... Until this decade, low- and middle-income countries were forced to wait 10–20 years – sometimes for more than a generation – before breakthrough health technologies were broadly available. Slightly more than a decade after the emergence of combination antiretroviral therapy, millions of individuals in resource-limited settings are now benefiting from these medications.

Global commitment to make HIV treatments available in resource-limited settings is bearing fruit. In only six years, the number of people receiving antiretroviral drugs in low- and middle-income countries has increased more than 10-fold. In settings where HIV was invariably fatal only a short time ago, introduction of life-preserving therapies has rejuvenated households, revived entire communities, and re-energized the broader response to the epidemic....

Notwithstanding these considerable achievements, substantially greater progress will be required to move towards universal access to HIV treatment and care. The number of new HIV infections continues to outstrip the increase each year in the number of people on antiretroviral drugs by 2.5 to 1. Thus, the long-term sustainability of even the current pace of treatment scale-up may be jeopardized.

...

Progress in Reducing HIV-related Illness and Death

The impact of antiretroviral drugs on the management of HIV infection has been startling, with improvements in health proving to be far more marked and enduring than anticipated when combination antiretroviral therapy first emerged in the mid-1990s. Recent studies in Denmark suggest that a young man newly diagnosed with HIV is likely to live an additional 35 years with available medications, a tripling of the life expectancy for people with HIV. In slightly more than a decade, the introduction of combination antiretroviral therapy has saved an estimated three million years of life in the United States alone.

...

The growing availability of antiretroviral drugs is lessening the burden of HIV-related mortality in low- and middle-income countries, as it did in high-income countries a decade ago. In rural South Africa, substantial declines in mortality were reported in 2006, as these drugs became increasingly available. After decades of increasing mortality, the annual number of AIDS deaths globally has declined in the past two years, in part as a result of the substantial increase in HIV treatment access in recent years.

...

Antiretroviral Management in Resource-limited Settings

As of December 2007, an estimated 3 million people in low- and middle-income countries were receiving antiretroviral drugs, which represents 31% of those who need the medications, and is a 45% increase over 2006. Increases in treatment coverage have been extraordinary in many countries. For example, in Namibia, where treatment coverage was less than 1% in 2003, 88% of individuals in need were on antiretroviral drugs in 2007. In Rwanda, antiretroviral therapy coverage increased from 1% in 2003 to almost 71% in 2007, aided by a 40-fold growth in the number of antiretroviral treatment sites. Antiretroviral therapy coverage in Thailand rose from 4% in 2003 to 61% in 2007.

...

Expanding Treatment Access: A Collective Endeavour

The rapid growth in antiretroviral therapy coverage represents one of the great success stories in recent global health history. Less than ten years ago, even as antiretroviral drugs were contributing to sharp declines in HIV-related morbidity and mortality in high-income countries, it was widely assumed that these life-preserving medications would remain unaffordable and thus unavailable in low-income countries, perhaps for decades.

In the case of HIV, alleviating the stark disparities in health-care access that typify global health practice has required the leadership and coordination of diverse stakeholders at global, regional, and national levels. In response to the WHO/UNAIDS "3 by 5" initiative,[3] national governments embraced the push to expand HIV treatment access, establishing ambitious targets and making extensive efforts to build national capacity and address obstacles to scale-up. Civil society has mobilized in support of universal treatment access, with particular leadership provided by people living with HIV. At the global level, the Political Declaration on HIV/AIDS, adopted at the UN General Assembly's High Level Meeting on HIV/AIDS in 2006, pledged to move towards universal access to HIV prevention, treatment, care, and support by 2010 – a goal that has obtained the strong support of key global and regional bodies, ranging from the G8 industrialized countries to the African Union and the Caribbean Community and Common Market.

---

[3] Launched in December 2003, the "3 by 5" initiative proposed a massive scale-up of antiretroviral therapy, sufficient to ensure that 3 million people would be on antiretroviral drugs by the end of 2005.

Leading donors have helped finance the expansion of access to treatment. PEPFAR [the U.S. President's Emergency Plan for AIDS Relief] aims to reach 2.5 million people with treatment by 2012. As of December 2007, the Global Fund [to Fight AIDS, Tuberculosis and Malaria] was supporting the delivery of antiretroviral drugs to 1.4 million people, which represents an increase of 88% from the previous year. UNITAID – a relatively new international mechanism for purchasing drugs that is funded by airline taxes – is playing a major role in scaling up paediatric treatment programmes and services to prevent mother-to-child transmission.

Many private companies are also helping to expand HIV treatment access. In Botswana, [for example,] the mining company Debswana entered into a formal partnership with the national government to accelerate treatment scale-up, by covering the delivery of antiretroviral drugs to its HIV-positive workers....

Numerous faith-based organizations are also playing a part in expanding treatment access, providing as much as 40% of all HIV-related health services in some countries....

People living with HIV have mobilized in countries throughout the world to support accelerated treatment scale-up and to promote treatment success.... [For example, a]fter meeting with representatives from 20 pharmaceutical companies, Ashar Alo, a leading network of people living with HIV in Bangladesh, forged an agreement to obtain lower prices for antiretroviral drugs and to establish a drug contribution programme.

———

In 1998, UNAIDS and the Office of the High Commissioner for Human Rights published the International Guidelines on HIV/AIDS and Human Rights.[4] The guidelines, which were updated in 2002, seek to develop effective national responses to the HIV/AIDS pandemic. Guideline 6 concerns access to medicines. It encourages states to, *inter alia*, provide access to antiretroviral medications at affordable prices. It also urges them to "incorporate to the fullest extent any safeguards and flexibilities" in international IP treaties "to the extent necessary to satisfy their domestic and international obligations in relation to human rights."[5] The content of those obligations is the subject of the next section of this chapter.

[4] OHCHR & UNAIDS, *International Guidelines on HIV/AIDS and Human Rights*, U.N. Doc. HR/PUB/06/9 (2006), *available at* http://data.unaids.org/Publications/IRC-pub07/jc1252-internguidelines_en.pdf.

[5] *Id.*, Guideline 6.

2.3. The Human Right to Health and the Emerging Right of Access to Medicines

International recognition of the right to health has existed since the founding of the modern human rights movement at the end of the Second World War. The Universal Declaration of Human Rights (UDHR) provides that everyone has "the right to a standard of living adequate for the health and well-being of himself and his family, including ... medical care."[6] And the Constitution of the World Health Organization (WHO), adopted two years earlier, proclaims in its preamble that "the enjoyment of the highest attainable standard of health is one of the fundamental rights of every human being without distinction of race, religion, political belief, economic or social conditions."[7]

Notwithstanding the widespread acceptance of the right to health, states, policymakers, and scholars continue to debate the content and contours of the right as well as the measures that governments must undertake to satisfy their obligations under international and domestic law. These debates have intensified over the last several years as a growing number of courts have adjudicated complaints alleging violations of the right to health in national constitutions, and as international bodies such as the Committee on Economic, Social and Cultural Rights (CESCR Committee) and the Special Rapporteur on the Right of Everyone to the Enjoyment of the Highest Attainable Standard of Physical and Mental Health have developed more precise frameworks for understanding the scope of the right. The materials that follow engage with these debates, first by considering the justifications for and critiques of the human right to health, and then by explaining the evolution of the right in international and national law, with a particular focus on access to medicines.

A. Justifications for and Critiques of the Human Right to Health

The following two articles offer competing perspectives on the right to health. The first, published by a human rights scholar before international experts and national courts began to focus intensively on the subject, offers foundational arguments concerning the scope of the right. The second article is a more recent critique of the right to health by the President of the Open Society Institute and the former Executive Director of Human Rights Watch.

---

[6] Universal Declaration of Human Rights, G.A. Res. 217A(III), at art. 25.1, U.N. GAOR, 3d Sess., 1st plen. mtg., U.N. Doc. A/810 (Dec. 12, 1948).

[7] Constitution of the World Health Organization, July 22, 1946, prmbl, *available at* http://www.who.int/governance/eb/who_constitution_en.pdf.

Virginia Leary, *The Right to Health in International Human Rights Law*, 1 HEALTH & HUM. RTS. 25, 28, 35–40 (1994)

On first hearing it, the phrase "right to health" strikes many as strange.... [It] seems to presume that government or international organizations or individuals must guarantee a person's good health. This interpretation is obviously absurd.... The term "right to health" is currently used in the context of human rights as short-hand, referring to the more detailed language contained in international treaties and to fundamental human rights principles.

. . .

What does rights discourse add to consideration of complex technical, economic, and practical issues involved in health care and status? ... The concept of a right to health as a human right emphasizes social and ethical aspects of health care and health status, as these aspects are embodied in principles underlying all international human rights. With that in mind, a rights-based perspective on health is developed in this section by focusing on the following elements of all rights and applying them to health status issues:

(1) Conceptualizing something as a right emphasizes its exceptional importance as a social or public goal. (Rights as "trumps.")
(2) Rights concepts focus on the dignity of persons.
(3) Equality or non-discrimination is a fundamental principle of human rights.
(4) Participation of individuals and groups in issues affecting them is an essential aspect of human rights.
(5) The concept of rights implies entitlement.
(6) Rights are interdependent.
(7) Rights are almost never absolute and may be limited, but such limitations should be subject to strict scrutiny.

Rights as Trumps

The use of rights language vis à vis social goals confers a special status on those goals. As Ronald Dworkin puts it, categorizing something as a right means that the right "trumps" many other claims or goods. A special importance, status, priority, is implied in categorizing something as a right. Therefore, the use of rights language in connection with health issues emphasizes the importance of health care and health status. To speak of a right to health does not mean that that right should always take priority over all other goods, claims, or other rights; but it does emphasize that health issues are of special importance given the impact of health on the life and survival of individuals....

Conceptualizing health status in terms of rights under-scores health as a social good and not solely a medical, technical, or economic problem.

Dignity as the Foundation of Human Rights

In the language of the Preamble to the Universal Declaration of Human Rights, "recognition of the inherent dignity and of the equal and inalienable rights of all members of the human family is the foundation of freedom, justice and peace in the world." The concept of rights grows out of a perception of the inherent dignity of every human being. Thus, use of rights language in connection with health emphasizes that the dignity of each person must be central in all aspects of health, including health care, medical experimentation, and limitations on freedom in the name of health. The focus must be on the dignity of the individual rather than the good of the collectivity. The utilitarian principle is rejected by a rights approach. The greater good of the greater number may not override individual dignity.

. . .

The Equality or Non-Discrimination Principle

Equality or non-discrimination is a fundamental principle of human rights law. . . . The rights approach, with its emphasis on non-discrimination (including on the grounds of limited economic resources) implies rejection of a solely market-based approach to the social good of health care and health status. Cost-containment and cost-benefit analyses in the health care allocation remain important but need not be determinative in matters of social goals relating to health.

. . .

It requires only cursory consideration to understand how frequently equality and prohibition of discrimination is violated in many aspects of health status. In most countries, the health status of racial or ethnic minorities is far worse than that of the majority population. . . . Women's health issues have been given less attention in medical research; women's health problems have attracted less interest than those from which men suffer; and many common cultural practices affect women more negatively than men.

. . .

Participation

Participation of individuals and groups in matters that affect them is essential to the protection of all human rights. Democracy and human rights are frequently linked in current rights discourse – and democracy means more than merely voting: it requires provision of information and informed participation....

Entitlement

The concept of a right implies entitlement to the subject of that right.... [T]he recognition of the right to health as an internationally guaranteed right ... gives legal and political legitimacy to the claims for its enjoyment. This does not necessarily imply resort to lawsuits, which may not always be the best means of asserting rights. Indeed, in some legal systems, social rights are considered non-justiciable. Other measures may be resorted to, such as administrative agencies or tribunals or creation of the role of ombudsman to respond to citizens' complaints. Audrey Chapman, in an American Association for the Advancement of Science publication on the right to health care, has commented,

> A rights approach offers a normative vocabulary that facilitates both the framing of claims and the identification of the right holder. This means that the addressees of the rights or duty-bearers [governments] ... have the duty to provide the entitlement, not to society in general, but to each member. This standing has very important implications for efforts to seek redress in cases where the entitlement is not provided or the right violated.

...

Interdependence of Human Rights

Human rights are interdependent. That is, particular rights may depend on other rights for their fulfillment.... Therefore, the right to health cannot be effectively protected without respect for other recognized rights. These include, in particular, both prohibition of discrimination, and the right of persons to participate in decisions affecting them.

Limitations on Rights

Rights are generally not absolute in national or international legal systems and may be subject to limitations on certain grounds. Protection of public health is one of the accepted grounds for which limitations are permitted in the International Covenant on Civil and Political Rights and in other human rights instruments. Under the Covenant, protection of public health is a permissible ground for limiting the rights to liberty of movement, freedom of religion, freedom of expression and the right to freedom of association.... Limitations on rights must be scrutinized to determine whether they are truly necessary. Under international human rights law, national decisions to limit rights may be over-seen by international monitoring committees, which can require states to provide adequate justifications for rights limitations.

Aryeh Neier, *Social and Economic Rights: A Critique*, 13/2 Hum. Rts. Brief 1, 1–3 (2006)

Let me first make clear that I favor a fairer distribution of the world's resources; however, I believe that the effort to achieve fairer distribution has to take place through the political process. For the most part ... it cannot take place through the assertion of rights. I do not think that rights are an abstract concept. I think they are a contract between a citizen and a state, or a citizen and her community, and that a citizen has to be able to enforce her side of that contract. Rights only have meaning if it is possible to enforce them. But there has to be some mechanism for that enforcement, and adjudication seems to be the mechanism that we have chosen. Therefore, from my standpoint, if one is to talk meaningfully of rights, one has to discuss what can be enforced through the judicial process.

...

The concern I have with economic and social rights is when there are broad assertions of the sort that appear in the Universal Declaration of Human Rights or that appear in the South African Constitution, which speak broadly of ... a right to health care. There, I think, we get into territory that is unmanageable through the judicial process and that intrudes fundamentally into an area where the democratic process ought to prevail.

... Economic and security matters ought to be questions of public debate. To withdraw either of them from the democratic process is to carve the heart out of that process. Everybody has an opinion on what should be done to protect the public's safety, and everybody has a view as to what is appropriate in the allocation of a society's resources and its economic burdens. Therefore, everybody ought to be able to take part in the discussion. It should not be settled by some person exercising superior wisdom, who comes along as a sort of Platonic guardian and decides this is the way it ought to be. These issues ought to be debated by everyone in the democratic process, with the legislature representing the public and with the public influencing the legislature in turn. To suggest otherwise undermines the very concept of democracy by stripping from it an essential part of its role.

... Whenever you get to these broad assertions of shelter or housing or other economic resources, the question becomes: What shelter, employment, security, or level of education and health care is the person entitled to? It is only possible to deal with this question through the process of negotiation and compromise. Not everybody can have everything. There have to be certain decisions and choices that are made when one comes to the question of benefits, and a court is not the place where it is possible to engage in that sort of negotiation and compromise. It is not the place where different individuals come forward and declare their interests and what they are willing to sacrifice for those interests. That is the heart of the political process; only the political process can handle those questions.

Consider the question of health care. One person needs a kidney transplant to save her life, another needs a heart-bypass operation, and still another needs life-long anti-retroviral therapy. All of these are life-saving measures, but they are expensive. Then there is the concern about primary health care for everyone. If you are allocating the resources of a society, how do you deal with the person who says they need that kidney transplant or that bypass or those anti-retroviral drugs to save their life when the cost of these procedures may be equivalent to providing primary health care for a thousand children? Do you say the greater good for the greater number, a utilitarian principle, and exclude the person whose life is at stake if they do not get the health care that they require? I do not believe that is the kind of thing a court should do. Rather, I think that many different considerations need to be taken into account, and that only through a process of negotiation can an outcome be reached that, although it might not satisfy everybody, allows society to grapple with questions that affect a whole community of people.

...

Part of my concern with this question of so-called economic and social rights is that I am a believer in very strong civil and political rights: the right to free speech, the right to assemble, the right not to be tortured, etc. Those rights have to mean exactly the same thing every place in the world. With social and economic "rights," however, it is inevitable that they are going to be applied differently in different places. That is, if you are talking about one country with extensive resources and one that is very poor, there is not going to be the same right to shelter or to health care. Resource allocation has to come into play in determining what is going to be provided, and it is appropriate that countries should deal with these matters in different ways depending upon their resources.

But suppose that one takes that same idea – that different stages of development mean different things for each country – and applies it to the concept of civil and political rights. Suppose China or Zimbabwe says it is not a developed country and therefore cannot provide the same civil and political rights as a developed country. If you introduce the idea that different stages of development mean different things as far as rights are concerned, it is not going to be possible to prevent that from carrying over into the realm of civil and political rights. Therefore, I think it is dangerous to allow this idea of social and economic rights to flourish.

Notes and Questions

1. What arguments does Virginia Leary advance in favor of the right to health? What are Aryeh Neier's objections to the recognition of this right? Which of his objections are responsive to the arguments that Leary advances?

2. In her discussion of "dignity as the foundation of human rights," Leary asserts that human rights law rejects the "utilitarian principle" that the "greater good of the greater number" can override the rights or needs of the individual. Would Neier agree or disagree with this assertion, and why?

3. Leary cites the prohibition on human medical experimentation as an example of human rights law's emphasis on human dignity. Although such experimentation "may result in good for the general populace, it must not violate the dignity of the individuals subjected to it." Does this example provide a persuasive justification for privileging individual rights over the collective good with respect to health care decisions in general? What consequences can you foresee from the adoption of such an approach?

4. Are the other six human rights "elements" that Leary discusses also inconsistent with the utilitarian principle? If not, how does one determine whether utilitarian concerns should be considered in defining the scope of the human right to health?

5. Which legal and political institutions are best suited to make decisions concerning health care entitlements? To resolve disputes concerning those entitlements? What response would you offer to the argument that judges lack the expertise and skills needed to address these issues?

6. Leary and Neier both stress the importance of individuals and groups participating in decision making involving health care issues. Yet they reach very different conclusions as to whether recognition of a right to health is compatible with democratic processes. Is it possible to reconcile their competing perspectives? Under what circumstances might a democracy with strong political institutions nevertheless decide that every individual should enjoy a judicially enforceable right to health care? How might such a democracy give effect to such a decision?

7. Assume for purposes of argument that a national constitution prohibits judges from adjudicating complaints alleging violations of the right to

health. What other institutions, if any, might be appropriate to resolve such complaints?

8. If the right to health is nonjusticiable and judicial remedies are unavailable to individuals whose rights have been violated, is there any justification for framing health concerns in human rights terms? What other values might be advanced by such a human rights framing?

B. The Normative Development of the Human Right to Health and of Access to Medicines

The right to health was mentioned by U.S. President Franklin Roosevelt in his famous "four freedoms" speech given during the early dark days of the Second World War. Roosevelt identified one of the four freedoms – "freedom from want" – as including "a healthy peacetime life for [the] inhabitants" of every nation.[8] Three years later, in his 1944 State of the Union address, Roosevelt called for an economic bill of rights that included "the right to adequate medical care and the opportunity to achieve and enjoy good health."[9]

As noted earlier, the right to health appears in Article 25 of the UDHR and, more capaciously, in the preamble to the WHO Constitution. It has since been incorporated into a multitude of global and regional human rights agreements[10] and two-thirds of national constitutions.[11] Among the most prominent of these instruments is Article 12 of the ICESCR, which

---

[8] Franklin D. Roosevelt, *The "Four Freedoms" Address*, 87 CONG. REC. 44, 46–47 (1941). The other three freedoms were freedom of speech and expression, freedom of religious worship, and freedom from fear. For additional discussion of "freedom from want" as it applies to the right to food, see Chapter 6.

[9] Franklin D. Roosevelt, *State of the Union Address to Congress*, 90 CONG. REC. 55, 57 (Jan. 11, 1944).

[10] Human rights treaties that protect the right to health include (1) Article 24 of the Convention on the Rights of the Child, which recognizes the right "to the enjoyment of the highest attainable standard of health and to facilities for the treatment of illness and rehabilitation of health"; (2) Article 5(e) of the Convention on the Elimination of All Forms of Racial Discrimination, which prohibits discrimination in "public health" and "medical care"; (3) Article 11 of Convention on the Elimination of All Forms of Discrimination against Women, which protects gender equality with respect to health and safety in working conditions, including reproductive health; (4) Article 10 of the Additional Protocol to the American Convention on Human Rights in the Area of Economic, Social, and Cultural Rights (the Protocol of San Salvador), which defines the "right to health" as "the enjoyment of the highest level of physical, mental and social well-being," and includes a detailed list of measures that states parties must adopt to "ensure" that right, including the "prevention and treatment of endemic, occupational and other diseases"; (5) Article 16 of the African Charter, which provides that "every individual shall have the right to enjoy the best attainable state of physical and mental health" and requires states to "take the necessary measures to protect the health of their people and to ensure that they receive medical attention when they are sick"; and (6) Article 11 of the European Social Charter, which recognizes the "right to protection of health."

[11] *See* Eleanor D. Kinney & Brian Alexander Clark, *Provisions for Health and Healthcare in the Constitutions of the Countries of the World*, 37 CORNELL INT'L L.J. 287, 291 (2004).

"recognize[s] the right of everyone to the enjoyment of the highest attainable standard of physical and mental health," and which requires states parties to take "steps ... to achieve the full realization of this right," including those necessary for

(a) The provision for the reduction of the stillbirth-rate and of infant mortality and for the healthy development of the child;
(b) The improvement of all aspects of environmental and industrial hygiene;
(c) The prevention, treatment and control of epidemic, endemic, occupational and other diseases;
(d) The creation of conditions which would assure to all medical service and medical attention in the event of sickness.[12]

In accordance with the principle of progressive realization applicable to all economic, social, and cultural rights in the ICESCR, states parties must "take steps" to achieve the right to health "to the maximum of its available resources, with a view to achieving progressively the full realization of the rights."[13] According to several commentators, the incremental, resource-dependent nature of the progressive realization approach undermines the universality of the right to health and provides insufficient guidance to states concerning their legal obligations.[14] In response to these criticisms and after reviewing numerous reports from states parties concerning Article 12, the CESCR Committee adopted, in 2000, a *General Comment* on the right to health. The *General Comment* has been highly influential on subsequent interpretations and analyses of the right by governments, judges, and commentators. We reproduce its key provisions below, emphasizing those clauses concerning access to medicines.

---

[12] International Covenant on Economic, Social and Cultural Rights, art. 12(2), *adopted* Dec. 16, 1966, S. Exec. Doc. D, 95–2 (1977), 993 U.N.T.S. 3 (entered into force Jan. 3, 1976) [ICESCR].

[13] *Id.* art. 2(1).

[14] *See, e.g.,* DAVID P. FIDLER, INTERNATIONAL LAW AND INFECTIOUS DISEASES 188 (1999) ("The text of [ICESCR] Article 12(2) is too general to provide insight into concrete actions States parties need to take."); Benjamin M. Meier & Larisa M. Mori, *The Highest Attainable Standard: Advancing a Collective Human Right to Public Health*, 37 COLUM. HUM. RTS. L. REV. 101, 114 (2005) ("Outside of the sweeping platitudes enunciated in national and international law, what specific entitlements does the individual right to health include? With countries differing greatly in available health resources, how is the 'highest attainable standard' of health defined?"); Brigit Toebes, *Towards an Improved Understanding of the International Human Right to Health*, 21 HUM. RTS. Q. 661, 661–62 (1999) ("It is by no means clear precisely what individuals are entitled to under the right to health, nor is it clear what the resulting obligations are on the part of states.").

General Comment No. 14, *The Right to the Highest Attainable Standard of Health* (art. 12), U.N. Doc. E/C.12/2000/4 (2000)

1. Health is a fundamental human right indispensable for the exercise of other human rights. Every human being is entitled to the enjoyment of the highest attainable standard of health conducive to living a life in dignity. The realization of the right to health may be pursued through numerous, complementary approaches.... Moreover, the right to health includes certain components which are legally enforceable.

2. The human right to health is recognized in numerous international instruments....

3. The right to health is closely related to and dependent upon the realization of other human rights, ... including the rights to food, housing, work, education, human dignity, life, non-discrimination, equality, the prohibition against torture, privacy, access to information, and the freedoms of association, assembly and movement. These and other rights and freedoms address integral components of the right to health.

. . .

5. The Committee is aware that, for millions of people throughout the world, the full enjoyment of the right to health still remains a distant goal. Moreover, in many cases, especially for those living in poverty, this goal is becoming increasingly remote. The Committee recognizes the formidable structural and other obstacles resulting from international and other factors beyond the control of States that impede the full realization of article 12 in many States parties.

. . .

12. The right to health in all its forms and at all levels contains the following interrelated and essential elements, the precise application of which will depend on the conditions prevailing in a particular State party:

(a) *Availability*. Functioning public health and health-care facilities, goods and services, as well as programmes, have to be available in sufficient quantity within the State party. The precise nature of the facilities, goods and services will vary depending on numerous factors, including the State party's developmental level....

(b) *Accessibility*. Health facilities, goods and services have to be accessible to everyone without discrimination.... Accessibility has four overlapping dimensions:

Non-discrimination: health facilities, goods and services must be accessible to all, especially the most vulnerable or marginalized sections of the population....

Physical accessibility: health facilities, goods and services must be within safe physical reach for all sections of the population, especially vulnerable or marginalized groups....

Economic accessibility (affordability): health facilities, goods and services must be affordable for all. Payment for health-care services ... has to be based on the principle of equity, ensuring that these services, whether privately or publicly provided, are affordable for all, including socially disadvantaged groups. Equity demands that poorer households should not be disproportionately burdened with health expenses as compared to richer households.

Information accessibility: accessibility includes the right to seek, receive and impart information and ideas concerning health issues....

(c) *Acceptability*. All health facilities, goods and services must be respectful of medical ethics and culturally appropriate, i.e. respectful of the culture of individuals, minorities, peoples and communities....

(d) *Quality*. Health facilities, goods and services must also be scientifically and medically appropriate and of good quality. This requires, *inter alia*, skilled medical personnel, scientifically approved and unexpired drugs and hospital equipment, safe and potable water, and adequate sanitation.

...

Article 12.2 (c). The Right to Prevention, Treatment
and Control of Diseases

16. "The prevention, treatment and control of epidemic, endemic, occupational and other diseases" (art. 12.2 (c)) requires the establishment of prevention and education programmes for behaviour-related health concerns such as sexually transmitted diseases, in particular HIV/AIDS, and those adversely affecting sexual and reproductive health, and the promotion of social determinants of good health, such as environmental safety, education, economic development and gender equity. The right to treatment includes the creation of a system of urgent medical care in cases of accidents, epidemics and similar health hazards, and the provision of disaster relief and humanitarian assistance in emergency situations. The control of diseases refers to States' individual and joint efforts to, *inter alia*, make available relevant technologies....

Article 12.2 (d). The Right to Health Facilities, Goods and Services

17. "The creation of conditions which would assure to all medical service and medical attention in the event of sickness" (art. 12.2 (d)), both physical

and mental, includes the provision of equal and timely access to basic preventive, curative, rehabilitative health services and health education; regular
screening programmes; appropriate treatment of prevalent diseases, illnesses,
injuries and disabilities, preferably at community level; the provision of essential drugs; and appropriate mental health treatment and care....

...

General Legal Obligations

30. While the Covenant provides for progressive realization ... it also
imposes on States parties various obligations which are of immediate effect ...
such as the guarantee that the right will be exercised without discrimination
of any kind (art. 2.2) and the obligation to take steps (art. 2.1) towards the full
realization of article 12. Such steps must be deliberate, concrete and targeted
towards the full realization of the right to health.

31. ... Progressive realization means that States parties have a specific and
continuing obligation to move as expeditiously and effectively as possible
towards the full realization of article 12.

32. ... There is a strong presumption that retrogressive measures taken in
relation to the right to health are not permissible. If any deliberately retrogressive measures are taken, the State party has the burden of proving that
they have been introduced after the most careful consideration of all alternatives and that they are duly justified by reference to the totality of the rights
provided for in the Covenant in the context of the full use of the State party's
maximum available resources.

33. The right to health, like all human rights, imposes three types or levels
of obligations on States parties: the obligations to *respect*, *protect* and *fulfil*.
In turn, the obligation to fulfil contains obligations to facilitate, provide and
promote. The obligation to *respect* requires States to refrain from interfering
directly or indirectly with the enjoyment of the right to health. The obligation to *protect* requires States to take measures that prevent third parties from
interfering with article 12 guarantees. Finally, the obligation to *fulfil* requires
States to adopt appropriate legislative, administrative, budgetary, judicial,
promotional and other measures towards the full realization of the right to
health.

Specific Legal Obligations

34. In particular, States are under the obligation to *respect* the right to health
by, *inter alia*, refraining from denying or limiting equal access for all persons ...
to preventive, curative and palliative health services; obligations to respect
include a State's obligation to refrain ... from marketing unsafe drugs....

35. Obligations to *protect* include, *inter alia*, the duties of States to adopt legislation or to take other measures ensuring equal access to health care and health-related services provided by third parties; to ensure that privatization of the health sector does not constitute a threat to the availability, accessibility, acceptability and quality of health facilities, goods and services; [and] to control the marketing of medical equipment and medicines by third parties....

36. The obligation to *fulfil* requires States parties, *inter alia*, to give sufficient recognition to the right to health in the national political and legal systems, preferably by way of legislative implementation, and to adopt a national health policy....

...

International Obligations

...

39. ... States parties have to respect the enjoyment of the right to health in other countries, and to prevent third parties from violating the right in other countries, if they are able to influence these third parties by way of legal or political means, in accordance with the Charter of the United Nations and applicable international law. Depending on the availability of resources, States should facilitate access to essential health facilities, goods and services in other countries, wherever possible and provide the necessary aid when required. States parties should ensure that the right to health is given due attention in international agreements.... In relation to the conclusion of other international agreements, States parties should take steps to ensure that these instruments do not adversely impact upon the right to health. Similarly, States parties have an obligation to ensure that their actions as members of international organizations take due account of the right to health....

...

Core Obligations

43. In *General Comment No. 3*, the Committee confirms that States parties have a core obligation to ensure the satisfaction of, at the very least, minimum essential levels of each of the rights enunciated in the Covenant, including essential primary health care. These core obligations include at least the following obligations:

(a) To ensure the right of access to health facilities, goods and services on a non-discriminatory basis, especially for vulnerable or marginalized groups;

(b) To ensure access to the minimum essential food which is nutritionally adequate and safe, to ensure freedom from hunger to everyone;

(c) To ensure access to basic shelter, housing and sanitation, and an adequate supply of safe and potable water;

(d) To provide essential drugs, as from time to time defined under the WHO Action Programme on Essential Drugs;

(e) To ensure equitable distribution of all health facilities, goods and services;

(f) To adopt and implement a national public health strategy and plan of action, on the basis of epidemiological evidence, addressing the health concerns of the whole population ....

...

47.... If resource constraints render it impossible for a State to comply fully with its Covenant obligations, it has the burden of justifying that every effort has nevertheless been made to use all available resources at its disposal in order to satisfy, as a matter of priority, the obligations outlined above. It should be stressed, however, that a State party cannot, under any circumstances whatsoever, justify its non-compliance with the core obligations set out in paragraph 43 above, which are non-derogable.

48. Violations of the right to health can occur through the direct action of States or other entities insufficiently regulated by States. The adoption of any retrogressive measures incompatible with the core obligations under the right to health, outlined in paragraph 43 above, constitutes a violation of the right to health. Violations through *acts of commission* include the formal repeal or suspension of legislation necessary for the continued enjoyment of the right to health or the adoption of legislation or policies which are manifestly incompatible with pre-existing domestic or international legal obligations in relation to the right to health.

49. Violations of the right to health can also occur through the omission or failure of States to take necessary measures arising from legal obligations. Violations through *acts of omission* include the failure to take appropriate steps towards the full realization of everyone's right to the enjoyment of the highest attainable standard of physical and mental health, the failure to have a national policy on occupational safety and health as well as occupational health services, and the failure to enforce relevant laws.

Violations of the Obligation to Respect

50. Violations of the obligation to respect are those State actions, policies or laws that contravene the standards set out in article 12 of the Covenant

and are likely to result in bodily harm, unnecessary morbidity and preventable mortality. Examples include the denial of access to health facilities, goods and services to particular individuals or groups as a result of de jure or de facto discrimination; the deliberate withholding or misrepresentation of information vital to health protection or treatment; the suspension of legislation or the adoption of laws or policies that interfere with the enjoyment of any of the components of the right to health; and the failure of the State to take into account its legal obligations regarding the right to health when entering into bilateral or multilateral agreements with other States, international organizations and other entities, such as multinational corporations.

Violations of the Obligation to Protect

51. Violations of the obligation to protect follow from the failure of a State to take all necessary measures to safeguard persons within their jurisdiction from infringements of the right to health by third parties. This category includes such omissions as the failure to regulate the activities of individuals, groups or corporations so as to prevent them from violating the right to health of others; the failure to protect consumers and workers from practices detrimental to health, e.g. by employers and manufacturers of medicines or food ....

Violations of the Obligation to Fulfil

52. Violations of the obligation to fulfil occur through the failure of States parties to take all necessary steps to ensure the realization of the right to health. Examples include the failure to adopt or implement a national health policy designed to ensure the right to health for everyone; insufficient expenditure or misallocation of public resources which results in the non-enjoyment of the right to health by individuals or groups, particularly the vulnerable or marginalized....

. . .

Remedies and Accountability

59. Any person or group victim of a violation of the right to health should have access to effective judicial or other appropriate remedies at both national and international levels. All victims of such violations should be entitled to adequate reparation, which may take the form of restitution, compensation, satisfaction or guarantees of non-repetition....

60. The incorporation in the domestic legal order of international instruments recognizing the right to health can significantly enhance the scope and effectiveness of remedial measures and should be encouraged in all cases. Incorporation enables courts to adjudicate violations of the right to health, or at least its core obligations, by direct reference to the Covenant.

A rapid evolution of the normative content of the right to health occurred in the decade following the adoption of *General Comment No. 14* in 2000. A confluence of several factors – the spread of global pandemics such as HIV/AIDS, malaria, and tuberculosis, a growing awareness of the adverse consequences of those pandemics, and an expanding list of antiretroviral drugs for treating HIV/AIDS – has engendered repeated assertions that the right to health encompasses a right of access to livesaving medicines. Statements affirming such a right of access appear in, *inter alia*, declarations adopted by the U.N. General Assembly in 2001 and 2006; resolutions of the Human Rights Council and its predecessor, the Commission on Human Rights, adopted in 2001, 2002, 2003, and 2005; reports by the Special Rapporteur on the Right to Health; a 2003 *General Comment* by the U.N. Committee on the Rights of the Child; and a 2008 resolution of the African Commission on Human and Peoples' Rights.[15] Commentators have bolstered these statements

---

[15] *See, e.g., U.N. Declaration of Commitment on HIV/AIDS*, G.A. Res. 33/2001, para. 15, U.N. GAOR, 26th Special Sess. (June 25–27, 2001) (recognizing "that access to medication in the context of pandemics such as HIV/AIDS is one of the fundamental elements to achieve progressively the full realization of the right of everyone to the enjoyment of the highest attainable standard of physical and mental health"); Human Rights Council, Res. 12/24, U.N. Doc. A/HRC/RES/12/24 (Oct. 2, 2009), para. 1 (stating that "access to medicines is one of the fundamental elements in achieving progressively the full realization of the right of everyone to the enjoyment of the highest attainable standard of physical and mental health"); Comm'n on Human Rights, *Access to Medication in the Context of Pandemics Such as HIV/AIDS*, para. 3(a), U.N. Doc. E/CN.4/RES/2002/32 (Apr. 22, 2002) (containing a materially identical statement concerning "access to medication in the context of pandemics such as HIV/AIDS"); U.N. Special Rapporteur on the Right of Everyone to the Highest Attainable Standard of Physical and Mental Health, *Addendum: Mission to the World Trade Organization*, para. 18, U.N. Doc. E/CN.4/2004/49/Add.1 (Mar. 1, 2004) (*prepared by* Paul Hunt) [Special Rapporteur, *Mission to the WTO*] ("The right to health is an inclusive right, extending not only to timely and appropriate health care, including access to essential medicines, but also to the underlying determinants of health, such as access to safe and potable water and adequate sanitation."); Comm. on the Rights of the Child, *General Comment No. 3: HIV/AIDS and the Rights of the Child*, para. 28, U.N. Doc. CRC/GC/2003/3 (Mar. 17, 2003) [*General Comment No. 3*] ("The obligations of States parties under the Convention extend to ensuring that children have sustained and equal access to comprehensive treatment and

with analyses that draw upon other human rights, including the right to life, the right to share in the benefits of scientific progress, and the right to nondiscrimination.[16]

Notwithstanding the large number of affirmations of a right of access to medicines, the precise scope of the right, and its relationship to patent protection, remain somewhat ambiguous.[17] Numerous documents assert a universal right of access to pharmaceuticals and medical technologies without, however, expressly indicating whether those drugs and technologies are protected by patents or what the consequences of such protection, if any, might be. Illustrative is a 2003 resolution of the Human Rights Commission, which

> 4. *Further calls upon* States to pursue policies, in accordance with applicable international law, including international agreements acceded to, which would promote:
> (*a*) The availability in sufficient quantities of pharmaceutical products and medical technologies used to treat pandemics such as HIV/AIDS, tuberculosis and malaria....;
> (*b*) The accessibility and affordability for all without discrimination, including the most vulnerable or socially disadvantaged groups of the population, of pharmaceutical products or medical technologies used to treat pandemics such as HIV/AIDS....;
> (*c*) The assurance that pharmaceutical products or medical technologies used to treat pandemics such as HIV/AIDS ... are scientifically and medically appropriate and of good quality;
>
> 5. *Calls upon* States, at the national level, on a non-discriminatory basis, in accordance with applicable international law, including international agreements acceded to:
> (*a*) To refrain from taking measures which would deny or limit equal access for all persons to preventive, curative or palliative pharmaceutical products or medical technologies used to treat pandemics such as HIV/AIDS....;
> (*b*) To adopt and implement legislation or other measures, in accordance with applicable international law, including international agreements acceded

---

care, including necessary HIV-related drugs"); Afr. Comm'n on Human and Peoples' Rights, *Resolution on Access to Health and Needed Medicines in Africa*, Res. 141 (XXXXIIII)08 (2008) (recognizing "that access to needed medicines is a fundamental component of the right to health and that States parties to the African Charter have an obligation to provide where appropriate needed medicines, or facilitate access to them").

[16] *See, e.g.,* Zita Lazzarini, *Making Access to Pharmaceuticals a Reality: Legal Options under TRIPS and the Case of Brazil*, 6 Yale Hum. Rts. & Dev. L.J. 103, 117–18 (2003); Alicia Yamin, *Not Just a Tragedy: Access to Medications as a Right under International Law*, 21 B.U. Int'l L.J. 325, 329–51 (2003).

[17] A few of these documents refer favorably to the 2001 Doha Declaration on the TRIPS Agreement and Public Health, a document whose origins and consequences we discuss in greater detail later.

to, to safeguard access to such preventive, curative or palliative pharma-ceutical products or medical technologies from any limitations by third parties;

(c) To adopt all appropriate positive measures, to the maximum of the resources allocated for this purpose, to promote effective access to such preventive, curative or palliative pharmaceutical products or medical technologies....[18]

A few of the documents listed in the previous paragraph address the issue of patented medicines indirectly. For example, the *General Comment on HIV/AIDS and the Rights of the Child* asserts that the Convention on the Rights of the Child requires states parties to "ensur[e] that children have sustained and equal access to ... HIV-related drugs" (including, presumably those protected by patents), and it urges such states to "negotiate with the pharmaceutical industry in order to make the necessary medicines locally available at the lowest costs possible."[19] Similarly, the U.N. General Assembly's *Declaration of Commitment on HIV/AIDS* recognizes "that the cost, availability and afford-ability of drugs and related technology are significant factors [relating to access to medicines] and that there is a need to reduce the cost of these drugs and technologies in close collaboration with the private sector and pharma-ceutical companies."[20]

Perhaps the most extensive discussion of the relationship between intellec-tual property protection and access to medicines appears in a 2004 report of the Special Rapporteur on the Right to Health:

43. The exclusion of competitors as a result of the grant of a patent can ... be used by patent holders as a tool to increase the price of pharmaceuticals. High prices can exclude some sections of the population, particularly poor people, from accessing medicines. Given that the right to health includes an obliga-tion on States to provide affordable essential medicines according to the WHO essential drugs list, intellectual property protection can lead to negative effects on the enjoyment of the right to health. In other words, in some cases intel-lectual property protection can reduce the economic accessibility of essential medicines....

44. Neglected diseases and very neglected diseases are human rights issues. In particular, very neglected diseases – those diseases overwhelmingly or exclusively occurring in developing countries, such as river blindness and sleeping sickness – receive little research and development, and very lit-tle commercially-based research and development in wealthy countries. The

[18] Comm'n on Human Rights, *Access to Medication in the Context of Pandemics Such as HIV/AIDS, Tuberculosis and Malaria*, paras. 4–5, U.N. Doc. E/CN.4/Res/2003/29 (Apr. 22, 2003).

[19] *General Comment No. 3, supra* note 15, para. 28.

[20] *U.N. Declaration of Commitment on HIV/AIDS, supra* note 15, para. 24.

possibility of recouping research and development costs by excluding compe-tition from the market through the use of intellectual property rights assumes that there is a market for new medicines in the first place. The fact that very neglected diseases are suffered overwhelmingly by poor people in poor countries underlines that there is no or little market potential for medicines fighting these diseases, simply because the sufferers are unable to pay. Intellectual property protection does not provide an incentive to invest in research and development in relation to very neglected diseases.[21]

Notes and Questions

1. The 2004 report of the Special Rapporteur identifies two ways that IP protection may adversely affect the availability of and access to medicines. First, such protection increases the costs of pharmaceuticals, making them unaffordable to segments of the population who could have paid for the drugs had they been sold at their marginal cost of production. As the U.K. Commission on Intellectual Property Rights has observed:

> The importance of prices of medicines to poor consumers in developing coun-tries is perhaps obvious. But it is worth emphasising that if a sick person has to pay more for a pharmaceutical product as a result of a patent, it means that he or she will have less to spend on other essentials of life such as food or shelter. Alternatively, foregoing the medicine because it is unavailable or unaffordable may result in long term ill health, or death. That is why it is essential to consider the impact of the introduction of an IP regime on prices, while recognising that prices are affected by many factors. These include purchasing power, competi-tion and market structure, responsiveness of demand to price and government price controls and regulations.[22]

Second, patent protection channels private research and development toward new drugs that are likely to generate significant revenues for pharmaceutical firms. Conversely, it creates little incentive to develop drugs that have lim-ited market potential, for example, because a small number of individuals are affected by a disease, or because the purchasers, although numerous, are overwhelmingly poor and do not have the means to pay the supracompeti-tive prices that enable the firms to recoup their research costs. According to the U.K. Commission:

> Pharmaceutical research by the private sector is driven by commercial consid-erations and if the effective demand in terms of market size is small, even for the most common diseases such as TB and malaria, it is often not commercially worthwhile to devote significant resources to addressing the needs.... This nec-essarily leads to a research agenda led by the market demand in the markets of

---

[21] Special Rapporteur, *Mission to the WTO, supra* note 15, paras. 43–44.
[22] Commission on Intellectual Property Rights, *supra* note 2, at 36.

the developed world, rather than by the needs of poor people in the developing world, and thus a focus mainly on non-communicable disease.[23]

We return to these two distinct dimensions of the intersection of patents and the right to health in later sections of this chapter.

2. Which provisions of *General Comment No. 14* are relevant to patent protection for pharmaceuticals? What actions does the *General Comment* require of states parties to increase access to patented medicines?[24]

3. Does *General Comment No. 14* impose legal obligations on private drug manufacturers? In answering this question, consider the *Human Rights Guidelines for Pharmaceutical Companies in Relation to Access to Medicines*,[25] adopted by the Special Rapporteur on the Right to Health and discussed in greater detail in Chapter 1. Does the existence of these guidelines, adopted in August 2008, bolster or undercut the assertion that private pharmaceutical companies have legal obligations relating to the human right to health?

4. Paragraph 43 of *General Comment No. 14* recognizes a "core obligation" for states parties to provide "essential drugs, as from time to time defined under the WHO Action Programme on Essential Drugs." Since 1977, the WHO has published a Model List of Essential Medicines. Revised every two years by a committee of experts, the Model List has guided the development of national essential medicines lists that "address the priority health care requirements of a population." Pharmaceuticals on the WHO Model List are selected through "an evidence-based process" that considers "disease prevalence, evidence of safety and efficacy, and comparative cost-effectiveness."[26] The most recent version of the list, published in 2010, contains more than 350 medicines for the treatment of infectious diseases including HIV/AIDS, malaria, and tuberculosis, as well as chronic diseases such as cancer and diabetes, and medicines relating to reproductive health.[27] Although not legally binding, the WHO list of essential medicines is highly influential. "For example, major nongovernmental organizations and United Nations agencies limit the drugs that they purchase for donation to those on the list."[28]

---

[23] *Id.* at 32.

[24] *See, e.g.,* Jamie Crook, *Balancing Intellectual Property Protection with the Human Right to Health*, 23 BERKELEY J. INT'L L. 524, 536 (2005); Yamin, *supra* note 16, at 350–59.

[25] U.N. Special Rapporteur on the Right of Everyone to the Enjoyment of the Highest Attainable Standard of Physical and Mental Health, *Human Rights Guidelines for Pharmaceutical Companies in Relation to Access to Medicines*, UN Doc. A/63/263, pmbl. para. i & Guideline 26 (Aug. 11, 2008) (*prepared by* Paul Hunt) [*Pharmaceutical Company Guidelines*].

[26] World Health Organization, *Essential Medicines List*, Fact Sheet No. 325 (June 2010), *available at* http://www.who.int/mediacentre/factsheets/fs325/en/print.html.

[27] *Id.*

[28] S. P. Kishore & B. J. Herbstman, *Adding a Medicine to the WHO Model List of Essential Medicines*, 85 CLINICAL PHARMACOLOGY & THERAPEUTICS 237, 237 (2009).

Only a handful of the pharmaceuticals on the Model List are protected by patents. According to a 2004 study, only 17 of the 319 medicines on the list in 2003 were patented in developing countries. Of these, 12 were antiretroviral drugs recommended by WHO as first- and second-line treatments for HIV/ AIDS.[29] The small number of patent-protected medicines on the Model List has generated considerable criticism. According to one commentator, the list "is replete with antiquated and increasingly ineffective drugs" and includes "less than 2 per cent (21) of the 1,377 drugs indicated for global diseases" in the last quarter of the twentieth century – many of which are protected by patents.[30] Similarly, a leading NGO proponent of access to medicines has urged WHO to "reassess the role that cost – especially as reflected under current patent medicine pricing regimes – plays in" excluding patent-protected drugs from the Model List.[31]

What are the implications of the preceding information for the right to health as interpreted in *General Comment No. 14*? Do states parties have an obligation to provide access to medicines *not* included on the WHO Model List of Essential Medicines? Which provisions of the *General Comment* help to answer this question?[32] Consider the small number of patent-protected drugs included on the Model List. What measures must states adopt to satisfy their obligations to "respect, protect, and fulfill" the right to health concerning such medicines? Could a state refuse to grant a patent for such drugs? Would such a position be consistent with the TRIPS Agreement? (We consider this question in greater detail in the next section after reviewing TRIPS patent protection rules.) If patent-protected drugs are effective in treating infectious and chronic diseases, why would the WHO exclude such drugs from its Model List?

5. Review the text of Human Rights Commission Resolution 2003/29 excerpted earlier. Does the resolution recognize a broader right of access to medicines than the right articulated in *General Comment No. 14*? Does it recognize a broader right of access to pharmaceuticals protected by patents? What is the legal significance of the phrase "in accordance with applicable international law, including international agreements acceded to," which appears at the beginning of paragraphs 4 and 5 of the resolution?

[29] Amir Attaran, *How Do Patents and Economic Policies Affect Access to Essential Medicines in Developing Countries?*, 23 HEALTH AFF. 155, 155 (2004).

[30] Maxwell R. Morgan, *Medicines for the Developing World: Promoting Access and Innovation in the Post-TRIPS Environment*, 64 U.T. FAC. L. REV. 45, 71–72 (2006).

[31] Letter from James Packard Love, Consumer Project on Technology, to Margaret Chan, Director-General, WHO (Dec. 1, 2006) (requesting that the WHO review of the Essential Drugs List (EDL) as it relates to patented products), *available at* http://www.cptech.org/ blogs/ipdisputesinmedicine/2006/12/letter-asking-who-review-of-essential.html.

[32] *See* Yamin, *supra* note 16, at 360.

The United States was the only country that abstained when the Commission adopted its first resolution on access to medicines and HIV/AIDS in 2001. It objected to a statement (repeated in subsequent resolutions) that states must adopt legislation or other measures to "safeguard access" to pharmaceutical products "from any limitations by third parties." The United States "maintained that by questioning 'the validity of internationally agreed protections of intellectual property rights', the text was 'simply put, bad public health policy.'"[33] The European Union voted in favor of the resolution but "expressed its understanding that 'no provisions in this resolution can be interpreted as undermining or limiting existing international agreements, including in the field of intellectual property.'"[34] Do you agree with the U.S. position that the Commission's resolution challenges the validity of patent protection for pharmaceuticals? Or are you more persuaded by the EU's assessment?

2.4. Patent Protection for Pharmaceuticals and Revising the TRIPS Agreement to Enhance Access to Medicines

The TRIPS Agreement is the leading multilateral treaty regulating the protection of inventions, including pharmaceutical patents. In Chapter 1, we describe the negotiations leading to the adoption of TRIPS in 1994, the changes that the treaty wrought for international IP protection and enforcement, and its implications for developing countries in particular. Here, we focus on TRIPS patent protection rules and on the flexibility mechanisms in the treaty that permit WTO member states to promote public health and increase access to medicines.[35]

A. An Overview of TRIPS Patent Provisions Relating to Access to Medicines

TRIPS requires that patents be available for all "inventions" in all fields of technology if they are "new, involve an inventive step and are capable of industrial application."[36] The breadth of this language and the treaty's negotiating

---

[33] Michael J. Dennis, Current Development, *The Fifty-Seventh Session of the UN Commission on Human Rights*, 96 Am. J. Int'l L. 181, 191 & n.65 (2002).

[34] *Id.* at 191 & n.66.

[35] TRIPS Article 8, which sets forth the treaty's "principles," expressly authorizes WTO member states to adopt measures "to protect public health and nutrition, and to promote the public interest in sectors of vital importance to their socio-economic and technological development." Agreement on Trade-Related Aspects of Intellectual Property Rights art. 8, Apr. 15, 1994, 1869 U.N.T.S. 299 [TRIPS Agreement]. The scope of this provision remains unclear, however, inasmuch as Article 8 also provides that such measures must be "consistent with the provisions of this Agreement." *Id.*

[36] *Id.* art. 27.1. Patent applications must also adequately disclose the invention such that a person of similar technical skill could carry out the invention.

history make plain that patent protection extends to both pharmaceutical products and processes.[37] The extension of patents to drug products and processes marked a significant expansion of international patent rules. Prior to the adoption of TRIPS, approximately fifty countries did not recognize any patent protection for pharmaceuticals. Other nations, such as India, recognized patents for the process of making a new drug, but not the resulting product. Governments justified both positions on public health grounds as a way to promote low-cost access to new medicines.[38] Under TRIPS, however, "so long as an invention meets the technical requirements of patentability, a patent must be granted for an inventive product, including a pharmaceutical compound, even if it would negatively impact the accessibility of drugs."[39] To ease the transition to full patent protection for new drugs, TRIPS provided a ten-year period – which ended in 2005 – during which developing and least-developed countries were not required to recognize pharmaceutical product patents.[40]

Even after the end of this transition period, governments retain some discretion to tailor patent requirements to public health needs. By adopting a narrow definition of novelty, for example, they can exclude some types of medicines from patentability.[41] These include newly discovered uses of existing medicines (so-called second use patents)[42] and new forms of known substances that do not enhance "efficacy."[43] In addition, states may exclude

---

[37] See DANIEL GERVAIS, THE TRIPS AGREEMENT: DRAFTING HISTORY AND ANALYSIS 218–19 (2d ed. 2003).

[38] See Carlos M. Correa, *Patent Rights*, in CARLOS M. CORREA & ABDULQAWI A. YUSUF (EDS.), INTELLECTUAL PROPERTY AND INTERNATIONAL TRADE: THE TRIPS AGREEMENT 227, 229 (2008); Cynthia M. Ho, *A New World Order for Addressing Patent Rights and Public Health*, 82 CHI.-KENT L. REV. 1469, 1475–76 (2007).

[39] Ho, *supra* note 38, at 1476.

[40] TRIPS Agreement, *supra* note 35, art. 65(4). Developing countries were required to provide so-called mailbox provisions for such patents as well as exclusive marketing rights. *Id.* art. 70(8) & (9). For additional discussion, see GERVAIS, *supra* note 37, at 349, 365–66.

[41] *See, e.g., Constitutionality of "Pipeline" Patents Challenged*, WORLD INTELL. PROP. REP. (No. 601) (BNA), June 1, 2009 (describing constitutional challenge to a Brazilian patent law enabling foreign pharmaceutical companies to patent "drugs that already were patented in other countries"; the government argued that such patents "did not respect a key requirement for patents in Brazil, namely that they must be for new products or processes").

[42] *E.g.*, Andean Community Decision 486, art. 21 (stating that "products or processes already patented and included in the state of the art … may not be the subject of new patents on the sole ground [that the product was] put to a use different from that originally contemplated by the initial patent"). For an analysis of this provision, see Laurence R. Helfer, Karen J. Alter & M. Florencia Guerzovich, *Islands of Effective International Adjudication: Constructing an Intellectual Property Rule of Law in the Andean Community*, 103 AM. J. INT'L L. 1, 28–30 (2009).

[43] The Patents (Amendment) Act, No. 15 of 2005, § 3(d) (prohibiting, in relevant part, patents on "the mere discovery of a new form of a known substance which does not result in the

"diagnostic, therapeutic and surgical methods for the treatment of humans and animals."[44]

TRIPS also specifies the economic exploitation rights of patent owners, which include the right to exclude others from making, using, selling, offering to sell, or importing the patented invention into a country where it is protected. These rights must subsist for a period of twenty years calculated from the date of filing an application to register the patent. As a practical matter, however, the term of protection may be several years shorter for patented medicines, which must undergo a separate government approval process, usually by a public health ministry or similar agency, before the drug may be marketed or sold to the public.

One exploitation right relevant to access to medicines was a topic of contentious debate among TRIPS negotiators – whether a patent owner can prevent the importation of patented products (including pharmaceuticals) that it has authorized for sale in another country. This question relates to another issue upon which governments divided: whether patent rights are "exhausted" at the national, regional, or international level. A worldwide exhaustion rule would allow a country to acquire patented medicines from another nation in which they had previously been sold with the patentee's consent, a practice known as "parallel importation." A national exhaustion rule, by contrast, would preserve the patent owner's exclusive rights in all other countries in which the drug had not previously been sold. As scholars have noted, an international exhaustion rule and the parallel importation associated with it

> favor[s] consumer interests and access to medicine, because countries are free to import products from the country where they are legitimately sold for the lowest possible price. Pharmaceutical manufacturers are strongly opposed to international exhaustion since their business model relies upon price differentiation amongst different countries. If consumers could freely buy the cheapest product available, companies would not be able to discriminate amongst different markets.[45]

---

enhancement of the known efficacy of that substance"). For an analysis of this provision, see Amy Kapczynski, *Harmonization and Its Discontents: A Case Study of TRIPS Implementation in India's Pharmaceutical Sector*, 97 CAL. L. REV. 1571 (2009).

[44] TRIPS Agreement, *supra* note 35, art. 27.3(a). TRIPS also permits a state to exclude a particular invention from patentability if it concludes that the prevention of commercial exploitation of the invention within its territory "is necessary to protect *ordre public* or morality, including to protect human ... life or health, ..." provided, however, that no exclusion is permitted "merely because the exploitation is prohibited by [the state's] law." *Id.* art. 27.2. On its face, this provision suggests that states have broad discretion to restrict patents that restrict access to medicines. However, "to date countries do not seem to have attempted to utilize this provision to exclude subject matter from patentability for the purposes of promoting public health." Ho, *supra* note 38, at 1478.

[45] Ho, *supra* note 38, at 1501.

TRIPS is deliberately ambiguous on the legality of parallel imports, stating only that nothing in the treaty "shall be used to address the issue of exhaustion of intellectual property rights" in WTO dispute settlement proceedings.[46] The 2001 Declaration on TRIPS and Public Health, discussed in greater detail below, clarifies that each WTO member state is "free to establish its own regime for such exhaustion without challenge."[47]

In addition to setting forth rules for patentability, term of protection, and economic exploitation, TRIPS contains two types of exceptions and limitations to patents. First, Article 30 of the treaty authorizes "limited exceptions" to exclusive rights provided that such exceptions "do not unreasonably conflict with a normal exploitation of the patent and do not unreasonably prejudice the legitimate interests of the patent owner, taking account of the legitimate interests of third parties."[48] In *Canada – Patent Protection of Pharmaceutical Products*,[49] a dispute settlement panel issued the only WTO decision to date concerning the exceptions clause in Article 30. The panel considered a complaint against two provisions of Canada's patent law. The first permitted generic drug producers to use patented pharmaceuticals to obtain regulatory approval of generic medicines before the patent term expired. The second authorized the stockpiling of generic drugs during the patent term so that the drugs could be released immediately after the expiration of the patent. Canada adopted both provisions to encourage the prompt marketing of generic drugs. The WTO panel interpreted the patent exceptions clause as having three distinct and cumulative requirements. Applying this standard, the panel held that the regulatory review exception, but not the stockpiling exception, was consistent with TRIPS.[50]

Second, Article 31 of TRIPS permits governments to issue compulsory licenses that authorize the use of a patented product or process without the patent owner's consent but subject to the payment of "adequate remuneration."[51] Numerous procedural requirements govern the issuance of such licenses. In general, the state must first attempt to negotiate with the patent owner for a voluntary license. This requirement "may be waived by a Member in the case of a national emergency or other circumstances of

[46] TRIPS Agreement, *supra* note 35, art. 6.
[47] WTO, Ministerial Declaration on the TRIPS Agreement and Public Health, para. 5(d), WT/MIN(01)/DEC/W/2 (Nov. 14, 2001) [Public Health Declaration].
[48] TRIPS Agreement, *supra* note 35, art. 30.
[49] WTO, WT/DS114/R (Mar. 17, 2000).
[50] For additional analysis, see Robert Howse, *The Canadian Generic Medicines Panel: A Dangerous Precedent in Dangerous Times*, 3 J. WORLD. INTELL. PROP. 493 (2000); Ho, *supra* note 38, at 1481–84.
[51] TRIPS Agreement, *supra* note 35, art. 31; *see* Correa, *supra* note 38, at 245–52.

extreme urgency or in cases of public non-commercial use."[52] Other restrictions include considering the "individual merits" of each compulsory license, limiting the duration and scope of the license to its authorized purpose, and enabling a court or other independent body to review the license and the amount of the royalty awarded.[53]

Article 31(f) is a particularly controversial clause. It provides that uses under a compulsory license must be "predominantly for the supply of the domestic market." For countries with little or no local pharmaceutical manufacturing capacity (typically developing or least developed nations) the declaration of a national health emergency – for example, in response to widespread HIV/AIDS infections – has little practical benefit. Such countries cannot produce generic drugs themselves. And the terms of Article 31(f) largely prohibit supply from another country in which a compulsory license has been granted.

As the Doha round of trade negotiations was getting underway in the WTO in 2001, this specific problem attracted considerable attention, as did more general concerns about the high prices of patented medicines for infectious diseases such as malaria, tuberculosis, and HIV/AIDS, and the aggressive efforts by some industrialized nations and pharmaceutical companies to enforce patent rights. As a condition of agreeing to launch the new trade talks, developing countries successfully pressed for the adoption of a Declaration on TRIPS and Public Health. The Declaration clarifies that TRIPS "can and should be interpreted and implemented in a manner supportive of WTO Members' right to protect public health and, in particular, to promote access to medicines for all."[54] It allows least developed countries to defer until 2016 the obligation in TRIPS to extend patent protection to pharmaceutical products. And it affirms the right of all countries to issue compulsory licenses to produce low-cost drugs in national health emergencies, while acknowledging that states with insufficient domestic manufacturing capabilities cannot make effective use of such licenses.

The Declaration directed the TRIPS Council[55] to remedy the latter problem and facilitate the export of generic drugs to poor countries with limited or no local manufacturing capacity. In 2003, the Council adopted a decision waiving the domestic use requirement for compulsory licenses. The waiver was subject, however, to several complex procedures and notification rules

---

[52] TRIPS Agreement, *supra* note 35, art. 31(b).
[53] For analysis, see Correa, *supra* note 38, at 245–52; NUNO PIRES DE CARVALHO, THE TRIPS REGIME OF PATENT RIGHTS 315–71 (2d ed. 2005).
[54] Public Health Declaration, *supra* note 47, para. 4.
[55] For a discussion of the TRIPS Council and its activities, see Chapter 1.

applicable to both exporting and importing WTO member states, both of which must issue a compulsory license.[56] In 2005, the Council agreed to make the waiver permanent by adopting a formal amendment to TRIPS – Article 31*bis* – that will become effective when ratified by two-thirds of the WTO's 153 member states.[57] Pending the amendment's entry into force, the 2003 waiver provisions will remain in effect.

Many commentators and NGOs initially hailed the 2001 Public Health Declaration as a major breakthrough for access to medicines. More recent assessments of the Declaration, and in particular of the 2003 waiver and 2005 amendment, have been more equivocal. Scholars have characterized the waiver and amendment as "saddled with unnecessary administrative hurdles" that make the export of generic versions of patented drugs neither "simple [n]or expeditious."[58] Moreover, even if governments with limited capacity master the intricacies of the formal legal regime, numerous practical obstacles stand in the way of effectively utilizing the system:

> First, exporting countries must amend their own patent legislation to produce generic drugs solely for export to countries that need them. In the face of a strong pharmaceutical lobby, this may be a difficult task for exporting countries to undertake. Second, because compulsory licensing under the importing/ exporting scheme was once prohibited by the TRIPS agreement, the effects of past sanctions for engaging in such practices has lingering effects which make developing countries reluctant to seek out exporting countries. Finally, under the current scheme of compulsory licensing proposed by the ... waiver, remuneration costs to the patent holder are to be paid by the exporting country, creating little incentive for such countries to participate in the new compulsory licensing scheme.[59]

There is yet another reason why some developing nations may have eschewed issuing compulsory licenses pursuant to the waiver regime – concern that such licenses may violate the TRIPS Plus regional or bilateral treaties that

---

[56] For an analysis of the 2003 waiver and its negotiating history, see Frederick M. Abbott, *The WTO Medicines Decision: World Pharmaceutical Trade and the Protection of Public Health*, 99 AM. J. INT'L L. 317, 326–48 (2005).

[57] World Trade Organization, *Members Accepting Amendment of the TRIPS Agreement*, *available at* http://www.wto.org/english/tratop_e/TRIPs_e/amendment_e.htm (last visited Mar. 31, 2010) (stating that 29 WTO members, including Canada, China, and India, as well as the European Community, had accepted the amendment as of March 2010).

[58] Frederick M. Abbott & Jerome H. Reichman, *Doha Round's Public Health Legacy: Strategies for the Production and Diffusion of Patented Medicines under the Amended TRIPS Provisions*, 10 J. INT'L ECON. L. 921, 921, 932 (2007).

[59] Jessica L. Greenbaum, *TRIPS and Public Health: Solutions for Ensuring Global Access to Essential AIDS Medication in the Wake of the Paragraph 6 Waiver*, 25 J. CONTEMP. HEALTH L. & POL'Y 142, 151–52 (2008).

these countries have ratified.[60] Several such treaties incorporate patent protection rules more stringent than those found in TRIPS. As Professors Abbott and Reichman have explained, the patent provisions of these agreements "follow a common template" that includes:

- extend[ing] the scope of patent protection to cover new uses of known compounds ...;
- provid[ing] patent term extensions to offset regulatory delay;
- limit[ing] the scope of permissible exceptions to patent rights; ...
- prohibit[ing] effective granting of marketing approval by the health regulatory authority during the patent term without the consent or acquiescence of patent holders; ...
- prohibit[ing] parallel importation (in some cases); and
- limit[ing] the grounds for granting compulsory licensing (in higher income countries).[61]

The combined effect of these and other TRIPS Plus treaty provisions has been to "significantly strengthen the position" of foreign pharmaceutical firms and "thereby to erect barriers to the introduction of generic pharmaceutical products" in ratifying countries.[62]

---

* * * Issues in Focus * * *

Proponents of the WIPO Development Agenda (discussed in greater detail in Chapter 1) have on several occasions addressed the need to facilitate access to essential medicines. When the Group of Friends of Development launched the Development Agenda in 2004, its submission to the WIPO General Assemblies referenced the Doha Declaration on the TRIPS Agreement and Public Health. The submission characterized the Declaration as "an important milestone," which "recognize[s] that the TRIPS Agreement ... should operate in a manner that is supportive of and does not run counter to the public health objectives of all countries."[63]

---

[60] As described in Chapter 1, "TRIPS Plus" treaties contain more expansive IP protection rules than those found in TRIPS. The U.S. and EU have negotiated such treaties with developing nations to expand IP protection rules at a faster pace than is possible within the WTO.

[61] Abbott & Reichman, *supra* note 58, at 963.

[62] *Id.*

[63] *Proposal by Argentina and Brazil for the Establishment of a Development Agenda for WIPO, presented to* WIPO General Assembly, WO/GA/31/11 (Aug. 27, 2004), *available at* http://www.wipo.int/meetings/en/doc_details.jsp?doc_id=31737.

Subsequently, several WIPO member states called for measures "ensur[ing] that technical assistance activities provided to developing and least developed countries are able to implement the pro-development provisions of the TRIPS Agreement, for example, Articles 7, 8, 30, 31 and 40, in addition to subsequent pro-development decisions, such as the Doha Declaration on the TRIPS Agreement and Public Health."[64] These states also argued that "norm-setting activities" at WIPO should be "fully compatible with and actively support other international instruments that reflect and advance development objectives, in particular Human Rights international instruments."[65]

Curiously, none of the forty-five recommendations adopted when WIPO approved the Development Agenda in 2007 mentions the term "health," "medicine," "Doha," or "human rights," notwithstanding the fact that these issues were extensively discussed during nearly a dozen meetings between 2004 and the adoption of the recommendations in 2007. Nonetheless, several recommendations use broad language that is consistent with promoting access to medicines and with support for the Declaration on TRIPS and Public Health. For example, Recommendation No. 10 urges WIPO "to promote fair balance between intellectual property protection and the public interest."[66] Other recommendations reference TRIPS flexibilities[67] and emphasize the need to "tak[e] into account the priorities and the special needs of developing countries, especially LDCs."[68]

A more indirect reference to access to medicines appears in the recommendation urging WIPO to "intensify its cooperation" with international organizations, such as the World Health Organization (WHO) and the WTO, to achieve "maximum efficiency in undertaking development programs."[69] This suggests that norm setting and other activities in WIPO should be consistent with developments in these organizations, which, as we describe later in this chapter, are analyzing the relationship between patents and access to essential medicines and proposing new ways to promote medical innovation.

---

[64] WIPO, Provisional Comm. on Proposals Related to a WIPO Development Agenda (PCDA): First Session, *Summary by the Chair*, 3 (Feb. 20–24, 2006), *available at* http://www.wipo.int/meetings/en/details.jsp?meeting_id=9643.

[65] *Id.* at 6.

[66] WIPO, The 45 Adopted Recommendations under the WIPO Development Agenda, para. 10, *available at* http://www.wipo.int/ip-development/en/agenda/recommendations.html.

[67] *Id.*, paras. 14, 16, 17, 19, 20, 22, 36, 40, 45.

[68] *Id.*, para. 13.

[69] *Id.*, para. 40.

B. Recent Examples of Compulsory Licenses to Promote Access to Medicines

The legal and practical issues described previously have also influenced negotiations between governments and pharmaceutical firms over the price of patented medicines and the issuance of compulsory licenses to produce generic drugs for domestic markets and for export to other eligible WTO member states. The following materials summarize national experiences concerning compulsory licenses in Thailand, Brazil, Canada, and Rwanda.

Cynthia M. Ho, *Patent Breaking or Balancing?: Separating Strands of Fact from Fiction under TRIPS*, 34 N.C. J. INT'L L. & COM. REG. 371, 412–19 (2009)

. . .

Thailand has a national mandate to provide universal access to essential medicine to all its citizens pursuant to the National Health Security Act of 2002 and access to antiretrovirals for all AIDS patients since 2003.... The WHO and the World Bank predict that Thailand will face dramatic price increases in treating their HIV population because HIV patients normally become resistant to initial treatments and need to switch to newer, patented drugs....

Thailand issued compulsory licenses to achieve its mandate of providing access to essential drugs, including antiretroviral drugs that cannot otherwise be provided despite increases in the public health budget after years of negotiation with patent owners that failed to yield price cuts beyond the level of currency appreciation. Although Thailand asserts that it engaged in prior negotiations with the patent owners, each of its compulsory licenses stated that it could grant compulsory licenses without prior negotiations in the case of public use based on the "right to ... protect ... public health" as supported by the Doha Public Health Declaration. The licenses were issued to cover only Thai citizens who are supported by government funded insurance and not the small percent of Thai citizens who are capable of paying the premium patent prices for the drugs....

On November 29, 2006, Thailand issued a compulsory license to its Government Pharmaceutical Organization (GPO) on Merck's patented drug Efavirenz..., an effective first line treatment for AIDS that has fewer adverse side effects, including life-threatening side effects, than the generic antiretroviral Nevirapine. Thailand's license stated that it was for non-commercial purposes and for the public interest to help achieve its policy of universal access to antiretrovirals for the 500,000 Thai citizens that need them for long-term use. The compulsory license also stated that the high cost of Efavirenz without a license resulted in many Thai patients having inadequate access. The compulsory license was expected to halve the treatment cost so that more patients could be covered with the eventual goal of having all new patients treated with Efavirenz initially, just as patients are treated in developed countries.

A Thai compulsory license on the AIDS drug Kaletra was issued to the GPO on January 25, 2007. Kaletra is a patented combination of two antiretrovirals that is often used for patients that become resistant to basic formulations of HIV medications, such as Efavirenz. The Thai government estimated that around ten percent of patients require second-line treatments such as Kaletra within the first few years, or else such patients will die. The Kaletra license was designed to support an increasing number of patients and thus save more lives. Prior to the compulsory license, Kaletra was priced at $2200 per patient per year by patent owner Abbott, a cost that is close to the yearly income of a Thai citizen.

On the same day, January 25, 2007, Thailand issued a compulsory license to the GPO for Bristol Myers' anti-platelet drug Plavix, a drug useful for treating heart disease. According to the license, heart disease is one of the top three causes of death in Thailand and although some non-drug preventative measures could be taken there is a need for drug treatment to prevent unnecessary mortality. Without the license only twenty percent of government insured patients could access the medicine, which is inconsistent with the Thai policy of providing universal coverage of essential medicine.

. . .

Even though controversy never subsided regarding the initial licenses, Thailand continued to explore additional compulsory licenses. In June 2007, Thailand established two exploratory committees to consider possible compulsory licenses on cancer medications considered necessary for the universal healthcare scheme. At the same time, Thailand was pressured against perceived broad use of compulsory licenses by E.U. Trade Commissioner Peter Mandelson, as well as by the U.S. Ambassador to Thailand, Ralph Boyce. Thailand began negotiations for lower prices on patented cancer drugs in October 2007. Although initial signs were promising, the negotiations eventually broke down in December 2007.

Thailand then issued licenses on four cancer drugs in January 2008, on the eve of a change in government administration. Thailand asserted that they were necessary because cancer is currently the number one cause of death in Thailand, and most effective cancer treatments are patented, not covered on the Thai List of Essential Drugs due to their high cost, and thereby inaccessible to Thai citizens. Thailand asserted that cancer is no less serious than HIV/AIDS, accounting for 30,000 deaths a year with 100,000 new cases diagnosed each year. Moreover, Thailand noted that the licenses were critical to prevent either severe economic hardship, including bankruptcy or certain death, without treatment.

However, unlike the initial compulsory licenses, Thailand delayed implementation of the signed licenses to enable continued negotiations. The continued negotiations yielded a successful outcome in one case; patent owner Novartis agreed to provide its drug Glivec at no cost to Thai citizens meeting certain income requirements, and Thailand revoked the license on Glivec. On the other hand, Thailand was not satisfied with the prices of other patented drugs. Although the other patent owners offered discounts of up to one third the original price, Thailand stated that it would impose a compulsory license unless patent owners offered prices no more than five percent higher than those offered by generic competitors.

On February 7, 2008 … the new Thai Public Health Minister announced that he would re-evaluate the decision to issue licenses on the cancer drugs. Also of relevance was an attempt to clarify Thailand's position with the United States in hopes of avoiding negative economic repercussions, including loss of trade preferences under the Generalized System of Preferences as well as potential trade sanctions if listed on the Special 301 Report. Some American pharmaceutical companies had requested that Thailand be given Priority Foreign Country status, which is the most severe trade category and is most likely to result in trade sanctions.

. . .

Ultimately, Thailand decided not to revoke any of the compulsory licenses issued on cancer drugs despite being told that the continued imposition of licenses threatened to impact Thailand's international trade. Some suggested that cancelling the licenses would be inconsistent with the Thai Constitution and other laws requiring the government to provide low-cost drugs. Thailand has also resisted the suggestion that it promise to forgo the option of compulsory licenses in the future, stating that to do so would be considered a "neglect of duty or failure to exercise the rights established by the law to safeguard public interest and public health.…"

Robert Bird & Daniel R. Cahoy, *The Impact of Compulsory Licensing on Foreign Direct Investment: A Collective Bargaining Approach*, 45 Am. Bus. L.J. 283, 309–12, 315–16 (2008)

. . .

… Brazil has made significant steps toward solving public health problems while using its compulsory licensing statute as an asset. Brazil, like many countries, suffers from a spreading AIDS epidemic. However, the Brazilian government has responded by providing aggressive prevention services and free access to antiretroviral drugs for over ten years.… Roughly 600,000, or one percent of the adult population, are infected with the disease.…

Why has Brazil been so successful? The primary reason has been the government's early implementation of an aggressive anti-AIDS program. Launched in 1983 when the scientists in Brazil first isolated the HIV virus, Brazil's anti-AIDS program has provided extensive support services to infected people.… This program has grown to provide 159,000 infected Brazilians with free antiretroviral drugs and support services.

Antiretroviral drugs, however, potentially come only at a steep price. Brazil's skillful negotiation with pharmaceutical companies as well as its savvy use of its compulsory licensing statute has allowed the government to provide these drugs on a broad scale. Prior to TRIPS, Brazilian patent laws did not provide protection for pharmaceutical … products.… After the enactment of TRIPS, Brazil enacted [Industrial] Property Law number 9.279, which went into effect on May 15, 1997. This law recognized the relevant TRIPS provisions, including patent protection for pharmaceutical drugs and processes.…

Embedded in the 1997 law are Brazil's compulsory licensing statutes.… For example, Article 71 states that, through an act of the Federal Executive Authorities, a compulsory license may be granted in cases of "national emergency or public interest." Then Brazilian President Fernando Henrique Cardoso reinforced this provision through an Executive Decree. While President Cardoso limited "national emergency" to conditions of "imminent public danger," he also declared that matters of public health were of public interest, suggesting pharmaceutical drugs are a particular focus of compulsory licensing statutes.

. . .

Brazil could defend the compulsory license because, although Brazil is a developing country, it has the resources to develop the technology necessary to manufacture pharmaceuticals. Brazil can thus more readily implement a compulsory license than its poor neighbors, giving threats to compulsory licensing a greater sense of immediacy and importance.…

… Brazil has used a three-pronged attack in order to protect its compulsory license. First, Brazil produces locally any HIV drugs that are not subject to patent protection in Brazil because they predate legal protection. Second, if the needed drugs are covered by Brazilian patents, then the Brazilian government attempts to negotiate a deal with the patent holder for a lower price that would allow the Brazilian government to provide the drugs to citizens for free. Over the past ten years Brazil has successfully negotiated deep discounts for different kinds of antiretroviral and other drugs from a variety of pharmaceutical enterprises. Only when these negotiations fail does Brazil threaten to issue a compulsory license for the needed drugs. Brazil has successfully used this threat to secure an affordable price for antiretroviral drugs, and other countries have taken notice.

Vera Zolotaryova, Note, *Are We There Yet? Taking "TRIPS" to Brazil and Expanding Access to HIV/AIDS Medication*, 33 Brook. J. Int'l L. 1099, 1110–12 (2008)[70]

…

In furthering its campaign to provide affordable HIV/AIDS treatment, Brazil has used the threat of issuing a compulsory license as a means of negotiating lower prices with drug companies. In 2001, Merck responded to Brazil's recent threat to issue a compulsory license by reducing the price of Stocrin, an HIV/AIDS medication. In August of the same year, Swiss pharmaceutical company Roche also agreed to lower the price of its AIDS-fighting drug Viracept by forty percent, in response to Brazil's threat to issue a compulsory license. Similarly, in 2003, Merck agreed to lower the price of ARV Kaletra after Brazil's threat to issue a compulsory license for the drug. This pattern of threats and negotiations clearly demonstrates that Brazil's threats to issue compulsory licenses for HIV/AIDS medications have resulted in lowering the costs of many essential drugs for the government's HIV/AIDS program.

B. The Recent Controversy: Brazil and Merck

Despite Brazil's previous success in negotiating with pharmaceutical companies, the cost of Brazil's HIV/AIDS program has almost doubled in the last several years, partially due to the increased demand for second-line HIV/

---

[70] © 2008 *Brooklyn Journal of International Law*. This article was originally published in the *Brooklyn Journal of International Law*, Volume 33, Issue 3. Reprinted with permission.

AIDS medication. At current prices, the annual cost of Merck's Efavirenz for the Brazilian government was $42 million, at $1.59 per pill. Brazil's health ministry claimed that they could import a generic version of the drug from India at a price of $0.45 per pill. Since 2006, Brazil's Ministry of Health has attempted to negotiate with Merck for a price reduction. Brazil stated that it wanted to pay the price for the drug that Merck currently offered to countries in similar income levels as Brazil. On April 25, 2007, Brazil took the first step in the compulsory licensing process by declaring Efavirenz in "the public interest." After the Health Ministry rejected Merck's offer of $1.10 per pill, the Brazilian government took the final step in its compulsory licensing process by issuing a license to import the generic version of the drug from India while paying Merck royalties of 1.5%. The government claimed that the generic drug would permit an annual savings of $30 million on their anti-AIDS program. In justifying this unprecedented action, Brazil's president stated that he was not willing to sacrifice the health of his country's citizens for the sake of world trade.

––––––––––

George Tsai, Note, *Canada's Access to Medicines Regime: Lessons for Compulsory Licensing Schemes under the WTO Doha Declaration*, 49 Va. J. Int'l L. 1063, 1075–79 (2009)

. . .

Shortly after the implementation of the 30 August Decision, the Canadian government responded to pressures by Canadian civil organizations and the UN Special Envoy on HIV/AIDS in Africa by committing, in September 2003, to enact Canadian legislation, enabling compulsory licensing for export to developing countries and LDCs. In May 2004, Canada amended its patent laws to reflect the WTO decision, becoming one of the first member nations to do so. These amendments were codified in [Canada's Access to Medicines Regime (CAMR)].... The CAMR legislation ... sets forth the process for obtaining a compulsory license for export.... Compliance with CAMR is governed by the therapeutic products directorate of Health Canada, the agency to which a manufacturer applies for export authorization under CAMR.

. . .

On July 17, 2007, Rwanda became the first country to notify the WTO that it intended to take advantage of the compulsory licensing provisions of the 30 August Decision, paragraph 6 of the Doha Declaration, and Article 31 of the TRIPS Agreement by importing the generic HIV/AIDS cocktail drug Apo TriAvir from Canada. The production and export of this drug was the first – and currently the only – use of the CAMR legislation since its adoption in 2004....

Rwanda has been and is currently experiencing an HIV/AIDS epidemic. Of the country's total population of approximately 9.3 million people, an estimated 200,000 are infected with HIV or AIDS. As of 2007, only around 44,000 patients were receiving antiviral treatment. The high infection rate, combined with the country's lack of doctors and hospitals, cycle of poverty, and history of civil war, makes the need for help to fight the HIV/AIDS epidemic urgent.

In December 2004, Canadian generic pharmaceutical manufacturer Apotex committed to and began development of a "fixed-dose" combination of three HIV/AIDS antiviral drugs: zidovudine, lamivudine, and nevirapine. These three original drugs were still under Canadian patent protection; the patents were held by pharmaceutical groups Glaxo-SmithKline (GSK), Shire, and Boehringer Ingelheim. Apotex's new "cocktail" drug – Apo TriAvir – cost about forty cents per pill, compared to roughly twenty dollars for the patented version. Apotex planned to export 260,000 packages of Apo TriAvir, which is enough to treat 21,000 HIV/AIDS patients for one year.

Apotex faced numerous hurdles in its pursuit of a compulsory license for Apo TriAvir under CAMR. Initially, at the time that Apotex proposed Apo TriAvir in 2004, neither it nor any other "combination" or "cocktail" drug was included in Schedule 1 of the Patent Act, the exhaustive list of all of the pharmaceutical products that qualified for generic manufacture under CAMR. The schedule was thereby amended ... to include the combination of zidovudine, lamivudine, and nevirapine in 2005, and Apo TriAvir subsequently received manufacturing approval from Health Canada in August 2006 to begin manufacturing the drug.

The second substantial challenge that Apotex faced, following Health Canada's approval of Apo TriAvir, was negotiating for voluntary licenses from GSK, Shire, and Boehringer Ingelheim for use of their patented drugs. Section 21.04(3)(c) of CAMR requires an applicant to demonstrate that it "sought from the patentee ... a license to manufacture and sell the pharmaceutical product for export to the country or WTO member named in the application on reasonable terms and conditions and that such efforts have not been successful." Exact criteria for what sort of negotiations will satisfy the CAMR requirement are not stated. Negotiations between Apotex and the three manufacturers stalled, and Apotex ultimately failed to obtain a voluntary license from any of the manufacturers.

The final major obstacle that Apotex faced came from the Rwandan end of the transaction. Even after clearing all of the domestic hurdles imposed by CAMR, Apotex still had to win a Rwandan government tender for the purchase of Apo TriAvir (required by Rwandan law for import of generics). Apotex had to beat out other potential generics manufacturers vying for the contract.

The following synopsis clarifies the unfolding of events leading up to the export of Apo TriAvir to Rwanda under CAMR. Nine months after the 30 August Decision, in May 2004, Canada enacted CAMR. Seven months later, in December 2004, Apotex agreed to produce a fixed-dose combination generic drug for HIV/AIDS; such a drug did not exist at the time in Canada. After another nine months, in September 2005, the Canadian Parliament amended Schedule 1 of the Canadian Patent Act to include the fixed-dose combination of zidovudine, lamivudine, and nevirapine. Health Canada finally approved Apo TriAvir almost a year later in August 2006. Apotex then sought to fulfill CAMR's voluntary license negotiation requirements; Boehringer and GSK received formal requests for a voluntary license on May 11, 2007. Apotex claimed that the patent holders were intentionally stalling the negotiations, although the patent holders denied as much. Meanwhile, in July 2007, Rwanda notified the WTO that it planned to import Apo TriAvir under CAMR.

... The Canadian government ... granted a compulsory license on September 20, 2007. In October 2007, Canada notified the WTO of the grant of the compulsory license and of its intention to export Apo TriAvir to Rwanda. Apotex did not actually receive Rwanda's final tender approval – winning the bid to supply Rwanda with the generic drug – until May 2008, and the first and only package of Apo TriAvir to reach Rwanda to date was shipped on September 23, 2008, more than five years after the WTO's implementing decision.

Notes and Questions

1. Brazil and Thailand issued compulsory licenses for the domestic production of generic versions of patented medicines. In contrast, Canada and Rwanda issued compulsory licenses for the export of generic drugs to a country with insufficient pharmaceutical manufacturing capacity pursuant to the 2003 WTO waiver. What other differences can you identify in the licensing practices of these countries?[71]

---

[71] See Vera Zolotaryova, Note, *Are We There Yet? Taking "TRIPS" to Brazil and Expanding Access to HIV/AIDS Medication*, 33 BROOK. J. INT'L L. 1099, 1122–24 (2008).

2. The Doha Declaration on TRIPS and Public Health clarifies the reference in TRIPS Article 31 to emergencies that justify the issuance of compulsory licenses. Paragraph 5 of the Declaration provides that "each [WTO] member has the right to determine what constitutes a national emergency or other circumstances of extreme urgency, it being understood that public health crises, including those relating to HIV/AIDS, tuberculosis, malaria and other epidemics, can represent a national emergency or other circumstances of extreme urgency." In addition to clarifying that "public health crises" can represent national emergencies "or other circumstances of extreme urgency," Paragraph 5 provides that compulsory licenses can be granted under domestic law without prior negotiation with the patent owner. One commentator has argued that this approach "leave[s] the door wide open for abuses by allowing WTO Members absolute subjective power in determining whether to issue a compulsory license."[72] Do you agree with this concern? If so, what alternative approaches would you recommend?

3. Do the compulsory licenses issued by Brazil and Thailand comply with the procedural requirements in TRIPS Article 31, summarized in subsection A of this section? If you were counsel to a pharmaceutical manufacturer, what arguments would you raise to challenge the legality of the compulsory licenses? If you were an attorney in the Brazilian or Thai foreign or health ministries, what arguments would you raise to defend the legality of the licenses? Would you raise arguments based on human rights?[73]

4. Formal legal arguments do not exhaust the interactions between human rights and intellectual property. Arguments grounded in political claims and morality are also critically important, as is the development of "soft law" principles that may later ripen into legally binding rules. What political or moral arguments might be made in opposition to or in defense of the compulsory licenses described previously? Do these arguments complement the legal arguments, or are they in tension with a strictly legal analysis of the relevant treaty texts?

Viewed from one perspective, compulsory licenses reflect a compromise between two categorical opposing positions – one that gives patent owners

---

[72] Jamie Feldman, Note, *Compulsory Licenses: The Dangers behind the Current Practice*, 8 J. Int'l Bus. & L. 137, 163 (2009).

[73] *See* Robert Bird & Daniel R. Cahoy, *The Impact of Compulsory Licensing on Foreign Direct Investment: A Collective Bargaining Approach*, 45 Am. Bus. L.J. 283, 309–12, 314 (2008) (explaining that "the Brazilian government also leveraged its role as a developing country leader to present a resolution to the United Nations Human Rights Commission" that "called for making appropriate medicines available at accessible prices and that access to AIDS treatment was a human right").

exclusive control over their inventions without regard to the social consequences of that decision during the patent term, and the other that provides the widest possible access to medicines at the lowest possible cost without regard to whether doing so reduces the incentives for medical research or compensates inventors for their time, effort, and expense. Compulsory licenses are, in other words, *modus vivendi* that avoid, on a case by case basis, conflicts between patents and the right to health. Such "agreements to disagree" have clear benefits. But do they also have costs? Might they obfuscate more fundamental issues concerning the appropriate relationship between human rights and intellectual property? If so, might it be preferable for states to defy existing IP protection rules openly and argue that such defiance is consistent with, or even required by, the dictates of international human rights law?

5. Consider the following response by one of the pharmaceutical companies whose patented medicines were produced in Thailand pursuant to a compulsory license:

> One important problem with issuing compulsory licenses is that patent owners may retaliate by withdrawing other drugs from the marketplace.... After Thailand issued a compulsory license on Abbott's HIV drug Kaletra, Abbott announced that it was withdrawing its application to sell seven new drugs in Thailand including its new HIV drug, Aluvia, that was well-suited to Thailand's climate. Abbott's action is believed to be the first such retaliation by a drug company to a compulsory license; prompting substantial criticism, calls for boycotts, and protests at Abbott's shareholder meeting. Although Abbott eventually decided to register Aluvia and offer it at a discounted rate to Thailand, it has not changed its position on the other drugs.[74]

Does Abbott's withdrawal of its application to market patented drugs in Thailand violate TRIPS? Does the withdrawal violate the ICESCR? Is it inconsistent with the Human Rights Guidelines for Pharmaceutical Companies in relation to Access to Medicines, discussed in Chapter 1? Is the withdrawal an economically wise decision? What legal and political responses are available to the Thai government?

6. For several years after TRIPS' entry into force in 1995, no country issued compulsory licenses for antiretroviral drugs. Beginning in 2002, developing and middle-income countries began to issue such licenses, mostly for patented medicines for HIV/AIDS. In addition to Brazil, Rwanda, and Thailand, those countries include Ghana (2005), Indonesia (2004), Malaysia (2004), Mozambique (2004), Zambia (2004), and Zimbabwe (2002).[75] Why

[74] Ho, *supra* note 38, at 443–44.
[75] Consumer Project on Tech., *Examples of Health-Related Compulsory Licenses, available at* http://www.cptech.org/ip/health/cl/recent-examples.html (last visited Mar. 31, 2010).

might several countries have started to issue compulsory licenses at around the same time? Is it relevant that the ten-year transition period in TRIPS, during which developing countries could refrain from recognizing patents for pharmaceutical products, expired at the beginning of 2005?

7. What qualifies as "adequate remuneration" for purposes of TRIPS' compulsory licenses rules? If more than one country issues a compulsory license for the same patented drug, should all governments issuing compulsory licenses pay the same royalty fee to the pharmaceutical company that owns the patent on that drug?

8. Is a negotiated license a more advantageous alternative for patent owners than a compulsory license? Consider the following assessment:

> LDCs [less developed countries] are demanding prices offered to other, differently situated LDCs. Pharmas like Merck & Co. and Abbott have negotiated in good-faith with individual LDCs like Malaysia, Thailand, and Brazil, and ultimately offered prices based on individual LDCs' abilities to pay. LDCs, however, are aware of the prices other LDCs receive, and as was the case where Brazil sought Thailand's Efavirenz price, have been demanding the lowest price offered any LDC – irrespective of the economic standing on which the price is based. Under the current [regime], there is the potential for better situated LDCs, like Brazil, to insist on paying for medicines according to the pricing precedents set by Pharmas in negotiations with truly impoverished, like those in Sub-Saharan Africa. This seemingly abusive use of pricing precedents may result in better-situated LDCs receiving prices disproportionately low compared to their ability to pay.[76]

9. As noted earlier, Article 30 of TRIPS authorizes "limited exceptions to the exclusive rights conferred by a patent, provided that such exceptions do not unreasonably conflict with a normal exploitation of the patent and do not unreasonably prejudice the legitimate interests of the patent owner, taking account of the legitimate interests of third parties." Could Brazil or Thailand justify the production of generic versions of patented HIV/AIDS medications pursuant to Article 30? Could Canada?[77] What are the advantages and disadvantages associated with invoking Article 30 as the basis for producing generic drugs?

10. The Doha Declaration on TRIPS and Public Health affirms that each WTO member state is "free to establish its own regime for such exhaustion without challenge." In principle, this provision permits states to import patented medicines previously distributed in another country with the consent

---

[76] Riadh Quadir, Note, *Patent Stalemate? The WTO's Essential Medicines Impasse between Pharmas and Least Developed Countries*, 61 RUTGERS L. REV. 437, 462 (2009).

[77] *See* Abbott & Reichman, *supra* note 58, at 957–58.

of the patent owner. As a practical matter, how effective is such parallel importation likely to be in increasing access to medicines? What practical obstacles to parallel importation are foreseeable?[78]

11. How effective is the 2003 waiver decision as illustrated by its implementation in Canada and Rwanda? Is it relevant that, as of the end of 2009, only one country – Rwanda – had issued a compulsory license to import generic copies of patented medicines pursuant to the waiver? In what other ways might the waiver's effectiveness be measured?[79]

---

* * * Issues in Focus * * *

India is a major producer and exporter of generic versions of patented medicines. Generic drugs shipped from India to other developing nations are often routed through a third country. Since the fall of 2008, European Union (EU) customs authorities have, on more than twenty occasions, seized shipments of generic medicines in transit to developing nations on suspicion that they are "counterfeit" products. The seizures were made in response to complaints by pharmaceutical companies that hold patents for the drugs in countries, such as Germany and the Netherlands, where the transshipments occurred. The seized drugs were held for up to eight months before being released. In one instance, customs officials returned the drugs to India.[80]

European Council Regulation 1383/2003 authorizes the "detention" and "suspension release" of goods that EU customs officials suspect of infringing certain intellectual property rights.[81] The regulation applies not only to goods

---

[78] *See* Keith E. Maskus, Final Report to World Intellectual Property Organization, *Parallel Imports in Pharmaceuticals: Implications for Competition and Prices in Developing Countries* (2001), *available at* www.wipo.int/export/sites/www/about-ip/en/studies/pdf/ssa_maskus_pi.pdf; Peggy B. Sherman & Ellwood F. Oakley, *Pandemics and Panaceas: The World Trade Organization's Efforts to Balance Pharmaceutical Patents and Access to AIDS Drugs*, 41 AM. BUS. L.J. 353 (2004).

[79] *Compare* George Tsai, Note, *Canada's Access to Medicines Regime: Lessons for Compulsory Licensing Schemes under the WTO Doha Declaration*, 49 VA. J. INT'L L. 1063, 79 (2009), *with* Abbott & Reichman, *supra* note 58, at 947–49. *See also* Daniel Pruzin, *Lamy Defends TRIPS/Medicines Pact in Face of Lack of Use by Poor Countries*, WTO REPORTER No. 133 (July 15, 2009).

[80] John W. Miller & Geeta Anand, *India Prepares EU Trade Complaint*, WALL ST. J., Aug. 6, 2009; Nirmalya Syam, *Seizures of Drugs in Transit: Why Europe's Law and Actions Are Wrong*, SOUTH BULLETIN, Sept. 22, 2009, at 3.

[81] *See* Council Regulation (EC) 1383/2003, art. 4, 2003 O.J. (L 196) 7 [Regulation 1383/2003] (concerning customs action against goods suspected of infringing certain intellectual property rights and the measures to be taken against goods found to have infringed such rights); Xavier Seuba, *Border Measures Concerning Goods Allegedly Infringing Intellectual Property*

cleared for entry into the EU but also to goods transshipped through an EU member state.[82] According to Article 10, the law of the country where a seizure occurs determines whether the good infringes an intellectual property right.[83] Applying this rule, EU customs officials have detained drugs that were not patented either in India or in the countries of final destination but that were protected by patents in the place of transshipment. To avoid future seizures, Indian generics manufacturers have incurred additional costs to reroute shipments to transit hubs outside the EU.[84]

The legality of seizing generic medicines in these circumstances is questionable. Article 51 of the TRIPS Agreement mandates procedures that enable IP owners to apply to customs authorities "for the suspension ... of the release into free circulation" of "counterfeit trademark or pirated copyright goods" where the owner "has valid grounds for suspecting" that the goods are infringing.[85] Article 51 permits but does not require such procedures in the case of patents, which customs officials may be ill equipped to identify as infringing.[86] And a footnote clarifies that "there shall be no obligation to apply such procedures ... to goods in transit."[87] These provisions must be read in light of TRIPS Article 41, which sets forth rules applicable to all IP enforcement actions, including border measures. Article 41(1) provides that enforcement procedures "shall be applied in such a manner as to avoid the creation of barriers to legitimate trade and to provide for safeguards against their abuse."[88] The EU regulations are also in tension with the foundational principle of territoriality, according to which the existence and scope of intellectual property protection depends upon each country's national legislation.[89]

Rights: The Seizures of Generic Medicines in Transit, 4–6 (Int'l Centre for Trade & Sustainable Dev., Working Paper, Jun. 2009), *available at* http://ictsd.net/i/publications/53747/.

[82] Regulation 1383/2003, *supra* note 81, third recital, art. 1.1; Seuba, *supra* note 81, at 5.

[83] Regulation 1383/2003, *supra* note 81, art. 10. The regulation contemplates that "proceedings [will be] initiated to determine whether an intellectual property right has been infringed." *Id.* art. 13(1). Presumably, such determinations are to be made by a court, although the regulation is silent on this point. The regulation also permits destruction of seized goods without a determination of infringement in certain cases upon the request of the intellectual property right holder. *Id.* art. 11(1). Such cases do not, however, include situations in which destruction of the goods is contested. *Id.* art. 13.2.

[84] Miller & Anand, *supra* note 80.

[85] TRIPS Agreement, *supra* note 35, art. 51.

[86] *Id.*; *see* GERVAIS, *supra* note 37, at 312.

[87] TRIPS Agreement, *supra* note 35, art. 51 & n.13.

[88] *Id.* art. 41; *see also id.* art. 8 (recognizing that "appropriate measures" consistent with TRIPS "may be needed to prevent the abuse of intellectual property rights by right holders or the resort to practices which unreasonably restrain trade").

[89] Seuba, *supra* note 81, at 13–17.

There are thus strong arguments that seizing lawfully manufactured generic drugs not intended for "release into free circulation" in the EU creates "barriers to legitimate trade" in generic medicines in contravention of TRIPS.[90] India challenged the seizures before the TRIPS Council on these and other grounds. It also argued that the seizures "ran counter to … the resolution 2002/31 of the Commission on Human Rights on the right to enjoy the highest standard to physical and mental health."[91] In May 2010, India and Brazil filed requests for consultations against the EU, the first step in convening a WTO dispute settlement panel to address the TRIPS-compatibility of the seizures.[92]

2.5. Human Rights Approaches to Closing the "Global Drug Gap" Created by Patented Pharmaceuticals

As stated earlier in this chapter, patent protection can adversely affect access to medicines – and thus the human right to health – in two distinct ways: first, by increasing the cost of pharmaceuticals and thus limiting their availability to individuals unable to afford the monopoly price charged by patent owners, and second, by channeling private firms to research treatments for diseases prevalent in industrialized countries whose affluent populations offer lucrative markets for new drugs and medical technologies. The confluence of these two trends is a "global drug gap"[93] in which new drugs remain mostly unavailable to a majority of the world's population, which resides in developing and least developed countries.[94] A different way to express the same idea is the "10/90 disequilibrium" – the finding that "only 10 percent of the global health research is devoted to conditions that account for 90 percent of the global disease burden."[95]

---

[90] Commentators have also argued that the seizures contravene Article V of GATT 1994. *See* Syam, *supra* note 80, at 4–5.

[91] India – Intervention at WTO TRIPS Council on Public Health Dimension of the TRIPS Agreement (Mar. 3, 2009), *available at* http://keionline.org/node/309.

[92] World Trade Organization, *available at* http://keionline.org/node/309. World Trade Organization, Request for Consultation by India, WT/DS408/1 (May 19, 2010). For further analysis, see Shashank P. Kumar, *International Trade, Public Health, and Intellectual Property Maximalism: The Case of European Border Enforcement and Trade in Generic Pharmaceuticals*, 5 GLOBAL TRADE & CUSTOMS J. 155 (2010).

[93] Michael R. Reich, *The Global Drug Gap*, 287 SCIENCE 1979 (2000).

[94] As of 2008, more than 5.6 billion people – more than 80% of the total world population of nearly 6.7 billion – lived in developing countries. World Bank, *World Development Indicators: Population* (2008), *available at* http://siteresources.worldbank.org/DATASTATISTICS/Resources/POP.pdf.

[95] Médecins sans Frontières, Access to Essential Medicines Campaign & Drugs for Neglected Diseases Working Group, *Fatal Imbalance: The Crisis in Research and Development for*

In analyzing these disparities, the WHO has distinguished among three types of diseases:

> *Type I diseases* are incident in both rich and poor countries, with large numbers of vulnerable population in each. Examples of communicable diseases include measles, hepatitis B, [and certain influenza viruses,] and examples of noncommunicable diseases abound (e.g., diabetes, cardiovascular diseases, and tobacco-related illnesses).... Many vaccines for Type I diseases have been developed in the past 20 years but have not been widely introduced into the poor countries because of cost. *Type II diseases* [also known as "neglected diseases"] are incident in both rich and poor countries, but with a substantial proportion of the cases in the poor countries.... HIV/AIDS and tuberculosis are examples: both diseases are present in both rich and poor countries, but more than 90 percent of cases are in the poor countries.... *Type III diseases* [also known as "very neglected diseases"] are those that are overwhelmingly or exclusively incident in the developing countries, such as African sleeping sickness (trypanosomiasis) and African river blindness (onchocerciasis). Such diseases receive extremely little R&D, and essentially no commercially based R&D in the rich countries.[96]

Compulsory licenses, analyzed in detail earlier, authorize the production of generic copies of patented medicines, mostly for the treatment of Type II (neglected) diseases. Such licenses address the first component of the global drug gap by reducing the costs of those medicines in countries in which the generics are sold. Such licenses do not, however, remediate the gap's second component, since they can be applied only to drugs and medical technologies already in existence. As one commentator has pointedly stated, little is gained by "enshrining a right to healthcare access in international proclamations ... if that healthcare does not exist in the first place [because] pharmaceutical companies ... have little incentive to produce drugs which may be sorely needed in developing countries."[97]

Seen from this perspective, the two components of the global drug gap are interrelated. Mechanisms that reduce the price of existing medicines do not encourage pharmaceutical companies to research new treatments for neglected and very neglected diseases (and in fact may discourage them from doing so).[98] Conversely, redirecting medical innovation to the health

Drugs for Neglected Diseases 10 (2001), *available at* http://www.msf.org/source/access/2001/fatal/fatal.pdf.

[96] WHO, Commission on Macroeconomics and Health, *Macroeconomics and Health: Investing in Health for Economic Development* 78 (Dec. 20, 2001) (*presented by* Jeffrey D. Sachs), *available at* http://www.emro.who.int/cbi/pdf/CMHReportHQ.pdf.

[97] Siddartha Rao, *Closing the Global Drug Gap: A Pragmatic Approach to the Problem of Access to Medicines*, 3 J. LEGAL TECH. RISK MGMT. 1, 16 (2008).

[98] Mary Moran et al., *Neglected Disease Research and Development: How Much Are We Really Spending?*, 6 PLoS MED. e30 (2009), *available at* http://www.plosmedicine.org/article/

conditions of the world's poor does not, without more, ensure that the impoverished will have access to the fruits of that research. To be effective and compatible with human rights standards, therefore, proposals to close the global drug gap should encompass both of its core components. In addition, the proponents of such proposals should also consider the extent to which patents, as compared to other factors, reduce access to medicines and thus adversely affect the human right to health.

This section considers these issues in depth. We begin with an overview of debates over how patent protection contributes to the global drug gap. We then discuss the ways in which international human rights law might contribute to closing that gap. We identify several arguments and strategies, grounded in human rights law, that governments officials, civil society groups, courts, and commentators have invoked regarding access to medicines. These arguments and strategies include (1) reframing public perceptions of morally and legally acceptable behavior, (2) providing a mechanism to compel governments to provide access to lifesaving drugs, and (3) revising national health care systems and social safety nets in which access to medicine regimes are embedded. The section concludes with an overview and assessment of alternative proposals to restructure patent protection rules to encourage research of neglected diseases and to increase access to the treatments that result from that research.

A. Are Patents a Barrier to Access to Medicines?

There are many impediments to providing individuals in developing countries with access to essential medicines. These include widespread poverty, insufficient government financing of health care, poor infrastructure (including inadequate health care facilities, lack of appropriately trained medical personnel, and deficient distribution and supply systems), duties and tariffs on imported drugs, political opportunism by some government officials, and broader sociocultural determinants of health.[99]

Where patents rank on this list of barriers to access has engendered spirited debate, a debate that is not well served by the paucity of detailed country-specific research on the effects of patents and other potential or actual barriers. Scholars who assert that patent protection has little effect

info:doi/10.1371/journal.pmed.1000030; *see also* Drugs for Neglected Diseases Initiative, Vision and Mission, *available at* http://www.dndi.org/overview-dndi/vision-mission.html (last visited Mar. 31, 2010) (identifying malaria, visceral leishmaniasis, sleeping sickness, and Chagas disease as "most neglected diseases").

[99] *See, e.g.,* Rao, *supra* note 97, at 18–20; Morgan, *supra* note 30, at 67–75.

on access highlight the fact that only a handful of the drugs on the WHO Model List of Essential Medicines are patented, that access remains limited even for off-patent drugs, and that public spending for health care is so meager in many countries that their governments would be unable to purchase drugs even at their marginal costs of production.[100] Other commentators have criticized the findings of these studies. They cite evidence that newer and more effective drugs – such as first- and second-line retroviral medicines for HIV/AIDS – are widely patented even in poor countries, and that pharmaceutical firms actively seek patents in higher-income developing countries – such as China, India, and South Africa – that have larger markets and manufacturing capacity for domestic use or export.[101] They also highlight the 2005 expiration of TRIPS' transition periods for pharmaceutical products as evidence that barriers to access will increase in the near future.[102]

One way to reconcile these competing positions is to refocus the debate away from the relative contribution of patents versus other factors in creating barriers to access, and to focus instead on how to limit the impediments that patents do impose. To be sure, "removing the patent barrier will not miraculously produce access to medicines. There will still be a need for funding for the drugs, for effective health systems, and for wise selections of medicines."[103] Yet the lower the price of pharmaceuticals, the greater their affordability to impoverished populations. The key challenge is how to expand affordability while also taking into account other barriers to access and maintaining incentive structures to reward medical research and innovation.

[100] See Attaran, supra note 29, at 155–63; Amir Attaran & Lee Gillespie-White, Do Patents for Antiretroviral Drugs Constrain Access to AIDS Treatment in Africa?, 286 J. AM. MED. ASS'N 1886, 1887–88 (2001). These arguments have, unsurprisingly, been endorsed by pharmaceutical companies. See Ellen t'Hoen, TRIPS, Pharmaceutical Patents, and Access to Essential Medicines: A Long Way from Seattle to Doha, 3 CHI. J. INT'L L. 27, 43 (2002) (describing the use of the Attaran-White study by pharmaceutical companies); Crook, supra note 24, at 530 (stating that "pharmaceutical corporations have a financial interest in framing this humanitarian crisis as one of poverty rather than affordability").

[101] See Morgan, supra note 30, at 73–75. In South Africa, for example, more than 95% of antiretroviral drugs are patented. Eric Goemaere et al., Do Patents Prevent Access to Drugs for HIV in Developing Countries?, 287 J. AM. MED. ASS'N 841 (2002).

[102] Morgan, supra note 30, at 75 (stating that "for new medicines developed from 2005 onward, when pharmaceutical product patents will be available in virtually all Member states of the WTO, the supply of low-cost versions of such new products in developing countries will be threatened by the greatly reduced possibility of generic substitution" in the form of imports from other WTO member states).

[103] Sean Flynn, Legal Strategies for Expanding Access to Medicines, 17 EMORY INT'L L. REV. 535, 539 (2003).

B. Human Rights Contributions to Closing the Global Drug Gap

The human right to health provides a useful framework for addressing these difficult issues.[104] As described in *General Comment No. 14*, excerpted earlier, the right to health treats access to essential medicines as only one facet of a broader cluster of issues relating to the availability, accessibility, acceptability, and quality of national health care systems and the determinants of health more generally. It also conceptualizes health in relation to other human rights, such as the right to life and the right to enjoy the benefits of scientific progress and their applications. A human rights framework thus shifts the focus of analysis in several ways. First, it reframes existing legal discourses that privilege legal rules protecting intellectual property over those protecting individual rights and social values. Second, it provides a mechanism to hold governments accountable for providing at least minimal levels of health care. And third, it emphasizes the need to restructure incentives for medical research and innovation toward the treatment of neglected diseases and the health needs of the world's poor. The materials that follow explore these issues. We also consider recent proposals to revise legal rules and institutions, including patent protection, in ways that enhance access to medicines.

The following article explains how arguments based on human rights changed public perceptions of the relationship between patent protection and health in South Africa, setting the stage for a broader reframing of national and international legal rules and institutions (including the TRIPS Agreement) and an increase in litigation to compel governments to increase access to medicines. The key catalyst for these developments was the *Pharmaceutical Manufacturer's Association (PMA)* case[105] – a lawsuit filed by a group of pharmaceutical companies against a South African statute that authorized compulsory licenses and parallel importation of patented medicines in response to the country's growing HIV/AIDS pandemic.[106]

---

[104] *See* WHO, Comm'n on Intell. Prop. Rights, Innovation and Pub. Health, *Public Health, Innovation and Intellectual Property Rights* 12 (2006) (characterizing the schema of *General Comment No. 14* as "fram[ing] the problem in a way that points to particular gaps and challenges ... and to appropriate remedies"), *available at* http://www.who.int/intellectualproperty/documents/thereport/ENPublicHealthReport.pdf.

[105] *Pharmaceutical Manufacturer's Association v. The President of South Africa (PMA)* 2000 (2) SA 674 (CC) (S. Afr.).

[106] UNAIDS, *Sub-Saharan Africa AIDS Epidemic Update Regional Summary 2007* at 3, U.N. Doc. UNAIDS/08.08E/JC1526E (Mar. 2008) ("With an estimated 5.5 million ... people living with HIV, South Africa is the country with the largest number of infections in the world. The country's Department of Health estimates that 18.3% of adults (15–49 years) were living with HIV in 2006."), *available at* http://data.unaids.org/pub/Report/2008/JC1526_epibriefs_subsaharanafrica_en.pdf.

Lisa Forman, *"Rights" and Wrongs: What Utility for the Right to Health in Reforming Trade Rules on Medicines?*, 10 HEALTH & HUM. RTS. 37, 39, 43–45 (2008)

What role, if any, could the right to health play in reforming trade-related intellectual property rights and assuring greater accountability from corporate and state actors regarding global access to medicines? ... I suggest that the AIDS medicine experience and the seminal corporate litigation in South Africa in 2001, in particular, point to the transformative potential of the right to health to raise the priority of public health needs in trade-related intellectual property rights, and to advance access to critical health interventions in resource-poor settings.

...

The Legal, Normative, and Discursive Power of Rights

The human right to health provides a different account of government duties on medicines that significantly re-prioritizes public needs for medicines. The provision of essential medicines is seen to place a core duty on governments that cannot be traded for private property interests or domestic economic growth. The right's potential is therefore to provide a means of achieving a more public-health-oriented formulation, implementation, and interpretation of trade rules by domestic courts, governments, and the WTO alike, and perhaps even a mechanism to assist efforts to amend the TRIPS agreement itself.

...

Seven years ago, there was little hope that AIDS medicines could become widely accessible in the developing world. The drugs cost approximately US$15,000 a year. WHO's and UNAIDS's official position was that, given high drug costs and the need for effective prevention, treatment was not a wise use of resources in poorer countries. This shadowed a broader policy consensus that cost-effectiveness demanded a brutal triage in which prevention of HIV/AIDS was funded instead of treatment, an ethically questionable choice in a gross pandemic that had already infected almost 28 million people in sub-Saharan Africa. As a result, there was no international funding for developing countries to purchase drugs, and companies gave extremely limited price concessions. The idea that poor people in Africa should receive expensive state-of-the-art AIDS drugs was viewed as naïve and unrealistic, and arguments for lower-priced medicines were viewed as proposing an unacceptable violation of corporate patents and international trade rules. Generally, access to these drugs in developing countries was around 5% of HIV-positive persons, and in sub-Saharan Africa, the vast epicentre of the global pandemic, access was considerably under 1%.

Yet millions of people were dying from AIDS in sub-Saharan Africa every year, at the same time that antiretroviral medicines had begun to slash AIDS-related illness and death in the West and transform the very nature of the disease. To those on the frontlines of the pandemic, this lack of access primarily on the basis of price did not seem logical, appropriate, or ethically defensible. Rather, it seemed to be a shocking prioritization of property interests over the health and welfare needs of much of the African continent, in service of little more than profit – a global crisis not just of health but of morality. A dramatic global battle for AIDS medicines ensued, coalescing around moral arguments and human rights claims for medicines and mass actions by social networks of health and human rights activists. This battle challenged drug pricing, legal interpretations of TRIPS, and corporate contestation of TRIPS flexibilities.

The tipping point of this struggle appeared to come in 2001, in the PMA case in South Africa. Between 1997 and 2001, the US and 40 pharmaceutical companies used trade pressures and litigation to prevent the South African government from passing legislation (the "Medicines Act") to gain access to affordable medicines. South Africa, then, as now, had one of the world's largest HIV epidemics. In 2000, the US withdrew its trade pressures after Al Gore was embarrassed by AIDS advocates during his presidential campaign. However, the pharmaceutical companies went to court in South Africa. The industry claimed that South Africa's legislation (and the parallel importing it authorized) breached the TRIPS agreement and South Africa's constitutional property protection. It also argued that the proposed act threatened the industry's incentive to innovate new medicines. In response, the South African government denied that the litigation either posed any serious threats to PMA's intellectual property rights or conflicted with TRIPS and the Constitution. It is notable that in the early court documents, there was little focus by either side on HIV/AIDS medicines or human rights arguments. The situation changed in April 2001, when the Treatment Action Campaign (TAC), a South African treatment advocacy group, joined the government's case, and in detailed affidavits set out to show the weakness of corporate arguments about the TRIPS legality of the legislation, and the research- and development-based necessity of opposing it. South Africa's constitutional framework greatly assisted activist claims, particularly because of its entrenchment of a justiciable right to access health care services, as well as constitutional rules on the limitation of rights that demand strong justifications for any restrictions of core dignity and life interests. Using this framework, TAC brought human rights arguments drawn from international and domestic law, arguing that the right to health provided constitutional authority for the legislation itself and was a legal interest that should be prioritized over corporate property rights. TAC also presented extensive empirical research that undercut corporate claims about the cost of research and development, and its link to innovation, as well as personal testimony from poor people unable to buy medicines to illustrate the human costs of the litigation.

In addition, working with activists around the world, TAC and other South African human rights groups organized an extraordinary level of public action concurrent with the case. On the day the case began, an international day of action was held with demonstrations in 30 cities across the world. A petition opposing the litigation signed by 250 organizations from 35 countries was published in Business Day, a national South African newspaper. The international aid group *Médecins Sans Frontières* initiated an international petition that collected 250,000 signatures and persuaded the European Union and Dutch governments to pass resolutions calling for the case to be dropped, followed by the German and French governments. WHO not only stated its support for South Africa's defense of the litigation, but also provided legal assistance. In the days before the hearing, Nelson Mandela, the former South African president, criticized the pharmaceutical companies for charging exorbitant prices on AIDS drugs, attracting considerable media attention. This confluence of activism and media coverage attracted an extraordinary amount of global censure against the corporations, which recognized that they had far more to lose through reputational damage than through any outcomes to which the Medicines Act could possibly lead. In April 2001, the pharmaceutical companies withdrew their case.

The litigation and surrounding media furor precipitated a discernable shift in how the appropriateness of TRIPS and patents in poor countries came to be seen. Even mainstream publications such as the *Washington Post* and *Time* began to question the legitimacy of corporate action to protect patents in developing countries, and, indeed, of the intellectual property system itself. Yet the case appeared to have broader normative effects. Closely following its conclusion, what looks like a norm cascade began, with a sharp upsurge at the UN in international statements on treatment as a human right and on state obligations to provide [antiretroviral medicines (ARV)]. This process moved later that year to the WTO in a Declaration on TRIPS and Public Health, issued at the Doha Ministerial Conference. In language redolent of human rights and the right to health, the declaration articulated that WTO members had "the right to protect public health and, in particular, to promote access to medicines for all"; and "the right" to do so using TRIPS flexibilities such as compulsory licensing and parallel imports.

These rhetorical commitments were matched by considerable policy and price shifts. Due to the combination of pressure, concessions, and the availability of generic alternatives from India (which was not yet bound by TRIPS' [pharmaceutical patent rules]), drug prices in many low-income countries dropped from US$15,000 to US$148 – $549 per annum. Global funding mechanisms were created, such as the Global Fund to Fight HIV/AIDS, Tuberculosis and Malaria, the US President's Emergency Plan for AIDS Relief (PEPFAR), and the World Bank Multi-Country HIV/AIDS Program for Africa. In 2002, WHO adopted the goal of placing 3 million people on ARV and, in late 2005, shifted upwards to the goal of achieving universal access to treatment by 2010, a goal similarly adopted by the UN General Assembly and by the G8 as part of a comprehensive plan of assistance for Africa. In 2008, at the 61st World Health Assembly, WHO member states adopted a global strategy and plan of action on public health, innovation, and intellectual property explicitly based on recognizing the right to health and promoting a country's right to use TRIPS flexibilities to the fullest. In six years, access to ARVs in sub-Saharan Africa increased from under 1% to 28%. In 2006 and 2007, AIDS mortality decreased for the first time, partly due to the scaling up of ARV treatment services.

Implications for Rights and Trade

Rights-based discourse, litigation, and action appear to have played significant roles in shifting policy, price, and perception around AIDS medicines. In the PMA case, discursive arguments and empirical evidence in the litigation, accompanied by mass action and media attention, ensured growing reputational damage for the industry. Without this coercive pressure, the companies were unlikely to have withdrawn the litigation. However, the PMA case also illustrates how social action and rights discourse persuaded a global collective of the legitimacy of the rights claim for medicines and of the immorality of the corporate positions. This not only assured the collective disapproval that became so important to ensuring the corporate withdrawal of its litigation, but also led to a far broader global acceptance of the rights claim and a shift in perspectives on the moral necessity of ensuring access to AIDS medicines in Africa.

Notes and Questions

1. The theoretical approach applied in *"Rights" and Wrongs* is the constructivist school of international relations theory. Constructivism posits that norms and ideas shape the identity and behavior of states and nonstate actors, influencing international and domestic policy outcomes. Norms that achieve these results do so because of their intrinsic qualities and the values they embody. This approach has strong appeal for scholars who seek to understand how respect for human rights has increased over time. According to two leading constructivist theorists, human rights norms evolve in a "life cycle" comprised of three stages – norm emergence, norm acceptance after a "tipping point" is reached, and norm internalization:

> At the first stage in [the life cycle] model, norms emerge through persuasion by norm entrepreneurs who reframe state and public perceptions. They are successful when the "new frames resonate with broader public understandings and are adopted as new ways of talking about and understanding issues." The tipping point comes when a critical mass adopts the norm, leading to the second stage, when norms cascade through combined coercion and persuasion. The final stage of normative internalization occurs when norms "acquire a taken-for-granted quality and are no longer a matter of broad public debate."[107]

In which stage of the norm "life cycle" is the *Pharmaceutical Manufacturers Association* case? What aspects of the case made it well suited to serve as a catalyst for challenging pharmaceutical industry claims about the importance of strong patent protection in developing countries?

2. As noted earlier in this chapter, a right to health appears in some form in two-thirds of the world's national constitutions. Among the most well known is Article 27 of the 1996 Constitution of South Africa, which provides in relevant part:

(1) Everyone has the right to have access to ... (a) health care services....
(2) The state must take reasonable legislative and other measures, within its available resources, to achieve the progressive realization of each of these rights.
(3) No one may be refused emergency medical treatment.

---

[107] Lisa Forman, *"Rights" and Wrongs: What Utility for the Right to Health in Reforming Trade Rules on Medicines?*, 10 HEALTH & HUM. RTS. 37, 39, 43 (2008) (quoting Martha Finnemore & Kathryn Sikkink, *International Norm Dynamics and Political Change*, 52 INT'L ORG. 887, 897, 895 [1998]).

The Constitutional Court of South Africa has issued groundbreaking decisions recognizing the justiciability of the right to health and adjudicating the constitutional claims of individuals and groups.[108] Yet in the initial phases of the *Pharmaceutical Manufacturers Association* case, Lisa Forman notes that "there was little focus by either side on HIV/AIDS medicines or human rights arguments." Why might the government of South Africa – the defendant in the lawsuit – not have raised arguments based on the right to health in the constitution and in human rights treaties that the country had ratified?

3. What strategies and arguments did nongovernmental organizations such as the Treatment Action Campaign (TAC) use to develop an alternative framing of the link between patents and the right to health? Why were these strategies and arguments effective, even in the face of resistance by the well-resourced and politically influential pharmaceutical industry?[109]

4. In *"Rights" and Wrongs*, Lisa Forman identifies a link between human rights and the 2001 Doha Declaration on TRIPS Agreement and Public Health, analyzed earlier in this chapter. Do you agree with Forman that the Declaration contains "language redolent of human rights and the right to health"? What other interests might the references to "rights" in the Declaration be intended to protect? In addition to explicit references to human rights, how else might one measure the influence of human rights arguments in the WTO? More generally, does the fact that WTO member states responded to concerns regarding access to medicines *within* the trade regime undermine the claim that intellectual property should be analyzed in other venues, such as the U.N. human rights system?

5. In the years following the withdrawal of the *Pharmaceutical Manufacturers Association* case, TAC has continued to advocate and litigate for increased access to HIV/AIDS medications in South Africa. In 2000, Boehringer Ingelheim, the manufacturer of nevirapine – a patented antiretroviral drug that reduces the likelihood of HIV transmission from mother to child during childbirth – agreed to provide a five-year supply of the drug to the government without charge. In 2001, TAC challenged the government's decision to limit the availability of nevirapine in the public health system to a small number of research and training sites and its failure to "plan and implement

---

[108] *See, e.g., Minister of Health v. Treatment Action Campaign & Others*, 2002 (10) BCLR 1033 (CC) (S. Afr.); *Soobramoney v. Minister of Health*, 1998 (1) SA 765 (CC) (S. Afr.).

[109] *See* Andrew T. F. Lang, *The Role of the Human Rights Movement in Trade Policy-Making: Human Rights as a Trigger for Social Learning*, 5 N.Z. J. PUB. & INT'L L. 77, 89 (2007); Susan K. Sell, *TRIPS and the Access to Medicines Campaign*, 20 WIS. INT'L L.J. 481, 496–97 (2002); Susan K. Sell & Aseem Prakash, *Using Ideas Strategically: The Contest between Business and NGO Networks in Intellectual Property Rights*, 48 INT'L STUD. Q. 143, 160–67 (2004).

an effective, comprehensive and progressive programme for the prevention of mother-to-child transmission of HIV throughout the country."[110] In its response, the government argued, in part, that it had limited the drug's availability to locations where trained personnel were available to provide counseling and testing for pregnant mothers and to deliver "a 'package' of care for mother and infant." Extending these services throughout the public health care system, the government contended, would require a significant outlay of resources.[111]

In a 2002 judgment, the Constitutional Court held that the government's policy was unreasonable and thus violated, *inter alia*, Article 27 of the Constitution. It ordered the government to remove restrictions preventing nevirapine from being made available at all public hospitals and clinics. It also required the government "to take reasonable measures to extend the testing and counselling facilities to hospitals and clinics throughout the public health sector beyond the test sites to facilitate and expedite the use of nevirapine for the purpose of reducing the risk of mother-to-child transmission of HIV."[112] Implementation of the Constitutional Court's ruling in the Treatment Action Campaign has extended over several years:

> TAC returned to court in late 2002 to obtain a contempt judgment against the Minister of Health and one province. By August 2003, five of [South Africa's nine] provinces and the national health department still had not accepted the drug company's offer of free supplies of nevirapine. [The organization again] returned to court in 2004 seeking to make public the government's undisclosed timetables for implementation. A new plan for providing antiretroviral therapy to South Africans living with HIV was drafted in 2006 and announced in 2007, this time with input from civil society leaders, including [TAC]. The United Nations Programme on HIV/AIDS ("UNAIDS") reported that anti-retroviral coverage for the prevention of mother-to-child-transmission had increased from 15 percent to 57 percent in the country between 2004 and 2006. HIV infection rates among pregnant South Africans attending antenatal clinics remained constant at around 30 percent.[113]

What insights do the Treatment Action Campaign case and its implementation suggest for the debates, summarized previously, over the relative importance of patents versus other factors as barriers to access to medicines? Should the Constitutional Court have found a violation of Article 27 of the

---

[110] *Minister of Health v. Treatment Action Campaign*, 2002 (10) BCLR 1033 (CC) at para. 5 (S. Afr.).

[111] *Id.* para. 51.

[112] *Id.* para. 95.

[113] Louis Henkin et al., Human Rights 1448 (2d ed. 2009) (citing UNAIDS, *Report on the Global AIDS Epidemic* 41, U.N. Doc. UNAIDS/08.25E/JC1510E [Aug. 2008]).

Constitution if the manufacturer of nevirapine had *not* provided the government with a free supply of the drug? If so, what should the court have ordered the government to do to remedy the violation?

6. Litigation concerning the right to health in general and access to medicines for HIV/AIDS in particular has increased markedly over the last decade. The trend is especially pronounced in Central and South America, regions "characterized by rights-rich constitutions, high social exclusion, and systemic failures of representation by the political branches of government."[114]

In one of the earliest cases, in the late 1990s, nearly 170 HIV-infected individuals filed a complaint against the Venezuelan Ministry of Health and Social Action. The plaintiffs alleged that the failure of the country's public health care system to provide antiretroviral drugs violated the rights to life, health, liberty, and security of the person; the right to equality; and the right to enjoy the benefits of science and technology as guaranteed by the Venezuelan constitution and international law. The plaintiffs sought an order to compel the government to provide them with the medications.

In 1999, the Supreme Court of Venezuela ruled for the plaintiffs.[115] The court based its decision on the rights to life and health and the right to enjoy the benefits of science and technology. It rejected the defense of insufficient resources and ordered the ministry to seek the necessary budget allocations to provide antiretroviral medications for all similarly situated HIV-infected individuals in the country. In particular, the court ordered the ministry to:

- regularly supply antiretroviral drugs as prescribed and take measures necessary to ensure uninterrupted supply;
- cover all tests necessary for using antiretroviral drugs and for treating opportunistic infections;
- provide medications necessary for treating opportunistic infections;
- develop a policy of information, treatment and comprehensive medical assistance for people living with HIV or AIDS who are eligible for social assistance; and

---

[114] Alicia Ely Yamin & Oscar Parra-Vera, *How Do Courts Set Health Policy? The Case of the Colombian Constitutional Court*, 6 Pub. Library of Science Med. 147, 149 (2009); *see also* Hans V. Hogerzeil et al., *Is Access to Essential Medicines as Part of the Fulfillment of the Right to Health Enforceable through the Courts?*, 368 Lancet 305, 307 (2006) (analyzing "73 cases from 12 low- and middle-income countries," 90% of which were in Latin America).

[115] *Cruz del Valle Bermúdez v. Ministerio de Sanidad y Asistencia Social*, expediente no. 15,789 (Corte Suprema de Justicia, July 15, 1999) (Venezuela), *translated in* David P. Fidler, International Law and Public Health: Materials on and Analysis of Global Health Jurisprudence 316–26 (2000).

- undertake research on HIV and AIDS in Venezuela, for the purpose of developing programmes and infrastructure to prevent HIV transmission and provide care for those infected.[116]

In subsequent decisions, the Venezuelan courts extended this ruling, finding the government in violation of the constitution for failing to provide additional antiretroviral medications, laboratory tests, and treatments for opportunistic infections associated with HIV/AIDS.[117]

In what ways do the Venezuelan cases differ from the Treatment Action Campaign case discussed earlier? Is the wider scope of the Venezuelan Supreme Court's order justifiable? If so, on what basis? Are there any risks associated with robust judicial oversight of national health care policies?[118] Would it be appropriate for a court to order the government to provide potentially lifesaving treatment for a disease such as leukemia that had been deliberately excluded from the health care system because of its high cost?[119]

7. Litigation concerning access to medicines has also occurred in the Inter-American human rights system. In *Jorge Odir Miranda Cortez et al. v. El Salvador*,[120] more than two dozen HIV-infected individuals alleged that El Salvador had violated, *inter alia*, the rights to life and health protected by the American Convention on Human Rights by failing to provide antiretroviral drugs to prevent their death and improve their quality of life. The Inter-American Commission on Human Rights issued a precautionary measures order requesting the government to provide the medications on an interim basis. In March 2001, the Commission declared the complaint admissible. Shortly thereafter, the Supreme Court of El Salvador issued a ruling in a related case ordering the Salvadoran Social Security Institute to provide the requested antiretroviral therapy. The government agreed to do so and the proceedings before the Inter-American Commission ended in a friendly settlement. Although the Commission never issued a decision on the merits, the case "contributed to treatment activism throughout the region, complementing high-profile cases before a number of domestic courts."[121]

---

[116] *Id.* (summarized in UNAIDS, *Courting Rights: Case Studies in Litigating the Human Rights of People Living with HIV* 66, U.N. Doc. UNAIDS/06.01E (Mar. 2006) [*Courting Rights*]).

[117] *Courting Rights, supra* note 116, 67–68; Mary Ann Torres, *The Human Right to Health, National Courts and Access to HIV/AIDS Treatment: A Case Study from Venezuela.* 3 CHI. J. INT'L L. 105 (2002).

[118] *See* Siri Gloppen, *Litigation as a Strategy to Hold Governments Accountable for Implementing the Right to Health,* 10 HEALTH & HUM RTS. 21, 24 (2008).

[119] *See* Hogerzeil et al., *supra* note 114, at 310 (discussing such a case from Costa Rica).

[120] *Jorge Odir Miranda Cortez et al. v. El Salvador,* Case 12.249, Inter-Am. C.H.R., Report No. 29/01, OEA/Ser.L/V/II.111, doc. 20 rev. 284 (2000).

[121] *Courting Rights, supra* note 116, at 71.

In addition to using human rights arguments to reframe public perceptions and to bolster lawsuits seeking to compel governments to provide
access to medicines, scholars and advocates have also turned to human rights
when developing proposals to restructure the incentives for medical innovation to focus attention on the treatment of neglected diseases and the health
needs of the world's poor. The following essay, authored by the philosopher
Thomas Pogge, highlights the shortcomings of the existing patent system and
develops an alternative innovation framework inspired in part by human
rights concerns.

Thomas W. Pogge, *Human Rights and Global Health: A Research Program*, 36 METAPHILOSOPHY 182, 184–94, 197 (2005)

Some eighteen million human beings die prematurely each year from medical
conditions we can cure – this is equivalent to fifty thousand avoidable deaths
per day, or one-third of all human deaths. Hundreds of millions more suffer
grievously from these conditions....

. . .

This essay outlines how one crucial obstacle to a dramatic reduction in the
global disease burden can be removed by giving medical innovators stable
and reliable financial incentives to address the medical conditions of the
poor. My aim is to develop a concrete, feasible, and politically realistic plan
for reforming current national and global rules for incentivizing the search
for new essential drugs. If adopted, this plan would not add much to the
overall cost of global health-care spending. In fact, on any plausible accounting, which would take note of the huge economic losses caused by the present
global disease burden, the reform would actually save money. Moreover, it
would distribute the cost of global health-care spending more fairly across
countries, across generations, and between those lucky enough to enjoy good
health and the unlucky ones suffering from serious medical conditions.

. . .

The existing rules for incentivizing pharmaceutical research are morally
deeply problematic. This fact, long understood among international health
experts, has come to be more widely recognized in the wake of the AIDS
crisis, especially in Africa, where the vital needs of poor patients are pitted
against the need of pharmaceutical companies to recoup their research-and-
development investments. Still, this wider recognition does not easily translate into political reform. Some believe (like Churchill about democracy) that

the present regime is the lesser evil in comparison to its alternatives that have any chance of implementation. And others, more friendly to reform, disagree about what the flaws of the present system are exactly and have put forward a wide range of alternative reform ideas. What is needed now is a careful comparative exploration of the various reforms that have been proposed by academics, nongovernmental organizations (NGOs), and politicians as well as in the media, with the aim of formulating and justifying a specific alternative that is clearly superior to the present regime.

...

In addition, this plan must be politically feasible and realistic. To be *feasible* it must, once implemented, generate its own support from governments, pharmaceutical companies, and the general public (taking these three key constituencies as they would be under the reformed regime). To be *realistic*, the plan must possess moral and prudential appeal for governments, pharmaceutical companies, and the general public (taking these three constituencies as they are now, under the existing regime). A reform plan that is not incentive compatible in these two ways is destined to remain a philosopher's pipe dream.

Bringing new, safe and effective life saving medications to market is hugely expensive, as inventor firms must pay for the research and development of new drugs as well as for elaborate testing and the subsequent approval process. In addition, newly developed medical treatments often turn out to be unsafe or not effective enough, to have bad side effects, or to fail getting government approval for some other reason, which may lead to the loss of the entire investment.

Given such large investment costs and risks, very little innovative pharmaceutical research would take place in a free-market system....

The classic solution, also enshrined in the TRIPS regime ..., corrects this market failure through patent rules that grant inventor firms a temporary monopoly on their inventions, typically for twenty years from the time of filing a patent application. With competitors barred from copying and selling any newly invented drug during this period, the inventor firm can sell it at the profit-maximizing monopoly price well above, and often very far above, its marginal cost of production. In this way, the inventor firm can recoup its research and overhead expenses plus some of the cost of its other research efforts that failed to bear fruit.

This solution corrects the market failure (undersupply of medical innovation), but its monopoly feature creates another. During the patent's duration, the profit-maximizing sale price of the invented medicine will be far above its marginal cost of production. This large differential is collectively irrational by impeding many mutually beneficial transactions between the inventor firm and potential buyers who are unwilling or unable to pay the monopoly price but are willing and able to pay substantially more than the marginal cost of production. If modified rules could facilitate these potential transactions, then many patients would benefit and so would the drug companies, as they would book additional profitable sales and typically also, through economies of scale, reduce their marginal cost of production. Such a reform would not merely avoid a sizable economic loss for the national and global economies. It would also avoid countless premature deaths and much severe suffering worldwide that the present patent regime engenders by blocking mutually advantageous sales of essential medicines.

There are two basic reform strategies for avoiding this second market failure associated with monopoly pricing powers. I will refer to these as the differential-pricing and public-good strategies, respectively. The *differential-pricing strategy* comes in different variants. One would have inventor firms themselves offer their proprietary drugs to different customers at different prices, thereby realizing a large profit margin from sales to the more affluent without renouncing sales to poorer buyers at a lower margin. Another variant is the right of governments, recognized under TRIPS rules, to issue compulsory licenses for inventions that are urgently needed in a public emergency. Exercising this right, a government can force down the price of a patented invention by compelling the patent holder to license it to other producers for a set percentage (typically below 10 percent) of the latter's sales revenues.... It has often been suggested that poor countries should assert their compulsory licensing rights to cope with their public-health crises, particularly the AIDS pandemic.

Differential-pricing solutions are generally unworkable unless the different categories of buyers can be prevented from knowing about, or from trading with, one another. In the real world, if the drug were sold at a lower price to some, then many buyers who would otherwise be willing and able to pay the higher price would find a way to buy at the lower price. Selling expensive drugs more cheaply in poor developing countries, for example, would create strong incentives to divert (for example, smuggle) this drug back into the more affluent countries, leading to relative losses in the latter markets that outweigh the gains in the former. Anticipating such net losses through diversion, inventor firms typically do not themselves try to overcome the second market failure through differential pricing, resist pressures to do so, and fight attempts to impose compulsory licensing upon them. As a result, differential pricing has not gained much of a foothold, and many poor patients who would be willing and able to purchase the drug at a price well above the marginal cost of production are excluded from this drug because they cannot afford the much higher monopoly price. While such exclusion is acceptable for other categories of intellectual property (for example, software, films, and music), it is morally highly problematic in the case of essential medicines.

To be sure, insofar as a government does succeed, against heavy pressure from pharmaceutical companies and often their home governments, in exercising its right to issue compulsory licenses, any net losses due to diversion are simply forced upon the patent holders. But such compulsory licensing, especially if it were to become more common, brings back the first market failure of undersupply: Pharmaceutical companies will tend to spend less on the quest for essential drugs when the uncertainty of success is compounded by the additional unpredictability of whether and to what extent they will be allowed to recoup their investments through undisturbed use of their monopoly pricing powers.

In light of these serious problems, I doubt that the differential-pricing strategy can yield a plan for reform that would constitute a substantial improvement over the present regime. So I am proceeding, for now, on the assumption that an exploration of the *public-good strategy* is more promising, that is, more likely to lead to the formulation of a reform plan that would avoid the main defects of the present monopoly-patent regime while preserving most of its important benefits. The great difficulty to be overcome lies in devising the best possible reform plan....

We may think of such a reform plan as consisting of three components. First, the results of any successful effort to develop (research, test, and obtain regulatory approval for) a new essential drug are to be provided as a public good that all pharmaceutical companies may use free of charge. This reform would eliminate the second market failure (associated with monopoly pricing powers) by allowing competition to bring the prices of new essential drugs down close to their marginal cost of production. Implemented in only one country or a few countries, this reform would engender problems like those we have found to attend differential-pricing solutions: Cheaper drugs produced in countries where drug development is treated as a public good would seep back into countries adhering to the monopoly-patent regime, undermining research incentives in the latter countries. The reform should therefore be global in scope, just as the rules of the current TRIPS regime are. The first reform component, then, is that results of successful efforts to develop new essential drugs are to be provided as public goods that all pharmaceutical companies anywhere may use free of charge.

Implemented in isolation, this first reform component would destroy incentives for pharmaceutical research. This effect is avoided by the second component, which is that, similar to the current regime, inventor firms should be entitled to take out a multiyear patent on any essential medicines they invent but, during the life of the patent, should be rewarded, out of public funds, in proportion to the impact of their invention on the global disease burden. This reform component would reorient the incentives of such firms in highly desirable ways: Any inventor firm would have incentives to sell its innovative treatments cheaply (often even below their marginal cost of production) in order to help get its drugs to even very poor people who need them. Such a firm would have incentives also to see to it that patients are fully instructed in the proper use of its drugs (dosage, compliance, and so on), in order to ensure that, through wide and effective deployment, they have as great an impact on the global disease burden as possible. Rather than ignore poor countries as unlucrative markets, inventor firms would moreover have incentives to work together toward improving the health systems of these countries in order to enhance the impact of their inventions there. In addition, any inventor firm would have reason to encourage and support efforts by cheap generic producers (already well established in India, Brazil, and South Africa, for example) to copy its drugs, because such copying would further increase the number of users and hence the invention's favorable impact on the global disease burden. In all these ways, the reform would align and harmonize the interests of inventor firms with those of patients and the generic drug producers – interests that, under the current regime, are diametrically opposed. The reform would also align the moral and prudential interests of the inventor firms who, under the present regime, are forced to choose between recouping their investments in the search for essential drugs and preventing avoidable suffering and deaths.

This second component of a plausible public-good strategy realizes yet one further tremendous advantage over the status quo: Under the current regime, inventor firms have incentives to try to develop a new medical treatment only if the expected value of the temporary monopoly pricing power they might gain, discounted by the probability of failure, is greater than the full development and patenting costs. They have no incentives, then, to try to develop treatments that few people have a need for and treatments needed by people who are unable to afford them at a price far above the marginal cost of production. The former category contains treatments for many so-called orphan diseases that affect only small numbers of patients. The latter category contains many diseases mainly affecting the poor, for which treatments priced far above the marginal cost of production could be sold only in small quantities. It may be acceptable that no one is developing software demanded only by a few and that no one is producing music valued only by the very poor. But it is morally problematic that no treatments are developed for rare diseases, and it is extremely problematic, morally, that so few treatments are developed for medical conditions that cause most of the premature deaths and suffering in the world today.

Even if common talk of the 10/90 gap is now an overstatement, the problem is certainly real: Malaria, pneumonia, diarrhea, and tuberculosis, which together account for 21 percent of the global disease burden, receive 0.31 percent of all public and private funds devoted to health research. And diseases confined to the tropics tend to be the most neglected: Of the 1,393 new drugs approved between 1975 and 1999, only thirteen were specifically indicated for tropical diseases and five out of these thirteen actually emerged from veterinary research.

Rewarding pharmaceutical research on the basis of its impact on the global disease burden would attract inventor firms toward medical conditions whose adverse effects on humankind can be reduced most cost effectively. This reorientation would greatly mitigate the problem of neglected diseases that overwhelmingly affect the poor. And it would open new profitable research opportunities for pharmaceutical companies.

One might worry that the second component of the reform would also reduce incentives to develop treatments for medical conditions that, though they add little to the global disease burden (on any plausible conception thereof), affluent patients are willing to pay a lot to avoid. But this worry can be addressed, at least in part, by limiting the application of the reform plan to essential drugs, that is, to medicines for diseases that destroy human lives. Drugs for other medical conditions, such as hair loss, acne, and impotence, for example, can remain under the existing regime with no loss in incentives or rewards.

Incorporating this distinction between essential and nonessential drugs into the reform plan raises the specter of political battles over how this distinction is to be defined and of legal battles over how some particular invention should be classified. These dangers could be averted by allowing inventor firms to classify their inventions as they wish and then designing the rewards in such a way that these firms will themselves choose to register under the reform rules any inventions that stand to make a real difference to the global disease burden. Such freedom of choice would also greatly facilitate a smooth and rapid phasing in of the new rules, as there would be no disappointment of the legitimate expectations of firms that have undertaken research for the sake of gaining a conventional patent. The reform plan should be *attractive* for pharmaceutical companies by winning them new lucrative opportunities for research into currently neglected diseases without significant losses in the lucrative research opportunities they now enjoy – and by restoring their moral stature as benefactors of humankind.

This second reform component requires a way of funding the planned incentives for developing new essential medicines, which might cost some US$45–90 billion annually on a global scale. The third component of the reform plan is then to develop a fair, feasible, and politically realistic allocation of these costs, as well as compelling arguments in support of this allocation.

While the general approach as outlined may seem plausible enough, the great intellectual challenge is to specify it concretely in a way that shows it to be both feasible and politically realistic. This is an extremely complex undertaking that involves a formidable array of multiply interdependent tasks and subtasks. Here one main task, associated with the second component, concerns the design of the planned incentives. This requires a suitable measure of the global disease burden and ways of assessing the contributions that various new medical treatments are making to its reduction. When two or more different medicines are alternative treatments for the same disease, then the reward corresponding to their aggregate impact must be allocated among their respective inventors on the basis of each medicine's market share and effectiveness.

More complex is the case (exemplified in the fight against HIV, tuberculosis, and malaria) of "drug cocktails" that combine various drugs that frequently have been developed by different companies. Here the reform plan must formulate clear and transparent rules for distributing the overall reward, based on the impact of the drug cocktail, among the inventors of the drugs it contains. And it must also include specific rules for the phase-in period so as not to discourage ongoing research efforts motivated by the existing patent rules. It is of crucial importance that all these rules be clear and transparent, lest they add to the inevitable risks and uncertainties that complicate the work of inventor firms and sometimes discourage them from important research efforts. This task requires expertise in medicine, statistics, economics, and legal regulation.

Another main task, associated with the third component, concerns the design of rules for allocating the cost of the incentives as well as the formulation of good arguments in favor of this allocation. Effective implementation of the reform requires that much of its cost be borne by the developed countries, which, with 16 percent of the world's population, control about 81 percent of the global social product. This is feasible even if these countries, after retargeting existing subsidies to the pharmaceutical industry in accordance with the reformed rules, still had to shoulder around US$70 billion in new expenditures. This amount, after all, is only 0.27 percent of the aggregate gross national income of the high-income countries, or US$70 for each of their residents. To make this planned spending increase realistic, the taxpayers and politicians of the high-income countries need to be given compelling reasons for supporting it.

The plan can be supported by prudential considerations. For one thing, the taxpayers of the more affluent countries gain a substantial benefit for themselves in the form of lower drug prices. Under the current regime, affluent persons in need of essential drugs pay high prices for them, either directly or through their contributions to commercial insurance companies. Under the projected scheme, the prices of such drugs would be much lower, and their consumers, even the richest, would thus save money on drugs and/or insurance premiums. To be sure, such a shifting of costs, within affluent countries, from patients to taxpayers would benefit less-healthy citizens at the expense of the healthier ones. But such a mild mitigation of the effects of luck is actually morally appealing – not least because even those fortunate persons who never or rarely need to take advantage of recent medical advances still benefit from pharmaceutical research that affords them the peace of mind derived from knowing that, should they ever become seriously ill, they would have access to cutting-edge medical knowledge and treatments.

A second prudential argument is that, by giving poor populations a free ride on the pharmaceutical research conducted for the benefit of citizens in the affluent countries, we are building goodwill toward ourselves in the developing world by demonstrating in a tangible way our concern for the horrendous public-health problems these populations are facing. This argument has a moral twin: In light of the extent of avoidable mortality and morbidity in the developing world, the case for giving the poor a free ride is morally compelling.

These last twin arguments have wider application. The reform plan would not merely encourage the same sort of pharmaceutical research differently but would also expand the range of medical conditions for which inventor firms would seek solutions. Under the current regime, these firms understandably show little interest in tropical diseases, for example, because, even if they could develop successful treatments, they would not be able to make much money from selling or licensing them. Under the alternative regime I suggest we design, inventor firms could make lots of money by developing such treatments, whose potential impact on the global disease burden is enormous. Measles, malaria, and tuberculosis each kill well over a million people per year, mostly children, and pneumonia kills more than these three combined. New drugs could dramatically reduce the impact of these diseases.

But, it may be asked, why should we citizens of the high-income countries support a rule change that benefits others (poor people in the developing world) at our expense? Viewed narrowly, underwriting such incentives for research into widespread but currently neglected diseases might seem to be a dead loss for the affluent countries.

Taking a larger view, however, important gains are readily apparent: The reform would create top-flight medical-research jobs in the developed countries. It would enable us to respond more effectively to public-health emergencies and problems in the future by earning us more rapidly increasing medical knowledge combined with a stronger and more diversified arsenal of medical interventions. In addition, better human health around the world would reduce the threat we face from invasive diseases. The recent SARS outbreak illustrates the last two points: Dangerous diseases can rapidly transit from poor-country settings into cities in the industrialized world...; and the current neglect of the medical needs of poor populations leaves us unprepared to deal with such problems when we are suddenly confronted with them. Slowing population growth and bringing enormous reductions in avoidable suffering and deaths worldwide, the reform would furthermore be vastly more cost effective and also be vastly better received by people in the poor countries than similarly expensive humanitarian interventions we have undertaken in recent years and the huge, unrepayable loans our governments and their international financial institutions tend to extend[ ] to (often corrupt and oppressive) rulers and elites in the developing countries. Last, but not least, there is the important moral and social benefit of working with others, nationally and internationally, toward overcoming the morally preeminent problem of our age, which is the horrendous, poverty-induced and largely avoidable morbidity and mortality in the developing world.

...

In the world as it is, some eighteen million human beings die each year from poverty-related causes, mostly from communicable diseases that could easily be averted or cured. Insofar as these deaths and the immense suffering of those still surviving these diseases are avoidable, their victims are deprived of some of the objects of their human rights – for example, of their "right to a standard of living adequate for the health and well-being of himself and of his family, including food, clothing, housing and medical care and necessary social services" (UDHR, Article 25; cf. ICESCR, Articles 11–12).

If these victims are so deprived, then who or what is depriving them, violating their human rights? Several factors, national and global, substantially contribute to the deprivations they suffer. As I have been arguing, one important such factor is the way pharmaceutical research into drugs and vaccines is incentivized under the current rules of the TRIPS Agreement as supplemented by various bilateral agreements the United States has been pursuing.

With this background, we can look once more at the question of why we citizens of the high-income countries should support a reform of the global health system that benefits others (poor people in the developing world) at our expense.... We ought to support such a reform, even if it involves significant opportunity costs for us, because it is necessary for rendering minimally just ... the rules of the world economy considered as one scheme. Minimal justice in this sense is compatible with these rules being designed by, and with their greatly and disproportionately benefiting, the governments and corporations of the developed countries. However, minimal justice is not compatible with these rules being designed so that they result in a much higher incidence of extreme poverty and in much higher mortality and morbidity from curable diseases than would be reasonably avoidable.

Notes and Questions

1. Does the proposal that Thomas Pogge advances meet the standard he sets of being "politically feasible and realistic"? Would you support the proposal if you were (a) a member of the United States Congress or a European Union official? (b) a multinational pharmaceutical company with a research portfolio that includes the development of new drugs for HIV/AIDS? (c) a middle-income resident of the United States or an EU member state? (d) a member of an NGO that advocates expanding access to medicines? (e) the government of a country that provides a robust socialized medicine system within which the cost of pharmaceuticals is already subsidized by taxpayers?

2. Pogge estimates that funding the research and development of new medicines to treat diseases that afflict the world's poor populations would require between U.S. $45 and U.S. $90 billion annually, the majority of which would be borne by industrialized countries. To provide additional context for assessing these costs, consider the following:

> In 2001 ... the total estimated global spending on health research by the public sector was nearly US $47 billion. Of this amount, nearly US $29 billion (61%)

was spent in the United States, predominantly by the NIH [National Institutes of Health]. The amount spent by the public sector in developing countries is estimated at US $2.5 billion.

. . .

The significant fact about public funding of R&D is that its focus is predominantly shaped by domestic priorities. Thus, the priorities for public sector R&D funding in developed countries will necessarily be shaped by their own disease burden … and on finding solutions that reflect the resources they have available for new methods of diagnosis, prevention and treatment.…

There is some developed country interest in international health, dating back to the beginning of the 20th century for former colonial powers such as France and the United Kingdom. In these cases, the infrastructure for research on diseases mainly affecting developing countries remains strong, with links existing between researchers in several parts of the developing world. Thus, for example, the Medical Research Council in the United Kingdom maintains a significant portfolio of research relevant to developing countries. In 2002–2003, the Medical Research Council spent an estimated £22.5 million on research relevant to developing countries, representing over 6% of its total expenditure. The NIH in the United States was specifically empowered to conduct research on tropical diseases in 1993, whereas previously any international research was required to be specifically of benefit to United States citizens. [One study] estimated that the share of R&D expenditure on tropical diseases by the NIH had increased to as much as US$ 1 billion (4% of total R&D) in 2004, whereas in the 1990s the share averaged well under 1% of a much smaller total investment.[122]

3. Pogge discusses two ways to correct the market failure created by the patent monopoly – different pricing strategies and public goods strategies. Pricing strategies segment the market for a patented drug and set different prices for each market, thereby expanding access to consumers otherwise unable to afford the drug. Differential pricing strategies can be either voluntary or mandated by law. They can be ex ante schemes in which prices are set in advance of a drug's distribution, or ex post mechanisms in which the price is adjusted after sale in a particular market. (Compulsory licenses are an example of ex post differential pricing.) Some differential pricing arrangements also aim to increase pharmaceutical firm profits, such as where a firm would not otherwise have sold the drug in developing countries. Differential pricing schemes depend upon some mechanism to keep different markets separate to prevent arbitrage – buying drugs in bulk at a low price in country "A" and selling at a higher price in country "B." Examples of differential pricing strategies include the following[123]:

---

[122] WHO, Comm'n on Intell. Prop. Rights, Innovation and Pub. Health, *supra* note 104, at 42–44.
[123] *See id.* at 111–14, 121–23.

a. Setting drug prices according to some measure of national wealth or consumer income in each country of sale, rather than selling the drug at a uniform global price.
b. Discount pricing schemes for certain categories of customers (especially government agencies or nongovernmental organizations) in particular countries.
c. Limiting the sales price of patented medicines in designated nations to the price of generic equivalents.
d. Issuing voluntary licenses to the generic drug industry in lower income countries.
e. Pooling arrangements in which multiple purchasers act collectively to purchase medicines at a reduced cost.
f. Patent buy-outs, in which government agencies purchase the patent owner's exclusive rights at a reduced price.
g. Agreements by pharmaceutical companies not to enforce patents in certain countries.
h. Pharmaceutical company drug donation programs.
i. Compulsory licenses issued pursuant to TRIPS Article 31 (discussed in detail in subsection 2.4).

Why is Pogge pessimistic that differential pricing strategies "can yield a plan for reform that would constitute a substantial improvement over the present regime"? If the public goods strategy that Pogge proposes were adopted, would it be feasible to continue compulsory licensing as set forth in the TRIPS Agreement, or would such licenses need to be curtailed?

4. Consider the three-part public goods proposal that Pogge favors, which rewards private innovation from public funds in proportion to the degree to which it alleviates the global disease burden. Aside from concerns about cost or political feasibility, in what ways does this proposal improve upon the existing innovation system?[124] What are the proposal's drawbacks from an innovation perspective? Would the proposal have different consequences for research relating to the three diseases categories identified by WHO and described at the beginning of Section 2.5?

5. What role does patent protection play in Pogge's proposal? What functions would international law and international institutions perform?

6. Over the last several years, WHO has actively studied the global drug gap and the mechanisms that might be employed to close it. In 2003, the World Health Assembly (WHA), WHO's legislative arm, called for the creation of a

---

[124] *See id.* at 88.

commission of independent experts "to collect data and proposals from different actors involved and produce an analysis of intellectual property rights, innovation and public health, including the question of appropriate funding and incentive mechanisms for the creation of new medicines and other products against diseases that disproportionately affect developing countries."[125] The Commission on Intellectual Property Rights, Innovation and Public Health issued its report to the organization – which we excerpt below – in 2006. In the same year, the WHA established the Intergovernmental Working Group on Public Health, Innovation and Intellectual Property with a mandate to develop a global strategy and work program on these issues.[126] Following the submission of the working group's report in 2008, the WHA approved a resolution adopting a Global Strategy and Plan of Action on Public Health, Innovation and Intellectual Property.[127] The resolution, which reaffirms the right to health as a fundamental right, "aims to promote new thinking on innovation and access to medicines" with regard to diseases that disproportionately affect developing countries. The many detailed recommendations set forth in the strategy include prioritizing research and development needs; building innovative capacity and technology transfer; improving delivery and access; and revising the "application and management of intellectual property to contribute to innovation and promote public health."[128]

7. In its 2006 report, the WHO Commission on Intellectual Property Rights, Innovation and Public Health summarized a variety of existing and proposed innovation mechanisms that incorporate public goods strategies similar to those described in the article by Pogge. These mechanisms included the following:

> *Orphan drug schemes.* In orphan drug schemes, there is an offer of limited additional market exclusivity (along with other tax and funding benefits) to promote the development of drugs to treat diseases that affect relatively few people (less than 200 000 in the United States). The United States Orphan Drug Act of 1983 resulted in more than 1238 orphan drug designations from the United States [Food and Drug Administration] FDA as of May 2003, of which 238 had received marketing approval. This is a 10-fold increase on the rate of development of orphan drugs before the Orphan Drug Act. Some have

---

[125] World Health Assembly, Res. WHA 56.27, *Intellectual Property Rights, Innovation and Public Health* (May 28, 2003).

[126] World Health Assembly Res. WHA 59.24, *Public Health, Innovation, Essential Health Research and Intellectual Property Rights: Towards a Global Strategy and Plan of Action* (May 27, 2006).

[127] World Health Assembly, Res. WHA 61.21, *Global Strategy and Plan of Action on Public Health, Innovation and Intellectual Property* (May 24, 2008).

[128] *Id.* paras. 13, 27–44.

proposed a number of modifications to orphan drug legislation in the United States or Europe to provide a greater stimulus for diseases mainly affecting developing countries. The pharmaceutical industry has suggested the idea of tropical diseases drug legislation, based principally on the package of orphan drug incentives.

...

Tax credits. An element of orphan drug schemes is the provision of tax credits.... Some governments, such as that of the United Kingdom, have introduced specific additional tax credits to boost research on, for instance, HIV/AIDS, TB and malaria. The evidence is mixed on the effectiveness of tax credits in boosting R&D on diseases where the market is uncertain, although there is evidence that general tax credits have an impact on market-driven R&D....

Scheme for transferable intellectual property rights. The proposal for transferable intellectual property rights (TIPRs) seeks to overcome the lack of a market by allowing the reward for innovation to come from a patent extension on an unrelated product in a developed country market. Thus, a company that develops a drug for a notified disease may be rewarded by an extension of the patent term on an existing product (e.g. a "blockbuster" drug).

...

Transferable fast-track review scheme. A variation on the TIPR proposal is to spur private sector involvement in the development of treatments for neglected diseases by offering companies fast-track regulatory review status on a product with a substantial potential market in the developed world. This would be a variation on current procedures of regulatory authorities, which allow fast-tracking for products that meet certain criteria of potential therapeutic benefit. This proposal might allow entry to the market a year or two earlier than otherwise possible. In one version, this scheme is operated simply as an auction and thus becomes a way of raising money which can then be spent as desired on R&D in the public or private sectors....

Reward systems. The central idea in the proposals for reward systems is that patents on products would be bought out, or replaced altogether, by governmental payments in relation to a calculation of the incremental therapeutic value of the product.[129] By this means, it is argued, priorities for innovation could be more closely related to public health priorities, and the product could then be made available at production costs, excluding those of R&D. This could have the important effect that, while the incentive for innovation is retained, the loss in economic efficiency through the distorting effect of patents on prices is avoided.

...

[129] [Prizes are one form of reward system. *See* James Love & Tim Hubbard, *The Big Idea: Prizes to Stimulate R&D for New Medicines*, 82 CHI.-KENT L. REV. 1519 (2007) – Eds.]

A variation on these comprehensive proposals is to introduce a reward scheme specifically targeted at products to meet the needs of developing countries. The intention would not be to supplant patents, but to supplement them by offering a reward for products to tackle diseases that affect developing country populations where, because market incentives are deficient, patents are not an effective incentive. Thus, the implementing authority could set a high value on products that would have a correspondingly high public health impact in these countries.... A different approach is provided by the advance purchase commitment proposal, which seeks to mimic the market by guaranteeing the purchase at a future date of, for example, a new vaccine in a pre-established quantity and price. The vaccine would have to meet specific criteria for efficacy. The same principle could also apply to treatments, or indeed diagnostics. The intention is to replicate the potential rewards of a minor blockbuster drug as an incentive to induce companies to invest in R&D. In addition, commitments would be built into the contractual arrangements to oblige a price reduction once the guarantee expired.

...

Medical R&D treaty.... The basic idea behind the proposed treaty is that governments would commit themselves to spending a certain proportion of national income on medical R&D in a number of ways. The proposal seeks to introduce more eclectic and innovative means of financing R&D, underpinned by a global commitment by governments, embodied in a treaty, to spend agreed proportions of national income on medical R&D [for neglected diseases and other public health priorities].[130]

How do these mechanisms compare to the proposal that Pogge advocates? In making this comparison, consider the following perspectives: (1) incentives for innovation into neglected diseases, (2) cost, (3) political feasibility, and (4) administrative feasibility.

8. Over the last decade, more than eighty public-private partnerships (PPPs) have formed to focus on the development of treatments for HIV/ AIDS, malaria, tuberculosis, and other neglected infectious diseases. Prominent partnerships include the Drugs for Neglected Disease Initiative (DNDi), the Medicines for Malaria Venture (MMV), and the Global Alliance for TB Drug Development (TB Alliance). PPPs – whose members include various combinations of private philanthropies, international organizations, pharmaceutical companies, universities, national governments, and NGOs – seek to harness the strengths of both public and private research strategies. Their benefits include

(1) integrating and coordinating multiple industry and academic partners and contractors along the drug development pipeline; (2) allocating public and

[130] WHO, Comm'n on Intell. Prop. Rights, Innovation and Pub. Health, *supra* note 104, at 86–90.

philanthropic funds to the "right" kinds of R&D projects from a public health perspective...; and (3) managing neglected-disease drug portfolios, including selection and termination of projects based on their relative merits.[131]

In addition, PPPs provide opportunities for larger pharmaceutical companies to focus on neglected diseases. "Rather than pursue fully-fledged R&D programmes which are unlikely to meet companies' economic and financial criteria, companies can set up relatively low cost R&D programmes" that focus on "early stage R&D in the expectation that the expensive clinical trials phase, and some of the early stage research, may be subsidized by a public-private partnership."[132] Recent studies suggest that PPPs are succeeding where earlier efforts have failed. A 2005 study identified sixty-three new drug research initiatives for neglected diseases. Of these, sixteen were developed by private pharmaceutical companies alone and forty-seven by PPPs. Eighteen of the sixty-three drugs were in clinical trials, half of these in late-stage trials.[133]

According to one commentator, the proliferation of PPPs has occurred "largely in the *absence* of significant new government incentives and generally without public intervention."[134] Instead, private foundations have contributed three-quarters of the funding for these hybrid initiatives. (The Bill and Melinda Gates Foundation, the largest single contributor, is responsible for more than 60 percent of total nonprofit funding.) What do these facts suggest about the need for additional reform proposals, such as those described above?

C. Implications for Other Intellectual Property Rights

Among all the issues in which human rights and intellectual property intersect, the right to health and pharmaceutical patents have generated the most high-profile and high-stakes controversies. What implications do these controversies have for other intersections between human rights and intellectual property, such as the right to food and plant variety protection, the right to education and copyrights, and freedom of expression and trademarks? We explore these questions in detail in the remaining chapters of this book. For now, however, consider the statement by Pogge that "exclusion is acceptable

---

[131] Mary Moran, *A Breakthrough in R&D for Neglected Diseases: New Ways to Get the Drugs We Need*, 2 PLoS Med e302 at 830 (2005), *available at* http://www.plosmedicine.org/article/info:doi/10.1371/journal.pmed.0020302.

[132] WHO, Comm'n on Intell. Prop. Rights, Innovation and Pub. Health, *supra* note 104, at 72–73.

[133] *See id.* at 71–72; *see also* Taiwo A. Oriola, *Strong Medicine: Patents, Market, and Policy Challenges for Managing Neglected Diseases and Affordable Prescription Drugs*, 7 CAN. J. L. & TECH. 57, 103–07 (2009).

[134] Moran, *supra* note 131, at 829.

for other categories of intellectual property (for example, software, films, and music)," even if it is unacceptable for essential medicines. Should exclusion rules vary for different types of intellectual property? Before answering this question, consider this analysis of the "life cycle" of a copyrighted work:

> A copyrighted work is born when an idea is conceived and initially expressed and fixed; it is then brought to the market and matures. Sooner or later its glory days fade away (perhaps with some chances for a potential comeback), until it is ultimately forgotten in the archives of cultural relics.... At the early stage of a work's life cycle, its value (or at this stage the potential value) may lie predominantly in the ideas expressed therein. At this stage, other works embodying the same ideas but expressing them in a slightly different manner can function as very close substitutes. We can assume, for example, that at the time Mickey Mouse was developed, the idea of an antromorphic mouse as a cartoon character expressed with Mickey's distinct appearance and voice easily could be replaced by another antromorphic mouse with a different appearance and voice, or another antromorphic animated creature. The commercial viability of the work at this stage is highly susceptible to competition from other similar (even if not identical) works. As the work matures, however, its commercial success tends to depend less on the intrinsic value of the ideas and their specific expression and more on complementary inputs provided by other coproducers, as well as on exogenous factors, such as the word of critics and the work's ability to represent shared identities of groups' members or to become a shared cultural focal point for meaningful social interactions. At that stage, the work is much less likely to be susceptible to substitution effects, although its popularity may make it attractive for follow-on creators to build upon.... At both stages the first work's copyright owner might invoke her copyright to fend off the competitor, or stake a claim in the competitor's profits. But while at the early stage, fending off the competitor by accepting an infringement claim against her may be beneficial because it directly preserves the incentive to invest, using copyright law to protect [the work at the later state] may be less socially desirable.[135]

Should legal protections for intellectual property rights decline over time? Under what circumstances would it be desirable to encourage the creation of substitutes for existing copyrighted works, inventions, or brands? Does the concept of substitutability described in the quoted passage help to explain why Pogge distinguishes between patented medicines and other forms of intellectual property in evaluating the propriety of the right to exclude?

---

[135] Ariel Katz, *Substitution and Schumpeterian Effects over the Life Cycle of Copyrighted Works*, 49 Jurimetrics J. 113, 116 (2009); *see also* Justin Hughes, *Fair Use across Time*, 43 UCLA L. Rev. 775 (2003).

Chapter 3

Creators' Rights as Human Rights and the Human Right of Property

3.1. Introduction

Key international human rights instruments recognize that "authors" – those responsible for creating works that are typically protected by intellectual property rights – are the beneficiaries of human rights. Analysis of the inter sections between human rights and intellectual property cannot therefore be entirely concerned with the potential of human rights to constrain intellectual property. Even if the human rights of creators are not equivalent to intellectual property rights, a disjunction we analyze later in this chapter, the recognition in international human rights law that creators have a right to the protection of the "moral and material interests" resulting from any scientific, literary, or artistic "production" of which he or she is the author – to paraphrase Article 27(2) or the 1948 Universal Declaration of Human Rights (UDHR) and Article 15(1)(c) of the International Covenant on Economic, Social and Cultural Rights (ICESCR) – certainly complicates reliance on human rights to limit intellectual property.

Human rights protections for those who do creative work date from the beginning of the international human rights movement. The drafting of the UDHR in the years immediately following World War II was broadly contemporaneous with the 1948 American Declaration on the Rights and Duties of Man, which likewise recognizes the right of everyone "to the protection of his moral and material interests as regards his inventions or any literary, scientific or artistic works of which he is the author."[1]

---

[1] American Declaration of the Rights and Duties of Man, O.A.S. Res. XXX, art. 13(2), *reprinted in* Basic Documents Pertaining to Human Rights in the Inter-American System, OEA/Ser.L.V/II.82 doc.6 rev.1 at 17 (1992) [American Declaration], *available at* http://www.hrcr.org/docs/OAS_Declaration/oasrights.html.

The protection of intellectual endeavor through the vehicle of human rights law brings to the discussion of intellectual property a different theoretical framework from that suggested by the announcement in the Preamble to the TRIPS Agreement – that "intellectual property rights are private rights."[2] Characterizing intellectual property as a matter of private rights is consistent with instrumentalist approaches to creativity and innovation, which view intellectual property as a means to further socioeconomic ends. In this chapter, we explore whether it makes a difference to the relationship between human rights and intellectual property if creators' economic and moral productions are viewed as both human rights *and* as intellectual property rights.

The chapter's first section focuses on the texts of the relevant articles in the pertinent international instruments in order to analyze the obligations they impose and the kinds of legal and normative arguments that they make available to individuals and organizations that are interested in enhancing the rights of those who engage in creative work. We then survey the drafting history of Article 15(1)(c) of the ICESCR, and the earlier statements guaranteeing creators' human rights on which Article 15(1)(c) was based, particularly Article 27(2) of the UDHR. Next, we discuss the *General Comment* on Article 15(1)(c) published by the UN Committee on Economic, Social and Cultural Rights in 2005.[3] *General Comment No. 17*, now a key point of reference for analysis of the normative content of Article 15(1)(c), emphasizes both similarities and differences between the protections afforded to creators by human rights and intellectual property regimes. At the outset, it is important to note that *General Comment No. 17* did not consider in detail the other parts of Article 15(1), the rights to take part in cultural life and to enjoy the benefits of scientific progress and its applications. As we discuss later in this chapter and in Chapter 4, the jurisprudence on these aspects of Article 15 is only beginning to emerge. Until we have a fuller exegesis on creators' rights in the context of its accompanying obligations, our understanding of the scope of creators' rights will necessarily be incomplete.

To explore the potential implications of creators' human rights for the domestic law reform agenda, the chapter then considers three proposals for

---

[2] Agreement on Trade-Related Aspects of Intellectual Property Rights, pmbl., Apr. 15, 1994, 1869 U.N.T.S. 299 [TRIPS Agreement]. *See generally*, Laurence R. Helfer, *Regime Shifting: The TRIPS Agreement and New Dynamics of International Intellectual Property Lawmaking*, 29 Yale J. Int. L. 1 (2004) [Helfer, *Regime Shifting*].

[3] Comm. on Econ., Soc. & Cultural Rights, *General Comment No. 17: The Right of Everyone to Benefit from the Protection of the Moral and Material Interests Resulting from Any Scientific, Literary or Artistic Production of Which He Is the Author*, art. 15(1)(c), U.N. Doc. E/C.12/2005 (Jan. 12, 2006) [*General Comment No. 17*].

reforming copyright law that have been pursued (principally) in the U.S. academic literature: (1) limiting the reproduction right, a proposal that has been directed specifically at musical works; (2) constraining the adaptation, or "derivative work," right; and (3) resurrecting copyright formalities. We use these proposals as case studies: they offer an opportunity to consider whether creators' human rights might impose constraints on domestic law reforms that are of a different character from the more familiar constraints imposed by international intellectual property law. An important substantive issue explored in these case studies, particularly the third, is whether human rights obligations have the potential to "domesticate" some of the obligations that are imposed by international intellectual property law. Intellectual property treaties typically require member states to accord rights to authors and inventors who are nationals of, or who have their habitual residence in, *other* member nations; human rights obligations, in contrast, also require states to protect the rights of their citizens and others over whom the state has jurisdiction. Accordingly, we explore whether the overlap between creators' human rights and intellectual property might make it more difficult to sustain some of the distinctions between the treatment of domestic and foreign works that international intellectual property law currently permits.

Finally, we consider possibilities for protecting the works of creators and innovators through the human right of property as set forth principally in the First Protocol to the European Convention on Human Rights. The European Court of Human Rights has recently held that the right of property extends to the intellectual property interests of corporations as well as individuals. These rulings create points of tension with other human rights norms, most importantly those, such as freedom of expression, that may act as limits on expansive intellectual property protection standards.

3.2. Definitional Issues

In this chapter, we use the terms "creators' human rights" and "creators' rights" interchangeably to denote the protections afforded to the products of intellectual endeavors by international human rights instruments such as the UDHR and the ICESCR. Creators' rights must be distinguished from "intellectual property rights," by which we mean rights that are recognized in intellectual property law treaties, such as the TRIPS Agreement and the Berne Convention, and in domestic intellectual property laws.

Human rights instruments refer to the "moral and material interests" of scientific, literary, or artistic "productions," without identifying either (1) the mechanisms by which productions are to be protected, or (2) the relationship between productions and the facts, ideas, products of nature, basic principles of science, and other materials in the public domain. Domestic intellectual property systems, in contrast, maintain reasonably clear distinctions between different legal vehicles for protection, such as "copyright" or "authors' rights," "patents," "trademarks," "design rights," and so on. In addition, such systems generally do not define the public domain as such. Rather, the public domain, as traditionally conceived, emerges by negative implication from the vast amount of materials – such as those listed previously – that are exempted from intellectual property protection and from works whose term of protection has expired.[4]

In other respects, the human rights instruments seem more detailed than the intellectual property instruments. For example, under human rights law, protections are extended to "literary, scientific, or artistic works." This phrase appears to echo Article 2(1) of the Berne Convention, which refers to "productions in the literary, scientific and artistic sphere."[5] The American Declaration contains slightly more delineation: it refers to "inventions" as well as "works." Even here, however, the use of the terms "scientific" *and* "literary" "works" is suggestive of a different kind of heuristic structure from that adopted in the intellectual property context. Copyright law, for example, does not typically distinguish between protections afforded to works based on their subject matter: rights usually attach to "works." Although the full title of the Berne Convention (the "Berne Convention for the Protection of Literary and Artistic Works") appears to differentiate between "literary and artistic works," its first article eschews any such distinction. It specifies that, "[t]he expression 'literary and artistic works' shall include every production in the literary, scientific and artistic domain, whatever may be the mode or form of its expression[.]"

In one of the very early analyses of the significance of creators' human rights for the intellectual property system, François Desselmontet states that "to some extent, the Universal Declaration and the [ICESCR] mark the apex of the French vision of literary and artistic property, as opposed to the Anglo-American 'mercantalist' view as ensconced in . . . TRIPS."[6] Other commentators

4   *See* Tyler T. Ochoa, *Origins and Meanings of the Public Domain*, 28 U. DAYTON L. REV. 215, 217 (2002). Recent scholarship contests this conception of the public domain as negative space and instead promotes the public domain as a positive resource of immense richness that must be preserved. *See* JAMES BOYLE, THE PUBLIC DOMAIN: ENCLOSING THE COMMONS OF THE MIND, xiv–xv (2008).

5   *See* Sam Ricketson, *Intellectual Property and Human Rights*, in STEPHEN BOTTOMLEY & DAVID KINLEY (EDS.), COMMERCIAL LAW AND HUMAN RIGHTS 187, 190 (2002).

6   François Desselmontet, *Copyright and Human Rights*, in JAN J. C. CABEL & GERARD J. H. M. MOM (EDS.), INTELLECTUAL PROPERTY AND INFORMATION LAW: ESSAYS IN HONOUR OF HERMAN COHEN JEHORAM 113, 114 (1998).

have suggested that moral rights – strongly protected within continental European copyright traditions – are closest to the core of the human rights protections for creators.[7] Desselmontet's analysis also appears to be reinforced by TRIPS' characterization of intellectual property rights as "private rights." We should avoid concluding too readily, however, that this concept of creators' rights – as distinct from mercantilist conceptions – exists *in opposition* to broader societal interests, and that, for this reason alone, creators' human rights occupy a distinct territory from intellectual property rights.

The international intellectual property system is not solely concerned with economic imperatives. Article 6*bis* of the Berne Convention, for example, mandates protection of authors' moral rights: specifically, "the right to claim authorship of the work and to object to any distortion, mutilation or other modification of, or other derogatory action in relation to, the said work, which would be prejudicial to his honor or reputation." Under Article 6*bis*, moral rights endure "independently of the author's economic rights, and even after the transfer of the said rights." To emphasize the economic character of intellectual property rights, to the exclusion of other values, also risks creating or, at least, perpetuating a false dichotomy between "private" intellectual property rights and broader societal values and interests. "Private" property does not reflect an absence of concern with the general public good. As many property theorists have emphasized, private property regimes generally develop when the social benefits of removing things from the commons outweighs the costs associated with doing so.[8] The purpose of copyright, even in Anglo-American legal systems, is to promote the public good through the provision of appropriately tailored private rights. And the *droit d'auteur* systems, which arose in continental Europe, typically protect a duality of interests: they protect authors' moral rights while also making extensive provision for their economic interests. Even in the more instrumentally focused Anglo-American regimes, natural rights have always been an important subtext of justifications for intellectual property protection.[9] In sum, if human rights protections for creators embody principles derived

---

[7] Ort Fischman Afori, *Human Rights and Copyright: The Introduction of Natural Law Considerations into American Copyright Law*, 14 FORD. INTELL. PROP. MEDIA & ENT. L. J. 497, 524 (2004) (suggesting that "the center of copyright as a human right lies in the moral rights arena").

[8] *See, e.g.*, Carol Rose, *Crystals and Mud in Property Law*, 40 STAN. L. REV. 577 (1988).

[9] Jane Ginsburg warns against viewing *droit d'auteur* and copyright systems as radically distinct, and notes that from the beginning of each tradition moral rights and utilitarian concerns have influenced both the content of the law and its philosophical foundations. Jane C. Ginsburg, *A Tale of Two Copyrights: Literary Property in Revolutionary France and America*, in BRAD SHERMAN & ALAIN STROWEL (EDS.), OF AUTHORS AND ORIGINS: ESSAYS IN COPYRIGHT LAW 131 (1994).

from the *droit d'auteur* tradition, they do so as a matter of emphasis rather than of sharp delineation.

The Solemn Declaration adopted by the Assembly of the Berne Union in 1986 is one context in which the two legal traditions are brought together. The Declaration asserts that "copyright is based on human rights and justice and ... authors, as creators of beauty, entertainment and learning, deserve that their rights in their creations be recognized and effectively protected both in their country and in all other countries of the world."[10] A leading commentator has cited this statement to refute the conclusion that intellectual property rights "have no human rights dimension and are purely legal rights."[11]

In each of the human rights instruments in which creators' rights are set forth, the right to benefit from the fruits of creativity follows a statement of rights to participate in cultural life and to benefit from advancements in knowledge. For example, Article 27(1) of the UDHR provides that "[e]veryone has the right freely to participate in the cultural life of the community, to enjoy the arts and to share in scientific advancement and its benefits." Creators' rights are thus inextricably linked to a larger cluster of cultural rights. As Daniel Bécourt puts it, "The Universal Declaration considers copyright to be a human right in itself, within the more general context of the right to culture."[12] The link between these two sets of rights is clearest in the American Declaration. After announcing the right of "everyone" to participate in cultural life and to benefit from creativity, the Declaration reinforces the connection by announcing: "*He likewise* has the right to the protection of his moral and material interests."[13]

3.3. Drafting History of UDHR Article 27 and ICESCR Article 15(1)(c)

Audrey Chapman, *Approaching Intellectual Property as a Human Right: Obligations Related to Article 15(1)(c)*, 35 COPYRIGHT BULL. 4, 10–13 (2001)

The drafters of the UDHR and ICESCR decided to recognize the intellectual property claims of authors, creators, and inventors as a human right. Why

---

[10] Solemn Declaration by the Assembly of the Berne Union of September 9, 1986 (kindly supplied by Boris Kokin, Senior Legal Counsellor, Copyright Law Division, World Intellectual Property Organization [Geneva]) (on file with authors).

[11] Duncan Mathews, *Intellectual Property Rights, Human Rights and the Right to Health*, in WILLEM GROSHEIDE (ED.), INTELLECTUAL PROPERTY AND HUMAN RIGHTS: A PARADOX 118, 120 (2010).

[12] Daniel Bécourt, *Copyright and Human Rights*, 32 COPYRIGHT BULL. 13, 14 (1998). We discuss the right to enjoy the benefits of scientific progress and its applications in Chapter 4.

[13] American Declaration, *supra* note 1, art. 13(2) (emphasis added).

did they decide to do so? How did they conceptualize this right? And was it just accidental that drafters of both documents link the intellectual property claims of authors and creators with the rights to participate in cultural life and to enjoy the benefits of scientific progress and its applications, or did they understand the three to be intrinsically interconnected?

According to Johannes Morsink's account of the drafting history of Article 27 of the UDHR, there was not much disagreement over the notion of the right of everyone to enjoy the benefits of scientific advances and to participate in cultural life. In contrast, the discussion of intellectual property issues evoked considerably more controversy. This pattern was to reoccur when the United Nations Economic and Social Council (ECOSOC) took up the drafting of a covenant on human rights based on the UDHR. A review of the travaux préparatoire of the drafting committee for the UDHR operating under the aegis of the United Nations Commission on Human Rights indicates that the initial discussions of author's rights introduced by the French delegation were concerned primarily with two issues. The first was the moral right of an author to control alteration and other misuses of the creation. The second was the right of authors and creators to remuneration for their labour. An important factor influencing the inclusion of author's rights as a basic human right was that the American Declaration on the Rights and Duties of Man adopted earlier in the year (1948) contained a provision on intellectual property. Article 13 of the American Declaration states that: every person has the right to take part in the cultural life of the community, to enjoy the arts, and to participate in the benefits that result from intellectual progress, especially scientific discoveries. He likewise has the right to the protection of his moral and material interests as regards his inventions or any literary, scientific or artistic works of which he is the author.

Mexican and Cuban members of the UDHR drafting committee, supported by the French delegation, introduced language on author's rights so as to harmonize the Universal Declaration with the American Declaration. The Mexican representative argued that the United Nations needed the moral authority to protect all forms of work, intellectual as well as manual, so as to safeguard intellectual production on an equal basis with material property. (Provisions of the draft of the UDHR already recognized the right to work.)

The provision on intellectual property was rejected in the Commission on Human Rights but passed in the Third Committee. It survived objections that intellectual property was not properly speaking a basic human right. Others also argued that intellectual property needed no special protection beyond that afforded generally by property rights (already in Article 17 of the Universal Declaration), as well as claims by other members of the drafting committee that special protection for intellectual property entailed an élitist perspective. Apparently the motives of those who voted for adoption of the intellectual property provision were mixed. Some voted for the provision on the "moral rights" issue. Others sought to support efforts to internationalize copyright law, already given a boost by the Berne International Copyright Convention, adopted earlier that year.

The text of Article 15 of the ICESCR closely resembles Article 27 of the UDHR. Like the UDHR it has three components dealing with right to culture, scientific advancement, and intellectual property. However, there was nothing automatic about carrying over the three provisions of the UDHR. The drafting of the Covenant involved heated debate about whether to include the intellectual property provision.

In 1951, when the Commission was beginning to consider the inclusion of economic, social and cultural rights provisions into a single planned draft covenant on human rights, [the United Nations Educational, Scientific and Cultural Organization] UNESCO presented the Commission with draft language of a proposed provision on cultural rights.

UNESCO provided two different versions of the proposed article, one longer and more comprehensive than the other. Both the longer and shorter drafts contained language about rights to culture, scientific advancement, and intellectual property. A year later, in May 1952, the Commission took up this provision again, this time in the context of a separate Covenant on Economic, Social and Cultural Rights. The French delegation resubmitted a provision containing intellectual property protection. But the American delegation, still represented by Eleanor Roosevelt, argued that the issue was too complex to be dealt with in the Covenant. Her position was supported by the United Kingdom and Yugoslavia. The UNESCO representative again advocated for including an intellectual property provision in the Covenant. In the discussion, the Chilean delegation raised the issue of the disadvantage of underdeveloped countries stemming from their inability to take out patents and thereby compete in scientific research. The Australian representative argued that it was inadvisable to provide for the protection of the author without also considering the rights of the community. At this stage, the provision on author's rights was rejected.

Thus the draft Covenant submitted to the twelfth session of the Third Committee of the General Assembly by the Commission on Human Rights in the autumn of 1957 lacked the language of what was to become 15(1)(c) recognizing the rights of authors and creators. In the initial discussions, there was strong support for the provisions related to the right to take part in cultural life and to enjoy the benefits of scientific progress, but not for author's rights. The French delegation again argued in favour of the inclusion of an intellectual property provision. The representative of UNESCO advised that intellectual property rights be restored. Statements of support also came from a variety of delegations on the grounds of encouraging culture and science and not dropping a principle already recognized in the Universal Declaration. The USSR and the socialist bloc, reflecting their socialist interests and the dynamics of the Cold War, however, strongly objected to incorporating the provision on intellectual property. They argued that the people's right to benefit from science should not become intermixed with property rights.

The representative of the Soviet Union claimed that author's rights were too complicated and varied to draw up a clause that would be valid for all States. The socialist bloc's opposition to property rights had already played a major role in the decision of the Covenant's drafting committee to drop the text of Article 17 of the UDHR recognizing the right to tangible forms of property in the Covenant.

The Uruguayan and Costa Rican delegates co-sponsored an amendment reinserting the intellectual property provision arguing for it on several grounds: the UDHR already recognized this right; by incorporating the provision the work of UNESCO in this area would be given new impetus and prestige; the right of the author and the right of the public were complementary, not opposed; and respect for the right of the author would assure the public of the authenticity of works presented to it. A statement by the Israeli delegate went further. He argued that "it would be impossible to give effective encouragement to the development of culture unless the rights of authors and scientists were protected."

In the end, of course, the arguments of those defending author's rights won the day. The final vote on the provision was 39 to 9 with 24 delegations abstaining.

This history underscores four points. The first is the relatively weak claims of intellectual property as a human right. The provision on author's rights was included in the UDHR and the Covenant only after considerable discussion and controversy. In both cases the intellectual property components of articles were supported primarily because of their instrumental character in realizing other rights, which were seen as having a stronger moral basis.

The second point is that the three provisions of Article 15 in the ICESCR were viewed by drafters as intrinsically interrelated to one another. Three major human-rights instruments – the American Declaration, the UDHR, and the Covenant – enumerate these rights as components of a single article. The rights of authors and creators are not just good in themselves but were understood as essential preconditions for cultural freedom and participation and access to the benefits of scientific progress.

The third point is that human rights considerations impose conditions on the manner in which author's rights are protected in intellectual property regimes. To be consistent with the provisions of Article 15, intellectual property law must assure that intellectual property protections complement, fully respect, and promote other components of Article 15. Put another way, the rights of authors and creators should facilitate rather than constrain cultural participation on the one side and broad access to the benefits of scientific progress on the other.

And fourthly, the discussion of the intellectual property provisions did not provide a conceptual foundation for interpreting this right. To put the matter another way, the drafters did not delineate the scope and limits of author's rights. Considerations at all levels of drafting focused primarily on whether an intellectual property provision should be included and not its substance and implications.

---

* * * Issues in Focus * * *

Creators' human rights add an important, and hitherto largely ignored, element to debates about the character of intellectual property rights, particularly copyright. International copyright law is typically characterized as involving a division between authors' rights (or *droit d'auteur*) systems and copyright systems. In the latter, copyrights are instrumentalist tools to serve socioeconomic ends. Copyright systems began in England, and then migrated to the countries of the British Commonwealth and the United States. The authors' rights tradition, which is more closely affiliated with natural rights, is rooted in the civil law system and prevails in the nations of continental Europe and their former colonies in Latin America, Africa, and Asia.[14] As noted previously, these distinctions are sometimes a matter of emphasis rather than sharp delineation: The two great traditions have, from their beginnings, shared a number of common ideals, and they are becoming increasingly merged as a result of the internationalization of copyright law.[15]

A human right to benefit from one's creative productions arguably casts new emphasis on the role and vulnerabilities of individual creators. Recognition of human rights obligations connects creative work to the grounding of all human rights in the dignity of the human person. As the Notes that follow explore, in the development of this human right, government representatives

---

[14] PAUL GOLDSTEIN, INTERNATIONAL COPYRIGHT 3 (2001).

[15] *See generally* Gillian Davies, *The Convergence of Copyright and Authors' Rights – Reality or Chimera?*, 26 I.I.C. 964 (1995).

highlighted the role of the individual as an "intellectual worker, artist, scientist or writer." (This perspective was not uniformly endorsed, however.) In later parts of this chapter, we explore the domestic legal and policy issues that follow from this emphasis. Concern for the special circumstances of creators has also been expressed in domestic constitutions. For example, the Constitution of Venezuela stipulates that "cultural workers" must be included in the social security system, "to provide them with a dignified life, recognizing the idiosyncrasies of cultural work, in accordance with law."

The foregoing analysis emphasizes the distinction between the human rights protections that attach to creative *works* and those relevant to creative *workers*. As we explore later, creative workers can be particularly vulnerable, and be targets of human rights abuses, precisely because of their creative endeavors.

Notes and Questions

1. Is there a human right to benefit from all scientific advances? Would it make more sense to limit the right to scientific advances that are related in some respect to other human rights obligations, such as advances in food production, or in technologies associated with improving human health and well-being? Why do "material and moral interests" need to be singled out for special protection at all? With respect to copyright, for example, why would it not have been adequate to set forth general obligations in areas such as education, literacy, and freedom of expression and leave it to individual states to determine how these rights should be realized? If protection of authors' moral and material interests is the best vehicle for realizing these rights, would states inclined to do so not inevitably adopt and develop a copyright system anyway? And, if protections for authors' moral and material interests are *not* the best vehicle for realizing these other rights, does their recognition in international human rights instruments constrain opportunities for states to find the best way to do so? If so, is this a problem?

2. As noted previously, creators' rights form part of a broader set of cultural rights, including the right to participate in cultural life, the right to enjoy culture, and the right to benefit from scientific advances.[16] Why does participation in "culture" raise human rights issues? In modern economies, why is it not more appropriate to regard cultural products simply as marketplace

---

[16] *See generally* IMRE SZABÓ, CULTURAL RIGHTS (1974); ELSA STAMATOPOULOU, CULTURAL RIGHTS IN INTERNATIONAL LAW: ARTICLE 27 OF THE UNIVERSAL DECLARATION OF HUMAN RIGHTS AND BEYOND (2007).

commodities? Does the role of culture differ across societies, and, if so, can it genuinely be claimed that participation in cultural life represents a universal value? Article 8 of the Universal Declaration on Cultural Diversity (promulgated by UNESCO) describes "cultural goods and services" as "vectors of identity, values and meaning [that] must not be treated as mere commodities or consumer goods."[17] What, if anything, does this characterization add to your analysis? And do you agree that the description in Article 8 is adequately justified by the characterization itself? Put another way, why are "vectors of identity" *not* "mere" consumer goods?

3. Cultural rights feature in a number of national constitutions. For example, Article 27(5) of the Constitution of Belgium provides: "Everyone has the right to lead a life in conformity with human dignity. To this end, the laws, decrees and rulings ... guarantee, taking into account corresponding obligations, economic, social and cultural rights, and determine the conditions for exercising them. These rights include notably: ... (5) the right to enjoy cultural and social fulfillment."[18] The Constitution of the Bolivarian Republic of Venezuela,[19] adopted in 1999, includes a number of detailed provisions on the protection of intellectual property rights and, within the same general context, also recognizes the rights to participate in cultural life and education:

Chapter VI Culture and Educational Rights:

> Article 98: Cultural creation is free. This freedom includes the right to invest in, produce and disseminate the creative, scientific, technical and humanistic work, as well as legal protection of the author's rights in his works. The State recognizes and protects intellectual property rights in scientific, literary and artistic works, inventions, innovations, trade names, patents, trademarks and slogans, in accordance with the conditions and exceptions established by law and the international treaties executed and ratified by the Republic in this field.

> Article 99: Cultural values are the unrenounceable property of the Venezuelan people and a fundamental right to be encouraged and guaranteed by the State, efforts being made to provide the necessary conditions, legal instruments, means and funding. The autonomy of the public administration of culture is recognized, on such terms as may be established by law. The State guarantees the protection and preservation, enrichment, conservation and restoration of the cultural tangible and intangible heritage and the historic memories of the nation. The assets constituting the cultural heritage of the nation are inalienable,

---

[17] UNESCO, *Universal Declaration on Cultural Diversity*, UNESCO Doc. 31C/Res.25 (Nov. 2, 2001), *available at* http://unesdoc.unesco.org/images/0012/001271/127160m.pdf.

[18] *La Constitution Belge, translated in* Rüdiger Wolfrum & Rainer Grote (Eds.), Constitutions of the Countries of the World (2005).

[19] *Available at* http://www.analitica.com/bitblioteca/venezuela/constitucion_ingles.pdf.

not subject to distrait or to statute of limitations. Penalties and sanctions for damage caused to these assets shall be provided for by law.

Article 100: The folk cultures comprising the national identity of Venezuela enjoy special attention, with recognition of and respect for intercultural relations under the principle of equality of cultures. Incentives and inducements shall be provided for by law for persons, institutions and communities which promote, support, develop or finance cultural plans, programs and activities within the country and Venezuelan culture abroad. The State guarantees cultural workers inclusion in the Social security system to provide them with a dignified life, recognizing the idiosyncrasies of cultural work, in accordance with law.

Are the rights protected in the Venezuelan constitution mutually inconsistent or in tension with each other? Are they capable of immediate application by courts?

4. In a seminal work on cultural rights,[20] Imre Szabó discussed the significance of the UDHR's apparent singling out of authors' rights for special treatment. One issue that Szabó identifies is the problem of the assimilation of copyright and cultural rights without clarifying the relationship between them. This topic is also addressed by *General Comment No. 17*, which we consider in more detail later in this chapter. Szabó observed that copyright is the subject of a distinct international legal regime and is mentioned in several national constitutions. He concludes: "A so very divergent protection of a right, of its different ramifications within the limits of a single right, can hardly be durable and does not further the *shaping of the right to culture as an increasingly homogeneous right*."[21] In other words, the diversity of domestic approaches to copyright might detract from the recognition and protection of the cultural rights set forth in UDHR Article 27. Given the increasing uniformity among domestic copyright regimes in response to the developments analyzed in Chapter 2, does this concern continue to be salient? Is the observation also relevant in the patents context?

5. René Cassin, one of the architects of the post–Second World War human rights system, believed that all human beings possess the ability and desire to engage in creative activity. Does this imply that Article 27(2) of the UDHR responds to, and is protective of, a fundamental human trait?[22]

---

[20] SZABÓ, *supra* note 16.

[21] *Id.* at 47.

[22] *See* Paul L. C. Torremans, *Copyright (and Other Intellectual Property Rights) as a Human Right*, in PAUL TORREMANS (ED.), INTELLECTUAL PROPERTY AND HUMAN RIGHTS 195, 198 (2008) (citing Cassin, *L'intégration, parmi les droits fondamentaux de l'homme, des droits des créateurs des oevres de l'espirit, in* MÉLANGES MARCEL PLAISANT: ETUDES SUR LA PROPRIÉTÉ INDUSTRIELLE, LITTÉRAIRE ET ARTISTIQUE 229 [1959]).

6. As Johannes Morsink recounts in his study of the drafting history of the UDHR (discussed in the extract of Audrey Chapman's article), the word "freely" was inserted into the first sentence of Article 27 following a suggestion by the Peruvian delegate to the drafting conference, José Encinas.[23] Encinas argued that it was "not enough for the Declaration to state that everyone has the right to participate in the cultural, artistic and scientific life of the community."[24] He believed that the UDHR should also state "the right to do so in that complete freedom without which there could be no creation worthy of man."[25] Encinas saw a connection between freedom of thought and the freedom to create. As Morsink recounts: "An earlier article ... dealt with freedom of thought; it seemed pertinent now to recognize freedom of creative thought, in order to protect it from harmful pressures which were only too frequent in recent history."[26] Encinas' amendment was adopted by a vote of thirty-eight to zero, with two abstentions.[27]

7. The term "freely" did not migrate from the UDHR into Article 15(1)(a) of the ICESCR. It does, however, appear in the more recent United Nations Convention on the Rights of the Child (UNCROC). Article 31 of the UNCROC provides:

1. States Parties recognize the right of the child to rest and leisure, to engage in play and recreational activities appropriate to the age of the child and to participate freely in cultural life and the arts.

2. States Parties shall respect and promote the right of the child to participate fully in cultural and artistic life and shall encourage the provision of appropriate and equal opportunities for cultural, artistic, recreational and leisure activity.

The UNCROC does not make specific provision for the protection of children's artistic or other creative productions. It does, however, set forth guarantee of the right to freedom of expression in Article 13, accompanied by a number of limitations:

1. The child shall have the right to freedom of expression; this right shall include freedom to seek, receive and impart information and ideas of all kinds, regardless of frontiers, either orally, in writing or in print, in the form of art, or through any other media of the child's choice.

---

[23] JOHANNES MORSINK, THE UNIVERSAL DECLARATION OF HUMAN RIGHTS 218 (1999).
[24] Id.
[25] Id. (citation omitted).
[26] Id. (citation omitted).
[27] Id.

2. The exercise of this right may be subject to certain restrictions, but these shall only be such as are provided by law and are necessary: (a) For respect of the rights or reputations of others; or (b) For the protection of national security or of public order (ordre public), or of public health or morals.

As we discuss in more detail in Chapter 5, the UNCROC also makes detailed provision for rights in the education context, which may have significant implications for the scope of copyright protection.

8. During the drafting of the UDHR, the Mexican delegate, Campos Ortiz, defended Article 27(2) by invoking "rights of the individual as an 'intellectual worker, artist, scientist or writer'."[28] In contrast, the Australian delegate, Alan Watt, asserted that "the indisputable rights of the intellectual worker could not appear beside fundamental rights of a more general nature, such as freedom of thought, religious freedom or the right to work,"[29] sentiments that echoed earlier concerns voiced by delegates from India and the United Kingdom, who felt that no group should be singled out for special attention.[30] The Chinese delegate, Pen-Chun Chang, argued that the purpose of the paragraph was "not merely to protect creative artists but to safeguard the interests of everyone"; for that reason, "literary, artistic and scientific works should be made accessible to the people directly in their original form," which "could only be done if the moral rights of the creative artist were protected."[31] Does this history, and that recounted by Audrey Chapman, support or detract from the conclusion of one commentator that Article 27(2) of the UDHR is a "*declaration of copyright* raised … to the rank of a 'human right'"?[32]

9. The right to benefit from "the protection of the moral and material interests resulting from … scientific, literary or artistic production[s]" implicates a much wider set of controversies surrounding recognition of "property" itself as a human right.[33] Do any of the delegates' concerns described in the previous Notes reflect the same general concerns about protecting property as a human right?[34] (Note that although UDHR Article 17 protects "the right to own property" and proscribes "arbitrar[y] depriv[ations]

---

[28]   *Id.* at 221.

[29]   *Id.*

[30]   *Id.* at 220.

[31]   *Id.* at 222.

[32]   Szabó, *supra* note 16, at 46 (original emphasis).

[33]   *See generally* Margaret Davies, Property: Meaning, History, Theories 16 (2007).

[34]   For further discussion of the drafting history, *see* Peter Yu, *Reconceptualizing Intellectual Property Interests in a Human Rights Framework* 40 U.C. Davis L. Rev. 1039, 1060–1069 (2007).

of … property," neither the International Covenant on Civil and Political Rights nor the ICESCR protects property rights.) As the discussion of Article 27(2) progressed, some delegates shifted attention to the "special character of the moral interests under discussion."[35] Is it sensible to protect the intellectual output of creators but not to protect other forms of property? We discuss the human right of property, as it applies to intellectual property, later in this chapter.

10. Should creators' human rights distinguish between copyrights and patents? Consider the U.S. constitutional context. In *Federalist 43*, James Madison noted that "the copyright of authors has been solemnly adjudged, in Great Britain, to be a right of common law."[36] This characterization perhaps implies that, in the United States, copyright protections are antecedent to the constitutional structure. Patent rights, in contrast, more clearly depended on the specific constitutional grant that empowered Congress to enact patent laws. Does this fact make it more difficult to sustain human rights claims for the material interests of inventors?[37] Does it make sense to protect the moral interests of inventors?

11. Does protection of creators' "moral and material interests" necessarily require the maintenance of a system of *proprietary* rights? The general language of Article 27(2) of the UDHR seems quite different from the specific protections for property in Article 17: "(1) Everyone has the right to own property alone as well as in association with others. (2) No one shall be arbitrarily deprived of his property." Would protection through other legal rules, such as tort law, adequately protect creators' rights? Is it relevant to your answer that, until the latter part of last century, most common law countries did not protect authors' moral rights through copyright law? In Australia, protection of moral rights was not included in the federal copyright statute until 2000.[38] The United States has never enacted comprehensive moral rights protections but has provided limited protections for works of visual art.[39] Without bespoke moral rights protections, authors in common law

---

[35] *See* MORSINK, *supra* note 23, at 221.
[36] Whether Anglo-American common law protections extended to published works has been a matter of considerable controversy. *See* Jane C. Ginsburg, "Une Chose Publique"? *The Author's Domain and the Public Domain in Early British, French and U.S. Copyright Law*, 65 CAM. L.J. 636 (2006). The U.S. Supreme Court eventually held that even if common law rights in published works subsisted under English common law, that law was not incorporated into the law of the American colonies. *Wheaton v. Peters*, 33 U.S. (8 Pet.) 591 (1834).
[37] *Cf.* Rochelle Cooper Dreyfuss, *Patents and Human Rights: Where Is the Paradox?* in GROSHEIDE, *supra* note 11.
[38] Copyright Amendment (Moral Rights) Act, 2000 (Austl.).
[39] Visual Artists Rights Act of 1990, 17 U.S.C. § 106A (U.S.).

countries have invoked a variety of legal theories, with varying degrees of success, to vindicate their reputational interests, including the torts of passing off and defamation.[40]

12. Since World War II, the United States has been ascendant in the creation and marketing of patent- and copyright-protected products.[41] From a self-interested economic perspective, did it make sense for the United States to oppose the adoption of Article 27?

13. Does recognizing human rights for creators necessarily imply that there exists a hierarchy between those rights and any limitations that the public international law of intellectual property itself permits?[42] For instance, if creators' rights enjoy the "primacy" that is often claimed for other human rights, might this inhibit the development of further exceptions consistent with the "flexibilities" in the TRIPS Agreement?[43]

14. The potential risk that creators' rights pose to efforts to use human rights to constrain the expansion of intellectual property protection standards has provoked a variety of responses. (We discuss this issue in more detail in Chapter 1.) At the most general level, one response has been to question whether any benefits that might accompany recourse to human rights as a basis for *constraining* intellectual property rights are likely to be outweighed by the risks.[44] This might imply that human rights' role in intellectual property law and policy ought to be quite modest. It also been suggested that the lack of consensus as to the inclusion of creators' human rights recognition in international human rights instruments reduces their significance.[45] To assess whether invoking human rights in the intellectual property context will do more harm than good it is necessary to have a detailed sense of the obligations imposed by creators' human rights. The following section discusses the interpretation of Article 15(1)(c) of the ICESCR by the Committee on Economic, Social and Cultural Rights.

---

[40] *See* Gerald Dworkin, *The Moral Rights of the Author: Moral Rights and the Common Law Countries*, 19 Colum.-VLA J.L. & Arts 229 (1995).

[41] *See generally* B. Zorina Khan, The Democratization of Invention: Patents and Copyrights in American Economic Development, 1790–1920 (2005).

[42] For an important early analysis of the inconsistencies between human rights and intellectual property, see Ruth Gana, *The Myth of Development, the Progress of Rights: Human Rights to Intellectual Property and Development*, 18 Law and Policy 315 (1996).

[43] On the scope of those permissible limitations, see WTO, Ministerial Declaration on the TRIPs Agreement and Public Health, WT/MIN(01)/DEC/W/2 (Nov. 14, 2001) [Public Health Declaration].

[44] *See, e.g.*, Margaret Chon, *Intellectual Property and the Development Divide*, 27 Cardozo L. Rev. 2821 (2006); *see also* Kal Raustiala, *Density and Conflict in International Intellectual Property Law*, 40 U.C. Davis L. Rev. 1021 (2007).

[45] *See, e.g.*, Peter Yu, *Reconceptualizing Intellectual Property Interests in a Human Rights Framework*, 40 U.C. Davis L. Rev. 1039, 1060–1069 (2007).

3.4. *General Comment No. 17*: An Overview

The principal authoritative source for analysis of the content and scope of creators' human rights is now *General Comment No. 17*, which the Committee on Economic, Social and Cultural Rights published in 2005.[46] As we discuss in Chapter 1, *General Comments* provide general guidance on the meaning of specific treaty articles or specific human rights issues. They serve as focal points for change in national legal systems and provide a standard against which the Committee can review states' compliance with the Covenant. They also provide a general interpretive jurisprudence on the ICESCR, which is less easily developed by the Committee's scrutiny of treaty compliance through the examination of and commentary on periodic reports filed by individual states parties.

General Comment No. 17 is a lengthy, densely worded, and somewhat repetitive document of fifty-seven paragraphs divided into six parts: (1) an introductory section that explains the basic premises of the Committee's analysis; (2) a close textual reading of Article 15(1)(c)'s "normative content"; (3) a section outlining states' legal obligations, including general, specific, core, and related obligations; (4) an analysis of actions or omissions that would violate the article; (5) a section on how authors' rights are to be implemented at the national level; and (6) a short discussion of the obligations of nonstate actors and intergovernmental organizations.

Most significantly, the detailed interpretation of Article 15(1)(c) set forth in the *General Comment* suggests that the Committee views the scope of creators' rights to be far more circumscribed than the rights guaranteed by the public international law of intellectual property. At a number of points, the document emphasizes that the right set forth in Article 15(1)(c), while being protective of authors' moral and material interests, "does not necessarily coincide with what is referred to as intellectual property rights under national legislation or international agreements."[47] To this end, the *General Comment* identifies a number of conceptual distinctions between intellectual property rights and human rights: "human rights are fundamental as they are inherent to the human person as such, whereas intellectual property rights are first and foremost means by which States seek to provide incentives for inventiveness and creativity, encourage the dissemination of creative and innovative productions as well as the development of cultural identities, and preserve the integrity of scientific, literary and artistic productions for the benefit of

---

[46] *General Comment No. 17, supra* note 3.
[47] *Id.* para. 2.

society as a whole."[48] The document also characterizes intellectual property rights as being "generally of a temporary nature" and notes that they "can be revoked, licensed or assigned to someone else."[49] Moreover, "while under most intellectual property systems, intellectual property rights, often with the exception of moral rights, may be allocated, limited in time and scope, traded, amended and even forfeited, human rights are timeless expressions of fundamental entitlements of the human person."[50] Here, the document appears to foreground a key distinction between the "primary" protections that intellectual property rights afford to "business and corporate interests and investments" and the safeguards that human rights offer to "the personal link between authors and their creations and between peoples, communities, or other groups and their collective cultural heritage, as well as their basic material interests which are necessary to enable authors to enjoy an adequate standard of living."[51]

The *General Comment* persistently links creators' human rights to the protection of "a zone of personal autonomy in which authors can achieve their creative potential, control their productive output, and lead independent intellectual lives that are essential requisites for any free society."[52] Creators' rights are also closely related to the personality of the individual author and to communal interests in cultural heritage. Significantly, these rights do not necessarily encompass the same pecuniary interests as are covered by intellectual property law; rather, "material interests" are instead tied to the ability of creators to enjoy an *adequate* standard of living. In striking contrast, the *General Comment* categorically excludes nonlegal persons from the protections of Article 15(1)(c).

In addition to analyzing the normative content of Article 15(1)(c), the *General Comment* also considers the connections between creators' rights and other guarantees in the ICESCR:

> The right to benefit from the protection of the moral and material interests resulting from one's scientific, literary and artistic productions seeks to encourage the active contribution of creators to the arts and sciences and to the progress of society as a whole. As such, it is intrinsically linked to the other rights recognized

---

[48] *Id.* para. 1.
[49] *Id.* para. 2.
[50] *Id.*
[51] *Id.*
[52] Laurence R. Helfer, *Collective Management of Copyright and Human Rights: An Uneasy Alliance*, in Daniel J. Gervais (Ed.), Collective Management of Copyright and Related Rights 85, 97 (2006) [Helfer, *Collective Management*]; *see also* Laurence R. Helfer, *Toward a Human Rights Framework for Intellectual Property*, 40 U.C. Davis. L. Rev. 971, 987–1001 (2007).

in article 15 of the Covenant, i.e. the right to take part in cultural life (art. 15, Para. 1 (a)), the right to enjoy the benefits of scientific progress and its applications (art. 15, Para. 1 (b)), and the freedom indispensable for scientific research and creative activity (art. 15, para. 3). The relationship between these rights and Article 15, paragraph 1 (c), is at the same time mutually reinforcing and reciprocally limitative.... As a material safeguard for the freedom of scientific research and creative activity, guaranteed under article 15, paragraph 3 and article 15, paragraph 1 (c), also has an economic dimension and is, therefore, closely linked to the rights to the opportunity to gain one's living by work which one freely chooses (art. 6, para. 1) and to adequate remuneration (art. 7 (a)), and to the human right to an adequate standard of living (art. 11, para. 1). Moreover, the realization of article 15, paragraph 1 (c), is dependent on the enjoyment of other human rights guaranteed in the International Bill of Human Rights and other international and regional instruments, such as the right to own property alone as well as in association with others, the freedom of expression including the freedom to seek, receive and impart information and ideas of all kinds, the right to the full development of the human personality, and rights of cultural participation, including cultural rights of specific groups.[53]

The distinction drawn by the *General Comment* between the right in Article 15(1)(c) and the instrumentalist approach of the intellectual property regime is also reflected in a section of the *General Comment* titled "Specific Legal Obligations," which explains the tripartite duties to respect, protect, and fulfill:

30. States parties are under an obligation to *respect* the human right to benefit from the protection of the moral and material interests of authors by, inter alia, abstaining from infringing the right of authors to be recognized as the creators of their scientific, literary or artistic productions and to object to any distortion, mutilation or other modification of, or other derogatory action in relation to, their productions that would be prejudicial to their honour or reputation. States parties must abstain from unjustifiably interfering with the material interests of authors, which are necessary to enable those authors to enjoy an adequate standard of living.

31. Obligations to *protect* include the duty of States parties to ensure the effective protection of the moral and material interests of authors against infringement by third parties.... Similarly, States parties are obliged to prevent third parties from infringing the material interests of authors resulting from their productions. To that effect, States parties must prevent the unauthorized use of scientific, literary and artistic productions that are easily accessible or reproducible through modern communication and reproduction technologies, e.g. by establishing systems of collective administration of authors' rights or by adopting legislation requiring users to inform authors of any use made of their productions and to remunerate them adequately. States parties must ensure that third parties adequately compensate authors for any unreasonable prejudice suffered as a consequence of the unauthorized use of their productions.

[53] *General Comment No. 17, supra* note 3, para. 4.

32. With regard to the right to benefit from the protection of the moral and material interests resulting from any scientific, literary or artistic production of indigenous peoples, States parties should adopt measures to ensure the effective protection of the interests of indigenous peoples relating to their productions, which are often expressions of their cultural heritage and traditional knowledge. ... States parties should respect the principle of free, prior and informed consent of the indigenous authors concerned and the oral or other customary forms of transmission of scientific, literary or artistic production; where appropriate, they should provide for the collective administration by indigenous peoples of the benefits derived from their productions.

33. States parties in which ethnic, religious or linguistic minorities exist are under an obligation to protect the moral and material interests of authors belonging to these minorities through special measures to preserve the distinctive character of minority cultures.

34. The obligation to *fulfil* (provide) requires States parties to provide administrative, judicial or other appropriate remedies in order to enable authors to claim the moral and material interests resulting from their scientific, literary or artistic productions and to seek and obtain effective redress in cases of violation of these interests. States parties are also required to *fulfil* (facilitate) the right in article 15, paragraph 1 (c), e.g. by taking financial and other positive measures which facilitate the formation of professional and other associations representing the moral and material interests of authors, including disadvantaged and marginalized authors, in line with article 8, paragraph 1 (a), of the Covenant. The obligation to *fulfil* (promote) requires States parties to ensure the right of authors of scientific, literary and artistic productions to take part in the conduct of public affairs and in any significant decision-making processes that have an impact on their rights and legitimate interests, and to consult these individuals or groups or their elected representatives prior to the adoption of any significant decisions affecting their rights under article 15, paragraph 1 (c).

The *General Comment* insists that authorial rights cannot be "isolated from the other rights recognized in the Covenant."[54] States parties are thus obliged to strike an "adequate balance" between their obligations under Article 15(1) (c) and other rights in the Covenant "with a view to promoting and protecting the full range of rights guaranteed in the Covenant."[55] States parties should also "ensure that their legal or other regimes for the protection of the moral and material interests resulting from one's scientific, literary or artistic productions constitute no impediment to their ability to comply with their core obligations in relation to the rights to food, health and education, as well as to take part in cultural life and to enjoy the benefits of scientific progress and its applications, or any other rights enshrined in the Covenant."[56]

[54] *Id.* para. 35.
[55] *Id.*
[56] *Id.*

The *General Comment* reasons that "ultimately" intellectual property is "a social product [that] has a social function,"[57] a view that appears to share some common ground with the instrumentalist perspective on intellectual property rights discussed earlier in this chapter. Consistent with that view, states have an obligation to prevent uses of intellectual property that result in socially deleterious outcomes. In particular, they "have a duty to prevent unreasonably high costs for access to essential medicines, plant seeds or other means of food production, or for schoolbooks and learning materials, from undermining the rights of large segments of the population to health, food and education."[58]

Notwithstanding its length and complexity, the *General Comment* leaves a number of important issues unresolved. First, it does not discuss the pre-existing materials that creators draw upon when engaging in artistic and scientific endeavors, including facts, ideas, products of nature, and works whose term of intellectual property protection has expired. However, key passages of the *General Comment* suggest – with one possible exception – that the Committee's understanding of creators' human rights presupposes the existence of a robust public domain.

For example, the *General Comment* asserts that "the private interests of authors should not be unduly favoured and the public interest in enjoying broad access to their productions should be given due consideration."[59] This statement reflects a concern with striking a balance between creators' rights and those of the wider public, a balance whose considerations include preservation of the public domain. Additionally, the Committee devotes an entire paragraph to the word "resulting" to "stress" that creators "only benefit from the protection of such moral and material interests which are *directly generated* by their scientific, literary or artistic productions."[60] When read together, these passages imply the existence of "knowledge, truths ascertained, conceptions, and ideas"[61] that fall outside the protection of creators' human rights. In this regard, the Committee's analysis is consistent with fundamental systemic characteristics of intellectual property laws, which are also premised upon the existence of a robust public domain.[62]

---

[57] *Id.*

[58] *Id.*

[59] *Id.* para. 35.

[60] *Id.* para. 17 (emphasis added).

[61] *Int'l News Serv. v. Associated Press*, 248 U.S. 215, 250 (1918) (Brandeis, J., dissenting).

[62] *See generally* BOYLE, *supra* note 4; *see also* James Grimmelmann, *The Internet Is a Semicommons*, 78 FORDHAM L. REV. 2799, 2813 (2010) ("All creativity is influenced and inspired by what has come before; all innovation incrementally builds on past inventions.").

The one potential exception to this conclusion relates to the "knowledge, innovations and practices" of indigenous communities. The Committee does not define this phrase, nor explain how it relates to existing intellectual property paradigms. As a result, it is uncertain whether the *General Comment* contemplates protection for indigenous knowledge and related practices that intellectual property systems would place in the public domain.[63] We address this topic in more detail in Chapter 7.

A second unexplored topic in the *General Comment* also concerns indigenous communities. As explained earlier, the Committee grounds Article 15(1)(c) in a "zone of personal autonomy" for creators and a commitment to protecting their independent intellectual lives. How this grounding intersects with the rights of indigenous peoples is uncertain. As we discuss in Chapter 7, many indigenous peoples assert a conception of selfhood that is not one of atomized individualism but of connection with a wider group, such as a tribal structure or an extended family. For some indigenous communities, therefore, human rights protection of a zone of *personal* autonomy may have less salience. This may explain why the *General Comment*'s discussion of states parties' obligations to protect indigenous creativity includes elements – such as "the principle of free, prior and informed consent" and "oral or other customary forms of transmission of scientific, literary or artistic production"[64] – that appear nowhere else in the document.

A third issue that *General Comment No. 17* does not adequately address is how states parties are to balance Article 15(1)(c) against other provisions of the ICESCR (such as the rights to food, health, education, and to enjoyment of the benefits of scientific progress and its applications), or how they are to realize the accompanying proscriptions against creators' rights imposing barriers to the realization of those rights. This problem is exacerbated by the opacity of the *General Comment*'s analysis of the specific content of the moral and material interests that states must respect, protect, and fulfill.

The document provides a few specific suggestions concerning these issues. For example, the document links "material interests" to the right to an "adequate standard of living," apparently implying a right to compensation from unauthorized "reproduction."[65] The document also notes that "moral"

---

[63] *See generally* Anupam Chander & Madhavi Sunder, *The Romance of the Public Domain*, 92 CAL. L. REV. 1331, 1331–32 (2004) (arguing that the "romance of the commons" – the belief that because a resource is "open to all by force of law, it will indeed be equally exploited by all" – may "justify forms of property uncommon in Western legal traditions").

[64] *General Comment No. 17, supra* note 3, para. 32.

[65] "In particular, States parties must prevent third parties from infringing the right of authors to claim authorship of their scientific, literary or artistic productions, and from distorting,

interests concern protection of an author's "honor or reputation," in contrast, for example, to the economic rights that are accorded by copyright. However, the document lacks detailed information on exactly what these interests are or how governments are to take them into account.

The issue of rights balancing also implicates a fourth insufficiently analyzed subject – the permissible limitations on creators' rights. According to the *General Comment*, limitations on the rights protected in Article 15(1)(c) must be "determined by law, in a manner compatible with the nature of these rights, must pursue legitimate aims, and must be strictly necessary for the promotion of the general welfare in a democratic society." In addition, such limitations must "be proportionate, meaning that the least restrictive measures must be adopted when several types of limitations may be imposed."[66] This language is considerably more exacting than the "three-step test" by which domestic law exceptions and limitations must typically be tested for compliance with international intellectual property instruments.[67] Viewed in context, however, the more exacting standard may be understandable: according to the analysis set forth in the *General Comment*, the scope of creators' human rights is significantly narrower than that of intellectual property rights. Moreover, the close connection that the Committee draws between creators' rights and the inherent dignity of all persons would also seem to justify adoption of a more exacting standard. We explore these issues further in Chapter 8.

---

* * * Issues in Focus * * *

At different times in history, and still today in a number of places, the freedom to be a creative professional has been contingent at best, and sometimes categorically denied. Censorship of authorial and scientific activity is a notorious tool of oppression.[68] In a number of countries, authors are not secure in their ability to create and to earn a living from creative work safe from governmental

---

mutilating or otherwise modifying, or taking any derogatory action in relation to such productions in a manner that would be prejudicial to the author's honour or reputation. Similarly, States parties are obliged to prevent third parties from infringing the material interests of authors resulting from their productions." *General Comment No. 17, supra* note 3, para. 31.

[66] *Id.* paras. 22, 23.

[67] TRIPS Agreement, *supra* note 2, art. 13 ("Members shall confine limitations or exceptions to exclusive rights to certain special cases which do not conflict with a normal exploitation of the work and do not unreasonably prejudice the legitimate interests of the right holder.")

[68] *See* S. C. Jansen & B. Martin, *Exposing and Opposing Censorship: Backfire Dynamics in Freedom-of-Speech Struggles*, 10 PACIFIC JOURNALISM REV. 29–45 (2004).

interference, suppression, or persecution.[69] In many nations, authors continue to be exiled, executed, assassinated, and threatened into silence. Subtler forms of attack occur when the national government in question exerts pressures to enforce a censorship policy that is unwritten and unspoken and that the government outwardly disavows. Economic controls are sometimes used to suppress creative activity. For example, an author who finds herself on a "gray list"[70] does not encounter outright censorship by the governing body of her home country, but instead finds that she cannot get her work published by large publishers or that she cannot appear on television or be heard on the radio. Unknown writers are particularly vulnerable: they can be arrested or exiled, and their work seized or destroyed. Government bodies can also suppress authorial freedom in the opposite manner, by recruiting authors, particularly those who have found fame, to serve the interests of the state. This has allowed governments to control literary production while they continued to feign adherence to democratic precepts such as free expression.

Clear links exist between these abuses and other established human rights, such as rights to be free from torture and arbitrary imprisonment and the right to freedom of expression. In addition, governmental suppression of creative work directs attention to the connection between the human rights of creators and the operation of markets that support creative endeavor. As the analysis in the *General Comment* suggests, the question "how does the creative worker get paid?" can itself be characterized as a human rights issue. Of course, no formulation of a human right for creators can fully insulate authors and scientists from the various forms of oppression experienced by those who do creative and intellectual work. Even so, marketplace mechanisms such as intellectual property might, in some circumstances, enable creators to secure an income beyond the reach of the state.[71] Markets help writers find a paying audience for their work. Under some political regimes, these private sources of income may be more protective of creators' rights than alternative means of payment, such as government-controlled systems of patronage, which might be accompanied by opportunities for abuse.[72] If so, acknowledging and

---

[69] Claude Brulé, *Sun and Storm*, 32 COPYRIGHT BULL. 4, 5 (1998); *see also* Jonathan Jansen, *Intellectuals under Fire*, 18 CRITICAL ARTS 163 (2004); H. Gafaiti, *Between God and the President: Literature and Censorship in North Africa*, DIACRITICS, Summer 1997, at 59, 68.

[70] A state could also exert control over the literary market by refusing to buy an author's books and so use its monopoly status to dictate which works were published, and which works were publicly disseminated. Brulé, *supra* note 69, at 5.

[71] *See generally* Neil Weinstock Netanel, *Copyright and a Democratic Civil Society*, 106 YALE L.J. 283 (1996).

[72] *See* Cohen Jehoram, *Freedom of Expression in Copyright Law*, [1984] EUR. INTELL. PROP. REV. 1.

protecting creators' human rights may in some cases also invite recognition of ways that markets – created and sustained by economic vehicles such as intellectual property rights – can protect creative workers from government censorship and, in so doing, further a human rights agenda.

Notes and Questions

1. One commentator has observed that, in Article 15(1)(c), "copyright is not directly expressed as a human right, but rather as a natural limitation on freedom of expression."[73] Is there any textual support for this view in the ICESCR or in the *General Comment*?

2. As noted previously, legal persons such as corporations and other business associations are excluded from the scope of the protections afforded by Article 15(1)(c):

> The Committee considers that only the "author," namely the creator, whether man or woman, individual or group of individuals, of scientific, literary or artistic productions, such as, inter alia, writers and artists, can be the beneficiary of the protection of article 15, paragraph 1 (c). This follows from the words "everyone," "he" and "author," which indicate that the drafters of that article seemed to have believed authors of scientific, literary or artistic productions to be natural persons, without at that time realizing that they could also be groups of individuals. Under the existing international treaty protection regimes, legal entities are included among the holders of intellectual property rights. However, as noted above, their entitlements, because of their different nature, are not protected at the level of human rights.[74]

However, the *General Comment* also articulates a set of specific obligations to protect indigenous groups within the ambit of this right: "With regard to the right to benefit from the protection of the moral and material interests resulting from any scientific, literary or artistic production of indigenous peoples, States parties should adopt measures to ensure the effective protection of the interests of indigenous peoples relating to their productions, which are often expressions of their cultural heritage and traditional knowledge."[75]

What textual support does Article 15(1)(c) provide for recognizing the rights of indigenous groups? Is it relevant, as the Committee notes, that the drafters of the Covenant did not "at that time realiz[e that authors] could also

---

[73] Jan Rosén, *Copyright and Freedom of Expression in Sweden: Private Law in a Constitutional Context*, in PAUL TORREMANS (ED.), COPYRIGHT LAW: A HANDBOOK OF CONTEMPORARY RESEARCH 355, 358 (2007).

[74] *General Comment No. 17, supra* note 3, para. 7.

[75] *Id.* para. 32.

be groups of individuals"? What accounts for the distinction drawn between indigenous peoples and other groups or corporate entities? Is the answer suggested by the phrase "expressions of their cultural heritage and traditional knowledge" a sufficient basis for such a distinction? Can the Committee's explanation be amplified by reference to broader themes contained in the *General Comment*? We return to the topic of indigenous peoples' rights in Chapter 7.

3. Even though the obligation to respect, protect, and fulfill creators' moral and material interests does not extend to corporations, could individual authors nevertheless be protected in respect of corporate vehicles chosen by them to exploit their material interests? The *General Comment* does not specifically address this issue. The document explains that states parties' obligations may extend to "taking financial and other positive measures which facilitate the formation of professional and other associations representing the moral and material interests of authors, including disadvantaged and marginalized authors," and that member states may be required to "establis[h] systems of collective administration of authors' rights."[76] Might the choices that authors make as to the most appropriate economic vehicles for securing their material interests be acknowledged and protected through the document's references to systemic "rule of law" protections? The *General Comment* notes, for example, that "accountability, transparency and independence of the judiciary" are "essential to the effective implementation of all human rights."[77]

4. The importance of appropriate procedural safeguards for protecting legal rights has been recognized by the European Court of Human Rights in the copyright law context. *Nemec v. Slovakia*[78] concerned a copyright infringement case that was filed in 1990 and dragged on for approximately ten years. The copyright owners based their claims on Article 6(1) of the European Convention on Human Rights, which provides in material part: "In the determination of his civil rights and obligations..., everyone is entitled to a ... hearing within a reasonable time by [a] ... tribunal." The Court's observations on the issue of delay were as follows:

> The Court accepts that the case is of a certain complexity and that the applicants contributed to the length of the proceedings in that they had challenged the judge dealing with their case and also an expert appointed by the District Court. These factors alone do not, however, account for the overall length of the period under consideration.

---

[76] On the relationship between human rights and collective rights management within the European human rights framework, see Helfer, *Collective Management, supra* note 52, at 91.

[77] *General Comment No. 17, supra* note 3, para. 48.

[78] *Nemec v. Slovakia*, No. 48672/99 (Eur. Ct. H.R. Nov. 15, 2001) (admissibility decision).

As to the conduct of the authorities, the Court notes that the president of the Bratislava City Court admitted delays in the proceedings between 4 August and 2 December 1993. Furthermore, the Bratislava III District Court took more than nine months to decide on the defendant's request of 13 February 1995 that the interim judgment of 5 December 1994 be amended. The appellate court decided on the defendant's appeal of 18 January 1996 on 13 June 1996, *i.e.* after almost five months.

The next hearing in the case was held on 2 July 1997 which is more than ten months after the Bratislava City Court's judgment of 13 June 1996 had been served. The Court finds that such a long delay cannot be justified by the mere fact that during this period the case was allocated to another judge due to restructuring of the Bratislava III District Court as at that time the case was pending for more than six years.

The Court further notes that the parties submitted documents to the District Court on 16 July and 5 August 1997 respectively and that the latter held the next hearing on 3 June 1998, *i.e.* after some ten months. Another ten months elapsed between 27 August 1999, when the applicants challenged the judge dealing with the case and appealed against the decision ordering them to pay an advance on the expert's fees and 30 June 2000, when the Bratislava Regional Court decided on these issues in two separate sets of proceedings. Finally, the Court notes that the expert was requested to submit the opinion on 27 October 2000, and it does not appear from the documents available that such an opinion has been submitted.

Having regard to all the evidence before it the Court finds that the above delays and periods of inertia, if counted against the overall duration of the period under consideration, cannot be regarded as compatible with the "reasonable time" requirement. There has accordingly been a violation of Article 6(1) of the [European] Convention.

An important innovation in the TRIPS Agreement was the inclusion of obligations relating to the national enforcement of intellectual property rights. Article 41(2) of TRIPS, for instance, provides that "procedures concerning the enforcement of intellectual property rights shall be fair and equitable. They shall not be unnecessarily complicated or costly, or entail unreasonable time-limits or unwarranted delays." Does the *Nemec* case support the claim that the enforcement provisions of TRIPS reflect human rights commitments? Does *General Comment No. 17*?

5. In writings in the 1980s and early 1990s, Philip Alston, among others, drew attention to the "vagueness" of many of the rights in the ICESCR, a "lack of clarity as to their normative implications," and an "underdeveloped justiciability" of such rights.[79] These are perennial concerns in the economic,

---

[79]   Philip Alston, *No Right to Complain about Being Poor: The Need for an Optional Protocol to the Economic Rights Covenant*, in Asbjørn Eide & Jan Helgesen (Eds.), The Future

social, and cultural rights context. Is this characterization apposite in the context of Article 15(1)(c)? Do the problems to which Alston refers endure after the publication of the *General Comment*?

6. In addition to the international human rights instruments already discussed, creators' rights are also guaranteed by the 1951 UN Convention on the Status of Refugees.[80] Article 14 provides:

> In respect of the protection of industrial property, such as inventions, designs or models, trade marks, trade names, and of rights in literary, artistic, and scientific works, a refugee shall be accorded in the country in which he has his habitual residence the same protection as is accorded to nationals of that country. In the territory of any other Contracting State, he shall be accorded the same protection as is accorded in that territory to nationals of the country in which he has his habitual residence.

Why might these protections have been added to this treaty?[81] When answering this question, consider the typical bases on which intellectual property treaties accord rights to foreigners.

3.5. Domestic Law Reform and Creators' Human Rights: Three Case Studies

International intellectual property law imposes constraints on domestic law reform agendas. For example, one of the early cases arising out the TRIPS Agreement held that certain aspects of a U.S. law reform agenda in the copyright field – which allows certain small businesses to play broadcast music in their premises without paying a license fee – were inconsistent with the obligations of the United States under TRIPS.[82] Creators' human rights also potentially restrict what domestic law reform agendas are able to achieve.

OF HUMAN RIGHTS PROTECTIONS IN A CHANGING WORLD 79, 86 (1991). Since 1990, the Committee on Economic, Social and Cultural Rights has considered whether to create an Optional Protocol to the ICESCR authorizing the Committee to receive and examine communications from individuals or groups alleging violations of one or more rights protected in the Covenant. After many years of deliberation and debate, the U.N. General Assembly unanimously adopted the text of an Optional Protocol in December 2008. The Protocol was opened for signature in September 2009. Arne Vandenbogaerde & Wouter Vandenhole, *The Optional Protocol to the International Covenant on Economic, Social and Cultural Rights: An Ex Ante Assessment of Its Effectiveness in Light of the Drafting Process*, 10 HUM. RTS. L. REV. 207 (2010).

[80] 1951 Convention on the Status of Refugees, July 28, 1951, 189 U.N.T.S. 150.

[81] See JAMES HATHAWAY, THE RIGHTS OF REFUGEES UNDER INTERNATIONAL LAW 830–33 (2005).

[82] Panel Report, United States – Section 110(5) of the U.S. Copyright Act, WT/DS 160/R (June 15, 2000) [Section 110(5) Panel Report].

These rights also carry significant normative and rhetorical weight, a point that may be particularly relevant for economic, social, and cultural rights, given the enduring controversies over their status, a topic that we analyze elsewhere in this book.[83]

Copyright law provides a useful context in which to explore these issues. In a number of jurisdictions, copyright has become an especially contested and controversial topic. Some commentators and civil society groups consider that copyrights are too strong, last too long, and inappropriately constrain the creative activities of others and the right to freedom of expression. At least two scholars have invoked the term "war" to describe these controversies.[84] Many distinguished commentators have advanced a variety of suggestions for reforming the law in the light of these concerns. Here, we consider three possible reforms: limiting the reproduction right for musical works, curtailing the derivative work right, and resurrecting formalities.

Each of these proposals should be tested against the obligations imposed by international intellectual property law. The proposals might also usefully be evaluated in the light of international human rights obligations. Lastly, the materials also provide an opportunity to evaluate the application of the principles developed in *General Comment No. 17* in concrete settings.

A. Limiting the Reproduction Right for Musical Works

The reproduction right is basic to copyright law. It protects one of the core principles in every copyright system – that the copyright owner has the exclusive right to make copies of his or her work. Proposals to jettison or limit the reproduction right respond in part to recent changes in distribution technologies that have radically altered the economics of dissemination of copyright-protected works.

Technological changes have been particularly important in the music context, as the wide variety of distribution networks – some operating under licenses, but many others not – clearly shows. Some commentators have suggested that authors of musical works and sound recordings (the latter are protected in many jurisdictions through "neighboring" or "related" rights) no longer need a reproduction right.[85] They argue that new technologies, especially the Internet, make reproduction and distribution of copyright-protected

---

[83] *See, e.g.*, Chapters 2 and 6. This point is particularly pertinent for law reform proposals advanced in the U.S. context: the United States has not yet ratified the ICESCR.

[84] Peter K. Yu, *The Escalating Copyright Wars*, 32 Hofstra L. Rev. 907 (2004); Jessica Litman, *War Stories*, 20 Cardozo Arts & Ent. L.J. 337 (2002).

[85] *See, e.g.*, Raymond S. R. Ku, *The Creative Destruction of Copyright: Napster and the New Economics of Digital Technology*, 69 U. Chi. L. Rev. 269 (2002).

works almost costless – or, more accurately, the cost is distributed across the very many users of the networks. As a result, there is no need for copyright law to protect exclusive reproduction and distribution rights and, thereby, provide economic incentives for these activities. Added to this, many contemporary musical artists now derive a significant proportion of their income from concerts and merchandizing, in addition to the income derived from sales of copies of their works. According to one proposal, musical artists would continue to earn income from live performances and merchandizing, but income formerly derived from the reproduction right would be replaced by distributions from a new tax on computer and other electronic equipment.[86]

There is some support for these proposals. Hardware and media levies have been adopted in some jurisdictions,[87] and many owners of musical works rely heavily on collective rights management.[88] Nevertheless, the exclusive reproduction right remains a fundamental obligation of international intellectual property law, one that applies even to those fortunate authors who can earn a living from merchandizing, concert sales or royalties distributed by collecting societies. Jettisoning the reproduction right entirely for a specific category of works would appear to conflict with these guarantees.[89]

---

[86] *Id.* Many other distinguished commentators have explored variations on, or abolition of, traditional copyright models for compensating authors. *See, e.g.,* WILLIAM W. FISHER, PROMISES TO KEEP: TECHNOLOGY, LAW AND THE FUTURE OF ENTERTAINMENT (2004); Neil Netanel, *Impose a Non Commercial Use Levy to Allow Free Peer-to-Peer File Sharing,* 17 HARV. J. L. & TECH. 1, 4 (2003); Jessica Litman, *Sharing and Stealing,* 27 HASTINGS COMM. & ENT. L. J. 1 (2004). The United States has adopted a (very limited) levy system in the music context. *See* Audio Home Recording Act of 1992, 17 U.S.C. §§ 1001–10 (2006). For an analysis contesting the viability of compensation systems based on taxation and levies (but concluding that most unauthorized distribution of musical works via peer-to-peer [P2P] networks should nevertheless be permitted), *see* Henry Pettit Jr., *New Architectures for Music: Law Should Get Out of the Way,* 29 HASTINGS COMM. & ENT. L.J. 259 (2007). The issue has become more complex in recent years with the merging of the reproduction and public performance right. For instance, in some circumstances, a digital phonorecord delivery might be functionally equivalent to a public performance even though it is not perceived contemporaneously with the delivery. The economic implications of jettisoning the reproduction right may be significantly affected by how courts characterize these "disseminations" of copyright-protected works. *Cf. U.S. v. American Society of Composers, Authors, & Publishers,* __ F.3d __, 2010 WL 3749292 (2d Cir. Sept. 28, 2010) (in the digital context, to implicate the public performance right, the perception of a public performance must be simultaneous with its transmission).

[87] For example, Article 5(2)(b) of the EU Copyright Directive allows member states to "provide for exceptions or limitations to the reproduction right" of the copyright owner in the case of private copying, as long as the rights holders receive "fair compensation." Council Directive 29/EC, art. 5(2)(b), on the Harmonization of Certain Aspects of Copyright and Related Rights in the Information Society, 2001 O.J. (L 167) at 10–19.

[88] *See generally* Helfer, *Collective Management, supra* note 52, at 85.

[89] *See* Berne Convention, Article 9(1): "Authors of literary and artistic works protected by this Convention shall have the exclusive right of authorizing the reproduction of these works, in

Does the recognition of creators' human rights add anything to this analysis? Recall that the *General Comment* recognized a link between creators and the ability to make a living from creative activities. Composers who performed music would still be compensated directly for their performances (and, presumably, from royalties derived from the granting of blanket licenses to live performance venues), and all composers would be compensated from hardware and media levies, which may be more lucrative for some copyright owners than enforcing the reproduction right directly.[90] Nevertheless, the opportunity for sales of copies and phonograms to contribute to an author's livelihood would be foreclosed entirely.

The proposal to limit the reproduction right may also have disparate consequences for different types of creators. Some composers achieve considerable fame by performing their music: for them, significant sources of income would remain intact. But for composers who are not so fortunate, income from merchandizing rights and, perhaps, performances, is unlikely to be meaningful. For the latter group in particular, the proposal may be in some tension with human rights law. As the *General Comment* emphasizes, there is a strong normative connection between creators' rights and the "opportunity to gain one's living by work which one freely chooses."[91] Proposals to limit the

---

any manner or form." The proposal may also be inconsistent with copyright owners' exclusive rights of making their works available to the public that is set forth in more recent international instruments. See WIPO Performances and Phonograms Treaty, adopted May 20, 2002, 36 I.L.M. 76; WIPO Copyright Treaty, adopted Mar. 6, 2002, 36 I.L.M. 65.

In this chapter, we do not examine these proposals in the light of the "three-step test" against which exceptions and limitations to the exclusive rights of copyright owners are required to be tested. That test is set forth in Article 13 of the TRIPS Agreement, which provides: "Members shall confine limitations or exceptions to exclusive rights to certain special cases which do not conflict with a normal exploitation of the work and do not unreasonably prejudice the legitimate interests of the right holder." Assuming that these proposals were adopted by a nation whose obligations under TRIPS had tolled, and that they applied to both foreign and domestic origin works, it may be quite difficult to show that the proposals pass muster under the three-step test. All of them constrain core economic rights of copyright owners – the reproduction right, the adaptation right, and the protection of works without regard to compliance with formalities. In addition, only the first of the three proposals (jettisoning the reproduction right) would appear to be limited with reference to genre – musical works. This limitation is very unlikely to be a sufficient basis for showing that the exception was confined to "certain special cases." *See generally* Section 110(5) Panel Report, *supra* note 82 (finding that an exception to the broadcast right failed the three-step test where the exception largely applied to musical works generally that were broadcast in businesses whose premises were of limited and defined dimensions).

[90] *See, e.g.,* FISHER, *supra* note 86, at 203.

[91] *General Comment No. 17, supra* note 3, para. 4. This may give rise to particularly difficult problems for composers who, for some reason, cannot perform in "live venues," such as composers suffering from stage fright or repetitive strain injury. We are grateful to Professor Peter Yu for this observation.

reproduction right may jeopardize at least part of that livelihood. To put the position more concretely, consider a composer who suffers from a disability, which makes live performances impossible. How would this individual's right to the material interests resulting from his or her compositions be realized if the reproduction right were foreclosed?

These tensions do not, however, necessarily equate with a breach of creators' human rights. Individual nations have a large measure of flexibility in how they realize their obligations with regard to social, economic, and cultural rights. Furthermore, *General Comment No. 17* does not specify the sources of funds that are relevant to securing authors' incomes. And it recognizes that collective management of rights may be a necessary vehicle for securing the fruits of creative work. Given the prohibitive transaction costs associated with individualized enforcement of copyrights, efficient and fair collective rights management and, perhaps, hardware and media levies, may be the only realistic way to guarantee the material interests of creators protected by ICESCR Article 15(1)(c).[92]

Even so, the text of the *General Comment* at least alerts us to the possibility that human rights issues may be implicated by requiring composers to derive income *only* from performances, merchandizing, and levies and *not* from direct sales of copies. This possibility might be relevant to policymakers who favor domestic law reforms that take into account both international intellectual property law and human rights law. It might also provide a platform on which activists and artists rights organizations might argue that policymakers should consider alternative income sources for creators disproportionately burdened by the reform proposals. The differential impact on certain classes of composers and musicians highlights a related concern: extraordinarily successful artists who can afford to forgo income from the reproduction right may well be in the minority. Focusing on the human rights dimensions of those *not* in this privileged group foregrounds the practical consequences of law reform proposals on the livelihood of all creators, including those who are economically vulnerable or suffering from disabilities.

B. Restricting the Scope of the Derivative Work Right

Potential tensions between human rights and limiting sources of creators' income also arise in the context of a second law reform proposal: restricting the derivative works right. A number of U.S. commentators have criticized the scope of copyright owners' exclusive right to create derivative works.[93]

---

[92] *See generally* Helfer, *Collective Management, supra* note 52.
[93] *See, e.g.,* JESSICA LITMAN, DIGITAL COPYRIGHT 22 (2001).

According to one analysis, the First Amendment to the U.S. Constitution demands replacement of this right with a right to share in profits from the exploitation of derivative works prepared by others.[94] (We discuss issues raised by the human right to freedom of expression in more detail in Chapter 4.) According to this proposal, the copyright owner would keep the reproduction right, but she would not be able choose among different parties who might want to use the underlying copyright-protected work to make a derivative work. The copyright owner would be entitled to share in the profits from paid performances but would have no basis to object, or to receive any remuneration if, for example, an amateur dramatic society performed her work and did not charge admission, or if it charged only what was required to cover the production costs.

Once again, international intellectual property law is likely to impede realization of this reform proposal. The suggestion that authors should not have an exclusive derivative works right is facially inconsistent with the Berne Convention's requirement that authors of literary or artistic works have the right to authorize the making of adaptations of their works.[95] Curtailing the derivative work right could also deprive authors of an important source of income and thus implicate the human rights analyzed in *General Comment No. 17*. For authors who derive a significant portion of their livelihood from royalties and license fees, in contrast to those whose principal income sources are foundation grants, patronage, or academic salaries and the like, the financial benefits of exploiting derivative works can be considerable. For a modestly successful writer, for example, the sale of a film option can provide rent or mortgage payments needed to complete and sell the next work. To be sure, it is difficult to assess in the abstract how the fees for licensing derivative works might be affected by replacement of the exclusive derivative work right with a right to share in the profits from unauthorized adaptations. It seems more than plausible, however, that the price that the copyright owner could demand for her work would be depressed by the increased competition from these adaptations.

Denying creators control over the promulgation of derivative works might also impinge upon their moral rights, which are protected by Article 6*bis* of the Berne Convention.[96] As we have seen, protection of authors' moral rights marks an important point of intersection between the protections

---

[94] Jed Rubenfeld, *The Freedom of Imagination: Copyright's Constitutionality*, 112 YALE L.J. 1 (2002).

[95] Berne Convention, art. 12.

[96] *Id.* art. 6*bis*.

afforded by intellectual property instruments and human rights guarantees.[97] As the drafting history discloses, the connection between human rights and moral rights was advanced in support of the inclusion of Article 27(2) in the UDHR. At least one commentator has suggested that the connections that exist between authors and their works, which form the conceptual basis for protecting moral rights, establish the very foundation for recognizing human rights associated with authorship.[98]

The *General Comment*'s assertion – that protection of authors' moral interests encompasses the right "to object to any distortion, mutilation or other modification of, or other derogatory action in relation to, their productions that would be prejudicial to their honor or reputation"[99] – appears to be broadly consistent with the protections of moral rights set forth in Article 6*bis*.[100] But it is worth remembering that moral rights protections that are articulated in international intellectual property instruments are significantly more constrained than they might have been. The drafting history of the moral rights protections in the Berne Convention shows that the final text of Article 6*bis* was a product of significant compromise. Some nations sought a more expansive provision that protected the subjective integrity of the work, emphasizing how authors themselves might respond to changes to their works. In the end, in large part through the diplomatic efforts of the United Kingdom, the drafters agreed to a diluted form of moral rights protection. For example, the use of the phrase "prejudicial to their honor or reputation" appears to limit the coverage of Article 6*bis* to affronts that can be objectively measured.[101]

The *General Comment* does not clarify whether the moral rights guarantees of human rights law add anything to the protections already afforded by international intellectual property law – whether, for example, the "moral" interests in Article 15(1)(c) encompass uses of works that cause *subjective* harms to the creator, or whether the injunction to balance "the private interests of authors" against other human rights, such as freedom of expression, might

---

[97] *See generally* Gana, *supra* note 42, 318–323.

[98] Michel Vivant, *Authors' Rights, Human Rights* 174 REVUE INTERNATIONALE DU DROIT D'AUTEUR 60 (1997).

[99] *General Comment No. 17, supra* note 3, para. 13.

[100] "Independently of the author's economic rights, and even after the transfer of the said rights, the author shall have the right to claim authorship of the work and to object to any distortion, mutilation or other modification of, or other derogatory action in relation to, the said work, which would be prejudicial to his honor or reputation." Berne Convention, art. 6*bis*.

[101] 1 SAM RICKETSON & JANE GINSBURG, INTERNATIONAL COPYRIGHT AND NEIGHBOURING RIGHTS: THE BERNE CONVENTION AND BEYOND 589–99 (2005).

permit unauthorized "modifications" that, notwithstanding a claim of subjective harm, involve critiques of the author's work. Nothing in the Committee's analysis suggests that a human rights approach to moral rights is confined to an objective concept of prejudice to the author's honor or reputation. At this stage, however, the precise scope of moral rights protections afforded by international human rights law is, like many other substantive issues, impossible to delineate fully. Even so, the close connection between authors and their creative works that is emphasized in emerging human rights jurisprudence may provide policymakers with another substantive basis for scrutinizing law reform proposals aimed at constraining authors' exclusive right to prepare derivative works.

C. Resurrecting Copyright Formalities

A number of distinguished commentators have suggested a third type of reform of domestic intellectual property law – reviving compliance with formalities as a condition for securing or retaining copyright protection.[102] A key motivation for this suggestion is a concern with the possible chilling effect of difficulties in securing licenses for copyright-protected works. The removal of formalities as a necessary condition for securing or maintaining copyright protection precludes the possibility of establishing a comprehensive or reliable copyright register that subsequent authors could search in order to establish the provenance of preexisting copyright-protected works that the authors might want to use in their new creative endeavors. The development of an efficient licensing scheme is made more difficult because copyright owners often cannot be found easily, with the result that creative activity that utilizes preexisting works may be stifled. This may also have implications for freedom of expression: the transaction costs associated with securing a license for the use of the work, absent a comprehensive and efficiently searchable register, may cause potential authors wishing to use the earlier material to forgo the intended use. As a result, these subsequent authors might be unable to "speak" as they originally intended.

At the same time, the absence of any system that conditions the subsistence or maintenance of copyrights on compliance with formalities has the effect of enhancing the security of copyright owners' title. In the past, U.S. copyright law provided a notorious illustration of how formalities could impede authors' ability to keep their copyrights and continue to derive income from

---

[102] *See* William Landes & Richard Posner, *Indefinitely Renewable Copyright*, 70 U. CHI. L. REV. 471 (2003); *see also* Christopher Sprigman, *Reform(aliz)ing Copyright*, 57 STAN. L. REV. 485 (2004).

them. Under earlier copyright laws, publication without affixing a copyright notice could effect a "divestive publication," consigning the work to the public domain.[103] Even if the first term was secured, enjoyment of the "renewal term" was, prior to important amendments to the Copyright Act in 1992,[104] conditioned on registration of that term. Failure to register had the effect of shortening protection to an initial term of twenty-eight years, a very brief period compared with many other nations' laws.[105]

Whichever side one comes down on in the formalities debate as a policy matter, as a matter of black-letter international intellectual property law the resurrection of formalities for all works would be impermissible. Prohibiting the use of formalities as preconditions for subsistence of copyright was one of the significant achievements of the Berne Convention. Successive drafts of the Convention gradually evolved away from permitting the protection of copyright to be conditioned on compliance with formalities, such as registration or publication with notice.[106] For formalities to be revived for all works, both the Berne Convention and the TRIPS Agreement in which it is incorporated would need to be changed – a politically implausible prospect that risks unraveling of intellectual property's incorporation into the world trade regime. Whatever one's views on the merits of this outcome, it is surely relevant to the cost/benefits analysis that should accompany domestic law reform proposals of this kind.

---

[103] *See generally Estate of Martin Luther King, Jr., Inc. v. CBS, Inc.*, 194 F.3d 1211 (11th Cir. 1999). As Sprigman explains, the formalities in the first federal copyright statute, the Copyright Act of 1791, Act of May 31, 1790, ch. 15, 1 Stat. 124, had three principal effects: failure to comply could result in the work's not being copyrighted at all, being unenforceable, or being terminated at the end of the first term. Sprigman, *supra* note 102, at 493. Later enactments imposed requirements as to the recordation of all transfers or assignments of copyrights. Failure to comply with these requirements could lead to a transfer being adjudged fraudulent and void against parties who subsequently dealt with the copyright in prescribed ways. Act of June 30, 1834, ch. 157, 4 Stat. 778 (1834).

[104] Copyright Renewal Act of 1992, Pub. L. No. 102–307, 106 Stat. 264 (1992) (providing for the automatic renewal of pre-1978 works in their first term of copyright).

[105] The endurance of formalities within the U.S. copyright system was one of the principal reasons why the United States did not join the Berne Convention until 1988. Implementing legislation was passed in 1988, effective March 1, 1989. Berne Convention Implementation Act 1988, Pub. L. No. 100–568, 102 Stat. 2853 (codified at 17 U.S.C. § 116); *see* Jane C. Ginsburg & John M. Kernochan, *One Hundred and Two Years Later: The U.S. Joins the Berne Convention*, 13 COLUM. J. L. & ARTS 1 (1988).

[106] 1 RICKETSON & GINSBURG, *supra* note 101, at 321–22 (2005). In some jurisdictions, compliance with formalities continues to be advantageous. Under U.S. law, for example, significant remedial and procedural advantages still attach to registration. 17 U.S.C. § 412 (awards of attorneys fees and statutory damages conditioned on timely registration); PAUL GOLDSTEIN, GOLDSTEIN ON COPYRIGHT § 3:2–4 (3d ed., 2006).

A more modest version of the proposal would limit the application of formalities to domestic-origin works.[107] The Berne Convention, and, indeed, international intellectual property law generally, requires members states to apply the treaty's substantive protections (including the requirement that copyright may not be conditioned on formalities) only to foreign-origin works. Substantive obligations typically do not apply to works originating in the member state. Accordingly, it is permissible to discriminate against works that originated in one's own country. United States copyright law takes advantage of this provision. In broad outline, the law provides that a work must be registered prior to bringing an infringement action, but this condition does not apply to foreign-origin works.[108] The proposals explored earlier in this section might be similarly constrained if they were to jettison the reproduction right or constrain the derivative work right for domestic-origin works alone.

The three law reform proposals thus intersect with another major achievement of the international intellectual property system – the adoption of broad nondiscrimination rules.[109] In the copyright context, for instance, international agreements were animated by a concern that foreigners should be treated no worse than domestic authors.[110] "Most favored nation" rules enhance these national treatment obligations by requiring states to extend the benefits given to intellectual property proprietors in one country to those in other countries.[111] These now fundamental principles of international

---

[107] See 1 RICKETSON & GINSBURG, supra note 101, at 319 ("If local law does not otherwise provide a level of protection consistent with Berne minima, it must nonetheless adhere to these supranational norms when non-local Berne works are at issue.").

[108] See generally Ginsburg & Kernochan, supra note 105. The Supreme Court recently held that the registration requirement was not "jurisdictional." Reed Elsevier Inc. v. Muchnick,130 S. Ct. 1237 (2010). Although the Court's analysis of the implications of this holding was somewhat opaque, this presumably means that U.S. courts are not constitutionally precluded from adjudicating cases involving unregistered works. A U.S. district court recently held that conditioning the availability of statutory damages on registration for all works, whether of U.S. or foreign origin, was consistent with domestic law and did not violate any domestically applicable rule of international law. Football Ass'n Premier League Ltd. v. YouTube, Inc., 633 F. Supp. 2d 159 (S.D.N.Y. 2009).

[109] Famously, the European Court of Justice (albeit in the context of achieving economic harmonization within the European Union) has established a general nondiscrimination principle in the administration of intellectual property rights. See Case C-92/92, Phil Collins v. Imtrat Handelsgesellschaft; case C-326/92, EMI v. Patricia Im-und Export, 3 C.M.L.R. 773 (E.C.J. 1993).

[110] 1 RICKETSON & GINSBURG, supra note 101, at 674 et seq.

[111] Article 4 of the TRIPS Agreement sets forth the most favored nation obligation that is imposed on all members of the WTO: "With regard to the protection of intellectual property, any advantage, favour, privilege or immunity granted by a Member to the nationals of

intellectual property law do not, however, implicate a nation's discretion to treat domestic works *less favorably* than those of foreign origin.

Human rights law, in contrast, is not so limited. It is profoundly concerned with the treatment of all members of the human family, not the least with how a nation treats its own. Nondiscrimination, including nondiscrimination on the basis of national origin and "other status,"[112] is a foundational principle of international human rights law. If this principle were applied to creators' rights, human rights law might give rise to legal obligations that are more expansive than those imposed by international intellectual property laws.[113] In particular, creators' rights have the potential to "domesticate" international intellectual property law by requiring that its provisions be applied to local and foreign authors alike.[114]

However, because human rights for creators and intellectual property rights are ontologically distinct, it would be difficult to argue that human rights law domesticates international intellectual property law *in toto*. Rather, such a consequence would arise only where creators' human rights and international intellectual property laws overlap – a zone that, as previously

any other country shall be accorded immediately and unconditionally to the nationals of all other Members."

[112] *Cf.* ICESCR, art. 2. "The States Parties to the present Covenant undertake to guarantee that the rights enunciated in the present Covenant will be exercised without discrimination of any kind as to race, colour, sex, language, religion, political or other opinion, national or social origin, property, birth or other status." *See generally* HERSCH LAUTERPACHT, INTERNATIONAL LAW AND HUMAN RIGHTS (1950) (noting the recognition of the individual as the direct subject of international law). *Cf.* SIGRUN SKOGLY, BEYOND NATIONAL BORDERS: STATES' HUMAN RIGHTS AND OBLIGATIONS IN INTERNATIONAL COOPERATION 4, 11 (2006) (characterizing this "vertical" aspect of international human rights law, which was ushered in with the U.N. Charter in 1945, as the "traditional" approach to realization of human rights obligations).

[113] As Johannes Morsink recounts, some Latin American nations sponsored the inclusion of Article 27(2) of the UDHR precisely because they saw it as "a step toward the internationalization of copyright law." MORSINK, *supra* note 23, at 221. Interestingly, at the time of the negotiation of the text of UDHR, many Latin American nations were not signatories to the Berne Convention. They had, however, signed on to the American Declaration of the Rights and Duties of Man, which, as noted previously, included a copyright provision. *Id.* at 220. Accordingly, in this context, human rights protections had a temporal priority over the adoption of Berne Convention obligations.

[114] This has occurred, to a limited extent, in some jurisdictions. In France, for example, Article 27(2) of the UDHR has been invoked to extend national protections of moral rights to foreigners. *Société Roy Export Company Establishment et Charlie Chaplin v. Société Les films Roger Richebé*, 28 R.I.D.A. 133 (1960). Article 27 was also invoked by the Paris Tribunal de Grande Instance in the famous *Asphalt Jungle* case, where the court noted that "the author is the true creator" and that "French law conforms to the international legal order" as restated in Article 27(2). *Huston v. Turner Ent. Co.*, [1992] E.C.C. 334. *See* Desselmontet, *supra* note 6, at 114–115.

explained, is quite narrow.[115] Moreover, differential treatment of foreigners and citizens is ubiquitous in the organization of the nation state. For the domestication argument to be salient, therefore, it would be necessary to link any discrimination claim to specific obligations that human rights law imposes. For example, for a differential registration requirement to trigger human rights concerns, it would be important to provide detailed empirical data as to the requirement's practical consequences. What might initially be viewed as a minor or anodyne procedural hurdle could be quite burdensome in some contexts, such as for remote indigenous communities without reticulated power sources or Internet access.

We suggested previously that there may be links between creators' rights and both the reproduction right and the derivative work right, to the extent that each is closely connected to creators' ability to pursue a livelihood. In the formalities context, however, it would also be necessary to show that restoring copyright formalities, and conditioning the subsistence of copyright on compliance with them, would impede realization of authors' material or moral interests. In turn, this might require analysis of issues such as costs and convenience of the registration, whether there are barriers to accessing relevant technologies, whether the registration requirements are significantly more onerous for individual authors/owners (especially those of disadvantaged groups) as compared with corporate copyright owners, and so on. Human rights obligations could contribute to this debate, by focusing policymakers' attention on the specific burdens that law reform proposals might impose on creators.

As this brief discussion suggests, the full implications of obligations arising from creators' human rights is only beginning to emerge. Our understanding of these obligations also requires analysis of the other provisions of international instruments – particularly the right to share in cultural and scientific advances, and, as the *General Comment* emphasizes, rights such as freedom of expression, education, food, and health. Accordingly, much more work will need to be done before clear "human-rights-consistent" principles will emerge that would have the capacity to guide domestic law reform initiatives toward specific policy outcomes. What is reasonably certain, however, is that

---

[115] Some commentators appear to assume that the area of overlap is more extensive. For example, Asbjørn Eide reasons that the obligation in Article 15(1)(c) of the ICESCR "is contained" in a number of international intellectual property instruments, including the Universal Copyright convention. Asbjørn Eide, *Cultural Rights as Individual Human Rights*, in ASBJØRN EIDE ET AL. (EDS.), ECONOMIC, SOCIAL AND CULTURAL RIGHTS 229, 236 (1995). As the analysis of *General Comment No. 17* earlier in this chapter reveals, the analysis is more complex.

taking creators' rights seriously may require policymakers to look beyond the traditional preoccupations that have informed policy development in the intellectual property field, and to view law reform initiatives though a different kind of lens.

Notes and Questions

1. Referencing creators' human rights in law reform deliberations focuses attention on a set of issues that do not typically arise in the context of deliberations on intellectual property, including the vulnerability of people who do creative work and the connection between creativity and the dignity of the human person. There is some conceptual overlap between this way of approaching intellectual property issues and the "capabilities approach" to human rights that has been advanced in the work of a number of theorists, including Amartya Sen and Martha Nussbaum. A capabilities approach recognizes that "human abilities exert a moral claim that they should be developed,"[116] and it foregrounds the material circumstances necessary for the realization and flourishing of human capabilities. There may also be some cross-over between this set of ideas and the themes developed in *General Comment No. 17*, particularly the attention given there to securing authors' material interests. On the other hand, as Margaret Chon has argued, the capabilities approach to human rights may point toward constraining intellectual property protection, especially when such protection impedes other rights, including the right to an adequate education.[117]

2. Daniel Gervais has argued that "human rights approaches bring *values* back into the [copyright] system."[118] Elaborating on this point, he argues that "the emphasis on culture in human rights instruments allow one ... to acknowledge the limits of economic analysis and theory as a policy machine."[119] Exactly what values are put at stake by the three law reform proposals discussed in this section? Would identification of these values act as a counterweight to the law reform proposals – or might it give further support to them?[120]

---

[116] Martha Nussbaum, *Capabilities and Social Justice*, 4 INT'L STUDIES REV. 123, 132 (2002).

[117] *See* Margaret Chon, *Intellectual Property and the Development Divide*, 27 CARDOZO L. REV. 2821, 2874–2911 (2006).

[118] Daniel J. Gervais, *Intellectual Property and Human Rights: Learning to Live Together*, in INTELLECTUAL PROPERTY AND HUMAN RIGHTS, *supra* note 22, at 3, 15.

[119] *Id.*

[120] *See generally* Julie E. Cohen, *Creativity and Culture in Copyright Theory*, 40 U.C. DAVIS L. REV. 1151 (2007).

3. Within the United States, might a reform agenda for intellectual property law that focused on noneconomic concerns be constitutionally infirm? For example, would such an agenda be consistent with the constitutional prescription to "promote the progress of science and useful arts"?[121] The U.S. Supreme Court has indicated that legislation is not constitutionally infirm for being economically irrational.[122] But does this also permit the legislature to be *motivated* by noneconomic imperatives?

3.6. The Human Right of Property

The European Convention on Human Rights (ECHR) offers another basis in human rights law to protect the intellectual output of creators. In the European context, a leading commentator has asserted that the "fundamental rights basis" for copyright law rests in part on the "property clause" of the ECHR's First Protocol,[123] which provides:

> Every natural or legal person is entitled to the peaceful enjoyment of his possessions. No one shall be deprived of his possessions except in the public interest and subject to the conditions provided for by law and by the general principles of international law.

> The preceding provisions shall not, however, in any way impair the right of a State to enforce such laws as it deems necessary to control the use of property in accordance with the general interest or to secure the payment of taxes or other contributions or penalties.

The following materials review recent decisions of the European Court of Human Rights (ECtHR) in which individual creators alleged that the government's unauthorized use of their creative works violated Article 1 of the First Protocol.

Balan v. Moldova, App. No. 19247/03 (Eur. Ct. H.R. 2008)

[In this case, Balan, a photographer, alleged that his rights under Article 1 had been infringed as a result of the refusal by the Moldovan domestic courts to compensate him for an unlawful use of his work – a 1985 photograph of

---

[121] U.S. Const. art. I., § 8, cl. 8.

[122] *Eldred v. Ashcroft*, 537 U.S. 186, 209 n.16 (2003) (responding to and rejecting Justice Breyer's argument that the challenged legislation was economically irrational).

[123] *See* P. B. Hugenholtz, *Copyright and Freedom of Expression in Europe*, in Rochelle Cooper Dreyfuss, Harry First, & Diane Leheer Zimmerman (Eds.), Innovation Policy in an Information Age 343, 346 (2000). Hugenholtz also grounded the human rights for copyright in the ECHR's right of privacy. *Id.*

Soroca Castle, a well-known historical site in Moldova. In 1996 the Ministry of Internal Affairs of Moldova ("the Ministry") used the photograph as a background for national identity cards. Balan did not agree to this use of the photograph. When the government rebuffed his requests for compensation, he initiated court proceedings. The lower court issued a modest compensation award to Balan, the equivalent of just over US$550. However, the government continued to use the photograph on identity cards without permission, leading Balan to file a second complaint. The lower courts refused his request for additional compensation and for an order compelling the Ministry to enter into a contract with him for future use of the photograph. On appeal, the Supreme Court of Justice of Moldova confirmed Balan's intellectual property rights in respect of the photograph but refused his request for additional damages and other relief. The Supreme Court also held that, under the relevant provisions of the Moldovan Copyright and Related Rights Act, an identity card was an official government document that could not be subject to copyright. Balan challenged the courts' rulings before the ECtHR, which upheld his complaint.]

...

The Court reiterates that Article 1 of Protocol No. 1 to the Convention does not guarantee the right to acquire property. Moreover, "an applicant can allege a violation of Article 1 of Protocol No. 1 only in so far as the impugned decisions related to his 'possessions' within the meaning of this provision. 'Possessions' can be either 'existing possessions' or assets, including claims, in respect of which the applicant can argue that he or she has at least a 'legitimate expectation' of obtaining effective enjoyment of a property right. By way of contrast, the hope of recognition of a property right which it has been impossible to exercise effectively cannot be considered a 'possession' within the meaning of Article 1 of Protocol No. 1, nor can a conditional claim which lapses as a result of the non-fulfilment of the condition."

The concept of "possessions" referred to in the first part of Article 1 of Protocol No. 1 has an autonomous meaning which is not limited to ownership of physical goods and is independent from the formal classification in domestic law: certain other rights and interests constituting assets can also be regarded as "property rights," and thus as "possessions" for the purposes of this provision. The issue that needs to be examined in each case is whether the circumstances of the case, considered as a whole, confer on the applicant title to a substantive interest protected by Article 1 of Protocol No. 1.

In certain circumstances, a "legitimate expectation" of obtaining an "asset" may also enjoy the protection of Article 1 of Protocol No. 1 to the Convention.

Thus, where a proprietary interest is in the nature of a claim, the person in whom it is vested may be regarded as having a "legitimate expectation" if there is a sufficient basis for the interest in national law, for example where there is settled case-law of the domestic courts confirming its existence....

Application of These Principles to the Present Case

Whether the Applicant Had "Possessions"
The Court reiterates that Article 1 of Protocol No. 1 is applicable to intellectual property (see *Anheuser-Busch Inc. v. Portugal*). In the present case, the Court notes that the applicant's rights in respect of the photograph he had taken were confirmed by the domestic courts. Therefore, ... there was no dispute in the present case as to whether the applicant could claim protection of his intellectual property rights. In this connection, the Court takes note of the applicant's submission that he asked the courts to protect his already established right over the protected work by awarding him compensation, and not to establish his "property right" over such compensation. He had, in the Court's opinion, a right recognised by law and by a previous final judgment, and not merely a legitimate expectation of obtaining a property right.

The Court notes that the Supreme Court of Justice decided ... that identity cards ... could not be subject to the applicant's intellectual property rights.... However, the court only referred to identity cards and not to the photograph taken by the applicant, in respect of which there was no dispute. Moreover, [the Copyright Act] expressly distinguishes between the author's rights in respect of works created by him or her and the property right over the material object in which that creation is embodied. It follows that the finding of the Supreme Court of Justice that identity cards could not be subject to copyright had no bearing on the applicant's rights in respect of the photograph he had taken. This finding is confirmed by the fact that the domestic courts found, in the first set of proceedings, that the applicant's rights had been infringed. The courts awarded him compensation despite the Ministry's use of the photograph in an identical manner, that is as a background for identity cards.

In view of the above, the Court concludes that the applicant had a "possession" within the meaning of Article 1 of Protocol No. 1 to the Convention.

Whether There Has Been Interference
The Court reiterates that it is not its task to take the place of the national authorities who ruled on the applicant's case. It primarily falls to them to examine all the facts of the case and set their reasons out in their decisions.

In the present case, the Court does not see any reason for questioning the domestic courts' application of a law adopted specifically to regulate intellectual property rights issues and which came into force before the alleged violation of the applicant's rights.... The Court will therefore examine the case on the basis of the law as applied by the domestic courts.

...

It cannot be said, as argued by the Government, that the applicant tacitly accepted the use of his protected work without remuneration. On the contrary, by lodging a new court action he clearly expressed his view that such use was in violation of his rights. Moreover, the fact that he consistently claimed the protection of his right by asking the Ministry to conclude a contract with him and to pay him author's fees or compensation is evidence of the fact that he has continuously opposed unauthorised use of his protected work. It follows that the applicant's failure to request the prohibition of the unauthorised use of his work by the Ministry could not make such use lawful as unauthorised use was expressly prohibited by law and was opposed by the applicant.

In the light of the above, the Court finds that there has been interference with the applicant's property rights within the meaning of Article 1 of Protocol No. 1 to the Convention.

Whether the Interference Was "lawful"
[Under the legislation] the only means of extinguishing the author's right is a contract with the author or his or her successors, while the author's "moral rights" can never be transmitted to third persons. In addition, it is for the author of a protected work to decide which of the penalties provided by law he or she wants to apply in case of an infringement of his or her rights....

The Court notes that neither the domestic courts nor the Government referred to any specific provision in the [Copyright Act] which expressly provides for the termination of an author's rights in respect of his or her creation by virtue of a failure to prohibit its unauthorised use. [The legislation] refers to the right to ask for the prohibition of the unlawful use but does not attach any negative consequences to a failure to do so.

Purpose and Lawfulness of the Interference

...

... The Court must determine whether the interference with the applicant's rights was proportionate to the aims pursued.

The Court accepts that issuing identity cards to the population serves an undoubtedly important public interest. However, it is apparent that this socially important aim could have been reached in a variety of ways not involving a breach of the applicant's rights. For instance, another photograph could have been used or a contract could have been concluded with the applicant. The Court is unaware of any compelling reason for the use of the particular photograph taken by the applicant or of any impediments to the use of other materials for the same purpose. Indeed, the photograph taken by the applicant was no longer used as a background in identity cards after 1 May 2000, which confirms that the public interest could be served without violating the applicant's rights.

It follows that the domestic courts failed to strike a fair balance between the interests of the community and those of the applicant, placing on him an individual and excessive burden. There has, accordingly, been a violation of Article 1 of Protocol No. 1 to the Convention.

[The ECtHR then considered what reparations to award to Balan for the state's violation.]

...

The Court considers that the applicant must have been caused damage as a result of the infringement of his rights in respect of the photograph he had taken and the refusal of the domestic courts to award compensation for that violation, the more so seeing that the photograph had been reproduced on a large scale, despite the authorities' awareness of the unlawful character of such use. Moreover, the Court finds that the award in the applicant's favour made in [the first court proceedings] compensated him only for the infringement of his rights prior to the initiation [of those] proceedings and not for the subsequent use of the photograph taken by him.

In the light of the above and deciding on an equitable basis, the Court awards the applicant EUR 5,000 for pecuniary and non-pecuniary damage.

_____

Notes and Questions

1. The ECtHR applies a three-part framework to determine whether a violation of Article 1 of the First Protocol has occurred in cases involving intellectual property:

The analysis consists of three questions: First, does Article 1 apply to the intellectual property at issue, either because it is an existing possession or because the owner has a legitimate expectation of obtaining a future proprietary interest? If neither type of property exists, the government's conduct, however egregious, cannot violate Article 1. In contrast, if the EC[t]HR answers this question affirmatively, it must consider a second question: Has the government "interfered" with the possession? The absence of such an interference also requires a ruling for the respondent state. Conversely, the existence of an interference leads to a third and final question: Whether the interference is justified, i.e., has the state upset the fair and proportional balance that Article 1 requires between the interests of the public and the property owner's rights?[124]

Did the ECtHR faithfully apply each part of this framework in the *Balan* case? For example, is it self-evident that creative works such as photographs are protected by Article 1? Is the intangible nature of the rights in creative works relevant to answering this question? Is the degree of originality in the photograph of Soroca Castle a relevant concern? In addition, should the nature of the government's use of Balan's photograph – as the background for Moldova's national identity card – influence whether the state has failed to strike a "fair and proportional balance" between the creator's rights and the public interest? Does anything in the text of Article 1 support Moldova's position that it did not violate Balan's property right?

2. In discussing whether the government had interfered with the right of property, the ECtHR emphasizes that it cannot "take the place of the national authorities who ruled on the applicant's case" and that it "primarily falls to [those authorities] to examine all the facts of the case and set their reasons out in their decisions." Can these principles be reconciled with the ECtHR's damages award, which is roughly fifteen times the damages awarded by the Moldovan courts?

3. *Anheuser-Busch Inc. v. Portugal*[125] (cited in the *Balan* decision) involved a dispute between two corporations, the well-known American brewer and its longstanding Czech rival, Budějovický Budvar, over the exclusive right to market "Budweiser" beer in Portugal. In a dispute lasting for nearly two decades, the Portuguese courts ultimately canceled Anheuser-Busch's registration for the "Budweiser" trademark in favor of Budvar's registration for a competing appellation of origin, a type of geographical indication. Anheuser-Busch challenged the cancellation as a violation of its property rights. In 2007, a Grand Chamber of the ECtHR concluded that both registered trademarks and applications to register such marks fall within the ambit of the ECHR's

---

[124] Laurence R. Helfer, *The New Innovation Frontier? Intellectual Property and the European Court of Human Rights*, 49 Harv. Int'l L.J. 1, 11 (2008) [Helfer, *New Innovation Frontier*].

[125] *Anheuser-Busch Inc. v. Portugal*, No. 73049/01 (Eur. Ct. H.R. Grand Chamber Jan. 11, 2007).

property rights clause. On the particular facts presented, however, the court held that Portugal had not violated Article 1.

As is evident from this brief description, the ECtHR recognizes the property rights of multinational corporations as well as those of natural persons. Does the text of Article 1, reproduced at the beginning of this subsection, support this result? Is protecting the property rights of business entities consistent with the protection of other human rights? Consider the following proposal that the ECtHR adopt a "rule of law paradigm" to determine whether a restriction on intellectual property violates Article 1:

> Under a rule of law paradigm ... the EC[t]HR would treat intellectual property no differently than any other type of real, personal, or intangible property protected by Article 1. The Court would not consider the public-good qualities of intellectual property rights, nor would it concern itself with the social and cultural policies which justify the state's protection of those rights. Instead, it would find fault only with arbitrary government conduct, such as *ultra vires* actions [or the] failure to follow previously established rules and procedures.... The Court's scrutiny of national decisionmakers would thus be minimal and unobtrusive. It would allow governments unfettered discretion to fashion their domestic innovation and creativity policies as they see fit, provided that they adhere to previously established rules embodying those policies.[126]

Do you agree with the proposal? More generally, how active a role should the ECtHR play in shaping innovation and creativity policies in Europe? Should the court favor the rights of corporate intellectual property owners over the rights of individual users and consumers, or should it strike a distinctive human rights balance among the competing interests of these actors?

4. In a 2005 decision, *Dima v. Romania*,[127] the ECtHR considered the scope of the right of property in a copyright case in which a graphic artist brought an infringement action against the Romanian government in respect of designs for a new national emblem and seal. The artist developed the design in response to a competition that was held shortly after the fall of Romania's communist regime. The Parliament adopted a revised version of the design and listed Dima as the graphic designer in a statute published in Romania's official journal. The government did not, however, pay him for his work. Dima initiated proceedings in the Romanian courts against two private firms and a state-owned enterprise that had, at a profit, minted coins using the design. The artist was rebuffed by the Supreme Court of Justice, despite the

---

[126]	Helfer, *New Innovation Frontier, supra* note 124, at 37.
[127]	*Dima v. Romania*, No. 58472/00 (Eur. Ct. H.R. Nov. 16, 2005) (admissibility decision) (in French only).

court's acknowledgment that he had personally created the design. The court reasoned that the Parliament, which had commissioned the designs, was the author of the work. As an alternative ground, it held that state symbols could never be the subject of copyright.

Dima challenged these rulings as a violation of the right of property. The ECtHR rejected his complaint, principally on the basis that Dima had no rights to vindicate under Article 1 of the First Protocol because there was uncertainty as to the interpretation of national law (i.e., whether state symbols could be the subject of copyright) that was ultimately resolved against him. In so ruling, the ECtHR invoked its "limited power" to review allegations of legal or factual errors committed by national courts when interpreting domestic laws.

Is the ECtHR's approach in *Dima* consistent with the insistence in *General Comment No. 17*'s insistence that "States parties are obliged to prevent third parties from infringing the material interests of authors resulting from their productions" and that "States parties must ensure that third parties adequately compensate authors for any unreasonable prejudice suffered as a consequence of the unauthorized use of their productions"? The ECtHR signaled that its approach might have been different had the Romanian government retro-spectively applied intellectual property statutes with the effect of depriving Dima of vested property rights. The court also suggested that its review might have been more exacting had the Romanian courts had acted arbitrarily. In contrast to these concerns, the *General Comment* appears to be more focused on establishing a set of normative expectations as to initial entitlements to the moral and material interests resulting from creative work.[128]

5. The ECtHR has not addressed the deprivation of moral rights. Commentators are divided as to whether Article 1 of the First Protocol applies to moral rights.[129] The *General Comment*, in contrast, makes clear that the protections envisaged by Article 15(1)(c) extend to both moral and material interests. Suppose that a government misattributes authorship of a work or uses the work in a disparaging or distasteful context. Is a less def-erential attitude toward national courts' interpretation of domestic statutes warranted when moral rights are at issue?

---

[128] For additional analysis of *Dima*, see Helfer, *New Innovation Frontier*, *supra* note 124, at 14–18.

[129] *Compare* ALI RIZA ÇOBAN, PROTECTION OF PROPERTY RIGHTS WITHIN THE EUROPEAN CONVENTION ON HUMAN RIGHTS 149–50 (2004) (suggesting that the coverage extends only to economic interests), *with* Christophe Geiger, *"Constitutionalising" Intellectual Property Law? The Influence of Fundamental Rights on Intellectual Property in the European Union*, 37 I.I.C. 382, 383 & n.54 (2004) (suggesting that Article 1 extends to moral rights).

6. Another human rights treaty relevant in the European context is the Charter of Fundamental Rights of the European Union, Article 17(1) of which expressly includes protection of intellectual property in its statement of rights relating to property.

> 17(1) Everyone has the right to own, use, dispose of and bequeath his or her lawfully acquired possessions. No one may be deprived of his or her possessions, except in the public interest and in the cases and under the conditions provided for by law, subject to fair compensation being paid in good time for their loss. The use of property may be regulated by law in so far as is necessary for the general interest.
>
> (2) Intellectual property shall be protected.

Should any significance be accorded to the differences in syntax between the two parts of Article 17? That is, is it relevant that Article 17(2) does not state, "Everyone is entitled to own (etc.) intellectual property"? Is it significant that, unlike Article 17(1), Article 17(2) does not expressly make provision for limitations? What, if any, are the implications of characterizing the right in terms of "intellectual property" rather than a right to creators' "moral and material interests"?[130] The Charter entered into force in December 2009 with the adoption of the Treaty of Lisbon.[131] Even before that date, however, the Charter had been increasingly been invoked by the EU's political and judicial institutions, by the ECtHR, and by national courts in Europe.[132]

---

[130]   *See* Christophe Geiger, *Intellectual Property Shall Be Protected!? Article 17(2) of the Charter of Fundamental Rights of the European Union: A Mysterious Provision with an Unclear Scope*, 31 Eur. Intell. Prop. Rev. 113 (2009).

[131]   Matej Avbelj, *The Treaty of Lisbon: An Ongoing Search for Structural Equilibrium*, 16 Colum. J. Eur. L. 521 (2010).

[132]   *See, e.g., Bosphorus Hava Yollari Turizm ve Ticaret Anonim Sirketi v. Ireland*, No. 45036/98, 2005–VI Eur. Ct. H.R. para. 159 (Grand Chamber) ("Although not fully binding, the provisions of the Charter of Fundamental Rights of the European Union were substantially inspired by those of the Convention, and the Charter recognises the Convention as establishing the minimum human rights standards.").

Chapter 4

Rights to Freedom of Expression, to Cultural Participation, and to Benefit from Scientific Advancements

4.1. Introduction

Intellectual property rights can create scarcity[1] in some types of expression. For example, copyright owners can entirely suppress some forms of speech by seeking injunctions against those who want to express themselves by means of unauthorized uses of copyright-protected material. Alternatively, if license fees for such uses are required, the cost of particular expression increases, sometimes prohibitively. These actions implicate the right to freedom of expression – a right that is found in many international and regional human rights instruments and domestic constitutions. Limits on access to the manifestations and products of culture and science also implicate other rights and freedoms. Informed political participation, for example, requires access to information, such as news reports and other media – and many sources of such information can be protected by copyright.[2] These limits also implicate the human rights to participate in the cultural life of the community, to enjoy the arts, and to share in scientific advancement and its benefits – rights

---

[1] Intellectual property rights typically attach to "collective consumption goods ... which all enjoy in common ... the sense that each individual's consumption of such a good leads to no subtraction from any other individual's consumption of that good." Paul A. Samuelson, *The Pure Theory of Public Expenditure*, 36 REV. ECON. & STAT. 387, 387 (1954); *see also* Edwin C. Hettinger, *Justifying Intellectual Property*, 18 PHIL. & PUB. AFF. 31, 34 (1989). Information-embedded goods are often described as "nonrival." To create markets for these goods, the law intervenes by creating artificial scarcity though an array of different exclusive legal rights. *See generally* YOCHAI BENKLER, THE WEALTH OF NETWORKS 311 (2006).

[2] To the extent that copyright raises the cost of textbooks and other classroom materials, it has the potential to impede the realization of the human right to education. *See, e.g.*, Enyinna S. Nwauche, *The Judicial Construction of the Public Interest in South African Copyright Law*, 39 I.I.C. 917, 930 (2008) (noting that the right to education should be recognized as among the human rights that are furthered by the right to freedom of expression). We explore the relationship between copyright and education in Chapter 5.

that are set forth in Article 27 of the Universal Declaration of Human Rights (UDHR) and Article 15 of the International Covenant on Economic, Social, and Cultural Rights (ICESCR).

In this chapter, we first consider the range of philosophical rationales for the right to freedom of expression. We then survey some of the sources of the right in domestic, regional, and international law, and briefly consider rights to participate in culture and to benefit from scientific progress. Much of the analysis in the chapter considers ways that the right to freedom of expression has been invoked in judicial decisions relating to intellectual property. This analysis explores the intersection between two competing perspectives on the relationship between intellectual property and freedom of expression: first, intellectual property furthers freedom of expression values by encouraging speech; second, the right to freedom of expression imposes legal and normative limits on the scope of intellectual property rights. The first perspective reflects the view that intellectual property – copyright in particular – promotes speech through the incentives it provides to creators and those who invest in the dissemination of creative works. According to this perspective, free expression norms are "internalized" within the doctrines of copyright law. The second perspective reflects the view that the right to freedom of expression establishes a borderline beyond which intellectual property rights cannot – or should not – expand. This perspective is particularly salient in the context of newer theories of intellectual property, such as trademark dilution, where freedom of expression has been invoked as a basis for resisting seemingly exorbitant claims by intellectual property owners to control others' discourse. We observe similar concerns at the boundaries of patent law, where freedom of expression concerns are increasingly providing a platform for questioning, and perhaps resisting, the migration of patent rights into areas such as computer technology and biotechnology.

4.2. Rationales for the Right to Freedom of Expression

A "favorite topic for philosophers,"[3] freedom of expression is a vast and complex subject to which no brief summary can do justice. As Thomas Emerson notes in his foundational writings, "the problem of maintaining a system of freedom of expression in a society is one of the most complex any society has to face."[4]

[3]   Lawrence Alexander & Paul Horton, *Review Essay: The Impossibility of a Free Speech Principle*, 78 Nw. U. L Rev. 1319, 1321 (1983).
[4]   Thomas I. Emerson, *Toward a General Theory of the First Amendment*, 72 Yale L.J. 877, 889 (1963).

Perhaps the most enduring rationale for the right to freedom of expression is that it fosters a "marketplace of ideas." In his *Areopagitica* pamphlet, John Milton famously wrote: "Let [truth] and falsehood grapple; whoever knew truth put to the worst, in a free and open encounter?"[5] In like terms, John Mill reasoned that "since the general or prevailing opinion on any subject is rarely or never the whole truth, it is only by the collision of adverse opinions that the remainder of the truth had any choice of being supplied."[6] Elaborating on these themes, Justice Oliver Wendell Holmes[7] described the theory of the U.S. Constitution in terms of its commitment to "free trade in ideas – that the best test of truth is the power of the thought to get itself accepted in the competition of the market."[8]

Underlying such commitments is an assumption that truth will eventually percolate to the surface though the processes of societal discourse and free exchange of ideas, and, moreover, will prevail. As many commentators have observed, however, this assumption can seem decidedly sanguine, particularly so given obvious instances of "market failure" in various contexts in which speech occurs. In a more realist vein, Mill observed: "The dictum that truth always triumphs over persecution is one of those pleasant falsehoods which men repeat after one another till they pass into commonplaces, but which all experience refutes."[9] "Speech markets" – such as the traditional mass media – are heavily influenced by powerful clusters of commercial and political motivations. Within these markets, there is always the risk that "truth rarely catches up with a lie,"[10] as the U.S. Supreme Court once put the point. James Boyd White has suggested that there is a deep irony accompanying the marketplace of ideas metaphor. White argues that when this metaphor is

---

[5] JOHN MILTON, in T.H. WHITE (ED.), AREOPAGITICA: A SPEECH TO THE PARLIAMENT OF ENGLAND FOR LIBERTY OF UNLICENSED PRINTING 200 (1940).

[6] JOHN STUART MILL, ELIZABETH RAPPAPORT (ED.), ON LIBERTY 50 (Hackett Publ'g 1978) (1859). Mill did not believe that all speech should be beyond prosecution and was concerned that an individual's speech might be circumscribed where it led to a positive instigation to a "mischievous act." *See* THOMAS DAVID JONES, HUMAN RIGHTS: GROUP DEFAMATION, FREEDOM OF EXPRESSION AND THE LAW OF NATIONS 62 (1998).

[7] *Abrams v. United States*, 250 U.S. 616 (1919).

[8] *Id.* at 630.

[9] MILL, *supra* note 6, at 27; *see also* James Boyd White, *Free Speech and Valuable Speech: Silence, Dante, and the Marketplace of Ideas*, 51 UCLA. L. REV. 799, 812 (2004) (noting the tendency to *regulate* valuable speech, rather than leaving its truth value to be recognized within an unfettered marketplace). Identifying the problem of market failure does not, of course, solve the problem of calibrating governmental intervention into the marketplace – that is, identifying *ex ante* what a properly functioning marketplace might look like. *See generally* C. Erwin Baker, *Scope of the First Amendment Freedom of Speech*, 25 UCLA L. REV. 964 (1978).

[10] *Gertz v. Welch*, 418 U.S. 323, 344 (1974).

invoked, discourse tends to collapse into "slogans and clichés," and we fail to manifest those "qualities of mind and expression for which speech itself at its best is properly valued."[11] If marketplaces for speech were working as well as the theory promises we might do somewhat better in our discussions of the very topic that provides one of the most enduring rationales for this right.

A second set of justifications focuses more closely on the role of freedom of expression in political processes. Here, the argument is that democratic government requires citizens to be capable of assessing and evaluating the performance of elected officials. The free flow of information is critical to that task. In some iterations, this theory suggests that the right to question governmental action should endure (perhaps trump) even when speech has been restricted or regulated by legislation that has been enacted in accordance with democratic processes.[12] Some jurists conceive of this justification for the right to freedom of expression quite narrowly. For example, in the United States, Robert Bork has urged that the sole purpose served by the U.S. Constitution's guarantee of freedom of expression is to aid the political process, which suggests that these protections extend only to speech that is "expressly political."[13] "There is no basis for judicial intervention," he reasoned, "to protect any other form of expression, be it scientific, literary, or that variety of expression we call obscene or pornographic."[14]

Others have adopted a broader approach to the "democracy promoting" aspect of freedom of expression. Alexander Meikeljohn, for example, included a more diverse range of speech within the democracy-functioning justification: "people do need novels and dramas and paintings and poems," he reasons, "because they will be called upon to vote."[15] In other words, equipping citizens for democratic participation requires a diet that is broader than (manifestly) political speech. This rationale has been criticized for creating what Larry Alexander characterizes as a "capaciousness problem."[16] Alexander poses the question, "Who is to decide what the people need to know in order to perform the role of democratic citizen, and on what basis?"[17] To underscore this point, he posits a number of examples of speech that might – or might not – be

---

[11] White, *supra* note 9, at 814.
[12] FREDERICH F. SCHAUER, FREE SPEECH: A PHILOSOPHICAL ENQUIRY 40–44 (1982).
[13] Robert R. Bork, *Neutral Principles and Some First Amendment Problems*, 47 IND. L. REV. 1, 20 (1971).
[14] *Id.*
[15] Alexander Meiklejohn, *The First Amendment Is an Absolute*, 1961 SUP. CT. REV. 245, 263 (adapting language from Harry Kalven, *The Metaphysics of the Law of Obscenity*, 1960 SUP. CT. REV. 1, 15–16).
[16] LARRY ALEXANDER, IS THERE A RIGHT OF FREEDOM OF EXPRESSION? 138 (2005).
[17] *Id.*

characterized as "political": an advertisement claiming that a company treats workers well; warnings about the health risks of certain types of abortion procedures; information about genetically modified crops. Each of these could be characterized as political speech, but other labels could be equally appropriate, such as "commercial," "medical," or "scientific."[18] Some members of the judiciary have also identified similar problems with democracy-promoting rationales. As Justice Mokgoro, a member of the Constitutional Court of South Africa, put the point: "There is an inherent artificiality in categorising expression in principle as 'political' or not."[19]

"Individual self-realization" provides another set of justifications for the right to freedom of expression. Rationales grounded in individual autonomy contest the more "collectivist" focus of the democracy-promoting justifications. On this view, democratic government is (merely) a vehicle through which individual self-realization can be achieved. Accordingly, constitutional protections for freedom of expression must extend beyond the political arena and encompass speech that relates to all aspects of life: "Just as individuals need an open flow of information and opinion to aid them in making their electoral and governmental decisions, they similarly need a free flow of information and opinion to guide them in making other life-affecting decisions." Accordingly, "there is ... no logical reason for distinguishing the role speech plays in the political process."[20] This theory has found support in the domestic constitutional law of some nations. For example, in the Supreme Court of Canada, Justices L'Heureux-Dubé, Gonthier, and Bastarache have reasoned that individual self-fulfillment is one of the principles underlying freedom of expression, and that this conclusion supports a basic commitment to protecting all speech regardless of its "popularity, aesthetic or moral tastefulness or mainstream acceptance."[21] In the South African case previously mentioned, Justice Mokgoro expanded on these themes as follows:

> The most commonly cited rationale is that the search for truth is best facilitated in a free "marketplace of ideas." That obviously presupposes that both the supply and the demand side of the market will be unfettered. But of more relevance here than this "marketplace" conception of the role of free speech is the consideration that freedom of speech is a *sine qua non* for every person's right to realise her or his full potential as a human being, free of the imposition of heteronomous power. Viewed in that light, the right to receive others' expressions

---

[18] *Id.*
[19] *Case v. Minister of Safety and Security; Curtis v. Minister of Safety and Security*, (CCT20/95, CCT21/95) [1996] ZACC 7; 1996 (3) SA 617; 1996 (5) BCLR 608 (May 9, 1996), para. 23 (S. Afr.).
[20] Martin H. Redish, *The Value of Free Speech*, 130 U. Pa. L. Rev. 591, 604 (1982).
[21] *R. v. Sharpe*, [2001] 194 D.L.R. (4th) 1, para. 141 (Can.).

has more than merely instrumental utility, as a predicate for the addressee's meaningful exercise of her or his own rights of free expression. It is also foundational to each individual's empowerment to autonomous self-development.[22]

These contrasting perspectives have provoked a rich dialogue among commentators.[23] Collectivist approaches to expressive freedoms are, at least in part, a response to perceived inadequacies of the emphasis on individual autonomy in the analysis of the justifications for protecting expressive freedom. Moreover, to the extent that the personal autonomy justification provokes adoption of strong positions against regulation of speech, it has been criticized for failing to invoke empirical evidence that well-reasoned and carefully implemented government regulation would *not* be respectful of autonomy, or, at least, would be any less respectful than giving free rein to the marketplace of ideas.[24] In addition, theories grounded in personal autonomy may fail to take sufficient account of the material circumstances of the individuals whose ability to make autonomous choices is valorized by this set of rationales for protecting expressive freedoms. Entrenched inequalities may belie the autonomy-promoting justifications for the right to "free" expression,[25] particularly where an awareness of one's material circumstances makes certain options for one's life either unimaginable or unattainable. In addition, the personal autonomy rationale might not take sufficient account of ways that speech, particularly commercial speech, contributes to preference formulation, most typically through advertising.[26]

A further rationale for protecting expressive freedoms as a human right is suggested in the "capabilities" approach to human rights, which is advanced in some of the work by Amartya Sen and Martha Nussbaum.[27] Part of this project, particularly as espoused by Nussbaum, is to develop "working lists"[28] of human capabilities, to be generated through a process of empirical observations, which "can be convincingly argued to be of central importance in

---

[22] *Case*, (5) BCLR para. 26.

[23] *See* Robert Post, *Managing Deliberation: The Quandary of Democratic Dialogue*, 103 ETHICS 645 (1993).

[24] Susan T. Brison, *The Autonomy Defense of Free Speech*, 108 ETHICS 312, 334 (1998).

[25] *See* Meir Dan-Cohen, *Conceptions of Choice and Conceptions of Autonomy*, 102 ETHICS 221 (1992).

[26] *See* Brison, *supra* note 24, at 337; JOHN KENNEDY GALBRAITH, THE AFFLUENT SOCIETY 24 (4th ed. 1998).

[27] *See, e.g.*, Martha C. Nussbaum, *Capabilities and Human Rights*, 66 FORDHAM L. REV. 273 (1997) (exploring the relationship between the theory of "capabilities" advanced by Professors Nussbaum and Sen and the rhetoric and traditions of human rights).

[28] Professor Nussbaum's articulation of human capabilities is grounded in cross-cultural, empirical research. In her words, the project is "open-ended and humble; it can always be contested and remade." *Id.* at 286.

any human life, whatever else [a] person pursues or chooses."[29] Among these capabilities are a number that are closely associated with "senses, imagination, and thought." Nussbaum characterizes one set of human capabilities in the following terms:

> Being able to use the senses; being able to imagine, to think, and to reason – and to do these things in a "truly human" way, a way informed and cultivated by an adequate education, including, but by no means limited to, literacy and basic mathematical and scientific training. Being able to use imagination and thought in connection with experiencing and producing expressive works and events of one's own choice, religious, literary, musical, and so forth. Being able to use one's mind in ways protected by guarantees of freedom of expression and with respect to both political and artistic speech and freedom of religious exercise.[30]

The right to freedom of expression is thus positioned at the intersection of many different concepts and intellectual traditions. This diversity of perspectives and domestic, regional, and international sources suggests that it is likely to be unhelpful to approach challenges to intellectual property grounded in the "right to freedom of expression" in a monolithic way. This point has particular relevance when we move from the variety of philosophical justifications to consider the right to freedom of expression in different institutional and textual contexts.[31]

4.3. International, Regional, and Domestic Law Sources

The human right to freedom of expression appears in numerous legal, political, and institutional contexts. Different histories, traditions, and heuristic structures affect the character and content of the "right" in different contexts. The right to freedom of expression is a complex of related concepts, including freedom of the press, information rights, freedom of thought and opinion, and the right to receive information. The scope of the right is also shaped by the duties that accompany it, as well as by the limits that can be imposed on the right in some circumstances.

In U.S. constitutional discourse, there have been powerful assertions of the primacy of the right to freedom of speech. Consider this statement by Justice

---

[29] *Id.*

[30] *Id.* at 287.

[31] Cf. Ernst-Ulrich Petersmann, *The "Human Rights Approach" Advocated by the UN High Commissioner for Human Rights and by the International Labour Organization: Is It Relevant for WTO Law and Policy?*, in Ernst-Ulrich Petersmann (Ed.), Reforming the World Trading System: Legitimacy, Efficiency, and Democratic Governance 357, 370 (2005) (suggesting that international and domestic constitutional law should be regarded as "a functional unity for promoting and protecting human rights").

Cardozo: "Of that freedom one may say that it is the matrix, the indispensable condition, of nearly every other form of freedom. With rare aberrations a pervasive recognition of that truth can be traced in our history, political and legal."[32] Structurally and historically, the right to freedom of expression has a flavor of fundamentality within the U.S. legal and political context: it is a key part of the "first" amendment to the Constitution, and it was included within the U.S. constitutional framework long before the document reflected any kind of genuine commitment to many other fundamental rights, particularly the equality of all people.

In the international context, the right to freedom of expression is located within a broader set of civil, political, and socioeconomic rights. Moreover, unlike the U.S. constitution, international human rights law has reflected from the outset an urgent and *universal* commitment to human dignity and equality. Some national regimes also reflect the connection between the right to expressive freedoms and other rights. In this analysis, these rights, together with the right to freedom of expression, all "[underpin] an entitlement to participate in an ongoing process of communicative interaction that is of both instrumental and intrinsic value."[33]

With these ideas in mind, we move from broader conceptual themes to consider the content and scope of the right to freedom of expression in different international, regional, and domestic law instruments.[34] Even before any of the U.N.'s formal human rights documents had been written, it was the topic of a resolution of the U.N. General Assembly at its first session in 1946, which announced that "freedom of information is a fundamental human right and ... the touchstone of all the freedoms to which the United Nations is consecrated."[35] Two years later, the preamble to the UDHR recorded that "the advent of a world in which human beings shall enjoy freedom of speech and belief and freedom from fear and want has been proclaimed as the highest aspiration of the common people." Article 19 of the UDHR more specifically provides: "Everyone has the right to the freedom of opinion and expression; this right includes freedom to hold opinions without interference and to seek, receive and impart information and ideas through any media and regardless of frontiers."[36] The latter statement influenced the subsequent

---

[32] *Palko v. Connecticut*, 302 U.S. 319, 327 (1937).

[33] *Case v. Minister of Safety and Security; Curtis v. Minister of Safety and Security*, (CCT20/95, CCT21/95) [1996] ZACC 7; 1996 (3) SA 617; 1996 (5) BCLR 608 (May 9, 1996), para. 27.

[34] HENRY J. STEINER & PHILIP ALSTON, INTERNATIONAL HUMAN RIGHTS IN CONTEXT: LAW, POLITICS, MORALS 57 (2000).

[35] G.A. Res. 59(I), at 95, U.N. Doc. A/64/Add.1 (Dec. 14, 1946).

[36] Universal Declaration of Human Rights, G.A. Res. 217A(III), at 71, U.N. GAOR, 3d Sess., 1st plen. mtg., U.N. Doc. A/810 (Dec. 12, 1948). The contemporary history of the (complex

adoption of the right. Article 19 of the 1966 International Covenant on Civil and Political Rights (ICCPR), for example, provides more detail on what the right includes, and articulates a set of basic principles concerning permissible limitations[37]:

(1) Everyone shall have the right to hold opinions without interference.

(2) Everyone shall have the right to freedom of expression; this right shall include freedom to seek, receive and impart information and ideas of all kinds, regardless of frontiers, either orally, in writing or in print, in the form of art, or through any other media of his choice.

(3) The exercise of the rights provided for in paragraph 2 of this article carries with it special duties and responsibilities. It may therefore be subject to certain restrictions, but these shall only be such as are provided by law and are necessary: (a) For respect of the rights or reputations of others; (b) For the protection of national security or of public order (ordre public), or of public health or morals.

Regional human rights instruments also typically include a commitment to the right to freedom of expression. A particularly full statement appears in

and often fraught) development of the right to freedom of information at international law is usefully recounted in Erwin D. Canham, *International Freedom of Information*, 14 LAW & CONTEMP. PROBS. 589 (1949).

[37] G.A. Res. 2200A(XXI), at 52, U.N. GAOR Supp. No. 16, U.N. Doc. A/6316 (1966). The ICCPR contains a set of further obligations and principles that relate to limitations on the right to expressive freedoms. For example, Article 5.1 of the ICCPR provides: "Nothing in the present Covenant may be interpreted as implying for any State, group or person any right to engage in any activity or perform any act aimed at the destruction of any of the rights and freedoms recognized herein or at their limitation to a greater extent than is provided for in the present Covenant." Article 26 imposes a positive requirement to prohibit discrimination on the grounds of "political or other opinion." Article 17 requires member states to provide protections against arbitrary or unlawful interference with privacy, and against unlawful attacks on honor and reputation.

A commitment to the right to freedom of expression is integral to many other human rights instruments. For example, the 1969 International Convention on the Elimination of All Forms of Racial Discrimination obliges States Parties to guarantee the right of everyone, "without distinction as to race, color, or national or ethnic origin, to equality before the law," including rights to "freedom of thought, conscience and religion," and "freedom of opinion and expression." Art. 5, Dec. 21, 1965, 660 U.N.T.S. 195. It is also included in Article 13 of the 1989 United Nations Convention on the Rights of the Child, November 20, 1989, 1577 U.N.T.S. 3. The 1981 Convention on the Elimination of All Forms of Discrimination against Women incorporates the right to freedom of expression through a broad nondiscrimination principle: "States Parties shall take in all fields, in particular in the political, social, economic and cultural fields, all appropriate measures, including legislation, to ensure the full development and advancement of women, for the purpose of guaranteeing them the exercise and enjoyment of human rights and fundamental freedoms on a basis of equality with men." Art. 3, Sep. 3, 1981, 1249 U.N.T.S. 13.

Article 13 of the American Convention of Human Rights, which entered into force in 1978:

1. Everyone has the right to freedom of thought and expression. This right includes freedom to seek, receive, and impart information and ideas of all kinds, regardless of frontiers, either orally, in writing, in print, in the form of art, or through any other medium of one's choice.
2. The exercise of the right provided for in the foregoing paragraph shall not be subject to prior censorship but shall be subject to subsequent imposition of liability, which shall be expressly established by law to the extent necessary to ensure:
   a. respect for the rights or reputations of others; or
   b. the protection of national security, public order, or public health or morals.
3. The right of expression may not be restricted by indirect methods or means, such as the abuse of government or private controls over newsprint, radio broadcasting frequencies, or equipment used in the dissemination of information, or by any other means tending to impede the communication and circulation of ideas and opinions.
4. Notwithstanding the provisions of paragraph 2 earlier, public entertainments may be subject by law to prior censorship for the sole purpose of regulating access to them for the moral protection of childhood and adolescence.
5. Any propaganda for war and any advocacy of national, racial, or religious hatred that constitute incitements to lawless violence or to any other similar action against any person or group of persons on any grounds including those of race, color, religion, language, or national origin shall be considered as offenses punishable by law.

According to these provisions, the exercise of the right to freedom of expression may not be conditioned on the form of the relevant information: the Convention guarantees individuals the right to receive and impart the information "orally, in writing, in print, in the form of art, or through any other medium of [their] choice." As will be discussed later, the issue of the medium in which information is imparted has been important to debates about the interaction between copyright and the right to freedom of expression.

Another important regional instrument recognizing a right to freedom of expression is the European Convention on Human Rights (ECHR).[38]

---

[38] Convention for the Protection of Human Rights and Fundamental Freedoms, Sept. 3, 1953, 213 U.N.T.S. 221 [ECHR].

Article 10, which, as we discuss later, has been invoked in a number of cases involving intellectual property rights, provides:

1. Everyone has the right to freedom of expression. This right shall include freedom to hold opinions and to receive and impart information and ideas without interference by public authority and regardless of frontiers.
2. The exercise of these freedoms, since it carries with it duties and responsibilities, may be subject to such formalities, conditions, restrictions or penalties as are prescribed by law and are necessary in a democratic society, in the interests of national security, territorial integrity or public safety, for the prevention of disorder or crime, for the protection of health or morals, for the protection of the reputation or rights of others, for preventing the disclosure of information received in confidence, or for maintaining the authority and impartiality of the judiciary.

In domestic law, the First Amendment to the U.S. Constitution is among the most venerable statements of the right to freedom of expression. It provides, "Congress shall make no law ... abridging the freedom of speech, or of the press."[39] The basic principles captured by the First Amendment are now echoed in many other domestic constitutions.[40] More modern instruments build on these basic principles and add details that further delineate the scope of right, often drawing inspiration from international human rights instruments. Domestic articulations frequently also include specific limitations on the right. The Canadian Charter of Rights and Freedoms, for instance, lists "freedom of thought, belief, opinion and expression, including freedom of the press and other media of communication" among "fundamental freedoms."[41] The Canadian Charter also includes a "justified limitations clause," according to which rights may be "subject only to such reasonable limits prescribed by law as can be demonstrably justified in a free and democratic society."[42]

The freedom of expression clauses in other national constitutions are also noteworthy. For example, Article 16 of 1996 Constitution of the Republic of South Africa sets forth the right to freedom of expression in the following terms:

1. Everyone has the right to freedom of expression, which includes:
   a. freedom of the press and other media;
   b. freedom to receive or impart information or ideas;

---

[39] U.S. Const. amend. I.
[40] Many countries provide for freedom of speech in their domestic constitutions. *See, e.g.,* Ir. Const., 1937, art. 40(6)(1) (Ireland); Kenpō, art. 21 (Japan).
[41] Constitution Act Part I, 1982, Canada Act 1982, Schedule B, ch. 11 (U.K.), *as reprinted in* R.S.C., No. 44 (Appendix 1985).
[42] *Id.* art. 1.

    c. freedom of artistic creativity; and

    d. academic freedom and freedom of scientific research.

The South African Constitution explicitly excludes from protection a number of types of speech that have caused difficulties for other national constitutional systems: "propaganda for war," "incitement of imminent violence," and "advocacy of hatred that is based on race, ethnicity, gender or religion, and that constitutes incitement to cause harm."[43]

The Constitution of Venezuela offers even more detail on the content and context of the right, linking expressive freedoms to issues of censorship and education, as well as the citizen's own responsibility for his or her speech:

> Article 57: Everyone has the right to express freely his or her thoughts, ideas or opinions orally, in writing or by any other form of expression, and to use for such purpose any means of communication and diffusion, and no censorship shall be established. Anyone making use of this right assumes full responsibility for everything expressed. Anonymity, war propaganda, discriminatory messages or those promoting religious intolerance are not permitted. Censorship restricting the ability of public officials to report on matters for which they are responsible is prohibited.

> Article 58: Communications are free and plural, and involve the duties and responsibilities indicated by law. Everyone has the right to timely, truthful and impartial information, without censorship, in accordance with the principles of this Constitution, as well as the right to reply and corrections when they are directly affected by inaccurate or offensive information. Children and adolescents have the right to receive adequate information for purposes of their overall development.

The United Kingdom was once the paradigmatic example of a modern democracy lacking a Bill of Rights with explicit protection of freedom of expression. That changed with the domestic incorporation of most of the ECHR in the Human Rights Act of 1998 (U.K.), which entered into force in 2000. This Act, which requires courts to interpret laws consistently with the ECHR, including Article 10, the Convention's freedom of expression provision, reproduced earlier. The Act also requires government agencies to conform their conduct to the ECHR, unless doing so is rendered impossible by another act of Parliament.

Australia remains an important exception to these trends. It lacks bespoke parliamentary protections for freedom of expression. Australia's written constitution, while modeled in large part on that of the United States, does not

---

[43] S. Afr. Const. 1996, § 16.

include a Bill of Rights. The framers of the Federal Constitution believed that citizens' rights were "best left to the protection of the common law in association with the doctrine of parliamentary supremacy."[44] Bills of Rights, including protections for expressive freedoms, have, however, been adopted in Australia at the state and territory levels.[45] Conceptually, Australian courts have tended to characterize the constitutional guarantee as a "freedom" rather than a constitutional "right" – though the distinction between these two characterizations remains somewhat elusive.[46] In a series of cases from the 1990s, the High Court of Australia recognized that the system of "representative government" created by the Federal Constitution requires protection for certain kinds of political communication. This principle might even be relied upon to render federal enactments invalid.[47] Subsequent High Court cases appear to have retreated somewhat, preferring instead to ground the freedom in particular provisions of the Constitution – such as those that provide for federal elections – rather than in the more general principle of representative government.[48]

4.4. Rights to Participate in Culture and to Benefit from Scientific Progress

In Article 15(1)(a) and (b) of the ICESCR the following human rights are set forth: the rights "to take part in cultural life" and "to enjoy the benefits of scientific progress and its applications."[49] The remaining provisions of Article 15 add three further elements:

2. The steps to be taken by the States Parties to the present Covenant to achieve the full realization of this right shall include those necessary for the conservation, the development and the diffusion of science and culture.

[44] *Australian Capital Television v. Commonwealth*, (1992) 177 C.L.R. 106, 135–36 (Mason C.J.).

[45] Human Rights Act, 2004, c. 5 (Austl.) (enacted by Parliament of Australian Capital Territory); Charter of Human Rights and Responsibilities Act, 2006 (Victoria, Austrl.). In December 2008, the federal government tasked a high-level consultative group to examine whether a national bill of rights should be adopted. *See McClelland Names Human Rights Consultation Panel*, AUSTL. BROAD. CORP. (ABC) NEWS, Dec. 10, 2008.

[46] *See* Robert Burrell & James Stellios, *Copyright and Freedom of Political Communication in Australia*, in JONATHAN GRIFFITHS & UMA SUTHERSANEN (EDS.), COPYRIGHT AND FREE SPEECH: COMPARATIVE AND INTERNATIONAL ANALYSES 257, 262 (2005).

[47] *See, e.g., Nationwide News v. Wills* (1992) 177 C.L.R. 1.

[48] *See Lange v. Australian Broad. Corp.* (1997) 189 C.L.R. 529.

[49] Although Article 27(1) of the UDHR contains similarly worded commitments, there are a few terminological distinctions. Article 27(1) provides: "Everyone has the right freely to participate in the cultural life of the community [and] to enjoy the arts." On the significance of the omission of "freely" and the reference to "the community," *see* ECOSOC, Comm. on Econ., Soc. & Cultural Rights, *Background Paper: Cultural Life in the Context of Human Rights* 3, U.N. Doc. E/C.12/40/13 (May 9, 2008) (prepared by Yvonne Donders).

3. The States Parties to the present Covenant undertake to respect the freedom indispensable for scientific research and creative activity.
4. The States Parties to the present Covenant recognize the benefits to be derived from the encouragement and development of international contacts and co-operation in the scientific and cultural fields.

The normative content of this set of rights has been slow to emerge. Analysis of the relationship between intellectual property and this cluster of rights is even more underdeveloped. Quite recently, however, these rights have been emphasized in the context of the growing concern with finding human rights bases for limiting perceived excesses of intellectual property rights. The right to enjoy the benefits of science has been invoked as a counterweight to the expansion of intellectual property rights in technical fields, particularly patents. Likewise, the right to participate in culture might be understood as articulating a set of legal obligations and values that limit copyright protections, to the extent that those protections impose barriers (typically, but not exclusively, monetary barriers) to accessing copyright-protected cultural products.

As Audrey Chapman notes, the right to the benefits of science "is so obscure and its interpretation so neglected that the overwhelming majority of human rights advocates, governments, and international human rights bodies appear to be oblivious to its existence."[50] Recently, UNESCO has taken an interest in the normative content of the right to the benefits of scientific progress. In 2007 and 2009, meetings of experts sponsored by UNESCO were convened to consider the scope and interpretation of Article 15(1)(b). One outcome of these meetings was the 2009 *Venice Statement on the Right to Enjoy the Benefits of Scientific Progress and Its Applications*.[51] The *Venice Statement* addresses a large range of issues that are relevant to human existence, including food production, advances in medicine, and information technology. The document directly confronts the relationship between intellectual property rights and the right to enjoy the benefits of scientific progress and its applications in the following terms:

> The right to enjoy the benefits of scientific progress and its applications may create tensions with the intellectual property regime, which is a temporary

[50] Audrey R. Chapman, *Towards an Understanding of the Right to Enjoy the Benefits of Scientific Progress and Its Applications*, 8 J. HUM. RTS. 1, 1 (2009).
[51] UNESCO, Experts' Meeting on the Right to Enjoy the Benefits of Scientific Progress and Its Application, Venice, Italy, July 16–17, 2009, *Venice Statement on the Right to Enjoy the Benefits of Scientific Progress and Its Applications, available at* http://shr.aaas.org/article15/Reference_Materials/internationaldocuments.html [*Venice Statement*].

monopoly with a valuable social function that should be managed in accordance with a common responsibility to prevent the unacceptable prioritization of profit for some over benefit for all.[52]

Characterizing intellectual property as a "temporary monopoly," the document echoes the language used in *General Comment No. 17* issued by the Committee on Economic, Social, and Cultural Rights on Article 15(1)(c), the right of everyone to benefit from the protection of the moral and material interests resulting from any scientific, literary or artistic production of which he or she is the author.[53] The General Comment, which we consider in detail in Chapter 3, emphasizes that "intellectual property rights" are ontologically and normatively distinct from the human rights protected by Article 15(1) (c), and it stresses the need to balance the provisions of that article against other human rights, including those set forth in Articles 15(1)(a) and (b).

A number of other passages in the *Venice Statement* advert to points of intersection with intellectual property. For example, the document states:

> Science is not only about advancing knowledge of a specific subject matter, nor merely about procuring a set of data and testing hypotheses that may be useful for some practical purposes. It is also, at the same time, about enhancing the conditions for further scientific and cultural activity.[54]

The latter statement may have relevance for specific doctrines of patent law, including the ability of patents to privatize tools of basic research, such as mathematical algorithms and genetic material,[55] and the scope of exceptions that permit third parties to experiment using the patented invention.[56] The concern with enhancing conditions for future scientific activity may also implicate emerging controversies that concern the assertion of patent rights to preclude the testing of patented inventions in critical areas of human health, such as diagnostic medicine.[57]

---

[52] *Id.* para. 10.
[53] Comm. on Econ., Soc. & Cultural Rights, *General Comment No. 17: The Right of Everyone to Benefit from the Protection of the Moral and Material Interests Resulting from Any Scientific, Literary or Artistic Production of Which He Is the Author*, art. 15(1)(c), U.N. Doc. E/C.12/2005 (Nov. 21, 2005) [*General Comment No. 17*].
[54] *Venice Statement, supra* note 51, para. 8.
[55] *See infra* Part 4.5(C).
[56] In the U.S. context, *see Madey v. Duke University*, 307 F.3d 1351 (Fed. Cir. 2002) (narrowing the scope of the experimental use defense under U.S. patent law). *See also* Janice M. Mueller, *No "Dilettante Affair": Rethinking the Experimental Use Exception to Patent Infringement for BioMedical Research Tools*, 76 Wash. L. Rev. 1 (2001).
[57] *See* Brenda M. Simon, *Patent Cover-Ups*, 47 Hous. L. Rev. ___ (forthcoming 2011) (discussing the assertion of patent rights to impede diagnostic testing).

In its exposition of the normative content of the right, the *Venice Statement* sets forth the following "areas of contemporary controversy": "stem cell research, nanotechnologies, nuclear energy, GMOs, climate change, generic seeds that cannot be reused, cloning, ethics of science and technology, new technologies in the working environment."[58] The *Venice Statement* identifies a need for impact assessments in these areas. It is significant that in most, if not all, of these areas, intellectual property rights have a significant role to play in the development and financing of the underlying technologies.

Also relevant to intellectual property are the Statement's prescriptions concerning states' obligations "to respect the freedoms indispensable for scientific research and creative activity" including "freedom of thought" and the freedom "to hold opinions without interference, and to seek, receive, and impart information and ideas of all kinds."[59] As we discuss later in this chapter, in some circumstances intellectual property protection can make the rights to express opinions and receive information more difficult to realize. In addition, the duty of states to respect the right is described as including the obligation "to respect the freedom of the scientific community and its individual members to collaborate with others both within an across the country's borders, including the freed exchange of information, research ideas and results."[60] While this part of the document seems to focus most directly on the freedom to participate in scientific inquiry without government interference, intellectual property doctrines may be relevant to the ability to exercise this right. For example, if defenses and exceptions to patent rights are too narrowly conceived, experimental work using patented inventions may be impeded. The *Venice Statement* also explains that the obligation to "fulfill" this right includes the obligation to adopt a legal and policy framework and to establish institutions "to promote the development and diffusion of science and technology in a manner consistent with fundamental human rights" and "to promote access to the benefits of science and its applications on a nondiscriminatory basis."[61] States are also urged to "apply human rights–based approaches to their policies and activities in the field of science and technology" so as "to ensure that science and technology policy serve human needs in addition to economic prosperity."[62]

In sum, the *Venice Statement* asks governments and civil society to consider not only whether intellectual property protection results in an impediment

---

[58] *Venice Statement, supra* note 51, para. 13(c).
[59] *Id.* para. 14.
[60] *Id.*
[61] *Id.* para. 16.
[62] *Id.* para. 24.

to the advancement of science *per se* but also whether it hinders realization of the public's right to benefit from scientific advances.

In a detailed elaboration of the obligations embedded in the right to enjoy the benefits of scientific progress, Chapman writes:

> A human rights approach focuses on the status of the most disadvantaged rather than some societal average or the interests of the most advanced and affluent communities. Applied to the right to the benefits of scientific progress, this requires a form of affirmative action, that is, specific investments in science and technology likely to benefit those at the bottom of the economical and social scale. In undertaking the determinations of the benefits that are likely to accrue from investments into specific areas of science and technology, potential profits to investors and improvements in the standards of the affluent should count for much less than improving the status of the vulnerable and bringing them up to mainstream standards. In poor countries this commitment also means giving priority to the development, importation, and dissemination of simple and inexpensive technologies that can improve the life of the disadvantaged rather than the more complex and high-technology state-of-the-art innovations that disproportionately favor the educated and economically affluent individuals and regions.[63]

This call for distributive justice in the technological and scientific context challenges some of the normative assumptions underlying modern intellectual property regimes. Distributive justice concerns do not typically inform intellectual property's analytical frameworks. Patent law, for example, is almost invariably characterized as a policy tool whose principal aim is "to promote innovation, encourage the development of new technologies, and increase the fund of human knowledge."[64] A human rights focus contests these assumptions in various ways. The poorest and most vulnerable members of the human family do not always, or ever, benefit from the most sophisticated or advanced technologies. Their right to benefit from scientific progress cannot be reduced to the right to *wait* to benefit from any trickledown effects that may result from the aggregate increase in societal welfare flowing from the technological progress that intellectual property encourages. Chapman's analysis suggests that the distributive justice demands of this right must be more expansive (and more immediate) than the narrow utilitarian emphases that dominate in intellectual property law thinking. She writes: "the benefits of an intellectual property system tend at best to be long-term and tenuous while in the short-term, intellectual property protection increases the cost of development, especially since in the globalized economy

---

[63] Chapman, *supra* note 50, at 14.
[64] Dan L. Burk & Mark Lemley, *Policy Levers in Patent Law*, 89 Va. L. Rev. 1575, 1576 (2003).

the patents awarded and resulting payment for the use of these technologies go primarily to foreign multinational corporations."[65]

Aside from the reference to "tensions" between the exercise of this right and intellectual property, however, the *Venice Statement* offers no detailed analysis of the interaction between these two sources of law. The document's approach to intellectual property's contribution to the regulation of science and technology appears to be consistent with the "conflicts" model of interaction between human rights and intellectual property that we discuss in Chapter 1. An embedded assumption of this model is the primacy of human rights over intellectual property. Yet, as is frequently the case within the conflicts model, the *Venice Statement* offers no concrete guidance as to how the tensions are to be negotiated in the contemporary realpolitik of international and domestic legal regimes. Even more noteworthy is the document's lack of engagement with the human rights bases for protecting authors and scientists that are set forth in Article 15(1)(c) of the ICESCR, and, as we discuss in Chapter 3, in other human rights instruments as well. Article 15(1)(c) articulates a human rights basis for protecting at least some of the economic interests of scientists and authors. Given the ontological distinctions between these sources of human rights and "intellectual property rights," the rights set forth in Articles 15(1)(a) and (b) cannot, at least not within a human rights framework, be considered to have primacy over them.

Similar issues arise in the context of the right to participate in culture.[66] "Culture" and "rights to culture" are relevant to an extensive body of human rights law.[67] This is especially apparent when culture is understood in its anthropological sense, as encompassing aspects of life such as language, norms, values, beliefs, and practices that are specific to a certain human group and distinguish that group from others.[68] Article 15(1)(a) of the ICESCR

---

[65] Chapman, *supra* note 50, at 29.

[66] In May 2008, the Committee held a day of discussion devoted to Article 15(1)(a). Several submissions explored the relationship between culture and intellectual property. *See* Comm. on Econ., Soc. & Cultural Rights, Day of General Discussion on "The Right to Take Part in Cultural Life" (May 9, 2008), *available at* http://www2.ohchr.org/english/bodies/cescr/discussion090508.htm. In December 2009, the Committee issued *General Comment No. 21: Right of Everyone to Take Part in Cultural Life* (art. 15, para. 1 (a), of the International Covenant on Economic, Social and Cultural Rights) [*General Comment No. 21*].

[67] *See generally* Stephen Marks, *UNESCSO and Human Rights: The Implementation of Rights Relating to Education, Science, Culture and Communication*, 13 Tex. Int'l L.J. 35, 42 (1977).

[68] For example, protection of the rights to respect for family life and privacy, guaranteed by Articles 17(1) and 23(1) of the ICCPR, requires some analysis of what "family" means for a particular social group, an analysis that must often occur against the background of specific cultural norms that concern areas of life that are far more far-reaching than "high" culture

and its antecedent, Article 27(1) of the UDHR, add to this body of human rights law by treating the right to participate in culture as a right that must be protected for its own sake.

The framers of this right, as it was set forth in Article 27(1), appear to have had in mind a narrow view of culture that encompassed access to a preordained canon of "great" works that had previously been the sole preserve of cultural élites.[69] In general, the drafting history of Article 27(1) reveals little else as to the meaning or scope of the right to participate in cultural life. Most of the discussion focused on the companion right that is set forth in Article 27(2) (and, now, Article 15(1)(c) of the ICESCR), the right to benefit from the moral and material interests of creativity in the artistic and scientific fields.[70] Since this initial framing, however, studies by international agencies have elaborated on the content of the right to participate in culture. In the late 1960s UNESCO started to embrace a more expansive concept of culture in the context of this right, and, in 1976, it issued a *Recommendation on Participation by the People at Large in Cultural Life*, which characterized culture as "includ[ing] all forms of creativity and expression of groups and individuals."[71] Building upon UNESCO's intervention, the Committee on Economic, Social and Cultural Rights broadened the notion of culture embodied by this right, describing it as "the right of everyone to take part in cultural life which he or she considers pertinent, and to manifest his or her own culture."[72] Today, it is widely agreed that the concerns of cultural rights are much broader than consumer-based culture. As one commentator has put it, "cultural rights should accordingly be considered more than merely rights to enjoy a cultural product. Cultural rights are real human rights aimed at protecting an important part of human dignity."[73]

---

or other kinds of narrow conceptualizations of "culture." *See, e.g.*, Human Rights Comm., Communication No. 549/1993, *Hopu & Bessert v. France*, UN Doc. CCPR/C/60/D/549/1993/Rev.1 (1997) (the concept of "family" includes the concept of "family" as understood by the society in question).

[69] *See* Roger O'Keefe, *Cultural Life under the ICESCR*, 47 INT'L & COMP. L.Q. 904, 912 (1998).

[70] Yvonne Donders, *The Legal Framework of the Right to Take Part in Cultural Life*, in YVONNE DONDERS & VLADIMIR VOLODIN (EDS.), HUMAN RIGHTS IN EDUCATION, SCIENCE AND CULTURE: LEGAL DEVELOPMENTS AND CHALLENGES 231, 233 (2009).

[71] UNESCO, *Recommendation on Participation by the People at Large in Cultural Life*, para. I.3(a), UNESCO Doc. 19 C/Resolutions (1976).

[72] Comm. on Econ., Soc. & Cultural Rights, *Revised Guidelines Regarding the Form and Contents of Reports to Be Submitted by States Parties under Articles 16 and 17 of the International Covenant on Economic, Social and Cultural Rights*, at 88, para. 1, U.N. Doc. E/1991/23. (Articles 16 and 17 of the ICESCR, which are in Part IV of that document, concern states parties' reporting obligations.)

[73] Donders, *supra* note 70, 231.

In its recently published *General Comment No. 21: Right of everyone to take part in cultural life*, the Committee on Economic, Social and Cultural Rights characterized the phrase "cultural life" as "an explicit reference to culture as a living process, historical, dynamic and evolving, with a past, a present and a future,"[74] In the Committee's view, the concept of culture "must be seen not as a series of isolated manifestations or hermetic compartments, but as an interactive process whereby individuals and communities, while preserving their specificities and purposes, give expression to the culture of humanity."[75]

The *General Comment* explained the scope of the right in the following terms:

> There are, among others, three interrelated main components of the right to participate or take part in cultural life: (a) participation in, (b) access to, and (c) contribution to cultural life.
>
> (a) *Participation* covers in particular the right of everyone – alone, or in association with others or as a community – to act freely, to choose his or her own identity, to identify or not with one or several communities or to change that choice, to take part in the political life of society, to engage in one's own cultural practices and to express oneself in the language of one's choice. Everyone also has the right to seek and develop cultural knowledge and expressions and to share them with others, as well as to act creatively and take part in creative activity;
> (b) *Access* covers in particular the right of everyone – alone, in association with others or as a community – to know and understand his or her own culture and that of others through education and information, and to receive quality education and training with due regard for cultural identity. Everyone has also the right to learn about forms of expression and dissemination through any technical medium of information or communication, to follow a way of life associated with the use of cultural goods and resources such as land, water, biodiversity, language or specific institutions, and to benefit from the cultural heritage and the creation of other individuals and communities;
> (c) *Contribution to cultural life* refers to the right of everyone to be involved in creating the spiritual, material, intellectual and emotional expressions of the community. This is supported by the right to take part in the development of the community to which a person belongs, and in the definition, elaboration and implementation of policies and decisions that have an impact on the exercise of a person's cultural rights.[76]

Interestingly, *General Comment No. 21* contains almost no analysis of the relationship between cultural rights and intellectual property. The document does not mention the words "intellectual property," contains only

[74] *General Comment No. 21, supra* note 66, para 12.
[75] Id.
[76] *Id.* para. 15.

sparse references to *General Comment No. 17* on creators' rights (discussed in Chapter 3), and does not discuss whether intellectual property laws and treaties help or hinder the realization of the right to "be involved in creating ... intellectual ... expressions." The Committee also does not discuss whether the "access" and "participation" components of the right envisage uncompensated access to copyright protected works.[77] More broadly, the *General Comment* does not address the role of markets in the production of cultural goods. Indeed, one of the few passages that refer to the financial circumstances of those engaged in creative work suggests that government largesse is far more important than market mechanisms to the realization of the right.[78]

States parties' reports under the ICESCR provide some additional insights on these issues. The reports have referred to a broad range of laws and practices relating to Article 15, including measures taken to make culture more freely available, to promote creativity, and to disseminate creative results.[79] Reports have also provided information on cultural industries and cultural institutions, such as cinemas, theaters, libraries, and museums.[80] Some of these industries are based, at least in part, on intellectual property rights, particularly copyright. Cinema is the most obvious example. State practice thus provides support for treating intellectual property as an economic platform for certain cultural practices – a result that is perhaps in some tension with the analysis in *General Comment No. 21*.

Although scholars are beginning to map the relationship between the right to participation in culture and intellectual property,[81] there is not yet a detailed body of jurisprudence concerned with the relationship between the two bodies of law. As with the right to benefit from scientific progress, there has also been relatively little engagement with the implications of the human rights bases for protecting the moral and material interests of creators set forth in Article 27(2) of the UDHR and Article 15(1)(c) of the ICESCR. It is likely that

---

[77] At least one commentator has argued that the realization of the right to take part in cultural life requires the abolition of copyright. ECOSOC, Comm. on Econ., Soc. & Cultural Rights, *Background Paper: Cultural Life in the Context of Human Rights* 3, U.N. Doc. E/C.12/40/6 (May 9, 2008) (prepared by Joost Smiers).

[78] *General Comment No. 21*, *supra* note 66, para 52(d) (admonishing states parties to "grant assistance, financial or other, to artists, public and private organizations, including science academies, cultural associations, trade unions and other individuals and institutions engaged in scientific and creative activities").

[79] *See* Donders, *supra* note 70, 250.

[80] *Id.*

[81] *See* Lea Shaver, *The Right to Science and Culture*, 2010 WISC. L. REV. 121 (2010); Lea Shaver & Caterina Sganga, *The Right to Take Part in Cultural Life: On Copyright and Human Rights*, 27 WISC. INT'L L. REV. 637 (2009).

many of the issues that arise in the context of the right to freedom of expression will also arise in the context of the rights set forth in Article 15(1)(a) and (b). Because the relationship between the right to freedom of expression and intellectual property has been elaborated in some detail, that relationship is the principal focus of the remainder of this chapter. Other chapters that examine topics for which patents are particularly important, including the right to food and the right to health, also raise issues that are relevant to the right to benefit from scientific progress and its applications.

4.5. Intersections between Freedom of Expression and Intellectual Property

This section first considers the U.S. Supreme Court's major exegeses on the relationship between copyright and the First Amendment to the U.S. Constitution. It would be wrong, however, to assume that U.S. domestic principles are always coextensive with international commitments. As we discuss, however, international commitments may be more extensive in a number of respects. For example, some international treaties require access to information in a particular form; conversely, important strands of U.S. jurisprudence assume that copyright law's inability to privatize facts and ideas is sufficient to alleviate any free expression concerns. Moreover, U.S. constitutional principles concerning freedom of speech generally do not reach citizens' rights to information, such as the right to receive government information relevant, for example, to citizens' health and safety concerns. These divergences with international law notwithstanding, a discussion of U.S. domestic principles is useful if only because the First Amendment has been the catalyst for the fullest jurisprudential exploration of the relationship between freedom of expression and intellectual property, especially copyright.

After exploring the U.S. context in some detail, this section then turns to the somewhat more piecemeal, but continually evolving,[82] jurisprudence in Europe concerning freedom of expression as set forth in Article 10 of the ECHR. We also consider the emerging importance of expressive freedoms in trademark and patent law. Throughout this section, indeed, throughout this chapter, it is important to recognize that the concept of "freedom of expression" itself continues to evolve. Beginning as indictment of governmental suppression of speech, and, in some contexts, a moral indictment of secrecy,

---

[82] See generally Christophe Geiger, "Constitutionalising" Intellectual Property Law? The Influence of Fundamental Rights on Intellectual Property in the European Union, 37 INT'L REV. INTELL. PROP. & COMPETITION L. 71 (2006).

the concept is in some jurisdictions increasingly conceptualized as a tool to encourage regulatory efficiency (entitling individuals to receive information from public entities and some private economic actors) and the participation of citizens in political processes. These different perceptions of the right engender different responses to the challenges posed by the various interfaces with intellectual property.

A. Copyright
1. The First Amendment to the U.S. Constitution
The modern foundation for the U.S. Supreme Court's jurisprudence on the relationship between the First Amendment and copyright was established by the 1984 decision, *Harper & Row v. The Nation*.[83] The following statement of facts appears in Justice O'Connor's majority opinion:

> In February 1977, shortly after leaving the White House, former President Gerald R. Ford contracted with petitioners Harper & Row and Reader's Digest, to publish his as yet unwritten memoirs. The memoirs were to contain "significant hitherto unpublished material" concerning the Watergate crisis, Mr. Ford's pardon of former President Nixon and "Mr. Ford's reflections on this period of history, and the morality and personalities involved." In addition to the right to publish the Ford memoirs in book form, the agreement gave petitioners the exclusive right to license prepublication excerpts, known in the trade as "first serial rights." Two years later, as the memoirs were nearing completion, petitioners negotiated a prepublication licensing agreement with Time, a weekly news magazine. Time agreed to pay $25,000, $12,500 in advance and an additional $12,500 at publication, in exchange for the right to excerpt 7,500 words from Mr. Ford's account of the Nixon pardon. The issue featuring the excerpts was timed to appear approximately one week before shipment of the full length book version to bookstores. Exclusivity was an important consideration; Harper & Row instituted procedures designed to maintain the confidentiality of the manuscript, and Time retained the right to renegotiate the second payment should the material appear in print prior to its release of the excerpts.

> Two to three weeks before the Time article's scheduled release, an unidentified person secretly brought a copy of the Ford manuscript to Victor Navasky, editor of The Nation, a political commentary magazine. Mr. Navasky knew that his possession of the manuscript was not authorized and that the manuscript must be returned quickly to his "source" to avoid discovery. He hastily put together what he believed was "a real hot news story" composed of quotes, paraphrases, and facts drawn exclusively from the manuscript. Mr. Navasky attempted no independent commentary, research or criticism, in part because of the need for speed if he was to "make news" by "publish[ing] in advance of publication of

[83]   471 U.S. 539 (1985).

the Ford book." The 2,250-word article appeared on April 3, 1979. As a result of The Nation's article, Time canceled its piece and refused to pay the remaining $12,500.

Reversing a decision by the U.S. Court of Appeals for the Second Circuit, a majority of the Supreme Court held that *The Nation's* activities were not protected by copyright law's "fair use" defense. Under the Copyright Act of 1976,[84] if the defense is made out, the defendant's use is deemed not to infringe the copyright. To determine whether a use is fair, courts consider four factors listed in section 107 of the statute:

(1) the purpose and character of the use, including whether such use is of a commercial nature or is for nonprofit educational purposes;
(2) the nature of the copyrighted work;
(3) the amount and substantiality of the portion used in relation to the copyrighted work as a whole; and
(4) the effect of the use upon the potential market for or value of the copyrighted work.

In the following section of the opinion, Justice O'Connor discussed the relationship between the First Amendment and U.S. copyright law in considerable detail.

Respondents, however, contend that First Amendment values require a different rule under the circumstances of this case. The thrust of the decision below is that "[t]he scope of [fair use] is undoubtedly wider when the information conveyed relates to matters of high public concern." Respondents advance the substantial public import of the subject matter of the Ford memoirs as grounds for excusing a use that would ordinarily not pass muster as a fair use – the piracy of verbatim quotations for the purpose of "scooping" the authorized first serialization. Respondents explain their copying of Mr. Ford's expression as essential to reporting the news story it claims the book itself represents. In respondents' view, not only the facts contained in Mr. Ford's memoirs, but "the precise manner in which [he] expressed himself [were] as newsworthy as what he had to say." Respondents argue that the public's interest in learning this news as fast as possible outweighs the right of the author to control its first publication.

The Second Circuit noted, correctly, that copyright's idea/expression dichotomy "strike[s] a definitional balance between the First Amendment and the Copyright Act by permitting free communication of facts while still protecting an author's expression." No author may copyright his ideas or the facts he narrates. As this Court long ago observed: "[T]he news element – the information respecting current events contained in the literary production – is not the creation of the writer, but is a report of matters that ordinarily are *publici juris*; it is the history of the day." *International News Service v. Associated Press*, 248

---

[84] Pub. L. No. 94–553, 90 Stat. 2541 (1976) (codified at 17 U.S.C. § 101 et seq.).

U.S. 215 (1918). But copyright assures those who write and publish factual narratives such as "A Time to Heal" that they may at least enjoy the right to market the original expression contained therein as just compensation for their investment.

Respondents' theory, however, would expand fair use to effectively destroy any expectation of copyright protection in the work of a public figure. Absent such protection, there would be little incentive to create or profit in financing such memoirs, and the public would be denied an important source of significant historical information. The promise of copyright would be an empty one if it could be avoided merely by dubbing the infringement a fair use "news report" of the book.

Nor do respondents assert any actual necessity for circumventing the copyright scheme with respect to the types of works and users at issue here. Where an author and publisher have invested extensive resources in creating an original work and are poised to release it to the public, no legitimate aim is served by pre-empting the right of first publication. The fact that the words the author has chosen to clothe his narrative may of themselves be "newsworthy" is not an independent justification for unauthorized copying of the author's expression prior to publication. To paraphrase another recent Second Circuit decision: "[Respondent] possessed an unfettered right to use any factual information revealed in [the memoirs] for the purpose of enlightening its audience, but it can claim no need to 'bodily appropriate' [Mr. Ford's] 'expression' of that information by utilizing portions of the actual [manuscript]. The public interest in the free flow of information is assured by the law's refusal to recognize a valid copyright in facts. The fair use doctrine is not a license for corporate theft, empowering a court to ignore a copyright whenever it determines the underlying work contains material of possible public importance."

In our haste to disseminate news, it should not be forgotten that the Framers intended copyright itself to be the engine of free expression. By establishing a marketable right to the use of one's expression, copyright supplies the economic incentive to create and disseminate ideas. This Court stated in *Mazer v. Stein*, 347 U.S. 201, 219 (1954): "The economic philosophy behind the clause empowering Congress to grant patents and copyrights is the conviction that encouragement of individual effort by personal gain is the best way to advance public welfare through the talents of authors and inventors in 'Science and useful Arts.' "The immediate effect of our copyright law is to secure a fair return for an 'author's' creative labor. But the ultimate aim is, by this incentive, to stimulate [the creation of useful works] for the general public good."

It is fundamentally at odds with the scheme of copyright to accord lesser rights in those works that are of greatest importance to the public. Such a notion ignores the major premise of copyright and injures author and public alike. "[T]o propose that fair use be imposed whenever the 'social value [of dissemination] ... outweighs any detriment to the artist,' would be to propose depriving copyright owners of their right in the property precisely when they encounter those users who could afford to pay for it." And as one commentator has noted: "If every volume that was in the public interest could be pirated away by a competing publisher, ... the public [soon] would have nothing worth reading."

Moreover, freedom of thought and expression "includes both the right to speak freely and the right to refrain from speaking at all." We do not suggest this right not to speak would sanction abuse of the copyright owner's monopoly as an instrument to suppress facts. But in the words of New York's Chief Judge Fuld: "The essential thrust of the First Amendment is to prohibit improper restraints on the *voluntary* public expression of ideas; it shields the man who wants to speak or publish when others wish him to be quiet. There is necessarily, and within suitably defined areas, a concomitant freedom *not* to speak publicly, one which serves the same ultimate end as freedom of speech in its affirmative aspect."

Courts and commentators have recognized that copyright, and the right of first publication in particular, serve this countervailing First Amendment value. In view of the First Amendment protections already embodied in the Copyright Act's distinction between copyrightable expression and uncopyrightable facts and ideas, and the latitude for scholarship and comment traditionally afforded by fair use, we see no warrant for expanding the doctrine of fair use to create what amounts to a public figure exception to copyright. Whether verbatim copying from a public figure's manuscript in a given case is or is not fair must be judged according to the traditional equities of fair use.

The U.S. Supreme Court revisited the issue of the relationship between the First Amendment and copyright law in 2003. In *Eldred v. Ashcroft*,[85] the petitioners mounted an array of constitutional challenges against the Sonny Bono Copyright Term Extension Act (CTEA),[86] a statute that added twenty years to the terms of existing copyright works and of works yet to be created. The constitutional challenge principally targeted the former set of term extensions. The challengers urged that copyright extension impinged upon freedom of expression, and, therefore, "heightened" judicial scrutiny of its constitutionality was required.[87] Addressing the challenges based on the First Amendment, Justice Ginsburg wrote:

Petitioners separately argue that the CTEA is a content-neutral regulation of speech that fails heightened judicial review under the First Amendment. We reject petitioners' plea for imposition of uncommonly strict scrutiny on a copyright scheme that incorporates its own speech-protective purposes and safeguards. The Copyright Clause and First Amendment were adopted close in time. This proximity indicates that, in the Framers' view, copyright's limited

---

[85] *Eldred v. Ashcroft*, 537 U.S. 186 (2003).
[86] Pub. L. No. 105–298, 112 Stat. 2827 (1998).
[87] As the term suggests, "heightened scrutiny" envisages a more rigorous assessment of a statute's enactment – in contrast to "rational basis scrutiny," the usual standard for testing the constitutionality of legislation, according to which all that is required is a rational basis for the enactment. As a leading constitutional theorist puts it, "rational basis" is a test that Congress "seldom flunks." Toni M. Massaro, *Constitutional Law as "Normal Science,"* 21 CONST. COMMENT. 547, 552 (2004).

monopolies are compatible with free speech principles. Indeed, copyright's purpose is to *promote* the creation and publication of free expression. As *Harper & Row* observed: "[T]he Framers intended copyright itself to be the engine of free expression. By establishing a marketable right to the use of one's expression, copyright supplies the economic incentive to create and disseminate ideas."

In addition to spurring the creation and publication of new expression, copyright law contains built-in First Amendment accommodations. First, it distinguishes between ideas and expression and makes only the latter eligible for copyright protection.

Second, the "fair use" defense allows the public to use not only facts and ideas contained in a copyrighted work, but also expression itself in certain circumstances.The fair use defense affords considerable "latitude for scholarship and comment," and even for parody, see *Campbell v. Acuff-Rose Music, Inc.*, 510 U.S. 569 (1994) (rap group's musical parody of Roy Orbison's "Oh, Pretty Woman" may be fair use).

The CTEA itself supplements these traditional First Amendment safeguards. First, it allows libraries, archives, and similar institutions to "reproduce" and "distribute, display, or perform in facsimile or digital form" copies of certain published works "during the last 20 years of any term of copyright ... for purposes of preservation, scholarship, or research" if the work is not already being exploited commercially and further copies are unavailable at a reasonable price. Second, Title II of the CTEA, known as the Fairness in Music Licensing Act of 1998, exempts small businesses, restaurants, and like entities from having to pay performance royalties on music played from licensed radio, television, and similar facilities. 17 U.S.C. § 110(5)(B).

The CTEA ... does not oblige anyone to reproduce another's speech[.] Instead, it protects authors' original expression from unrestricted exploitation. Protection of that order does not raise the free speech concerns present when the government compels or burdens the communication of particular facts or ideas. The First Amendment securely protects the freedom to make – or decline to make – one's own speech; it bears less heavily when speakers assert the right to make other people's speeches. To the extent such assertions raise First Amendment concerns, copyright's built-in free speech safeguards are generally adequate to address them. We recognize that the D.C. Circuit spoke too broadly when it declared copyrights "categorically immune from challenges under the First Amendment." But when, as in this case, Congress has not altered the traditional contours of copyright protection, further First Amendment scrutiny is unnecessary.[88]

---

* * * Issues in Focus * * *

The U.S. jurisprudence on the relationship between copyright law and the First Amendment to the U.S. Constitution takes the position that copyright law "internalizes" freedom of expression values. In other words, because

---

[88] *Eldred v. Ashcroft*, 537 U.S. 186, 218–21 (2003).

copyright law provides economic encouragement for individuals and business entities to create new works of authorship, copyright promotes speech. Many of the notes and questions that follow explore this assumption.

If that assumption reflects reality, it is important to identify with precision those aspects of copyright law that are speech-promoting. In the preceding quotation, Justice Ginsburg emphasized "copyright's built-in free speech safeguards" – the fair use defense and the idea/expression dichotomy – in rejecting a First Amendment challenge to a twenty-year extension of copyright protection. The first safeguard is largely a peculiarity of U.S. copyright law: most other nations do not have a broad fair use defense and have instead adopted more narrow defenses and exceptions that are tailored to specific situations, such as news reporting. The idea/expression dichotomy is a widely recognized international copyright norm. It is mandated by Article 9(2) of the TRIPS Agreement, which provides that "copyright protection shall extend to expressions and not to ideas, procedures, methods of operation or mathematical concepts as such." It is also true, however, that the idea/expression dichotomy is sometimes a variable standard that is applied differently in different legal contexts.[89]

If Justice Ginsburg is correct as a general matter, it follows that other domestic copyright laws must contain both of the embedded "safeguards" that exist in the United States – or their equivalents – to be consistent, at least presumptively, with the right to freedom of expression. If so, this conclusion may give rise to a set of important issues for other nations engaged in intellectual property law reform. Every country is obliged to act consistently with the human right to freedom of expression as set forth in its domestic laws and in any regional and international instruments that it has ratified. Justice Ginsburg's analysis may thus provide a set of human rights-based arguments in favor of developing a wider set of defenses to copyright law.

At the same time, it is also important to interrogate the basic assumption that underlies the internalization thesis. The questions that follow identify situations in which the premise might be contestable. In the domestic law reform context, for instance, it might be important to note that the U.S. Supreme Court provides no empirical analysis to substantiate the thesis. It would of course be difficult, if not impossible, to develop a precise empirical

---

[89] The idea/expression dichotomy has been firmly established in U.S. law since at least the 1897 decision of the Supreme Court in *Baker v. Selden*, 101 U.S. 99 (1879). However, in the cognate jurisdiction of the United Kingdom, the idea/expression dichotomy was slower to emerge. Indeed, in a 1994 case, a leading English judge, Sir Robin Jacob, referred to *Baker v. Selden* and opined, "I doubt that would have happened here." *Ibcos Computers Ltd. v. Barclays Mercantile Highland Finance Ltd.* [1994] F.S.R. 275, 292.

test that analyzes copyright law's effects on the amount, or indeed, the quality of expression that exists at any point in time. Even so, it could reasonably be asserted that more evidence is required before endorsing the assumption that copyright promotes speech. Moreover, there are specific contexts where copyright law, even when mediated by the idea/expression dichotomy and the fair use defense, directly affects the kinds of speech that some people may favor. An obvious example is where, in order to make one's point, it is necessary to use the exact written expression or audio-visual content. A rule prohibiting such usage in these contexts might interfere with the realization of the human rights discussed in this chapter.

The questions that follow also examine cases of parodies of copyright-protected works. This is a context in which U.S. courts have been particularly solicitous of free expression values. A key question for those thinking about copyright law through a human rights lens is whether special treatment for parodies sufficiently complies with obligations to protect the human right to free expression.

Notes and Questions

1. As the previous extracts indicate, U.S. courts have conventionally taken the view that copyright and freedom of expression are "harmonious and complementary concepts."[90] The idea that copyright "internalizes" freedom of expression frames contemporary discussion of copyright law's relationship with freedom of expression. As Justice Ginsburg's analysis in *Eldred v. Ashcroft* shows, this approach makes an appeal to the contemporaneity of the drafting of the First Amendment (1791) and the first federal Copyright Act (1790).[91] How convincing is the suggestion that this temporal proximity indicates that the Framers saw no tension between the two?[92] Is it relevant, for example, that the "fair use" principle had not been specifically developed in U.S. copyright law when the first federal copyright statute was enacted?[93]

2. If, as Justice Ginsburg suggested, fair use is one of copyright law's free speech accommodations, is the endurance of the fair use defense also necessary to the constitutionality of U.S. copyright law? Drawing on Justice

---

[90] *See generally* Pamela Samuelson, *Copyright and Freedom of Expression in Historical Perspective*, 10 J. INTELL. PROP. L. 319 (2003).

[91] U.S. Copyright Act 1790, 1 Stat. 124 (1790).

[92] *See generally* Lionel S. Sobel, *Copyright and the First Amendment: A Gathering Storm?*, 19 COPYRIGHT L. SYMP. 43, 70 (1971).

[93] *See generally* WILLIAM F. PATRY, THE FAIR USE PRIVILEGE IN COPYRIGHT LAW (1985).

Ginsburg's references to copyright's "traditional contours," Edward Lee has argued: "If Congress abrogated either doctrine or any other traditional First Amendment safeguard in copyright law, First Amendment scrutiny would be required, and such a change in copyright law would be unconstitutional."[94] To the extent that the First Amendment is broadly consistent with international and regional human rights guarantees of the right to freedom of expression, does this mean that if a nation's copyright law lacks a broad "fair use" exception (and almost all do), that nation's copyright laws are inconsistent with international law obligations to protect freedom of expression?

3. The "judicial immunization of traditional copyright from First Amendment scrutiny" has been characterized by one scholar as a "peculiar and pernicious anomaly."[95] Certainly, aspects of the Supreme Court's analysis of the relationship between U.S. Copyright Act and the First Amendment seem controversial. Consider, for example, the basic proposition that copyright is the engine of free expression, a dictum premised on the belief that copyright's restrictions on speech create markets that, in the end, encourage speech. The Supreme Court's analysis implies that for some types of speech to be "free" (at the very least, those that are produced in response to economic encouragements) they must, paradoxically, be paid for.[96] But in what other circumstances does the law legitimately restrict X's speech so that Y can speak? Note that the restriction might last a long time: under U.S. copyright law, for example, X might be required to wait until 70 years after Y has died before she can use Y's speech. Moreover, copyright's proscriptions do not necessarily focus on encouraging Y to speak at all: copyright's incentive structure is more obviously directed at protecting *others* who might speak some time in the future (again, encouraged by commercial incentives).

4. Consider the argument that "fair use" is a free speech "safeguard." There is a significant body of literature contesting the ability of fair use to preserve expressive freedoms,[97] which advances the view that fair use often "crumbles in the face of expansive assertions of copyright rights."[98] A

---

[94] Edward Lee, *Freedom of the Press 2.0*, 42 GA. L. REV. 309, 365 (2008).

[95] Neil Winestock Netanel, *Copyright and the First Amendment: What* Eldred *Misses – and Portends*, in PAUL TORREMANS & UMA SUTHERSANEN (EDS.), COPYRIGHT AND FREE SPEECH: COMPARATIVE AND INTERNATIONAL ANALYSES 127, 151 (2005).

[96] *See generally* Rebecca Tushnet, *Copyright as a Model for Free Speech Law: What Copyright Has in Common with Anti-Pornography Laws, Campaign Finance Reform, and Telecommunications Regulation*, 42 B.C. L. REV. 1 (2000).

[97] *See, e.g.*, Gideon Parchomovsky & Kevin Goldman, *Fair Use Harbors*, 93 VA. L. REV. 1483 (2007); PATRICIA AUFDERHEIDE & PETER JASZI, CTR. FOR SOC. MEDIA, UNTOLD STORIES: CREATIVE CONSEQUENCES OF THE RIGHTS CLEARANCE CULTURE FOR DOCUMENTARY FILM MAKERS (2004).

[98] Thomas F. Cotter, *Fair Use and Copyright Overenforcement*, 93 IOWA L. REV. 1271, 1274 (2008).

number of commentators have also identified a systemic imbalance in fair use doctrine: the positive externalities generated by one user's "use" of another's work (thereby contributing positively to aggregate social welfare) may significantly outweigh the value of the use to the individual user, which may, in turn, cause the copyright owner to expend greater resources to "block" the use[99] than would be deployed by an individual "fair user" to secure a license. To what extent does this sysmetic imbalance influence your assessment of whether fair use provides a safe harbor for the First Amendment?

5. Another argument advanced by the Supreme Court – that copyright and the First Amendment can be accommodated because of the idea/expression dichotomy – raises a number of intriguing issues that are relevant to the protections for speech provided by domestic and international law. Within the First Amendment's own terms, when a statute proscribes use of a particular form of expression and requires the speaker to use only the ideas embodied in the speech, why is this not a "law abridging the freedom of speech"? Are there situations where, to make one's point, it is necessary to use a particular (copyright-protected) expression, in its original form?[100] If so, how does it protect speech to require the speaker to use the second-best alternative? Is the analysis in *Eldred v. Ashcroft* consistent with treaty provisions (excerpted in Section 4.3 of this chapter) that emphasize the irrelevance of the form in which the speaker seeks to impart information? Consider, for example, the right set forth in Article 19 of the ICCPR, to be able to "impart information and ideas of all kinds … in writing or in print, in the form of art, or through any other media of his choice." Is it also significant that at least one U.S. court has eschewed the idea/expression dichotomy as a ground for distinguishing between protected and unprotected material in a photograph?[101] If this became established doctrine, would U.S. copyright law be (a) susceptible to heightened First Amendment scrutiny under *Eldred v. Ashcroft*? and/or (b) in tension with public international law rules protecting freedom of expression?

6. The idea/expression dichotomy has been incorporated into the public international law of intellectual property. Article 9(2) of the TRIPS

---

[99] See, e.g., Lydia Pallas Loren, *Redefining the Market Failure Approach to Fair Use in an Era of Copyright Permission Systems*, 5 J. INTELL. PROP. L. 1 (1997).

[100] Justice Ginsburg's analysis in *Eldred v. Ashcroft* does not appear to reach the situation where the *only* relevant use requires use of the copyright-protected material, rather than the ideas embodied in the material. In the music sampling context, some U.S. courts have interpreted the Copyright Act 1976 as precluding application of a *de minimis* principle that would excuse uses of small "clips" of sound recordings. See *Bridgeport Music v. Dimension Films*, 410 F.3d 792 (6th Cir. 2005).

[101] See *Mannion v. Coors Brewing Co.*, 377 F. Supp. 2d 444 (S.D.N.Y. 2005).

Agreement provides that "[c]opyright protection shall extend to expressions and not to ideas, procedures, methods of operation or mathematical concepts as such."[102] Consider again the approach to the idea/expression dichotomy in the context of photographs referred to in the previous Note. This case law appears to point in the opposite direction from the typical approach to the "merger" doctrine in U.S. copyright law. Under this doctrine, if ideas and expression merge (such that protecting the expression would have the effect of giving copyright protection to the underlying ideas),[103] the expression is designated to the public domain unless another legal vehicle, such as patent, continues to protect it. But in the context of copyright-protected photographs, U.S. courts have held that the inability to disaggregate ideas and expression renders everything protectable expression. Is this case law consistent with the TRIPS Agreement? Does TRIPS require that *every* type of protected expression be accompanied by unprotected ideas? If so, how would such an obligation be enforced?

7. Is the proposition that the First Amendment "bears less heavily when speakers assert the right to make other people's speeches" so axiomatic that no citation of authority in its support is required? (The Court provides none.) If there is an (implicit) appeal here to first principles, what are they? Are there circumstances where rote copying, even of copyright-protected material, might serve free speech interests?[104]

8. Citing *Campbell v. Acuff-Rose Music, Inc.*,[105] Justice Ginsburg noted that, in the U.S. context, fair use may accommodate uses of copyright works for the purposes of parody. *Sun-Trust Bank v. Houghton Mifflin Company*[106] concerned a copyright infringement action brought by the copyright owners of the American classic novel *Gone with the Wind* (GWTW) by Margaret Mitchell. The plaintiffs sought a temporary restraining order and preliminary injunction to stop the publication of a novel entitled *The Wind Done Gone* (TWDG), which was marketed as an "unofficial parody" of the original. On appeal, the U.S. Court of Appeals for the Eleventh Circuit held in favor of the defendants. In its analysis of the application of the fair use defense to parodies, the court stated:

> Before considering a claimed fair use defense based on parody ... the Supreme Court [in *Campbell*] has required that we ensure that "a parodic character may

---

[102] Agreement on Trade-Related Aspects of Intellectual Property Rights, art. 9, Apr. 15, 1994, 1869 U.N.T.S. 299 [TRIPS Agreement].

[103] *See Baker v. Selden*, 101 U.S. 99 (1879).

[104] *See* Rebecca Tushnet, *Copy This Essay: How Fair Use Doctrine Harms Free Speech and How Copying Serves It*, 114 Yale L.J. 535, 546 (2004).

[105] 510 U.S. 569 (1994).

[106] 268 F.3d 1257 (11th Cir. 2001).

reasonably be perceived" in the allegedly infringing work. The Supreme Court's definition of parody ... is somewhat vague. On the one hand, the Court suggests that the aim of parody is "comic effect or ridicule," but it then proceeds to discuss parody more expansively in terms of its "commentary" on the original. In light of the admonition in *Campbell* that courts should not judge the quality of the work or the success of the attempted humor in discerning its parodic character, we choose to take the broader view. For purposes of our fair-use analysis, we will treat a work as a parody if its aim is to comment upon or criticize a prior work by appropriating elements of the original in creating a new artistic, as opposed to scholarly or journalistic, work. Under this definition, the parodic character of *TWDG* is clear. *TWDG* is not a general commentary upon the Civil-War-era American South, but a specific criticism of and rejoinder to the depiction of slavery and the relationships between blacks and whites in *GWTW*. The fact that Randall chose to convey her criticisms of *GWTW* through a work of fiction, which she contends is a more powerful vehicle for her message than a scholarly article, does not, in and of itself, deprive *TWDG* of fair-use protection.

9. Why are parodies special? In a 2007 U.S. district court case,[107] Carol Burnett, a famous U.S. media personality and comedy star, brought a copyright infringement action against the makers of a popular television cartoon, which, in the words of the court, "routinely puts cartoon versions of celebrities in awkward, ridiculous, and absurd situations in order to lampoon and parody those public figures and to poke fun at society's general fascination with celebrity and pop culture." Ms Burnett objected to a section in an episode of the program that depicted one of her much-loved characters, the "Char Woman," as a janitor in a store purveying pornography and other "adult"-themed items. In a brief segment, an animated depiction of the char woman character appears "mopping the floor next to seven 'blow-up dolls,' a rack of 'XXX' movies, and a curtained room with a sign above it reading 'Video Booths." Characterizing the segment as a "parody" and dismissing Ms Burnett's claims, the court concluded: "the law, as it must in an open society, provides broad protection for the defendant's [television] segment."[108]

10. Does it follow from the examples in the previous two Notes that the more generously a nation's copyright laws excuse parodic uses the more open it is? In Australia, the federal copyright act was recently amended to make provision for "fair dealing for the purposes of parody and satire."[109]

---

[107]   491 F. Supp. 2d 962 (C.D. Cal. 2007).
[108]   *Id.* at 975.
[109]   Copyright Act of 1968 § 41A, as amended by Copyright Amendment Act 2006 (Cth.) ("A fair dealing with a literary, dramatic, musical or artistic work, or with an adaptation of a literary, dramatic or musical work, does not constitute an infringement of the copyright in the work if it is for the purpose of parody or satire."); *id.* § 133A ("A fair dealing with an audio–visual item does not constitute an infringement of the copyright in the item or

The drafters of this provision were aware of the application of the U.S. fair use defense in the parody context. Accordingly, it could be argued that the addition of "satire" was meant to amplify the provision made under U.S. law for parodies. The distinction between parody and satire appears to be part of the subtext in the passage quoted from the *Sun-Trust* case. The court of appeals appeared to distinguish between specific commentaries on the copyright owner's work (here, *Gone with the Wind*), which, in the circumstances of the case, would fall within the U.S. fair use defense, and "general commentary upon the Civil-War-era American South," which apparently would not. Will it always be easy to distinguish between parody and satire? If not, does the uncertainty as to which side of the line the defendant's work falls on have implications for the right to freedom of expression?[110] Even if such a line can be drawn, why is parody more important speech than satire? That is, why does a defendant's attempt to make a *general* social critique, rather than a specific critique of a copyright-protected work, deserve less protection? Is the discussion earlier in this chapter concerning the way that copyright creates markets for speech relevant to this question?

11. According to the U.S. approach to parody, the fair use analysis does not merely ask whether the defendant has created a work whose parodic character can reasonably be perceived. The use must also be "fair" as determined by an analysis of the four factors cited at the beginning of this subsection. In *Campbell*, which involved a "rap" version of the Roy Orbison classic song "O Pretty Woman," the Supreme Court emphasized that no single factor is dispositive, and that courts must evaluate and weigh them all. As for the first factor, the Court in *Campbell* rejected any presumption that a commercial use is unfair. (By negative implication, does this analysis also suggest that noncommercial uses are *not* presumptively *fair*?) Under this factor, the Court also emphasized the importance of the "transformative" character of the defendant's use of the plaintiff's work. In respect of parodies, however, less transformation might perhaps be tolerated because of the necessity to "conjure up" the original in the minds of the audience for the parody to work. This approach to the first factor contrasts with an earlier Supreme Court decision, *Sony Corp. of America v. Universal City Studios, Inc.*,[111]

---

in any work or other audio–visual item included in the item if it is for the purpose of parody or satire.").

[110] *See, e.g., Grayned v. City of Rockford*, 408 U.S. 104, 108 (1972) ("[W]here a vague statute 'abut[s] upon sensitive areas of basic First Amendment freedoms,' it 'operates to inhibit the exercise of [those] freedoms.' Uncertain meanings inevitably lead citizens to 'steer far wider of the unlawful zone' ... than if the boundaries of the forbidden areas were clearly marked.") (citations omitted).

[111] 464 U.S. 417 (1984).

which held a more obviously "consumptive" use of copyright-protected works – home videotaping of free-to-air television broadcasts for later viewing – to be a fair use.

How does the emphasis on the transformative character of the defendant's use relate to the underlying First Amendment concerns? Is this emphasis consistent with the "engine" of free speech concept, or are defendants required to do too much (transformative) work to avoid liability? More generally, is excusing "consumptive" uses consistent with freedom of expression principles? Is it consistent with the incentive structures underlying copyright law? Despite its emphasis on the transformative character of the defendants' use, *Campbell* did not hold the parodic version of the Orbison song to be a fair use. Instead, the Court remanded the case to develop the factual record concerning the damage to the derivative market for rap versions of the original song. The parties later reached a settlement that included an agreement to pay royalties to the copyright owner.

12. Other expansions of copyright law that occurred toward the end of last century were quickly followed by constitutional challenges, including challenges based on the First Amendment. Litigants have argued, for example, that the fair use defense is constitutionally required by the First Amendment.[112] Some support for this proposition might be derived from *Eldred*'s suggestion that the fair use defense is among the Copyright Act's First Amendment safeguards. This argument has been rejected, however, albeit in a case that predated the *Eldred* decision. In *Universal Studios, Inc. v. Corley*,[113] the Second Circuit confronted an argument that amendments to U.S. copyright law in the Digital Millennium Copyright Act (DMCA) unconstitutionally eliminated fair use. The DMCA's prohibitions on circumventing technological protection measures that control "access" to copyright-protected works are not subject to the fair use defense. The Second Circuit reasoned that "fair use has never been held to be a guarantee of access to copyrighted material in order to copy it by the fair user's preferred technique or in the format of the original."[114] Fair use does not, it would appear, require that the "fair user" be able to use the material in the most technologically convenient manner. Is this conclusion consistent with the right to freedom of expression as protected in international law?

---

[112] TyAnna K. Herrington, *The Interdependency of Fair Use and the First Amendment*, 15 COMPUTERS & COMPOSITION 125, 141 (1998) (asserting that fair use is the "lifeblood of the first amendment"); *see also* Dan L. Burk & Julie E. Cohen, *Fair Use Infrastructure for Copyright Management Systems*, 15 HARV. J.L. & TECH. 41 (2001).

[113] 273 F.3d 429, 459 (2d Cir. 2001).

[114] *Id.* at 458.

13. Until quite recently, the U.S. doctrine on the relationship between the First Amendment and copyright law could have been accurately captured by a district judge's single sentence dismissal of a constitutional challenge to an aspect of U.S. copyright law: "I see no need to expand upon the settled rule that private censorship via copyright enforcement does not implicate First Amendment concerns."[115] The case involved a challenge to a statute that restored the copyrights in foreign-origin works that had fallen into the public domain in the United States.[116] The plaintiffs included orchestra conductors, educators, performers, publishers, film archivists, and motion picture distributors, many of whom were required to pay royalties for works that were hitherto in the public domain in the United States. On appeal, however, the U.S. Court of Appeals for the Tenth Circuit signaled that the First Amendment continues to enjoy some enduring purchase in domestic copyright jurisprudence. The court accepted the argument that removal of works from the public domain departed from the "traditional contours" of U.S. copyright law. According to the court's interpretation of Justice Ginsburg's analysis in *Eldred v. Ashcroft*, this conclusion triggered heightened First Amendment scrutiny. The Tenth Circuit therefore remanded the case for further consideration of the statute's constitutionality.[117] On remand, the district court held that the statute was substantially broader than necessary to achieve the governmental purpose.[118] That decision was subsequently reversed by the Tenth Circuit, which held that the restoration of foreign copyrights – required by the TRIPS Agreement and the Berne Convention – was not contrary to the First Amendment.[119] The court characterized compliance with the treaties as furthering the government's "substantial interest in securing protections for American works in foreign countries" and "not burden[ing] substantially more speech than necessary to advance that interest."[120] The Tenth Circuit also rejected the plaintiffs' claim "that the First Amendment – either by itself or informed by any other provision of the Constitution – draws ... absolute, bright lines around the public domain."[121]

Suppose the work at issue is a twentieth-century orchestral masterpiece, such as Prokofiev's *Peter and the Wolf* – a foreign-origin work whose copyright

---

[115] *Golan v. Gonzales*, No. Civ-01-B-1854, 2005 WL 914754 at *17 (D. Colo. Apr. 20, 2005).
[116] The case concerned a challenge to the constitutionality of section 514 of the Uruguay Round Agreements Act ("URAA"), 17 U.S.C. §§ 104A, 109 (2006).
[117] 501 F.3d 1179 (10th Cir. 2007).
[118] *Golan v. Holder*, 611 F. Supp. 2d 1165 (D. Colo. 2009).
[119] *Golan v. Holder*, 609 F.3d 1076 (10th Cir. 2010).
[120] *Id.* at 1091, 1092.
[121] *Id.* at 1095.

had fallen into the public domain in the United States. Is the right to freedom of expression implicated because the work's U.S. copyright has been restored, obligating users to pay royalties to the copyright owner for activities such as public performances? Is the amount of the royalty demanded by the copyright owner a relevant concern? If so, how are courts to assess whether the size of the fee renders the law itself unconstitutional? Would a more "systemic" approach to these questions be more appropriate? For instance, what if it could be shown that works by more recent U.S. composers have a greater chance of being played by the nation's orchestras now that they are no longer "undercut" by European-origin works that were formerly in the public domain (which meant that no composers' royalties were payable)? Or must freedom of expression be analyzed seriatim – that is, on a "work-by-work" basis?

14. Whose rights are most salient? Consider section 110(11) of the U.S. Copyright Act, according to which the following action is deemed not to be an infringement of copyright:

> The making imperceptible, by or at the direction of a member of a private household, of limited portions of audio or video content of a motion picture, during a performance in or transmitted to that household for private home viewing, from an authorized copy of the motion picture, or the creation or provision of a computer program or other technology that enables such making imperceptible and that is designed and marketed to be used, at the direction of a member of a private household, for such making imperceptible, if no fixed copy of the altered version of the motion picture is created by such computer program or other technology.

This provision, which was adopted as the Family Movie Act of 2005,[122] allows families to "edit out" possibly offensive content, such as violence and profanity, from movies as they are viewed, and to support business models based around developing technologies to enable this kind of "editing" to occur. The statute arguably enhances viewers' expressive freedoms, to the extent that it confirms that viewing certain altered versions of copyright-protected material does not implicate the copyright owners' exclusive right to make derivative works. But does the statute not also impinge upon the expressive freedoms of the "authors" of the movies whose original artistic vision is modified in this way? Are these authors being forced to "speak" in ways that implicate their right to freedom of expression?

15. Broadly analogous issues underlie the protection of moral rights. For example, representatives of the Irish playwright Samuel Beckett persuaded

---

[122] Pub. L. No. 109–9, 119 Stat. 218, 223 (2005).

the Tribunal de Grand Instance (Paris) to prevent the staging of the famous play *Waiting for Godot* using female, rather than male, actors.[123] In *Turner Entertainment Company v. Huston*, the French Cour de Cassation held that televised screening of a colorized version of the John Huston movie *The Asphalt Jungle* infringed his moral rights.[124] In both instances, "authors" responsible for the original works were arguably being forced to "speak" in a manner that was different from their original conception. On the other hand, the cases also involved new – arguably expressive – versions of these works that were to be communicated to audiences who, presumably, sought to apprehend these works in their new guises. In rights conflicts such as these, whose rights should prevail?

16. Is the right to freedom of expression implicated when copyright owners seek to regulate technologies that facilitate the copying and dissemination of protected works? As Jane Ginsburg notes, there is a long history in the United States of courts declining to give copyright owners full protection where they seek to prohibit new dissemination technologies; however, courts have been rather more solicitous when copyright owners have instead sought to be compensated for infringements that these technologies enable.[125] Edward Lee has recently addressed the First Amendment issues that arguably arise when copyright owners seek to regulate such technologies. Drawing in part on the historical linkage between copyright law and protections for a "free," unregulated press, Lee argues that constitutional commitments to a free press require First Amendment scrutiny of secondary liability principles that hold the developers or purveyors of such technologies liable for infringements by end users.[126] What counterarguments might be advanced by copyright owners?

17. Recall the language of the Canadian Charter of Rights referenced in Section 4.3. Limits on "fundamental" rights, including the right to freedom of expression, may be "subject only to such reasonable limits prescribed by law as can be demonstrably justified in a free and democratic society." Is copyright law consistent with this prescription? Is it possible to answer this question at a general level, or does the question make sense only in the context of specific statutory provisions?

---

[123] Tribunal de grande instance [T.G.I.] [ordinary court of original jurisdiction] Paris (3rd chamber), Oct. 15, 1992, (1993) 155 R.I.D.A. 225 (Fr.).

[124] Cour de Cass. [CC] [highest court of ordinary jurisdiction], May 28, 1991, 149 R.I.D.A. 197 (Fr.); Cour d'appel [CA] [regional court of appeal] Versailles, Dec. 10, 1994, R.I.D.A. 256. (Fr.).

[125] Jane C. Ginsburg, *Copyright and Control over New Technologies of Dissemination*, 101 COLUM. L. REV. 1613 (2001).

[126] Lee, *supra* note 94.

18. U.S. law is by no means unique in its basic commitment to the position that copyright "internalizes" free speech values and principles. Sweden, for example, has been described as the European nation that offers copyright, or, rather, "authors' rights" the most profound constitutional support.[127] Article 2:19 of the Government Form of 1974 provides that "authors, artists and photographers shall own the rights to their works according to norms stated in statutory law." The Swedish Constitution appears to *require* the enactment of legislation protecting these rights. This contrasts with the U.S. Constitution, which merely *empowers* the U.S. Congress to do so.[128] Jan Rosen explains that the rationale for constitutional support of authors' rights in Sweden is found in copyright law's "considered purpose to promote 'the freedom of opinion.'"[129] Would you advocate inclusion of an explicit statement requiring protection of authors' rights in other national constitutions?

2. Article 10 of the European Convention on Human Rights

"The potential conflict between copyright and free speech has long been ignored in European law."[130] Bernt Hugenholtz, the author of this comment, notes a number of reasons for this, the most convincing of which, he suggests, is that copyright "already reflects" a balance between free speech and property rights. This is another assertion of the "internalization" thesis. According to Hugenholtz, copyright law interalizes this balance through principles and doctrine such as the concept of a work of authorship, the idea/expression dichotomy, the limited term of protection, and specific limitations or exceptions to the economic rights of copyright owners.[131]

Article 10 of the ECHR (quoted in Section 4.3) provides the principal framework for balancing copyright and the right to freedom of information

[127] Jan Rosen, *Copyright and Freedom of Expression in Sweden – Private Law in a Constitutional Context*, in PAUL TORREMANS (ED.), COPYRIGHT LAW: A HANDBOOK OF CONTEMPORARY RESEARCH 355, 364 (2007).

[128] U.S. CONST. art. I, § 8.

[129] Rosen, *supra* note 127, at 365.

[130] P. B. Hugenholtz, *Copyright and Freedom of Expression in Europe*, in ROCHELLE COOPER DREYFUSS, HARRY FIRST, & DIANE LEHEER ZIMMERMAN (EDS.), INNOVATION POLICY IN AN INFORMATION AGE 343, 350 (2000). In a more recent survey, Hugenholtz again confirmed that the position had not much changed. *See* Alain Strowel & François Tulkens, *Freedom of Expression and Copyright under Civil Law: Of Balance, Adaptation, and Access*, in JONATHAN GRIFFITHS & UMA SUTHERSANEN (EDS.), COPYRIGHT AND FREE SPEECH, COMPARATIVE AND INTERNATIONAL ANALYSES 287 (2005).

[131] Hugenholtz, *supra* note 130. Also relevant is the 2001 Directive on Copyright in the Information Society, which provides EU members with the option of including such an exception in their national laws. Council Directive 2001/29/EC, art. 5(2)(b), on the Harmonization of Certain Aspects of Copyright and Related Rights in the Information Society, 2001 O.J. (L 167) at 10 [Directive 2001/29/EC].

in European human rights jurisprudence. Article 10(1) is worded broadly. It refers simply to "expression" and does not single out for special protection particular actors or activities, such as the news media or press reports. The European Court of Human Rights (ECtHR) has not much concerned itself with definitional questions regarding the meaning of the word "expression."[132] As a result, "in very large measure, the law of free expression under the Convention is the law of Article 10(2),"[133] which articulates restrictions on that right. Facially, this marks an important contract with the First Amendment to the U.S. Constitution, which is articulated in absolute terms and contains no express limitations. In the European context, restrictions must be "prescribed by law," a stipulation that appears to encompass copyright laws.[134] Second, Article 10(2) provides that the right to freedom of expression may be "subject to ... restrictions ... for the protection of ... rights of others," which again appears to anticipate the existence and endurance of national copyright laws.[135] Limitations on the right must also be "necessary in a democratic society." The ECtHR has reasoned that the word "necessary" requires that there be a "pressing social need" for the restriction.[136] Several

---

[132] MARK JANIS, RICHARD KAY, & ANTHONY BRADLEY, EUROPEAN HUMAN RIGHTS LAW: TEXT AND MATERIALS 141 (2d ed. 2000).

[133] Id.

[134] The (former) European Commission of Human Rights also accepted that copyright laws were "prescribed by law" within the terms of Article 10. *Societe Nationale De Programmes France 2 v. France*, App. No. 30262/96 (Eur. Comm'n H.R. 1997), [*France 2*], *available at* http://cmiskp.echr.coe.int/tkp197/view.asp?action=html&documentId=676692&portal= hbkm&source=externalbydocnumber&table=F69A27FD8FB86142BF01C1166DEA39864 9 (last visited Mar. 31, 2010).

[135] Some commentators have suggested that "rights of others" includes intellectual property rights. *See* Strowel & Tulkens, *supra* note 130, at 290 n.7; *see also* Timothy Pinto, *The Influence of the European Convention on Human Rights on Intellectual Property Rights*, 24 EUR. INTELL. PROP. REV. 209, 217 (2002). A similar view has been adopted by the cour d'appel (Paris) in a case involving the works of Maurice Utrillo. *Utrillo*, Tribunal de grande instance [T.G.I.] [ordinary court of original jurisdiction] Paris, Feb. 23, 1999, No. 98/7053 (unpublished); cour d'appel [CA] [regional court of appeals] May 30, 2001, D. 2001, 2504 (Fr.). Professor Hugenholtz, *supra* note 130, notes that a contrary view, that the "rights of others" only includes fundamental rights recognized by the ECHR (as opposed to subjective rights adopted in national laws), is not reflected in the jurisprudence of the European Court of Human Rights. For instance in *Chappell v. United Kingdom*, 152-A Eur. Ct. H.R. (ser. A) (1989), an *Anton-Pillar* order (a type of "private search warrant" often used in intellectual property cases) was upheld as a legitimate exception under Article 8 of the ECHR, which also permits limitations directed at protecting the "rights and freedoms of others." The European Commission of Human Rights in the *France 2* case, *supra* note 134, also accepted that copyright law protects the rights of others.

[136] *Ergin v. Turkey*, 47 Eur. H.R. Rep. 829, 839 (2008).

domestic cases in Europe have held that copyright law is among the permitted restrictions anticipated by Article 10(2).[137]

The European Commission of Human Rights[138] has largely resisted engaging with any apparent tension between intellectual property rights and the right to freedom of information. For example, in *De Geïllustreerde Pers. N.V. v. The Netherlands*,[139] the Commission concluded that the refusal to license radio and television listings for use by commercial rivals was not inconsistent with Article 10. The case concerned the (highly regulated) Dutch broadcasting system, under which certain broadcasters were accorded transmission time by the Netherlands broadcasting authority, the Nederlandse Omroep Stichting ("NOS"). The governing legislation required licensed broadcasting organizations to make available to the NOS lists of the programs they proposed to broadcast. The NOS then sent aggregated program information to all of the broadcasting organizations, which were allowed to publish that information in their own program magazines. The broadcasting organizations were, pursuant to Article 23 of the 1967 Broadcasting Act, expressly precluded from publishing the complete program information in any other publication. Short summaries were, however, sent to some general magazines and were also sent to foreign magazines on a reciprocal basis. Article 22 of the Act specifically provided that any "reproduction or publication of lists or other statements of those programmes otherwise than on behalf of or with the authorisation" of the NOS constituted a breach of copyright that would result in civil liability.

The *De Geïllustreerde* litigation arose out of denial of the applicant's petition to publish "complete lists of television and radio programme data compiled for each week by the Netherlands Broadcasting Foundation (NOS) on information supplied by the various broadcasting organisations" in a weekly general interest magazine. The Commission analyzed the NOS's information monopoly conflicted with Article 10 of the ECHR as follows:

> It is clear from [Articles 22 and 23 of the 1967 Broadcast Act] that the reproduction and publication of the lists referred to is reserved exclusively to the established or prospective broadcasting organisations, or to the Foundation, and that anyone else is prevented from publishing these lists without the consent of the Foundation, unless it can be shown that the information so published has

---

[137]   *E.g., Copiepresse v. Google, Inc.*, Tribunal de Premiere Instances de Bruxelles [Court of First Instance] Brussels, Feb. 13, 2007, J.B.C. 7964 (Belg.), *available at* http://www.copiepresse. be/13–02–07-jugement-en.pdf.

[138]   The European Commission of Human Rights was abolished in 1998, after adoption of Protocol 11 to the European Convention on Human Rights.

[139]   App. No. 5178/71, 8 Eur. Comm'n H.R. Dec. & Rep. 5 (1977).

not been obtained directly or indirectly from any written work containing the programme data concerned. It is this exclusive right on publication which the applicant also calls a "monopoly" that is challenged in the present application.

The Commission has first considered the nature of the particular matter which the applicant company is seeking to impart. It is true that in the ordinary sense of the word information includes the expression of facts and of news and that television and radio programme data can be regarded as being either of them. The Commission considers therefore that the lists of programme data in question constitute "information," as opposed to "opinions" or "ideas," within the meaning of Art. 10 of the Convention. Indeed, this point is not in dispute between the parties.

However, in the opinion of the Commission, there are various special features concerning these programme data which must be taken into account when determining whether or not any restrictions imposed on their publication amount to an interference with the rights of the applicant under Art. 10 or the Convention.

In the first place, such lists of programme data are not simple facts, or news in the proper sense of the word. They are rather a compilation of facts and they are news in the sense that they provide an orientation guide for television viewers or radio listeners prior to or during a particular week with a view to assisting them in the selection of forthcoming programmes. The characteristic feature of such information is that it can only be produced and provided by the broadcasting organisations being charged with the production of the programmes themselves and that it is organised by the Foundation being the co-ordinating body of these organisations.

The Commission considers that the freedom under Art. 10 to impart information of the kind described above is only granted to the person or body who produces, provides or organizes it. In other words the freedom to impart such information is limited to information produced, provided or organized by the person claiming that freedom, being the author, the originator or otherwise the intellectual owner of the information concerned. It follows that any right which the applicant company itself may have under Art. 10 of the Convention has not been interfered with where it is prevented from publishing information not yet in its possession.

Furthermore, in the area of "information," i.e. in the area of facts and news as opposed to "ideas" and "opinions" the protection which Art. 10 of the Convention seeks to secure concerns the free flow of such information to the public in general.

However, there can be no question in the present case that the freedom of the press in general is threatened in the sense that the public is deprived of any specific information, i.e. in the present case, the programme data, by censorship or otherwise by reason of any undue State monopoly on news. On the contrary, every person in the Netherlands may inform himself about the forthcoming radio and television programmes through a variety of mass media representing various sections and tendencies of society. To that extent there is, in the Commission's opinion, no merit in the applicant company's claim that the public is prevented from receiving unbiased information about these programmes owing to the fact that it can only obtain such information by reading the broadcasting organisations' own magazines.

Of course, the Commission does not ignore that the applicant company might suffer considerable commercial disadvantages by reason of the fact that it is prevented from publishing these lists of programmed data. The Commission has noted the applicant company's submissions that, although the legislation in question imposed various restrictions on the contents and presentation of the "programme magazines" so as to prevent them from being competitive with the "general interest magazines," these legislative restrictions were in fact not complied with, and that consequently the "programme magazines" were real competitors of the "general interest magazines." According to the applicant company this had considerably affected the financial position of "general interest magazines," and had reduced sales.

Be that as it may, the Commission considers that the protection of the commercial interests of particular newspapers or groups of newspapers is not as such contemplated by the terms of Art. 10 of the Convention. These matters might perhaps raise an issue under this provision where a State fails in its duty to protect against excessive press-concentrations, but this obviously is not the position in the present case.

It follows that there has been, in the circumstances, no interference with any of the rights protected by Art. 10 (1) of the Convention, and that the Commission is therefore not required to examine the applicant company's complaints in the light of Art. 10 (2).

In a subsequent decision, *Societe Nationale de Programmes France 2 v. France*,[140] the Commission affirmed a judgment of the French Cour de Cassation holding that broadcasting pictures of frescoes by Edouard Vuillard in conjunction with a television program covering the reopening of a theater on the Champs-Elysées infringed Vuillard's copyrights. In the domestic litigation, a visual arts collecting society representing the Vuillard estate demanded, and eventually received, compensation for the use. The Commission accepted that the collecting society's claim to royalties was consistent with Article 10. More controversially, however, the Commission observed that it was normally not for the organs of the European Convention to adjudicate possible conflicts between the rights to communicate information freely and the rights of the authors of the communicated works.[141] Even so, the Commission went on to explain that the requirement to pay royalties did not generate a conflict with Article 10, and that this restriction was,

[140] *France 2 supra* note 134.
[141] "[La Commission] rappelle également qu'il n'appartient normalement pas aux organes de la Convention de régler, au regard du [art. 10(2)], les conflits susceptibles d'apparaître entre, d'une part, le droit de communiquer librement des informations et, d'autre part, le droit des auteurs dont les oeuvres sont communiquées."

within the terms of Article 10(2), necessary in a democratic society in order to protect the rights of others.[142]

At the domestic level, one of the fullest analyses of the relationship between copyright law and Article 10 is in the English decision *Ashdown v. Telegraph Group Ltd.*[143] The case concerned publication of a portion (approximately one fifth) of a confidential memorandum prepared by Lord (Paddy) Ashdown (referred to by the Court as "Mr. Ashdown") on October 21, 1997, at the time that he was leader of the Liberal Democrats, a major British political party. Approximately one quarter of the article consisted of a verbatim or almost-verbatim reproduction of the memorandum. The memorandum was an *aide memoir* prepared by Mr. Ashdown that disclosed, contrary to public denials by political leaders, that high-level meetings on the topic of constitutional reform continued between Mr. Ashdown and the Labour prime minister, Tony Blair, after the British Labour Party's landslide election victory in 1997. By some unknown means, a copy of the memorandum reached the hands of the political editor of the *Sunday Telegraph* newspaper. Mr. Ashdown contended that publication of the newspaper article infringed his copyright in the memorandum. The judge at first instance, Sir Andrew Morritt, Vice-Chancellor, gave judgment against the Telegraph Group on the copyright claim and granted a final injunction against any further infringement. He also directed the defendant to provide Mr. Ashdown with sufficient information to enable him to elect between damages and an account of profits.

The Vice-Chancellor rejected the Telegraph Group's contention that, when considering whether an actionable breach of copyright has occurred or the remedies appropriate in the event of such a breach, an English court must give separate consideration to the impact of Article 10. He observed that there had been no previous reported case, either in the European Court of Human Rights or in the courts of the United Kingdom, that had considered the interaction between freedom of expression and copyright. Although Lord Morritt accepted that Article 10 could be engaged in a claim for copyright infringement, he reasoned:

[142] "La Commission relève que la condamnation de la requérante à payer des dommages-intérêts trouve sa cause dans l'absence de paiement de la redevance due à l'auteur des fresques intégralement diffusées. Compte tenu des circonstances de l'espèce, la Commission considère qu'il était raisonnable, pour les juridictions saisies dans l'intérêt de l'auteur et de ses ayants droit, de tenir compte des droits de ceux-ci sur les oeuvres au demeurant librement diffusées par la requérante. En conséquence, la Commission estime que la restriction ou sanction litigieuse constituait une mesure nécessaire, dans une société démocratique, à la protection des droits d'autrui."
[143] [2001] EWCA (Civ) 1142 (Eng.).

It does not follow that because Article 10 is engaged the facts of each case have to be considered to determine whether the restriction imposed by the law of copyright goes further than what is necessary in a democratic society. Article 10.2 recognises that the exercise of the right to freedom of expression carries with it duties and responsibilities.

The Vice-Chancellor also observed that Article 10 cannot be relied on to create defenses to an alleged infringement over and above those for which the Copyright Act provides:

> The balance between the rights of the owner of the copyright and those of the public has been struck by the legislative organ of the democratic state itself in the legislation it has enacted. There is no room for any further defences outside the code which establishes the particular species of intellectual property in question.

Subsequently, the Court of Appeal for England and Wales dismissed an appeal by the newspaper and required the newspaper to pay 95 percent of Lord Ashdown's costs. The Court of Appeal's judgment, excerpted below, offers an extensive analysis of the relationship between copyright law and the right to freedom of expression. It begins with an analysis of the limits on freedom of expression in Article 10's second paragraph:

Ashdown v. Telegraph Group Ltd. [2001] EWCA (Civ) 1142 (Eng.)

The second paragraph of this Article is particularly significant. In a democratic society there are many circumstances in which freedom of expression must, of necessity, be restricted. In particular untrammelled exercise of freedom of expression will often infringe the "rights of others", both under the Convention and outside it. The right to respect for one's private life recognised by Article 8 is an example. More pertinent in the present context is the right recognised by Article 1 of the First Protocol [to the ECHR].

Telegraph Group submit that s.12 of the Human Rights Act is of importance when considering the contest between the remedies available for breach of copyright and the right to freedom of expression. That section provides:

(1) This section applies if a court is considering whether to grant any relief which, if granted, might affect the exercise of the Convention right to freedom of expression....

(4) The court must have particular regard to the importance of the Convention right to freedom of expression and, where the proceedings relate to material which the respondent claims, or which appears to the court, to be

journalistic, literary or artistic material (or to conduct connected with such material), to (a) the extent to which – (i) the material has, or is about to, become available to the public; or (ii) it is, or would be, in the public interest for the material to be published; (b) any relevant privacy code.

Telegraph Group contends that the Vice-Chancellor was wrong to reject the submission that "must have particular regard to" indicates that the Court should place extra weight on the matters to which the subsection refers. The requirement of s.2(1) of the Human Rights Act to take account of the [ECtHR] jurisprudence must apply to the interpretation of the Act itself. It seems to us that s.12 does no more than underline the need to have regard to contexts in which that jurisprudence has given particular weight to freedom of expression, while at the same time drawing attention to considerations which may nonetheless justify restricting that right.

The infringement of copyright constitutes interference with "the peaceful enjoyment of possessions." It is, furthermore, the interference with a right arising under a statute which confers rights recognised under international convention and harmonised under European law. There is thus no question but that restriction of the right of freedom of expression can be justified where necessary in a democratic society in order to protect copyright. The protection afforded to copyright under the 1988 Act is, however, itself subject to exceptions. Thus both the right of freedom of expression and copyright are qualified. This appeal raises the question of how the two rights fall to be balanced, when they are in conflict.

The Nature of Copyright

It is important to emphasise in the present context that it is only the form of the literary work that is protected by copyright. Copyright does not normally prevent the publication of the information conveyed by the literary work. Thus it is only the freedom to express information using the verbal formula devised by another that is prevented by copyright. This will not normally constitute a significant encroachment on the freedom of expression. The prime importance of freedom of expression is that it enables the citizen freely to express ideas and convey information. It is also important that the citizen should be free to express the ideas and convey the information in a form of words of his or her choice. It is stretching the concept of freedom of expression to postulate that it extends to the freedom to convey ideas and information using the form of words devised by someone else. Nonetheless there are circumstances, as we shall demonstrate in due course, where this freedom is important.

Restrictions on Copyright

The Vice-Chancellor ... drew attention to the fact that it is possible to identify 42 circumstances in which copying material does not infringe copyright. He concluded that each of these reflected circumstances in which freedom of expression was recognised and confirmed. In effect they were circumstances where freedom of expression trumped copyright protection. Two of these call for particular consideration in the circumstances of this case. The first is the defence of fair dealing that is provided by s.30 of the Copyright Act. So far as material, that section provides:

> Criticism, review and news reporting. 30(1) Fair dealing with a work for the purpose of criticism or review, of that or another work or of a performance of a work, does not infringe any copyright in the work.... (2) Fair dealing with a work (other than a photograph) for the purpose of reporting current events does not infringe any copyright in the work....

We agree that these provisions reflect freedom of expression in that, in the specific circumstances set out and provided that there is "fair dealing," freedom of expression displaces the protection that would otherwise be afforded to copyright.

The other restriction which requires consideration is the defence to a claim for breach of copyright that can be mounted on the basis of 'public interest.' This is not a statutory defence, but one which arises at common law, and which subsists by virtue of s.171(3) of the Copyright Act, which provides:

> Nothing in this Part affects any rule of law preventing or restricting the enforcement of copyright, on grounds of public interest or otherwise.

Telegraph Group argued that this provision enabled the Court to give effect to the right of freedom of expression at the expense of copyright, save where it was necessary in a democratic society that freedom of expression should give way. The Vice-Chancellor rejected this submission, holding that the defence of public interest is narrowly constrained under English law. This conclusion is one to which we shall have to give detailed consideration.

Remedies for Breach of Copyright

In this case the Vice-Chancellor granted Mr. Ashdown an injunction restraining any further infringement of the copyright in his work. An injunction has been said to be "a peculiarly suitable and, indeed, the normal remedy" for breach of copyright. It is, however, a discretionary remedy and subject to the principles governing the grant of an injunction, whether interlocutory or final, in other areas of our law.

Compensatory relief is also available for breach of copyright. The claimant has the option of seeking damages, which will reflect the loss caused to him by the breach, or an account of the profits made by the defendant from the use of the claimant's work.

Has the Human Rights Act Impacted on the Protection Afforded to Copyright?

We have already observed that in most circumstances, the principle of freedom of expression will be sufficiently protected if there is a right to publish information and ideas set out in another's literary work, without copying the very words which that person has employed to convey the information or express the ideas. In such circumstances it will normally be necessary in a democratic society that the author of the work should have his property in his own creation protected. Strasbourg jurisprudence demonstrates, however, that circumstances can arise in which freedom of expression will only be fully effective if an individual is permitted to reproduce the very words spoken by another.

Freedom of expression protects the right both to publish information and to receive it. There will be occasions when it is in the public interest not merely that information should be published, but that the public should be told the very words used by a person, notwithstanding that the author enjoys copyright in them. On occasions, indeed, it is the form and not the content of a document which is of interest.

Where the subject matter of the information is a current event, s.30(2) of the Copyright Act may permit publication of the words used. But it is possible to conceive of information of the greatest public interest relating not to a current event, but to a document produced in the past. We are not aware of any provision of the Copyright Act which would permit publication in such circumstances, unless the mere fact of publication, and any controversy created by the disclosure, is sufficient to make them 'current events.' This will often be a "bootstraps" argument of little merit....

For these reasons, we have reached the conclusion that rare circumstances can arise where the right of freedom of expression will come into conflict with the protection afforded by the Copyright Act, notwithstanding the express exceptions to be found in the Act. In these circumstances, we consider that the court is bound, insofar as it is able, to apply the Act in a manner that accommodates the right of freedom of expression. This will make it necessary for the Court to look closely at the facts of individual cases (as indeed it must whenever a "fair dealing" defence is raised). We do not foresee this leading to a flood of litigation.

The first way in which it may be possible to do this is by declining the discretionary relief of an injunction. Usually, so it seems to us, such a step will be likely to be sufficient. If a newspaper considers it necessary to copy the exact words created by another, we can see no reason in principle why the newspaper should not indemnify the author for any loss caused to him, or alternatively account to him for any profit made as a result of copying his work. Freedom of expression should not normally carry with it the right to make free use of another's work.

[The Court of Appeal then considered the scope of the "public interest" defense in copyright law.]

We prefer the conclusion ... that the circumstances in which public interest may override copyright are not capable of precise categorisation or definition. Now that the Human Rights Act is in force, there is the clearest public interest in giving effect to the right of freedom of expression in those rare cases where this right trumps the rights conferred by the Copyright Act. In such circumstances, we consider that the defence of public interest [can be] raised.

We do not consider that this conclusion will lead to a flood of cases where freedom of expression is invoked as a defence to a claim for breach of copyright. It will be very rare for the public interest to justify the copying of the form of a work to which copyright attaches. We would add that the implications of the Human Rights Act must always be considered where the discretionary relief of an injunction is sought, and this is true in the field of copyright quite apart from the ambit of the public interest defence.

[Endorsing the analysis by the Vice-Chancellor, the Court of Appeal next held that the newspaper could not rely on the defense of fair dealing for the purposes of criticism or review.]

On one of the ingredients required to establish a defence under s.30(2) of the Copyright Act [fair dealing for the purposes of reporting current events] the Judge found in favour of the Telegraph Group. He held that there was a reasonable prospect of the Sunday Telegraph establishing that the copying of the minute was for the purpose of reporting current events, those events including such matters as: "the continuing issue over the degree and nature of actual and planned co-operation between Labour and the Liberal Democrats" and the: "continuing saga over the role of and accuracy of information disseminated by the Prime Minister's press office."

... As this Court said in *Pro Sieben A.G. v. Carlton Television Ltd* [1999] 1 WLR 605 at 614G, the expression "reporting current events" should be interpreted liberally. The defence ... is clearly intended to protect the role of the media in informing the public about matters of current concern to the public. The meeting between the claimant, the Prime Minister and others in October 1997 was undoubtedly an event, and while it might be said that by November 1999 it was not current solely in the sense of recent in time, it was arguably a matter of current interest to the public. In a democratic society, information about a meeting between the Prime Minister and an opposition party leader during the then current Parliament to discuss possible close co-operation between those parties is very likely to be of legitimate and continuing public interest. It might impinge upon the way in which the public would vote at the next general election. The "issues" identified by the Sunday Telegraph may not themselves be "events," but the existence of those issues may help to demonstrate the continuing public interest in a meeting two years earlier.

For present purposes all that we have to decide is whether the Judge was right in holding that it was arguable that publication was for "the purpose of reporting current events." We are in no doubt that he was.

Fair Dealing

Where part of a work is copied in the course of a report on current events, the "fair dealing" defence ... will normally afford the Court all the scope that it needs properly to reflect the public interest in freedom of expression and, in particular, the freedom of the press. There will then be no need to give separate consideration to the availability of a public interest defence....

We have considered why it should ever be contrary to the public interest that a newspaper should have to pay compensation, or account for the profit made, when it makes unauthorised use of the work product of another. We have concluded that s.30 provides examples of situations where this may be justified, and that these are broadly in line with the Strasbourg jurisprudence in another area where freedom of expression has to be balanced against a justification for restricting that freedom which is recognised by Article 10.

In the field of defamation, the European Court of Human Rights has recognized that the awarding of damages by a public authority for press publication of defamatory statements may infringe Article 10, at least where the publication consists of balanced reporting on a matter of current public interest. The reason is that such liability may discourage the participation by the press in matters of public concern – *Bladet Tromso and Stensaas v. Norway* (1999) 29 EHRR 125. In *Tolstoy Miloslavsky v. United Kingdom* (1995) 20 EHRR 442, where individual but not press freedom of expression was in issue, the Court held that Article 10 was infringed, not because damages were awarded, but because the size of the damages was disproportionate to the legitimate aim of providing reasonable compensation for injury to reputation.

The fair dealing defense under s. 30 should lie where the public interest in learning of the very words written by the owner of the copyright is such that publication should not be inhibited by the chilling factor of having to pay damages or account for profits. When considering this question it is right to observe that, as damages are compensatory and not at large, they may produce a relatively mild chill.

Commercial competition: [The] Telegraph Group contended that its publication "in no or no appreciable way competed with any publication or publications which the Claimant might issue in the future." The Vice-Chancellor rejected this assertion, and we consider that he was right to do so. There was evidence, as he pointed out, that the publication in the *Sunday Telegraph* destroyed a part of the value of the memoirs that it had been Mr. Ashdown's intention to sell, and that he did, in fact, sell. Equally we are in no doubt that the extensive quotations of Mr. Ashdown's own words added a flavor to the description of the events covered that made the article more attractive to read and will have been of significant commercial value in enabling the *Sunday Telegraph* to maintain, if not to enhance, the loyalty of its readership.

Prior publication: The Vice-Chancellor rightly attached importance to the fact that the minute was secret and had been obtained by Telegraph Group without Mr. Ashdown's knowledge or approval.

The Amount and Importance of the Work Taken

Here again we consider that the Vice-Chancellor correctly found that this aspect of the test of fair dealing weighed against the defense of fair dealing. A substantial portion of the minute was copied, and it is reasonable to conclude, for the reasons given by the Vice-Chancellor at paragraph 29, that the most important passages in the minute were selected for publication.

All these considerations point in one direction and satisfy us that the Vice-Chancellor was correct to conclude that if the established authorities fell to be applied without any additional regard to the effect of Article 10, there was no realistic prospect that a defense of fair dealing would be made out.

Human Rights Impact: At this point, however, we believe that it is necessary to consider the impact of the public interest on the test of fair dealing. Are the facts of this case such that, arguably, the importance of freedom of expression outweighs the conventional considerations set out previously so as to afford the Telegraph Group a defense of fair dealing?

Is it arguable that it was necessary to quote verbatim the passages of which Mr. Ashdown was the author in order to convey to the readers of the *Sunday Telegraph* the authenticity of its reports of current events of public interest? [Counsel for the Telegraph Group] argued that it was. He contended that the subject matter of the article was of high public interest, concerning the potential composition of the government of the country. It related to an important meeting between the prime minister and other leading political figures, including Mr. Ashdown. It was true that the basic facts in the articles may have been published already in the *Financial Times*, the *Observer*, and the radio interview on *Resigning Issues*. But Mr. Ashdown's own words gave the factual material a detail and authority that were novel.

There had been previous publications that gave the public much of the information that was contained in the *Sunday Telegraph* articles. An article in the *Financial Times* dated 11 June 1999 reported that Mr. Ashdown and Mr. Blair had been "hatching a secret project the creation of a Lab-Lib coalition." On 26 September 1999 the political editor of the *Observer* told its readers:

> Tony Blair and Paddy Ashdown privately agreed to try to persuade Labour and the Liberal Democrats to go into the next election on a joint policy manifesto, before the LibDem leader stood down. Details of the scheme are due to be revealed in Ashdown's diaries. Downing Street is seeking assurances that the diaries will not be published until after the next election. The diaries, a highly detailed account of Ashdown's top secret contacts with Labour, are described as explosive by one senior Liberal Democrat who has seen extracts. The source said: "They were practising a massive deception on their respective parties."

There were a number of other newspaper articles to similar effect.

The accuracy of these accounts was challenged by Mr. Blair. In these circumstances we consider that, just as there is scope for argument that the *Sunday Telegraph*'s publication was the reporting of current events, so it is arguable that the Telegraph Group were justified in making limited quotation of Mr. Ashdown's own words, in order to demonstrate that they had indeed obtained his own minute, so that they were in a position to give an authentic account of the meeting. In this context the last of the criteria that we have just considered is of critical relevance. Can it be argued that the extensive reproduction of Mr. Ashdown's own words was necessary in order to satisfy the reader that the account given of his meeting with Mr. Blair was authoritative? We do not believe that it can. The statement by the *Sunday Telegraph* that they had obtained a copy of the minute coupled with one or two short extracts from it would have sufficed.

There may in law have been justification for the publication of the confidential information that was contained in the minute. That is not an issue that is before this court. We do not, however, consider that it is arguable that there was any justification for the extent of the reproduction of Mr. Ashdown's own words. It appears to us that the minute was deliberately filleted in order to extract colorful passages that were most likely to add flavor to the article and thus to appeal to the readership of the newspaper. Mr. Ashdown's work product was deployed in the way that it was for reasons that were essentially journalistic in furtherance of the commercial interests of the Telegraph Group. We do not consider it arguable that Article 10 requires that the Group should be able to profit from this use of Mr. Ashdown's copyright without paying compensation.

This appeal has been founded on the contention that the Vice-Chancellor erred in law in holding that the Telegraph Group had infringed the Copyright Act. No separate attack was made upon the exercise of his discretion in granting injunctive relief. It follows that we do not need to consider whether that relief was appropriate having regard to s.12 of the Human Rights Act and Article 10 of the Convention.

---

* * * Issues in Focus * * *

A key issue addressed in *Ashdown v. Telegraph Group Ltd.* concerned the scope of remedies available in a copyright infringement case. The English Court of Appeal emphasized that an injunction may not necessarily be granted to a successful plaintiff. Without such an injunction, copyright owners cannot stop the publication of copyright-protected material. The Court of Appeal also concluded, however, that it was consistent with the right to freedom of expression set forth in Article 10 of the European Convention on Human Rights to insist that copyright owners receive payment for the uses of this material. In essence, the court replaced a "property" rule with a "liability" rule.[144] The price for licensing certain copyrighted works in England will thus presumably be negotiated in the shadow of the possibility that a court may set the fee for the use through the imposition of a damages award. As explored in the Notes and Questions that follow, this approach intervenes in the copyright marketplace by helping to ensure that copyright owners cannot act as "holdouts" to preclude the distribution of protected material by users who seek a license for that purpose. This is not the same, however, as putting the copyright-protected material in the public domain.

Another theme explored in the Notes and Questions is the importance of context to assessing the extent to which intellectual property protection impinges on the right to freedom of expression. For instance, in the *De Geïllustreerde Pers* case, it is possible that the income derived from the radio and television listings was important to the economic viability of broadcasting stations in post–World War II Holland. From a systemic perspective, it might be important to analyze the right to freedom of information and its relevance to copyright law in light of the overall situation existing within the particular nation state at the relevant time.

The Notes and Questions also consider another body of law that may limit the scope of copyright protection: competition law. Competition law (often

---

[144] *See generally* Guido Calabresi & A. Douglas Melamed, *Property Rules, Liability Rules and Inalienability: One View of the Cathedral*, 85 HARV. L. REV. 1089 (1972).

referred to as in the U.S. as antitrust law) provides a legal basis for curbing the overreaching by intellectual property owners. Although this branch of law is principally concerned with ensuring that firms do not abuse dominant market positions, the practical effect of some competition law cases has been to put copyright-protected material in the public domain.

Notes and Questions

1. In *Ashdown*, the Court of Appeal recognized that it may not always be appropriate to grant an injunction in a copyright infringement case. Similarly, the U.S. Supreme Court has "consistently rejected invitations to replace traditional equitable considerations with a rule that an injunction automatically follows a determination that a copyright has been infringed."[145] The Court endorsed this approach in a case involving an electronic database containing articles from *The New York Times*, which contained articles by freelance writers whose contracts were silent as to the newspaper's right to claim copyright in the articles.[146] These observations as to the discretionary character of injunctive relief were made by the Court as a riposte to the claim that upholding the freelance writers' copyrights would leave "gaping" holes in the electronic record of history.[147] Another case where the Court confirmed that an injunction would not automatically issue was the *Campbell* decision, which, as noted previously, involved an assertion that the defendant's work was a "parody."[148] In *Dun v. Lumbermen's Credit Assn.*,[149] a 1908 case, the Court declined to overturn the Court of Appeals' decision not to grant an injunction in a case involving allegations of infringement of the copyright in "lists of merchants, manufacturers, and traders in the United States and the North American British possessions." Do these U.S. cases have any characteristics in common? Is there common ground between these cases and *Ashdown*?

2. Recall that the U.S. Supreme Court has endorsed the "internalization" thesis, which asserts that the idea/expression dichotomy strikes a "definitional balance" between copyright and the First Amendment. Copyright law achieves this balance, it is argued, by ensuring that only the author's original expression is privatized, and that the ideas remain in the public domain. As you engage with the European materials, it will be helpful to consider points

---

[145] *eBay Inc. v. MercExchange, L.L.C.*, 547 U.S. 388, 393–94 (2006).
[146] *N.Y. Times v. Tasini*, 533 U.S. 483, 505 (2001).
[147] *Id.*
[148] *Campbell v. Acuff-Rose Music, Inc.*, 510 U.S. 569, 578 n.10 (1994).
[149] 209 U.S. 20, 23–24 (1908).

of contrast and correspondence with the U.S. approach. How, for example, do courts in different jurisdictions view the "internalization" of freedom of expression (or information) by copyright law? Within the framework of the ECHR, the English Court of Appeal has recognized that the right to freedom of expression will sometimes require use of the actual words (expression) used by the copyright owner. On the surface, these approaches appear to be quite different. But does the U.S. approach to fair use achieve much the same thing as is suggested by the English court's (possibly) more permissive approach to the authorized use of copyright-protected expression? Contrariwise, could it be argued that the approach to the idea/expression dichotomy that is suggested by *Ashdown* is actually *less* protective of expressive freedoms than the U.S. approach? As the extract from *Ashdown* shows, the English court appeared to consider it generally appropriate for a defendant to *pay* for the use when an injunction does not issue, in order "to indemnify the author for any loss caused to him, or alternatively account to him for any profit made as a result of copying his work." Does this dictum suggest that the commercial importance of the memorandum might outweigh the freedom of expression values at stake?

   3. A 2003 case before French Cour de Cassation concerned a fleeting, but apparently integral, reproduction of twelve paintings by Maurice Utrillo in a TV report on a museum exhibition about the artist. Notwithstanding a reference to Article 10 of the ECHR, the French court upheld a decision requiring the broadcaster to pay compensation for intentionally screening the paintings.[150] Advancing an approach that is broadly similar to that of the English Court of Appeal in *Ashdown*, Professors Strowel and Tulkens have argued that "the true underlying question in [the *Utrillo*] case is whether it was indispensable for the broadcaster to display the paintings in the manner in which it did in order to inform the public of the exhibition.... The opinion of the French court appears quite restrictive, but it is also clear that the broadcaster was invoking the right of the public to avoid payment to the copyright holders. A financial rather than an access issue was thus lurking in the background."[151] The suggestion, which also appears to be consistent with the European Commission's analysis in the Vuillard frescoes case, is that attempts to obtain compensation for copyright infringement do not in themselves trigger Article 10. If "freedom of expression should not normally carry with it the right to make free use of another's work," as the court in

---

[150] *Utrillo*, premiere chamber civile [Cass. 1e civ.] [First Civil Chamber of the Cour de Cassation] Nov. 13, 2003 (unreported), JCP éd. G 2004, II 10080.

[151] Strowel & Turlkens, *supra* note 130, at 306.

Ashdown indicated, are there any circumstances where such compensation claims might raise free expression concerns? Would – or should – it make a difference to the analysis if the defendant is not the owner of a major newspaper, but is instead (a) a fledgling online political blog; (b) an established political magazine that has fallen on hard times; or (c) a web site version of an established newspaper, where the web site version is owned by a subsidiary corporation and runs at a loss? Is "indispensible" the appropriate threshold in each example?

4. The ECtHR has developed the "margin of appreciation" doctrine to provide a modicum of discretion to democratically elected national governments that apply and interpret the Convention. The court has emphasized that such deference is appropriate because it is not always as well-equipped as national actors to strike an appropriate balance among competing interests in complex areas of law and policy.[152] In assessing whether officials have overstepped their margin of appreciation, the ECtHR considers, among other factors, whether a measure taken in the general interest bears a reasonable relationship of proportionality to the governmental aim pursued.[153] Does the prevailing approach to assessing the potential impact of copyright on freedom of expression – that the payment of, or demand for, compensation for the use of protected works does not normally implicate Article 10 – introduce a kind of "economic proportionality" principle to the copyright marketplace? If so, how should this principle apply if the defendant attempted to secure a license and was refused, or if the price demanded by the copyright owner was disproportionately higher than the market value of the license (assuming its market value can be established)?

5. A possible interpretation of the emerging European jurisprudence is that copyright owners are being put on notice that they may be unable to assert their copyrights to the extent ordinarily permitted by law if their demands are unreasonable, taking into account other factors, including whether the defendant's use is "necessary." Conventionally, the law allows property owners both to set their own price for property they seek to alienate and to refuse to sell at all. At the interface between human rights and intellectual property, however, is the right to freedom of expression coming to impose a set of "human rights parameters" around the operation of the copyright marketplace, warning copyright owners to keep their demands "in proportion" in the light of all the circumstances? Consider a copyright infringement claim

---

[152] *See generally* Y. ARAI-TAKAHASHI, THE MARGIN OF APPRECIATION DOCTRINE AND THE PRINCIPLE OF PROPORTIONALITY IN THE JURISPRUDENCE OF THE ECHR (2002).

[153] Ernst-Ulrich Petersmann, *Human Rights, International Economic Law and "Constitutional Justice,"* 19 EUR. J. INT'L L. 769, 778 (2008).

challenging the unauthorized posting to a web site of internal corporate memoranda that identify flaws in electronic voting machines that the firm manufactures. How might the discussion of the various rationales for the right to freedom of expression that appears in Section 2.4 of this chapter inform analysis of the different interests at stake in this example?

6. In the *De Gueillustreerde Pers* decision, the Commission considered that the freedom under Article 10 to impart the television and radio program listings "is only granted to the person or body who produces, provides or organises it," a conclusion one leading commentator has described as "difficult to fathom."[154] What kind of "grant" did the 1967 Broadcasting Act make? Should the exclusive right to publish the listings be understood as a right that accompanies the statutory authorization to operate a broadcasting franchise?

7. The applicant in *De Gueillustreerde Pers* also alleged that the refusal to grant it a license was inconsistent with Article 14 of the ECHR, which provides: "The enjoyment of the rights and freedoms set forth in the Convention shall be secured without discrimination on any ground such as sex, race, color language, religion, political or other opinion, national or social origin, association with a national minority, property, birth or other status." The Commission concluded that the differential treatment received by different magazines was "not discriminatory on any ground ... within the meaning of article 14 of the Convention in conjunction with article 10, as it pursues a legitimate aim." The Commission explained this point in more detail:

> Under the Netherlands system broadcasting organizations, whilst performing a public service, are companies created under private law. Broadcasting time is allocated to them according to their membership and an indication of membership is given by the number of subscriptions to the broadcasting organisations' programme magazines. Furthermore, the profits from the subscriptions to the programme magazines contribute to the financing of the broadcasting activities of the organizations, although it appears that they are mainly financed by public funds deriving from television and radio licence fees and the yields of advertising.

> In this situation, the Commission considers that, apart from any other considerations, there are objective and reasonable grounds justifying the protection granted to programme magazines against competition from the general interest magazines.

Is any of this history also relevant to the application of Article 10? The Commission provided further contextual background in the initial paragraphs of its decision, which briefly recount some of the twentieth-century history of broadcasting in the Netherlands. As the Commission describes

---

[154] Hugenholtz, *supra* note 130, at 358.

it, the private-sector firms whose business concerned the transmission of wireless broadcasting in the 1920s "reflected the various cultural, political, spiritual and social sections of which Netherlands society was composed." In 1928, the Dutch broadcasting regulations were amended in a manner that was consistent with the private-sector origins of the broadcasting system. During the Second World War, however, the occupation authorities put an end to a broadcasting system that was based on free, private-sector organizations and established a state-owned enterprise that controlled broadcasting. Under the system that was established after the war, organizations that existed prior to the occupation resumed broadcasting. Broadcasting was then funded through the levying of a broadcasting fee. To raise additional operation funds, the broadcasting organizations had to "rely on contributions received from their members, either in the form of subscriptions to their weekly magazines, or as simple contributions." The 1967 Broadcasting Act, which largely confirmed these arrangements, was enacted after "long political debates." Should any account be taken of this history when assessing any potential conflict between copyright protection of the schedules and Article 10 of the ECHR?

8. In a series of important decisions, the European Court of Justice (ECJ) and the European Court of First Instance have held that the assertion of rights under a copyright may be limited by European Community (EC) competition law. *Radio Telefis Eireann v. European Commission Joined Cases C-241–249/91 P (Magill)*[155] arose out of a decision by an Irish court to enjoin the publication by Magill of a weekly television guide that contained all the listings of various television channels available in the reception area. Prior to the publication of the *Magill TV Guide*, there were no comprehensive weekly broadcast listings available in Ireland, unlike in other EC member states. Consumers who sought comprehensive program listings were required to buy three weekly television guides. Under the applicable Irish and U.K. law, program listings enjoyed copyright protection as literary works and as compilations. Magill also lodged a complaint with the European Commission of the EC (not to be confused with the similarly named European Commission of Human Rights) claiming that the broadcasting companies were violating EC competition law. Upholding the complaint, the Commission ruled in 1988 that the broadcasters were required to supply each other "and third parties on request and on a non discriminatory basis with their individual advance weekly programme listings and [to] permi[t] reproduction of those listings by such parties." The Commission also stated that any royalties for such reproductions

---

[155] [1995] All E.R. 416, [1995] F.S.R. 530.

"should be reasonable." The Court of First Instance subsequently ruled that the broadcasting companies were abusing a dominant position, a holding that the ECJ in turn upheld. In *IMS Health v. NDC Health*,[156] the ECJ again held that a refusal by an entity occupying a dominant position to license an intellectual property right such as to prevent the emergence of new products or services could constitute an abuse of a dominant market position. The TRIPS Agreement suggests that the copyright/competition law interface will continue to evolve.[157] Although TRIPS is silent about international and domestic human rights law, it expressly allows member states to constrain the anticompetitive effects of intellectual property rights.[158]

9. The facts of *Magill* and *De Geillustreerde* share some superficial similarities, but there are also some important differences: in the latter decision, for example, the state broadcasting agency was itself facilitating the production of aggregated listings, whereas in the circumstances described in *Magill*, no aggregated listing was available in the relevant market. Even so, as *Magill* and *IMS* illustrate, competition law's concern with the impediments that copyright law can impose on the emergence of new products shares common ground with some of the concerns underlying the right to freedom of expression. In many instances, anticompetitive behavior will impede potential competitors' production and dissemination of information-rich products. In Chapter 1, we described a "regime shift" in international law: the inability or unwillingness of international intellectual property law bodies to address human rights concerns triggered an examination of intellectual property and trade issues by international human rights bodies. Is it possible to characterize the invocation of competition law to curtail overreaching assertions of intellectual property rights as a nascent "regime shift" in another direction? That is, in European jurisprudence, is competition law a possible vehicle for "protecting" the right to freedom of expression from copyright law? As we indicated previously, leading commentators have identified the potential relevance of economic issues to the human rights/copyright interface. Does the concern expressed by the European Commission (raised particularly in the *Magill* case) to keep royalties at a reasonable level reinforce this insight?

---

[156] Case C-418/01, 1 E.C.R. 503 (2004).

[157] In *Microsoft v. Commission of the European Commission*, No. T-201/04. (Sept. 17, 2007), for instance, the Court of First Instance upheld most of a decision by the European Commission finding Microsoft to have infringed EC competition law by refusing to supply information that is relevant to the interoperability of Microsoft software with products that other firms might develop. For a discussion of more recent developments, *see* Nicholas Economides & Ioannis Lianos, *The Elusive Antitrust Standard on Bundling in Europe and in the United States in the Aftermath of the Microsoft Cases*, 76 ANTITRUST L.J. 483 (2009).

[158] TRIPS Agreement, *supra* note 102, art. 40.

10. Within the EC, copyright is supplemented by *sui generis* protection of databases, which is required by the 1996 Database Directive.[159] The Directive limits copyright protection to databases "which, by reason of the selection or arrangement of their contents, constitute the author's own intellectual creation."[160] In this, the Directive is consistent with the typical scope of protection that copyright law affords to original compilations. The *sui generis* protection that the Directive provides is more controversial. The principal criterion for protection is substantial quantitative or qualitative investment in obtaining, checking, or presenting the contents of the database.[161] The investment expended in gathering data substitutes for the originality requirement in copyright law. Under the Database Directive, the duration of rights can be extended beyond an initial fifteen-year term, presumably perpetually, if any substantial quantitative or qualitative change is made to the contents of the database.[162] The Directive protects against the unauthorized extraction or reutilization of the whole or a substantial part of the database.

Some commentators have characterized *sui generis* protection of databases as an "extravagant" form of copyright.[163] Controversy surrounding the database right has prevented the adoption of a multilateral treaty on the topic.[164] A frequently expressed fear is that exclusive rights in data "entai[l] setting up an economic barrier to all access to information."[165] Commentators have also drawn attention to the adverse implications for developing countries: "Setting up a monopoly over information through the *sui generis* right on databases not only jeopardizes access to information by developing countries, but also prevents the non-commercial sector from taking advantage of the free flow of information."[166] These concerns persist despite the inclusion in the European Database Directive of specific exceptions for the extraction of data for private purposes, for teaching and scientific research (if the source is indicated and the extraction is justified by the noncommercial character of these uses), and

---

[159] Council Directive 96/9/EC, On the Legal Protection of Databases, 1996 O.J. (L 77) 20 [European Database Directive].

[160] *Id.* art. 3.

[161] *Id.* art. 7.

[162] *Id.* art. 10.

[163] Séverine Dusollier, Yves Poullet & Mireille Buydens, *Copyright and Access to Information in the Digital Environment*, 34 COPYRIGHT BULL. 4, 7 (2000).

[164] The World Intellectual Property Organization has been unable to secure agreement at the international level to the adoption of such a treaty. *See Diplomatic Conference on Certain Copyright and Neighboring Rights Questions*, Geneva, Switz., Dec. 2–20, 1996, *available at* http://www.wipo.int/meetings/en/details.jsp?meeting_id=3010.

[165] Dusollier et al., *supra* note 163, at 7.

[166] *Id.* at 8.

for purposes of public security.[167] Are these exceptions sufficiently broad to address potential human rights concerns?

10. Recent evidence suggests that the European Database Directive has not been particularly effective in encouraging the production of databases, or, at best, that the results have been mixed.[168] This raises an interesting set of questions that are relevant to both utilitarian and human rights perspectives on the database right. From a utilitarian perspective, it questions the necessity for a *sui generis* database right that imposes an additional barrier to entry for other firms seeking to build on existing data collections. From a human rights perspective, the empirical evidence offers an interesting point of comparison with copyright. The preceding analysis suggests that copyright internalizes the principle of freedom of expression by encouraging more speech by authors. If the incentives underlying the *sui generis* right are not particularly strong and do not encourage the creation and maintenance of databases, this may provide an additional ground for challenging the *sui generis* right on freedom of expression grounds.

11. Privacy is another human right that intersects in complex ways with both copyright and the right to freedom of expression. Numerous U.N. and regional human rights instruments contain a provision protecting privacy. Among the most well known is Article 8 of the European Convention on Human Rights, which states that "[e]veryone has the right to respect for his private and family life, his home and his correspondence." The European Court of Human Rights has held that Article 8 recognizes "the fundamental importance of protecting private life from the point of view of the development of every human being's personality."[169]

Privacy concerns relating to intellectual property have been heightened by the increasingly pervasive delivery of copyrighted content in digital formats. Suppliers of such content have both the technological capacity and commercial motivations to collect, store, and analyze information about purchasers and licensees.[170] Similar concerns have also been triggered by

---

[167] European Database Directive, *supra* note 159, art. 9.

[168] Comm'n Eur. Cmtys., *First Evaluation of Directive 96/9/EC on the Legal Protection of Databases*, DG Internal Market and Services Working Paper, at 24 (Dec. 12, 2005) (noting that the sui generis right has had no proven impact on the production of databases), *available at* http://ec.europa.eu/internal_market/copyright/docs/databases/evaluation_report_en.pdf.

[169] *Von Hannover v. Germany*, App. No. 59320/00, 2004-VI ECHR (2004), para. 69; *see also P.G. & J.H. v. United Kingdom*, App. No. 44787/98, 2001-IX ECHR, para. 56 (stating that Article 8 "protects a right to identity and personal development").

[170] *Von Hannover*, *supra* note 169, para. 70 (asserting that "increased vigilance in protecting private life is necessary to contend with new communication technologies which make it possible to store and reproduce personal data").

copyright owners' demands that internet service providers disclose personal information about subscribers who are suspected of supplying, accessing, or downloading copyright-protected material without authorization.[171]

These issues have generally not been framed in the discourse of human rights, but they nevertheless touch upon the core justifications for protecting privacy in international human rights law.[172] In addition, the right to privacy connects to with some of the rationales for freedom of expression discussed previously in this chapter. As noted in Section 4.3, Martha Nussbaum emphasized the importance of the human capabilities approach to human rights of "being able to use the senses; being able to imagine; to think, and to reason- and to do these things in a truly human way." A number of privacy theorists emphasize the importance to human dignity and autonomy of engaging in these activities in the private sphere. In particular, privacy protects a zone of personal autonomy within which human beings can "imagine" and "reason" without the potentially chilling effect of others' scrutiny or judgment.[173]

Certain aspects of copyright law also protect, albeit implicitly, "imaginative engagement" with protected works. Typically, copyright law prohibits only the playing of works *in public*, the showing of works *in public*, the communication of works *to the public*, and so forth. Activities such as private performances and displays are not within the copyright owner's prerogatives. Private research, conducted within reasonable parameters, is also typically exempt. Are these accommodations in national copyright laws sufficiently capacious to protect the human right of privacy?

Dignity, autonomy, and respect for personality are also important values that underlie the protection of authors' rights. In French law, *droit moral* are often seen as expressing a basic truth about respect for authorial personality, a respect that persists after a work's publication and even after the author's death. Similarly, in German law, moral rights are also linked to the author's personality rights.[174] And Anglo-American copyright law has long protected common law rights in unpublished manuscripts. In their famous 1890 article, *The Right to Privacy*, Samuel Warren and Louis Brandeis characterized the common law copyright as an illustration of a broader common

---

[171] *See, e.g., EMI Records (Ireland) Ltd. v. Eircom Ltd.*, [2010] I.E.H.C. 108 (High Court of Ireland).

[172] *See generally* JILL MARSHALL, PERSONAL FREEDOM THROUGH HUMAN RIGHTS LAW? AUTONOMY, IDENTITY AND INTEGRITY UNDER THE EUROPEAN CONVENTION ON HUMAN RIGHTS (2009).

[173] *See generally* Jeffery L. Johnson, *Privacy and the Judgment of Others*, 23 J. VALUE INQUIRY 157 (1989).

[174] ELIZABETH ADENY, THE MORAL RIGHTS OF AUTHORS AND PERFORMERS 168, 122 (2006).

law commitment to protecting privacy, and each individual's "inviolate personality."[175]

A recent illustration of the interface between copyright and privacy involved the publication of extracts from the personal journals of the Prince of Wales. The court held that the publication was both an infringement of copyright and an invasion of the Prince's privacy: "The fact that the contents of the [journal] are not at the most intimate end of the privacy spectrum does not ... lessen the force of [the] claim. The claimant is as much entitled to enjoy confidentiality for his private thoughts as an aspect of his own 'human autonomy and dignity' as any other."[176]

In European jurisprudence, privacy rights must be balanced against the right to freedom of expression and its limitations that are set forth in Article 10 of the European Convention.[177] How should the right to freedom of expression be applied in the context of an unlicensed publication of extracts from personal papers? Is it possible for such a publication to be excused under a defense to copyright infringement (such as fair use or fair dealing) but nevertheless violate the right to privacy? As we saw previously, the U.S. Supreme Court has suggested that, in the copyright context, "fair use" accommodates freedom of speech prescriptions. Does fair use also strike an appropriate balance in a case involving an invasion of privacy?

B. Trademarks

Disputes about trademarks often "involve serious arguments about the defendant's right to engage in free speech."[178] It should thus not be surprising that freedom of expression issues have been invoked in trademark cases and in legal scholarship.[179]

To better appreciate how trademark protection might implicate the right to freedom of expression, it is necessary to consider the function of a trademark. As discussed in Chapter 1, trademarks, traditionally conceived, are

---

[175] Samuel D. Warren & Louis D. Brandeis, *The Right to Privacy* 4 HARV. L. REV. 193 (1890).

[176] *HRH Prince of Wales v. Associated Newspapers Ltd.*, [2006] EWCA 1776, at [70].

[177] *See, e.g., Campbell v. MGN Ltd.*, [2004] 2 A.C. 457.

[178] William McGeveran, *Four Free Speech Goals for Trademark Law*, 18 FORDHAM INTELL. PROP. MEDIA & ENT. L.J. 1205, 1205 (2008).

[179] *See* Lisa P. Ramsey, *Increasing First Amendment Scrutiny of Trademark Law*, 61 SMU L. REV. 381 (2008); Rochelle Cooper Dreyfuss, *Expressive Genericity: Trademarks as Language in the Pepsi Generation*, 65 NOTRE DAME L. REV. 397 (1990); Alex Kozinski, Essay, *Trademarks Unplugged*, 68 N.Y.U. L. REV. 960 (1993); Mark A. Lemley, *The Modern Lanham Act and the Death of Common Sense*, 108 YALE L.J. 1687 (1999); Jessica Litman, *Breakfast with Batman: The Public Interest in the Advertising Age*, 108 YALE L.J. 1717 (1999); *see also* KEMBREW MCLEOD, FREEDOM OF EXPRESSION®: OVERZEALOUS COPYRIGHT BOZOS AND OTHER ENEMIES OF CREATIVITY (2005).

"signs" that symbolize the goodwill in products and services. They represent the single source of products and services and help ensure that consumers can find the goods and services they want and avoid the goods and services they do not want. Trademarks help firms to internalize the costs of building up goodwill in their products and services. This is achieved by limiting the ability of others to use the marks in commerce. This is another kind of artificial scarcity that intellectual property law creates.

This description may suggest that the *only* communicative function of trademarks is to signal the origin of goods and services. Conventionally understood, trademarks accord rights to proprietors to the extent that their use of the mark serves this essential function. Accordingly, rights in a trademark do not protect the proprietor against simple reproduction of the trademark by other parties; trademark rights are only triggered if the reproduction also implicates the source-designating function of the mark. As the Supreme Court of the Republic of South Africa put the point "trade mark law does not give copyright-like protection."[180] The U.S. Supreme Court has also confirmed that a trademark "does not confer a right to prohibit the use of the word or words. It is not a copyright.... A trade-mark only gives the right to prohibit the use of it so far as to protect the owner's good will against the sale of another's product as his."[181] In its 1879 decision in *The Trade-Mark Cases*,[182] which held that certain criminal prohibitions against infringing trademarks were not authorized by the Copyright and Patent Clause of the U.S. Constitution, the U.S. Supreme Court explored the distinctions between copyright and trademark rights in some detail. The Court opined that under the Clause, "the writings which are to be protected are the fruits of intellectual labor, embodied in the form of books, prints, engravings, and the like,"[183] but a trademark "may be, and generally is, the adoption of something already in existence as the distinctive symbol of the party using it."[184] In broadly similar terms, the English Court of Appeal held in *Exxon Corp. v. Exxon Insurance Consultants Int'l Ltd.*,[185] that the trademark "EXXON" was not protected by copyright law, partly on the ground that the mark was not a literary "work," as it did not "afford either information and instruction, or pleasure in the form of literary enjoyment."[186]

---

[180] *Verimark (Pty.) Ltd. v. Bayerische Motoren Werke Aktiengesellschaft*, 2007 (6) SA 263 (SCA) at para. 5.
[181] Prestonettes, Inc. v. Coty, 264 U.S. 359 (1924).
[182] 100 U.S. 82 (1879).
[183] *Id.* at 94.
[184] *Id.* The U.S. trademark system has since its inception been a "use-based" rather than a registration system. Today, however, some inchoate trademark rights follow from the filing of an application to register, based on a bona fide intention to use the mark in commerce.
[185] [1982] R.P.C. 69.
[186] *Id.* (citing *Hollinrake v. Truswell*, [1894] 3 Ch. 420, 428 [Davey L.J.]).

Today, the distinction between copyright and trademark may not be quite as straightforward as these dicta suggest. Marketing departments and advertising agencies put enormous creative and other resources into the selection and development of attractive and engaging brands.[187] Moreover, as many commentators have pointed out, trademarks very often communicate far more than the "source" of goods and services; trademarks are used "not just to identify products but also to enhance or adorn them, even to create new commodities altogether."[188] Marketers know this too: trademarks' communicative functions, above and beyond their traditional source-designating functions, are critical to generating subjective brand loyalty. Later in this section, we note that some commentators have suggested that, as a result of modern marketing practices, trademarks are becoming much more like copyrights than early court decisions perhaps envisaged, a claim that gives rise to a set of intriguing questions about the kind of incentives that should be directed at trademark proprietors to encourage them to create interesting, emotionally compelling, and *expressive* brands.

Even if freedom of expression interests are implicated by the core trademark functions of preventing consumer confusion and deception, this fact is unlikely to have any practical significance for decisional law. There is a very strong public interest in prohibiting unlicensed uses of trademarks. If freedom of expression interests were raised in this context, this public interest is likely to justify any burden that trademark law imposes on expressive freedoms. Judge Alex Kozinski of the U.S. Court of Appeals for the Ninth Circuit put the point well: "So long as trademark law limits itself to its traditional role of avoiding confusion in the marketplace, there's little likelihood that free expression will be hindered. Whatever First Amendment rights you may have in calling the brew you make in your bathtub 'Pepsi' are easily outweighed by the buyer's interest in not being fooled into buying them."[189] As Judge Kozinski also noted, however, difficulties arise "once you get past the confusion rationale."[190]

It might be argued that *all* uses of trademarks that are unrelated to the confusion rationale are "expressive" and thus potentially implicate freedom of expression interests. Consider the following examples: the use of a sports team's insignia on a T-shirt,[191] a replica toy car version of a famous brand of car on which are affixed miniature versions of the original trademarks,[192]

---

[187] Graeme W. Austin, *Trademarks and the Burdened Imagination*, 69 Brook. L. Rev. 827 (2004).
[188] *See, e.g.*, Alex Kozinski, *Trademarks Unplugged*, 68 N.Y.U. L. Rev. 960, 961 (1993).
[189] *Id.* at 973.
[190] *Id.*
[191] *See, e.g.*, C-206/01, *Reed v. Arsenal Football Club*, 2002 E.C.R. I-10273.
[192] *See, e.g.*, C-48/05, *Adam Opel*, 2007 E.C.R. I-1017.

a comparative advertisement that references a competitor's trademark.[193] Defendants in cases in which the trademark owner sought to prohibit such uses would claim that they are using the original marks in ways that are not solely related to their source-designating functions. Purveyors of the T-shirts might suggest that they are allowing fans to "signal" their allegiance to a particular sports franchise; the model car could be said to merely "depict" the original; and comparative advertisements provide important commercial information to consumers. All of the decisional law examined in this section can be understood as engaging with the questions of whether and in what circumstances assertions of trademark rights inhibit uses of marks that are expressive in some sense.

1. The "Essential Function" of a Trademark

Case law on the essential function of a trademark helps to delineate a border around the property rights in trademarks, a border that is especially important for mapping the interface between intellectual property and the right to freedom of expression. A number of cases exploring this essential function have arisen in the context of the EC Trademark Directive,[194] which aims to harmonize domestic trademark law within the EC and, consistent with general EC economic policy, to remove barriers to the free movement of goods that might be created by disparities between national laws.[195]

In very broad terms, and in a variety of contexts, these cases are all asking, What is it that trademarks do? Where a defendant uses in the course of trade a mark that is identical with or similar to a registered trademark in respect of goods or services that are identical with or similar to those for which the mark is registered, the ECJ has said that the owner may only prevent use that affects or are likely to affect "the essential function of the trade mark, which is to guarantee to consumers the origin of the goods or services, by reason of a likelihood of confusion on the part of the public."[196] These deliberations on the essential function of trademarks are critical to appreciating the nature of the relationship between freedom of expression and trademark rights – even if the cases do not discuss freedom of expression directly. At bottom, these cases can be understood as standing for the proposition that trademark rights should only impose restrictions on uses of marks that implicate their essential functions; other expressive uses should be free. The cases also

---

[193] *See, e.g.,* C-533/06, *O2 Holdings Ltd. v. Hutchinson,* 3G U.K. Ltd., 2008 R.P.C. 33.
[194] First Council Directive 89/104/EEC, To Approximate the Laws of the Member States Relating to Trade Marks, 1989 O.J. (L40) 1 [Trade Mark Directive].
[195] *Arsenal,* 2002 E.C.R. I-10273, para. 3.
[196] *O2 Holdings,* 2008 R.P.C. 33, para. 57.

reveal, however, that determining where to draw the line between these uses is a decidedly fraught question.

The ECJ's 2002 decision in *Arsenal Football Club v. Matthew Reed*[197] concerned a trademark infringement action brought by the famous football club against a seller of unlicensed souvenirs and memorabilia. The defendant did not represent that his merchandise was licensed. On the contrary, he marketed his goods at stalls accompanied by signs that made it clear that the goods he was selling were unofficial products. The defendant submitted that the sale of the merchandise did not fall with the rights of the trademark owner because signs made it clear to prospective purchasers that his souvenirs goods were not from the same source as "official" goods. An English court asked the ECJ to determine whether these uses of the Arsenal mark denoted a "connection in the course of trade between the goods and the trademark proprietor" and were therefore infringing. The ECJ reasoned that such a connection existed, stating that the essential function of a trademark is to "guarantee the identity of origin of marked goods or services to the consumer or end user by enabling him, without any possibility of confusion, to distinguish the goods or services from others which have another origin." For the mark to fulfill this essential function, "it must offer a guarantee that all the goods or services bearing it have been manufactured or supplied under the control of a single undertaking which is responsible for their quality."[198] That function was implicated by the defendant's activities, notwithstanding the presence on the defendant's stall of signs communicating to purchasers that the goods were not official Arsenal products. The ECJ observed: "There is a clear possibility in the present case that some consumers, in particular if they come across the goods after they have been sold by [the defendant] and taken away from the stall where the notice appears, may interpret the sign as designating [Arsenal] as the undertaking of origin of the goods."[199] Accordingly, because the conduct was within the trademark's essential function, the plaintiff could prohibit commercial uses of the mark that indirectly expressed allegiance and loyalty to the sports team.

In other recent cases, however, the ECJ has not quite so readily concluded that expressive conduct may be prohibited by the assertion of trademark rights. A useful example is the 2007 *Adam Opel* decision, where a motor vehicle manufacturer sought to prohibit the use of its registered trademark by a manufacturer of scale-model replica cars. The defendant placed the trademark

---

[197] 2002 E.C.R. I-10273.
[198] *Id.* para. 48.
[199] *Id.* para. 57.

on the model cars themselves, on the front page of the user instructions accompanying each model, and on the front of the remote-control transmitter. The plaintiff had registered the mark for both motor vehicles and toys. The principal question referred to the ECJ was whether use as a trademark occurs "if the manufacturer of a toy model car copies a real car in a reduced scale." Significantly, the ECJ was not prepared to rule that the defendant's use of the trademark on the toy replicas *necessarily* affected the functions of the plaintiff's trademark, and it referred the case back to the German court to decide the point. The ECJ also noted that it would be open to that court to decide that consumers would perceive the toy car to be a depiction of the original motor vehicle.[200] If so, a court "would have to conclude that the use at issue ... does not affect the essential function of the Opel logo as a trade mark registered for toys."[201] The plaintiff also invoked prohibitions against trademark dilution, claiming that the use of the mark on the toy cars would "take[e] unfair advantage of" or be "detrimental" to the "distinctive character or the repute of the trade mark."[202] Again, the ECJ was not prepared to rule in the plaintiff's favor. The decision thus leaves considerable scope for national courts to treat depictions of trademarks as outside the essential functions of the mark, and thus as noninfringing.[203]

A more recent decision, *L'Oréal v, Bellure*,[204] points in the opposite direction. The case concerned comparative advertising. The defendant sold perfumes that were less expensive immitations of the plaintiff's famous perfume

---

[200] C-48/05, *Adam Opel*, 2007 E.C.R. I-1017. The Nuremberg District Court subsequently held that there was no trademark infringement. Landgericht Nürnberg-Fürth, May 11, 2007, NJOZ 2007, 4377.

[201] C-48/05, *Adam Opel*, 2007 E.C.R. I-1017, paras. 23–24.

[202] Trade Mark Directive, *supra* note 194, art. 5(2).

[203] The decision in *Adam Opel* to relegate the final decision as to whether defendant's conduct implicated the essential function of the mark shares considerable common ground with the ECJ's 2007 decision in *Céline SARL v. Céline SA*, [2007] E.C.R. I-7041, where it held that use of a business name that is identical to a registered trademark may implicate the essential function of the mark. However, in the course of so ruling, the ECJ left to the national court the task of deciding whether such use implicated the rights of the trademark owner, and whether the safe harbor in Article 6(1) of the Trade Mark Directive applies. Article 6(1) permits a third party to use his own name or address, "provided he uses them in accordance with honest practices in industrial or commercial matters." The ECJ instructed that, in determining whether conduct falls within the safe harbor, "account must be taken first of the extent to which the use of the third party's name is understood by the relevant public, or at least a significant section of that public, as indicating a link between the third party's goods or services and the trade-mark proprietor or a person authorised to use the trademark, and secondly of the extent to which the third party ought to have been aware of that." [2007] E.C.R. I-7041, para. 34.

[204] *L'Oréal SA v. Bellure NV* Case C-487/07, [2009] WLR (D) 203.

brands, such as Trésor and Miracle. The defendant's products were marketed with trade dress that imitated the plaintiff's packaging, but it was accepted that consumers would not confuse the defendant's products with those of the plaintiff. The case raises complex legal issues concerning the relationship between trademark rights and the specific prescriptions in the EC's Directive on misleading and comparative advertising.[205] For present purposes, the case is significant for the ECJ's recognition that the functions of a mark include both the essential functions of designating the source of products and "those of communication, investment or advertising."[206] In adopting this expansive approach, the ECJ's ruling indicates that trademarks can be infringed by a defendant's "free riding" on the image that has been created through the trademark owner's advertising and promotion.

Notes and Questions

1. Does the ECJ's jurisprudence on the essential function of a trademark correctly balance intellectual property rights and speech rights?

2. Drawing on ECJ case law, the Supreme Court of Appeal of South Africa has confirmed that trademark rights are not implicated by uses for "purely descriptive purposes," and, conversely, that such rights are engaged only where the unauthorized use "creates an impression of a material link between the product and the owner of the mark."[207] The leading case, *Verimark (Pty) Ltd. v. Bayerische Motoren Werke AktienGesellschaft*,[208] was an infringement action initiated by the owner of the trademark for BMW cars, which was registered for, among other things, cleaning and polishing preparations and vehicle polishes, in addition, of course, to being registered for the famous motor vehicles. The trademark owner objected to a television commercial for a different cleaning product marketed under the mark "Diamond Guard." The commercial featured BMW cars in the course of demonstrating the qualities of the cleaning product. The South African court declined to hold that BMW's trademark rights were implicated. For a unanimous court, Justice Harms wrote: "I am satisfied that any customer would regard the presence of the logo on the picture of the BMW car as identifying the car and being part and parcel of the car. It is the use of the car to illustrate Diamond Guard's

---

[205] Council Directive 84/450/EEC, Concerning Misleading and Comparative Advertising, 1984 O.J. (L 250) 17, *as amended by* Council Directive 97/55/EC, 1997 O.J. (L 290) 18).

[206] *L'Oréal SA v. Bellure NV* Case C-487/07, para. 58.

[207] *Verimark (Pty.) Ltd. v. Bayerische Motoren Werke Aktiengesellschaft*, 2007 (6) SA 263 (SCA), para. 7.

[208] *Id.*

properties rather than use of the trade mark. No-one, in my judgment, would perceive that there exists a material link between BMW and Diamond Guard or that the logo on the car performs any guarantee of origin function in relation to Diamond Guard."[209] The trademark did not, therefore, impose any legal impediment to the broadcasting of the television commercial.

2. Freedom of Expression and Trademark Doctrine

Some cases have involved a direct confrontation between trademark law and constitutional rights to freedom of expression. In this section, we consider two: one from the United States, the other from South Africa. The first case concerned a Maine statute that prohibited "dilution" of a trademark. The statute provided, "Likelihood of injury to business reputation or of dilution of a mark registered under this chapter ... shall be a ground for injunctive relief notwithstanding the absence of competition between the parties or the absence of confusion as to the source of the goods or services."[210] The key question confronted by the U.S. Court of Appeals for the First Circuit was whether the statute reached parodic uses of a trademark:

L.L. *Bean* v. Drake Publishers, 811 F.2d 26 (1st Cir. 1987)

Imitation may be the highest form of flattery, but plaintiff-appellee L.L. Bean, Inc. was neither flattered nor amused when *High Society* magazine published a prurient parody of Bean's famous catalog. Defendant-appellant Drake Publishers, Inc., owns *High Society*, a monthly periodical featuring adult erotic entertainment. Its October 1984 issue contained a two-page article entitled "L.L. Bea*m*'s Back-To-School-Sex-Catalog." (Emphasis added.) The article was labeled on the magazine's contents page as "humor" and "parody." The article displayed a facsimile of Bean's trademark and featured pictures of nude models in sexually explicit positions using "products" that were described in a crudely humorous fashion.

L.L. Bean sought a temporary restraining order to remove the October 1984 issue from circulation.

The district court [granted] Bean summary judgment with respect to the trademark dilution claim raised under Maine law. It ruled that the article had tarnished Bean's trademark by undermining the goodwill and reputation associated with the mark. Relying on two affidavits presented by appellee, the district court found that Bean had suffered harm from the publication of the

---

[209] *Id.* para. 8.
[210] Me. Rev. Stat. Ann. tit. 10, § 1530 (1981).

article. The court rejected Drake's claim that the Maine statute did not encompass allegations of tarnishment caused by parody. The court also held that enjoining the publication of a parody to prevent trademark dilution did not offend the First Amendment. An injunction issued prohibiting further publication or distribution of the "L.L. Beam Sex Catalog." After its motion for reconsideration was denied, Drake appealed the order enjoining further publication of the Sex Catalog. Anti-dilution statutes have developed to fill a void left by the failure of trademark infringement law to curb the unauthorized use of marks where there is no likelihood of confusion between the original use and the infringing use. The law of trademark dilution aims to protect the distinctive quality of a trademark from deterioration caused by its use on dissimilar products. The dilution injury "is the gradual whittling away or dispersion of the identity and hold upon the public mind of the mark or name by its use on non-competing goods." Schechter, *The Rational Basis of Trademark Protection*, 40 Harv.L.Rev. 813, 825 (1927). The overriding purpose of anti-dilution statutes is to prohibit a merchant of noncompetitive goods from selling its products by trading on the goodwill and reputation of another's mark.

A trademark owner may obtain relief under an anti-dilution statute if his mark is distinctive and there is a likelihood of dilution due to (1) injury to the value of the mark caused by actual or potential confusion, (2) diminution in the uniqueness and individuality of the mark, or (3) injury resulting from use of the mark in a manner that tarnishes or appropriates the goodwill and reputation associated with plaintiff's mark. There is no dispute that Bean's mark is distinctive. The basis for the district court's injunction was that Bean's trademark had been tarnished by the parody in defendant's magazine. We think this was a constitutionally impermissible application of the anti-dilution statute. The district court believed that if a noncommercial parody "would result in images of impurity in the minds of [consumers] ... [s]uch connotations would obviously tarnish the affirmative associations the mark had come to convey." It thus read the anti-dilution statute as granting a trademark owner the unfettered right to suppress the use of its name in any context, commercial or noncommercial, found to be offensive, negative or unwholesome. As one commentator has pointed out, there are serious First Amendment implications involved in applying anti-dilution statutes to cover noncommercial uses of a trademark:

> Famous trademarks offer a particularly powerful means of conjuring up the image of their owners, and thus become an important, perhaps at times indispensable, part of the public vocabulary. Rules restricting the use of well-known trademarks may therefore restrict the communication of ideas ... If the defendant's speech is particularly unflattering, it is also possible to argue that the trademark has been tarnished by the defendant's use. The constitutional

implications of extending the misappropriation or tarnishment rationales to such cases, however, may often be intolerable. Since a trademark may frequently be the most effective means of focusing attention on the trademark owner or its product, the recognition of exclusive rights encompassing such use would permit the stifling of unwelcome discussion.... Denicola, *Trademarks as Speech*, Wisc.L.Rev. at 195–96.

The district court's opinion suggests that tarnishment may be found when a trademark is used without authorization in a context which diminishes the positive associations with the mark. Neither the strictures of the First Amendment nor the history and theory of anti-dilution law permit a finding of tarnishment based solely on the presence of an unwholesome or negative context in which a trademark is used without authorization. Such a reading of the anti-dilution statute unhinges it from its origins in the marketplace. A trademark is tarnished when consumer capacity to associate it with the appropriate products or services has been diminished. The threat of tarnishment arises when the goodwill and reputation of a plaintiff's trademark is linked to products which are of shoddy quality or which conjure associations that clash with the associations generated by the owner's lawful use of the mark[.] The Constitution is not offended when the anti-dilution statute is applied to prevent a defendant from using a trademark without permission in order to merchandise dissimilar products or services. Any residual effect on First Amendment freedoms should be balanced against the need to fulfill the legitimate purpose of the anti-dilution statute. The law of trademark dilution has developed to combat an unauthorized and harmful appropriation of a trademark by another for the purpose of identifying, manufacturing, merchandising or promoting dissimilar products or services. The harm occurs when a trademark's identity and integrity – its capacity to command respect in the market – is undermined due to its inappropriate and unauthorized use by other market actors. When presented with such circumstances, courts have found that trademark owners have suffered harm despite the fact that redressing such harm entailed some residual impact on the rights of expression of commercial actors. The legitimate aim of the anti-dilution statute is to prohibit the unauthorized use of another's trademark in order to market incompatible products or services. The Constitution does not, however, permit the range of the anti-dilution statute to encompass the unauthorized use of a trademark in a noncommercial setting such as an editorial or artistic context.

The district court's application of the Maine anti-dilution statute to appellant's noncommercial parody cannot withstand constitutional scrutiny. Drake has not used Bean's mark to identify or market goods or services; it has used the mark solely to identify Bean as the object of its parody. The reading of the anti-dilution provision advanced by the district court would improperly

expand the scope of the anti-dilution statute far beyond the frontiers of commerce and deep into the realm of expression.

Our reluctance to apply the anti-dilution statute to the instant case also
stems from a recognition of the vital importance of parody. Although, as we
have noted, parody is often offensive, it is nevertheless "deserving of substantial
freedom-both as entertainment and as a form of social and literary criticism."

The district court's injunction falls not only because it trammels upon a
protected form of expression, but also because it depends upon an untoward
judicial evaluation of the offensiveness or unwholesomeness of the appellant's materials. . . .

Finally, we reject Bean's argument that enjoining the publication of appellant's
parody does not violate the First Amendment because "there are innumerable
alternative ways that Drake could have made a satiric statement concerning
'sex in the outdoors' or 'sex and camping gear' without using plaintiff's name
and mark." This argument fails to recognize that appellant is parodying L.L.
Bean's catalog, not "sex in the outdoors." The central role which trademarks
occupy in public discourse (a role eagerly encouraged by trademark owners),
makes them a natural target of parodists. Trademark parodies, even when
offensive, do convey a message. The message may be simply that business and
product images need not always be taken too seriously; a trademark parody
reminds us that we are free to laugh at the images and associations linked with
the mark. The message also may be a simple form of entertainment conveyed
by juxtaposing the irreverent representation of the trademark with the ideal-
ized image created by the mark's owner. . . . While such a message lacks explicit
political content, that is no reason to afford it less protection under the First
Amendment. Denying parodists the opportunity to poke fun at symbols and
names which have become woven into the fabric of our daily life, would constitute a serious curtailment of a protected form of expression.

Laugh It Off Promotions CC v. South African Breweries International (Finance) BV, 2006 (1) SA 144 (CC)

[In this case, the Constitutional Court of South Africa considered a similar set of issues involving parodies of trademarks. The plaintiff (respondent)
was the owner of a number of famous trademarks, described collectively
as the CARLING BLACK LABEL trademarks, which had been extensively
used by South African Breweries Ltd. (SAB), in conjunction with the marketing of alcoholic beverages, particularly beer. The defendant (the applicant

before the Constitutional Court) marketed T-shirts bearing a print that was "markedly similar, in lettering, colour scheme and background, to that of the respondent's CARLING BLACK LABEL trademarks." As the Court explained: "The only real difference was in the wording. The words 'Black Label' on the respondent's registered trade marks were replaced, on the T-shirt, with 'Black Labour'; the respondent's 'Carling Beer' was substituted with 'White Guilt'; and where [was] written 'America's lusty lively beer' and 'enjoyed by men around the World', the applicant had printed 'Africa's lusty lively exploitation since 1652' and 'No regard given worldwide', respectively." The applicant was a for-profit closely held company that sought to create a close association between its T-shirt designs and famous brands. It had marketed T-shirts making fun of at least eleven other brands, including Coca-Cola, Kentucky Fried Chicken, Shell, McDonalds, and Lego.

Carling, but apparently none of the other trademark owners, initiated proceedings against the applicant for trademark dilution, under the South African Trade Marks Act (the Act).[211] Section 34(1)(c) of the Act prohibited unauthorized use of a well-known mark that "would be likely to take unfair advantage or, or be detrimental to, the distinctive character or repute of the registered trademark, notwithstanding the absence of confusion or deception." Setting aside a decision in favor of the trademark owner, the Constitutional Court held that a dilution action could not be sustained in the light of domestic protections for freedom of expression set forth in section 16 of the South African Constitution.[212] Writing for a unanimous court, Justice Moseneke reasoned that the prohibition against trademark dilution in section 34(1)(c) needs to be viewed through the lens of constitutional protections for freedom of expression.]

Antidilution Protection and Free Expression
It is trite that under our constitutional democracy, the requirements of the section ought to be understood through the prism of the Constitution and specifically that of the free expression guarantee. The Supreme Court of Appeal (SCA), too, correctly recognized that a construction of the section is subject to the dictates of the Constitution and that its application must not unduly

---

[211] Trade Marks Act 194 of 1993 § 31(1)(c).

[212] "Freedom of expression. – (1) Everyone has the right to freedom of expression, which includes – (a) freedom of the press and other media; (b) freedom to receive or impart information or ideas; (c) freedom of artistic creativity; and (d) academic freedom and freedom of scientific research. (2) The right in subsection (1) does not extend to – (a) propaganda for war; (b) incitement of imminent violence; or (c) advocacy of hatred that is based on race, ethnicity, gender or religion, and that constitutes incitement to cause harm." S. AFR. CONST. 1996 § 16.

restrict a party's freedom of expression. However, in deciding the merits of the infringement claim it opted for a two-stage approach. In the first inquiry the court held that the message on the T-shirts amounts to an infringement because it is unfair and materially harmful to the repute of the trademarks. Only thereafter did the court inquire into and find that freedom of expression does not afford justification for the infringement. This approach appears to be premised on the reasoning that one must first find an infringement under the section and only thereafter determine whether the infringement is excused by an assertion of freedom of expression. This approach is flawed.

A finding of unfair use or likelihood of detriment to the repute of the marks hinges on whether the offending expression is protected under section 16(1) of the Constitution or not. If the expression is constitutionally protected, what is unfair or detrimental, or not, in the context of section 34(1)(c) must then be mediated against the competing claim for free expression. By determining the unfairness and detriment anteriorly, the SCA in effect precluded itself from properly taking into account the free expression guarantee claimed by the alleged infringer. The two-stage approach advocated by the SCA in effect prevents an understanding of the internal requirements of the section through the lens of the Constitution. The injunction to construe statutes consistently with the Constitution means that, where reasonably possible, the court is obliged to promote the rights entrenched by it. In this case the SCA was obliged to balance out the interests of the owner of the marks against the claim of free expression for the very purpose of determining what is unfair and materially harmful to the marks. It is to that task that I now turn.

Section 34(1)(c) falls to be construed bearing in mind the entrenched free expression right under section 16. The importance of freedom of expression has been articulated and underscored by this and other courts in this country and indeed in other open democracies and by its inclusion in international law instruments. Suffice it to repeat that freedom of expression is a vital incidence of dignity, equal worth and freedom. It carries its own inherent worth and serves a collection of other intertwined constitutional ends in an open and democratic society.

[O'Regan J] points out [in *South African National Defence Union v. Minister of Defence and Another* 1999 (4) SA 469 (CC)] that

These rights taken together protect the rights of individuals not only individually to form and express opinions, of whatever nature, but to establish associations and groups of like-minded people to foster and propagate such opinions. The rights implicitly recognise the importance, both for a democratic society and for individuals personally, of the ability to form and express opinions, whether individually or collectively, even where those views are controversial. The

corollary of the freedom of expression and its related rights is tolerance by society of different views. Tolerance, of course, does not require approbation of a
particular view. In essence, it requires the acceptance of the public airing of
disagreements and the refusal to silence unpopular views.

We are obliged to delineate the bounds of the constitutional guarantee of
free expression generously. Section 16 is in two parts: the first subsection sets
out expression protected under the Constitution. It indeed has an expansive
reach, which encompasses freedom of the press and other media, freedom
to receive or impart information or ideas, freedom of artistic creativity, academic freedom, and freedom of scientific research. The second part contains
three categories of expression that are expressly excluded from constitutional
protection. It follows clearly that unless an expressive act is excluded by section 16(2), it is protected expression. Plainly, the right to free expression in
our Constitution is neither paramount over other guaranteed rights nor lim-
itless. As Kriegler J in *S v. Mamabolo* puts it, "With us it is not a pre-eminent
freedom ranking above all others. It is not even an unqualified right." 2001 (3)
SA 409 (CC). In appropriate circumstances authorized by the Constitution
itself, a law of general application may limit freedom of expression.

It is so that the antidilution prohibition under section 34(1)(c) seeks, in effect,
to oust certain expressive conduct in relation to registered marks with repute. It
thus limits the right to free expression embodied in at least section 16(1)(a) to
(c) of the Constitution. We are, however, not seized with the adjudication of the
constitutional validity of the section. We must assume without deciding that
the limitation is reasonable and justifiable in an open and democratic society to
which our Constitution is committed. That in turn impels us to a construction
of section 34(1)(c) most compatible with the right to free expression. The anti-
dilution provision must bear a meaning that is the least destructive of other
entrenched rights and in this case free expression rights. The reach of the statutory prohibition must be curtailed to the least intrusive means necessary to
achieve the purpose of the section. Courts must be astute not to convert the
antidilution safeguard of renowned trademarks usually controlled by powerful
financial interests into a monopoly adverse to other claims of expressive conduct of at least equal cogency and worth in our broader society.

I agree with the SCA that properly read the section requires that an infringement of a trademark may occur only if "unfair advantage" or "unfair detriment"
is shown. Equally clear is that the detriment relied upon must not be flimsy or
negligible. It must be substantial in the sense that it is likely to cause substantial
harm to the uniqueness and repute of the marks. Therefore, on its terms the
section has internal limitations. It sets fairness and materiality standards. The
section does not limit use that takes fair advantage of the mark or that does not
threaten substantial harm to the repute of the mark, or indeed that may lead

to harm but in a fair manner. What is fair will have to be assessed case by case with due regard to the factual matrix and other context of the case. A court will have to weigh carefully the competing interests of the owner of the mark against the claim of free expression of a user without permission.

The exercise calls for an evaluation of the importance of the purpose, nature, extent, and impact of the limitation of free expression invoked against claims of unfair advantage or of likelihood of material detriment to a registered mark. In sum, in order to succeed the owner of the mark bears the onus to demonstrate likelihood of substantial harm or detriment, which, seen within the context of the case, amounts to unfairness. What remains is to settle the content of the substantial detriment the section envisages.

Likelihood of Detriment

Before us the applicant strenuously persisted in the contention that the respondent had not adduced facts to show that the offending use of its marks would be likely to be hurtful, in the economic and trade sense, to the repute of the marks. The respondent accepts, correctly so in my view, that, seen through the lens of the Constitution, the likely prejudice or detriment required by the section must be restricted to material harm in the commercial sense. The respondent, however, refutes the assertion that there is no evidence to demonstrate the probability of economic harm and argues, in its words, that "the likelihood of suffering economic harm as a consequence of the offending use is self-evident." The respondent elaborates that no right thinking South African would wish to be associated with the racially insensitive message conveyed by the applicant on the T-shirts. The racial slur, it submits, is likely to erode the exclusiveness of the mark, discourage people from purchasing the respondent's Black Label Beer, and adversely curtail SAB's opportunities to sponsor domestic sport.

It is clear that even without reference to the dictates of the Constitution our courts rightly tend to determine likelihood of detriment to the selling appeal of a mark in the light of established facts and not bald allegations. However, in the present case, the SCA dismissed this contention of the applicant out of hand and on the narrow basis that section 34(1)(c) does not require proof of actual loss but only the likelihood of loss.... In other words, it requires a probability of the occurrence of material loss. The SCA and the High Court appear to have approached the likelihood of detriment on the footing that the message on the T-shirts would probably create in the minds of consumers a particularly unwholesome, unsavoury and degrading association difficult to detach from the reputation of the respondent's marks. But the difficulty is that ordinarily probability is a matter of inference to be made from facts consistent with the inference. No such facts have been pleaded.

In my view, the inference of material detriment made by the SCA hinges solely on the meaning it has attached to the impugned publication on the T-shirts. Even accepting that meaning, as evidence it is at best scant and unconvincing as an indicator of substantial economic harm to the respondent's marks. It is appropriate to observe that the mere fact that the expressive act may indeed stir discomfort in some and appear to be morally reprobate or unsavoury to others is not ordinarily indicative of a breach of section 34(1)(c). Such a moral or other censure is an irrelevant consideration if the expression enjoys protection under the Constitution. Of course freedom of expression is not boundless but may not be limited in a manner other than authorised by the Constitution itself such as by the law of defamation. The constitutional guarantee of free expression is available to all under the sway of our Constitution, even where others may deem the expression unsavoury, unwholesome or degrading. To that extent ordinarily such meaning should enjoy protection as fair use and should not amount to tarnishment of the trade marks.

I hold that in a claim under section 34(1)(c), a party that seeks to oust an expressive conduct protected under the Constitution must, on the facts, establish a likelihood of substantial economic detriment to the claimant's mark. There is indeed much to be said for the contention that, in a claim based on tarnishment of a trade mark, the probability of material detriment to the mark envisaged in the section must be restricted to economic and trade harm. In essence the protection is against detriment to the repute of the mark; and not against the dignity but the selling magnetism of the mark. In an open democracy valuable expressive acts in public ought not to be lightly trampled upon by marginal detriment or harm unrelated to the commercial value that vests in the mark itself.

In the respondent's depositions there are no facts which deal with probability of trade or commercial harm. Its attitude is that the likelihood of harm is self evident. I simply do not agree. In my view, if anything the facts suggest otherwise. What is clear is that over decades the CARLING BLACK LABEL marks have and still enjoy considerable recognition and renown in our land. The marks make up a leading, in-the-face, beer brand selling billions of litres of beer nation-wide. There is not even the slightest suggestion that, from the time the T-shirts saw the light of day to the date the interdict proceedings were launched, there had been a real possibility of a reduction of its market dominance or compromised beer sales. Nor is there evidence of the likelihood of future commercial detriment. The number of T-shirts produced and sold or viewed by the public is unknown but is at best truly negligible. On the applicant's version only a few hundred T-shirts were sold. For instance there are no facts on sales beyond a coterie of media students and activists. I am unable to agree with the SCA that the reach of the offending use is irrelevant. In the context of a tarnishment claim, it is important in understanding likely harm relative to the selling power and popularity of the mark in question.

In contrast, SAB has deposed graphically to its awesome marketing machinery bolstered by impressive advertising spend on every conceivable medium including artefacts and, not least, T-shirts. Even accepting that the racial slur may be unsavoury there is no evidence that it has or is likely to attach to or tarnish the selling power of the mark. It is plain from the record that no evidence, direct or inferential, was adduced to establish likelihood of detriment either in the sense of unfavourable associations that have been created between the registered marks and the illustration on the T-shirts, or in the context of a likelihood of loss of sales by virtue of the reduced commercial magnetism of the mark. In theory and in live trade there is a direct link between the mark and sales. As it is often said, the mark actually sells the goods and it is the acquired asset that the section seeks to protect from tarnishment.

In effect we are invited to find a probability of material economic detriment to the respondent's marks of well-entrenched repute on conjecture alone. We must decline the invitation. It follows that the claim of the respondent for a final interdict against the applicant must falter.

Interpretation of the Message on the T-shirts and Fair Use Arguments

... The difficult issue is whether the interpretation of the offending message in this case yields more than one plausible meaning. Before us the respondent argued that like the SCA this Court must grasp the nettle and support only one plausible meaning of the message. The applicant and the amicus argue that the message lends itself to at least one other reasonable meaning being that the statement is a critical but parodic comment on the methods used by SAB to market its beer by targeting male workers and in particular black male workers and should therefore be protected as fair use under section 34(1)(c) read with the Constitution.

On its approach, the SCA found that in this matter, the constitutional freedom of expression was no justification for the unauthorised use of trade marks because the applicant used the message on the T-shirts in relation to goods or services and in the course of trade. It found that the T-shirts are marketable goods and not only a medium of communication and therefore the message does not deserve constitutional protection. The amicus however draws our attention to the clear duality of the roles of the T-shirts – to sell and to make a social statement. It is the expressive role, the amicus argues, which engages the constitutional protection and is worthy of its shield. To limit valuable communication to non-commercial enterprises would further marginalise alternative and competing voices in society. In this way voices of the best resourced would tend to prevail. But also it is important to keep in mind the purpose for which the marks have been appropriated. What is being sold is not another beer or other product under the guise or on the back of the registered marks. What is being sold is rather an abstract brand criticism. T-shirts are not much more than the medium of choice.

The SCA denied the applicant the constitutional protection of freedom of expression on the further ground that it has adequate alternative means of expression. The amicus makes the point that although this test is of well-established pedigree in US jurisprudence, the critical enquiry is the sufficiency of the alternative modes of expression for the particular communication at hand. Adequacy of lines of communication is relative to a myriad of variables such as the nature of the message, the target audience, the means of the author or creator of the message and so on. In each case such adequacy must be probed with utmost care and before a conclusion is reached that the use ought not to be protected as part of free speech.

Notes and Questions

1. It is difficult to overstate the potential significance of the *Laugh it Off* decision. The Constitutional Court of South Africa demanded that assertions of trademarks be analyzed in the light of their impact on the exercise of the right to freedom of expression set forth in that country's Constitution. For example, the Court's emphasis on the burden of proof has the potential to affect the power relationships between intellectual property owners and alleged infringers in the litigation context. In particular, intellectual property owners may find it more difficult to establish that the defendant's actions have actually caused harm to a trademark. In cases of doubt, the issue may be resolved in favor of freedom of expression values.

2. Did *Laugh It Off* turn on the quality of the evidence of the likelihood of dilution? The risk that the Constitutional Court's analysis might be understood in this way appears to have been among the reasons why one member of the Court, Justice Sachs, wrote a separate concurrence. Near the beginning of his judgment, Justice Sachs wrote:

> It would in my opinion be unfortunate if [the plaintiff – and the others targeted by the T-shirts] were left with the impression that their case failed simply because they did not back it up with clip-board evidence to prove a measure of detriment.

I believe the appeal should be upheld on more substantial grounds.... I believe that when balancing the different interests involved [the lower court] failed to appreciate why the parodic use of the trademark in the milieu in which Laugh It Off operated was central to its critical project. By de-contextualising both the nature of the mockery contained in the image and the context in which it was deployed, the [lower court] over-emphasised the fact that the T-shirts were sold at a profit, and attributed undue weight to the literal meaning of the words used. At the same time it gave far too little regard to the uniquely expressive weight of the parodic form used. The result was inappropriately to allow what were tenuous property interests to outweigh substantial expression rights.

What difference does it make to analyze the substantive trademark law through the lens of freedom of expression or to treat freedom of expression as a defense to trademark infringement?

3. In *Laugh It Off*, the Court's balancing exercise was undertaken in the context of a modern constitution whose framing occurred *after* the rise of the post–World War II human rights movement. In a number of different jurisdictions, commentators are beginning to explore what the "constitutionalizing" of intellectual property law means for the development of juridical technique and analysis.[213] Whereas constitutional issues in the United States draw principally on U.S. domestic legal sources, cases in other jurisdictions appear to draw more directly on human rights law – either through their incorporation into domestic constitutional frameworks or by reference to international law as a relevant source of legal principles. What differences do you detect differences in the analysis in *Laugh It Off* from the approach adopted in the U.S. cases extracted previously?

4. In the United States, Judge Pierre Leval of the U.S. Court of Appeals for the Second Circuit has criticized recourse to the First Amendment in trademark infringement cases and has urged that freedom of expression values are better preserved through traditional trademark doctrines:

It is a mistake to see the trademark law as a unidirectional rule – a one-way highway of exclusivity eventually blocked off by the First Amendment. To the contrary, the trademark law is a complex, integrated body of rules, which is deeply concerned with the protection of free expression. Trademark, like copyright, does indeed place limitations on speech. But, as in the case of copyright, it has always had as a central concern distinguishing between speech that should be suppressed and speech that should not. Merchants need a source-identifying mark; society requires freedom for certain kinds of messages. Trademark law developed as an integrated body of rules to balance the potential conflict. The trademark law itself is fashioned to protect free-speech interests that may justify uses of a trademark by persons other than its owner. Where the trademark

---

[213] Geiger, *supra* note 82; Enyinna S. Nwauche, *The Judicial Construction of the Public Interest in South African Copyright Law*, 39 INT'L REV. INTELL. PROP. & COMPETITION L. 917 (2008).

law, by its own terms, protects the unauthorized use of another's trademark, there is no need to turn to the Constitution to justify a judgment in the alleged infringer's favor.[214]

Is this the same kind of "internalization" thesis that we have seen earlier in the chapter in the copyright context? If not, how does the analysis differ?

5. William McGeveran has suggested that it is not so much decisional law that creates tensions between trademark law and the First Amendment; rather, impediments to expressive freedoms are caused by doctrinal uncertainty concerning the principal ground for finding trademark infringement (likelihood of confusion), poorly delineated defenses, and the slow speed with which cases progress through the courts.[215] McGeveran also observes that while "decided cases ... might suggest that all is well with free speech in trademark law ... the structure of trademark law ... pervasively chills expression without sufficient benefit in thwarting confusion."[216] What structural changes might be made to domestic trademark law to address these concerns?

6. The U.S. Supreme Court's decision in *San Francisco Arts & Athletics, Inc. v. U.S. Olympic Committee*[217] involved assertions of First Amendment protections against special rights to control the use of the "Olympic" mark that were accorded by a statute that did *not* ground liability on likelihood of confusion. The United States Olympic Committee and the International Olympic Committee had initiated proceedings against the San Francisco Arts & Athletics, Inc. (SFAA), which had promoted the "Gay Olympic Games" on its letterheads and mailings, in local newspapers, and on various merchandise sold to cover the costs of the event. The Supreme Court majority upheld a lower court decision against the SFAA and resisted challenges grounded in the First Amendment against the existence and assertion of special rights in the "OLYMPIC" mark. In dissent, Justice Brennan observed: "The danger of substantial regulation of noncommercial speech is diminished by denying enforcement of a trademark against uses of words that are not likely 'to cause confusion, to cause mistake, or to deceive.'"[218] The implication – that the First Amendment is safe from trademark law because trademark law prohibits only those uses of marks that are likely to cause confusion – appears to rely on trademark law's ability to differentiate between uses of marks that do and do not cause consumer confusion. Is this apparent faith in trademark law doctrines always warranted?[219]

---

[214] Pierre Leval, *Trademark: Champion of Free Speech*, 27 COLUM. J.L. & ARTS 187, 188–89 (2004).
[215] McGeveran, *supra* note 178.
[216] *Id.* at 1227.
[217] 483 U.S. 522 (1987).
[218] *Id.* at 564 (Brennan, J., dissenting) (citation omitted).
[219] *See generally* Austin, *supra* note 187.

7. As in copyright law, defenses can be particularly relevant to the scope of expressive freedoms in the trademark context. Since 2006, the U.S. federal trademark dilution statute has included a specific defense to trademark dilution for "fair use … including use in connection with … identifying and parodying, criticizing, or commenting upon the famous mark owner or the goods and services or the famous mark owner."[220] There is, however, no equivalent statutory defense to traditional trademark infringement. In *Mattel, Inc. v. MCA Records, Inc.*,[221] the U.S. Court of Appeals for the Ninth Circuit confronted a range of trademark-related claims brought against firms that produced, marketed, and sold a highly popular song with the title "Barbie Girl." The song made fun of the popular child's toy, the "Barbie Doll," along with the values that defendants believed were associated with the doll. In its analysis of the plaintiff's confusion-based liability theory, the Ninth Circuit adopted the approach of the Second Circuit in a case brought by the famous American movie star Ginger Rogers involving a movie with the title *Ginger and Fred*, an obvious reference to Ms. Rogers and her dancing partner, Fred Astaire. In the latter case, the Second Circuit held that "in general, the [federal trademark act] should be construed to apply to artistic works only where the public interest in avoiding consumer confusion outweighs the public interest in free expression."[222] The Second Circuit held that uses of trademarks in titles only implicates the trademark owner's rights where the title has no reference to the underlying work. Applying that test, the Ninth Circuit held that the defendant's use of BARBIE mark in the song title was clearly relevant to the contents of the song. The use was therefore noninfringing. Mattel also alleged a trademark dilution claim. Because the case was decided in 2002, the defendant could not rely on the 2006 amendments to the dilution statute that create a specific defense for parody. Even so, the Ninth Circuit rejected Mattel's claim, reasoning that a cause of action for dilution targeted only "commercial speech," which the court understood to include speech that merely proposed a commercial transaction. Because the song "Barbie Girl" was also expressive, it was not "purely commercial speech," and, in the Ninth Circuit's view, it fell outside the statutory prohibitions of dilution.[223] Would this case have been decided the same way by the judge who wrote the opinion in the *L.L. Bean* case, extracted previously?

8. Because the *Mattel* case could be resolved on other grounds, the Ninth Circuit did not have to consider whether the use of BARBIE fell within a

---

[220] 15 U.S.C. § 1125(c)(3)(ii) (2006).
[221] 296 F.3d 894 (9th Cir. 2002).
[222] *Rogers v. Grimaldi*, 875 F.2d 994, 999 (2d Cir. 1989).
[223] *Mattel, Inc. v. MCA Records, Inc.*, 296 F.3d 894, 899 (9th Cir. 2002).

doctrine known as "nominative fair use." This defense permits activities that involve "naming" the trademark or the trademark owner. For example, *New Kids on the Bock v. News Am. Publ'g Inc.*,[224] a case often credited for establishing the defense,[225] concerned a trademark infringement action initiated by the pop group "New Kids on the Block" against newspapers that had used the group's name in newspaper competitions. The district court had reasoned that the newspapers' First Amendment rights outweighed whatever damage might have been done to the trademark by an implication of endorsement. The Ninth Circuit approached the question in a different way. It avoided specific recourse to the First Amendment and held that where the most efficient way to refer to the trademark owner was to use its name (even if the name was also a trademark), a new three-step test should replace the likelihood of confusion analysis, directed at whether the defendants had made "nominative fair use" of the mark. To assert the nominative fair use defense successfully, the alleged infringer must show that (1) the product in question is not readily identifiable without use of the trademark, (2) only so much of the mark is used as reasonably necessary to identify the product, and (3) the user of the mark did nothing that would suggest sponsorship by the trademark holder. Is a defense of this kind sufficiently protective of First Amendment values, or does it instead illustrate McGovern's concerns with doctrinal uncertainties? In *Century 21 Real Estate Corp. v. Lendingtree, Inc.*[226] the U.S. Court of Appeals for the Third Circuit revisited the nominative fair use defense and slightly revised the Ninth Circuit's test. Most pertinently, the Third Circuit requires a trial court to ask: "Does the defendant's conduct or language reflect the true and accurate relationship between plaintiff and defendant's products or services?"[227] Is either approach any more protective of expressive freedoms than the other?

9. European case law provides examples of parodies of trademarks that were defended on freedom of expression grounds. For instance, in a recent German case, the court invoked the protections for artistic freedom included in the German Basic Law[228] as a ground for dismissing a trademark infringement action brought in respect of a postcard that parodied a well-known

---

[224] *New Kids on the Block v. News Am. Publ'g, Inc.*, 745 F. Supp. 1540, 1545 (C.D. Cal. 1990), *aff'd*, 971 F.2d 302 (9th Cir. 1992).

[225] Arguably the defense was first developed by the Ninth Circuit in *R.G. Smith v. Chanel, Inc.*, 402 F.2d 562 (9th Cir. 1968), although the term "nominative fair use" was not used. The case upheld the rights of traders producing cheaper versions of famous perfumes to identify the trademarked versions that they imitated.

[226] 425 F.3d 211 (3d Cir. 2005).

[227] *Id.* at 228.

[228] Art. 5(3) ("[1] Kunst und Wissenschaft, Forschung und Lehre sind frei. [2] Die Freiheit der Lehre entbindet nicht von der Treue zur Verfassung.")

mark used in the marketing of chocolate.[229] In general terms, defending an unlicensed use on parody grounds requires targeting the product or company identified by the mark rather than using the mark only to gain attention. Factors relevant to this analysis include the "form, length of time, intensity and addressees of the criticism, as well as the degree of truth, the reason for the criticism and the public interest in a dispute of the topic."[230]

An English decision in 2007 concerned an application for an interim injunction by the owners of the "MISS WORLD" trademark against a British television channel, Channel 4, which sought to transmit a television program under the name "Mr Miss World." The program followed the fortunes of an English competitor in a beauty pageant for transvestites and transsexuals that took place in Thailand in 2006, called "Miss International Queen." Relying on the *Laugh It Off* case, counsel for Channel 4 argued that the use of the "MISS WORLD" mark, or a mark similar to it, was protected by Article 10 of the ECHR. Mr. Justice Pumfrey quoted extensively from the *Laugh It Off* judgment and then observed:

> It is a truism that a registered trade mark's primary function is as an indicator of the origin of the goods or services with which it is associated. It is equally a truism that its protection does not cease there. It also acts as a guarantee of such quality as the trade mark owner is willing to associate with the mark. Thus, if the trade mark owner is in the habit of turning out high quality goods under his or her mark, that becomes part of the commercial value with which the mark is associated because the nature of the goodwill then becomes associated with the mark and becomes a relevant factor in considering what the mark actually protects.

> This is a difficult area and I do not wish to go into it more than necessary but I am worried that it is difficult to see where marginal detriment, which any detriment starts by being, to the goodwill or the repute of a mark becomes unmarginal. So, for example, if, untruthfully, a statement is made, whether satirically or whatever, damaging to the quality reputation with which the mark is associated, should the proprietor of the mark have a complaint on the footing that such damage is wholly related to the commercial value vested in the mark itself?

> My immediate reaction is that it is very difficult generally to disentangle commercial value, properly understood, from the goodwill and repute that is associated with the mark. This case must, I think, be viewed as a case in which the point that was made by the alleged infringement was so disconnected from the

---

[229] *Lila-Postkarte*, Bundesgerichtshof [BGH] [Federal Court of Justice] Feb. 3, 2005, I ZR 159/02 (F.R.G.).

[230] Marcus H. H. Luepke, *Taking Unfair Advantage or Diluting a Famous Mark – a 20/20 Perspective on the Blurred Differences between U.S. and E.U. Dilution Law*, 98 TRADEMARK REP. 789, 817 (2008).

ordinary function as an indication of origin and as an indicator of quality fulfilled by the mark, that it was fanciful to say that the mark qua mark was affected in any way. That is a finding of fact, not a proposition of law, and it is plainly a consideration which must be, so far as the guarantee conveyed by the South African Constitution is concerned, assessed as a question of fact in every case.

Now, the relief in the present case is not to restrain the showing of the programme at all but to restrain showing of the programme using with it the words "Mr Miss World". What is the function of these words divorced from the programme? That was vividly described, I think, by Miss Heal this morning as a spoof and a parody, a use of part of the vernacular or a byword which means a reputation and an attitude in sexual matters appropriate to the 1970s, but inappropriate to modern conditions. She says that that burden is carried simply by the words "Mr Miss World". It is, I think, for this reason that she has to accept that Miss World is readily recognizable as a brand in its own right. I am very doubtful as to the correctness of this argument.

The scope of the intervention of Article 10 in matters concerning registered trade marks is far from well worked out. Indeed, I think it is fair to say that it is almost completely unworked out. It is conceivable, I think, that a use such as that with which [*Laugh It Off*] was concerned would, in this country, equally give rise to questions under Article 10.

Whether that is right or not, I am, I am afraid, unpersuaded that it does so in this case. In my view the use of the words "Mr Miss World" is a useful and indeed ingenious shorthand intended to convey that we are here dealing with a beauty pageant for men as well as women and also for transsexuals. It may be that the true unpacking of a name will not become apparent to everybody until they have looked at the descriptive matter but once the descriptive matter is looked at then I think that the way in which the name is to be unpacked is quite apparent. That is all. It is essentially descriptive and it depends for its descriptive power upon the reputation that is attached to the words "Miss World".

Weighing all the relevant factors, Justice Pumfrey granted the interim injunctive relief sought by the trademark owner.[231]

10. Rochelle Dreyfuss has questioned whether firms need additional legal incentives to produce attractive or arresting trademarks. As Dreyfuss points out, firms already have powerful incentives to do so: the motivation to sell more goods or services.[232] Unlike in the copyright context, where the creative work is the "product," trademark proprietors do not need any further incentives to be creative. How persuasive is this critique?

11. A recent decision of the Supreme Court of Pennsylvania teaches that particular care may be needed in the drafting of trademark counterfeiting

---

[231] Further background on the interface between trademark law and Article 10 of the ECHR is provided in Andreas Rahmatian, *Trade Marks and Human Rights*, in Paul Torremans (Ed.), Intellectual Property and Human Rights 335, 337 (2008).

[232] Dreyfuss, *supra* note 179.

statutes, lest they offend constitutional protections for freedom of expression. *Commonwealth of Pennsylvania v. Omar*[233] involved criminal prosecutions for selling counterfeit clothing items bearing trademarks that had been applied without the trademark owners' permission. As written, the Pennsylvania statute criminalized "any unauthorized reproduction of intellectual property" or "intellectual property affixed to any item knowingly sold, offered for sale, manufactured or distributed or identifying services offered or rendered, without the authority of the owner of the intellectual property."[234] Over a strenuous dissent, the Court held that the statute was not restricted to conduct that was accompanied by an intention to sell products or services "deceptively"; rather, the statute prohibited *any* conduct involving the use of a mark to identify trademarked goods. So construed, the statute prohibited a large amount of constitutionally protected speech, including the use of the mark for purposes of protest. The court held the statute to be unconstitutionally overbroad and it quashed the counterfeiting convictions.

12. Megan Richardson has advanced the following analysis of the relationship between trademarks and speech:

> In a world where trade mark is replacing copyright "as the favoured form for protecting cultural texts" it can no longer be said, if ever it could, that trade marks exist only in relation to goods or services and have no meanings in themselves. The 20th century has seen popular culture take art, music and poetry into the "street" of film, radio, television, and now even more pervasively the internet. Ordinary people (including importantly children) have money and leisure and independence to devote to their entertainment – and they are prepared to spend these on things that draw them together, creating their own virtual communities based around a network of shared experiences. Now trade marks do more than "sell" goods and services, let alone distinguish their "origin" – still the *only* true function of trade marks according to trade mark law. Like them or not, trade marks tell stories. Their expressiveness is the basis of commercial activity, the trader-author the conduit of meaning, and the market-audience the monitor and arbiter of taste. And the combination of a vivid visual characterization and aural sound-bite effect makes them easy to remember (and difficult to forget) across the entire base of the population.... Yet our trade mark law traditionally operates under the umbrella that the great open commons of the English language require the protective mantle of regulation: "trade marks" should be narrowly defined and thresholds for registration set high in order that the language commons should remain in their pristine natural state; while at the other end infringement of a registered trade mark should be narrowly construed to avoid anything that smacks of copyright style protection....

---

[233] 981 A.2d 179 (Pa. 2009).
[234] 18 PA. CONS. STAT. § 4119(a).

[Observations by experts in sociolinguistics] identify important features of language not previously well understood: its adaptability in the face of cultural change, its inclination to borrow from myriad sources as well as its influence as a cultural device. They challenge the negative premise of the inherent distinctiveness construct, *viz* protection of the language commons, pointing to positive as well as negative influences of social discourse and context for language development. And they suggest the need to map not assume in advance. Thus they ... raise the prospect of trade marks emerging as a kind of language *of their own*. At the highest trade marks "carry a lot of symbolic freight. They do more than identify ... things. They reveal social hierarchies ... [and] acts of identity" – in short, they satisfy the sociolinguistic idea of what language is and should be. Current trade marks theories identify the value of trade marks as lying in their ability to identify "things." These theories might explain the law's focus on avoiding likely confusion as the most obvious threat to the identification function. But at best they offer only a plausible reason for anti-dilution rights in asserting a trade mark over time be harmed in its trade mark capacity – leaving them open to the critique of pandering to owner interests without clear social benefit. Sociolinguistics reveals trade marks that cross the threshold from commercial indicators to expressive devices to be not only more language-like, but more truly intellectual property like, than before supposed (and not simply in the impoverished sense of the intellectual effort expended in achieving distinctiveness, which ultimately became insufficient to sustain any broad notion of a registered trade mark as an exclusive property right). The utilitarian justification for copyright protection, lying in providing incentives for artistic and cultural development for the broader social benefit, can be extended to these new cultural items. For these trade marks, at least, infringement can be rationally extended to encompass uses that will likely blur or tarnish their expressive associations, reducing them to "the commonplace" or rendering them socially "unacceptable."[235]

What implications does Richardson's analysis have for the task of mapping the human rights-intellectual property interface? As has been suggested previously, in the copyright context it may be overly simplistic to view copyright protections as necessarily inconsistent with expressive freedoms. If trademarks are themselves expressive in ways that are not captured by traditional trademark doctrines and defenses, this may have normative implications for the scope of the public domain in trademark law. For instance, if copyright's incentive justification can extend to trademarks, does this mean that trademark owners now have an additional basis for objecting to uncompensated uses of trademarks – even where such uses by third parties further expressive freedoms? Does Richardson's analysis support the view that speech-protective doctrines, which thrust trademarks into the public domain, risk demoralizing the creative efforts and endeavors of trademark owners and their licensees? Is

[235] Megan Richardson, *Trade Marks and Language*, 26 SYDNEY L.R. 193, 195–96, 211–13 (2004).

it also relevant that many uncompensated uses of trademarks, like those of the defendants in *LL. Bean* and *Laugh It Off*, will very often parody the marks or their owners?[236] If, as in the copyright context, there is unlikely to be a market for these kinds of uses (because few intellectual property owners are willing to offer commercial licenses for parodies), would such uses genuinely compromise the creative efforts of trademark owners?

13. How should courts accommodate the interests of individuals who appreciate the "stability" of the meaning of a trademark or other types of cultural artifacts that are protected by intellectual property rights? Justin Hughes has described these as "audience interests," which, he suggests, are sometimes accorded insufficient attention in analysis of intellectual property rights, especially in critiques of their apparent expansion.[237] Consider the position of the fervent fan of a particular sports team, such as the Boston Red Sox. Recently, the U.S. Trademark Trial and Appeal Board sustained an opposition to registration of the mark SEX ROD – an obvious play on the mark RED SOX, which uses the same letters as the famous sports franchise mark – on the basis that it would be disparaging and because the applicant lacked a bona fide intention to use the SEX ROD mark in commerce.[238] Is it obvious whose expressive freedoms are implicated by this example, or whose rights should trump? The refusal to register the "SEX ROD" mark does not preclude use of the mark by the applicant – but the failure to register may diminish its commercial value. And, of course, if the applicant were to use the SEX ROD mark, it may face an infringement action brought by the owner of the RED SOX mark. Impediments to the use of SEX ROD would impinge on the applicant's expressive freedoms. But its use may also implicate the expressive freedom of the owner of the RED SOX mark by diminishing its control over how people apprehend the mark and the cultural meanings that accompany it. But should Red Sox fans also have audience interests not to have the RED SOX brand "tarnished" by its association with the SEX ROD mark? If so, how should fans' interests be accommodated in the context of the application to register a mark such as SEX ROD?

14. The SEX ROD case implicated a specific provision of the U.S. federal trademark statute that allows a trademark to be refused registration where it "consists of or comprises immoral, deceptive, or scandalous matter;

---

[236] Rosemary Coombe, *Authors, Inventors and Trademark Owners: Private Intellectual Property and the Public Domain*, 18 COLUM. J.L. & ARTS 191, 247–48 (1994); Sonia Katyal, *Semiotic Disobedience*, 84 WASH. L. REV. 489, 504 (2006).

[237] Justin Hughes, *Recoding Intellectual Property and Overlooked Audience Interest*, 77 TEX. L. REV. 923, 925–26 (1999).

[238] *Boston Red Sox Baseball Club L.P. v. Sherman*, 88 U.S.P.Q.2d 1581 (TTAB 2008).

or matter which may disparage … persons, living or dead, institutions, beliefs, or national symbols, or bring them into contempt, or disrepute."[239] The EC Trademark Directive also precludes registration of a trademark if it is "contrary to public policy or to accepted principles of morality."[240] The TRIPS Agreement, through its incorporation of relevant articles of the Paris Convention, similarly permits trademarks to be refused registration on public policy grounds or where a conflict exists with "accepted principles of morality."[241] In the U.S. context, at least, the policy reasons for such refusals are unclear.[242] The U.S. Trademark Trial and Appeals Board has, for instance, rejected the argument that registration of a trademark represents any governmental "imprimatur" of the mark.[243] A number of commentators have also explored whether the refusal to register a trademark implicates the right to freedom of expression.[244]

15. In a handful of recent European cases, the human rights implications of refusals to register a trademark have been explored in some detail.[245] A recent case arising under U.K. trademark law involved an application by a clothing store to register the mark "FCUK."[246] Invoking Article 10 of the ECHR, the appeal tribunal reasoned that a refusal to register could be justified only by demonstrating a pressing social need that is proportionate to the legitimate governmental aim pursued. Any doubt as to the applicability of the objection was to be resolved by upholding the right to freedom of expression and permitting the registration.[247] Are such cases properly concerned with expressive freedoms? Is the freedom of expression argument somewhat (and, perhaps, ironically) deflated by the reality that a refusal to register does not prevent *use* of the mark: indeed, without registration, offensive marks might be even more widely disseminated.[248] Moreover, even if it can be shown that a refusal

---

[239] 15 U.S.C. § 1052(a).

[240] Trade Mark Directive, *supra* note 194, art. 3(1)(f).

[241] TRIPS Agreement, *supra* note 102, art. 15(2) (permitting a member state to deny registration "on other grounds, providing that they do not derogate from the provisions of the Paris Convention (1967)"). The Paris Convention, art. 6*quinquies*(B)(iii), permits trademarks to be refused registration "when they are contrary to morality or public order."

[242] GRAEME B. DINWOODIE & MARK JANIS, TRADEMARKS AND UNFAIR COMPETITION: LAW AND POLICY 321 (2d ed. 2008) (examining various rationales).

[243] *In re Old Glory Condom Corp.*, 26 U.S.P.Q.2d 1216, 1220 n.3 (TTAB 1993).

[244] *See, e.g.*, Jeffrey Lefstin, Note, *Does the First Amendment Bar Cancellation of Redskins?*, 52 STAN. L. REV. 665 (2000); Jonathan Griffiths, *Is There a Right to an Immoral Trade Mark?*, *in* INTELLECTUAL PROPERTY AND HUMAN RIGHTS, *supra* note 231, at 309.

[245] *See generally* Griffiths, *supra* note 244.

[246] *French Connection Ltd.'s Trade Mark Registration*, [2007] ETMR 8.

[247] *See* Griffiths, *supra* note 244, at 317 (detailed discussion of the decision).

[248] *See, e.g.*, *French Connection Ltd.'s Trade Mark Registration*, [2007] ETMR 8, para. [54].

to register does impede the use of the mark, what kind of communication is being suppressed? Earlier in this section, we surveyed recent jurisprudence that has sought to delineate the essential function of a trademark. If a trademark's communicative function is (merely) to symbolize the goodwill in products and services, and, if that is the only "meaning" a trademark embodies, how is expression being suppressed when the commercial viability of a particular mark is limited by a refusal to register? For instance, the clothing store could have chosen a vast array of marks other than FCUK. How is the right to freedom of expression implicated when a firm is indirectly encouraged to make such a choice by a refusal to register the mark? If the right to freedom of expression is indeed implicated by such a refusal, does this bespeak some pessimism (or, perhaps, cynicism?) about the ability to "confine" the expressive character of trademarks to their traditional functions?

16. General limitations on the rights of trademark owners are also permitted under Article 17 of the TRIPS Agreement: Members "may provide limited exceptions to the rights conferred by a trademark, such as fair use of descriptive terms, provided that such exceptions take account of the legitimate interests of the owner of the trademark and of third parties." In contrast, limitations and exceptions to copyright and patent holders' exclusive rights must comply with the "three-step test," which varies slightly between the two fields.[249] In the trademarks context, there is no reference to "certain special cases" or the "normal exploitation" of the intellectual property right.[250] As we have seen, TRIPS also provides for further (and, in some cases, mandatory) exceptions in the context of other intellectual property rights, such as the prohibition in Article 9(2) against the extension of copyright to "ideas, procedures, methods of operation or mathematical concepts as such." Some scholars have suggested that, because the exceptions in the trademark context are narrower than is the case for copyright, the need for limitations to trademarks grounded in human rights is "of even greater importance."[251]

If permissible limitations on trademark rights are indeed more restrictive than those anticipated in other intellectual property contexts, does this support or detract from Judge Leval's suggestion, quoted earlier, that free expression values are better protected through doctrines and limitations that are "internal" to trademark law? Consider this question in the light of the basic substantive right ("legitimate interest") of trademark owners protected by TRIPS – namely, "the exclusive right to prevent all third parties not having

---

[249] *See* TRIPS Agreement, *supra* note 102, arts. 13 (copyright), 30 (patents).

[250] *Cf. id.* art. 30.

[251] Rahmatian, *supra* note 231, at 337.

the owner's consent from using in the course of trade identical or similar signs for goods or services which are identical or similar to those in respect of which the trademark is registered where such use would result in a likelihood of confusion."[252] Would it be consistent with TRIPS for a domestic court to analyze a likelihood of confusion case through the lens of free speech protections, as the South African Constitutional Court did when analyzing the dilution claims in *Laugh It Off*? The TRIPS Agreement stipulates that "in the case of the use of an identical sign for identical goods or services, a likelihood of confusion shall be presumed."[253] In disputes involving similar marks and/ or similar goods, might a domestic court require very strong evidence of likelihood of confusion as a way of (implicitly) taking free speech values into account while formally adhering to this presumption? Stated another way, would it be permissible for a court to invoke the right to freedom of expression as a basis for requiring a particularly strong showing of likelihood of confusion in any particular case, preferring to err on the side of treating the defendant's use as beyond the scope of the trademark owners' rights? Does Megan Richardson's analysis suggest that such an approach risks demoralizing trademark proprietors and insufficiently encouraging the kind of creative endeavor that is involved in building strong (and expressive) brands?

C. Patents

Freedom of expression issues have not typically arisen in the context of patents. As we explore in Chapters 2 and 6, tensions between patent law and human rights more often concern rights such as the right to health or the right to food. However, there have been two fairly recent developments in patent law that do appear to implicate the right to freedom of expression.

First, in the U.S. context, the Court of Appeals for the Federal Circuit has accepted that methods of doing business can be patentable subject matter. The leading case, *State Street Bank & Trust Co. v. Signature Financial Group, Inc.*,[254] upheld the patent in a system for managing a partner-fund financial services configuration. Some business method patents, particularly those that rely principally on mathematical concepts, are difficult to reconcile with the fundamental principle that mathematical algorithms are among the building blocks of technological development that should not be patented.[255]

---

[252] TRIPS Agreement, *supra* note 102, art. 16(1).
[253] *Id.*
[254] 149 F.3d 1368 (Fed. Cir. 1998).
[255] *See Mackay Radio & Tel. Co. v. Radio Corp. of Am.*, 306 U.S. 86, 94 (1939) ("While a scientific truth, or the mathematical expression of it, is not a patentable invention, a novel and useful structure created with the aid of knowledge of scientific truth may be.").

As a result, a number of scholars have claimed that the granting of business method patents is unconstitutional.[256] Some have raised freedom of expression concerns. For example, Jay Thomas has noted potential dangers of the shift away from industrial applicability as the touchstone for patentability.[257] Parts of his analysis implicate the relationship between patent rights and expressive freedoms. Thomas argues: "Disconnected from any physical apparatus, such patents will set forth not so much technical artifacts, but a broad category of proprietary modes of analysis, techniques and protocols from disciplines ranging from the social sciences to the law."[258] The privatization of "modes of analysis," human thoughts and behaviors, in these contexts arguably implicates expressive freedoms.[259] Thomas sets forth the following prescription:

> Restoring a patentability standard firmly grounded in industrial applicability, rather than equating technology with anything artificial, would enable us to maintain the integrity of our current patent system. Moreover, it would enable us to respect the boundary between the whole expression of our humanity and that small part of it that is properly called technological. However central to contemporary life and worthy of nurturing through the patent system, technology is but one manifestation of the human experience.[260]

In a recent decision, *Bilski v. Kappos*,[261] the Supreme Court had the opportunity to invalidate business method patents, but declined to do so. Even so, during oral argument of the case, some of the Justices expressed concern that expansive patent rights might suppress speech:

JUSTICE SOTOMAYOR: [A] patent limits the free flow of information. It requires licensing fees and other steps, legal steps. So you can't argue that your definition is improving the free flow of information.

MR. JAKES: Your Honor, I would, because of the disclosure requirement of the patent laws. It requires people to disclose their inventions rather than keeping them secret, so there is a second benefit to the patent system just other than encouraging people to invent, and that is to have that information get to the public generally. And in exchange for that –

---

[256]   *See, e.g.,* Malla Pollack, The Multiple Unconstitutionality of Business Method Patents: Common Sense, Congressional Consideration, and the Constitutional History, 28 RUTGERS COMPUTER & TECH. L.J. 61 (2002).

[257]   John R. Thomas, *The Patenting of the Liberal Professions*, 40 B.C. L. REV. 1139 (1999).

[258]   Thomas, *supra* note 257, at 1142.

[259]   Thomas F. Cotter, *A Burkean Perspective on Patent Eligibility*, 22 BERKELEY TECH. L.J. 855, 880–82 (2007).

[260]   Thomas, *supra* note 257, at 1185.

[261]   *Bilski v. Kappos*, 130 S. Ct. 3218 (2010).

JUSTICE SCALIA: Even though the public can't use it, right, until the patent expires?

MR. JAKES: Until the patent expires, if a valid patent issues on that, yes. But that's our system. We do give exclusive rights in exchange for that information being provided to the public.[262]

Biotechnology is a second area in which the granting of patents potentially implicates freedom of expression concerns. In the United States, a group of plaintiffs recently challenged the validity of patents that allegedly include methods of comparing human genes with genetic mutations associated with breast and ovarian cancer.[263] The complaint invited the court to reconsider the patentability of DNA sequences given that genes are the same whether they are inside or outside of the human body. The plaintiffs also challenged the patentability of gene sequences linked with human health. There is an obvious point of intersection here between the human right to health. In addition, the cases identify potential tensions between patents and speech.

From one perspective, patents are, at least in theory, "speech promoting."[264] Potential patentees often have a choice: they can keep the invention secret or seek patent protection.[265] (Inventions that are "self-disclosing" – that is, whose components or ingredients are not obvious on the face of the invention – may be a partial exception.) The *quid pro quo* underlying the patent system involves the exchange of exclusive rights, granted by the government, for the "disclosure" of the invention in the form of a written description, and, often, technical drawings, in the patent specification.[266] The litigation challenging the patentability of genetic material is motivated by a contrary perspective – that

---

[262] Transcript of Oral Argument at 14, *Bilski v. Kappos*, No. 08–964, 2009 WL 3750776 (U.S. Nov. 9, 2009).

[263] Information on the proceedings *available at* http://www.aclu.org/freespeech/gen/brca. html (last visited Mar. 31, 2010). In a recent ruling, a district court – found the challenged patents to be invalid, but avoided the plaintiffs' constitutional challenges. *See Association for Molecular Pathology v. U.S. Patent and Trademark Office*, 70 F.Supp.2d 181 (S.D.N.Y. 2010).

[264] *Cf.* Fiona Murry & Scott Stern, *Do Formal Intellectual Property Rights Hinder the Free Flow of Scientific Knowledge? An Empirical Test of the Anti-Commons Hypothesis*, 63 J. ECON. BEHAV. & ORG. 648 (2007) (identifying a decline in paper citations to patented technology after patents were granted); Timothy R. Holbrook, *Possession in Patent Law*, 59 SMU L. Rev. 123, 139–46 (2006) (noting that structural flaws in the patent system, including limitations on experimental use, inhibit the ability of a patent to perform a teaching function).

[265] *See Kewanee Oil Co. v. Bircron Corp.*, 416 U.S. 470, 480 (1974) (discussing the obligations imposed on patentees to disclose their inventions fully).

[266] *Aronson v. Quick Point Pencil Co.*, 440 U.S. 257, 262 (1979) ("[Patent law] promotes of inventions, to stimulate further innovation and to permit the public to practice the invention once the patent expires").

overbroad patents can chill expression. In particular, the complaint alleges that the challenged patents protect "pure information," the effect of which may be to prohibit research by others, and even some forms of genetic counseling and screening of cancer victims – issues also relevant to the right to benefit from scientific advancement disucssed in Section 4.4 of this chapter.

While this litigation at a preliminary stage, the recourse to the First Amendment in the context of a challenge to the validity of biotechnology patents is noteworthy. For the purposes of this book, its significance lies in foregrounding the potential confrontations between patents and human rights. It is too early to know whether freedom of expression issues will achieve a strong foothold in patent doctrine in the biotechnology context. It may transpire that patent doctrine develops the same kind of "internalization" thesis as has developed in the copyright context. That said, the recent developments described above suggest that challenges to patents grounded in expressive freedoms may receive a more welcome reception than may have been the case in the past.

Chapter 5

The Right to Education and Copyright
in Learning Materials

5.1. Introduction

Conceptually and textually, there exist venerable connections between education and intellectual property. These connections are particularly clear in the copyright context, which is the focus of this chapter. The first copyright statute, the English Statute of Anne of 1709, was entitled "An Act for the Encouragement of Learning."[1] Similarly, the Copyright Clause of the U.S. Constitution empowers the U.S. Congress to "to promote the progress of science" (or, in modern parlance, "knowledge") by creating a national copyright system. In the early years of the French Revolution, responsibility for the development of copyright law passed to the "Committee for Public Instruction," and by 1793, it was accepted that "enacting a copyright law formed part of a grander scheme of public education."[2]

At the outset, it is necessary to distinguish between realization of the human right to education and the belief that copyright's role is to facilitate learning. Copyright protection has always extended to educational materials. Since its beginnings, copyright law has been premised on the idea that the flourishing of private markets in copyright-protected works will promote learning. In contrast, the human right to education imposes public law obligations on governments, including the provision of free educational materials (particularly to primary school children).[3] The human right to education must therefore mean something other than the existence of markets for copyright-protected works, which anticipate that educational materials will

---

[1]   Copyright Act, 1709, 1710, 8 Ann., c. 19 (Eng.).
[2]   Jane C. Ginsburg, *A Tale of Two Copyrights*, 64 TUL. L. REV. 991, 1009 (1989).
[3]   *See generally* JOEL SPRING, THE UNIVERSAL RIGHT TO EDUCATION: JUSTIFICATION, DEFINITION, AND GUIDELINES (2000); Fons Coomans, *In Search of the Core Content of the Right to Education*, in AUDREY CHAPMAN & SAGE RUSSELL (EDS.), CORE OBLIGATIONS: BUILDING A FRAMEWORK FOR ECONOMIC, SOCIAL AND CULTURAL RIGHTS 217, 219 (2002).

be sold rather than distributed free of charge. Stated differently, the human right of access to educational materials cannot be determined solely by the ability to participate as a consumer in the markets that copyright laws create and sustain.[4]

When these early connections between copyright and learning were being articulated, education was anything but a universal entitlement guaranteed by the nation state. In the eighteenth century, when the framers of national copyright systems in Europe and the United States drew connections between copyright and learning, education remained a private matter for which parents and the church were principally responsible. This private conception of education was not much disrupted by the rise of Enlightenment ideals. Focusing principally on fashioning and justifying civil and political rights, documents such as the 1776 American Declaration of Independence and the 1789 French Declaration of the Rights of Man and of the Citizen did not mention education. The intellectual and political ideas embodied in these texts conceived of the state as a threat to civil liberties. Its role was to be minimized and certainly not amplified by the imposition of any government obligation to educate individuals.

During the nineteenth century, a shift in the state's role in education began to occur. State intervention might be warranted where necessary to protect children against actions that interfered with the educational opportunities made available by parents and the church.[5] But specific government responsibilities to provide education in the public sphere developed only with the rise of socialist conceptions of the welfare state and its accompanying obligations.[6] Along with the right to work and the right to social security, the right to education featured prominently in socialist constitutions and in socialist theories of human rights.[7]

---

[4] The United Nations Educational, Scientific and Cultural Organization (UNESCO) has cautioned against the adoption of market-based approaches to the realization of the human right to education in the following terms: "In so far as the 'right to lifelong learning' is understood to include a 'right' to continuing education, it would seem in practice to amount to little more than the 'right' of any citizen to participate, at his or her own expense, in the market for goods and services generally, with more or less encouragement from public funds depending on the situation in individual countries." UNESCO, *World Education Report 2000: The Right to Education: Toward Education for All Throughout Life* 60 (2000), *available at* http://www.unesco.org/education/information/wer/PDFeng/wholewer.PDF.

[5] Manfred Nowak, *The Right to Education*, in Asbjørn Eide et al. (Eds.), Economic, Social and Cultural Rights: A Textbook 189, 191 (1995). This theme is now reflected in the obligation imposed on states parties to "protect this right from encroachment by third persons." Coomans, *supra* note 3, at 227.

[6] Nowak, *supra* note 5, at 192.

[7] *Id.* The former U.N. Special Rapporteur Katrian Tomaševski observes that actual practice in Soviet states was, in fact, incompatible with the international human right to education.

The connections that initially existed between intellectual property and education were products of a specific worldview that valorized the private provision of edifying texts. A different kind of worldview informs the commitment to a universal right to education that is set forth in modern international human rights instruments. This world view, together with changes in the understanding of state obligations since copyright's inception, may in turn require a reconsideration of the relationship between education and intellectual property. In the education context, human rights guarantees challenge the abstract references to "learning," "public instruction," and "science" to which copyright's early framers appealed. A human rights approach may require us to ask, in very specific terms: *Whose* learning is encouraged? *Whose* knowledge has progressed?

Following a brief analysis of the rationales and justifications for a human right to education, this chapter examines the specific content of this right as it is set forth in major international human rights instruments. We then turn to the topic of copyright in textbooks and learning materials. The focus on textbooks and learning materials directly connects copyright to the right to education and provides a useful focal point for exploring the interface between human rights and intellectual property. There is empirical evidence that the provision of learning materials has a greater positive effect on learning outcomes than other educational inputs.[8] The provision of learning materials is also an integral part of the human right to education: the cost of those materials should not impede free access to education. Because copyrights are among the many inputs that go into the production of textbooks and learning materials, and because copyright may affect the price at which textbooks and learning materials can be provided, difficult tensions with the human right to education may arise.

A point on terminology: The human rights literature often uses the term "textbooks."[9] But the more generic term "learning materials" is more appropriate.[10] The latter term focuses attention on the principal educational

Katrian Tomaševski, *Unasked Questions about Economic, Social, and Cultural Rights from the Experience of the Special Rapporteur on the Right to Education (1998–2004): A Response to Kenneth Roth, Leonard S. Rubenstein, and Mary Robinson*, 27 HUM. RTS. Q. 709, 710 (2005).

[8] *See infra* Issues in Focus, pp. 333–334.

[9] See, *e.g.*, the analysis in the national reports under the U.N. Convention on the Rights of the Child, which is cited *infra* in Section 5.4.

[10] A variety of different terms are used in different contexts. The phrase "schoolbooks and learning materials" is used in *General Comment No. 17* issued by the Committee on Economic, Social and Cultural Rights on Article 15(1)(c) of the ICESCR on the right of everyone to benefit from the protection of the moral and material interests resulting from any scientific, literary or artistic production of which he or she is the author. (We discuss *General*

output: learning. Moreover, it leaves room for analysis of forms of "delivery" other than textbooks, including, where relevant, electronic formats or other tangible formats, such as "course packets."[11]

Notes and Questions

1. "Education" has a range of meanings. In its wider sense, it refers to the process by which a society endeavors to transmit beliefs, culture, and other values. In a narrower sense, it refers to learning in the context of teaching and instruction and the transmission of knowledge within formal educational settings. The "progress of science" that the U.S. Constitution anticipates will be "promote[d]" by the establishment of a national copyright system and the "encouragement of learning" to which the English Parliament referred in the Preamble to the Statute of Anne are consistent with the broader conception of education. In contrast, according to one leading commentator, the human right to education that is set forth in international human rights instruments "refers primarily to education in its narrower sense";[12] it "connotes teaching and instruction in specialised institutions" and envisages formal teaching or instruction, comprising primary, secondary, and higher education."[13] As you read the material that follows, consider whether this description aptly characterizes the human right to education.

2. In the United States, one of the sources for the "promote the progress" language of the U.S. Constitution's Copyright Clause was a proposal advanced at the 1787 Constitutional Convention for a federal power to "establish seminaries for the promotion of literature and the arts and sciences."[14] The proposal was ultimately rejected. Does this chapter in the history of U.S. copyright law provide additional support for the idea that, in the United States, the legislative power to craft copyright laws requires consistency with the

---

Comment No. 17 in detail in Chapter 3.) The phrase "textbooks and learning materials" is used in a major report on the production of textbooks that was prepared under the auspices of UNESCO. IAN MONTAGNES, UNESCO, TEXTBOOKS AND LEARNING MATERIALS 1990–99 (2000), *available at* http://unesdoc.unesco.org/images/0012/001234/123487e.pdf.

[11] The more generic term is also consistent with developments in copyright law. Whereas the early focus of copyright law was on tangible copies such as books, modern copyright systems are typically "media neutral." Copyright subsists regardless of the particular form in which the work is reproduced. *See, e.g.,* Jane C. Ginsburg, *From Having Copies to Experiencing Works: The Development of an Access Right in U.S. Copyright Law,* 50 J. COPYRIGHT SOC'Y U.S.A. 113 (2003).

[12] KLAUS DIETER BEITER, THE PROTECTION OF THE RIGHT TO EDUCATION BY INTERNATIONAL LAW 19 (2006).

[13] *Id.*

[14] *See* Dotan Oliar, *Making Sense of the Intellectual Property Clause: Promotion of Progress as a Limitation on Congress's Intellectual Property Power,* 94 GEO. L.J. 1771, 1806 (2006).

constitutional purpose of furthering the progress of knowledge?[15] The U.S. Supreme Court has not definitively ruled on whether the prefatory words in the Copyright Clause do indeed impose substantive constraints on legislative power.[16] The Court has instead deferred to the legislature's decision to create a copyright "system."[17]

3. The right to education is not only relevant to the provision of textbooks. As a discrete pedagogical topic, education *about* human rights is also relevant to the content of textbooks. Article 13 of the International Covenant on Economic Social and Cultural Rights (ICESCR), which we consider in detail in Section 5.3, requires education to "strengthen the respect for human rights and fundamental freedoms." Concerted international action has been directed toward the achievement of this goal. In December 2004, for example, the General Assembly of the United Nations proclaimed the World Program for Human Rights Education to advance the implementation of human rights education in all sectors.[18] What implications for curricular design follow from this obligation?[19]

5.2. The Right to Education: Justifications and Rationales

Of all internationally recognized socioeconomic rights, the human right to education appears to be among the least controversial.[20] Even so, there is no general agreement on what education is *for*. As one might expect, justifications and rationales for the right to education appeal to an array of different commitments and ideas.[21]

The right to education is an aspect of the primary commitment to the "inherent dignity" of all people that animates all human rights. The dignity rationale is captured by the inclusion of the right to education in Article 26 of

---

[15] *Id.*

[16] *Eldred v. Ashcroft*, 537 U.S. 186 (2003).

[17] *Id.* at 212 ("The 'constitutional command', we have recognized, is that Congress, to the extent it enacts copyright laws at all, create[s] a 'system' that 'promote[s] the Progress of Science.'" [citing *Graham v. John Deere Co.*, 383 U.S. 1, 6 (1996)]).

[18] The Office of the UN High Commissioner for Human Rights has provided information on the World Program for Human Rights Education, *available at* http://www2.ohchr.org/english/issues/education/training/programme.htm (last visited Mar. 31, 2010).

[19] Information on national initiatives in this context is *available at* http://portal.unesco.org/education/en/ev.php-URL_ID=1961&URL_DO=DO_TOPIC&URL_SECTION=201.html (last visited Mar. 31, 2010).

[20] Yoram Rabin, *The Many Faces of the Right to Education*, in DAPHNE BARAK-EREZ & AEYAL M. GROSS (EDS.), EXPLORING SOCIAL RIGHTS: BETWEEN THEORY AND PRACTICE 265, 266 (2007).

[21] *See* BEITER, *supra* note 12, at 26; SPRING, *supra* note 3, at 63–64.

the Universal Declaration of Human Rights (UDHR), the Preamble of which emphasizes "the inherent dignity and of the equal and inalienable rights of all members of the human family.... " A more direct connection between human dignity and the right to education is made by Article 13(1) of the ICESCR, which announces the agreement by all parties "that education shall be directed to the full development of the human personality and the sense of its dignity, and shall strengthen the respect for human rights and fundamental freedoms."

The Supreme Court of India has grounded the right to education in the right to life, guaranteed by Article 21 of the Indian Constitution.[22] Broadly interpreting this constitutional guarantee, the court has developed the concept of a right to live with human dignity, which

> must include protection of the health and strength of workers men and women, and of the tender age of children against abuse, opportunities and facilities of children to develop in a healthy manner and in conditions of freedom and dignity, *educational facilities*, just and humane conditions of work and maternity relief. These are the minimum requirements which must exist in order to enable a person to live with human dignity.[23]

Education also furthers other human rights values. In its *General Comment No. 13*, the Committee on Economic, Social and Cultural Rights characterized education as the "primary vehicle by which economically and socially marginalized adults and children can lift themselves out of poverty."[24] Education is also closely tied to public health and individual survival; as is widely acknowledged, a strong positive relationship exists between education and health outcomes, whether measured by death rates (mortality), illness (morbidity), health behaviors, or health knowledge.[25] And basic literacy

[22] Article 21 provides: "No person shall be deprived of his life or personal liberty except according to procedure established by law."

[23] *Bandhua Mukti Morcha v. Union of India*, (1984) 2 S.C.R. 67 (Bhagwati J.) (emphasis added); see also *Unni Krishnan, J.P. v. State of Andhra Pradesh*, (1993) 1 S.C.R. 594.

[24] Comm. on Econ., Soc. & Cultural Rights, *General Comment No. 13: The Right to Education*, para. 1, U.N. Doc. E/C.12/1999/10 (Dec. 8, 1999) [*General Comment No. 13*].

[25] Many studies affirm the close connection between education and health. *See, e.g.*, Institute of Public Health in Ireland, *Health Impacts of Education: A Review* 7–8 (2008), *available at* http://www.publichealth.ie/files/file/Health%20Impacts%20of%20Education.pdf (noting sources). The World Bank's 2007 annual report noted: "In all developing countries, but especially in the low-income regions of South Asia and Subsaharan Africa, immunization rates are higher among families whose mothers have some secondary education." World Bank, *World Development Report 2007: Development and the Next Generation* 5 [*World Development Report 2007*], *available at* http://www-wds.worldbank.org/external/default/ WDSContentServer/WDSP/IB/2006/09/13/000112742_20060913111024/Rendered/ PDF/359990WDR0complete.pdf.

and numeracy can provide a means for an individual to secure employment and, thereby, to satisfy other needs such as food and shelter.[26] Education is also critical to development programs[27] and to the realization of sustainable development.[28] As Ruth Okediji observes, "A well-informed, educated, and skilled citizenry is indispensable to the development process."[29]

Education is also connected to the idea of self-realization. Article 26(2) of the UDHR, for example, states that "education shall be directed to the full development of the human personality." The Universal Convention on the Rights of the Child (UNCROC) refers to education in the context of "the development of the child's personality, talents and mental and physical abilities to their fullest potential."[30] The Committee on Economic, Social and Cultural Rights has also emphasized that "education is not just practical: a well-educated, enlightened and active mind, able to wander freely and widely, is one of the joys and rewards of the human existence."[31]

These appeals to self-realization share common ground with human capabilities and human flourishing approaches to human rights. These approaches emphasize "being able to use the senses; being able to imagine, to think, and to reason – and to do these things in a 'truly human' way, a way informed and cultivated by an adequate education, including, but by no means limited to, literacy and basic mathematical and scientific training."[32] Gregory Alexander and Eduardo Peñalver have suggested that human flourishing involves "the capacity to make meaningful choices among alternative life horizons, to discern the salient differences among them, and to deliberate deeply about what is valuable within those available choices."[33] This premise echoes the Aristotelean concept of "practical reason," the "capacity of deliberating well about what is good and advantageous for oneself."[34] Assuming different life

---

[26] BEITER, *supra* note 12, at 27; Tomaševski, *supra* note 7, at 715 ("child labor cannot be eliminated unless education is free and compulsory").

[27] This is a persistent theme, for example, in the *World Development Report 2007, supra* note 25.

[28] Johannesburg Plan of Implementation, *in* World Summit on Sustainable Development, Johannesburg, S. Afr., Aug. 26–Sept. 4, 2002, *Report of the World Summit on Sustainable Development*, UN Doc. A/CONF.199/20.

[29] RUTH L. OKEDIJI, THE INTERNATIONAL COPYRIGHT SYSTEM: LIMITATIONS, EXCEPTIONS AND PUBLIC INTEREST CONSIDERATIONS FOR DEVELOPING COUNTRIES 2 (International Centre for Trade and Sustainable Development 2006), *available at* http://www.unctad.org/en/docs/iteipc200610_en.pdf.

[30] UNCROC art. 29(1)(a).

[31] *General Comment No. 13, supra* note 24.

[32] *See, e.g.,* Martha Nussbaum, *Human Rights and Capabilities*, 20 HARV. HUM. RTS. J. 21, 23 (2007).

[33] Gregory S. Alexander & Eduardo Peñalver, *Properties of Community*, 10 THEORETICAL INQUIRIES L. 127, 135 (2009).

[34] ARISTOTLE, NICOMACHEAN ETHICS Bk. VI, ch. 5, at 152 (Library of Liberal Arts 1962).

choices are in fact available (and too frequently they are not), an adequate education will surely make these choices more meaningful.

The right to education has also been characterized as an empowerment right. As such, it straddles different categories of human rights.[35] Consistent with the liberty concerns of civil and political rights, for example, education provides citizens with the tools to question and challenge government orthodoxy.[36] In addition, education makes basic democratic commitments, including the right to vote, more meaningful, by facilitating better understanding of the political questions that are at issue, a point that further underscores the requirement that education be provided without discrimination to all citizens.

The famous decision of the U.S. Supreme Court, *Brown v. Board of Education*,[37] reflects many of these themes. The Court's analysis also emphasized the role of education in achieving social cohesion. Holding that the "separate but equal" provision of state education for African-American children was unconstitutional, the Court characterized education as "the most important function of state and local governments," "the very foundation of good citizenship," and the "principal instrument in awakening the child to cultural values, in preparing him for later professional training, and in helping him to adjust normally to his environment."[38] The Court emphasized that education "is required in the performance of our most basic public responsibilities, even service in the armed forces."[39] Compulsory education and expenditure on public education were considered to manifest the nation's

[35] In *General Comment No. 11*, the U.N. Committee on Economic, Social and Cultural Rights noted: "[The right to education] has been variously classified as an economic right, a social right and a cultural right. It is all of these. It is also, in many ways, a civil right and a political right, since it is central to the full and effective realization of those rights as well. In this respect, the right to education epitomizes the indivisibility and interdependence of all human rights." Comm. on Econ., Soc. & Cultural Rights, *General Comment No. 11: Plans of Action for Primary Education (Article 14)*, para. 2, U.N. Doc. E/C.12/1999/4 (May 10, 1999) [*General Comment No. 11*]; see also, Katrina Tomaševski, *Removing Obstacles in the Way of the Right to Education: Right to Education Primers No. 1*, 5. (undated) [Tomaševski, *Primers No. 1*].

[36] Education can also equip citizens to question private sector practices in areas such as workplace policies. *See* JUDITH TENDLER, GOOD GOVERNMENT IN THE TROPICS (1998) (discussing a survey of managers and factory owners in northern Brazil who felt that a primary education (eight years) was helpful, but more than that was "dangerous" because it created workers who were less docile), *reprinted in* World Bank, *World Development Report 2004: Making Services Work for Poor People* 115 [*World Development Report 2004*], *available at* http://www-wds.worldbank.org/external/default/WDSContentServer/IW3P/IB/2003/10/07/000090341_20031007150121/Rendered/PDF/268950PAPER0WDR02004.pdf.

[37] 347 U.S. 483 (1954).

[38] *Id.* at 493.

[39] *Id.*

"recognition of the importance of education to ... democratic society."[40] Where a state has undertaken to provide the opportunity of education, that opportunity, the Court reasoned, is a right that must be made available to all on "equal terms."[41] The Court's analysis also emphasized the exercise of public responsibilities that education enables, such as participation in democratic society and the transmission of values, which, in turn, facilitate the preservation of culture and its continuity through generations.[42]

In a subsequent decision, the U.S. Supreme Court held that education is not a fundamental right that is explicitly or implicitly guaranteed by the United States Constitution. *San Antonio Independent School District v. Rodriguez*[43] concerned the system for funding education established by the state of Texas. Because Texas law relied on local property taxes as a principal source of funding for schools, the quality of education available varied considerably according to the wealth of the school district. The plaintiffs were a group of schoolchildren who argued that this differential treatment violated the Equal Protection Clause of the Fourteenth Amendment. In the following passage, a majority of the Court analyzed whether there exists a fundamental constitutional right to education:

> Education, of course, is not among the rights afforded explicit protection under our Federal Constitution. Nor do we find any basis for saying it is implicitly so protected. As we have said, the undisputed importance of education will not alone cause this Court to depart from the usual standard for reviewing a State's social and economic legislation. It is appellees' contention, however, that education is distinguishable from other services and benefits provided by the State because it bears a peculiarly close relationship to other rights and liberties accorded protection under the Constitution. Specifically, they insist that education is itself a fundamental personal right because it is essential to the effective exercise of First Amendment freedoms and to intelligent utilization of the right to vote. In asserting a nexus between speech and education, appellees urge that the right to speak is meaningless unless the speaker is capable of articulating his thoughts intelligently and persuasively. The "marketplace of ideas" is an empty forum for those lacking basic communicative tools. Likewise, they argue that the corollary right to receive information becomes little more than a hollow privilege when the recipient has not been taught to read, assimilate, and utilize available knowledge.
>
> A similar line of reasoning is pursued with respect to the right to vote. Exercise of the franchise, it is contended, cannot be divorced from the educational foundation of the voter. The electoral process, if reality is to conform to the

[40]   *Id.*
[41]   *Id.*
[42]   *Id.*
[43]   411 U.S. 1 (1973).

democratic ideal, depends on an informed electorate: a voter cannot cast his ballot intelligently unless his reading skills and thought processes have been adequately developed.

Since the right to vote, per se, is not a constitutionally protected right, we assume that appellees' references to that right are simply shorthand references to the protected right, implicit in our constitutional system, to participate in state elections on an equal basis with other qualified voters whenever the State has adopted an elective process for determining who will represent any segment of the State's population.

We need not dispute any of these propositions. The Court has long afforded zealous protection against unjustifiable governmental interference with the individual's rights to speak and to vote. Yet we have never presumed to possess either the ability or the authority to guarantee to the citizenry the most effective speech or the most informed electoral choice. That these may be desirable goals of a system of freedom of expression and of a representative form of government is not to be doubted. These are indeed goals to be pursued by a people whose thoughts and beliefs are freed from governmental interference. But they are not values to be implemented by judicial instruction into otherwise legitimate state activities.

Even if it were conceded that some identifiable quantum of education is a constitutionally protected prerequisite to the meaningful exercise of either right, we have no indication that the present levels of educational expenditures in Texas provide an education that falls short. Whatever merit appellees' argument might have if a State's financing system occasioned an absolute denial of educational opportunities to any of its children, that argument provides no basis for finding an interference with fundamental rights where only relative differences in spending levels are involved and where – as is true in the present case – no charge fairly could be made that the system fails to provide each child with an opportunity to acquire the basic minimal skills necessary for the enjoyment of the rights of speech and of full participation in the political process.[44]

Although the plaintiffs were unsuccessful in *Rodriguez*, the case remains important for present purposes because of its recognition of the connections between education, freedom of expression, and political participation. Ultimately, the Court concluded that to treat education as a fundamental right would be inconsistent with case law in which the Court had denied that there were fundamental rights to welfare benefits[45] and housing[46] within the U.S. constitutional framework. In addition, the Court considered the case to be a direct, and legally impermissible, attack on the manner in which Texas had chosen to raise and disburse state and local tax revenues.[47]

[44] *Id.* at 35–37.
[45] *Dandridge v. Williams*, 397 U.S. 471 (1970).
[46] *Lindsey v. Normet*, 405 U.S. 56 (1972).
[47] 411 U.S. at 40.

These conclusions reflect orthodox U.S. domestic constitutional doctrine.[48] A point to consider as we examine some of the major public international law instruments that articulate a human right to education is whether the same approach would be permissible under international law. As we shall see, many of the commitments accompanying the human right to education, particularly obligations to make education up to certain levels "free," directly implicate member states' decisions as to how to allocate resources.

5.3. The Right to Education in International Law

The treaty provisions articulating the right to education contain some of the most detailed and specific statements of all internationally protected human rights.[49] These include the UDHR, the ICESCR, and the UNCROC. A right to nondiscrimination in the context of education is also included in the Convention on the Elimination of All Forms of Racial Discrimination[50] and in the Convention on the Elimination of All Forms of Discrimination against Women.[51] The role of United Nations Educational, Scientific and Cultural Organization (UNESCO) is particularly important in the nondiscrimination context. A UNESCO Convention against Discrimination in Education was adopted in 1960.[52] The right to education is also included in a number of key regional human rights instruments.[53]

---

[48] It should be noted, however, that nearly all of the fifty states within the United States protect the right to education in some form in their state constitutions. *See* LOUIS HENKIN ET AL., HUMAN RIGHTS 1477, 1483–1501 (2d ed. 2009).

[49] We do not consider in any detail the Education for All (EFA) initiative, which was launched at the World Conference on Education for All in 1990 by UNESCO, UNDP, UNFPA, UNICEF, and the World Bank. Where appropriate, however, we cite research that has been conducted in conjunction with this initiative.

[50] International Convention on the Elimination of All Forms of Racial Discrimination, art. 5, Dec. 21, 1965, 660 U.N.T.S. 195 (*entered into force* Jan. 4, 1969).

[51] Convention on the Elimination of All Forms of Discrimination against Women, art. 10, Dec. 18, 1979, 1249 U.N.T.S. 13 (*entered into force* Sept. 3, 1981).

[52] Convention against Discrimination in Education, Dec. 14, 1960, 429 U.N.T.S. 93 (*entered into force* May 22, 1962). In key respects, this Convention goes further than the ICESCR. For instance, Article 3(e) requires states parties to give foreign nationals who reside in their territories the same access to education as that given to their own nationals. The ICESCR does not spell out this obligation. At the time of adopting the Convention, UNESCO also adopted a Recommendation against Discrimination in Education, which has been particularly influential for nations in which jurisdictional competence over education is not vested in national governments, but instead in states and territories. *See generally* BEITER, *supra* note 12, at 242.

[53] *See, e.g.,* African Charter on Human and Peoples' Rights, art. 11, June 27, 1981, 21 I.L.M. 58; Protocol to the Convention for the Protection of Human Rights and Fundamental Freedoms, art. 2, Mar. 20, 1952, 213 U.N.T.S. 262; European Convention for the Protection

Article 26 of the UDHR was the first of these instruments to announce a human right to education. It provides:

1. Everyone has the right to education. Education shall be free, at least in the elementary and fundamental stages. Elementary education shall be compulsory. Technical and professional education shall be made generally available and higher education shall be equally accessible to all on the basis of merit.

2. Education shall be directed to the full development of the human personality and to the strengthening of respect for human rights and fundamental freedoms. It shall promote understanding, tolerance and friendship among all nations, racial or religious groups, and shall further the activities of the United Nations for the maintenance of peace.

3. Parents have a prior right to choose the kind of education that shall be given to their children.

As the text of Article 26 reflects, "the" right to education comprises a number of different components.[54] First, Article 26 announces a universal commitment: the right is guaranteed to "everyone." The article then provides that elementary and fundamental education must be free, and technical and professional education must be generally available. The *World Declaration on Education for All*, a UNESCO document promulgated in 1990, defines "primary" education as education that is directed to satisfying "basic learning needs."[55]

of Human Rights and Fundamental Freedoms, Nov. 4, 1950, 213 U.N.T.S. 221; Charter of the Organization of American States, art. 49, Apr. 30, 1948, 119 U.N.T.S. 48. The right to education is also set forth in some 140 domestic constitutions. *See* Rabin, *supra* note 20. For example, the Constitution of India provides for a right to education in Articles 41 and 45, implementation and enforcement of which have occurred pursuant to the somewhat controversial 86th Amendment to the Constitution. INDIA CONST. arts. 41, 45; *see also* Vijayashri Sripati & Arun K. Thiruvengadam, *India: Constitutional Amendment Making the Right to Education a Fundamental Right*, 2 INT'L J. CONST. L. 148, 150 (2004) (discussing the opposition to the limited rights provided by the 86th Amendment). Many of the constitutions of Latin American nations also contain provisions on the right to education. UNESCO, *Right to Education: Latin America and the Caribbean*, *available at* http://portal.unesco.org/shs/en/ev.php-URL_ID=6844&URL_DO=DO_TOPIC&URL_SECTION=201.html (last visited Mar. 31, 2010). The Colombian Constitution offers an example: CONSTITUCIÓN POLÍTICA DE LA REPÚBLICA DE COLOMBIA DE 1991, artículo 67, *available at* http://pdba.georgetown.edu/Constitutions/Colombia/col91.html (last visited Mar. 31, 2010). In South Africa, the Constitution includes a provision granting a right to education in the Bill of Rights. S. AFR. CONST. 1996 § 29, *available at* http://www.info.gov.za/documents/constitution/1996/a108–96.pdf (last visited Mar. 31, 2010).

54 *See* Rabin, *supra* note 20, at 267.

55 World Declaration on Education for All art. 5. Article 26 of the UDHR references a right to "elementary" education. Other international instruments, including the ICESCR, UNCROC, generally refer to "primary" education.

This obligation anticipates the achievement of essential learning tools, such as literacy, oral expression, numeracy, and problem solving, along with basic learning content, including knowledge, skills, values, and attitudes.[56] "Fundamental" education addresses a particular set of social problems associated with the failure to complete basic primary education, an issue that may be particularly acute in the context of widespread movements of people across international borders, whether voluntary or forced.[57]

These commitments are consistent with a number of the rationales for the right to education discussed in the previous section. Article 26 emphasizes the development of the human personality and the strengthening of respect for human rights. As was noted earlier, the UDHR's Preamble reinforces the grounding of all rights in the inherent dignity of all people. Although Article 26 does not refer to dignity or nondiscrimination as such, nondiscrimination obligations are incorporated by Article 2 of the UDHR, which provides that "everyone is entitled to all the rights and freedoms set forth in [the UDHR], without distinction of any kind, such as race, colour, sex, language, religion political or other opinion, national or social origin, property, birth or other status." Like the UDHR's other provisions, education is subject to the limits specified in Article 29(2) – namely, "such limitations as are determined by law solely for the purpose of securing due recognition and respect for the rights and freedoms of others and of meeting the just requirements of morality, public order and the general welfare in a democratic society."

Articles 13 and 14 of the ICESCR contain a far more detailed elaboration of the human right to education:

Article 13

1. The States Parties to the present Covenant recognize the right of everyone to education. They agree that education shall be directed to the full development of the human personality and the sense of its dignity, and shall strengthen the respect for human rights and fundamental freedoms. They further agree that education shall enable all persons to participate effectively in a free society, promote understanding, tolerance and friendship among all nations and all racial, ethnic or religious groups, and further the activities of the United Nations for the maintenance of peace.

---

[56] BEITER, *supra* note 12, at 527.
[57] Primary education may not have been completed in a migrant's place of birth, for example, a situation that gives rise to international human rights obligations to provide fundamental education in the person's new country of domicile. In *General Comment No. 13*, the Committee on Economic, Social and Cultural Rights noted that fundamental education corresponds to basic education that is set forth in the *Declaration on Education for All*. See *General Comment No. 13, supra* note 24, para. 22.

2. The States Parties to the present Covenant recognize that, with a view to achieving the full realization of this right:
   (a) Primary education shall be compulsory and available free to all;
   (b) Secondary education in its different forms, including technical and vocational secondary education, shall be made generally available and accessible to all by every appropriate means, and in particular by the progressive introduction of free education;
   (c) Higher education shall be made equally accessible to all, on the basis of capacity, by every appropriate means, and in particular by the progressive introduction of free education;
   (d) Fundamental education shall be encouraged or intensified as far as possible for those persons who have not received or completed the whole period of their primary education;
   (e) The development of a system of schools at all levels shall be actively pursued, an adequate fellowship system shall be established, and the material conditions of teaching staff shall be continuously improved.

3. The States Parties to the present Covenant undertake to have respect for the liberty of parents and, when applicable, legal guardians to choose for their children schools, other than those established by the public authorities, which conform to such minimum educational standards as may be laid down or approved by the State and to ensure the religious and moral education of their children in conformity with their own convictions.

4. No part of this article shall be construed so as to interfere with the liberty of individuals and bodies to establish and direct educational institutions, subject always to the observance of the principles set forth in paragraph 1 of this article and to the requirement that the education given in such institutions shall conform to such minimum standards as may be laid down by the State.

Article 14

Each State Party to the present Covenant which, at the time of becoming a Party, has not been able to secure in its metropolitan territory or other territories under its jurisdiction compulsory primary education, free of charge, undertakes, within two years, to work out and adopt a detailed plan of action for the progressive implementation, within a reasonable number of years, to be fixed in the plan, of the principle of compulsory education free of charge for all.

A review of these provisions highlights several of the justifications for the right to education discussed earlier. Article 13(1) makes an *explicit* connection between education and "the sense of dignity" of the human personality. It also requires education to "enable all persons to participate effectively in a free society," a point implied, but not expressly stated, in the text of the UDHR. The reference in Article 13 to "enabl[ing]" participation in society directs attention to substantive outcomes. Education must include a practical orientation, which involves teaching students how to satisfy their practical needs in life.[58]

---

[58] BEITER, *supra* note 12, at 95.

Article 13(2) confirms and adds detail to the UDHR's commitment to the provision of free and compulsory primary education. Unlike the UDHR, however, it withholds imposing any obligation for free provision of "fundamental" education. Instead, Article 13(2)(d) requires the availability and accessibility of fundamental education to be encouraged or intensified as far as possible for those who have not received or completed primary education. Secondary education is to be generally available and accessible to all, an obligation that seems to anticipate that instruction at this level may not be rationed on the basis of availability of places. While higher education need not be made generally available, it must be "equally accessible to all" based on the objective criteria of accessibility. The practicalities of enforcement in the area of education are further underscored by Article 14, which imposes specific obligations to create and adopt detailed plans of action to provide free and compulsory education, where this had not already been achieved.

A further key set of statements on the right to education is found in the UNCROC. Many of the obligations in this convention repeat, or are generally in line with, the commitments to the right to education set forth in earlier instruments. That said, some of its specific obligations relating to education appear to be more diluted than those set forth in the ICESCR. For example, Article 28(1) requires states parties to "make" primary education compulsory and freely available to all, phraseology that perhaps signals progressive realization rather than an immediate obligation. In contrast, the "shall be" language used in Article 13 of the ICESCR reinforces the immediate duty to provide free and compulsory primary education. Even so, at a substantive level, this phraseology should not be taken as a muted international commitment to the right to education: the UNCROC also includes in Article 41 a provision stipulating application of other national or international laws if they are more favorable to the child.[59]

Key human rights obligations set forth in the ICESCR underscore the point that education is critical to the provision of basic needs that enhance the ability to participate in community life.[60] Article 13(1) of the ICESCR announces that "that education shall enable all persons to participate effectively in a free

---

[59] UNCROC, art. 41 ("Nothing in the present Convention shall affect any provisions which are more conducive to the realization of the rights of the child and which may be contained in: (a) The law of a State party; or (b) International law in force for that State.").

[60] Katrina Tomaševski observes: "An important obstacle to universalizing the right to education is a view that education is not indispensible for human survival nor required for subsistence, that families can function with children labouring rather than learning. The absence of education for victims of armed conflicts and disasters dooms them to remain recipients of assistance while preventing them from becoming self-sustaining." Tomaševski, *Primers No. 1, supra* note 35, at 30.

society."[61] This understanding is confirmed by Article 29 of the UNCROC, which recognizes the role of education in preparing the child for "responsible life in a free society."

The theme of empowerment is underscored in the approach to education in the context of group rights, sometimes referred to as "third-generation" rights. The rights of indigenous peoples illustrate the point. For example, Article 29 of the 1989 International Labor Organization (ILO) Convention No. 169[62] describes the aims of education as being "the imparting of general knowledge and skills that will help children belonging to the peoples concerned to participate fully and on an equal footing in their own community and in the national community."[63] Convention No. 169 also imposes obligations to cooperate in the development of educational programs[64] and to adopt educational measures applicable to all sectors of the community aimed at eliminating prejudices toward indigenous peoples. The latter may include ensuring history textbooks and other educational materials "provide a fair, accurate and informative portrayal of the societies and cultures of these peoples."[65]

These concepts are further developed in the United Nations Declaration on the Rights of Indigenous Peoples, adopted by the General Assembly in 2007.[66] The Declaration contains a number of provisions that link education to the protection of culture. Article 13 recognizes indigenous peoples' right to control the transmission of culture between generations, including the right to "transmit to future generations their histories, languages, oral traditions, philosophies, writing systems and literatures."[67] Article 14 of the Declaration announces the right of indigenous peoples "to establish and control their educational systems and institutions providing education in their own languages, in a manner appropriate to their cultural methods of teaching and learning" while also providing for the rights of indigenous individuals, "particularly children," to have the "right to all levels and forms of education [from] the State without discrimination."[68] Both of these provisions are more specific manifestations of the minority rights clauses of earlier human rights instruments.

[61] Id. art. 13(1).
[62] Convention Concerning Indigenous and Tribal Peoples in Independent Countries, June 27, 1989, 328 U.N.T.S. 247 (entered into force Sept. 5, 1991).
[63] Id. art. 26.
[64] Id. art. 27.
[65] Id. art. 31.
[66] Declaration on the Rights of Indigenous Peoples, G.A. Res. 61/295, art. 31, U.N. GAOR, 61st Sess., 107th plen. mtg., U.N. Doc. A/RES/61/295 (Sept. 13, 2007).
[67] Id. art. 13.
[68] Id. art. 14.

These include Article 27 of the ICESCR, which establishes a right of ethnic, religious, or linguistic minorities, "in community with the other members of their group," not to be denied the right to "enjoy their own culture, to profess and practice their own religion, or to use their own language." Commitments of this kind also find expression in Article 30 of the UNCROC:

> In those States in which ethnic, religious or linguistic minorities or persons of indigenous origin exist, a child belonging to such a minority or who is indigenous shall not be denied the right, in community with other members of his or her group, to enjoy his or her own culture, to profess and practise his or her own religion, or to use his or her own language.

5.4. The Provision of Learning Materials and the Human Right to Education

Human rights commentary includes numerous references to the provision of adequate textbooks and learning materials as a component of the human right to education. In its *General Comment No. 13*, the Committee on Economic, Social and Cultural Rights stated:

> Education in all its forms and at all levels shall exhibit the following interrelated and essential features: (a) Availability – functioning educational institutions and programmes have to be available in sufficient quantity within the jurisdiction of the State party. What they require to function depends upon numerous factors, including the developmental context within which they operate; for example, all institutions and programmes are likely to require buildings or other protection from the elements, sanitation facilities for both sexes, safe drinking water, trained teachers receiving domestically competitive salaries, *teaching materials*, and so on; while some will also require facilities such as *a library, computer facilities and information technology*.[69]

In its 2007 report, *A Human Rights Approach to Education for All*, UNESCO described the "provision of schools, teachers, books and equipment" as a "fundamental prerequisite of education,"[70] and a key factor in improving the overall quality of education.[71]

The availability and cost of textbooks and learning materials are relevant to the state's obligation to provide "free" primary education.[72] As Fons

---

[69] *General Comment No. 13, supra* note 24, para. 6 (emphases added).

[70] UNESCO, *A Human Rights-Based Approach to Education for All*, 56 (2007), *available at* http://unesdoc.unesco.org/images/0015/001548/154861E.pdf.

[71] *Id.* at 77.

[72] *See, e.g.*, ICESCR, art. 13(2)(a); UDHR, art. 26; UNCROC, art. 28. The international commitment to the progressive realization of free education beyond the primary level is also reflected in these clauses.

Coomans observes: "The degree to which primary education is really free is determined by a number of direct and indirect costs, such as ... expenses for textbooks and supplies."[73] The *quality* of textbooks and learning materials is also relevant to this obligation. The Committee on the Rights of the Child has similarly noted in *General Comment No. 1* on UNCROC Article 29(1), *The Aims of Education*, that "every child has the right to receive an education of good quality which in turn requires a focus on the quality of ... teaching and learning ... materials."[74]

The realization of these rights in practice, however, remains incomplete. Many studies confirm that the provision of learning materials to school-children is often inadequate.[75] A 2009 study affiliated with UNESCO found that "in many cases, children and teachers lack access to basic learning materials.... Over half of grade 6 pupils in many countries – including Malawi, Mozambique, Uganda and Zambia – did not have a single book."[76] These failures must be viewed in the context of equally significant short-falls concerning other aspects of the right to education, including dev-astatingly low attendance and completion rates, particularly among the poor.[77]

In its concluding observations on member state reports, the Committee on the Rights of the Child has often identified problems with the provi-sion of education materials. Commenting on a 2005 report by Albania, the Committee noted its "concer[n] at ... the lack of qualified teaching staff and teaching materials."[78] In the same year, it recommended that Algeria "allocate adequate financial, human, and technical resources in order to ... complete the ongoing reform of the educational system, including revision of the cur-ricula and learning methods in order to increase the quality of education and teaching materials."[79] Of Barbados, the Committee said in 1999 that it "remains concerned about practical implementation of the educational

---

[73] Coomans, *supra* note 3, at 228.

[74] CRC/GC/2001/1 (Apr. 17, 2001), para 22.

[75] Shobhana Sosale, in SHOBHANA SOSALE (ED.), *Introduction* to THE WORLD BANK, EDUCATIONAL PUBLISHING IN GLOBAL PERSPECTIVE: CAPACITY BUILDING AND TRENDS 1, 1 (1999) (quoting PERNILLE AKEROD, A GUIDE TO SUSTAINABLE BOOK PROVISION 16 (1997)).

[76] EFA Global Monitoring Report, *Overcoming Inequality: Why Governance Matters* 13 (2009), *available at* http://unesdoc.unesco.org/images/0017/001776/177683E.pdf.

[77] *See, e.g.*, World Bank, *World Development Report 2004, supra* note 36, at 111–12.

[78] U.N. Comm. on the Rights of the Child, *Concluding Observations: Albania*, § 60, U.N. Doc. CRC/C/15/Add.249 (Mar. 31, 2005).

[79] U.N. Comm. on the Rights of the Child, *Concluding Observations: Algeria*, § 67(b), U.N. Doc. CRC/C/15/Add.269 (Oct. 12, 2005).

reforms and of the policy to provide textbooks to all schoolchildren."[80] In 2001, the Committee said of the Dominican Republic: "The Committee welcomes the State party's efforts in the field of education ... but it remains concerned about ... children's limited access to materials and textbooks."[81] In the same year, the Committee expressed concern regarding "the limited availability of learning materials" in Georgia.[82] A drastic shortage of textbooks in India was noted in 2000,[83] and reiterated in 2004, when the Committee referred to "the insufficient number of trained teachers, schools, classrooms, and the lack of relevant learning material, which affect the quality of education."[84]

Expressions of concern about the provision of textbooks are not confined to developing or least-developed nations. In its 2006 concluding observations on Ireland, the Committee expressed its concern that the cost of learning materials imposed a "de facto" cost on parents.[85] Similar observations were made about Austria in 2000: "The Committee notes that budgetary austerity measures have affected the working of the school system, for example by introducing some family contributions for school books and enrichment activities."[86] And in 2002, the Committee noted a problem of "outdated textbooks" in Greek schools.[87]

---

* * * Issues in Focus * * *

In its *2004 Development Report, Making Services Work for Poor People,* the World Bank summarized research that examined the increases in test scores per dollar spent on a variety of different educational "inputs."[88] Although

---

[80] U.N. Comm. on the Rights of the Child, *Concluding Observations: Barbados,* § 27, U.N. Doc. CRC/C/15/Add.103 (Aug. 24, 1999).

[81] U.N. Comm. on the Rights of the Child, *Concluding Observations: Dominican Republic,* § 41, U.N. Doc. CRC/C/15/Add.150 (Feb. 21, 2001).

[82] U.N. Comm. on the Rights of the Child, *Concluding Observations: Georgia,* § 52, U.N. Doc. CRC/C/15/Add.124 (June 28, 2000).

[83] U.N. Comm. on the Rights of the Child, *Concluding Observations: India,* § 56, U.N. Doc. CRC/C/15/Add.115 (Feb. 23, 2000).

[84] U.N. Comm. on the Rights of the Child, *Concluding Observations: India,* § 64, U.N. Doc. CRC/C/15/Add.228 (Feb. 26, 2004).

[85] U.N. Comm. on the Rights of the Child, *Concluding Observations: Ireland,* § 58, U.N. Doc. CRC/C/IRL/CO/2 (Sept. 29, 2006).

[86] U.N. Comm. on the Rights of the Child, *Concluding Observations: Austria,* § 26, U.N. Doc. CRC/C/15/Add.98 (May 7, 1999).

[87] U.N. Comm. on the Rights of the Child, *Concluding Observations: Greece,* § 66(f), U.N. Doc. CRC/C/15/Add.170 (Feb. 1, 2002).

[88] World Bank, *World Development Report 2004, supra* note 36, at 116.

(a) **Northeast Brazil (1980s)**

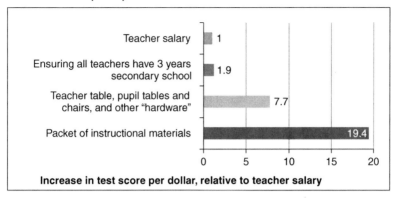

Increase in test score per dollar, relative to teacher salary

(b) **India (1990s)**

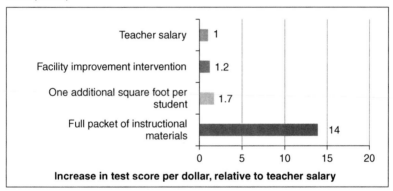

Increases in test scores per dollar spent on different inputs
(a) Northeast Brazil (1980s) and (b) India (1990s)

the focus of the World Bank's analysis was the relative benefit of increasing teacher salaries as compared with other inputs, the research results illustrate the comparative importance of instructional materials in improving educational outputs (here, measured by test scores). The studies do not, however, provide information about the copyright status of these "packet[s] of instructional materials."

5.5. Copyright in Textbooks and Learning Materials

For the present book, a key question is the extent to which copyright law impedes the provision of learning materials in a manner that is inconsistent with international human rights obligations. The source of the tension between intellectual property and the obligation to provide teaching and learning materials has been described by one scholar as follows: "The critical problem of potential conflicts arises from the fact that the educational materials, in which authors may have a material interest, are critical to the realization of the right to education."[89]

In the following passage, Margaret Chon explores this question in greater detail:

> Access to textbooks for students varies greatly between developed and developing countries. Textbooks are typically distributed to students "for free" in the United States as part of the system of public education. Even in the United States, which is one the most developed of the developed countries, textbooks can be out-of-date and in short supply. In the vast majority of developing countries, however, the state does not provide textbooks; students must purchase them out-of-pocket. The reasons for the lack of state provision include "rises in enrollment, economic recession, civil conflict, and pressing economic priorities in public health."[90] Additionally, structural adjustment policies have caused sacrifices across all public sector spending, especially education. "No nation chooses to have families cover school book costs on the basis of philosophy; rather it is a matter of exigency."[91]
>
> The price of textbooks can be very high relative to per capita income for a number of reasons. In the case of state owned or assisted publishing, these reasons include inefficient manufacturing methods, state monopolies, and favoritism. In the case of market-based textbook publishing, these reasons may include industry consolidation and lack of competition. Higher prices may be caused by the failure of multinational publishers to engage in differential pricing, so that a student in a developing country may pay a relatively high price for a book as a percentage of per capita GDP compared to a student in a developed country. Many developing countries, likewise, are "dominated by the major international languages, and this dominance places a further strain on limited publishing and other resources. It also makes these countries dependent on the nations which publish in the major international languages."[92] Moreover, the existence of minority languages within developing countries requires either de novo content creation or translation of existing materials that adds to the cost of textbook development.
>
> Reliance on trade books rather than textbooks does not solve the pricing or access issues. A literature-based approach to basic education is costly compared

---

[89] *See* Sharon E. Foster, *The Conflict between the Human Right to Education and Copyright*, in Paul Torremans (Ed.), Intellectual Property and Human Rights 287, 288 (2008).

[90] Stephen P. Heyneman, *The Role of Textbooks in a Modern System of Education: Towards High Quality Education for All*, in Cecilia Braslavsky (Ed.), Textbooks and Quality Learning for All: Some Lessons Learned from International Experiences (2006).

[91] *Id.*

[92] Philip G. Altbach, *Copyright in the Developing World*, in Joseph P. Farrell & Stephen P. Heyneman (Eds.), Textbooks in the Developing World: Economic and Educational Choice 3–5 (1989).

to a textbook-based approach. This is due to the lack of capacity and infra-structure to publish supplementary books, the expense of teacher training, and language difficulties including the challenge of multilingual nations. However, the limited book supply is "[p]erhaps the biggest obstacle to literacy using non-textbook reading materials alone."[93]

The combination of all these factors has led to severe access problems with respect to basic educational materials protected by copyright. The top-down way of understanding this problem is through the frequently invoked and suc-cinct term "piracy" with its heavy implication of blame and censure. However, a from below understanding is that this represents a failure in access to essential learning materials, combined with the necessary logic of an informal economy and cultural factors.[94]

A starting point for analyzing the human rights consequences of copyright protection for textbooks and learning materials should be the accommoda-tions that already exist in international copyright law for the provision of those materials. The principal international instrument that addresses these accommodations is the Appendix to the Berne Convention. The Appendix was adopted as part of the 1971 Paris Act of the Berne Convention.[95] It includes a complex set of provisions directed at facilitating bulk access to certain types of protected works – including educational materials – in devel-oping nations. The Appendix allows these nations to adopt a compulsory licensing scheme that limits copyright owners' control over reproduction and translation rights in these works.

The Berne Appendix does not cover broadcasting and communication rights, rights that are of particular importance in the education context.

---

[93] For all these reasons, Oliveira concludes that literature-based instruction may be cheaper and less dependent on government publishing, but that currently such instruction can only be effective as a supplement to textbooks, not a replacement for them. João Oliveira, *Textbooks in Developing Countries*, in VINCENT GREANEY (ED.), INT'L READING ASS'N, PROMOTING READING IN DEVELOPING COUNTRIES 78, 87 (1996) ("A broad choice of genre and subjects is important to engage a range of students' interests. In practice, the use of supplementary reading materials in developing countries means students read foreign books, typically pro-duced in developed countries and highly focused on fiction rather than on other genre[s] that may be more relevant to the students' experiences.").

[94] Margaret Chon, *Intellectual Property "from Below": Copyright and Capability for Education*, 40 U.C. DAVIS L. REV. 803, 824–827 (2007). We quote Chon's explanation of the meaning of "from below" in the Notes and Questions that follow this section.

[95] 1971 Appendix to the Paris Act Revision of the Berne Convention [Berne Appendix]. The Universal Copyright Convention (UCC) includes broadly parallel accommodations. Universal Copyright Convention arts. V*bis*-V*quater*, Sept. 6, 1952, as revised at Paris on July 24, 1971, 25 U.S.T. 1341, 943 U.N.T.S. 178. These accommodations were a principal topic for discussion at the July 1971 Conference for Revision of the Universal Copyright Convention. The report of the General Rapporteur of that Conference is reproduced at 19 J. COPYRIGHT SOC'Y U.S.A. 211 (1972).

These rights had been included in an earlier initiative, a Protocol to the Berne Convention, which was promulgated in conjunction with the 1967 Stockholm Conference. At that time, there was considerable pressure from developing countries for concessions in relation to their use of copyright-protected works.[96] Developed countries – the source of most published copyright-protected material – grudgingly acquiesced in these concessions; without them, the Berne Union might have collapsed. The Stockholm Protocol did not go into effect, however, since developed nations proved unwilling to ratify the instrument.[97] Binding concessions, albeit more limited ones than those set forth by the Stockholm Protocol, needed to wait until the adoption of the Paris Act in 1971. In part because the Berne Appendix was more limited in scope than the earlier Stockholm Protocol, its adoption was also less contentious.

Ruth Okediji explains the issues that motivated the adoption of the Appendix as follows:

> Bulk access – that is, access to multiple copies of a copyrighted work at affordable prices – goes directly to the right of an author to control the reproduction of the work. Most developing and least-developed countries have the requisite copying technologies to reproduce copyrighted works and supply the local market with cheap copies. [But t]here is also a second component to the access problem for developing countries and that is the availability of copies in local languages. The Berne Convention grants authors the exclusive right to translate their works, meaning that even if cheap copies were available for purchase locally, access would nevertheless be meaningless unless those copies were translated. The reproduction and translation rights thus operate in tandem as barriers to access in developing countries.[98]

Under the Berne Appendix, a national of an eligible developing country may apply for a compulsory license to translate or to reproduce covered works at a price that is reasonably related to that normally charged in the country for comparable works. This extends to the state itself and state-owned enterprises, but not, apparently, to other legal entities such as corporations and charitable organizations.[99] The circumstances in which states may issue such licenses are quite confined and highly complex. The Appendix provides for a three-year waiting period from the date of first publication of the work

---

[96] See 1 Sam Ricketson & Jane Ginsburg, International Copyright and Neighbouring Rights: The Berne Convention and Beyond 123 (2006).

[97] Id. at 131.

[98] Okediji, supra note 29, at 15.

[99] Cf. 2 Ricketson & Ginsburg, supra note 96, at 931 (discussing alternative interpretations, according to which corporations and charitable organizations are entitled to apply for a license under the Appendix).

before a translation license may be issued. A license to translate may only be granted if the work has not been published in a language in general use in that country by, or under the authority of, the owner of the translation right. The Appendix appears to preclude the issuing of a license if a translation into that language had been published within the three-year period anywhere in the world.[100] This waiting time may be shortened under limited circumstances.[101]

For a reproduction license, the waiting time is generally five years after publication of a particular edition of a copyright-protected work, if copies of this edition have not been distributed in the relevant country either (1) to the general public, or (2) in connection with systematic instructional activities, by or under the authority of the owner of the right of reproduction at a price reasonably related to the price that is normally charged in the country for comparable works. This waiting period is reduced to three years for scientific works but extended to seven years for works of poetry, fiction, music, and drama.[102]

A license to translate can be granted only for teaching, scholarship, and research purposes[103]; a license to reproduce is limited to "systemic instructional activities."[104] Furthermore, the Appendix gives a "grace period" (beyond the waiting period) to copyright owners, stating that no compulsory license can be issued if, during this grace period, the work is distributed in the developing country at reasonable prices (again, relative to prices in that country). In essence, where the owner of the reproduction and/or translation right chooses to make substantially the same work available at a reasonable price, any compulsory license terminates, subject to a right to sell copies already made under the license until the stock is depleted.[105] The Appendix also requires an applicant for a license to show that the copyright owner denied permission to reproduce or translate or that the copyright owner could not be located, and it imposes record-keeping and reporting obligations on parties who have attempted to locate the owner of the copyright.[106]

Reviewing these detailed interlocking provisions, Okediji observes that they are "intended to give the original owner every opportunity to supply that particular local market" and thus obviate the need for a compulsory license

---

[100] *Id.*
[101] *Id.* at 932. Shortened periods do not apply where the language in question is English, French, or Spanish.
[102] Berne Appendix, *supra* note 95, Art. 3(3).
[103] *Id.* art 2(5).
[104] *Id.* art. 3(2).
[105] *See, e.g., id.* art. 3(6).
[106] *Id.* art. 4(1)–(2).

in the first instance.[107] She concludes, however, that the Appendix has been "a dismal failure owing to unduly complex and burdensome requirements associated with its use."[108] Sam Ricketson and Jane Ginsburg concur, stating that "it is hard to point to any obvious benefits that have flowed directly to developing countries from the adoption of the Appendix."[109]

In the following extract, Margaret Chon discusses the need for a "substantive equality principle" that would inform the development of international copyright law in the education context. Chon analyzes accommodations for education in existing international instruments, including the Berne Appendix, in the light of this principle. She argues that substantive equality should inform the analysis of domestic-law exceptions to copyright and their compliance with "three-step test" that is set forth in Article 9(2) of the Berne Convention and Article 13 of TRIPS. According to the three-step test, member states "shall confine limitations or exceptions to exclusive rights to certain special cases which do not conflict with a normal exploitation of the work and do not unreasonably prejudice the legitimate interests of the right holder."[110] Chon also discusses the role of Article 10(2) of the Berne Convention, which provides: "It shall be a matter for legislation in the countries of the Union, and for special agreements existing or to be concluded between them, to permit the utilization, to the extent justified by the purpose, of literary or artistic works by way of illustration in publications, broadcasts or sound or visual recordings for teaching, provided such utilization is compatible with fair practice."

Margaret Chon, *Intellectual Property "from Below": Copyright and Capability for Education*, 40 U.C. DAVIS L. REV. 803, 828–33, 834–46 (2007)

Prevailing copyright practices and policies in the global book publishing industry have fostered inequality rather than addressed the glaring need to build domestic capacity in publishing or greater access to books published outside of a small national market. The net result is to promote unidirectional knowledge development and exchange in a manner that fails to benefit developing countries. As to the Berne Convention, several observers have recognized the glaring lack of transparency and functionality of the compulsory licensing provisions for educational use. These provisions

---

[107] OKEDIJI, *supra* note 29, at 29.
[108] *Id.*
[109] 2 RICKETSON & GINSBURG, *supra* note 96, at 957.
[110] Agreement on Trade-Related Aspects of Intellectual Property Rights, art. 13, Apr. 15, 1994, 1869 U.N.T.S. 299 [TRIPS Agreement].

were the result of a huge push by developing countries (arguably similar to the recent push in the WTO regarding TRIPS and public health) to shape copyright rules appropriate for the needs of developing countries, including more liberal translation rights, shorter duration of copyright, and use of works for broadcasting and educational purposes. The compromise, the 1971 Appendix to the Paris Act Revision of the Berne Convention (also known as the Berne Appendix), contains provisions so complex and arcane that very few developing countries have been able or willing to take advantage of them. Thus, instead of building capacity, the Berne Convention poses structural impediments to the creation of local publishing industries and to the translation of textbooks from the world's dominant languages into minority languages.

Others scholars have noted the anticompetitive nature of the global publishing industry. A pre-TRIPS analysis has also compared the copyright industries of the North to the OPEC cartel, with oligopolistic control over distribution and pricing and high barriers to entry resulting in sharp and systematic inequality of knowledge exchange.[111] Often, trade sanctions or structural adjustment conditions exacerbate the problem. For example, no small part of Korea's success as one of the four "Asian Tigers" is due to its government's deliberately weak copyright laws prior to TRIPS. Yet even before TRIPS, the United States Trade Representative put pressure on Korea for what it perceived to be violations of copyright. TRIPS has exacerbated the net movement of global rents towards developed countries. In addition to reducing flexibility in domestic regulatory strategies regarding global public goods, the benefits of TRIPS accrue overwhelmingly to publisher-rich countries such as the United States and the United Kingdom.

Reasons for higher textbook prices may include the inability or unwillingness of Berne developing member countries to engage robustly in the compulsory licensing provisions of the Berne Appendix[.] With narrow exceptions, the Berne Appendix does not allow a country issuing a license to print books domestically to extend that license to the publication of books outside of country with the purpose of importing them. Although permitted by Berne and TRIPS, parallel imports of cheaper editions of books from other countries may be banned by domestic law, underutilized, or foreclosed by TRIPS plus agreements.

---

[111] Philip G. Altbach, *The Subtle Inequalities of Copyright*, in PHILIP G. ALTBACH (ED.), COPYRIGHT AND DEVELOPMENT: INEQUALITY IN THE INFORMATION AGE 5 (1995) ("There is a kind of OPEC of knowledge in which a few rich nations and a small number of multinational publishers have a great deal of control over how and where books are published, the prices of printed materials, and the nature of international exchange of knowledge.").

Moreover, the conditions of education in many developing countries may not fall within the local exceptions for fair use or educational use. For example, under local South African copyright law, educational exceptions are limited to classroom use, and materials have to be used inside a classroom. Yet, in many rural schools, the teaching literally takes place outside and thus falls outside the exception. A relatively recent phenomenon is the expansion of the reprographic collection society model to parts of the developing world that have questionable capacity to participate in the exchange of royalty fees between reproduction rights organizations and user groups (mostly educational institutions).

Finally, most of the textbook publishing industry is concentrated in the developed countries. ... [M]any developing countries represent markets that are composed asymmetrically of users rather than producers. They also represent markets that, while perhaps altogether numerically large, are often individually neither profitable nor financially enticing to developed country producers. They are markets that are struggling to build domestic capacity and are not yet exporting globally. One big exception is India.

While publishers located in developed countries continue to engage in initiatives such as donation, differential pricing, publishing partnerships, and the like, there is consensus that much more needs to be done to ensure access to textbooks and to build local publishing capacity in developing countries....

Application of a Substantive Equality Norm to Copyright
and Capability for Basic Education

[A] substantive equality principle is needed in global IP norm-setting and norm-interpreting activities in order to facilitate access to essential information goods. This principle would be drawn from the key term "development" in relevant international IP foundational documents. This principle would take the form of an extra "thumb on the scale" of skepticism towards the enforcement of minimum rights expressed in multilateral or bilateral conventions as they pertain to certain types of development-sensitive categories. Conversely, this principle could express itself through a heightened embrace, as opposed to suspicion, of various exceptions and limitations expressed in these conventions. In either case, copyright norms would then be more responsive to the differently situated development concerns of various countries.

[The compulsory licensing provisions of the Berne Appendix have not only] proven to be unworkable and unfair throughout their thirty-five year existence, but also they explicitly cover educational use, which under the U.S. fair use doctrine is not a compensated use. Thus, users in developing countries, who are far less able to compensate copyright holders, are expected to provide equitable remuneration, whereas users in the United States may rely on uncompensated educational use in certain situations. From an IP from below perspective, this global structure is distributionally unjust.

What are possible alternatives? Some may lie in the area of specific exceptions and limitations, enacted in domestic legislation of member states or through bilateral, regional, or even multilateral agreements.... From a distributive justice standpoint, fair use is a choice in favor of access to a knowledge good that recognizes socially beneficial uses that may not always be better internalized by the rights holder. Leading commentators on fair use in the United States view educational fair use as a special fair use case, not only because it is listed as one of the categories within [the fair use statute] but also because of its positive spillover effects on society as a whole....

... From its inception, the term "teaching" in article 10(2) [of the Berne Convention] covered primary to tertiary levels of teaching.... In developing countries, a substantive equality principle would suggest the fullest expansion of this Berne-endorsed exception whenever possible. Among countries that have not yet enacted educational exceptions (or that even have curtailed the optimal policy space for educational exceptions to copyright provided by article 10(2)), these choices may reflect the lack of domestic institutional capacity to design appropriate policies as much as deliberate social policy. Where the former is the case, the domestic enactment of the broadest possible exception, including an illustration for teaching purposes, can begin to create access to works for educational purposes that may counterbalance the lack of bulk access to textbooks through the Berne Appendix....

Digital technology has tremendous potential to leverage information for development. The recent appearance of the $100 hand-cranked laptop, run on open source software, lends itself to a myriad of possibilities for nontextbook based distance education. The WIPO Copyright Treaty ("WCT") does not foreclose the enactment of further domestic exceptions and limitations to digital rights sounding in copyright....

Simultaneously, however, there are strong efforts by the copyright content industries in developed countries to expand digital rights.... WCT signatories are enacting technological protection measures required by article 11, such as the arguably draconian U.S. Digital Millennium Copyright Act. These multilateral efforts have generated bilateral offspring. For developing countries, any additional ratcheting up of protections in the digital environment "arguably constitute[s] a dead weight loss on already fragile economies" and should be viewed skeptically under a substantive equality paradigm.

Instead, the essential public goods nature of information should be viewed as a potential development asset. An IP from below approach views the potential for diffusion and dissemination of digital knowledge at almost zero marginal cost (once infrastructure is established) quite differently. These characteristics should be used to nurture and expand the basic literacy and educational capacity that are prerequisites to the creation of a functioning future copyright content market. Especially where the danger to copyright interests associated with mass distribution via digital networks is reduced (e.g., because the work is culturally specific or is in a language that is not widely read), networked digital technology can and should be linked to diffusion models of information access.

Countries should enact digital-specific educational exceptions where these are relevant and appropriate to their educational development policies. Arguably, these exceptions may even exceed the scope of the Berne Convention article 10(2). Open course content initiatives in the tertiary text-book arena indicate that market-based mechanisms for distribution are only one possible means for providing access to textbooks. Intergovernmental organizations and prestigious educational institutions are now providing content without charge. Private-public partnerships for library digitization projects are proliferating. These and other new digital initiatives have enormous potential to expand the informational universes of educational institutions.

Are there possible roadblocks to such educational exceptions posed by the so-called three-step tests? Berne Convention article 9(2) and its analogue in TRIPS article 13 set parameters for exceptions to rights under the respective treaties. Under a substantive equality principle, the interpretation of these norms should be generously construed in favor of development. The most generous interpretation, and one that is consistent with the drafting history of the Berne Convention, is that the "operation of [the educational exception] provisions within their specific sphere is unaffected by the more general provision in article 9(2), and that the uses allowed under them are therefore excluded from its scope." Another view is that article 10(2)'s requirement of "fair practice" is "essentially a question for national tribunals to determine in each particular instance," but is also possibly measured by the three-step test of article 9(2).[112] A substantive equality principle should lead a

---

[112] 1 RICKETSON & GINSBURG, *supra* note 96, at 789.

norm-interpreting body, such as a national court or WTO dispute settlement panel, to defer to the legislative intent regarding the "fair practice" nature of the educational exception. A WTO dispute settlement panel should similarly construe Berne Convention article 9(2) (which affects the reproduction right only) and TRIPS article 13 (which applies to exceptions to all rights) to allow the broadest possible exceptions to promote access to educational materials for purposes of development. Thus, domestic educational exceptions enacted in developing countries pursuant to article 10(2) would be consistent with the three-step test, in light of TRIPS articles 7 and 8, which refer to development.

To the extent that there is any conflict between an educational exception and TRIPS article 13, an educational exception would comport with the first step ("certain special cases") under one WTO panel ruling if it is "clearly defined and … narrow in its scope and reach." However, even if it is not clear, a norm interpreter should inquire into the public policy purpose of the exception. An analysis of a particular educational exception should push beyond the question of simply whether the exception is clearly defined. Under a substantive equality principle, a decision maker should explicitly consider and defer to a developing country's stated policy of promoting education for development. This interpretive approach would contrast, again, with a differently weighted application of the three-step test towards exceptions of developed countries and disputes between them over the scope of such exceptions.

Especially where schools are short on books, libraries have an important role in expanding educational access to copyrighted works through domestic exceptions and limitations. While there is some uncertainty in developed countries over whether library exceptions pass the three-step tests of the Berne Convention and TRIPS, a dispute settlement panel should apply the substantive equality principle to such domestic library exceptions enacted pursuant to article 10(2) in developing countries. If there is evidence that they are linked with the development objectives of promoting access to basic education, then there should be more deference with respect to their legitimacy.…

Pragmatically … it would not require much in terms of technical assistance or capacity building to draft and implement model exceptions for educational fair practice. Coupled with a substantive equality principle in norm interpretation, these legal initiatives should easily be Berne and TRIPS-compliant. They would not completely supplant the need for a revision of the Berne Appendix, nor would they solve the tremendous need for other restructuring efforts of the global IP regime. Nonetheless, they would go some way in remedying the indifference of the current structure to development concerns.

Notes and Questions

1. In the preceding extracts, Margaret Chon develops a concept she describes as "IP from below." She explains this concept as follows:

> IP from below highlights the needs of users in both developed and developing countries for knowledge goods that are accessible and affordable, particularly for purposes of basic human development. Thus, IP from below promotes a bottom-up approach to innovation capacity-building, especially for global sectors that are not technologically privileged. The term "from below" also dovetails with the term "Global South" that is increasingly being used to denote that subset of developing countries that are located below the equator and also below the median in terms of development indicators, whether measured by Gross National Income or Human Development Index. By contrast, a top-down approach to capacity-building in IP emphasizes building capacity to comply with international IP's minimum standards, which in turn are thought to generate domestic innovative capacity through foreign direct investment, licensing, and technology transfer.[113]

2. As discussed previously, the Berne Appendix has been criticized as unduly complex and burdensome. This may explain why so few developing and least-developed countries have issued compulsory licenses pursuant to the Appendix. These hurdles notwithstanding, might these countries nevertheless have a legal obligation under the relevant international human rights instruments to issue compulsory licenses pursuant to the Appendix for copyrighted learning materials that are not widely available in their respective national markets?

3. What are the contours of the "substantive equality principle" that Chon advocates? What justifications does she offer in support of the norm? How, precisely, would the adoption of a substantive equality norm change existing legal doctrines, and in which contexts? Does the norm further the right to education set forth in the international human rights instruments reviewed in Section 5.3 of this chapter?

4. Chon asserts that "it would not require much in terms of technical assistance or capacity building to draft and implement model exceptions for educational fair practice." Imagine that you are an attorney adviser to the

---

[113] Chon, *supra* note 94, at 813.

parliamentary drafting committee in a developing country. Several legislators have asked you to draft a proposal to revise the country's copyright statute to encourage use of copyrighted learning materials in educational settings. On which legal sources would you draw to justify your proposals? What provisions would you include in such a proposal and why? In answering this question, be sure to review the text of Article 10(2) of the Berne Convention and Article 13 of the TRIPS Agreement.

5. Ruth Okediji offers a number of proposals to reform the Berne Appendix:

> The Appendix must be reformed to reflect changing conditions in developing countries and also to facilitate a more expedient process for utilizing compulsory licensing to gain bulk access. Such reform should include at a minimum: (1) the elimination of the waiting period and the grace periods; (2) the elimination of notification to the owner prior to issuing the license; (3) eliminating the economies of scale problem by allowing simultaneous application for the translation and reproduction licenses under the same conditions; and (4) expanding the scope for which the license is issued to extend beyond teaching, education and research."[114]

Do these suggestions go far enough? Would they satisfy the requirements of the human right to education? Before you conclude that the Berne Appendix is a failure, would it be helpful to determine whether the Appendix has, despite its shortcomings, actually encouraged publishers to make their works available at appropriate prices?

6. Andrew Rens has advocated the adoption of international treaty provisions on minimum exceptions and limitations for education.[115] Rens urges that standardized minimum exceptions would be consistent with and further the aims of the WIPO Development Agenda, an initiative we discuss in Chapter 1. Would you support such an initiative?

7. What is the relevance of creators' human rights to the analysis of the following question: Does a state breach the right to education when its copyright law creates and enforces property rights that make it more difficult to provide textbooks and other learning materials to school-age children? The obligation to prevent creators' rights from becoming impediments to the realization of other human rights obligations, including education, was addressed by the Committee on Economic, Social and Cultural Rights in *General Comment No. 17* on Article 15(1)(c) of ICECR.[116] Article 15(1)(c),

---

[114] OKEDIJI, *supra* note 29, at 29.

[115] Andrew Rens, *Implementing WIPO's Development Agenda: Treaty Provisions on Minimum Exceptions and Limitations for Education*, in JEREMY DE BEER (ED.), IMPLEMENTING WIPO's DEVELOPMENT AGENDA 158 (2009).

[116] U.N. Doc. E/C.12/GC/17 (Jan. 12, 2006).

which we discuss in more detail in Chapter 3, announces a human "right of everyone to benefit from the protection of the moral and material interests resulting from any scientific, literary or artistic production of which he or she is the author." While there is considerable common ground between this right and intellectual property rights, the Committee emphasized that the human right guaranteed by Article 15(1)(c) and intellectual property rights are not necessarily equivalent. The Committee also noted that states parties should ensure that regimes for protecting this right "constitute no impediment to their ability to comply with their core obligations in relation to the rights to food, health and education." According to the Committee, member states "have a duty to prevent unreasonably high costs for access to ... schoolbooks and learning materials, from undermining the rights of large segments of the population to ... education."[117]

The thresholds referred to in the *General Comment* warrant further analysis. Initially, the *General Comment* states that intellectual property must impose "no impediment" to the realization of other rights. Later, the *General Comment* specifies that states must "prevent unreasonably high cost for access to ... schoolbooks and learning materials." The Committee does not explain the distinction in terminology or the (possible) discrepancy between these standards. One plausible interpretation is that "unreasonably high costs [that] ... undermin[e] the rights of large segments of the population to ... education" are, at least in this context, the legally relevant "impediment[s]." More generally, the analysis in this section of the *General Comment* is consistent with one of the principal themes of the document: the necessity for balance between the "material" interests that are protected by Article 15(1)(c) and other human rights, including the right to education. In addition, creators' rights must be balanced against the other the clauses in Article 15, including the rights to take part in cultural life and to enjoy the benefits of scientific progress and its applications. The *General Comment* does not, however, explain how these balances are to be achieved.[118]

8. Is copyright a limitation on human rights of the kind that is permitted, for example, by Article 29(2) of the UDHR, that is, a limitation that is "determined solely by law for the purposes of securing due recognition and respect for the rights and freedoms of others"? Does it make sense to put the question in such generalized terms? If not, what further contextual detail might

---

[117] *Id.* para. 35.
[118] *See* Foster, *supra* note 89; Laurence Helfer, *Toward a Human Rights Framework for Intellectual Property*, 40 U.C. DAVIS L. REV. 971 (2007).

be relevant to developing a set of questions that more subtly probe the relationship between human rights and intellectual property in the education context?

5.6. Other Impediments to the Provision of Learning Materials

Copyright is only one of many "inputs" that go into the production of learning materials. Suppose a government wanted to provide primary school children with reprinted chapters of a foreign textbook, adapted to local circumstances.[119] It would likely need to purchase the materials, such as paper and ink, as well as services, such as printing skills. And it might also be required to pay a license fee for the copyright-protected material. In many nations, the government would need to negotiate the many institutional, geo-political, and commercial barriers that may impede efficient publication and distribution of books. The preceding extracts from Margaret Chon's analysis mention impediments to the provision of learning materials other than copyright. The following extract explores in more detail the considerable array of structural impediments to the provision of adequate learning materials to school-age children in developing and least-developed nations.

UNESCO, Textbook and Learning Materials, 1990–99 (2000)[120]

The constraints that public- and private-sector publishers faced [in the provision of textbooks] at the end of the decade [1990–1999] were little changed from those they faced in 1990, although the increasing role of the private sector and concern about cost recovery resulted in some reconfigurations. Inconsistencies or weaknesses in government were more significant, for example, to private publishers than to a public institution that might be part of the problem. The route towards liberalization had many roadblocks.

Government

Government policy was often inconsistent – not only because of changes in leadership but because of conflicts between government departments.

---

[119] Here, we assume that the government wants to involve itself in direct provision of textbooks, rather than contracting with a third-party supplier. On the dangers of nationalization of the production of textbooks, see SPRING, *supra* note 3, at 62 (discussing the use of textbooks to promulgate national propaganda).

[120] Reproduced by permission of UNESCO. While this report was prepared under the auspices of UNESCO, UNESCO specifically notes that the report does not necessarily reflect UNESCO's views.

Publishers had to deal with several departments, few of them directly concerned with textbooks. The Ministry of Education normally had the leading role, but the Ministry of Industry might be concerned with protecting domestic printing and manufacture; the Ministry of Trade might be regulating the import and export of paper, machinery and books; the Ministry of Finance possibly regulated the availability of foreign currency, and imposed taxes and tariffs; the Ministry of Agriculture might have some say in the importation of raw materials; and the Ministry of Culture might set language policies, and regulate publishing and printing. Some countries, among them Ghana and Zambia, waived taxes on imported printing goods meant for book publishing, but in other countries local printers and publishers had to pay tax and duties on imported raw materials such as paper at the same time as competitive foreign-produced books were imported duty-free. More fundamentally, few countries in the developing world had coherent policies for publishing development or the provision of learning materials. [One study] found that lack of funding is often exaggerated as a cause for failure in providing basic learning materials and that other problems are more fundamental. Textbooks did not get the attention they required. Few decision-makers or managers understood publishing or even the difference between publishing and printing, and few gave proper recognition to those in the civil service, or outside it, who did have publishing expertise. As a result, the design of programmes was left to educators who had little awareness of the professional skills required to produce and distribute quality learning materials successfully, of possible institutional needs for reorganization, staffing and budgeting, of the economics of educational publishing or of the difficulties of marrying educational concerns with the concerns of commercial publishing. From ignorance of the totality and complexity of the book chain, textbooks were treated as simple commodities and planners concentrated only on manuscript development and production. Furthermore, some consultants who had been retained to advise on textbook projects had no interest in seeing local publishing industries develop and ministries were often reluctant to surrender control of textbook provision even when the need was pointed out....

In those countries that were in transition from public to private provision of learning materials, inconsistency and unprofessionalism were apt to be compounded by confusion. Few countries made five- or ten-year plans for the change. Some failed to spell out clearly the roles of the players, the timing of change or the operational details of each phase. The capacity of the private sector was not always taken into account or the need to rebuild publishing skills that had atrophied under state monopoly. If local publishers could not respond to an abrupt transition, the way was opened to foreign ones. In

Zambia, for example, the failure of the state monopoly and rapid liberalization led to a renewal of British transnational domination of the market.

Educational statistics remained unreliable and usually outdated. Under such circumstances it was difficult for governments to project requirements or for publishers to determine print runs. Data available from the United Republic of Tanzania indicate the discrepancies in supply and demand that can occur as a result of inadequate information, in this case in a period of increasing private-sector publication and continuing centralized public procurement. Variations of this magnitude can be financially disastrous to commercial publishers. So can unexpected cuts to education budgets by national legislatures. In the Philippines, for example, publishers who had lobbied for privatization were dismayed when they discovered how small the annual funding would be in comparison with the anticipated market. Failures in communication within government further hindered efforts to improve the availability of learning materials. Policies might be communicated so imprecisely that recipients were uncertain what they were expected to do, and as a result did not implement new policies or did so incorrectly. Even clearly-worded policies did not reach the schools, or were not believed when they did arrive.

Few government officers appreciated the time it takes to write, edit, test and print textbooks. As a result many contracts allowed unrealistically short times from signing to delivery. The resulting textbooks were apt to suffer in quality or would have to be brought in from outside the country. Political instability, authoritarian governments and war weakened or destroyed both educational and publishing facilities in the most unfortunate countries.

Finance

As devaluation and inflation drove up the cost of imported raw materials, the commercial school book publishers who were being encouraged by the new policies of liberalization and decentralization continued to have great difficulty in finding capital and credit. Investors found publishing unattractive because of low returns and high risk. Banks were reluctant to extend loans because sales revenue in publishing was notoriously unpredictable and few publishers had sufficient collateral or assets. Concessional credit from the World Bank and other international and regional finance institutions, available for agriculture and some other industries, was not extended to book publishing. If loans could be negotiated, interest rates throughout most of the developing world were high – commonly, from 23 to 40 per cent per year. One bank in Ghana did offer loans to publishers but none took up the opportunity because the annual interest rate was 45 per cent.

If publishers were able to borrow money at lower rates abroad, they faced the further possible hazard of devaluation. Some in the United Republic of Tanzania went bankrupt after devaluation of the shilling, when the loans they had negotiated in foreign currency had to be repaid. On a positive note, Nigeria established an Education Trust Fund, analogous to its long established agricultural development banks, to provide soft loans not only to institutions but to publishers, printers, artists, and others involved in producing learning materials.

Payment for textbooks was nearly always slow. Publishers might wait six months or a year for their money, making it even more difficult for them to produce books for the new school year. In Nigeria, the state and federal governments owed publishers considerable amounts of money for books delivered, in some cases, in the previous decade. Governments occasionally discriminated against local publishers, in effect depreciating what capital the publishers had. In Romania, international publishers were invited to bid on textbook provision and guaranteed payment in hard currency. Local publishers, in contrast, were paid in local currency in the amount established at the time of contract, regardless of any decline in value of the currency by the time books were delivered and payment was finally made. One publisher calculated that his loss from currency instability amounted to 60 per cent in the case of a civics textbook. Joint ventures between local and foreign publishers were discouraged because the foreign partner would receive its share only in local currency. The Ministry of Education further hampered liberalization by establishing unrealistic times for printing and delivery and for teachers to assess competing books.

The capital required to bid on major projects restricted the ability of local companies to participate in major projects funded by the international banks. In Indonesia, private companies were allowed to publish books in a number of fields formerly reserved for the government-owned Balai Pustaka. In practice, only large firms were able to compete. The government issued an invitation in 1999 for bids for textbooks and teachers' guides at the junior secondary level in biology, physics and English. Publishers had to pay 1.5 million rupiahs (about US$220) per subject to obtain the bidding documents. They had further to demonstrate their financial soundness and resources, and prove that they had been operating for at least four years with an important part of their business being the publishing and/or distribution of educational books. This was a year after the collapse of the Indonesian economy and only the biggest of publishers were able to qualify.

In a similar instance two or three years earlier, a West African distributor found it impossible to participate in a World Bank project that involved four textbooks and teachers' guides for the following reasons. It had to find CFA

50,000 (about US$100) to acquire the tender documents, a bank guarantee of 2.5 per cent of the value of the tender and a staff housing tax clearance equal to 1.5 per cent of the salary of each member of the staff. If successful, it would have had to provide CFA 9.8 million (about US$20,000), about 5 per cent of the value of the contract, in guarantees. The company would also have had to demonstrate that it had been financially healthy for some years and had assets worth at least four times the value of the contract sum. The government would advance 30 per cent of the contract price, but only subject to a bank's guarantee. The requirements in this case, coming from both the government and the Bank, effectively doubled the guarantees normally required by the World Bank.

Market Size

Not every country was large enough to support a competitive publishing industry. This was evidently true of small island nations, such as those of the Pacific and Caribbean. It was equally true of many other countries. Of the thirty-seven in sub-Saharan Africa, only two or three were thought to have a domestic market large enough to support a book industry, even in primary-level textbooks. In Central and Eastern Europe, the Soros Foundation considered a country in which 7 million people spoke the same language to be a large publishing market, but only ten of the twenty-two former communist countries in which the foundation was active met that criterion. In the other countries print runs and talent pools were smaller and the cost per copy higher. Even the relatively successful book industries of Kenya and Zimbabwe together could draw on a market that was only about one-twentieth of a small European country such as Norway, Denmark or the Netherlands – countries that had a single language and a much better infrastructure. Local markets were further reduced by photocopying and pirated editions. In most countries, families had limited disposable income for books, including textbooks. Markets could be expanded by export where there was a common language, as in Latin America. Elsewhere, the barriers mentioned previously worked to restrict publishers to their own countries.

Distribution

It was no easier to reach isolated rural schools at the end of the decade than at its beginning. In the United Republic of Tanzania, for example, official figures in 1994 indicated that more than 16 million textbooks had been delivered to district storerooms over the previous five years. Had all reached the schools, that should have resulted in a textbook: pupil ratio of 1:3 or 1:4. A trial survey that year found that the true ratio was closer to 1:9, with extreme variations between schools and districts. Many books didn't reach the schools, and some that did were kept in school storerooms "due to uncertainty over supply." Some books produced by the state were being bought by parents in the market. Liberalization simply increased the problem if the state was not undertaking responsibility for distribution. Bookstores were scarce outside the main centres and in many countries even well-established religious or family retail bookstore chains were diversifying, with books as only a minor item. In Latin America, it was said, no publishing house had a distribution network capable of delivering books to every school in every corner of the country, and in many instances books bought by the government simply remained in government warehouses. Kenya sought to resolve the problem by consolidating school orders for textbooks at the district level and then ordering the books from local booksellers, thereby strengthening the retail sector of the book trade and reducing the discrepancies that occurred under central procurement.

Production

Paper remained the principal expense. Some countries, such as Mozambique, had to depend on foreign printing for lack of domestic capacity. In general, the constraints previously noted prevailed.

Human Resources

The lack of professionally trained staff continued to hamper state and private publishers in most countries. Large publishing companies did a certain amount of training in-house, however, as did transnationals. In general, the greatest need was in publishing management and marketing, although more training was also needed in textbook development, editing, design and evaluation.... Training received new attention in the 1990s and a number of initiatives were taken. The most ambitious was the African Publishing Institute, which was established in 1992 with the help of several funding agencies, both governmental and nongovernmental organizations. The Institute held occasional workshops in its early years. In 1999 it was scheduled to run twenty-two national and regional training workshops throughout the continent, on a variety of topics, and in English, French or Portuguese depending on the country. Workshops are held in co-operation with national publishing associations, using local trainers in accord with a comprehensive syllabus in book publishing and management. The Asian Cultural Center for UNESCO, supported by the Japanese Ministry of Education and the Japan Book Publishers Association, organized annual courses in various aspects of publishing and book promotion for publishing staff in Asia and Oceania, as it had since 1967. El Centro Regional para el Fomento del Libro en América Latina y el Caribe (CERLALC), an international organization created under an agreement between the government of Colombia and UNESCO, offered training courses in book-related topics and published training handbooks for book professionals. UNESCO sponsored training workshops in other countries and, through the International Institute for Educational Planning (IIEP), supported the development and publication of a series of training modules in textbook planning and publishing in Spanish, French, English and Arabic, available in print and for a time as an interactive course on the Internet....

Notes and Questions

1. In the light of the various impediments to the provision of textbooks described in the UNESCO Report, how should the burdens of the subsistence of copyright be assessed? What, if anything, does the Report suggest about the urgency of reforming the Berne Appendix?

2. As we discuss in Chapter 1, a draft Treaty on Access to Knowledge and Technology[121] (A2K treaty) has been circulating in a variety of civil society fora for several years. Among academics, NGOs, and other interest groups, the A2K treaty has been highly influential in current discussions about how to develop exceptions and limitations in international intellectual property law.[122] The draft text treats those exceptions and limitations as mandatory. In contrast, international intellectual property instruments generally view exceptions and limitations as permissive and as matters to be determined by domestic law.[123] Exceptions and limitations in the A2K treaty specifically

---

[121] A2K treaty, *available at* http://www.cptech.org/a2k/.

[122] As one scholar explains: "A treaty on access to knowledge was first proposed as part of discussions about the World Intellectual Property Organization's Development Agenda. Civil society organizations began suggesting issues that could be protected by such a treaty, and a coalition of 'medical researchers, educators, archivists, disabled people, and librarians from industrialized and developing nations' began to form. The discussion that ensued yielded a variety of suggestions about the kinds of access such a treaty should protect, ranging from exceptions and limitations on copyright to research funding. The drafting of the Treaty was thus a constitutive process, bringing together advocates from a variety of different fields and providing an important opportunity for these constituencies to identify and discuss what issues should have central importance in A2K advocacy efforts." Molly Beutz Land, *Protecting Rights Online*, 34 YALE J. INT'L L. 1, 39 (2009).

[123] *See* P. Bernt Hugenholtz and Ruth Okediji, *Conceiving an International Instrument on Limitations and Exceptions to Copyright: Final Report* 3 (2008), *available at* http://www.iprsonline.org/resources/IntLE_HugenholtzOkediji.pdf (stating that "despite over a century of

directed to education issues include (1) the use of extracts of copyright-protected works in conjunction with not-for-profit teaching and scholarship, including by educational institutions as "secondary readings for enrolled students;" and (2) the use of works by educational institutions as primary instructional materials, "if those materials are not made readily available by right-holders, provided that in case of such use the right-holder shall be entitled to equitable remuneration."[124]

The A2K treaty would also require libraries, archivists, and educational institutions to be permitted to make copies of copyright-protected works for the purposes of education, preservation, or research where these works are not "currently the subject of commercial exploitation."[125] The document states that these exceptions are to be deemed "special cases that do not conflict with a normal exploitation of the work and do not unreasonably prejudice the legitimate interests of the right-holder," language that tracks the "three-step test" of the TRIPS Article 13 and Berne Article 9(2). The aim is to remove any doubt that these exceptions pass muster under international intellectual property law.

Perhaps most controversially, the A2K treaty would require parties to implement a general exception to copyright law, "applicable in special cases where the social, cultural, educational or other developmental benefit of a use outweigh the costs imposed by it on private parties."[126] Other limitations would privilege specific uses of copyright-protected works, including certain types of performances by educational institutions and for distance learning,[127] and would include a broad first sale right to enable libraries to lend works "without further transaction fees to be paid by the library."[128]

What is the likely relevance of the legal innovations contained in the A2K treaty to the realization of the human right to education, given the many practical difficulties of providing of learning materials in developing nations and the access to public domain materials that would otherwise be available?[129]

---

international norm setting in the field of copyright, L&E's [limitations and exceptions] have largely remained 'unregulated space'").

[124] A2K treaty, art. 3(1)(a)(iv).

[125] *Id.* art. 3(1)(a)(iv).

[126] *Id.* art. 3(1)(d). In its current draft, this article includes, in square parentheses, the following proviso: "providing for equitable remuneration to the copyright owner in appropriate circumstances."

[127] *Id.* art. (3)(2)(b)(1)–(2).

[128] *Id.* art. 3(4).

[129] *See* Land, *supra* note 122, at 42–43; *see also* Anupam Chander & Madhavi Sunder, *The Romance of the Public Domain*, 92 CAL. L. REV. 1331 (2004).

3. Molly Beutz Land has noted a number of areas for "collaboration" between human rights and the A2K agenda. Most pertinently for the present study, she observes:

> Additional avenues of collaboration might include access to educational, scientific, and legal materials, including the equitable distribution of technology necessary to ensure such access. Educational materials might be unavailable both because of copyright laws and because of the state's lack of resources and commitment necessary to ensure access. Access to information and communication technologies is a central issue of concern for A2K advocates; human rights advocates might emphasize the way in which such access can be considered an underlying determinant of many economic, social, and cultural rights. Access to legal information would be of interest to both movements given the overlap of their respective substantive areas of expertise. Access to legal materials is a critical component in ensuring participation in political processes, an issue of central concern for human rights advocates. A2K advocates, in turn, would be interested in this issue because of the way in which states are using copyright laws to restrict access to legal authority.[130]

Scrutinize these observations in the light of the rationales for the right to education discussed in Section 5.2 of this chapter. To which set of rationales are these observations most relevant?

5.7. Mapping the Interface between Copyright and the Right to Education

The extracts from the UNESCO Report raise difficult questions of factual causation. Given the many economic and structural impediments to the provision of learning materials, what real difference are revisions of international or domestic copyright law likely to make? Some might argue that, compared with these impediments, the subsistence of copyright in learning materials is largely irrelevant. In some nations, for example, other "input" barriers may be so overwhelming that reforming copyright law would seem like tinkering at the margins. Even so, analysis of the relationship between human rights and intellectual property must also take account of situations in which intellectual property law may make a real difference to the provision of learning materials, and, in turn, the realization of the human right to education.

It might be useful, therefore, to analyze further the relationship between human rights and intellectual property in circumstances where doing so could plausibly influence substantive outcomes. A persistent theme in this book is the need to move beyond generalized clashes between intellectual

---

[130] Land, *supra* note 122, at 23–24.

property and human rights, and to focus concretely on the impediments that specific types of intellectual property impose to the realization of particular human rights. This kind of focus may help us build a more robust normative framework, one that allows us to analyze the connection between intellectual property and human rights in sharply different contexts.

In Chapter 8, we elaborate on this framework in greater detail. Here, we seek to identify as precisely as possible how copyright impedes the realization of the right to education and the provision of learning materials. To be sure, copyright law gives powerful legal rights to authors and publishers. These legal rights impose individual duties on the rest of us. We are obliged not to perform the acts that are within the exclusive rights of the copyright owner, including the duties not to reproduce, distribute, or translate copyright-protected works.[131] A human rights focus helps us to see that refraining from *any* of these activities in the case of textbooks and other learning materials imposes additional social costs: it may impede realization of a human right. Accordingly, in the education context, the duties imposed by copyright law may need to be narrowed to avoid such costs.

Any analysis of the burdens imposed by intellectual property should also take account of the precise character of the legal impediments imposed by the relevant intellectual property rights. In the education context, for example, it is useful to recall that copyright is an incomplete monopoly. This means that different copyright-protected works are often substitutes for each other, even if they contain substantially the same information and/or substantially the same ideas. Stated more concretely, copyright itself will almost never impede the production of substitute textbooks.[132] In industrialized

---

[131] Our analysis draws on an important series of articles by Jeremy Waldron. In these writings, Waldron draws attention to the individual predicaments of those on whom duties are imposed by recognition of the property rights of others. In the intellectual property context, Waldron's work provides a useful framework for analyzing the practical significance of the duties that are imposed by intellectual property rights. *See* Jeremy Waldron, *Property, Justification and Need*, 6 Can. J.L. & Juris. 185 (1993); Jeremy Waldron, *Community and Property – for Those Who Have Neither*, 10 Theoretical Inquiries L. 161 (2009). In an important article from 1993, Waldron explored the relevance of his analysis in the context of other property rights. Jeremy Waldron, *From Authors to Copiers: Individual Rights and Social Values in Intellectual Property*, 68 Chi.-Kent L. Rev. 841 (1993). Waldron, in turn, draws on the classic Hohfeldian analysis of the relationship between rights and duties. *See* W.N. Hohfeld, Fundamental Legal Conceptions (1920).

[132] The contours of the idea/expression dichotomy in the educational context are sometimes difficult to draw, as they are in other contexts, and some of the analysis in the case law is unsatisfactory. For example, a U.S. court has held that standardized test questions can be infringed by questions that test essentially the same mathematical concepts. *Educ. Testing Servs. v. Katzman*, 793 F.2d 533 (3d Cir. 1986).

nations, this fact is reflected in the wide range of textbooks available in every conceivable subject area.

Fundamental copyright doctrines support this result. Particularly relevant here is the idea/expression dichotomy that is found, among other sources, in Article 9(2) of the TRIPS Agreement.[133] Copyright creates private property rights in *particular* expressions, but ideas (e.g., basic mathematical principles) are left in the public domain for others to use. In this respect, copyright contrasts with other intellectual property rights, such as patents. A patent gives the patent owner exclusive rights over equivalent inventions. So, in some areas, such as the provision of pharmaceuticals analyzed in Chapter 2, there may only be one available treatment for a particular disease – a treatment that is protected by a patent. In contrast, copyright does not, as such, impede governments or private actors from commissioning their own textbooks in any area of the school curriculum, even if the new works draw directly on the ideas set forth in works that have already been published. Absent verbatim copying or substantial appropriation of an original selection and arrangement, these substitute textbooks would be noninfringing. Moreover, a government seeking to satisfy its human rights obligations in the education context could, where the domestic law allows, commission the production of textbooks on a work-for-hire basis, pay the author a single fee, and allow all publishers to reproduce, translate, and distribute the work without charge. Thus, copyright has certain structural characteristics that may, in some instances, reduce the severity of the duties otherwise imposed on others by the subsistence of exclusive rights in textbooks and learning materials.

Analysis of the human rights implications of the subsistence and enforcement of copyrights should not end there, however. Establishing that copyright does not, in the abstract, impede the development of viable alternative texts says nothing about a state's actual capacity to take advantage of these structural characteristics. Scrutinizing copyright through a human rights lens, with an appropriate sensitivity to the duties imposed by the subsistence of copyright, directs attention to how the burdens imposed by these duties intersect with the economic, political, and social particularities of different nation states. This, in turn, raises a number of more fine-grained questions the answers to which are likely to vary from jurisdiction to jurisdiction. For example:

- Do governments and private parties have the capacity to take advantage of structural aspects of copyright law; for example, are there individuals whom the government can commission to produce alternative textbooks?

[133] TRIPS Agreement, *supra* note 110, art. 9(2) ("Copyright protection shall extend to expressions and not to ideas, procedures, methods of operation or mathematical concepts as such.").

- If there is a lack of capacity or other impediments, to what extent would they be mitigated by the compulsory licenses for textbooks and learning materials authorized by the Berne Appendix?
- If the Berne Appendix would assist in the provision of textbooks and learning materials, are governments and private parties well positioned to take advantage of the flexibilities that it provides?
- Are textbooks and learning materials affordable as a practical matter? Do prices vary for learning materials at different educational levels? (Recall, in this context, the requirements of Articles 13 and 14 of the ICESCR.)
- Are existing learning materials available that are not protected by copyright? If such materials are available, for example, under a Creative Commons license, how accessible are they *in reality*? (We discuss the Creative Commons in Chapter 1.) Is delivery of educational materials in electronic format a realistic alternative, given the relevant material and technological circumstances?

It may be more difficult to justify enforcing copyright to the extent otherwise permissible in countries that lack the capacity to facilitate the provision of learning materials by one or more of the mechanisms discussed previously in this section. The absence of such capacity vitiates one of the major structural characteristics of copyright law – the presence in the same market of substitute works that embody the same idea in a different form or expression.[134] In such a situation, copyright gets closer to being an absolute monopoly in practice, if not in principle, and could become tantamount to a grant of rights that is far stronger than envisaged by international copyright instruments and norms. In these circumstances, the duties imposed by copyright law – the duty not to copy, disseminate, translate, and so forth – would be particularly burdensome.

The analysis sketched here suggests that limitations on the scope of copyright should be regarded as particularly appropriate where such limitations directly assist in the realization of a human right and, *in addition*, other factors are present, such as the absence of the capacity to ensure that substitute works are available. Importantly, this approach does not imply that copyright must give way merely because its subsistence increases the price at which specific educational materials can be provided. Most, if not all, copyright protection would be swept away on that basis – an outcome at odds with copyright's foundational purpose of advancing learning. Instead, this approach invites

---

[134] *See* Ariel Katz, *Substitution and Schumpeterian Effects over the Life Cycle of Copyrighted Works*, 49 JURIMETRICS J. 113 (2009). For a more detailed discussion of this issue, see Section 2.5(C) of Chapter 2.

an inquiry into the effects of a particular mix of legal, economic, and political constraints on the provision of learning materials in specific factual milieux.

***

* * * Issues in Focus * * *

In a June 2009 "3D," an NGO concerned with trade and human rights issues published a report on the impact of copyright rules on access to education in the Philippines.[135] It analyzed the provision of educational materials through the lens of Article 28 of the UNCROC. As we noted earlier, this Article imposes obligations concerning the right to education that draw upon earlier articulations of this right in the UDHR and the ICESCR.

> In line with its obligations under Article 28(1) of the [UNCROC], we encourage the Filipino government to use available flexibilities under the Berne Convention and the TRIPS Agreement to ensure copyright legislation supports access to text books and other teaching materials at all educational levels. To achieve this goal, we recommend that the government extends the list of limitations and exceptions within the Intellectual Property Code to include detailed provisions for all aspects of educational activities. This should include a provision allowing the government to grant compulsory licenses to ensure the supply of affordable text books. As a State Party to the [UNCROC], the Filipino government has the obligation to take the right to education into account when negotiating and implementing multilateral, bilateral and regional trade agreements. It should therefore conduct impact assessments before negotiating such agreements to ensure that the copyright provisions they include do not impede children's access to educational materials. Further, we encourage the Filipino government to make sure that future legislation related to copyright for works on the internet fully takes into account the right to education. If the government asks for international technical assistance to implement the WIPO Copyright Treaty, this should be done in accordance with Article 28(3) of the [UNCROC] and facilitate "access to scientific and technical knowledge and modern teaching methods."

Notes and Questions

1. There is a growing worldwide movement aimed at providing free online versions of textbooks in electronic formats.[136] In what ways do the availability

---

[135] 3D, *The Philippines: Impact of copyright rules on access to education* (June 2009), *available at* http://www.3dthree.org/pdf_3D/3DCRC_PhilippinesJun09.pdf.

[136] Relevant Web sites include http://textbookrevolution.org/; http://www.freeloadpress.com/; http://www.math.gatech.edu/~cain/textbooks/onlinebooks.html; http://digg.com/tech_news/ Hundreds_of_Free_Textbooks_on_one_website; http://homepages.nyu.edu/~jmg336/html/ mathematics.html.

of these versions affect the question of whether the scope of copyright should be limited so as to ensure that learning materials are appropriately available? What further information, if any, do you need, in order to answer this question?

Many civil society groups are involved in this movement. One recent initiative is the *Cape Town Open Education Declaration: Unlocking the Promise of Open Educational Resources*,[137] adopted in September 2007. The aim of the meeting that produced the Declaration was to accelerate efforts to promote open resources, technology, and teaching practices. Although not specifically grounded in the human right to education, many of the initiatives that the Declaration proposes are directed at ensuring access to educational materials. Specifically, the document sets forth three strategies to increase the reach and impact of open educational resources:

1. Educators and learners: First, we encourage educators and learners to actively participate in the emerging open education movement. Participating includes: creating, using, adapting and improving open educational resources; embracing educational practices built around collaboration, discovery and the creation of knowledge; and inviting peers and colleagues to get involved. Creating and using open resources should be considered integral to education and should be supported and rewarded accordingly.

2. Open educational resources: Second, we call on educators, authors, publishers and institutions to release their resources openly. These open educational resources should be freely shared through open licences which facilitate use, revision, translation, improvement and sharing by anyone. Resources should be published in formats that facilitate both use and editing, and that accommodate a diversity of technical platforms. Whenever possible, they should also be available in formats that are accessible to people with disabilities and people who do not yet have access to the Internet.

3. Open education policy: Third, governments, school boards, colleges and universities should make open education a high priority. Ideally, taxpayer-funded educational resources should be open educational resources. Accreditation and adoption processes should give preference to open educational resources. Educational resource repositories should actively include and highlight open educational resources within their collections.

Do these strategies adequately address human rights obligations concerning access to learning materials? If not, what would you add?

---

[137] *Available at* http://www.capetowndeclaration.org/.

2. Article 7 of TRIPS provides that the protection and enforcement of intellectual property rights should, among other things, "contribute … to the transfer and dissemination of technology, to the mutual advantage of producers and users of technological knowledge and in a manner conducive to social and economic welfare, and to a balance of rights and obligations." What arguments can be made that Article 7 is relevant to the right to education, and, in addition, to the claim that copyright needs to be limited to ensure that learning materials are provided in a manner that is consistent with this right?

Chapter 6

The Human Right to Food, Plant Genetic Resources, and Intellectual Property

6.1. Introduction

The intersection of intellectual property and the human right to food raises contentious and unresolved issues of international law and politics. Analysis of these issues is made even more challenging by two distinct but related developments – (1) the diversity and complexity of the rules and institutions that regulate the creation, ownership, and exploitation of plant genetic resources (PGRs) for food and agriculture and of the biotechnologies used to manipulate them, and (2) the expansion, over the last quarter century, of the normative content of the human right to food and of intellectual property rights for plant-related innovations.

The first development – the diversity and complexity of the legal and institutional landscape – stems from the fact that the international rules governing PGRs and agrobiotechnologies include not only multilateral intellectual property agreements, the International Covenant on Economic Social and Cultural Rights (ICESCR), and customary human rights law, but also treaties, declarations, and resolutions adopted under the auspices of the World Trade Organization (WTO), the Food and Agriculture Organization (FAO), the Convention on Biological Diversity, the Commission on Genetic Resources for Food and Agriculture, and regional organizations such as the European and African Unions and the Andean Community. Scholars have labeled this dense thicket of overlapping rules and institutions as a "regime complex" for PGRs. And they have explained how the existence of multiple negotiating forums within the complex enable governments and public interest NGOs to shift from one venue to another and to select the venue most conducive to advancing their preferred legal and policy outcomes.[1]

---

[1] Laurence R. Helfer, *Regime Shifting: The TRIPS Agreement and New Dynamics of International Intellectual Property Lawmaking*, 29 YALE J. INT'L L. 1 (2004) [Helfer, *Regime*

The second development concerns the expansion of intellectual property protection for plant-related innovations and the concomitant evolution of the human right to food. Plant-specific intellectual property protection rules trace their origins to lobbying by commercial plant breeders in the United States and Europe in the first quarter of the twentieth century.[2] But the internationalization of those rules occurred only in the 1960s with the creation of the Union internationale pour la protection des obtentions végétales (UPOV), an international organization dedicated to protecting new plant varieties. Moreover, unlike some other areas of intellectual property, the proper scope and modalities of protection for plant-related innovations remain unresolved and highly contested.

The evolution of the human right to food is more recent and even more unsettled. This right (sometimes described as the freedom from hunger) has long been recognized as part of international human rights law. But the precise content of the right started to coalesce only in the last decade following the publication, in 1999, of a *General Comment* on the right to food by the Committee on Economic Social and Cultural Rights; the appointment, in 2001, of a Special Rapporteur on the Right to Food to submit annual reports to the U.N. Human Rights Commission (now the Human Rights Council); and the adoption by the FAO, in 2004, of Voluntary Guidelines to Support Progressive Realization of the Right to Adequate Food. As a formal matter, the legal analyses contained in these documents are nonbinding, although they are often viewed as highly persuasive because of their expert provenance. What remains uncertain, however, is the extent to which the normative statements of these bodies have modified international law, either for the more than 150 states parties to the ICESCR or for the smaller number of nonparties for which the right to food is obligatory only to the extent it has ripened into international custom.

This chapter considers how the human right to food may contribute to a reconceptualization of intellectual property protection for plant-related innovations. We do not claim that such protection violates the right to food – a position taken by some international expert bodies and commentators. Instead, we explore ways that intellectual property and the right to food can coexist in the same policy space. We also identify several ways in which

Shifting]; Kal Raustiala & David Victor, *The Regime Complex for Plant Genetic Resources*, 58 INT'L ORG. 277 (2004). For a recent analysis, *see* REGINE ANDERSEN, GOVERNING AGROBIODIVERSITY: PLANT GENETICS AND DEVELOPING COUNTRIES (2008).

[2] *See, e.g.*, Mark D. Janis & Stephan Smith, *Technological Change and the Design of Plant Variety Protection Regimes*, 82 CHI.-KENT L. REV. 1557 (2007); Mark D. Janis & Jay P. Kesan, *U.S. Plant Variety Protection: Sound and Fury . . . ?*, 39 HOUSTON L. REV. 727 (2002).

a human rights–focused analysis of PGRs and plant-related intellectual property rights generates prescriptions for redirecting national innovation policies in ways that enhance states' ability to respect, protect, and ensure the right to food.[3]

Section 6.2 reviews the justifications for, and the normative evolution of, the human right to food and intellectual property protection for PGRs, emphasizing rules that are situated at the interface of the two legal regimes. Section 6.3 analyzes a specific controversy that arises at that intersection – the increasingly pervasive use of genetically modified seeds in India. Throughout the chapter, we consider the extent to which intellectual property protection rules, as contrasted with other factors, are barriers to the realization of the right to food. We also suggest different ways in which intellectual property protection might be restructured to achieve human rights ends.

6.2. The Evolution of the Right to Food and of Intellectual Property Protection for Plant-Related Innovations

A The Right to Food

The founders of the human rights movement recognized the right to adequate food as a fundamental entitlement of all human beings and as a correlative obligation of all governments. Yet debate continues as to the content and legally binding character of this right. As recently as 2002, a U.N. General Assembly resolution simultaneously (and ambiguously) "reaffirm[ed] the right of everyone to have access to safe and nutritious food" and "encourage[d] all States to take steps with a view to achieving progressively the full realization of the right to food, including steps to promote the conditions for everyone to be free from hunger and, as soon as possible, to enjoy fully the right to food."[4] Given the "controverted position" that the right to food occupies "in the pantheon of global human rights,"[5] we first review the justifications for and critiques of this right and then explain its evolution in international law.

1. Justifications for and Critiques of the Human Right to Food

More than a decade before governments and international bodies began to give serious attention to developing the normative content of the right to

---

[3] For a comprehensive discussion that reaches similar conclusions, *see* HANS MORTEN HAUGEN, THE RIGHT TO FOOD AND THE TRIPS AGREEMENT: WITH A PARTICULAR EMPHASIS ON DEVELOPING COUNTRIES' MEASURES FOR FOOD PRODUCTION AND DISTRIBUTION (2007).

[4] The Right to Food, G.A. Res. 56/155, paras. 2, 4, U.N. Doc. A/RES/56/155 (Feb. 15, 2002).

[5] David Marcus, *Famine Crimes in International Law*, 97 AM. J. INT'L L. 245, 249 (2003).

food, scholars in law and philosophy debated the antecedent question of whether a right to food or to be free from hunger can be said to exist.

Robert L. Bard, *The Right to Food*, 70 Iowa L. Rev. 1279, 1289 (1985)

. . .

Not only does no right to food exist, but it is unlikely that one can be established. That is, both poor and wealthy nations are unlikely to subject themselves to law-based claims of either their own citizens or foreign governments pertaining to access to food. The reluctance of wealthy nations to accept any *formal* economic or welfare obligations toward the poor not only is well established by conduct, but is inherent in the existing international political order. Poor countries have long been trying to persuade or coerce the rich to make formal commitments to share the rich nations' advantages.... Western nations have resisted such efforts, and they will likely continue to resist. As previously noted, asserting a duty on the rich to guarantee adequate food for the poor is a welfare concept, and few nations have achieved a guaranteed, minimally accepted life for their people. Extending it to foreigners is grossly utopian. This does not mean that individual nations will not recognize obligations to less fortunate nations, only that they will refuse to accept this as a legally imposed obligation. Nation-states will insist on a right to retain absolute discretion in determining the level of their contribution to world welfare requirements.

Economically developed countries would not be alone in their resistance to the establishment of a right to food. Third World countries might be happy to impose legal requirements on other nations toward themselves, but they will strongly resist any legal norms that obligate them to their own citizens.

Amartya Sen, *The Right Not to Be Hungry*, in Philip Alston & Katarina Tomaševski (Eds.), The Right to Food 69, 69–71 (1984)[6]

Do people have a right to be free from hunger? This is asserted often enough, but what does it stand for? It is, of course, tempting to say: Nothing at all.

---

[6]   [Amartya Sen's analyses of human rights in general, including "the right not to be hungry," have evolved and gone beyond what is presented in this article, published in 1982, from which this is an extract. While there is no conflict between the two analyses, Sen's later presentation in chapter 17 ("Human Rights and Global Imperatives") of The Idea of Justice (Harvard University Press and Penguin, 2009) gives a fuller analysis of the claims related to human rights in general, including the right not to be hungry in particular.-Eds.]

But that piece of sophisticated cynicism provides not so much a penetrating insight into the practical affairs of the world, but merely a refusal to investigate what people mean when they assert the existence of rights that, for much of humanity, are plainly not guaranteed by existing institutional arrangements.

It is useful to begin with Ronald Dworkin's distinction[7] between "background rights" and "institutional rights":

> Any adequate theory will distinguish, for example, between background rights, which are rights that provide a justification for political decisions by society in the abstract, and institutional rights, that provide a justification for a decision by some particular and specified political institution....

A system of social security that guarantees to everyone a minimum income sufficient to buy enough food can be seen to make the right to be free from hunger an institutional right, provided it could be assumed that the decision-making within the family would lead to the income being expended for that purpose rather than some other. For a great many countries, however, such social security arrangements do not exist, and if the right in question is asserted in the context of such countries as well, they would clearly not be institutional rights but merely background rights.

But sometimes the assertion would seem to be even weaker than what could be called background right[s] in the sense of arguing that "the people as a whole would be justified in amending the Constitution" to make these claims institutional. Franklin Roosevelt's 1941 speech on "a world founded upon four *essential* freedoms," including "freedom from want ... everywhere in the world," was, in fact, quite unrevolutionary in its constitutional implications, despite the enormity of the "freedom" in question. Its importance rested primarily in acknowledging a shift in the political climate as a result of which the issues of hunger and want would enjoy an unprecedented standing in post-War discussion of public policy.

Dworkin's distinction between "concrete" and "abstract" rights must also be considered in this context. "An abstract right is a general political aim the statement of which does not indicate how the general aim is to be weighted or compromised in particular circumstances against the other political aims." The kinds of rights Dworkin mainly concentrates on in his examples are political in the narrower sense, but the distinction is quite general. The right to be free from hunger may be treated as an abstract right when the "trade-offs" with other objectives are not specified and other features of concrete application kept somewhat vague.

---

[7] Sen is referring to arguments made in RONALD DWORKIN, TAKING RIGHTS SERIOUSLY (1977).

The right to be free from hunger has different status in different countries, varying from being concrete, institutional rights (in countries with elaborate social security systems with specified priorities) to abstract, background rights (in countries in which such rights are accepted without institutional translation and without even concrete specification of priorities). I would now like to argue that the rights related to being free from hunger can take an even "remoter" form than an abstract, background right, *without* being empty of content ....

A *metaright* to something x can be defined as the right to have *policies* $p(x)$ that genuinely pursue the objective of making the right to x realisable. As an example, consider the following "Directive Principle of State Policy" inserted in the Constitution of India when it was adopted in 1950: "The state shall, in particular, direct its policy towards securing ... that the citizens, men and women equally, have the right to an adequate means of livelihood."

The wording was careful enough to avoid asserting that such a right already exists, but saying only that policy should be directed to making it possible to have that as a right. If *this* right were accepted, then the effect will not be to make the "right to an adequate means of livelihood" real – even as an abstract, background right – but to give a person the right to demand that policy be directed towards securing the objective of making the right to adequate means a realisable right, even if that objective cannot be immediately achieved. It is a right of a different kind: not to x but to $p(x)$. I propose to call a right to $p(x)$ a *metaright* to x.

Why do we need a different category of metarights given the very weak form of rights captured by Dworkin's concept of abstract, background rights? The reason is that the two general categories of rights and metarights deal with different subjects of entitlement. Corresponding to an institutional right to x (e.g., to a public arrangement for two meals a day for all), a background right permits one to claim that the state must see to it that x be achieved, and if it isn't, then to claim, as Dworkin puts it, "that the people as a whole would be justified to amending the Constitution ... or perhaps in rebelling or overthrowing the present form of government entirely." A metaright to x does not yield this claim. It concentrates not on the achievement of x, which might be currently unachievable, but on the pursuit of policies that would help to make x achievable in the future. Even an *abstract, background* right is concerned with x rather than with $p(x)$, which is the focus of attention of a metaright to x. The justification for amendment, rebellion, overthrowal, etc., would arise from the absence of such policy measures $p(x)$ rather than from the absence of achieved x.

It is not difficult to see why metarights of this kind have a particular relevance for economic aims such as the removal of poverty or hunger. For many countries where poverty or hunger is widespread, there might not exist *any* feasible way whatsoever by which freedom from them could be guaranteed for all in the very near future, but policies that would rapidly lead to such freedom do exist. The metaright for freedom from hunger is the right to such a policy, but what lies behind that right is ultimately the objective of achieving that freedom.

There are, of course, ambiguities as to ways of checking whether the measures taken by the government amount to a policy $p(x)$ aimed at securing a certain right x. There may be various ways of moving to x, at different speeds. Standards of acceptability are eminently arguable. But such ambiguities of specification are not unusual in dealing with rights in general. Debates on whether or not an abstract "right to free speech or dignity or equality" – to to quote Dworkin's example – is being violated, need not be any less intricate than debates on whether or not a set of public measures amount to a policy directed towards securing the abolition of starvation. Indeed, sometimes it is patently clear that the policies pursued are *not* thus directed.

A metaright to x as a right to $p(x)$ can, of course, also be either institutional or background, and either concrete or abstract. The "Directive Principle" of the Indian Constitution that was quoted did not make this metaright an institutional one, nor concrete in terms of specified priorities. So it is best viewed as an abstract, background metaright. There is, however, no difficulty in conceiving of the same right being made institutional and concrete, permitting any individual to sue the government for not pursuing, with the required amount of urgency, a policy that is genuinely aimed at achieving the right to adequate means.

The rights related to adequate means could, thus, vary from being concrete, institutional rights to abstract, background metarights. Even the last is not vacuous since it can provide a ground for protest, or rebellion aimed at overthrowal of the government, if the metaright is systematically ignored by the government, but it is, of course, in some ways, a good deal weaker than rights of other specification. The point of this section has been to identify the variety of forms in which rights related to adequate means could arise. The content of these rights would vary tremendously depending on the particular form, and it is important to be clear about what is or is not asserted by a particular formulation of a right of this kind.

----

2. The Normative Evolution of the Human Right to Food

As suggested in the essay by Sen, recognition of adequate food as a human right first rose to prominence during the Second World War. In 1941, U.S. President Franklin Roosevelt identified "freedom from want" as one of "four freedoms" that would define the postwar international order.[8] In an address to Congress three years later, Roosevelt elaborated upon this freedom as including "the right to earn enough to provide adequate food … [and t]he right of every farmer to raise and sell his products at a return which will give him and his family a decent living."[9] The drafters of the 1948 Universal Declaration on Human Rights (UDHR) employed similar language, recognizing in Article 25 that "everyone has the right to a standard of living adequate for the health and well-being of himself and of his family, including food.…"[10]

These articulations of the right to food remained in the realm of non-binding norms and aspirations. Codification of the right did not occur until the adoption of the ICESCR in 1966.[11] Article 11 of the Covenant continued and extended the earlier formulations but adapted them to the realities of a legally binding treaty. States parties "recognize[d] the right of everyone to an adequate standard of living for himself and his family, including adequate food." But they also qualified and softened that obligation by agreeing to "take appropriate steps to ensure the realization of this right, recognizing to this effect the essential importance of international co-operation based on free consent."[12] Article 11 also recognized, for the first time, a separate but related legal norm – "the fundamental right of everyone to be free from hunger" – with respect to which states parties obligated themselves to take,

> individually and through international co-operation, the measures, including specific programmes, which are needed:
>
> (a) To improve methods of production, conservation and distribution of food by making full use of technical and scientific knowledge, by disseminating

---

[8] The other three freedoms were freedom of speech and expression, freedom of religious worship, and freedom from fear.

[9] These rights were among those included in what Roosevelt described as the "second bill of rights." Franklin D. Roosevelt, *State of the Union Address to Congress*, 90 Cong. Rec. 55, 57 (Jan. 11, 1944).

[10] Universal Declaration of Human Rights, art. 25.1, G.A. Res. 217A(III), U.N. GAOR, 3d Sess., 1st plen. mtg., U.N. Doc. A/810 (Dec. 12, 1948).

[11] International humanitarian law, in particular the Third and Fourth Geneva Conventions, includes provisions concerning access to food for prisoners of war and civilians during armed conflicts. *See* Laura Niada, *Hunger and International Law: The Far-Reaching Scope of the Human Right to Food*, 22 Conn. J. Int'l L. 131, 168–70 (2006).

[12] International Covenant on Economic, Social and Cultural Rights, art. 11.1, *adopted* Dec. 16, 1966, S. Exec. Doc. D, 95–2 (1977), 993 U.N.T.S. 3 (entered into force Jan. 3, 1976) [ICESCR].

knowledge of the principles of nutrition and by developing or reforming agrarian systems in such a way as to achieve the most efficient development and utilization of natural resources;

(b) Taking into account the problems of both food-importing and food-exporting countries, to ensure an equitable distribution of world food supplies in relation to need.[13]

Article 11 gives more extensive treatment to the human right to food than any other international treaty.[14] But it nevertheless leaves unresolved many important issues about the meaning and scope of that right. In recognition of this omission, the 1996 World Food Summit adopted a declaration and plan of action that called for "clarif[ication of] the content of the right to adequate food and the fundamental right of everyone to be free from hunger[, giving] particular attention to implementation and full and progressive realization of this right as a means of achieving food security for all."[15]

This request precipitated a response from the Committee on Economic, Social and Cultural Rights. For more than a decade, the Committee had reviewed information from states parties concerning their implementation of Article 11. In 1999, the Committee drew upon those experiences to draft a *General Comment* that clarifies and amplifies the meaning of that article.[16] *General Comment No. 12* proceeds from the basic premise that the right to adequate food is realized when everyone – especially socially vulnerable groups and the impoverished – "has physical and economic access at all times to adequate food or means for its procurement."[17] Recognizing that "adequacy" varies with "prevailing social, economic, cultural, climatic, ecological and other conditions," the Committee nevertheless defines the "core content" of the right as requiring "the availability of food in a quantity and quality sufficient to satisfy the dietary needs of individuals, free from adverse substances, and acceptable within a given culture."[18] Availability, in turn, refers to the ability to feed oneself directly from the land or natural

---

[13] ICESCR, art. 11.2.

[14] Specific aspects of the right to food are also referenced in Article 12.2 of the Convention on the Elimination of all Forms of Discrimination against Women (recognizing the right to "adequate nutrition during pregnancy and lactation") and Article 24 of the Convention on the Rights of the Child (requiring states parties "[to] combat disease and malnutrition … through the provision of adequate nutritious foods and clean drinking-water").

[15] World Food Summit, Rome, Italy, Nov. 13–17, 1996, *Rome Declaration on World Food Security*, Objective 7.4, U.N. Doc. WFS 96/3, *available at* http://www.fao.org/docrep/003/w3613e/w3613e00.htm.

[16] Comm. on Econ., Soc. & Cultural Rights, *General Comment No. 12: The Right to Adequate Food*, U.N. Doc. E/C.12/1999/5 (May 12, 1999) [*General Comment No. 12*].

[17] *Id.* para. 6.

[18] *Id.* paras. 7, 8.

resources, or by means of well-functioning distribution, processing, and market-based systems.[19]

Having defined these foundational concepts, the *General Comment* sets out a three-part typology of state obligations – to respect, to protect, and to fulfill. The duty to "respect" requires states to avoid actions that prevent individuals from gaining access to adequate food. The obligation to "protect" requires states to take measures to prevent private actors – including business enterprises – from depriving others of access to adequate food. The duty to "fulfill" incorporates both a duty to facilitate and a duty to provide. The duty to "facilitate" requires states to strengthen access to, and utilization of, resources and means for individuals to ensure their livelihood. The duty to "provide" requires states to supply adequate food when individuals and groups cannot do so themselves for reasons beyond their control, such as natural disasters.[20]

In keeping with the leitmotif of progressive realization that infuses all of the ICESCR, the Committee recognizes that some measures at each level of the three-part typology "are of a more immediate nature, while other measures are more of a long-term character."[21] It also acknowledges that "the most appropriate ways and means of implementing the right to adequate food will inevitably vary significantly from one State party to another" and that each state has "a margin of discretion in choosing its own approaches" to implementation.[22] Nevertheless, the Committee also identifies instances when a state's actions or omissions rise to the level of violations of Article 11. Such violations arise, most notably, from the failure "to ensure the satisfaction of, at the very least, the minimum essential level required to be free from hunger." Additional specific actions identified as violations include the repeal or suspension of legislation necessary for the continued enjoyment of the right to food; the adoption of laws or policies that are manifestly incompatible with preexisting legal obligations relating to the right to food; and the failure to regulate activities of individuals or groups so as to prevent them from violating the right to food of others.[23]

The adoption of *General Comment No. 12* in 1999 increased the international visibility of the right to food and triggered a fresh round of initiatives within the U.N. human rights system, three of which we

[19] *Id.* para. 12.
[20] *Id.* para. 15.
[21] *Id.* para. 16.
[22] *Id.* para. 21.
[23] *Id.* paras. 17, 19.

highlight here. First, in April 2000, the Commission on Human Rights appointed a Special Rapporteur on the right to food with a mandate (1) to collect and analyze information on "all aspects of the realization of the right to food"; (2) to cooperate with governments, NGOs, and international organizations "on the promotion and effective implementation of the right to food, and to make appropriate recommendations on the realization thereof"; and (3) to identify "emerging issues related to the right to food worldwide."[24] In the ensuing decade, the Special Rapporteur has published annual reports that identify obstacles to realizing the right to food, undertaken missions to examine how different countries implement the right, and issued recommendations on subjects such as extraterritoriality, the regulation of transnational corporations, food sovereignty, and the world food crisis.[25]

Recent reports by the Special Rapporteur have drawn upon a second major initiative – the Voluntary Guidelines to Support the Progressive Realization of the Right to Adequate Food in the Context of National Food Security.[26] Adopted by the FAO Council and approved by all FAO member states in 2004, the Voluntary Guidelines reaffirm the ICESCR Committee's tripartite framework of state duties to respect, protect, and fulfill the right to adequate food. Applying this framework, the Guidelines provide advice to governments on implementing the right to adequate food, including issues such as economic development, market systems, domestic institutions, access to resources such as land, labor, water, and genetic resources, food safety, consumer protection, nutrition, international food aid, and natural and human-made disasters.[27]

A third development that has arisen since the *General Comment*'s adoption concerns national right to food campaigns. Human rights advocates have launched such campaigns in countries including Brazil, India, South Africa, and New Zealand. In addition to drawing upon the work of the

---

[24] Comm'n on Human Rights, Res. 2000/10, U.N. Doc. E/CN.4/RES/2000/10 (Apr. 17, 2000).

[25] *See* Office of the U.N. High Comm'r for Human Rights, Special Rapporteur on the Right to Food, *available at* http://www2.ohchr.org/english/issues/food/annual.htm (last visited Mar. 31, 2010).

[26] FAO, *Voluntary Guidelines to Support the Progressive Realization of the Right to Adequate Food in the Context of National Food Security* (2005), *available at* http://www.fao.org/docrep/meeting/009/y9825e/y9825e00.htm.

[27] *See* Nicole Trudcau, *Global Guidelines for Feeding the World's Hungry*, 1 HUM. RTS. BRIEF 33 (2004). The *Voluntary Guidelines* were approved by 200 delegates from 90 countries. FAO Conference, Rome, Italy, Nov. 19–26, 2005, *Voluntary Guidelines to Support the Progressive Realization of the Right to Adequate Food in the Context of National Food Security*, U.N. Doc. C 2005/INF/11, *available at* ftp://ftp.fao.org/docrep/fao/Meeting/009/J5874e.pdf.

international bodies described previously, several of these campaigns invoke national constitutions, at least twenty of which reference the right to food or related rights.[28]

Notes and Questions

1. To appreciate the importance that many governments, public interest NGOs, and commentators attach to the human right to food, consider the following statistics:

> Almost sixty percent of annual deaths worldwide – roughly 36 million – are a direct or indirect result of hunger and nutritional deficiencies. More than 840 million people worldwide are malnourished. Over ninety-five percent live in the developing world. 153 million of them are children under the age of five. Hunger is both a cause and consequence of poverty. Hungry workers produce less and therefore earn less. In turn, their poverty exacerbates their hunger. Malnourishment is also the largest single contributor to disease. Undernourished mothers give birth to underweight children who are more susceptible to diseases that lead to their premature deaths. Children who are sick and hungry also do poorly in school. As a result they are more likely to end up as unskilled laborers, who do not earn enough to feed themselves or their families. The cycle of poverty, disease, and hunger continues.[29]

2. What are the differences among "background," "institutional," "concrete," and "abstract" rights proposed by Ronald Dworkin and discussed in the essay by Amartya Sen? Does the right to food lie within one or more of these categories and, if so, which ones?

3. What arguments does Bard advance against the establishment of a right to food? Are you persuaded by those arguments? Does Sen's claim that the food is a *metaright* – that is, a "right to have *policies* $p(x)$ that genuinely pursue the objective of making the right to x realizable" – provide a persuasive rejoinder to Bard's objections?

4. As explained previously, recognition of the right to adequate food dates back to the founding of the international human rights movement. Yet the right received little attention until the late 1990s, at which point international bodies such as the ICESCR Committee and the Special Rapporteur on the right to adequate food made rapid progress in defining the contours of the right and the modalities for its domestic implementation. What might explain this sudden increase in interest in the right to food and the rapid normative evolution that followed?

---

[28] Smita Narula, *The Right to Food: Holding Global Actors Accountable under International Law*, 44 Colum. J. Transnat'l L. 691, 696 & nn. 4–7 (2006).

[29] *Id.* at 698–99.

5. Several commentators have criticized Article 11 of the ICESCR as poorly drafted, making it difficult to define the content of the obligations it imposes or the relationship between the "right to adequate food" in Article 11.1 and the "fundamental right to be free from hunger" in Article 11.2. Indeed, according to one leading scholar and former member of the ICESCR Committee:

> any attempt to distil from article 11 ... any grand design for a comprehensive, ordered, operational approach to implementation of the right to food, either at the national or international level is misplaced.... [T]he provisions of article 11 are in some respects both insufficiently detailed and sufficiently confused as to ensure that any such exercise would be largely speculative and ultimately frustrating.[30]

To what extent should Article 11's lack of clarity influence the Committee's interpretation in *General Comment No. 12*? If Article 11 does not offer a coherent understanding of the right to food, is it appropriate for the Committee to provide one? Before answering this question, consider that the Committee's mandate includes "mak[ing] suggestions and recommendations of a general nature on the basis of its consideration of [state party] reports."[31]

6. Assuming that some elaboration of Article 11's terse and opaque text is necessary, does *General Comment No. 12* depart too far from that text? What additional information is relevant to answering this question? The fact that *General Comments* are not, in themselves, legally binding? The fact, as some commentators contend, that the *General Comment No. 12* "adopt[ed] alternatives that were considered and rejected by the negotiators"[32] of the ICESCR? The fact that the 2004 Voluntary Guidelines incorporate significant portions of the *General Comment*'s analysis?

7. Can you determine, based on the materials set forth previously, whether the right to adequate food has acquired the status of customary international law? If not, what additional information would help you to answer this question? What consequences can you foresee if the right to adequate food is determined to be legally binding as a matter of international custom?

---

[30] Philip Alston, *International Law and the Human Right to Food*, in PHILIP ALSTON & KATARINA TOMAŠEVSKI (EDS.), THE RIGHT TO FOOD 9, 49 (1984).

[31] ECOSOC Res. 1985/17, U.N. Doc. E/RES/1985/17 (May 28, 1985).

[32] Michael J. Dennis & David P. Stewart, *Justiciability of Economic, Social, and Cultural Rights: Should There Be an International Complaints Mechanism to Adjudicate the Rights to Food, Water, Housing, and Health?*, 98 AM. J. INTL'L L. 462, 494 (2004).

8. The obligations to respect, protect, and fulfill, described in *General Comment No. 12*, are distinctive features of economic and social rights jurisprudence and academic discourse. To help grasp the distinctions among these concepts and their practical applications, consider the following excerpt from the first report of the Special Rapporteur on the right to food:

Respect

27. A State that respects the right to food of the people living in its territory should ensure that every individual has permanent access at all times to sufficient and adequate food, and should refrain from taking measures liable to deprive anyone of such access. An example of a practice that violates this right is when a Government at war with part of its own population deprives the part of the population it sees as "hostile" of access to food. Another example of non-observance of the right to food by a Government ... is the tragedy of Bar-el-Ghazal, where tens of thousands of people died of starvation in 1998. Muraheleen militia supported by the Government [of Sudan] pursued a counter-insurgency strategy characterized ... by the following human rights violations: looting of grain, abduction of women and children as spoils of war, burning of crops and homes, killing of civilians and cattle-rustling. The Special Rapporteur backs the conclusions of an NGO working in the region that "but for these human rights abuses, there would have been no famine in the Sudan in 1998." The case cited is a clear violation of the obligation to respect the right to food.

Protection

28. The second obligation that States must meet is to protect the right to food. Under this obligation, they must ensure that individuals and companies do not deprive people of permanent access to adequate and sufficient food.... In most cases, access to food is a question of affordability, and therefore income. This second obligation imposes a number of duties on the State, such as the duty to promote production, redistributive taxation and social security or to combat corruption.

29. The question of agrarian reform is particularly important in this respect. Several social movements around the world are currently campaigning to force their Governments to fulfil this second obligation. One of them is the Landless Rural Workers' Movement (MST) in Brazil, a country where 1 per cent of landowners own 46 per cent of all farmland and where 4.5 million peasant families have no land at all. According to the Secretary-General of UNCTAD, Mr. Rubens Ricupero, there has been no proper agrarian reform in Brazil since Portuguese colonization in the sixteenth century. MST, which was founded in

1984, peacefully reclaims and occupies arable lands that are not being farmed. Since 1984, it has reclaimed over 8 million hectares of uncultivated lands and settled more than 300,000 people there. Its production and marketing coopera-tives are independent and provide schooling for children and adults, employing 1,000 teachers. MST is campaigning to persuade the Brazilian Government to "protect" the right to food.

Fulfilment

30. The State's third obligation is to "fulfil" the right to food.... An appeal by a State for international humanitarian aid, when it is itself unable to guarantee the population's right to food, comes under this third obligation. States which, through neglect or misplaced national pride, make no such appeal or delib-erately delay in making it (as in the case of Ethiopia under the dictatorship of Haile Menguistu in the early 1980s) are violating this obligation. To take another example, a terrible famine was ravaging the Democratic People's Republic of Korea in the early 1990s: ... several NGOs made a massive effort there, espe-cially after 1995, but it gradually became clear that most of the international aid was being diverted by the army, the secret services and the Government. The NGO Action against Hunger stopped its aid at that point because of "lack of access to the victims of hunger".[33]

After reviewing this description, which of the three duties – respect, protect, and fulfill – is likely to be the most difficult for a state to satisfy and why? Put yourself in the position of an elected member of a national legislature. In that capacity, would you find the elaboration of these three duties helpful in realizing the right to adequate food? What measures would you undertake to realize this right? For example, would you favor any of the following: (a) adding the right to food to your country's constitution, (b) creating a new administrative agency to take responsibility for monitoring and coordinat-ing the government's food policies, (c) redistributing privately owned land to landless peasants or farmers, and (d) some combination of these strategies? Would your answer to these questions change if you were a legislator in an industrialized country such as Japan as compared to a developing country in sub-Saharan Africa?

9. Review the text of Article 11 of the ICESCR quoted previously. Which of the obligations described in that article might be relevant to intellectual property protection of PGRs?

---

[33] U.N. Special Rapporteur on the Right to Food, *Report to U.N. Commission on Human Rights*, 10–11, U.N. Doc. E/CN.4/2001/53 (Feb. 7, 2001) (*prepared by* Jean Ziegler) [Special Rapporteur, *2001 Right to Food Report*].

B. Intellectual Property Protection for PGRs

Contestations over the appropriate ownership rules for PGRs – sometimes colorfully referred to as the "seed wars" – have raged for more than two decades.[34] These disputes encompass three distinct types of plant genetic materials for food and agriculture: (1) those found in their natural or "raw" state (often referred to as *in situ*), (2) those held in global seed banks (known as *ex situ* PGRs), and (3) those that have been "worked" through human innovation (such as new plant varieties, isolated plant genes, or genetically modified plants). States, international organizations, public interest NGOs, and commentators have disputed whether PGRs in each of these three categories should be subject to individual, group, or government ownership or, conversely, should be treated as part of the common heritage of humanity and freely accessible to all.

This section analyzes the international legal rules governing these three types of PGRs. We first summarize the policy rationales for recognizing plant variety protection and plant patents and review the multilateral agreements that require such legal protections. We then examine the legal rules and policy objectives that are in tension with intellectual property protection for plant-related innovations.

1. Justifications for and Critiques of Intellectual Property Protection for PGRs

Commentators who favor recognizing exclusive rights in plant-related innovations justify patents and plant breeders' rights in familiar instrumentalist terms. According to this instrumentalist logic, legal protection of new plant varieties and genetically modified plants encourages commercial plant breeders and biotechnology firms to invest the resources, labor, and time needed to improve food and feed crops. Without a grant of exclusive rights, this argument continues, third parties would free ride on these improvements, reducing the incentive to innovate. The genetic material within plants that determines their distinctive and commercially valuable features is naturally self-replicating. Such self-replication makes innovations embodied in biological material particularly susceptible to unauthorized commercial exploitation. Intellectual property protection for plant-related innovations reduces free riding and enables breeders and

---

[34] KEITH AOKI, SEED WARS: CONTROVERSIES AND CASES ON PLANT GENETIC RESOURCES AND INTELLECTUAL PROPERTY (2008); Jack Kloppenburg, Jr., & Daniel Lee Kienman, *Seed Wars: Common Heritage, Private Property, and Political Strategy*, 95 SOCIALIST REV. 6 (1987).

firms to recoup the costs of their innovative activities involving biological resources.[35]

The grant of exclusive rights in PGRs is also justified by reference to the benefits it provides to society as a whole. Such rights, their proponents claim, provide an incentive for private research in agrobiotechnology and plant breeding and reduce the need for governments to fund or subsidize these activities. And they encourage development of seeds and plants with new and beneficial traits or characteristics – such as higher yields, increased productivity, toleration of droughts or poor soil conditions, and (in the case of genetically modified crops) nutritional enhancements. An international system of intellectual property protection for PGRs expands these benefits by encouraging the transborder distribution of improved plant materials. If biotechnology firms and commercial breeders can protect their innovations outside their countries of origin, they will be more likely to make their new varieties available to farmers, consumers, and researchers in other states.[36]

Opponents of intellectual property protection for PGRs challenge these claims on several grounds. One objection is that private sector research is overwhelmingly directed to developing innovations and technologies "suitable for the major commercial agricultural input markets in the temperate-zone production environments of North America and Europe." In contrast, commercial innovators have shown far less interest in "tackling the critical problems of the poor [or the] crops [such as tropical maize, sorghum, millet, cassava, groundnut, oilseed, and sweet potato] ... that provide the bulk of their food supply and livelihoods."[37]

A second and more fundamental objection is that genetic diversity is eroded rather than enhanced by granting exclusive economic rights in plant-related innovations. According to this view, the very same societal benefits that intellectual property protection allegedly engenders – new crops with desirable characteristics – are in fact detrimental to sustainable food and

---

[35] See, e.g., W. LESSER, THE ROLE OF INTELLECTUAL PROPERTY RIGHTS IN BIOTECHNOLOGY TRANSFER UNDER THE CONVENTION ON BIOLOGICAL DIVERSITY 6–8 (ISAAA Briefs No. 3, 1997), available at http://www.isaaa.org/Publications/Downloads/ Briefs%203.pdf; ORG. FOR ECON. CO-OPERATION AND DEV. (OECD), INTELLECTUAL PROPERTY, TECHNOLOGY TRANSFER AND GENETIC RESOURCES: AN OECD SURVEY OF CURRENT PRACTICES AND POLICIES (1996), available at www.oecd.org/dataoecd/60/11/ 1947170.pdf.

[36] LESSER, supra note 35, at 8, 10; Kerstin Mechlem & Terri Raney, Agricultural Biotechnology and the Right to Food, in FRANCESCO FRANCIONI (ED.), BIOTECHNOLOGIES AND INTERNATIONAL HUMAN RIGHTS 131, 132–33 (2007).

[37] Mechlem & Raney, supra note 36, at 145.

agriculture. Farmers purchase commercial seed lines from agrobiotech-nology firms because their uniform genetic traits purportedly increase the quality and quantity of their harvests. In fact, opponents contend, reliance on commercial seeds and propagating materials actually diminishes genetic diversity in several ways. First, it reduces the incentive of farmers to experiment with informal plant breeding techniques to create new varieties adopted to local growing conditions. Second, even those farmers interested in such experimentation are prevented from doing so by the exclusive rights that protect genetically modified plants and seeds. And third, the genetic uniformity of commercial seeds and plants – even those with highly beneficial traits – reduces their ability to adapt to pests and diseases as compared to wild or informally bred varieties.[38]

It would be useful to evaluate these competing claims empirically. Unfortunately, there are few comprehensive studies that analyze the effects of intellectual property protection on plant genetic diversity or research relating to beneficial plant characteristics.[39] Many empirical analyses focus on only one or two countries (usually industrialized nations), are based on only a few years of data, or rely on anecdotal evidence.[40] As a result, the accuracy or broader applicability of the studies' findings is often contested. Notwithstanding the lack of conclusive empirical evidence, the competing arguments for and against exclusive rights in PGRs have, as we now explain, shaped the evolution of international intellectual property protection rules over the last two decades.

2. The Evolution of Intellectual Property Protection for PGRs
Two multilateral treaty systems – the UPOV and the TRIPS Agreement – regulate intellectual property protection for plant-related innovations. We

---

[38] See, e.g., AOKI, supra note 34, at 23–25; CAREY FOWLER, UNNATURAL SELECTION xiii (1994).

[39] See, e.g., Deepthi Elizabeth Kolady & William Lesser, Does Plant Variety Protection Contribute to Crop Productivity? Lessons for Developing Countries from US Wheat Breeding, 12 J. WORLD INTELL. PROP. 137, 138 (2009) ("Particularly little is known of the operation and effects of PVP [plant variety protection] in developing countries, in part because implementation in many major countries is too recent to have discernable effects."); Brian D. Wright & Philip G. Pardey, Changing Intellectual Property Regimes: Implications for Developing Country Agriculture, 2 INT'L J. TECH. & GLOBALISATION, 93, 105 (2006) ("Definitive evidence on the effects of IPR on agricultural research will not be available soon, if ever.").

[40] See LAURENCE R. HELFER, FAO LEGAL OFFICE, INTELLECTUAL PROPERTY RIGHTS IN PLANT VARIETIES: INTERNATIONAL LEGAL REGIMES AND POLICY OPTIONS FOR NATIONAL GOVERNMENTS 21–29 (2004) [HELFER, IPRS IN PLANT VARIETIES]; Mechlem & Raney, supra note 36, at 139.

begin with the international rules governing plant variety protection and then discuss patent protection of genetically modified plants.

a. Plant Variety Protection

With respect to new plant varieties, the 1978 and 1991 Acts of the UPOV provide a *sui generis* system tailored to the needs of commercial plant breeders.[41] The two Acts have a similar structure to other multilateral intellectual property agreements reviewed in Chapter 1. They define the protected subject matter, eligibility requirements, terms of protection, exclusive rights, and exceptions and limitations to those rights.

A plant variety[42] is eligible for protection under the 1978 and 1991 Acts if it is (1) new,[43] (2) distinct from other varieties by virtue of its qualitative and quantitative characteristics, (3) uniform with regard to the specific features of its sexual reproduction or vegetative propagation, and (4) stable, such that the variety's essential characteristics persist even after repeated reproduction or propagation.[44] Some commentators have criticized these four requirements – in particular uniformity and stability – as discouraging the genetic diversity required for sound agricultural practices, especially "in risk-prone areas [where there] is an advantage to have a higher degree of variability in the fields."[45] The UPOV eligibility rules thus provide one of the principal

---

[41] The first UPOV Act was adopted in 1961, principally by European countries seeking to protect plant breeders in national and foreign markets. International Convention for the Protection of New Varieties of Plants, Dec. 2, 1961, 815 U.N.T.S. 89 [UPOV 1961]. The UPOV was later revised in acts adopted in 1972, 1978, and 1991. International Convention for the Protection of New Varieties of Plants, Dec. 2, 1961, as revised at Geneva on Nov. 10, 1972, and on Oct. 23, 1978, 1861 U.N.T.S. 281 [UPOV 1978]; International Convention for the Protection of New Varieties of Plants, Dec. 2, 1961, as revised at Geneva on Nov. 10, 1972, on Oct. 23, 1978, and on Mar. 19, 1991 [UPOV 1991]. The latter two acts are the most important and most widely ratified by UPOV member states. UPOV 1991 entered into force in 1998 and UPOV 1978 was closed to future accessions on that same date.

[42] UPOV 1991 defines a plant "variety" as a "plant grouping within a single botanical taxon of the lowest known rank" that can be "defined by the expression of the characteristics resulting from a given genotype or combination of genotypes; distinguished from any other plant grouping by the expression of at least one of the said characteristics; and considered as a unit with regard to its suitability for being propagated unchanged." UPOV 1991, Art. 1(vi). No definition of "variety" appears in UPOV 1978, which gives the states parties to that act greater discretion to define the characteristics of plant groupings that qualify for protection.

[43] Although the focus of the UPOV conventions is on new plant varieties created through commercial breeding methods, the treaties also require protection of discovered plant varieties. See UPOV 1978, art. 6.1(a); UPOV 1991, art. 1(iv).

[44] UPOV 1978, art. 6; UPOV 1991, arts. 6–9.

[45] Dan Leskien & Michael Flitner, Intellectual Property Rights and Plant Genetic Resources: Options for a Sui Generis System 51 (Issues in Genetic Resources No. 6, 1997).

bases for the criticisms of intellectual property protection of PGRs described earlier in this chapter.

If a variety meets these four eligibility requirements, the 1978 Act confers upon the breeder that created it the exclusive right to engage in the following activities: (1) production of the variety's propagating materials for purposes of commercial marketing, (2) the offering for sale of such materials, and (3) the marketing of the materials.[46] The 1991 Act substantially expands these exclusive rights to include (1) reproducing the protected variety, (2) conditioning it for propagation, (3) exporting and importing the variety, and (4) stocking it for any of these purposes.[47]

Two important exceptions and limitations to these exclusive rights – a breeders' exemption and a farmers' privilege – define the scope of intellectual property protection in the UPOV Acts and, as a consequence, the human rights implications of plant variety protection rules. The 1978 Act takes a capacious view of these exceptions and limitations. In contrast, the 1991 Act significantly narrows both provisions and thus substantially expands the economic controls that plant breeders can exercise.

With regard to the breeders' exemption, the 1978 Act permits second-generation breeders to create and to market new plant varieties based upon a protected variety without the permission of the latter variety's owner.[48] Like its predecessor, the 1991 Act also allows breeders to use protected plant varieties to create new varieties. However, the later exemption does not apply to new varieties that are "essentially derived" from those protected varieties.[49] The drafters added this provision to deter second-generation breeders from making merely cosmetic changes to existing varieties and then applying for intellectual property protection. In practice, however, disagreements over the definition of minimum genetic distance between first- and second-generation varieties has narrowed the breeders' exemption and expanded the exclusive rights of first-generation breeders.

The farmers' privilege has experienced a similar diminution. The 1978 Act's focus on commercial exploitation implicitly allows the noncommercial

---

[46] UPOV 1978, art. 5. UPOV 1978 does not require member states to extend these exclusive rights to harvested material or other marketed products. Protection lasts for fifteen years, with the exception of vines, forest trees, fruit trees, and ornamental trees, which are protected for no less than eighteen years.

[47] UPOV 1991, art. 14. All of the exclusive rights in UPOV 1991 apply not only to propagating material but also to harvested material, where the harvest has been obtained through the unauthorized use of the propagating material and the breeder has not had a reasonable opportunity to exercise his or her right in relation to that material. *Id.*

[48] UPOV 1978, art. 5.3.

[49] UPOV 1991, arts. 14.5, 15.

use of protected materials without the breeder's authorization. This exception benefits farmers who purchase the seeds of protected varieties. The scope of the privilege varies considerably across national jurisdictions. Some 1978 Act countries allow farmers to plant seeds saved from prior purchases on their own landholdings, while others permit them not only to replant but also to trade or sell limited quantities of seeds to other farmers, a practice often referred to as "brown bagging."[50] The 1991 Act contains an express farmers' privilege, but one that is more limited in scope. Farmers may save seeds for future use "on their own holdings," but only "within reasonable limits and subject to the safeguarding of the legitimate interests of the breeder."[51] Farmers may not sell or exchange seeds with other farmers, a limitation that some commentators have criticized as contrary to farming practices in many developing nations, where seeds are exchanged to facilitate crop and variety rotation.[52]

The UPOV Acts are the only multilateral treaties exclusively focused on intellectual property protection for plant varieties. But their significance has recently been overshadowed by the TRIPS Agreement. Article 27.3 of TRIPS sets forth the treaty's rules concerning plant-related innovations:

> Members may also *exclude from patentability* ... (b) *plants* and animals other than microorganisms; and essentially biological processes for the production of plants or animals other than non-biological and microbiological processes. However, *Members shall provide for the protection for plant varieties either by patents or by an effective* sui generis *system or by any combination thereof.*[53]

---

[50] Leskien & Flitner, *supra* note 45, at 61; Int'l Dev. Res. Ctr., Crucible II Group, Seeding Solutions – Volume 2: Options for National Laws Governing Control over Genetic Resources and Biological Innovations 170 (2001) [Seeding Solutions – Volume 2], *available at* http://www.idrc.org.sg/en/ev-9434-201-1-DO_TOPIC.html.

[51] UPOV 1991, art. 15.2.

[52] Leskien & Flitner, *supra* note 45, at 60; Jayashree Watal, Intellectual Property Rights in the WTO and Developing Countries 141 (2000). In addition, some commercial breeders have asserted that the "reasonable limits" restriction in UPOV 1991 requires states to restrict the acreage and quantity of seed and species subject to the farmers' privilege, while the requirement to safeguard breeders' "legitimate interests" requires farmers to pay some form of remuneration to the breeder for their privileged acts. *See* Int'l Seed Fed'n, *Position Paper on Farm Saved Seed* (May 3, 2001), *archived at* http://web.archive.org/web/20031219131731/www.worldseed.org/Position_papers/FSSe.htm. The latter assertion is controversial, however, and has not been enacted in the national laws of all UPOV 1991 member states. *Compare* Council Regulation 2100/94, Community Plant Variety Rights, 1994 O.J. (L 227) 1 (EC) (requiring such payments except for small farmers) *with* Plant Varieties Protection Act of 1994, 7 U.S.C. § 2543 (no payments required).

[53] Agreement on Trade-Related Aspects of Intellectual Property Rights, art. 27.3(b) (emphasis added), Apr. 15, 1994, 1869 U.N.T.S. 299 [TRIPS Agreement].

Two points about Article 27.3(b) are noteworthy. First, the article does not mention the 1978 and 1991 Acts of the UPOV. The absence of such a reference stands in contrasts to other fields of intellectual property (such as patents, trademarks, and copyrights) with respect to which TRIPS incorporates the standards of protection in preexisting treaties (such as the Paris and Berne Conventions).[54] As a result of this omission, nothing in TRIPS requires WTO member states to ratify either UPOV Act or to enact national plant breeders' laws consistent with either Act's requirements. However, several bilateral and regional "TRIPS Plus"[55] treaties do contain one or both of these requirements.[56] Second, Article 27.3(b) contemplates protection of plant varieties using one of three approaches: (1) patents, (2) an effective *sui generis* system, or (3) a combination of these approaches. Thus, unlike most other TRIPS provisions, the article grants WTO members discretion to choose the manner of protection of new plant varieties and expressly contemplates that such discretion may be exercised in different ways by different countries.

Precisely how much discretion WTO member states possess has been a subject of considerable debate. Much of the controversy results from uncertainty as to the meaning of the phrase "effective *sui generis* system." The term *sui generis* means "of its own kind" or "unique," a definition that does little to clarify which distinctive systems are compatible with TRIPS. A careful analysis of the treaty's object and purpose, however, reveals that national plant variety protection laws must include four core elements to qualify as an "effective *sui generis* system" within the meaning of Article 27.3(b). Such laws must (1) apply

[54] Although the drafting history of TRIPS does not explain this markedly different treatment of plant varieties, it seems likely that compliance with UPOV was not required because so few WTO members were party to UPOV and those who were could not agree upon which of its two most recent acts should serve as the standard for protection.

[55] These treaties are known by the appellation "TRIPS Plus" because they (1) contain intellectual property protection standards more stringent than those found in TRIPS, (2) obligate developing countries to implement TRIPS before the end of its specified transition periods, or (3) require such countries to accede to or conform to the requirements of other multilateral intellectual property agreements. GRAIN, *Bilateral Agreements Imposing TRIPS-Plus Intellectual Property Rights on Biodiversity in Developing Countries* (2008), *available at* http://www.grain.org/rights_files/TRIPS-plus-march-2008.pdf; David Vivas-Eugui, *Regional and Bilateral Agreements and a Trips-Plus World: The Free Trade Area of the Americas* (Quaker U.N. Office, TRIPS Issue Papers No. 1, 2003), *available at* http://www.quno.org/geneva/pdf/economic/Issues/FTAs-TRIPS-plus-English.pdf.

[56] For example, the draft U.S.-Colombia Free Trade Agreement, the 2007 U.S.-Peru Free Trade Agreement, the 2004 DR-CAFTA (applicable to Costa Rica, El Salvador, Guatemala, Honduras, Nicaragua, and the Dominican Republic), the 2002 U.S.-Chile Free Trade Agreement, the 2000 U.S.-Jordan Free Trade Agreement, the 2000 EU-Mexico Free Trade Agreement, and certain Euro-Mediterranean Association agreements mandate UPOV as the appropriate mechanism to protect plant breeders' rights. The treaties also require these countries to ratify the UPOV 1991 within specified periods. *See* GRAIN, *supra* note 55.

to plant varieties in all species and botanical genera; (2) grant plant breeders either an exclusive right to control particular acts with respect to those varieties, or, at a minimum, grant a right to remuneration when third parties engage in those acts; (3) provide national and most-favored nation treatment to breeders in other WTO member states; and (4) establish procedures that enable breeders to enforce the rights granted to them by such laws.[57]

Once WTO members adopt these four mandatory requirements, they are free to model their plant variety protection laws on the 1991 UPOV Act, the 1978 UPOV Act, the patent provisions of TRIPS, or some combination of these standards.[58] Each of these approaches achieves, in a different way, the principal policy rationale for extending intellectual property protection to PGRs: to create incentives for biotechnology firms and plant breeders to develop and market plant-related innovations. WTO members also have discretion to deviate from these standard approaches and tailor *sui generis* protection to the needs of their agricultural industries and farming sectors. Such modifications may, for example, (1) revise the eligibility requirements for new plant varieties, (2) impose additional conditions on the grant of protection for such varieties, or (3) alter the scope of exclusive rights or exceptions and limitations.

b. Patent Protection for Plant-Related Innovations

The creation of new plant varieties by commercial plant breeders is not the only way that intellectual property intersects with PGRs for food and agriculture. Other plant-related innovations derived from PGRs include isolated and purified genes and transgenic plants. The patent provisions of the TRIPS Agreement regulate these plant-related innovations. TRIPS requires WTO members to grant patents in all fields of technology for "inventions" that are "new, involve an inventive step and are capable of industrial application."[59]

---

[57] LESKIEN & FLITNER, *supra* note 45, at 26; HELFER, IPRs IN PLANT VARIETIES, *supra* note 40, at 56–60.

[58] States that are members of both the WTO and either the 1991 or 1978 UPOV act have somewhat less discretion, however, inasmuch as they must comply with both sets of treaty obligations. For a more detailed analysis of the discretion that these dual-treaty countries possess, *see* HELFER, IPRs IN PLANT VARIETIES, *supra* note 40, at 65–80.

[59] TRIPS Agreement, art. 27.1. As explained earlier, Article 27.3(b) permits members to refuse to grant patents for new plant varieties. In addition, Article 27.2 permits members to exclude from patentability those inventions whose commercial exploitation within their territory "is necessary to protect *ordre public* or morality, including to protect ... plant life or health or to avoid serious prejudice to the environment." Notwithstanding these discretionary exclusions, several industrialized countries, including the United States, Japan, Australia, New Zealand, Sweden, and the United Kingdom, permit plant breeders to obtain patent protection in new varieties provided that the eligibility requirements for a patent have been met. WATAL, *supra* note 52, at 149.

TRIPS does not define "invention," thus leaving the precise meaning of that term to national patent laws. All such laws recognize that inventions cannot be mere discoveries of natural phenomena or naturally occurring substances. The trend in industrialized countries, however, is to award patents for isolated and purified natural substances, including the polynucleotides deoxyribonucleic acid (DNA) and ribonucleic acid (RNA).[60] For example, Article 3.2 of the EU Directive on the Legal Protection of Biotechnological Inventions states that "biological material which is isolated from its natural environment or produced by means of a technical process" may be patentable.[61] As a result, "a very thin line separates invention from discovery in those countries."[62] In the United States, however, patents for isolated RNA and DNA sequences have been called into question by a recent appellate ruling which suggests that many applications for inventions of this kind may be rejected on "obviousness" grounds.[63]

Many developing countries refuse to grant patents in isolated or purified genetic material, often as a result of moral or cultural opposition to private ownership of PGRs.[64] For example, Article 15(b) of Decision 486 of the Andean Community, a five-member integration pact in the Andes region of South America, excludes from the definition of inventions "biological material, as existing in nature, or able to be separated, including the genome or germplasm of any living thing."[65] A country's refusal to recognize patents for isolated or purified plant genes is compatible with TRIPS provided that the exclusion does not extend to modified or artificial plant gene sequences, which often

---

[60] See Carlos M. Correa, *Patent Rights*, in CARLOS MARÍA CORREA & ABDULQAWI YUSUF (EDS.), INTELLECTUAL PROPERTY AND INTERNATIONAL TRADE: THE TRIPS AGREEMENT 227, 235 (2008) ("In the United States an isolated and purified form of a natural product can be patented.... Under these principles, the patenting of natural genes has become possible. Claims in this case normally refer to an isolated DNA sequence, DNA constructs, and new transformed plants derived from it, although claims often include natural DNA sequences without limitations."); *see also* CARLOS M. CORREA, TRADE RELATED ASPECTS OF INTELLECTUAL PROPERTY RIGHTS: A COMMENTARY ON THE TRIPS AGREEMENT 272–73 (2007); LESKIEN & FLITNER, *supra* note 45, at 8.

[61] Council Directive 98/44/EC, art. 3.2, 1998 O.J. (L 213) 13, 18.

[62] Correa, *Patent Rights*, *supra* note 60, at 235.

[63] *In re Kubin*, 561 F.3d 1351 (Fed. Cir. 2009); *see* Michael J. Stimson, *Is the Gene Patenting Party Over? Biotechnology Patents after In Re Kubin*, 28 BIOTECHNOLOGY L. REP. 329, 330–31 (2009) (stating that *Kubin* "brings into question the patentability of polynucleotide inventions and the validity of issued patent claims to polynucleotides" and potentially "every invention involving biotechnology, a highly developed field with many other established methods in addition to isolating DNA").

[64] *See, e.g.*, COMM'N ON INTELL. PROP. RIGHTS, INTEGRATING INTELLECTUAL PROPERTY RIGHTS AND DEVELOPMENT POLICY 59 (2002) (noting that "private ownership of substances created by nature is wrong, and inimical to cultural values in different parts of the world").

[65] Andean Community Decision 486, Art. 15(b). For additional examples, *see* CORREA, TRADE RELATED, *supra* note 60, at 186; WATAL, *supra* note 52, at 155–56.

vary significantly from naturally occurring substances and thus are properly classified as inventions.[66] In part for this reason, several "TRIPS Plus" treaties require developing countries to extend patent protection to transgenic plants that meet the requirements for patentability set forth in TRIPS.[67]

Once a patent is awarded, the owner of the patented product or process enjoys a broad panoply of exclusive rights. As provided in TRIPS Article 28, these include the right to prevent third parties from making the product, using the process, or using, offering for sale, selling, or importing for those purposes the patented product or the product obtained by the patented process. Countries that extend patent protection to plant-related innovations are thus required to protect products composed of genetically modified plants and processes (including biological processes) for the production of such plants.[68] In addition, although there is some uncertainty over whether traditional plant breeding methods can be protected by process patents, several industrialized countries have protected such methods.[69]

As compared to limitations on plant breeders' rights permitted by the UPOV Acts, the limitations on a patent owner's exclusive rights permitted under TRIPS are far narrower. Article 30 of TRIPS permits "limited exceptions" that do not "unreasonably conflict with a normal exploitation of the patent" and "do not unreasonably prejudice the legitimate interests of the patent owner, taking account of the legitimate interests of third parties." This standard precludes WTO members from adopting many of the limitations permitted under plant variety protection laws, such as the breeders' exemption and the farmers' privilege. These privileges are absent from the patent laws of several industrialized countries. For example, the United States does not recognize a farmers' privilege in its utility patent statute. Although such an exception appears in Article 11 of the European Union's 1998 Biotechnology Directive (conditioned upon the payment of equitable remuneration except for small farmers), at least one commentator has questioned whether that exception is compatible with Article 30, because such an exception unreasonably prejudices the "legitimate interests" of the patent owner.[70]

---

[66] LESKIEN & FLITNER, *supra* note 45, at 9.

[67] *See, e.g.,* Keith E. Maskus, *Intellectual Property Rights,* in JEFFREY J. SCHOTT (ED.), TRADE RELATIONS BETWEEN COLOMBIA AND THE UNITED STATES 145, 151 (2006) (stating that a provision in the U.S.-Colombia Free Trade Agreement that requires Colombia to "undertake all reasonable efforts to make ... patent protection available" for new plant varieties "is aimed primarily at ensuring that transgenic plants, especially those arising from biotechnological research, will be eligible for patents in Colombia").

[68] LESKIEN & FLITNER, *supra* note 45, at 22.

[69] *Compare* CORREA, INTELLECTUAL PROPERTY RIGHTS, THE WTO AND DEVELOPING COUNTRIES: THE TRIPS AGREEMENT AND POLICY OPTIONS 187 (2000) *with* Janis & Kesan, note 2, at 981.

[70] WATAL, *supra* note 52, at 155 n.62.

* * * Issues in Focus * * *

As the preceding discussion reveals, there are significant differences between the two forms of intellectual property – plant variety protection and patents – applicable to plant genetic resources. The eligibility requirements for plant variety protection are not onerous. But the scope of protection is quite narrow, in that exclusive rights are modest and exceptions and limitations to those rights are relatively robust. Patents strike a very different balance. Eligibility requirements are high and often difficult to meet. Once granted, however, a patent conveys broad rights to exclude third parties from exploiting the patented invention. In addition, the TRIPS Agreement, per Article 27.3(b), gives WTO member states discretion to protect plant varieties "either by patents or by an effective *sui generis* system or by any combination thereof." As a result, a state may decide that either or both forms of protection provide the appropriate level of incentives to encourage plant-related research and innovation within its territory. The following table compares the major differences among the three principal international instruments.

Comparison of Principal Differences among Plant Variety Protections Required by UPOV 1978 Act, UPOV 1991 Act, and TRIPS-compatible Patent Laws

Subject	Breeders' rights in UPOV 1978 Act	Breeders' rights in UPOV 1991 Act	TRIPS-compatible patent laws
Eligibility for protection	Plant varieties that are novel, distinctive, uniform, and stable.	Plant varieties that are novel, distinctive, uniform, and stable.	Plant varieties, plants, seeds, and enabling technologies that are novel, involve an inventive step, and are capable of industrial application.
Minimum exclusive rights in propagating material	Production for purposes of commercial marketing; offering for sale; marketing; repeated use for the commercial production of another variety.	Production or reproduction; conditioning for the purposes of propagation; offering for sale; selling or other marketing; exporting; importing or stocking for any of these purposes.	Making the patented product, using the patented process or using, offering for sale, selling, or importing for those purposes the patented product or the product obtained by the patented process.

Minimum exclusive rights in harvested material	No such obligation, except for ornamental plants used for commercial propagating purposes.	Same acts as above if harvested material obtained through unauthorized use of propagating material and if breeder had no reasonable opportunity to exercise his or her right in relation to the propagating material.	Making the patented product, using the patented process or using, offering for sale, selling, or importing for those purposes the patented product or the product obtained by the patented process.
Breeders' exemption	Mandatory. Breeders free to use protected variety to develop a new variety.	Permissive. But breeding and exploitation of variety "essentially derived" from an earlier variety require the right holder's authorization.	Generally not recognized, although compatibility with TRIPS not yet tested.
Farmers' privilege	Implicitly allowed under the definition of minimum exclusive rights.	Permissive within reasonable limits and subject to safeguarding the legitimate interests of the right holder.	Generally not recognized, although compatibility with TRIPS not yet tested.
Additional exceptions to exclusive rights	None specified.	Acts done privately and for noncommercial purposes, acts done for experimental purposes.	Research and experimentation. All exemptions must comply with three-part test of TRIPS Article 30.
Minimum term of protection	18 years for trees and grapevines; 15 years for all other plants.	25 years for trees and grapevines; 20 years for all other plants.	20 years from date the patent application filed.

3. Legal Rules and Policy Objectives in Tension with Intellectual Property Protection for Plant-Related Innovations

Having identified the principal international agreements that govern intellectual property protection for PGRs and associated technologies, we now consider legal rules and policy objectives that are in tension with exclusive rights for plant-related innovations and explore the policy arguments that underlie those rules and objectives.

a. Farmers' Rights

"Farmers' rights" seek to acknowledge the contributions that indigenous or small-scale farmers, particularly in developing countries, have made to the preservation and improvement of PGRs. Unlike natural resources such as coal and oil, PGRs are conserved and managed by the women and men who

cultivate wild plant varieties (also known as landraces or traditional culti-
vars) that help to ensure the genetic diversity needed to maintain healthy
agricultural systems. The following passage describes some of the conservation and management practices that farmers undertake:

> Farmers in developing countries routinely select-out mutant, high-yielding,
> or otherwise high-quality seed for testing and experimentation.... Such farm-
> ers (mostly women) regard harvested seed as their initial source of variation
> from which they can undertake their own plant breeding. Interesting mate-
> rial is tested in tiny plots adjacent to the home. Often, promising germplasm is
> exchanged with neighbours and tested against different slopes and soils in the
> community. The most promising material is multiplied and incorporated into
> the seed stock for the next planting.

> Community plant breeding can produce radical changes in the field, but it is
> more likely to be a gradual process that allows the diversity of farmers' varieties
> in the field to evolve over time. Nevertheless, the germplasm in the field does
> change somewhat every year, and yield and quality improvements are recorded
> in various ways by the farmer-breeders themselves....

> An important element in community plant breeding is the exchange of "exotic"
> germplasm among farming communities.... Every country and culture can
> point to a long history of customary seed exchange – sometimes linked to reli-
> gious practices and other times associated with markets or celebrations. The
> exchange process is a major opportunity for introducing significantly new
> seeds. It is this process that sped maize through many of the growing regions of
> Africa in a few generations and allowed sweet potatoes to spread through East
> Asia and the Pacific in less than a hundred years.[71]

In addition to promoting genetic diversity and the distribution of food crops,
informal cultivation practices preserve raw genetic materials for future innovation by commercial plant breeders and biotechnology firms. But whereas
these private actors obtain proprietary rights to compensate them for the
time and expense of innovation, no system of remuneration rewards farmers
for their efforts. The concept of farmers' rights is therefore intended to serve
as a counterweight to intellectual property protection by compensating the
upstream input providers who preserve the public domain plant materials
that make downstream innovations possible.[72]

Precisely how farmers' rights should be defined and implemented remains a
point of contention among public interest NGOs and governments. One recent
commentary offers the following "minimum definition" of farmers' rights:

> Farmers' rights consist of the customary rights that farmers have had as stew-
> ards and innovators of agro-biodiversity since the dawn of agriculture to save,

---

[71] Seeding Solutions – Volume 2, *supra* note 50, at 130.
[72] Helfer, *Regime Shifting, supra* note 1, at 36–37.

grow, share, develop, and maintain plant varieties; and of their legitimate rights to be rewarded and supported for their contribution to the global pool of genetic resources as well as to the development of commercial varieties of plants, and to participate in decision making on issues that may affect these rights.[73]

The most extensive treatment of farmers' rights in a legal instrument appears in Article 9 of the International Treaty on Plant Genetic Resources for Food and Agriculture (ITPGR).[74] Article 9 recognizes "the enormous contribution that the local and indigenous communities and farmers of all regions of the world, particularly those in the centres of origin and crop diversity, have made and will continue to make for the conservation and development of plant genetic resources which constitute the basis of food and agriculture production throughout the world."[75] After acknowledging these contributions, Article 9 provides as follows:

9.2 The Contracting Parties agree that the responsibility for realizing Farmers' Rights, as they relate to plant genetic resources for food and agriculture, rests with national governments. In accordance with their needs and priorities, each Contracting Party should, as appropriate, and subject to its national legislation, take measures to protect and promote Farmers' Rights, including:

(a) protection of traditional knowledge relevant to plant genetic resources for food and agriculture;
(b) the right to equitably participate in sharing benefits arising from the utilization of plant genetic resources for food and agriculture; and
(c) the right to participate in making decisions, at the national level, on matters related to the conservation and sustainable use of plant genetic resources for food and agriculture.

9.3 Nothing in this Article shall be interpreted to limit any rights that farmers have to save, use, exchange and sell farm-saved seed/propagating material, subject to national law and as appropriate.[76]

Commentators analyzing Article 9 have identified two different approaches to farmers' rights. The "ownership approach" seeks to reward farmers for

---

[73] Regine Andersen, *Protecting Farmers' Rights in the Global IPR Regime: Challenges and Options for Developing Countries*, 2 (Policy Brief, South Asia Watch on Trade, Economics & Environment (SAWTEE)) (2007), *available at* http://www.sawtee.org/pdf/Farmers%20 Rights_IPR%20Regime_Regine.pdf.

[74] International Treaty on Plant Genetic Resources for Food and Agriculture, Nov. 3, 2001 [ITPGR], *available at* http://www.fao.org/docrep/011/i0510e/i0510e00.htm. An earlier nonbinding FAO resolution defined farmers' rights as "rights arising from the past, present and future contributions of farmers in conserving, improving and making available plant genetic resources, particularly those in centers of origin/diversity." Farmers' Rights, FAO Res. 5/89, (Nov. 11–20, 1989).

[75] ITPGR, art. 9.1.

[76] *Id.* arts. 9.2, 9.3.

the genetic materials that commercial plant breeders and the seed industry obtain from their fields. Proponents of this approach seek "to ensure equitable sharing of benefits arising from the use of agro-biodiversity and to establish an incentive structure for continued maintenance of this diversity." In contrast, the "stewardship approach" focuses on "the rights that farmers must be granted in order to enable them to continue as stewards and innovators of agro-biodiversity. The idea is that the legal space required for farmers to continue with this role must be upheld and that farmers ... should be rewarded and supported for their contributions."[77]

b. Regulating Access to PGRs in Nature and in Global Seed Banks

Commercial plant breeders and biotechnology firms require access to existing stocks of seeds and plant germplasm for research and subsequent commercial development. Access issues arise for plant genetic materials located in their natural state (*in situ* PGRs) as well as in international networks of seed banks (*ex situ* PGRs).

With respect to *in situ* PGRs, a number of countries, especially those rich in biodiversity, have enacted national or regional laws to regulate third-party access. These laws enable governments to demand compensation or technology transfers as the *quid pro quo* for access to the genetic resources subject to their sovereign control. For example, Andean Community Decision 391 creates a Common Regime on Access to Genetic Resources.[78] This regional legislation establishes detailed rules that include "conditions for just and equitable participation in the benefits of access" and "mechanisms for the transfer of know-how and technology, including biotechnology" into the region.[79] The specific terms of access, benefit sharing, and technology transfer are memorialized in agreements entered into between the entity (usually a government) that owns or controls the plant materials and the party (whether private or public) that seeks to access them.[80]

A different set of access issues arise with regard to *ex situ* collections of plant germplasm, including seed banks affiliated with the Consultative Group on International Agricultural Research (CGIAR). CGIAR is an informal

---

[77] Andersen, *supra* note 73, at 2.

[78] Andean Community Decision 391, Common Regime on Access to Genetic Resources (July 2, 1996), *available at* http://www.comunidadandina.org/INGLES/normativa/D391e.htm.

[79] *Id.* arts. 2(a), 17(c)

[80] *Id.* arts. 32–37; *see also* Claudio Chiarolla, *Plant Patenting, Benefit Sharing and the Law Applicable to the Food and Agriculture Organisation Standard Material Transfer Agreement,* 11 J. WORLD INTELL. PROP. 1 (2008); Carlos M. Correa, *Considerations on the Standard Material Transfer Agreement under the FAO Treaty on Plant Genetic Resources for Food and Agriculture,* 9 J. WORLD INTELL. PROP. 137 (2006).

association of public and private donors founded in 1971 that supports a global network of agricultural research centers. The centers affiliated with CGIAR store and conserve seeds and plant propagating materials outside their natural habitat for future use by farmers, researchers, and breeders.[81] The seed banks hold these materials "in trust for the benefit of the international community" and cannot seek intellectual property protection for the materials themselves or for related information.[82] The same restrictions on intellectual property protection are contained in the material transfer agreements with third parties to the seed banks transfer germplasm in their collections.[83] As a result of these provisions, CGIAR research centers treat the seeds and plant materials under their control as part of the public domain.[84]

c. "Biopiracy" and Intellectual Property Protection of Raw Plant Materials

Restrictions on access to *in situ* and *ex situ* PGRs are linked to broader controversies surrounding attempts to secure intellectual property protection for raw plant materials. Multilateral treaties and national laws do not authorize private ownership of unimproved plant materials in the public domain. However, in several widely publicized cases in the 1990s, plant breeders and other commercial entities obtained intellectual property protection for plant materials transferred from the CGIAR seed collections or found in the wild. It is unclear whether these protections were the result of inadvertence, insufficient or inaccurate information provided by the intellectual property applicants, or national laws that limit the sources to which intellectual property agencies refer to determine whether materials are in the public domain. Also disputed in some cases was whether the claimants sought proprietary rights in raw plant materials themselves or in isolated and purified gene sequences.[85]

[81] *See* Elisabeth Rosenthal, *Near Arctic, Seed Vault Is a Fort Knox of Food*, N.Y. TIMES, Feb. 29, 2008.

[82] Agreement between [name of Centre] and the Food and Agriculture Organization of the United Nations (FAO) Placing Collections of Plant Germplasm under the Auspices of FAO, Art. 3 (1994), *reprinted in* BOOKLET OF CGIAR CENTRE POLICY INSTRUMENTS, GUIDELINES AND STATEMENTS ON GENETIC RESOURCES, BIOTECHNOLOGY AND INTELLECTUAL PROPERTY RIGHTS 2, 3 (Version 2, July 2003), *available at* http://www.cgiar.org/corecollection/docs/sgrp_policy_booklet_2003.pdf.

[83] *Id.* art. 10 (requiring centers to impose the same restrictions in material transfer agreements with third parties).

[84] *CGIAR: Research & Impact, Genebanks and Databases*, *available at* http://www.cgiar.org/impact/genebanksdatabases.html (last visited Mar. 31, 2010) (stating that CGIAR research centers and seed banks "together maintain over 650,000 samples of crop, forage and agroforestry genetic resources in the public domain").

[85] *See* GRAHAM DUTFIELD, INTELLECTUAL PROPERTY RIGHTS, TRADE AND BIODIVERSITY 50 (2000); Rural Advancement Found. Int'l, *An Inquiry into the Potential for Plant Piracy*

Efforts to claim intellectual property protection in raw or unimproved PGRs have been labeled as "biopiracy." Biopiracy, which is not a legal term of art, is commonly used to describe any act by which a commercial entity seeks intellectual property protection over biological resources, including plant genes and plant varieties in the public domain, that are seen as "belonging" to developing states or to indigenous communities.[86] Some commentators, however, applied the label more broadly to plant innovations whose source materials were obtained in violation of a national access law or a material transfer agreement, or whose owners have not provided compensation or technology transfers to the public or private entities that granted access to those source materials.[87]

Notes and Questions

1. Consider the three types of PGRs analyzed in the preceding sections of this chapter: (1) *in situ* PGRs in their natural or raw state, (2) *ex situ* PGRs in CGIAR seed banks, and (3) PGRs found in new plant varieties, isolated plant genes, or genetically modified plants. Which of these categories has the strongest claim to intellectual property protection based on the policy rationales described in Section 6.2(B)(1)? Is there a plausible policy justification for granting intellectual property protection to a researcher who discovers a previously unknown plant variety growing in the wild? Does your answer to this question depend upon the specific circumstances in which the researcher made the discovery? Does it depend upon whether the "discovery ... of mutations or variants in a population of cultivated plants is ... of great economic importance for agriculture"?[88]

2. As described previously, Article 27.3(b) of the TRIPS Agreement provides WTO member states with the option to protect plant varieties by means of an "effective *sui generis* system." Although the flexibility that this provision offers is not unlimited, it gives governments considerable discretion to

through International Intellectual Property Conventions, Plant Breeders Wrongs (1999), *available at* http://www.etcgroup.org/upload/publication/400/01/occ_plant.pdf. Where private firms have received a patent or plant variety protection for raw PGRs in the public domain, governments and public interest NGOs have sometimes succeeded in petitioning the intellectual property authorities in other nations to nullify legal recognition that they had previously granted. Michael Blakeney, *Protection of Plant Varieties and Farmers' Rights*, 24 EUR. INTELL. PROP. REV. 9, 12 (2002).

[86] CEAS Consultants (Wye) Ltd, Ctr. for European Agric. Studies, Final Report for DG TRADE Eur. Comm.: Study on the Relationship between the Agreement on TRIPS and Biodiversity Related Issues 78 (2000); *see also* CORREA, TRADE RELATED, *supra* note 60, at 172.

[87] Neil D. Hamilton, *Who Owns Dinner: Evolving Legal Mechanisms for Ownership of Plant Genetic Resources*, 28 TULSA L.J. 587, 600–01 (1993).

[88] SEEDING SOLUTIONS – VOLUME 2, *supra* note 50, at 139.

adjust plant variety protection laws to take into account local conditions. Consider the following advice that one of us has provided as to how countries might tailor national plant variety protection rules to their domestic agricultural needs:

> States with large-scale agriculture or plant breeding industries are likely to benefit by adopting relatively robust IPR [intellectual property rights] protection, with a broad array of exclusive rights, an expansive list of protected material and relatively limited exceptions and limitations (with the possible exception of a breeders' exemption, which breeders' advocacy groups have described as essential to promoting plant-related innovations). Such strong protections will facilitate exports of harvested products, imports of propagating materials and investment by foreign firms.

> States with agricultural systems that are domestically focused or rely upon the cultivation of traditional varieties by small-scale farmers face a different set of interests and incentives. Their populations are likely to prefer relatively weak IPR protection with a broad farmers' privilege that permits farmers to both save and exchange seeds. Protection that is too weak is not advisable, however, as it will discourage foreign breeders from importing seeds or other propagating material (which may be an important component of the nation's food supply) and may deter investment by foreign businesses or researchers for whom IPR protection is essential.

> States with mixed agricultural economies may benefit from adopting different levels of protection tailored to the needs of their domestic industries. For example, they may adopt different standards of protection for commercial and noncommercial breeders, with higher standards for the former to compensate them for their investment of capital and distribution costs. They may also permit protection of the same variety with both a breeders' right and a patent (for example, in countries where both classical breeding methods and methods making use of genetic manipulation are prevalent). Conversely, such states may adopt different and exclusive standards for specific varieties. Strong IPR protection in the form of a patent may be used to encourage the creation of new ornamental and high-value export crops without harming domestic consumers, whereas breeders' rights may be used for other species where the state seeks to balance IPR protection against the interests of farmers.[89]

Are these recommendations compatible with the legal requirements of TRIPS Article 27.3(b)? If you were a government official in each of the three types of countries described in this excerpt, would you support these recommendations?

In addition to these macro-level issues, the discretion afforded by Article 27.3(b) allows states to modify the UPOV model of intellectual property protection for new plant varieties. After reviewing the critiques of intellectual

---

[89] HELFER, IPRs IN PLANT VARIETIES, *supra* note 40, at 75–76.

property protection for PGRs and the discussion of the legal rules and policy goals in tension with such protection, what specific modifications, if any, would you propose to the UPOV model? For example, would you alter the eligibility requirements for protecting new plant varieties, and if so how? (Recall that, under the UPOV Acts, a new plant variety is eligible for protection if it is (1) new and (2) has uniform characteristics that are (3) distinct from other varieties and are (4) stable over multiple generations of plant reproduction.) Would you favor the inclusion of a provision that makes a new variety eligible for protection only if the breeder can demonstrate that the variety has more beneficial characteristics than other similar protected varieties or varieties in the public domain?[90] Which actors and interests groups are likely to support or oppose these changes?

3. One of the major battles in the "seed wars" of the last quarter century concerns where to draw the line between PGRs in the public domain and those that can be privatized. On one side of this battle are advocates of a global commons regime that allows researchers, plant breeders, and farmers free and unfettered access to all three types of PGRs analyzed in this section. Arrayed against them are proponents of a private property approach who seek to encourage plant-related innovations in agriculture and biotechnology by granting intellectual property rights to any PGRs that have been modified through human intervention – including isolated and purified plant genes.

The two groups have advanced different (and often inconsistent) international rules that reflect their policy preferences. Advocates of intellectual property protection have lobbied for patent and plant variety protection in treaties such as the TRIPS and the UPOV, whose provisions are described previously. Proponents of an open access regime, in contrast, advanced a different approach in a different international venue. They established a Commission on Genetic Resources for Food and Agriculture that in 1983 adopted a declaration known as the International Undertaking on Plant Genetic Resources. The Undertaking provided that *all* PGRs – naturally occurring plants, germplasm in seed banks, and cultivated plant varieties – were the "heritage of mankind and consequently should be available without restriction" for scientific research, plant breeding, and conservation.[91] The Undertaking was only a nonbinding statement of principles. But it was opposed by the United States and some European governments on the grounds that it conflicted with the UPOV and national patent laws.

---

[90] *Id.* at 71–73.
[91] FAO Conference, Rome, Italy, Nov. 5–23, 1983, *Report: International Undertaking on Plant Genetic Resources*, Art. 1, U.N. Doc. C/83/REP.

An uneasy peace (or at least a truce) in the seed wars was finally achieved in 2001 with the adoption of the International Treaty on Plant Genetic Resources for Food and Agriculture (ITPGR).[92] The ITPGR establishes a novel institutional mechanism to facilitate the exchange of seeds and plant materials for research, breeding, and training – a new "multilateral system" of public domain PGRs to which member states and their nationals will be granted "facilitated access."[93] The multilateral system is composed of genetic material from sixty-four food and feed crops that account for the bulk of human nutrition and that are held in government and CGIAR seed banks.[94] In exchange for access to this communal seed treasury, private parties that incorporate materials from the multilateral system into downstream commercial products must pay a percentage of their profits into a trust account whose proceeds will be used to promote benefit sharing and conservation of PGRs.[95]

The governments that negotiated the ITPGR reached consensus on these basic institutional principles. But they disagreed about where to mark the boundary between public and proprietary genetic resources. The treaty's drafters understood that a tension exists between a principle of open access to genetic resources and the grant of proprietary rights in those resources. Specifically, they recognized that the treaty's success hinged on allowing private parties to commercialize innovations based on the raw genetic materials acquired from the multilateral system. Only through such commercialization would sufficient revenue be generated to fund the treaty's benefit-sharing and conservation objectives. On the other hand, the multilateral system itself would be threatened if large parts of the public domain seed treasury could be privatized through the grant of intellectual property protection.

---

[92] The treaty entered into force on June 29, 2004. As of March 2010, 123 countries were parties to the treaty. FAO, International Treaty on Plant Genetic Resources for Food and Agriculture, *available at* http://www.fao.org/Legal/TREATIES/033s-e.htm (last visited Mar. 31, 2010). The United States signed the ITPGR in 2002, and President George W. Bush transmitted it to the U.S. Senate in 2008. Treaty on Plant Genetic Resources for Food and Agriculture, S. Treaty Doc. 110–19, 110th Cong. (2008). As of September 2010, the treaty had not been ratified.

[93] ITPGR, arts. 10–13.

[94] ITPGR, Annex I (listing thirty-five food and twenty-nine animal feed crops).

[95] Payments are mandatory when the commercialized product has limits on its availability for use in further research and breeding, and voluntary when the product is freely available for such purposes. Other benefit sharing mechanisms provided for in the ITPGR include the exchange of information, access to and transfer of technology, capacity building, and sharing of benefits arising from commercialization. Philippe Cullet, *The International Treaty on Plant Genetic Resources for Food and Agriculture* (Int'l Envtl. L. Res. Ctr. (IELR), Briefing Paper No. 2003–2), *available at* http://www.ielrc.org/content/f0302.htm.

The core of the debate focused on whether to bar patents for isolated and purified plant genes extracted from seeds contained in the common seed pool. After lengthy negotiations, the delegates adopted Article 12.3(d), which provides that access to the multilateral system will only be provided on condition that "recipients shall not claim any intellectual property or other rights that limit the facilitated access to [PGRs], or their genetic parts or components, in the form received from the Multilateral System."[96] This same prohibition must be included in the material transfer agreements executed by anyone accessing the PGRs in the multilateral system.[97]

Does the ITPGR strike an appropriate balance between preserving the PGRs in the public domain and providing incentives for plant-related innovations? Does the treaty's structure imply that such innovations are more likely to result from intellectual property protection than from other sources, such as public financing or university research? Does the ITPGR resolve concerns raised by those who allege that intellectual property protection for PGRs is a form of "biopiracy"?

What is the correct interpretation of Article 12.3(d)? In particular, to what extent must a seed's genetic blueprint be modified so that the resulting genetic material is no longer "in the form" received from the multilateral system and thus eligible for patent or plant variety protection? Would a new plant variety derived from the genetic material of a seed contained in a CGIAR seed satisfy this standard? Would an isolated and purified gene extracted from such a seed (assuming that it otherwise met the eligibility requirements for a patent)?[98] In answering these questions, what relevance, if any, should be attached to the following "interpretive statement" made by the European Community and its member states when ratifying the ITPGR: "The European Community interprets Article 12.3(d) ... as recognising that plant genetic resources for food and agriculture or their genetic parts or components which have undergone innovation may be the subject of intellectual property rights provided that the criteria relating to such rights are met."[99]

4. What are the links between "farmers' rights" and the right to adequate food? Are farmers' rights a component of the right to food? Related to that right? Should the right to food encompass not only the provision of

---

[96] ITPGR, art. 12.3(d).

[97] Id. art. 12.4; see Charles Lawson, Intellectual Property and the Material Transfer Agreement under the International Treaty on Plant Genetic Resources for Food and Agriculture, 31 EUR. INTELL. PROP. REV. 244 (2009).

[98] For a discussion of the treaty's negotiating history, see HELFER, IPRs IN PLANT VARIETIES, supra note 40, at 87–91.

[99] FAO, International Treaty on Plant Genetic Resources for Food and Agriculture: Declarations, http://www.fao.org/Legal/TREATIES/033s-e.htm (last visited Mar. 31, 2010).

minimum levels of sustenance but also the process by which food is produced, for example, by corporate conglomerates or smallholder farmers? (Recall in this context President Franklin Roosevelt's statement that "freedom from want" includes the "the right of every farmer to raise and sell his products at a return which will give him and his family a decent living.") More generally, do farmers' rights implicate other human rights, such as the right to culture or labor rights?

5. Alternatively, should farmers' rights be understood as a type of intellectual property right analogous to patents and plant variety protection? Do they fit within the rubric of "private rights" referenced in the preamble of the TRIPS Agreement? As described previously, farmers' informal breeding techniques, such as selecting plants on the basis of desirable characteristics, occur incrementally over years or even generations. What challenges does this pose for protecting farmers' rights as a form of intellectual property?

6. If farmers' rights are neither human rights nor intellectual property rights, is the term "farmers' rights" a misnomer? Why would advocates seeking legal recognition of farmers' contributions to plant genetic diversity adopt this phrase? How might existing intellectual property protection rules be modified to give effect to the policy objectives underlying farmers' rights? Note that the funds in the trust account established by the ITPGR will be used in part to promote the conservation of PGRs by farmers in developing countries.

6.3. Specific Controversies Involving the Right to Food and Intellectual Property Protection for PGRs

Having analyzed the legal rules and policy objectives relating to the right to food and intellectual property protection for plant-related innovations, we now turn to a discussion of specific controversies that lie at the intersection of the two legal regimes. We begin with a review of how expert and political bodies within the United Nations human rights system have addressed this intersection and then provide an in-depth analysis of the right to food and genetically modified seeds in India.

A. The Response to Expanding Intellectual Property Protection for PGRs in the United Nations Human Rights System
The expansion of intellectual property protection standards and enforcement mechanisms in the TRIPS Agreement and in other treaties adopted over the last fifteen years has created points of tension with international human rights law, including the right to adequate food. These tensions have existed at least since the establishment of the UPOV in the early 1960s. Prior to the

entry into force of TRIPS, however, they received little attention from the political and expert bodies of the U.N. human rights system.

Several of these political and expert bodies – whose activities include adopting nonbinding declarations, resolutions, recommendations, and reports concerning a vast array of human rights topics – were established under the auspices of the U.N. Charter. Others were created by a specific human rights treaty. Included in the first group are the Commission on Human Rights (replaced in 2006 by the Human Rights Council), the Sub-Commission on the Promotion and Protection of Human Rights (replaced in 2006 by the Human Rights Council Advisory Committee), the U.N. High Commissioner for Human Rights (the High Commissioner), and Special Rapporteurs and working groups. The treaty-based expert body most active in intellectual property issues is the Committee on Economic, Social and Cultural Rights, whose *General Comment* on the right to food is reviewed at the beginning of this chapter. (For additional discussion of the U.N. human rights system, see Chapter 1.)

Several of these political and expert bodies have adopted nonbinding declarations and interpretive statements that analyze the intersection of the right to food and intellectual property protection for plant-related innovations. Attention to these issues first arose in the Sub-Commission. In July 2000, an NGO consortium composed of the Lutheran World Federation, the Habitat International Coalition, and the International NGO Committee on Human Rights in Trade and Investment submitted a document titled "The WTO TRIPS Agreement and Human Rights" to the Chair of the Sub-Commission.[100] The statement contained "forceful language" that directly challenged the compatibility of TRIPS with states' human rights obligations.[101] In debating a subsequent resolution on TRIPS, Sub-Commission members moderated somewhat the tone of their discussions. The final, unanimous resolution they adopted on "Intellectual Property Rights and Human Rights" stated that "actual or potential conflicts exist between the implementation of the TRIPS Agreement and the realization of economic, social and cultural rights."[102] These conflicts cut across a wide swath of legal terrain, including

---

[100] Habitat Int'l Coalition & Lutheran World Fed'n, *The Realization of Economic, Social and Cultural Rights*, 6, U.N. Doc. E/CN.4/Sub.2/2000/NGO/14 (July 28, 2000) (statement submitted to U.N. Comm'n on Human Rights, 52d Sess.) (urging the Sub-Commission to "reassert the primacy of human rights obligations over the commercial and profit-driven motives upon which agreements such as TRIPS are based").

[101] David Weissbrodt & Kell Schoff, *A Human Rights Approach to Intellectual Property Protection: The Genesis and Application of Sub-Commission Resolution 2000/7*, 5 MINN. INTELL. PROP. REV. 1 (2003).

[102] ECOSOC, Sub-Comm'n on the Promotion and Protection of Human Rights, Res. 2000/7, at 2, U.N. Doc. E/CN.4/Sub.2/2000/L.20 (Aug. 11, 2000) [2000 Sub-Comm'n IP Resolution].

"the consequences for the enjoyment of the right to food of plant variety rights and the patenting of genetically modified organisms, 'bio-piracy' and the reduction of communities' (especially indigenous communities') control over their own genetic and natural resources and cultural values."[103] To address these conflicts, the Sub-Commission requested four different sets of actors – national governments, intergovernmental organizations, U.N. human rights bodies, and NGOs – to analyze the intersection of human rights and intellectual property and to recognize "the primacy of human rights obligations over economic policies and agreements."[104]

U.N. human rights bodies responded to the Sub-Commission's invitation by devoting increased attention to intellectual property issues, including the relationship between plant-related innovations and the right to food. For example, the Committee on Economic, Social and Cultural Rights, in its 2005 *General Comment No. 17* on creators' human rights analyzed in detail in Chapter 3, stated:

> States parties should ... ensure that their legal or other regimes for the protection of the moral and material interests resulting from one's scientific, literary or artistic productions constitute no impediment to their ability to comply with their core obligations in relation to ... the right[] to food.... States parties thus have a duty to prevent unreasonably high costs for access to ... plant seeds or other means of food production ... from undermining the rights of large segments of the population to ... food.[105]

This passage from the *General Comment* considers intellectual property as a limitation on the right to food only with regard to the royalties that farmers (and, eventually, consumers) pay to purchase seeds and plant materials. By contrast, statements by Special Rapporteur on the Right to Food Jean Ziegler engage more directly with intellectual property protection for plants and seeds.[106] In a 2001 report, the Special Rapporteur noted

> the problem of patents taken out by northern multinational [corporations] on plants growing in the south and the related question of the universal protection given to such patents by the WTO. The right to food implies not only

---

[103] *Id.; see also id.* para. 2 (noting conflicts between TRIPS and, *inter alia*, "the right to food").

[104] *Id.* para. 3.

[105] U.N. Comm. on Econ., Soc. & Cultural Rights, *General Comment No. 17: The Right of Everyone to Benefit from the Protection of the Moral and Material Interests Resulting from Any Scientific, Literary or Artistic Production of Which He Is the Author*, art. 15(1)(c), para. 35, U.N. Doc. E/C.12/GC/17 (Jan. 12, 2006) [*General Comment No. 17*].

[106] In a 2001 resolution, the Sub-Commission requested the Special Rapporteur "to include in [his] reports a review of the implication of the TRIPS Agreement for the realization of the rights falling within [his] mandate." ECOSOC, Sub-Comm'n on the Promotion and Protection of Human Rights, Res. 2001/21, *Intellectual Property and Human Rights*, para. 12, U.N. Doc. E/CN.4/Sub.2/RES/2001/21 (Aug. 16, 2001).

access to food, but also access to the means of producing it. International patents held by northern multinationals, combined with their universal protection and [TRIPS], deprive poor farmers of access to the means of growing their food.[107]

Similarly, in a 2003 report analyzing transnational corporations and the right to food, the Special Rapporteur stated that he had received numerous requests from public interest NGOs

> to examine the human rights obligations of transnational corporations in the context of their increasing control of the food sector, from production to the processing and marketing of food. For example, many [NGOs] raised concerns regarding increasing concentration in and monopoly control over the global market for agricultural seed, in particular the genetically modified seed market, which is dominated by the Monsanto corporation. Although it is generally agreed that genetically modified seeds can in some conditions bring higher yields, NGOs are concerned that increasing control over seeds by a few agroalimentary corporations will eventually reduce competition, reduce choice and may lead to higher prices for seeds. Many organizations ... are also concerned that current biotechnology research is driven by commercial imperatives and does not focus on the food security needs of the poorest.[108]

Special Rapporteur Ziegler continued this theme in his 2004 report:

> NGOs and farmers are particularly concerned about technologies that prevent seeds from regenerating and the use of intellectual property rights over seeds, which require farmers to purchase new seeds every year, threatening their independence and capacity to generate their own seed stocks. A marked paradigm shift has occurred from a system seeking to foster food security on the basis of the free exchange of knowledge, to a system seeking to achieve the same goal on the basis of the private appropriation of knowledge.... The Special Rapporteur believes that whilst the patent rights of corporations must be protected, the rights of small farmers must also be protected.[109]

Olivier De Schutter, appointed by the Human Rights Council in 2008 to replace Jean Ziegler as the Special Rapporteur on the Right to Food, has continued to emphasize the relationship between the right to food and intellectual property protection for plant-related innovations. In a speech delivered at the High-Level Conference on World Food Security at FAO in June 2008, De Schutter stated:

> One specific concern ... related to the role of the private sector ... is the potential obstacle strong patent rights may represent for the availability of

---

[107] Special Rapporteur, *2001 Right to Food Report, supra* 33, para. 73.
[108] U.N. Special Rapporteur on the Right to Food, *Report to U.N. General Assembly*, para. 29, U.N. Doc. A/58/330 (Aug. 28, 2003) (prepared by Jean Ziegler).
[109] U.N. Special Rapporteur on the Right to Food, *Report on the Right to Food*, para. 39, U.N. Doc. E/CN.4/2004/10 (Feb. 9, 2004) (prepared by Jean Ziegler).

quality seed. Many developing countries are facing a critical shortage of quality seed. Wherever necessary, consistent with Article 15 of the [ICESCR] and *General Comment No. 17*, . . . a balance may have to be struck between the intellectual property rights of corporations holding patents on seeds, and the need to ensure that agricultural inputs remain affordable for smallhold farmers and that they receive a fair remuneration from their work.[110]

A more comprehensive treatment of these issues appeared in the Special Rapporteur's 2009 report to the U.N. General Assembly, titled *Seed Policies and the Right to Food: Enhancing Agrobiodiversity, Encouraging Innovation.*[111] Analyzing the relationship between commercial and informal seed systems in the context of the right to food, the Special Rapporteur stated:

> These obligations [to respect, protect, and fulfill the right to food] apply both to the regulation of commercial seed systems and to the preservation and enhancement of informal or traditional farmers' seed systems. The separation of seed production and improvement from farming and the emergence of biotechnologies has led to a commercial seed system on which farmers are increasingly dependent. That system has to be regulated in order to ensure that farmers have access to inputs on conditions which are reasonable, thus helping them to achieve an adequate standard of living; and [it] should ensure that the innovations leading to improved varieties and to new plant resources benefit all farmers, including the most vulnerable and marginalized among them. This follows both from article 11(2)(a) of the [ICESCR, which imposes on States parties an obligation "to improve methods of production . . . of food by making full use of technical and scientific knowledge"]; and from the right of everyone to enjoy the benefits of scientific progress and its applications, recognized in Article 15, para. 1 (b) of the Covenant, which could be relied upon in order to justify recognizing a right of access of farmers to seeds which are not in open access. But States also should ensure that informal, non-commercial seed systems can develop: they should not interfere with such systems without adequate justification; they should protect such systems from interference by third parties; and they should proactively ensure that these systems can expand, despite the pressure imposed by the commercial seed system. Only a balanced approach between these two sets of obligations will ensure that the farmers will be in a position to make a fully free and informed choice between these systems, which are alternative ways for them to pursue their livelihoods.[112]

---

[110] Olivier De Schutter, U.N. Special Rapporteur on the Right to Food, Address at High-Level Conference on World Food Security: *The Challenges of Climate Change and Bioenergy* (June 3–5, 2008).

[111] U.N. Special Rapporteur on the Right to Food, *Report to U.N. General Assembly*, U.N. Doc. A/64/170 (July 23, 2009) (prepared by Olivier De Schutter) [Special Rapporteur, 2009 Right to Food Report].

[112] *Id.* para. 7.

The Special Rapporteur also criticized "the current intellectual property rights regime [as] suboptimal to ensure global food security today."[113] To remedy this situation so as to ensure that intellectual property rights and national seed policies are "compatible with and conducive to the realization of the right to adequate food," the Special Rapporteur recommended that all states, *inter alia*:

- Make swift progress towards the implementation of farmers' rights defined in article 9 of the [ITPGR] ...;
- Consider using antitrust legislation in order to combat ... [the] abuse of dominant position by ... seed companies [by] the setting of prices at levels which may be unjustifiably high and unaffordable to poor farmers;
- [For countries] that "have not implemented the TRIPS Agreement yet, prepare right-to-food impact assessments prior to doing so....;
- Ensure that protection of patent-holders or plant breeders' rights does not discourage innovation in the name of rewarding it, by introducing barriers to the use of patented material. In particular, States should not allow patents on plants and should establish research exemptions in legislation protecting plant breeders' rights. If States do allow patents on plants, they should establish research exemptions based on article 30 of [TRIPS];

...

- [E]ncourage innovative mechanisms such as patent pools, clearing houses and open source experiments in order to overcome barriers to research on patented material ...;

...

- Put in place mechanisms ensuring the active participation of farmers in decisions related to the conservation and sustainable use of plant genetic resources ...;
- Increase the resources allocated to public agricultural research and create new incentives for the private sector, in order to encourage research into the crops that benefit poor farmers in developing countries.[114]

---

[113] Press release, Current Intellectual Property Rights Regime Suboptimal for Global Food Security, According to U.N. Expert on Food, (Oct. 21, 2009), *available at* http://www2. ohchr.org/english/issues/food/docs/GA_press_release_21102009.pdf.

[114] U.N. Special Rapporteur on the Right to Food, *Seed Policies and the Right to Food: Enhancing Agrobiodiversity and Encouraging Innovation, Interim Report Delivered to the General Assembly*, U.N. Doc. A/64/170 (July 23, 2009).

Notes and Questions

1. How do the U.N. human rights bodies characterize the relationship between the right to food and intellectual property protection for new plant varieties? Do they view the two fields as in conflict or as attempting to achieve complementary goals? How, if at all, have the views of these bodies evolved over time? Consider the following statement by Hans Morten Haugen:

> Neither the WTO Agreement nor the TRIPS Agreement prevents any State from adopting legislation or measures to safeguard the interests of the marginalized people involved in agriculture. Rather, the fact that issues like farmers' rights or traditional or community intellectual property rights were not subject to TRIPS negotiations, implies that States are free to adopt legislation in these areas. They can also adopt any relevant measure in order to ensure the realization of the right to food. The only condition is that these laws or measures do not negatively affect the realization of TRIPS, meaning that the TRIPS provisions cannot be given effect.
>
> . . .
>
> The requirement in Article 2.1 of the [ICESCR] that States shall "take steps" "through all appropriate means" and "to the maximum of its available resources" could be more difficult to implement for technology-poor developing countries, as the implementation of TRIPS might affect their available resources – at least in the short term.... Moreover, for developing countries, the substantive requirements of the TRIPS Agreement imply that these countries are obliged to implement patent protection before their economic and technical capacity would naturally foster the adoption of legislation for such protection. The implementation of the TRIPS provisions might [therefore] divert attention and resources away from implementing the rights of the [ICESCR] as expeditiously and effectively as possible. More difficult implementation is not a precondition for identifying treaty conflict, however.[115]

Is this statement consistent with the analysis of the Special Rapporteurs discussed previously?

2. Most food and feed crops grown by small-scale farmers in developing countries are not protected by patents or plant breeders' rights. As a result, these farmers are free to save and exchange seeds and to select crops with beneficial qualities for informal breeding and replanting. Does the widespread availability of these crops undermine the concern that small-scale farmers will become dependent on commercial seed varieties protected by intellectual property rights? Such farmers are not, after all, required to purchase the seed lines marketed by multinational corporations. In considering

---

[115] HAUGEN, *supra* note 3, at 437, 442.

your answer to this question, review the following statement by the Special Rapporteur on the Right to Food:

> The standard argument ... is that farmers are not obliged to purchase plant variety protection (PVP)-protected seed just because it is made available. This, however, presupposes that farmers have real alternatives to acquiring their seed from the commercial system. Yet the coexistence between farmers' seed systems – operating at local or community levels between farmers, and mostly informal – and commercial seed systems is sometimes problematic. Public authorities have supported the expansion of commercial seeds not only through plant variety protection schemes, but also through the use of input subsidies and via the diffusion of selected seeds in rural extension networks. Farmers often receive commercial varieties as part of a package that includes credit (often vouchers), seed, fertilizer and pesticide. In many cases, acceptance of such packages is the only way farmers can access credit in rural areas. They need to accept the whole package in order to do so. In addition, traditional varieties [cultivated by farmers] are often excluded from government-approved seed lists that countries maintain under their seed regulations, and they are seldom included in seed distribution programmes subsidized by governments. The end result is a progressive marginalization or disappearance of local varieties.[116]

Are you persuaded by the Special Rapporteur's response? What additional information might help you to determine whether the informal, noncommercial seed systems used by small-scale farmers in developing countries are threatened by the distribution of commercial seed varieties protected by intellectual property rights?

3. World wide expenditures for agricultural research and development (R&D) totalled $40 billion in 2000, the latest year for which global aggregate data are available. Of this amount, $23 billion was funded by governments and $17 billion was funded by the private sector. Industrialized and high-income countries accounted for 57 percent of government-funded agricultural research worldwide, with Brazil, China, and India accounting for 43 percent of the remaining public expenditures by developing countries.[117] The global statistics for private agricultural R&D are more skewed. Private firms accounted for roughly one-third of the $40 billion invested in agricultural research worldwide. But little of this research took place in developing countries. "The overwhelming majority ($12.6 billion, or 91 percent of the global total) was conducted in developed countries. In the less-developed countries,

---

[116] Special Rapporteur, 2009 Right to Food Report, *supra* note 111, para. 36.

[117] Ruben G. Echeverria & Nienke M. Beinteme, *Mobilizing Financial Resources for Agricultural Research in Developing Countries, Trends and Mechanisms*, 4–8 (Global Forum on Agricultural Research, June 2009), *available at* http://www.fao.org/docs/eims/upload//261898/mobilizing%20financial%20resources%20for%20AR4D.pdf.

where public funds are still the major source of support, the private share of research was just 8.3 percent."[118]

4. Consider the following two statements concerning "spillovers" of agricultural research and technologies across national borders:

The history of agricultural development shows that agricultural technology need not be home-grown; over the years it has been bought, borrowed, and stolen. For instance, in the late 18th century, Thomas Jefferson, risking the death penalty, smuggled rice seeds out of Italy in the lining of his coat to encourage cultivation of the crop in South Carolina. Agricultural innovations move across borders, both by design and by accident. These technology spillovers imply both international market failures and a case for multinational government action to correct them.[119]

. . .

Spillovers of results from public agricultural R&D across geopolitical boundaries are positive externalities that give rise to distortions in incentives to undertake certain types of research.... Spillovers mean lower benefits to the innovating country as well as innovator benefits being less than global benefits. For example, innovations in the California almond industry might well give rise to a lower world price of almonds, which diminishes the benefits to California from its innovations (redistributing them towards interstate or international consumers). This effect is even greater if other countries such as Australia and Spain also can adopt the new technology, exacerbating the price-depressing effect. As California does not count the benefits (or costs) to overseas (or even interstate) producers and consumers, it will underinvest in almond research from a global standpoint.[120]

What relevance do these statements have for the relationship between the human right to food and intellectual property protection for plant-related innovations? Do the statements identify a rationale for stronger intellectual property protection, or, conversely, do they suggest the need to reduce such protection to encourage transborder flows of research relating to agrobiotechnology? More specifically, what relevance, if any, do Thomas Jefferson's actions in the eighteenth century have to contemporary debates about intellectual property protection for plant genetic resources for food and agriculture?

5. According to some commentators,[121] developing countries have long benefited from spillovers of agricultural technologies from industrialized

---

[118] Julian M. Alston & Philip G. Pardey, *Developing-Country Perspectives on Agricultural R&D: New Pressures for Self-Reliance?*, in PHILIP G. PARDEY ET AL. (EDS.), AGRICULTURAL R&D IN THE DEVELOPING WORLD: TOO LITTLE, TOO LATE? 11, 20 (2006).

[119] *Id.* at 16.

[120] Julian M. Alston, *Spillovers*, 48 AUSTL. J. AGRIC. & RESOURCE ECON. 315, 333–34 (2002).

[121] Alston & Pardey, *supra* note 118, at 24–25.

nations. Such reliance may be decreasing as a result of three interrelated developments:

- The types of technologies being developed in the rich countries may no longer be as readily applicable to less-developed countries as they were in the past: the agenda in richer countries is shifting away from areas like yield improvement in major crops to other crop characteristics and even to nonagricultural production concerns like health and nutrition and the environment.
- Applicable technologies developed in richer countries may not be as readily accessible because of intellectual-property protection of privately owned technologies: many biotech companies have little or no interest in developing technologies for less-developed country applications; and even where they have such technologies available, they are often not interested in pursuing potential markets in less developed countries, for a host of reasons.
- Those technologies that are applicable and available are likely to require more substantial local development and adaptation, which call for more sophisticated and more extensive forms of scientific research and development than in the past: for instance, more advanced skills in modern biotechnology or conventional breeding may be required to take advantage of enabling technologies or simply to make use of less-finished [plant] lines that must be tailored to local production environments.[122]

If the preceding predictions are accurate, do they provide a basis for revising plant patent and plant variety protection rules? What revisions would you favor and why?

B. Genetically Modified Seeds and the Right to Food in India

In this section, we consider the intersection of intellectual property protection for plant-related innovations and the human right to food in India. Since the mid-1990s, both intellectual property and human rights have assumed greater salience for India's government and its large and rapidly expanding population. We first review recent legal and policy developments and then raise issues and questions for further analysis.

1. The Protection of Plant Varieties and Farmers' Rights Act, 2001, and the Seeds Bill, 2004

India has been a member of the WTO since the organization's inception, and the country's entertainment, pharmaceutical, software, and agriculture

---

[122] *Id.*

industries are increasingly seeking intellectual property protection for their creative works and inventions.[123] With regard to plant-related innovations, India has attempted to satisfy its obligations under the TRIPS Agreement by enacting the Protection of Plant Varieties & Farmers Rights Act, 2001 (PPVFA)[124] and by proposing new legislation, the Seeds Bill, 2004.[125] The aim of both statutes is to establish an "effective *sui generis* system" for new plant varieties that both satisfies the requirements of TRIPS Article 27.3(b) and balances the interests of commercial plant breeders, farmers, and indigenous communities. The following article summarizes the key provisions of both laws.

Srividhya Ragavan & Jamie Mayer O'Shields, *Has India Addressed Its Farmers' Woes? A Story of Plant Protection Issues*, 20 Geo. Int'l Envtl. L. Rev. 97, 113–21, 124–26 (2007)

. . .

A. The Effectiveness of India's Protection of Plant Varieties & the 2004 Farmers' Rights Act

The central tenet of the PPVFA is to address India's national concerns about protecting the rights of traditional farming communities, while at the same time promoting plant breeding by vesting intellectual property protection. Thus, the PPVFA lumps plant varieties into three protectable categories: (a) New Varieties, (b) Extant Varieties, which refer to existing varieties discovered for the first time, and (c) Farmers' Varieties, based on community property concepts....

1. New Variety
A variety is eligible for protection provided it is novel, distinct, uniform, and stable. The[se] requirement[s ... are] similar to UPOV.

---

[123] *See, e.g.,* Ayan Roy Chowdhury, *The Future of Copyright in India*, 3 J. Intell. Prop. L. & Prac. 102 (2008); Janice M. Mueller, *The Tiger Awakens: The Tumultuous Transformation of India's Patent System and the Rise of Indian Pharmaceutical Innovation*, 68 U. Pitt. L. Rev. 491 (2007); Janice M. Mueller, *Biotechnology Patenting in India: Will Bio-Generics Lead a "Sunrise" Industry to Bio-Innovation?*, 76 UMKC L. Rev. 437 (2007).

[124] The Protection of Plant Varieties and Farmers' Rights Act, No. 53 of 2001, India Code (2001), *available at* http://indiacode.nic.in/fullact1.asp?tfnm=200153 [PPVFA].

[125] The Seeds Bill, 2004, No. 52, Acts of Parliament, 2004 [Seeds Bill, 2004]. The Indian cabinet approved amendments to the bill in June 2008. *New Seeds Bill Seeks a Quality Harvest*, Economic Times (India), June 27, 2008. The amendments regulate the quality of seeds and planting materials to ensure availability to farmers and to prevent the sale of spurious and poor quality seeds. *Id.* The text of the 2008 amendments is not yet publicly available.

The distinction of PPVFA lies in the registration regime, which enables protection for new varieties while at the same time recognizing the role of local farmers. For instance, every application for registration must include a denomination of the variety and describe (1) the geographical origin of the material, and (2) all information regarding the contribution of the farmer, community, or organization in the development of the variety. Further, the application must state that all genetic or parental material used to develop the variety has been lawfully acquired. Moreover, section 40 requires the breeder to disclose information "regarding the use of genetic material conserved by any tribal or rural families in the breeding or development of such [new] variety." The information in the application is meant to facilitate benefit sharing, a system discussed below, introduced to protect farmers rights. Unlike UPOV, the PPVFA bears a set of public interest exceptions to registration of a new variety. A new variety, for instance, becomes unregisterable if it is likely to deceive the public, hurt the religious sentiments of any class or section of Indians, or cause confusion regarding the variety's identity....

While the farmer's role is protected by the benefit sharing arrangement, the breeders' rights are protected using a combination of exclusive rights and harsh penalties for infringement. The owner-breeder retains exclusive commercial rights over the variety, once registered, including licensing, production, sales, marketing, distribution, and importing and exporting. The statute tries to deter infringement by providing stringent penalties, at rupees 50,000 (roughly US $1400) or imprisonment for a minimum of three months, which is also meant to offer breeders the incentive to innovate without fear of infringement.

2. Extant Variety

The introduction of farmers' variety and extant variety is meant to balance breeders' rights with rights of other players in agricultural trade. The *extant variety* typology itself was introduced to protect traditional knowledge and indigenous rights. The extant variety register serves as a compilation of matters known and existing in the public domain. In essence, an extant variety encompasses a farmers' variety, or a variety about which there is common knowledge....

Considering that the extant variety register is a log of materials in the public domain, the registration requirements are not rigorous. For instance, extant varieties need not be novel, although the requirements of distinctiveness, uniformity, and stability are regulated by administrative notifications. By making farmers' variety a subset of extant variety, the PPVFA encourages farmers to register varieties they have cultivated for years to ensure that they are not appropriated. . . .

An extant variety may be registered by a breeder, farmer, a community of farmers, a university, or a public sector. Although a breeder can register an extant variety, he is not entitled to exclusive rights over the variety. Section 28 of the Act provides that the Government, as the owner of the extant varieties, enjoys the rights to determine their production, sale, marketability, distribution, importation or exportation. The objective is to protect biodiversity by empowering the government to negotiate with entities that require biodiversity materials for creating biotechnology innovations. . . .

3. Farmers' Variety

The PPVFA defines "farmers" from a community rights perspective as those who "cultivate crops by cultivating the land," and those who supervise cultivation directly or indirectly through other people, or anyone who "conserves and preserves, severally or jointly, with any other person ... through selection and identification of their useful properties."

A "farmers' variety" is one "which has been traditionally cultivated and evolved by the farmers in their fields, or is a wild relative or land race of a variety about which the farmers posses the common knowledge." The emphasis on common knowledge strengthens community rights – a concept ignored by UPOV. . . .

The manner of stylizing protection of farmers' variety reflects a keen sense of consideration for community and traditional rights by including provisions for benefit sharing, community compensation, immunity from prosecution for innocent infringement, and the creation of a Gene Fund to collect breeders' annual fees. Each of the rights ... not only represents a deviation from UPOV, but also showcases rights contoured to suit unique national conditions.

. . .

4. Other Deviations from UPOV

The most significant features of the PPVFA lie in areas where it deviates from UPOV. As discussed below, these deviations contribute toward increasing the effectiveness of PPVFA.

a. Protecting Biodiversity

The PPVFA emphasizes traditional farming practices to protect biodiversity. Farmers are encouraged under the statute to conserve and improve genetic land resources. The statute establishes a Gene Fund to reward farmers whose existing variety or material is used as a source to create a new variety. The Gene Fund is a common fund created by the Central Government for the benefit of the farmers. Monies collected as royalties, funds collected towards benefit sharing, and other sums that become due to farmers will be credited into the Gene Fund. The Central government will use the fund towards "expenditures for supporting the conservation and sustainable use of genetic resources including in-situ and ex-situ collections and for strengthening the capability of [villages] for carrying out such projects."

. . .

b. Right to Resow

The PPVFA's *sui generis* stamp is showcased by allowing farmers to retain their traditional right to save and re-use seeds from their harvests. A farmer may "save, use, sow, re-sow, exchange, share or sell his produce" including non-branded seed, even if it is a protected variety. With a view to facilitating the use of the right by farmers, section 18 further specifies that every application for a new variety be submitted along with an affidavit swearing that the protected variety does not contain any gene or gene sequence involving terminator technology. The caveat to re-saving is that the farmer cannot use the breeder's brand name when reselling second generation produce....

. . .

d. Benefit Sharing

"Benefit sharing" refers to the concept of sharing a proportion of the benefits accruing to a breeder of a new variety with qualifying claimants who could be indigenous groups, individuals, or communities. The concept of benefit sharing is close to the community rights concept detailed above. The statute mandates that before registering any new variety, the statutory authority should invite claims for benefit sharing. Persons or groups can respond based on two criteria: a) the extent and/or nature of use of genetic material in the development of the new variety, and b) the commercial utility and demand in the market of the new variety. Only citizens of India or firms or organizations formed or established in India are eligible to claim benefits.

. . .

e. Compensation for Spurious Seed

To protect farmers from overly optimistic breeders, the Act requires breeders to disclose the expected performance. Should the varieties fail to perform as disclosed, farmers, as consumers, may seek compensation from the breeder.

A statutory authority determines whether the breeder has made spurious claims, and thus, whether the farmer is entitled to compensation. The objective is to ensure that quality is not compromised in the zeal to market new varieties....

...

B. The Seeds Bill, [2004]

[With a view to compliment the PPVFA, the Ministry of Agriculture introduced a Seeds Bill ... to encourage seed trade, to promote the seed industry, boost exports, and protect seed quality.]

...

The Bill requires commercial producers and dealers of seed to register all marketable seed.... The problem is, since there is no requirement for disclosure of the status of the protected seeds, when the Seeds Bill interacts with the PPVFA, farmers may not know that some of branded seeds are not protected by intellectual property rights. If they are not aware of the status as protected or otherwise, farmers may avoid brown bagging seeds that are in fact in the public domain.

Furthermore, the Bill requires all dealers of seeds to be registered. Generally, over 80% of all seed used in India is grown, saved, stored, exchanged and bartered by local farmers. Considering that dealing with seeds was considered a natural right of farmers for centuries, the Seed Bill may be unsuccessful in getting all small farmers to register.[126]

The Seeds Bill's biggest flaw is that it has not been fully harmonized with the PPVFA. The bill does not take into account the complexities that result from the benefit sharing arrangements proposed by the PPVFA. Hence, the bill has not fully addressed the issue of whether registered seeds of an existing variety and farmers' variety can be sold without sharing the benefits with

---

[126] The scope of the Seeds Bill's registration provision is somewhat uncertain. Section 1(3) of the bill states that, except as otherwise provided, the statute shall apply to "every producer of seed except when the seed is produced by him for his own use and not for sale." Section 22.1, in turn, provides that "every person who desires to carry on the business of selling, keeping for sale, offering to sell, bartering, import or export or otherwise supply any seed by himself, or by any other person on his behalf must be registered as a dealer." However, Section 43.1 limits the scope of the registration requirement in the following terms: "Nothing in this Act shall restrict the right of the farmer to save, use, exchange, share or sell his farm seeds and planting material, except that he shall not sell such seed or planting material under a brand name or which does not conform to the minimum limit of germination, physical purity, genetic purity prescribed" by procedures set forth elsewhere in the statute. Seeds Bill 2004, *supra* note 125.

the community or the farmers. Similarly, the Seeds Bill, unlike the PPVFA, does not embody a provision for pre-grant opposition to register seeds.

As for public interest exceptions, the bill specifies that registration may be refused or cancelled in the public interest. The bill, however, lacks a provision to control price and regulate supply of seeds under public interest conditions, unlike the PPVFA which has a relatively detailed compulsory licensing provision. Moreover, the bill provides for a possible maximum term of 36 years of protection. Although registration under the bill does not grant any intellectual property protection, it confers the right to market the seed. Considering this, a 36 year period of market protection … seems egregious.

· · ·

In short, the Seeds Bill is a shoddy piece of legislation that fails to tie in several aspects of the Seed trade with the PPVFA. To the extent that one of the objectives of the Seeds Bill is to maintain a balance between farmers and breeders, the provision fails for want of clarity. The Seed Bill creates an unnecessary parallel system of registration along with the PPVFA. Creating a parallel system can result in negating the entitlements and protections previously granted to farmers under the PPVFA.

----

2. Constitutional Protection of the Right to Food and the Review of India's 2008 Report to the Committee on Economic, Social and Cultural Rights

The human right to food occupies a prominent place in Indian society. More than two thirds of India's inhabitants live in rural areas and depend on agriculture for their livelihoods.[127] Improvements in production and distribution of foodstuffs over the past several decades have ended the famines that once plagued the country. By the government's own admission, however, these improvements have "had only a marginal effect on the chronic hunger and malnutrition prevailing in some parts of the country among some social groups," the most vulnerable of whom include "women across income groups, children, [and] rural landless poor."[128]

---

[127] Special Rapporteur on the Right to Food, *Mission to India*, para. 5, *Report to ECOSOC Comm'n on Human Rights*, U.N. Doc. E/CN.4/2006/44/Add.2 (Mar. 20, 2006) (prepared by Jean Ziegler) [Special Rapporteur, *Mission to India*].

[128] ECOSOC, *Implementation of the International Covenant on Economic, Social and Cultural Rights: Periodic Reports Submitted by States Parties under Articles 16 and 17 of the Covenant, Combined Second, Third, Fourth and Fifth Periodic Report of India*, para. 352, U.N. Doc. E/C.12/IND/5 (May 1, 2007) (*prepared by* India) [India ICESCR Report].

The Supreme Court of India has responded to these problems by recognizing the right to food as a component of the right to life protected by the Indian Constitution and enforceable through domestic litigation. As the Special Rapporteur on the Right to Food explained in a report describing the results of his mission to India in 2005:

> In the year 2000 the press reported on people dying from starvation, especially in the drought-stricken regions of Rajasthan, while food rotted in the government storage facilities. Reports suggested that food was being thrown into the sea or exported internationally at highly subsidized prices to reduce storage costs rather than being distributed to the hungry and starving. With growing public outrage at the paradox of starvation amidst overflowing foodstocks, this led to a ground-breaking public interest litigation being launched by People's Union for Civil Liberties (PUCL) against the Government before India's Supreme Court. PUCL petition argued that the right to food was part of the right to life of all Indian citizens and demanded that the country's food stocks be used without delay to prevent hunger and starvation. Interim orders of the Supreme Court ordered assistance be extended to those at risk of starvation. It ordered the full implementation of all the food-based schemes across India.... This landmark case has brought the issue of the right to food as a human right back into public debate.[129]

The right to food also featured prominently in the 2008 review of India's report to the Committee on Economic, Social and Cultural Rights.[130] The report analyzed in detail the achievements and shortcomings of the country's food and agricultural systems. As part of that analysis, the government credited the PPVFA as "taking a big step forward. The Act recognizes the role of farmers as cultivators and conservers and the contributors of traditional, rural and tribal communities to the country's biodiversity and food security by listing the farmer's rights in a separate chapter."[131] The report also included a brief reference to the Seeds Bill, 2004 as part of India's other initiatives to secure the right to food,[132] and it noted that an amendment to the Patents Act,

---

[129] Special Rapporteur, *Mission to India, supra* note 128, para. 16 (analyzing *People's Union for Civil Liberties v. Union of India*, Writ Petition (Civil) No. 196 of 2001 (India May 2, 2003) (interim order), *available at* http://www.escr-net.org/usr_doc/Interim_Order_of_May_2.doc).

[130] Article 16 of the ICESCR requires states parties to submit reports describing "the measures which they have adopted and the progress made in achieving the observance of the rights recognized herein." A discussion of the state reporting process of U.N. human rights treaties appears in Chapter 1.

[131] India ICESCR Report, *supra* note 128, para. 393; *see also id.* para. 777 (stating that the PPVFA "gives rights to farmer entitling them [to] benefit sharing for the use of bio-diversity conserved by the farming community").

[132] *Id.* para. 394.

1970 had been proposed "to provide for product patents in food products ... to comply with the WTO-TRIPS regime."[133]

Several NGOs submitted information to the ICESCR Committee in response to India's report. Included among them was the following submission from "Trade – Human Rights – Equitable Economy (3D)," a not-for-profit organization based in Geneva, Switzerland that aims to develop trade, intellectual property, and economic policies that are consistent with human rights. 3D's submission analyzed the consequences of Indian farmers' widespread adoption of Bt cotton, a genetically engineered cotton variety developed by Monsanto, a U.S.-based agrobiotechnology firm, that reduces or eliminates the need to spray cotton plants for bollworms.[134]

Trade – Human Rights – Equitable Economy (3D), Trade-Related Intellectual Property Rights, Livelihoods and the Right to Food – India 3–4 (Mar. 2008) http://www.3dthree.org/pdf_3D/3DIndiaIPfoodCESCR2008.pdf

. . .

In paragraph 351 of its report to the [ICESCR] Committee, India notes that it has taken a range of measures to promote self-sufficiency in the production of food grains. These efforts could be undermined if the country permits concentration of seeds sales in the hands of a few companies instead of facilitating the saving, exchanging and re-sowing of seeds by farmers themselves.

Genetically Modified Seeds and Farmer Suicides

This concentration of seeds in a few hands can already be witnessed. Monsanto has patents over GM [genetically modified] cotton all over the world and they own the patent on Bt cotton. Monsanto in partnership with Indian based Mahyco company is the owner of the four varieties of Bt cotton approved for use in India. The company asserted that the Bt variety of cotton seed can result in higher yield than the hybrid indigenous variety of cotton

---

[133] *Id.* para. 520. The amendments later were later codified in the India Patent Act (2005), a statute that includes many of the flexibilities in TRIPS to tailor international patent rules to the country's innovation needs. For an insightful analysis of the act and its application to patented medicines, *see* Amy Kapczynski, *Harmonization and Its Discontents: A Case Study of TRIPS Implementation in India's Pharmaceutical Sector*, 97 CAL. L. REV. 1571 (2009).

[134] Monsanto created the variety by introducing the *Bacillus thuringiensis* (Bt) gene into an existing variety of cotton. The new variety produces a toxin that kills bollworm larvae and prevents them from feeding on the plants. The Intellectual Property Office (India) granted two patents covering Bt cotton in 2000. Anitha Ramanna, *Bt Cotton and India's Policy on IPRs*, 7 ASIAN BIOTECH. & DEV. REV. 43, 44–50 (2005).

seeds. Further, Monsanto said that by using Bt cotton variety farmers may no longer have to expend on spraying pesticides to ward off pests and this in turn would save them significant costs. Thus, cotton farmers in India shifted gradually to Bt cotton variety.

Initially Bt variety – planted since 2002 in some parts of India – resulted in higher yield. Consequently more Indian farmers took to Bt variety of cotton seeds. In 2005, approximately 1.26 million hectares was under Bt cotton cultivation and as per the central government estimation, in 2006 nearly 3.28 million hectares were under Bt cotton cultivation. But with the Bt variety of cotton seeds, farmers could no longer save seeds and resow them on their lands. The farmers had to buy new cotton seeds from Mahyco-Monsanto each year at a price fixed by the company, and that price has gone up.[135] Mahyco Monsanto Biotech is now charging 1850 Rs. [Rupees] per 450 gram pack of Bt cotton seeds as compared to Rs. 38 charged in China for the same quantity. In India, the price for non-Bt cotton variety is at Rs. 450 to 500.

As more and more farmers began to use Bt cotton seeds from Monsanto, they were no longer left with their own indigenous variety of cotton seeds. And as a result of increased demand for Bt cotton variety, seed dealers have moved to sell more Bt cotton seeds than local or non-Bt variety of cotton, thus reducing the options for farmers, and jeopardizing long-term biological diversity.

While Bt variety of cotton seeds resulted in high yield in the initial years of its introduction, the yields gradually started to taper off and failed miserably in later years. The main reason for this is that Bt cotton seeds were not suited to varied weather conditions prevalent in India. Further the Bt cotton variety in the long run resulted in higher use of pesticides as it was unable to ward off the various pests that infest the cotton plants in India: throughout the country, Bt cotton crops have been attacked by "Lalya" or "reddening," a disease unseen before, which affected the GM acreage more than the non-Bt cotton crop. This resulted in a vast majority of cotton farmers spending substantial amount of money buying seeds and pesticides. According to a study, in the recent years, the gross margin for non-Bt farmers worked out to be Rs. 10,880 per hectare, while the margin for Bt farmers was merely Rs. 1435.

---

[135] [The price of Bt cotton seeds includes a "technology fee" that is based on a location-specific calculation of the cost savings to farmers from reduced pesticide use. Rhea Gala, *GM Cotton Fiascos around the World* (Inst. of Sci. in Soc'y, Report Jan. 26, 2005), *available at* http://www.i-sis.org.uk/GMCFATW.php. Increases in the technology fee prompted three state governments in India to limit the sales price of the company's genetically modified seeds. Manoj Mitta, *3 States Fix Price of Monsanto's Bt Cotton Seeds*, TIMES OF INDIA, June 1, 2006.—Eds.]

Besides, controlling the price of patented transgenic seeds, companies selling GM seeds typically require farmers to sign an agreement with the company.[136] Such agreements contain provisions that allow the farmer to use only the company-prescribed fertilizer in order to get a good yield and may also prohibit the farmer from saving and re-sowing the transgenic seeds.... This increased cost of seeds and restrictive agreements could impact agriculture and may in general affect access to food. The already poor rural farmers are further impoverished as they are driven into debt from trying to adopt farming inputs, paying royalties to the seed companies and buying seed each year.

The failure or low yield coupled with high input costs has left farmers in a debt trap and with reduced income, thereby affecting their income levels and access to adequate food. As a result of the high price of Bt cotton seeds and the failure of Bt cotton in various parts of India, thousands of farmers have committed suicide in the last few years.

A new development is particularly worrying: India has recently allowed field trials of GM varieties of rice, brinjal and groundnut. In addition to individual suffering, experience with GM seeds so far in India visibly undermines traditional agriculture, impedes sustainability and diversity, and contributes to the loss of traditional knowledge and culture, contrary to the [ICESCR]. India should thus tread cautiously before allowing new such crops.

...

Seed Bill 2004

[A] draft Seed Bill ... is currently before the Indian Parliament. If passed, it could drastically affect farmers' rights, impacting farmers' access to seeds and potentially raise the costs of food production. While the PPVFR allows the farmers to freely exchange seeds, the Seeds Bill 2004 would make it mandatory for every person who intends to sell or barter seeds to obtain registration certificate. In addition, the Seed Bill enables the period of intellectual property protection to be doubled, which means the seeds could be protected for 30 years, thus extending the monopoly of the owner of the seeds.

Whereas the PPVFR has provision for compulsory license to be issued if seeds are not sufficiently available in the market or if the seed prices are high, the Seed Bill fails to provide any such protection to the farmer; the Bill

---

[136] [Farmers who grow Bt cotton must sign a Technology Use Agreement with Monsanto that prohibits them from saving seeds for replanting or transferring them to other framers and requires them to pay damages and the company's legal fees for breaching the agreement. Gala, *supra* note 135.—Eds.]

contains no mechanism to regulate seed supply or seed price. This will enable seed companies to set high prices for seeds, and will leave the government no means to control the price even if the public interest so warrants. It could also mean that seed providers are under no obligation to ensure a reasonable seed supply to farmers. The proposed Seed Bill could thus hinder farmers' access to affordable seeds and thus to food, contrary to the right to food.

In May 2008, the ICESCR Committee questioned representatives of the Indian government about its report and, as it does for every states party, completed its review with a set of concluding observations.[137] In a section of the observations titled "Principal Subjects of Concern," the Committee stated that it was

> deeply concerned that the extreme hardship being experienced by farmers has led to an increasing incidence of suicides by farmers over the past decade. The Committee is particularly concerned that the extreme poverty among small-hold farmers caused by the lack of land, access to credit and adequate rural infrastructures, has been exacerbated by the introduction of genetically modi-fied seeds by multinational corporations and the ensuing escalation of prices of seeds, fertilisers and pesticides, particularly in the cotton industry.[138]

The Committee also urged India "to take all necessary measures to address the extreme poverty among small-holding farmers and to increase agricultural productivity as a matter of priority." It urged the government to achieve these goals by, among other measures,

> providing state subsidies to enable farmers to purchase generic seeds which they are able to re-use, with a view to eliminating their dependency on multina-tional corporations. The Committee also recommends the State party to review the Seed Bill (2004) in light of its obligations under the Covenant and draw the attention of the State party to para. 19 of the Committee's *General Comment No.12* on the right to adequate food (1999).[139]

---

[137] ECOSOC, *Concluding Observations: India*, U.N. Doc. E/C.12/IND/CO (May 2008).

[138] *Id.* para. 29.

[139] *Id.* para. 69. As explained in Section 6.2(A)(2) of this chapter, paragraph 19 of the *General Comment* states that "violations of the right to food can occur through the direct action of States or other entities insufficiently regulated by States," including "the formal repeal or suspension of legislation necessary for the continued enjoyment of the right to food; denial of access to food to particular individuals or groups …; adoption of legislation or policies which are manifestly incompatible with preexisting legal obligations relating to the right to food; and failure to regulate activities of individuals or groups so as to prevent them from violating the right to food of others. *General Comment No. 12, supra* note 16, para. 19.

Notes and Questions

1. As summarized in the article by Ragavan and O'Shields, the PPVFA recognizes three distinct categories of plant varieties: new varieties, extant varieties, and farmers' varieties. Do small-scale farmers in India have a financial incentive to register extant plant varieties? Are there any nonmonetary incentives to register? Conversely, can you identify any risks to farmers associated with such registration?

2. Ragavan and O'Shields assert that the PPVFA "represents a deviation from UPOV." What are the costs and benefits of such a deviation? Is the PPVFA an improvement over the UPOV in assisting India in realizing the human right to food? Which of the statute's provisions further human rights objectives?

3. The PPVFA requires plant breeders to share benefits with indigenous groups, individuals, or communities that have contributed to the development of the new variety in some fashion. Only Indian citizens, firms, and organizations are eligible to claim such benefits. Does this restriction violate TRIPS' national treatment requirement? Does it violate the nondiscrimination provisions of human rights treaties such as the ICESCR? Do other provisions of the treaties justify such treatment? Consider in particular Articles 1 and 2 of the ICESCR:

Article 1

1. All peoples have the right of self-determination. By virtue of that right they freely determine their political status and freely pursue their economic, social and cultural development.
2. All peoples may, for their own ends, freely dispose of their natural wealth and resources without prejudice to any obligations arising out of international economic co-operation, based upon the principle of mutual benefit, and international law. In no case may a people be deprived of its own means of subsistence....

Article 2

. . .

2. The States Parties to the present Covenant undertake to guarantee that the rights enunciated in the present Covenant will be exercised without discrimination of any kind as to race, colour, sex, language, religion, political or other opinion, national or social origin, property, birth or other status.
3. Developing countries, with due regard to human rights and their national economy, may determine to what extent they would guarantee the economic rights recognized in the present Covenant to non-nationals.

4. Women make substantial contributions to preserving plant genetic resources, genetic variation, and traditional knowledge of farming communities in developing nations. According to a recent study:

> In many countries, it is primarily women who save and manage seed. Up to 90% of planting material used in smallholder agriculture is seed and germplasm which women have produced, selected and saved. Women also have a key role in growing and preserving underutilised species, which do not satisfy a large proportion of the world's food needs, but which communities use to supplement their diets.... Women also play an important role in preserving the genetic diversity of many species because they have particular preferences. For example, Andean women choose a variety of potato that has the characteristics they want for cooking. Rwandan women are reported to grow more than 600 varieties of beans and Peruvian Aguaruna women plant more than 60 varieties of manioc. Yemeni women select and plant seeds of varieties with the characteristics they prefer, such as colour, size, genetic stability, disease tolerance, palatability and good processing qualities.[140]

According to the Special Rapporteur on the Right to Food, "the replacement of farmers' seed systems [with] commercial seeds systems may ... shift decision-making about which crops to grow and to sell to men."[141] Would such a shift violate the nondiscrimination clause of the ICESCR reproduced in the previous note? Would it violate the following provisions of CEDAW?

Article 1

For the purposes of the present Convention, the term "discrimination against women" shall mean any distinction, exclusion or restriction made on the basis of sex which has the effect or purpose of impairing or nullifying the recognition, enjoyment or exercise by women, irrespective of their marital status, on a basis of equality of men and women, of human rights and fundamental freedoms in the political, economic, social, cultural, civil or any other field.

Article 14

. . .

2. States Parties shall take all appropriate measures to eliminate discrimination against women in rural areas in order to ensure, on a basis of equality of men and women, that they participate in and benefit from rural development and, in particular, shall ensure to such women the right ...

---

[140] Gabriela Mata & Adél Anna Sasvári, *Integrating Gender Equality and Equity in Access and Benefit-Sharing Governance through a Rights-Based Approach*, in JESSICA CAMPESE ET AL. (EDS.), RIGHTS-BASED APPROACHES: EXPLORING ISSUES AND OPPORTUNITIES FOR CONSERVATION 251, 254 (2009).

[141] U.N. Special Rapporteur on the Right to Food, *Seed Policies and the Right to Food: Enhancing Agrobiodiversity, Encouraging Innovation, Background Document to Report to U.N. General Assembly (U.N. Doc. A/64/170)* (Oct. 2009) (prepared by Olivier De Schutter), *available at* http://www.keinpatent.de/uploads/media/seed_policies.pdf [Special Rapporteur, 2009 Right to Food Background Document].

(g) To have access to agricultural credit and loans, marketing facilities, appropriate technology and equal treatment in land and agrarian reform as well as in land resettlement schemes.

5. Are you persuaded by 3D's objections to the Seed Bill, 2004? Commentators have expressed other concerns regarding the Seeds Bill. According to one observer, the bill's requirement that all seeds sold in India

> conform to the minimum limit of germination, physical purity and genetic purity ... is an onerous obligation when understood in the context in which most farmers operate in India. As ... many farmers are poor and illiterate, they do not possess the technical information related to genetic purity and the minimum limit of germination of a seed. Therefore, it will be difficult for the farmers to find out whether their seeds satisfy these requirements or not.... Mandatory imposition of such onerous obligations indirectly restricts the right of farmers to sell or barter seeds.[142]

What other concerns does the Seeds Bill, 2004 raise with regard to the human right to food and farmers' rights? How might India address these concerns while advancing its goals of "encourag[ing] seed trade to promote the seed industry, boost exports, and protect seed quality"?

6. Significant controversy surrounds the increasingly widespread planting of genetically modified Bt cotton in India. According to a 2009 report by the International Service for the Acquisition of Agri-biotech Applications (ISAAA), an agricultural industry-funded NGO, Bt cotton has generated numerous economic benefits for resource-poor farmers in the country:

> In 2008, 5 million small farmers in India planted and benefited from 7.6 million hectares of Bt cotton, equivalent to 82% of the 9.3 million hectare national cotton crop, the largest in the world.... The Bt cotton story in India is remarkable, with an unprecedented 150-fold increase in adoption between 2002 and 2008. In the short span of six years, 2002 to 2007, Bt cotton has generated economic benefits of US$3.2 billion, halved insecticide requirements, contributed to the doubling of yield and transformed India from a cotton importer to a major exporter. Socio-economic surveys confirm that Bt cotton continues to deliver significant and multiple agronomic, economic, environmental and welfare benefits to farmers and society.[143]

The Indian government has been a strong supporter of Bt cotton. Its agencies have approved a large number of new hybrid varieties, including one domestically developed variety.[144] By contrast, civil society groups that oppose

---

[142] Prabhash Ranjan, *Recent Developments in India's Plant Variety Protection, Seed Regulation and Linkages with UPOV's Proposed Membership*, 12 J. WORLD INTELL. PROP. 219, 237 (2009).

[143] INT'L SERV. FOR THE ACQUISITION OF AGRI-BIOTECH APPLICATIONS, BIOTECH CROPS IN INDIA: THE DAWN OF A NEW ERA 1 (2009), *available at* http://www.isaaa.org/resources/publications/the_dawn_of_a_new_era/download/default.asp.

[144] *See id.* at 11–15.

genetically modified food and crops have accused the agricultural industry and the government of wildly exaggerating Bt cotton's benefits and obscuring its negative health consequences for poor farmers. The following two excerpts are illustrative of the arguments that these groups have raised.

> Conflicting accounts of the success/failure of Bt cotton have been coming from India for several years now. Monsanto claims that Bt cotton is great for Indian farmers, giving increased sales etc., but carefully conducted research shows the opposite to be the case: massive crop failures and uncontrollable pest infestations were also reported. And while politicians, seeking to appear progressive and patriotic, praised the "advantages" of biotech, the farmers have resorted to, at times, violent protest and suicide because of losses incurred through using the GM varieties.[145]
>
> * * *
>
> In AP [Andhra Pradesh], across various hybrids and varieties, the Bt cotton growers earned in 2006–7 just about 9% more than non Bt farmers who followed Non Pesticide Management (NPM) practices.... In spite of the fact that NPM farmers spent more on fertilizers than Bt farmers, their total Cost of Cultivation was still 11% less than the cost borne by Bt farmers.... In 2006–2007, NPM farmers spent 41% less on pest management than Bt farmers. While Bt farmers spent Rs.1051 per acre, the NPM farmers needed to spend just about Rs.625 per acre to save their crops from pests.... Bt Cotton has [also] brought never-before-seen diseases for cotton farmers[, including root rot].... After experiencing all the above effects of Bt cotton, thousands of cotton farmers ... are scared of sowing Bt cotton. But they are deprived of all other options in AP. All the good cotton hybrids have miraculously been made to disappear through a sleight of hand by the seed industry.[146]

An article published in 2006 by economists affiliated with the International Food Policy Research Institute (IFPRI) – an agricultural research center funded by governments, private foundations, and international and regional organizations – attempted to evaluate these competing claims. It assessed "47 peer-reviewed articles that have applied stated economics methods to measure the farm-level impacts of Bt cotton in developing agriculture from 1996."[147] The authors of the article summarized their assessment of the studies' findings as follows:

---

[145] Rhea Gala, *GM Cotton: Corruption, Hype, Half-truths and Lies* (Inst. of Sci. in Soc'y, Report Jan. 21, 2005), *available at* http://www.i-sis.org.uk/GMCCHHTAL.php.

[146] Media Release, A.P. Coalition in Defence of Diversity, *Farmyard Truths and Industry Lies* (July 30, 2007).

[147] Melinda Smale et al., *Bales and Balance: A Review of the Methods Used to Assess the Economic Impact of Bt Cotton on Farmers in Developing Economies*, 9 J. Agrobiotech. Mgmt. & Econ. 195 (2006).

The overall balance sheet, though promising, is mixed. Economic returns are highly variable over years, farm type, and geographical location. They depend on initial practices, pest infestations, seed costs, and other attributes of farmers and farm production. Thus, findings cannot be generalized. One hypothesis emerges strongly from the cross-case comparison of studies: institutional and marketing arrangements for supplying the technology and marketing the product may be the single most important determinant of Bt impact at the farm-level, even when the trait is shown to be effective.[148]

In 2008, IFPRI researchers released another study that "provide[d] a comprehensive review of evidence on Bt cotton and farmer suicides." Drawing on "information from published official and unofficial reports, peer-reviewed journal articles, published studies, media news clips, magazine articles, and radio broadcasts from India, Asia, and international sources from 2002 to 2007," the study evaluated "whether or not there has been a resurgence of farmer suicides, and the potential relationship suicide may have with the use of Bt cotton." After reviewing these materials, the study's authors concluded:

> We first show that there is no evidence in available data of a "resurgence" of farmer suicides in India in the last five years. Second, we find that Bt cotton technology has been very effective overall in India. However, the context in which Bt cotton was introduced has generated disappointing results in some particular districts and seasons. Third, our analysis clearly shows that Bt cotton is neither a necessary nor a sufficient condition for the occurrence of farmer suicides. In contrast, many other factors have likely played a prominent role. Nevertheless, in specific regions and years, where Bt cotton may have indirectly contributed to farmer indebtedness, leading to suicides, its failure was mainly the result of the context or environment in which it was planted.[149]

7. Evaluate the ICESCR Committee's concluding observations on India in light of the information summarized in note 6.

(a) Should the Committee have conducted an investigation of the controversies surrounding Bt cotton before citing the use of genetically modified cotton as a "principal subject of concern" regarding the right to food? Does the Committee have the authority or the resources to undertake such an investigation? (See Chapter 1 for additional information on the ICESCR Committee and other U.N. human rights treaty bodies.) More generally, how should the Committee respond when the human rights implications of new technologies are uncertain or contested?

---

[148] *Id.* at 209.

[149] Guillaume P. Gruère et al., *Bt Cotton and Farmer Suicides in India: Reviewing the Evidence*, at vi (Int'l Food Policy Research Inst., Discussion Paper 808, 2008), *available at* http://www.ifpri.org/publication/bt-cotton-and-farmer-suicides-india.

(b) Was the Committee justified in expressing concern about the suicides of poor farmers? In identifying Bt cotton as a factor contributing to those self-inflicted deaths?

(c) Consider the measures that the Committee urged India to undertake to alleviate poverty among small-holding farmers. These included "state subsidies to enable farmers to purchase generic seeds which they are able to re-use, with a view to eliminating their dependency on multinational corporations." Assume for purposes of argument that the claimed benefits of Bt cotton are in fact true. Is there nevertheless a legal basis in the ICESCR for the Committee's recommendation? If you were an official in the Indian agriculture ministry, what information would help you to decide whether to use the ministry's limited budget to subsidize the purchase generic or IP-protected seeds?

8. Plans are currently under way in India to introduce a Bt variety of brinjal, also known as eggplant and aubergine. According to a recent ISAAA report:

Brinjal is a very important common man's vegetable in India. After potato, it ranks as the second highest consumed vegetable in India, along with tomato and onion. A total of 1.4 million small, marginal and resource-poor farmers grow brinjal on 550,000 hectares annually in all the eight vegetable growing zones throughout India. It is an important cash crop for poor farmers.... Brinjal was one of the first vegetable crops adopted by farmers as hybrids, which occupied more than 50% of the brinjal planted area of 550,000 hectares in 2007, the balance being planted with open pollinated varieties. Brinjal is marketed in different sizes, shapes and colors to meet consumer preferences. Of the global production of 32 million tons of brinjal produced on 2 million hectares worldwide annually, India produces 8 to 9 million tons, equivalent to one quarter of the global production, which makes India the second largest producer of brinjal in the world, after China. Brinjal is a hardy crop that yields well under stress conditions, including drought. Productivity [in India] has increased from 12.6 tons per hectare in 1987–88, to 15.3 tons per hectare in 1991–92, to 16.5 tons per hectare in 2005–06....

Brinjal is prone to attack by many insect-pests, and diseases; by far the most important of which is the fruit and shoot borer (FSB), for which resistance has not been identified and thus it causes significant losses of up to 60 to 70% in commercial plantings, [reducing marketable yields]. Due to the fact that FSB larvae remain concealed within shoots and fruits, insecticide applications, although numerous, are ineffective. [Repeated applications of insecticide have resulted in residues on some brinjal sold to consumers.]

Bt brinjal has been under development by Mahyco [a subsidiary of Monsanto] for the last 8 years. It has undergone a rigorous science-based regulatory approval process in India and is currently at an advanced stage of consideration for deregulation by the Indian regulatory authorities.... The studies submitted to the regulatory authorities confirm that Bt brinjal offers the opportunity to simultaneously provide effective control of the most important pest of brinjal, FSB, decrease insecticides for this important insect-pest by 80%, and more than double the yield over conventional hybrids and open-pollinated varieties, thereby providing significant advantages for farmers and consumers alike.[150]

The study identifies three reasons to support the introduction of Bt brinjal in India:

> Firstly, it is likely to be the first biotech food crop commercialized in India.... Secondly, Bt brinjal technology has been generously donated by its private sector developer, Mahyco, to public sector institutes in India, Bangladesh and the Philippines for incorporation in open-pollinated varieties of brinjal for the use of small resource-poor farmers. Thirdly, sharing of knowledge and experience of the regulation process for Bt brinjal in India could greatly simplify and lighten the regulatory burden in Bangladesh and the Philippines by eliminating duplication of the significant effort already expended by India, thereby contributing to the important goal of harmonizing regulations between countries.[151]

Public interest NGOs that oppose government approval of the genetically modified eggplant have cited a study that have identified "a serious risk for human and animal health" from Bt brinjal:

> The GM aubergine is unfit for consumption. That's the verdict of French scientist Professor Gilles-Eric Seralini of the Committee for Independent Research and Information on Genetic Engineering (CRIIGEN), who carried out the first ever independent assessment of Monsanto-Mahyco's dossier on toxicity tests submitted to the Indian regulatory authorities.
>
> Professor Seralini, commissioned by Greenpeace India to undertake the assessment, said his key findings were statistically significant differences between groups of animals fed GM and non-GM brinjal in the raw data, which were discounted rather than used to raise food safety concerns and to call for further investigation. Although the differences were not reported in the dossier summaries, they remained visible in the raw experimental data. These differences, seen by Monsanto-Mahyco, were deemed biologically irrelevant, and disregarded on the grounds that they were within a wide 'reference' group of brinjal types.[152]

In light of this information, what are the human rights implications of introducing Bt brinjal in India? How do the benefits and risks differ from the

---

[150] Bhagirath Choudhary & Kadambini Gaur, *The Development and Regulation of Bt Brinjal in India (eggplant/aubergine)*, at x–xii (Int'l Serv. for the Acquisition of Agri-biotech Applications, Brief No. 38, 2009), *available at* http://www.isaaa.org/resources/publications/briefs/38/default.html.

[151] *Id.* at x.

[152] Press release, Inst. of Sci. in Soc'y, *Bt Brinjal Unfit for Human Consumption* (Feb. 9, 2009) (*prepared by* Sam Burcher), *available at* http://www.i-sis.org.uk/Bt_Brinjal_Unfit.php.

those associated with Bt cotton? Consider in particular the three factors cited in the ISAAA report concerning the importance of introducing genetically modified eggplant varieties in India.

9. Genetically modified food and feed crops are widely planted in the United States. "About 85 percent of corn and canola and 91 percent of soybean acreage this year was sown with biotech seed. Few food products in the supermarket lack at least some element derived from these crops, including oils, corn syrup, corn starch and soy lecithin."[153] The pervasiveness of gene-altered crops has raised concerns about contamination of organically grown crops and created demands for more stringent labeling rules:

> Farmers who want to plant without using biotechnology are often surrounded by neighbors whose fields are sown with genetically modified crops. And manufacturers who want to avoid genetically engineered crops and their byproducts find that increasingly difficult to do.
>
> Pollen from a biotech field may be carried by wind or insects to fertilize plants in a nonbiotech plot. At harvest and afterward, biotech and nonbiotech crops and their byproducts are often handled with the same farm equipment, trucks and so on. If the equipment is not properly cleaned, the two types of foodstuffs can mix.
>
> While federal organic regulations bar farmers from planting genetically engineered seed, they are silent on what should be done about issues like pollination from nearby biotech crops. Few regulations govern foods labeled "natural," but retailers say consumers of those products want them to be free of genetically engineered ingredients.[154]

What human rights concerns, if any, do the preceding facts raise?

10. Controversies involving genetically modified seeds are one facet of a broader concern with the consolidation of the agrobiotechnology industry. According to a 2009 report by the International Assessment of Agricultural Knowledge, Science and Technology for Development (IAASTD),[155] "the top 10 agribusiness companies (all based in Europe, the US or Japan) represent

---

[153] William Neuman, *"Non-GMO" Seal Identifies Foods Mostly Biotech-Free*, N.Y. TIMES, Aug. 29, 2009, at C1.

[154] *Id.*

[155] Launched by the World Bank and FAO in 2002, the IAASTD is a global consultative process involving governments, international organizations, the private sector, and civil society groups that analyzes how agricultural knowledge, science, and technology can help to reduce hunger and poverty, improve rural livelihoods and human health, and promote equitable, socially, environmentally, and economically sustainable development. The assessment resulted in a global report and five subglobal reports that draw upon the work of hundreds of experts from all regions of the world. *See* Int'l Assessment of Agric. Knowledge, Sci. & Tech. for Dev., *Overview and Structure, available at* http://www.agassessment.org/index.cfm?Page=Overview&ItemID=3 (last visited Mar. 31, 2010).

half of the world's commercial seed sales. These ten firms increased their control of biotechnology patents to over 50% in 2000."[156] The report acknowledges that the relatively stable market share these firms possess may encourage agricultural R&D. But it also identifies several negative consequences that private sector concentration may engender:

> The major concerns are (1) industrial concentration reduces the amount and the productivity of research because R&D expenditures are consolidated and narrowly focused; (2) concentrated markets create barriers to new firms and quell creative startups; (3) concentration allows large firms to gain substantial monopolistic power over the food industry, making food supply chains vulnerable to market maneuvers.... This ... brings into question whether large biotech firms can be relied on to conduct research with an eye on the public good as well as their own profit margins. There is additional concern that the anticompetitive impacts of concentration have led to higher seed prices.[157]

The consequences of private sector consolidation for agricultural R&D relevant to developing countries is a particular area of concern:

> The growing private sector has focused on widely commercialized, competitive crops that are well protected by legal or technical IPR. This has meant that tropical crops, crops for marginal areas (and other public goods attributes, such as safety, health, and environmental protection), and "orphan crops" have remained outside the orbit of private investment. This will remain a problem until an incentive is created for private firms to work on marginal crops or funding for these important crops is increased in public institutions.[158]

In response to these concerns, several initiatives have been launched to focus on the needs of poor and small-scale farmers. They include public-private partnerships (many involving international seed banks in the CGIAR network) as well as private philanthropies.[159] Among the most active philanthropic initiatives is the Alliance for a Green Revolution in Africa (AGRA), established in 2006 by the Bill and Melinda Gates Foundation and the Rockefeller Foundation. Currently chaired by the former U.N. Secretary-General Kofi Annan, AGRA is "a partnership-based organization" that works across Africa "to help millions of small-scale farmers and their families lift

---

[156] INT'L ASSESSMENT OF AGRIC. KNOWLEDGE, SCI. & TECH. FOR DEV. (IAASTD), AGRICULTURAL AT THE CROSSROADS (GLOBAL REPORT) (2009), *available at* http://www.agassessment.org/index.cfm?Page=doc_library&ItemID=14.

[157] *Id.* at 94.

[158] *Id.* at 96; *see also* R. Naylor et al., *Biotechnology in the Developing World: A Case for Increased Investments in Orphan Crops*, 29 FOOD POL'Y 15 (2004), *available at* http://execdeanagriculture.rutgers.edu/pdfs/goodman-091.pdf.

[159] For a list of these initiatives, *see* IAASTD, *supra* note 156, at 96–97.

themselves out of poverty and hunger. African-led and Africa-based, AGRA develops programs aimed at implementing practical solutions to significantly boost smallholder farm productivity and incomes while safeguarding the environment and promoting equity."[160] Its programs aim to be "comprehensive in that they address challenges all along the agricultural value chain: covering seeds, soil health, water, markets, and agricultural education."[161] According to a 2009 report,[162] AGRA's Programme for Africa's Seed Systems (PASS) has achieved a number of accomplishments:

> *Funding fellowship programs* in plant breeding at nine African universities, which are currently hosting 67 MSc and 46 PhD Fellows. Some 20 percent of the PhD students are women, as are nearly 30 percent of the MSc students....
>
> *Bolstering networks of crop breeders of cassava, maize, beans, and rice.* AGRA has funded regional meetings of crop breeders, bringing together over 200 practitioners to discuss their methods and share their results....
>
> *Funding Farmer-Participatory Crop Breeding, resulting so far in the release of 68 improved crop varieties.* AGRA has made 47 crop improvement grants to leading national program plant breeders to work collaboratively with farmers in breeding locally adapted and high-yielding varieties. Their new varieties have increased farmers' yields of crops such as cassava, bean, sorghum, and maize....
>
> In May 2009, the Malian Ministry of Agriculture announced the release of seven new maize hybrids, through work funded by AGRA. These are the very first hybrid maize varieties to be released in Mali, and among the first in all of West Africa. These varieties are based on International Maize and Wheat Improvement Center (CIMMYT) germplasm, and as such are in the public domain and can be freely shared....
>
> *Holding more than 2,000 on-farm trials and 500 field days.* These activities have demonstrated the effectiveness of improved seeds and crop management to one million smallholder farmers, and created a groundswell of demand for superior seed, modern inputs and better farming practices.
>
> Strengthening the private seed sector through grants to 24 promising small- and medium-sized seed companies and cooperatives, nearly doubling their production of improved seed. One of these cooperatives is the Busia Women's Producers Association, comprising 200 small-sized women's groups with a total membership of 5,000 farmers in Eastern Uganda. Its members produce and disseminate improved groundnuts and cassava to smallholder farmers, augmenting their food security.[163]

---

[160] Alliance for a Green Revolution in Africa (AGRA), *Frequently Asked Questions, available at* http://www.agra-alliance.org/section/about/faq#01 (last visited Mar. 31, 2010).

[161] *Id.*

[162] AGRA, AGRA: Early Accomplishments, Foundations for Growth (June 2009).

[163] *Id.* at 7–9.

As discussed throughout this book, international human rights law is primarily concerned with the responsibilities of governments, not private parties. Nevertheless, governments have an obligation to "protect," which, as described in the ICESCR Committee's *General Comments*, requires officials to prevent private actors – including corporations and other business entities – from depriving others of protected rights and freedoms. How should governments "protect" the right to food in response to the concentration of private agrobiotechnology industry described previously? Should they establish new public research initiatives? Contribute additional funding to the CGIAR? Revise plant variety protection rules to encourage innovation relating to orphan crops? Does the ICESCR Committee's *General Comment* on the right to food, summarized in Section 6.2(A)(2) of this chapter, provide guidance for governments to select from among these or other approaches?

More provocatively, do the apparent successes of private philanthropies such as AGRA suggest that governmental efforts to promote research involving orphan crops are likely to be minimal? If so, would it be preferable to create new international human rights standards directly applicable to private industry (and, perhaps, to private philanthropies)? If so, how might such standards be developed? Does the evolution of the right of access to patented medicines (discussed in Chapter 2) suggest any helpful analogies?

11. The concluding section of this chapter has focused on the human rights implications of genetically modified seeds protected by intellectual property rights. However, it is important to recall a point emphasized in other chapters, namely, that innovation and creativity policies and access to knowledge goods (be they pharmaceuticals, schoolbooks, or seeds) are only two among many factors relevant to the realization of human rights. As Special Rapporteur Olivier De Schutter has explained in analyzing the role of seed policies in realizing the human right to food:

> While seeds policies have an important role to play in the realization of the right to food, they are only part of a much larger challenge governments face in supporting agriculture. At least as important ... are improving the organization of farmers, the dissemination of knowledge about good soil management practices, crop rotation and combination, or ... the management of water.... Too much emphasis may have been put in the past on providing inputs to farmers, and that governments have sometimes neglected other forms or support to agriculture, often more appropriate, in particular, to smallscale farmers.[164]

---

[164] Special Rapporteur, 2009 Right to Food Background Document, *supra* note 141, at 3.

Chapter 7

Indigenous Peoples' Rights and Intellectual Property

7.1. Introduction

During the past several decades, in a variety of international and domestic fora, indigenous peoples have asserted the right to recognition of and control over their culture and traditional knowledge in areas such as biodiversity, medicines, and agriculture. As we discuss in Chapter 1, the increased attention given to the rights of indigenous peoples by U.N. agencies in the 1990s[1] was among the catalysts that encouraged international human rights bodies to address intellectual property issues.[2] This topic has generated a significant amount of commentary and analysis and continues to be the focus of numerous initiatives by international agencies and national governments. It is but one of a large array of human rights issues concerning indigenous peoples that have arisen in recent years.[3]

Indigenous peoples live in more than sixty nations, and studies have estimated their total number world wide as 300 million.[4] They are among the most economically destitute members of the human family and have frequently experienced adverse treatment, including forced assimilation, destruction of their cultures, racism, and loss of lands and resources to colonizers, governments, and commercial entities.[5] Indigenous peoples consider

---

[1] See Erica-Irene Daes, *Intellectual Property and Indigenous Peoples*, 95 AM. SOC'Y INT'L L. PROC. 143, 147 (2001).

[2] See Laurence R. Helfer, *Toward a Human Rights Framework for Intellectual Property*, 40 U.C. DAVIS L. REV. 971, 982 (2007).

[3] As one scholar has noted, "indigenous peoples have arguably come to represent one of the most influential, and well recognized, parties of a global civil movement committed to the pursuit of justice." Mauro Barelli, *The Role of Soft Law in the International Legal System: The Case of the United Nations Declaration on the Rights of Indigenous Peoples*, 58 INT'L & COMP. L.Q. 957, 957 (2009).

[4] *Id.* at 968.

[5] See S. James Anaya, *International Human Rights and Indigenous Peoples: The Move Toward the Multicultural State*, 21 ARIZ. J. INT'L & COMP. L. 13, 17–18 (2004) [Anaya, *Multicultural State*].

themselves to be "the historical successors of the peoples and nations that existed on their territories before the coming of the invaders of these territories, who eventually prevailed over them and imposed on them colonial or other forms of subjugation, and whose historical successors now form the predominant sectors of society."[6] For the purposes of this chapter, we use the term "indigenous peoples" to refer to peoples who possess their own cultural patterns, social institutions, and legal systems (albeit to different degrees); who claim a historical continuity with precolonial societies; and who are determined to preserve and transmit to future generations their ancestral territories and identities as a basis for their continued existence as peoples.[7]

Debate over indigenous peoples' intellectual property rights is situated in a matrix of legal and political ideas, sources, and traditions. The topic "traverses not only the boundaries between properties – real, personal, and intellectual – but also the boundaries between international, domestic, and tribal law."[8] Our aim in this chapter is to examine points of intersection between intellectual property laws and human rights in respect of indigenous knowledge, creativity, and cultural productions.[9] First, we summarize the human

---

[6] ECOSOC, Sub-Comm'n on Prevention of Discrimination & Prot. of Minorities, *Study of the Problem of Discrimination against Indigenous Populations*, para. 376, U.N. Doc. E/CN.4/Sub.2/1986/7/Add.4 (1987) (final report, last part, prepared by José Martínez Cobo) [Cobo Report]. We recognize that controversy surrounds the definitions of "indigenous" and "indigeneity." The Working Group on Indigenous Populations considered the possibility of establishing a working definition of the term "indigenous" at its second session (E/CN.4/Sub.2/AC.4/1983/CRP.2; E/CN.4/Sub.2/1983/22, paras. 109–119) but subsequently concluded that justice would best be served by allowing the scope of this concept to evolve over time. A number of commentators have questioned the salience of this term in debates over the scope of legal rights. *See, e.g.*, Michael H. Davis, *Some Realism about Indigenism*, 11 CARDOZO J. INT'L & COMP. L. 815 (2003); Jeremy Waldron, *Indigeneity? First Peoples and Last Occupancy*, 1 N.Z. J. PUB. L. 55 (2003) (questioning the salience of the concept in the context of political struggles). The concept of indigeneity has recently been invoked in some surprising contexts. A political party in the United Kingdom, the British National Party, consistently refers to "the Scots, Irish, English and Welsh people [as] the indigenous people of the British Isles." They base this designation on "the accepted international definition [according to which] the term 'indigenous people' is used to describe any ethnic group of people who inhabit a geographic region with which they have the earliest known historical connection." British National Party, *Immigration: Labour Party Is Guilty of Breach of UN Declaration on Indigenous Peoples' Rights* (Oct. 24, 2009), *available at* http://bnp.org.uk/2009/10/immigration-labour-party-is-guilty-of-breach-of-un-declaration-on-indigenous-peoples%E2%80%99-rights/.

[7] *See* Cobo Report, *supra* note 6, para. 379.

[8] Kristen A. Carpenter, Sonial K. Katyal & Angela R. Riley, *In Defense of Property*, 118 YALE L.J. 1022 (2009).

[9] This chapter does not provide a comprehensive analysis of indigenous peoples' intellectual property issues. Many excellent studies of that topic already exist. *See, e.g.*, SILKE VON LEWINSKI (ED.), INDIGENOUS HERITAGE AND INTELLECTUAL PROPERTY: GENETIC RESOURCES, TRADITIONAL KNOWLEDGE AND FOLKLORE (2004); MARY RILEY (ED.), INDIGENOUS INTELLECTUAL PROPERTY RIGHTS: LEGAL OBSTACLES AND INNOVATIVE SOLUTIONS (2004).

rights instruments that establish the public international law foundations for indigenous peoples' rights. We then examine human rights protections that are relevant to indigenous intellectual property issues, including the 2007 United Nations Declaration on the Rights of Indigenous Peoples (2007 Indigenous Peoples Declaration).[10] In a separate section, we discuss the non-binding declarations, resolutions, and statements that indigenous peoples have themselves disseminated concerning intellectual property.[11] These documents sit alongside instruments that form part of the "official" international human rights system. We then consider an array of potential legal vehicles for protecting indigenous peoples' intellectual property, drawing on recent analysis by the World Intellectual Property Organization (WIPO).[12]

As WIPO's involvement in this issue attests, intellectual property norms are critically important to the human rights of indigenous peoples. Some courts have attempted to accommodate indigenous claims within existing intellectual property principles. As an illustration, we provide extracts from a leading Australian decision, *John Bulun Bulun v. R. & T. Textiles Pty Ltd.*[13] We conclude the chapter with a brief discussion of how the interface of intellectual property and human rights can contribute to ongoing debates and analysis relating to the rights of indigenous communities.

Before proceeding, we emphasize that care is needed with definitional terms in this area.[14] The conceptual and heuristic structure of indigenous

[10] Declaration on the Rights of Indigenous Peoples, G.A. Res. 61/295, art. 32(2), U.N. GAOR, 61st Sess., 107th plen. mtg., U.N. Doc. A/RES/61/295 (Sept. 13, 2007).

[11] *See, e.g.,* Charter of the Indigenous-Tribal Peoples of the Tropical Forests, Penang, Malaysia (1992); Mataatua Declaration on Cultural and Intellectual Property Rights of Indigenous Peoples (1993) [*Mataatua Declaration*]; Kari-Oca Declaration and the Indigenous Peoples' Earth Charter, Kari-Oca, Brazil (1992). These documents are reproduced in DARREL A. POSEY & GRAHAM DUTFIELD, BEYOND INTELLECTUAL PROPERTY: TOWARDS TRADITIONAL RESOURCE RIGHTS FOR INDIGENOUS PEOPLES AND LOCAL COMMUNITIES (1996).

[12] *See* JANE E. ANDERSON, LAW, KNOWLEDGE, CULTURE: THE PRODUCTION OF INDIGENOUS KNOWLEDGE IN INTELLECTUAL PROPERTY LAW 174–76 (2009). WIPO's current involvement in the topic represents a significant change from past practice. *See* Special Rapporteur of the Sub-Comm'n on Prevention of Discrimination and Prot. of Minorities, *Final Report: Protection of the Heritage of Indigenous People*, U.N. Doc. E/CN.4/Sub.2/1995/26 (June 21, 1995) (prepared by Erica-Irene Daes) (containing Draft Principles and Guidelines on the Protection of the Heritage of Indigenous Peoples) [Special Rapporteur, *Protection of the Heritage*]. The report recounts that WIPO "maintained that its activities do not include the protection of the heritage of indigenous peoples, and therefore would appreciate that all references to WIPO in the draft guidelines be deleted." WIPO also "expressed its unwillingness to assume ... additional responsibilities." *Id.* paras. 12, 29.

[13] *John Bulun Bulun & Anor v. R. & T. Textiles Pty Ltd.*, [1998] FCA 1082.

[14] *See generally* Terri Janke, *Our Culture: Our Future: Report on Australian Indigenous Cultural and Intellectual Property Rights*, 14 (Austl. Inst. of Aboriginal & Torres Strait Islander Studies & the Aboriginal & Torres Strait Islander Comm'n, 1998) [*Our Culture: Our Future*], *available at* http://www.frankellawyers.com.au/media/report/culture.pdf.

intellectual property is not necessarily the same as that underpinning existing intellectual property laws. The intellectual property possessed by indigenous peoples draws from knowledge that predates colonial contact[15] and
can change and adapt through time. In general terms, such "traditional
knowledge" has been described as the "understanding or skill possessed by
indigenous peoples pertaining to their culture and folklore, their technologies, and their use of native plants for medicinal purposes."[16] "Traditional
cultural expressions," a term we also use in this chapter, include religious
rituals, sacred objects, rites of passage, songs, dances, myths, stories, and
folklore, which can also evolve over decades and centuries.[17] We use these
terms mindful of the claims of indigenous groups that their rights extend
to defining for themselves the extent and characteristics of their intellectual
property.[18]

---

* * * Issues in Focus * * *

In recent years, there have been several high-profile cases applying intellectual
property laws and concepts in ways that are at odds with the belief systems of
indigenous peoples and the rights they claim in traditional knowledge.

In 1986, a U.S. scientist, Loren Miller, was granted a patent as the
"inventor" of ayahuasca, a traditional Amazon healing vine also used in
sacred ceremonies.[19] Over a decade earlier, Miller had received samples
of ayahuasca from an Ecuadorian tribe.[20] Miller cultivated the plant in
Hawaii and called it "Da Vine." The Coordinating Body of Indigenous
Organizations of the Amazon Basin and the Amazon Coalition objected to
Miller's patent. With the help of the Center for International Environmental
Law, they filed a request to reexamine the patent. The U.S. Patent and

---

[15] *Id.*

[16] Steven R. Munzer & Kal Rustiala, *The Uneasy Case for Intellectual Property Rights in Traditional Knowledge*, 27 CARDOZO ARTS & ENT. L.J. 37, 38 (2009).

[17] *Id.* at 48.

[18] Such a claim was set forth, for example, in the first operative article of the 1993 Mataatua Declaration, adopted at the First International Conference on the Cultural and Intellectual Property Rights, which was held in New Zealand in 1993. *See Mataatua Declaration supra* note 11. The right to define "intellectual property" is also asserted in the *Julayinbul Statement on Indigenous Intellectual Property Rights* from November 27, 1993, at Jingarra, in the north-eastern coastal region of Australia. The full text of the *Julayinbul Statement* is included in Appendix 5 of *Our Culture: Our Future, supra* note 14 [*Julayinbul Statement*].

[19] Srividhya Ragavan, *Protecting Traditional Knowledge*, 2 MINN. INTELL. PROP. REV. 1, 9 (2001); *see also* Leanne M. Fecteau, *The Ayahuasca Patent Revocation: Raising Questions About Current U.S. Patent Policy*, 21 B.C. THIRD WORLD L.J. 69, 84 (2001).

[20] Fecteau, *supra* note 19, at 84.

Trademark Office granted the request and, in November 1999, rejected Miller's patent because Da Vine was "identical to other specimens of aya-huasca found in U.S. herbarium collections," thereby violating patent law's novelty requirement.[21]

In the early 1990s, the U.S. Department of Commerce, on behalf of the Centers for Disease Control and Prevention, submitted an application seek-ing to patent tissue from a woman of the Guaymai tribe of Panama.[22] The cell line from the woman's tissue was thought to have antiviral qualities.[23] The Rural Advancement Foundation International (RAFI) became aware of the pending patent and notified the Guaymai people. The tribe did not know that a cell sample had even been taken. With the help of RAFI, the Guaymai demanded the patent application be withdrawn. They issued the following statement: "It's fundamentally immoral, contrary to the Guaymai view of nature, and our place in it ... to patent human material. ... [I]t violates the integrity of life itself and our deepest sense of morality."[24] Submitting to inter-national pressure, the Centers for Disease Control and Prevention eventually withdrew the application.[25]

The numerous medicinal uses of the neem tree have been known in India for more than 2,000 years.[26] The seeds of the tree contain the chemical azadirachtin, an effective agricultural insecticide and fungicide. Because of its commercial value, an international chemical company, W. R. Grace, applied for a patent for azadirachtin. In 1994, the European Patent Office granted the patent, but India immediately disputed Grace's ownership.[27] After years of challenges and appeals, the European Patent Office revoked the patent in 2000, finding that it "lacked novelty because the use of neem extract as a fungicide by Indian farmers constituted prior use."[28]

Two African plants, katempfe and the serendipity berry, contain sweet-ening proteins that potentially have great commercial value.[29] Thaumatin,

---

[21] *Id.*

[22] Cyril R. Vidergar, *Biomedical Patenting: Permitted, but Permissible?*, 19 Santa Clara Computer & High Tech. L.J. 253, 266 (2001).

[23] *Id.*

[24] *Id.* at 267 (*quoting* Philip L. Bereano, *Patent Pending: The Race to Own DNA*, Seattle Times, Aug. 27, 1995, at B5).

[25] *Id.*

[26] Kari Moyer-Henry, *Patenting Neem & Hoodia: Conflicting Decisions Issued by the Opposition Board of the European Patent Office*, 27 Biotech. L. Rep. 1, 4 (2008).

[27] Munzer & Raustiala, *supra* note 16, at 50; *see also* Moyer-Henry, *supra* note 26, at 5.

[28] Moyer-Henry, *supra* note 26, at 5. The European proceeding resulted in the cancellation of the patent for the European nations specified in the application. It did not affect the status of patent rights and applications in other nations. *Id.*

[29] Sandra Blakeslee, *Supersweetner Found*, N.Y. Times, Mar. 5, 1985, at C8.

the protein derived from katempfe, is significantly sweeter than sugar[30] but contains no calories.[31] Similarly, monellin, the protein derived from the serendipity berry, is thought to be the second sweetest substance on earth.[32] Although Africans had been using the plants specifically for their sweetening abilities, a U.S. university and a Japanese firm were able to obtain patents for thaumatin and monellin that included any transgenic plant containing the derived sweetening proteins.[33] Apparently no arrangements were made to return part of the benefits to communities in Africa.[34]

At the 2004 U.S. Grammy Awards, the hip-hop/funk duo "OutKast" performed their song "Hey Ya!" to popular and critical acclaim. The performance featured choreography in which scantily clad backup dancers – dressed in buckskin bikinis, with long braids and feathers in their hair[35] – hit their open mouths in an apparent imitation of a traditional Plains tribe war cry.[36] The performance provoked numerous complaints by Native American communities. "Complaints ranged from a feeling of violation over the use of Indian symbols reserved for ceremonial purposes to anger over the perpetuation of 'tomahawk-and-tipi stereotypes.'"[37] The melody used to introduce the "Hey Ya!" song at the Grammy performance was a sacred Navajo (Dine) "Beauty Way" song. Navajo leaders complained that it was improper for OutKast to use the song for entertainment purposes.[38] Ironically, the performers have been vocal critics of unlicensed downloading of copyright-protected material. Yet, as Angela Riley has explained, intellectual property law makes "an important distinction between the unauthorized downloading of 'Hey Ya!' … and the appropriation of the Navajo 'Beauty Way' song: the former is protected by copyright law, and the latter is not. In fact, no law currently exists to protect against OutKast's appropriation of Native culture, Native symbols, Native dance, or Native music."[39]

---

[30] *See id.* (noting that thaumatin is "100,000 times sweeter than table sugar and 600 times sweeter than aspartame"); *see also* Naomi Roht-Arriaza, *Of Seeds & Shamans: The Appropriation of the Scientific & Technical Knowledge of Indigenous & Local Communities*, 17 Mich. J. Int'l. L. 919, 923 (1996).

[31] Rhot-Arriaza, *supra* note 30, at 923.

[32] Blakeslee, *supra* note 29, at C8.

[33] Rhot-Arriaza, *supra* note 30, at 923.

[34] *Id.* at 923–24.

[35] For a detailed account of the facts, *see* Angela R. Riley, *"Straight Stealing": Toward an Indigenous System of Cultural Property Protection*, 80 Wash. L. Rev. 69, 70–72 (2005).

[36] *Id.*

[37] *Id.* at 71 (citing sources).

[38] *Id.* at 71–2 (quoting Anthony Lee, Sr., president of the Navajo Medicine Man Association).

[39] *Id.* at 72.

7.2. International Human Rights Law Relating to Indigenous Peoples

International human rights law has developed a dual approach to protecting the rights of indigenous peoples. On the one hand, numerous declarations and studies affirm that indigenous peoples are guaranteed the same rights as all other members of the human family.[40] This point is underscored by Article 1 of the 2007 Indigenous Peoples Declaration, which affirms that "indigenous peoples have the right to the full enjoyment, as a collective or as individuals, of all human rights and fundamental freedoms as recognized in the Charter of the United Nations, the Universal Declaration of Human Rights and international human rights law."

On the other hand, as James Anaya, Special Rapporteur on the situation of human rights and fundamental freedoms of indigenous peoples, explains in a 2008 Report to the Human Rights Council,[41] international bodies have long interpreted human rights instruments to take account of the distinctive concerns of indigenous communities and their members.[42] For example, since the 1980s, the U.N. Human Rights Committee has advanced a broad interpretation of provisions in the International Covenant on Civil and Political Rights (ICCPR) that concern the integrity of indigenous culture, including such privacy and family rights; the rights of persons belonging to ethnic, religious, or linguistic minorities; and rights to land and resources.[43] The Committee on the Elimination of Racial Discrimination has interpreted the nondiscrimination norm in the Convention on the Elimination of All Forms of Racial Discrimination[44] as protecting aspects of indigenous cultural identity and language, economic and social development, effective participation,

---

[40]   U.N. Special Rapporteur on the Situation of Human Rights and Fundamental Freedoms of Indigenous Peoples, *Report to Human Rights Council*, para. 20, U.N. Doc. A/HRC/9/9 (2008) (prepared by S. James Anaya), *reprinted in* S. James Anaya, *The Human Rights of Indigenous Peoples, in Light of the New Declaration, and the Challenge of Making Them Operative: Report of the Special Rapporteur on the Situation of Human Rights and Fundamental Freedoms of Indigenous People* (Aug. 5, 2008) (unpublished manuscript), *available at* http://ssrn.com/abstract=1242451 [Anaya, *Report of the Special Rapporteur*].

[41]   *Id.*

[42]   The history of the development of human rights norms concerning indigenous peoples from the principles and human rights obligations set forth in international human rights instruments is traced in Patrick Thornberry, Indigenous Peoples and Human Rights 116–241 (2002). *See also* S. James Anaya, Indigenous Peoples in International Law 39–71 (2d ed. 1996).

[43]   Anaya, *Report of the Special Rapporteur, supra* note 40, para. 22 (citing U.N. High Comm'r for Human Rights, Human Rights Comm., *General Comment No. 23, The Rights of Minorities (Article 27)*, paras. 24–25, U.N. Doc. CCPR/C/21/Rev.1/Add5 [Apr. 8, 1994]).

[44]   International Convention on the Elimination of All Forms of Racial Discrimination, Dec. 21, 1965, 660 U.N.T.S. 195.

and rights over lands, territories, and resources.[45] In particular, the committee has called on states to

(a) Recognize and respect indigenous distinct culture, history, language and way of life as an enrichment of the State's cultural identity and to promote its preservation;

(b) Ensure that members of indigenous peoples are free and equal in dignity and rights and free from any discrimination, in particular that based on indigenous origin or identity;

(c) Provide indigenous peoples with conditions allowing for a sustainable economic and social development compatible with their cultural characteristics;

(d) Ensure that members of indigenous peoples have equal rights in respect of effective participation in public life and that no decisions directly relating to their rights and interests are taken without their informed consent;

(e) Ensure that indigenous communities can exercise their rights to practise and revitalize their cultural traditions and customs and to preserve and to practise their languages.[46]

Anaya explains that this statement by the Race Discrimination Committee "extends to indigenous peoples the same notion of respect for cultural integrity that developed within international law in other contexts some time ago."[47]

The work of other treaty bodies is similar. The Committee on Economic, Social and Cultural Rights, for example, has derived specific normative implications for indigenous peoples from several of the rights in the International Covenant on Economic, Social and Cultural Rights (ICESCR), including rights to adequate housing, to adequate food, to education without discrimination, to the highest attainable standard of health, to water, to share in culture, and to benefit from scientific progress.[48] Likewise, the Committee on the Rights of the Child has focused on the needs and circumstances of indigenous children,[49] basing its analysis on specific provisions in the Convention on the Rights of the Child that guarantee the rights of indigenous children to their own cultures, religions, and languages.[50]

---

[45] Anaya, *Report of the Special Rapporteur, supra* note 40, para. 23.

[46] U.N. Comm. on the Elimination of Racial Discrimination, *General Recommendation XXIII: Indigenous Peoples*, para. 4, U.N. Doc. CERD/C/51/misc 13/Rev 4 (1997).

[47] Anaya, *Multicultural State, supra* note 5, at 19.

[48] Anaya, *Report of the Special Rapporteur, supra* note 40, para. 23.

[49] *Id.* para. 24.

[50] United Nations Convention on the Rights of the Child, arts. 29–30, Nov. 20, 1989, 1577 U.N.T.S. 3 (1989).

A number of declarations and programmatic statements made in the context of United Nations issue-specific conferences are also relevant to the rights of indigenous peoples. These include the following statement in the Vienna Declaration and Programme of Action from the 1993 World Conference on Human Rights:

> The World Conference on Human Rights recognizes the inherent dignity and the unique contribution of indigenous people to the development and plurality of society and strongly reaffirms the commitment of the international community to their economic, social and cultural well-being and their enjoyment of the fruits of sustainable development. States should ensure the full and free participation of indigenous people in all aspects of society, in particular in matters of concern to them. Considering the importance of the promotion and protection of the rights of indigenous people, and the contribution of such promotion and protection to the political and social stability of the States in which such people live, States should, in accordance with international law, take concerted positive steps to ensure respect for all human rights and fundamental freedoms of indigenous people, on the basis of equality and non-discrimination, and recognize the value and diversity of their distinct identities, cultures and social organization.[51]

Special Rapporteur Anaya's study also refers to important initiatives at the regional level, especially the pathbreaking role played by the Inter-American Commission on Human Rights and the Inter-American Court of Human Rights in developing a rich and detailed jurisprudence concerning the rights of indigenous peoples in the Americas.[52] These bodies have interpreted key provisions in the American Declaration of the Rights and Duties of Man[53] and the American Convention on Human Rights[54] concerning rights to life, to property, and to political participation in light of the distinctive circumstances of indigenous peoples.[55] There have also been important initiatives by the African Commission on Human and Peoples' Rights, including the establishment of a working group on indigenous peoples and communities.[56]

---

[51] World Conference on Human Rights, June 14–25, 1993, *Vienna Declaration and Programme of Action*, U.N. Doc. A/CONF.157/23 (July 12, 1993).

[52] Anaya, *Report of the Special Rapporteur*, *supra* note 40, para. 28.

[53] American Declaration of the Rights and Duties of Man, O.A.S. Res. XXX, *reprinted in* Basic Documents Pertaining to Human Rights in the Inter-American System, OEA/Ser.L.V/II.82 rev.9 (2003).

[54] American Convention on Human Rights, Nov. 22, 1969, O.A.S.T.S. No. 36, 1144 U.N.T.S. 143.

[55] Anaya, *Report of the Special Rapporteur*, *supra* note 40, para. 28; *see also* Jo M. Pasqualucci, *International Indigenous Land Rights: A Critique of the Jurisprudence of the Inter-American Court of Human Rights in Light of the United Nations Declaration on the Rights of Indigenous Peoples*, 27 Wis. Int'l L.J. 51 (2009).

[56] Anaya, *Report of the Special Rapporteur*, *supra* note 40, para. 29.

The International Labour Organization (ILO) Convention Concerning Indigenous and Tribal Peoples in Independent Countries (ILO Convention No. 169)[57] is another source of international obligations. Adopted in 1989, ILO Convention No. 169 has been ratified by twenty-two countries, including most Latin American nations. The treaty expressly protects indigenous peoples' rights in many key areas that international and regional instruments address only implicitly: cultural integrity, consultation, and participation; self-government; autonomy; rights to land, territory, and resources; and non-discrimination. It also recognizes the rights of indigenous *peoples*, not just of individuals who happen to be indigenous.[58]

Taken together, the activities in the United Nations, the ILO, and regional human rights systems described above have led to a "gradual crystallization of a universal common understanding of the minimum content of the rights of these people as a matter of international law and policy."[59] These developments have also served as sources of inspiration for the 2007 Indigenous Peoples Declaration. In the following extract, Anaya discusses the content and implications of the Declaration in further detail.

S. James Anaya, *Report of the Special Rapporteur on the Situation of Human Rights and Fundamental Freedoms of Indigenous Peoples*, Human Rights Council, ninth session, agenda item 3, A/HRC/9/9 (2008)

The Character and General Content of the Declaration

35. The [2007 Indigenous Peoples' Declaration] was adopted by General Assembly resolution 61/295 by an overwhelming majority of Member States, with 143 voting in favour, 4 against and 11 abstaining. While the explanatory statements of the four States that voted against adoption of the Declaration (Australia, Canada, New Zealand, and United States of America) showed disagreement with the wording of specific articles or concerns with the process of adoption, they also expressed a general acceptance of the core principles and values advanced by the Declaration.

36. ... Far from affirming special rights per se, the Declaration aims at repairing the ongoing consequences of the historical denial of the right to self-determination and other basic human rights affirmed in international instruments of general applicability.

---

[57] Sept. 5, 1991, 72 ILO Official Bull. 59, 28 I.L.M. 1382 (1989).
[58] James Anaya, *Indigenous Law and Its Contribution to Global Pluralism*, 6 Indigenous L.J. 3, 6 (2007) [Anaya, *Indigenous Law*].
[59] *Id.*

37. The Declaration affirms in its article 3 the right of indigenous peoples to self-determination.... Reflecting the state of contemporary international law in relation to this principle as well as the demands of indigenous peoples themselves, the affirmation of self-determination in the Declaration is deemed compatible with the principle of territorial integrality and political unity of States (art. 46(1)).

38. The Declaration reaffirms basic individual rights to equality and non-discrimination, life and personal integrity and freedom, and nationality and access to justice; and it calls for special attention to specific rights and needs of indigenous elders, women, youth, children and persons with disabilities (art. 22(1).) At the same time, the Declaration affirms rights of a collective character in relation to self-government and autonomous political, legal, social and cultural institutions; cultural integrity, including cultural and spiritual objects, languages and other cultural expressions; lands, territories and natural resources; social services and development; treaties, agreements and other constructive arrangements; and cross-border cooperation.

39. Together with affirming the aspects of self-determination related to maintaining spheres of autonomy, the Declaration also reflects the common understanding that indigenous peoples' self-determination at the same time involves a participatory engagement and interaction with the larger societal structures in the countries in which they live. In this connection, the Declaration affirms indigenous peoples' right "to participate fully, if they so choose, in the political, economic, social and cultural life of the State" (art. 5); and to be consulted in relation to decisions affecting them, with the objective of obtaining their prior, free and informed consent (art. 19).

40. The Declaration does not affirm or create special rights separate from the fundamental human rights that are deemed of universal application, but rather elaborates upon these fundamental rights in the specific cultural, historical, social and economic circumstances of indigenous peoples. These include the basic norms of equality and non-discrimination, as well as other generally applicable human rights in areas such as culture, health or property, which are recognized in other international instruments and are universally applicable.

41. Albeit clearly not binding in the same way that a treaty is, the Declaration relates to already existing human rights obligations of States, as demonstrated by the work of United Nations treaty bodies and other human rights mechanisms, and hence can be seen as embodying to some extent general principles of international law. In addition, insofar as they connect with a pattern of consistent international and State practice, some aspects of the provisions of the Declaration can also be considered as a reflection of

norms of customary international law. In any event, as a resolution adopted by the General Assembly with the approval of an overwhelming majority of Member States, the Declaration represents a commitment on the part of the United Nations and Member States to its provisions, within the framework of the obligations established by the United Nations Charter to promote and protect human rights on a non-discriminatory basis.

. . .

43. The United Nations Declaration reflects the existing international consensus regarding the individual and collective rights of indigenous peoples in a way that is coherent with, and expands upon, the provisions of ILO Convention No. 169, as well as with other developments, including the interpretations of other human rights instruments by international bodies and mechanisms. As the most authoritative expression of this consensus, the Declaration provides a framework of action towards the full protection and implementation of these rights.

Mechanisms to Operationalize the Rights Affirmed
in the Declaration on the Rights of Indigenous Peoples

44. The seventh preambular paragraph of the Declaration emphasizes the "urgent need to respect and promote the inherent rights of indigenous peoples." Like any other human rights instrument does, the Declaration confers a pivotal role to State actors in the promotion and protection of the rights affirmed therein. The central role of the State is further reinforced by the essentially reparative orientation of the instrument, which requires States to take affirmative measures to attack the systemic problems that indigenous peoples face in the enjoyment of their human rights in ways that are consistent with their specific cultural characteristics and their own expressed wishes.

. . .

46. The kind of State action required to operationalize the rights affirmed in the Declaration ... entails an ambitious programme of legal and policy reform, institutional action and reparations for past wrongs, involving a myriad of State actors within their respective spheres of competence. [A] spirit of cooperation and mutual understanding between States and indigenous peoples is a theme throughout the Declaration, including in the provision which underlines the value of historical and modern treaties or compacts as mechanisms to advance relations of cooperation between indigenous peoples and States (art. 37).

47. The positive or special measures required to operationalize the Declaration need to reach the existing local institutional arrangements and policy frameworks, which in some cases may have to be reformed to accommodate the particular needs of indigenous peoples, as underlined in the Declaration. Depending on the local context, specific policies, programmes and institutions may be required to promote the concerted action of government agencies regarding indigenous peoples. In those countries where they already exist, their terms of reference and goals should be framed by rights and principles affirmed in the Declaration.

...

Legal Reform and Judicial Action

50. Implementing the Declaration will normally require or may be facilitated by the adoption of new laws or the amendment of existing legislation at the domestic level, as envisaged by article 38 of the Declaration which calls for appropriate "legislative measures." Also normally required will be new regulatory frameworks, which in most countries are still lacking or are insufficient.

51. This is true, for instance, in relation to the provisions of the Declaration regarding indigenous peoples' rights to "autonomy or self-government in matters relating to their internal and local affairs" (art. 4) and to "maintain and strengthen their distinct political, legal, economic, social and cultural institutions" (art. 5), including in the administration of justice (arts. 34–35). Indigenous systems of autonomy or self-government carry a number of implications for broader State governance that have not been fully acknowledged in most countries, where indigenous autonomy or self-government still operates de facto and without the proper legal guarantees. The same holds true in relation to indigenous rights over their lands, territories and natural resources, as affirmed in articles 26 to 28 and related provisions of the Declaration. While these rights are generally recognized in many countries, their realization implies a whole package of legal and administrative transformations, particularly regarding property and natural resources law and administration.

53. In a number of cases, the recognition of indigenous peoples and their rights as mandated by the Declaration may require changes of a constitutional nature. Based on this understanding, the Declaration has already been used as a normative reference in recent or ongoing constitutional revision processes, such as in Bolivia, Ecuador and Nepal.

54. Domestic courts also play a key role in operationalizing the rights of indigenous peoples as affirmed in international standards.

55. Bridging this gap requires the concerted, goal-oriented action of a myriad of governmental actors within the scope of their respective fields of competence, and involves a mixture of political will, technical capacity, and financial commitment.

Mainstreaming and Awareness-Raising

56. While the operationalization of the Declaration requires State action in the form of policies, programmes, institutions and legal reforms that are specific to indigenous peoples, the principles and rights set forth in the Declaration should be mainstreamed into the different operative sectors of government, and should be taken into consideration in the wider policy-making processes and in the establishment of programmatic priorities.

---

* * * Issues in Focus * * *

The emergence of indigenous peoples' human rights challenges fundamental structural elements of the international legal system. Most obviously, the right to self-determination challenges the sovereignty of nation states, especially in jurisdictions with unified national governments such as the "Crown-in-Parliament" Westminster system of democracy.[60] Conceptually – and, increasingly, legally – indigenous human rights claims are grounded on the idea that unitary notions of sovereignty are incomplete, and that indigenous peoples are also sources of power that exist alongside the nation state. At both the international and domestic levels, demands for self-determination – as well as solidarity among indigenous peoples physically located within different jurisdictions – question the dominant perception of the nation state as the lynchpin of the international legal order. As James Anaya has stated:

> The model that is emerging from the interplay of Indigenous demands and the authoritative responses to those demands is one that sees Indigenous peoples as simultaneously distinct from, yet part of, the social fabric of the states in which they live, as well as parts of other units of social and political interaction that might include Indigenous confederations or transnational associations.[61]

Indigenous peoples' rights claims have also contributed to the rise of collective rights, causing a shift in dominant paradigms of international law. The growth of the human rights movement beginning in the middle of the twentieth century was itself a profound shift in the "law of nations" toward greater

---

[60] See PAUL McHUGH, THE MĀORI MAGNA CARTA: NEW ZEALAND AND THE TREATY OF WAITANGI 15 (1991).

[61] Anaya, *Indigenous Law, supra* note 58, at 6.

recognition of individuals as subjects of international law. Indigenous peoples' claims, in turn, call into question the now well established focus of the human rights movement on the duties of the state toward the individual. These claims can thus be understood at least in part as challenging the state/individual dichotomy that is a foundational premise of international human rights law.[62]

These small but perceptible shifts in the conceptual underpinnings of international law also have important implications for intellectual property issues. Just as indigenous human rights claims unsettle the individual-state dichotomy in human rights law, they also challenge the individualist focus of intellectual property law. Indigenous claims often focus on the role of the group in creative processes that may develop through the accretion of innumerable individual contributions occurring over many generations. As an example of this collective focus, consider the following statement by Banduk Marika, a member of the Rirratjingu clan in northern Arnhem Land in Australia:

> My artwork ... is known as the "Djanda Sacred Waterhole." The image is an image which belongs to my clan, the Rirratjingu, and forms part of the mythology of the Djangkawu creation story. The image is of great importance to my clan and also has importance to clans in the neighbouring areas, which have rights in this image.[63]

Some nations' laws contain specific provisions to address this type of creativity. In the Philippines, for example, the 1997 Indigenous Peoples Rights Act protects the "community intellectual property rights" of indigenous peoples. These rights are very broadly defined and include past, present, and future manifestations of their cultures, such as archaeological and historical sites, designs, ceremonies, technologies, visual and performing arts, literature, and religious and "spiritual properties"; science and technology, such as "human and other genetic resources, seeds, medicines, health practices, vital medicinal plants, animals, minerals, indigenous knowledge systems and practices, resource management systems, agricultural technologies, knowledge of the properties of fauna and flora, and scientific discoveries"; and "language, music, dance, script, histories, oral traditions, conflict resolution mechanisms, peace building processes, life philosophy and perspectives and teaching and learning systems."[64]

---

[62] *Id.* at 9.
[63] Affidavit of Banduk Marika, 1994 (*cited in* World Intellectual Property Org. (WIPO), *Minding Culture: Case Studies on Intellectual Property and Traditional Cultural Expression*, 11, Doc. WIPO/GRTKF/STUDY/2 (2003) (*prepared by* Terri Janke)).
[64] Rules and Regulations Implementing, Rep. Act No. 8371, § 10, rule VI (*quoted in* Coenraad Visser, *Culture, Traditional Knowledge, and Trademarks: A View from the South*, in GRAEME B. DINWOODIE & MARK D. JANIS [EDS.], TRADEMARK LAW AND THEORY: A HANDBOOK OF CONTEMPORARY RESEARCH 464, 467 [2008]).

Notes and Questions

1. The 2007 Indigenous Peoples Declaration is a nonbinding instrument. As such, it is an example of an increasingly important mode of international norm generation known as "soft law,"[65] a broad category that includes declarations, resolutions, model rules, statements of principles, codes of conduct, and other nonbinding documents.[66]

2. What are the advantages and disadvantages of adopting an international instrument on the rights of indigenous peoples as a nonbinding declaration rather than attempting to forge a legally binding treaty? According to one scholar:

> Soft law ... may provide more immediate evidence of international support and consensus than a treaty. This is so because, even once agreed upon, a treaty will have to wait the necessary number of ratifications before entering into force. For indigenous peoples, instead, it was crucial that, after more than twenty years of negotiations, the final instrument could be instantly effective. This is so because urgent action is key to the protection of their rights. In addition, the possibility of entering reservations on fundamental provisions may weaken importantly the idea of international support, which, instead, represented a crucial factor in the context of indigenous rights.[67]

What other reasons might explain the decision to adopt the 2007 Indigenous Peoples Declaration as a soft law instrument? Consider in this context the issues addressed in the preceding Issues in Focus. As you review the materials in the section that follows, consider the implications of including specific protections for indigenous peoples' intellectual property rights in a "soft law" instrument rather than a treaty.

7.3. Human Rights, Self-Determination, and the Protection of Indigenous Peoples' Intellectual Property

Arguably the most central human rights issue for indigenous peoples is the right to self-determination, a right that in principle allows a "people"

---

[65] *See generally* Rosemary J. Coombe, *Protecting Traditional Environmental Knowledge and New Social Movements in the Americas: Intellectual Property, Human Right, or Claims to an Alternative Form of Sustainable Development?*, 17 FLA. J. INT'L L. 155, 118–19 (listing other examples of soft laws that are relevant to the protection of traditional knowledge and noting that these are "routinely reiterated by state and intergovernmental bodies as best practices for state conduct").

[66] *See generally* C.M. Chinkin, *The Challenge of Soft Law: Development and Change in International Law*, 38 INT'L & COMP. L.Q. 850, 851 (1989).

[67] Barelli, *supra* note 3, at 966 (internal citation and quotations omitted).

to determine freely its political status and pursue its economic, social, and cultural development.[68] Intellectual property is directly relevant to self-determination claims, in particular the cultural, technological, and economic development of indigenous peoples.

Both the ICESCR and the ICCPR set forth a right to self-determination that is relevant to indigenous intellectual property issues. The text of the first article in each instrument announces: "All peoples have the right of self-determination. By virtue of that right they freely determine their political status and freely pursue their economic, social and cultural development." The Covenants then elaborate on what might be described as the "economic" side of this right. Article 1(2) of both instruments provides: "All peoples may, for their own ends, freely dispose of their natural wealth and resources without prejudice to any obligations arising out of international economic co-operation, based upon the principle of mutual benefit, and international law. In no case may a people be deprived of its own means of subsistence." The instruments then oblige member states to "promote the realization of the right of self-determination" and to "respect that right, in conformity with the provisions of the Charter of the United Nations."[69] On their face, these provisions appear to provide capacious self-determination rights for indigenous communities. As Hurst Hannum has explained, however, "self-determination in the era of decolonization was based primarily on territory, not human beings. Despite frequent proclamations that all 'peoples' had the right to self-determination, it was colonial territories that were granted independence, not their peoples."[70]

A more productive source of indigenous self-determination claims, including those relevant to intellectual property, is found in Article 27 of the ICCPR. Article 27 provides that "in those States in which ethnic, religious or linguistic minorities exist, persons belonging to such minorities shall not be denied the right, in community with the other members of their group, to enjoy their own culture, to profess and practice their own religion or to use their own language."[71] (Because of its emphasis on the

---

[68] Peter-Tobias Stoll & Anja von Hahn, *Indigenous Peoples, Indigenous Knowledge and Indigenous Resources in International Law,* in INDIGENOUS HERITAGE AND INTELLECTUAL PROPERTY, *supra* note 9, at 5, 12.

[69] ICESCR, art. 1; ICCPR, art.1.

[70] Hurst Hannum, *Minorities, Indigenous Peoples, and Self-Determination,* in LOUIS HENKIN & JOHN LAWRENCE HARGROVE (EDS.), HUMAN RIGHTS: AN AGENDA FOR THE NEXT CENTURY 1, 5 (1994).

[71] *See generally* ANNA MEIJKNECHT, TOWARD INTERNATIONAL PERSONALITY: THE POSITION OF MINORITIES AND INDIGENOUS PEOPLES IN INTERNATIONAL LAW 135 (2001) (noting the "hybrid" character of Article 27: while Article 27 does not protect groups as such, and can

universality of human rights, the Universal Declaration of Human Rights (UDHR) does not contain specific provisions concerning the rights of minorities.[72]) Although the characterization of indigenous peoples as minorities is controversial,[73] the U.N. Human Rights Committee has interpreted Article 27 as providing a legal basis for indigenous peoples' right to self-determination.[74] Commentators have also cited Article 27 in support of the right of indigenous peoples to exist as distinct cultures, a right that encompasses economic and political institutions, land use patterns, language and religious practices, and connections to ancestral and communal lands.[75] The Human Rights Committee also envisions Article 27 as protecting the economic components of "culture,"[76] as is suggested by decisions that reference "traditional means of livelihood of minorities" and "adaptation of those means to the modern way of life and ensuing technology."[77] General guarantees of nondiscrimination are also relevant in this context.[78] The existence, continued flourishing, and protection of indigenous culture may be impeded by discrete or systemic prejudice, put into operation through governmental policies and laws.[79]

therefore be characterized as an individual right to belong to a minority group, meaningful exercise of this right requires, and is premised upon, the existence of the collectivity).

[72] See Martin Scheinin, *Indigenous Peoples' Rights under the International Covenant on Civil and Political Rights*, in JOSHUA CASTELLINO & NIAMH WALSH (EDS.), INTERNATIONAL LAW AND INDIGENOUS PEOPLES 3, 4 (2005).

[73] *Id.*

[74] See U.N. Human Rights Comm., Annual Report 1990, *Ominayak and the Lubicon Lake Band v. Canada*, U.N. Doc. A/45/40, Bd. II, App. A (1999) (Cree Indians' right to self-determination).

[75] Anaya, *Multicultural State, supra* note 5, at 25.

[76] *See, e.g.,* U.N. Human Rights Comm., Report, *Ivan Kitok v. Sweden* (Communication No. 197/1985), Supl. No. 40 (U.N. Doc. A/43/40) (July 27, 1988) (affirming the extension of article 27 to reindeer herding rights of member of Sami people) (*cited in* Scheinin, *supra* note 72, at 6); U.N. Human Rights Comm., Report, *Illmari Länsman v. Finland No. 1*, Supl. No. 40 (U.N. Doc. A/50/40) (noting that interference with the sustainability of the indigenous or minority community constitutes interference with the right protected by Article 27) (*cited in* Scheinin, *supra* note 72, at 7).

[77] U.N. Human Rights Comm., Report, at 11–29, para. 9.6, *Apirana Mahuika et al. v. New Zealand* (Communication No. 547/1993), U.N. Doc. A/56/40 (Vol. II) (Oct. 27, 2000).

[78] *See* Stoll & von Hahn, *supra* note 68, at 20; Patrick Thornberry, *The Convention on the Elimination of Racial Discrimination, Indigenous Peoples and Cast/Descent-Based Discrimination*, in INTERNATIONAL LAW AND INDIGENOUS PEOPLES, *supra* note 72, at 17; *see also* ANAYA, *supra* note 42, at 97 (noting general acceptance of the customary international law principle that states are enjoined not to promote or condone systemic racial discrimination).

[79] *See, e.g.,* Judith M. Maxwell, *Ownership of Indigenous Languages: A Case Study from Guatemala*, in INDIGENOUS INTELLECTUAL PROPERTY RIGHTS: LEGAL OBSTACLES AND INNOVATIVE SOLUTIONS, *supra* note 9, at 173.

Additional guarantees for indigenous peoples are found in ILO Convention No. 169. Although the Convention does not expressly mention folklore, traditional knowledge, or intellectual property, a number of its provisions are relevant to these topics. For instance, Article 23 refers to "handcrafts, rural and community-based industries, and subsistence economy and traditional activities" and specifies that these "shall be recognized as important factors in the maintenance of ... cultures and in ... economic self-reliance and development." In addition, Article 13 requires all states to "respect the special importance for the cultures and spiritual values of the peoples concerned of their relationship with [their] land." ILO Convention No. 169 does not, however, address the nexus between self-determination, land rights, and traditional knowledge.

Nonbinding international instruments do address this nexus. In 1995, the Sub-Commission on Prevention of Discrimination and Protection of Minorities promulgated a set of Principles and Guidelines for the Protection of the Heritage of Indigenous Peoples.[80] The document stipulated that, to be effective, "protection of indigenous peoples' heritage should be based broadly on the principle of self-determination, which includes the right and the duty of indigenous peoples to develop their own cultures and knowledge systems, and forms of social organization."[81] It also adopted a broad definition of the heritage of indigenous peoples that directly implicates intellectual property issues:

> 11. The heritage of indigenous peoples is comprised of all objects, sites and knowledge the nature or use of which has been transmitted from generation to generation, and which is regarded as pertaining to a particular people or its territory. The heritage of an indigenous people also includes objects, knowledge and literary or artistic works which may be created in the future based upon its heritage.

> 12. The heritage of indigenous peoples includes all moveable cultural property as defined by the relevant conventions of UNESCO; all kinds of literary and artistic works such as music, dance, song, ceremonies, symbols and designs, narratives and poetry; all kinds of scientific, agricultural, technical and ecological knowledge, including cultigens, medicines and the rational use of flora and fauna; human remains; immoveable cultural property such as sacred sites, sites of historical significance, and burials; and documentation of indigenous peoples' heritage on film, photographs, videotape, or audiotape.

> 13. Every element of an indigenous peoples' heritage has traditional owners, which may be the whole people, a particular family or clan, an association or

---

[80] *See* Special Rapporteur, *Protection of the Heritage, supra* note 12.

[81] *Id.* at para. 2. Interestingly in light of its subsequent involvement in indigenous intellectual property issues, WIPO was unwilling to assume any responsibilities relating to the Principles and Guidelines. *Id.* at paras. 12, 29.

society, or individuals who have been specially taught or initiated to be its custodians. The traditional owners of heritage must be determined in accordance
with indigenous peoples' own customs, laws and practices.

The document made a number of specific recommendations for reform of
domestic legal regimes, particularly in the area of intellectual property:

> 25. National laws should guarantee that indigenous peoples can obtain prompt,
> effective and affordable judicial or administrative action in their own languages
> to prevent, punish and obtain full restitution and just compensation for the
> acquisition, documentation or use of their heritage without proper authoriza-
> tion of the traditional owners.

> 26. National laws should deny to any person or corporation the right to obtain
> patent, copyright or other legal protection for any element of indigenous peo-
> ples' heritage without adequate documentation of the free and informed con-
> sent of the traditional owners to an arrangement for the sharing of ownership,
> control, use and benefits.

> 27. National laws should ensure the labelling and correct attribution of
> indigenous peoples' artistic, literary and cultural works whenever they are
> offered for public display or sale. Attribution should be in the form of a trade-
> mark or an appellation of origin, authorized by the peoples or communities
> concerned.

> 28. National laws for the protection of indigenous peoples' heritage should
> be adopted following consultations with the peoples concerned, in particular
> the traditional owners and teachers of religious, sacred and spiritual knowl-
> edge, and, wherever possible, should have the informed consent of the peoples
> concerned.

> 29. National laws should ensure that the use of traditional languages in
> education, arts and the mass media is respected and, to the extent possible, pro-
> moted and strengthened.[82]

The Principles and Guidelines also made several detailed stipulations concerning the activities of artists, writers and performers:

> 46. Artists, writers and performers should refrain from incorporating elements
> derived from indigenous heritage into their works without the informed con-
> sent of the traditional owners.

> 47. Artists, writers and performers should support the full artistic and cul-
> tural development of indigenous peoples, and encourage public support for
> the development and greater recognition of indigenous artists, writers and
> performers.

> 48. Artists, writers and performers should contribute, through their individ-
> ual works and professional organizations, to the greater public understanding

---

[82] *Id.* at paras. 25–29.

and respect for the indigenous heritage associated with the country in which they live.[83]

The 2007 Indigenous Peoples Declaration provides an express textual basis for indigenous peoples to exercise control over their intellectual property. Article 11 of the Declaration provides:

> 1. Indigenous peoples have the right to practise and revitalize their cultural traditions and customs. This includes the right to maintain, protect and develop the past, present and future manifestations of their cultures, such as archaeological and historical sites, artefacts, designs, ceremonies, technologies and visual and performing arts and literature.
>
> 2. States shall provide redress through effective mechanisms, which may include restitution, developed in conjunction with indigenous peoples, with respect to their cultural, intellectual, religious and spiritual property taken without their free, prior and informed consent or in violation of their laws, traditions and customs.

Article 24 is also relevant to this issue. It provides that "indigenous peoples have the right to their traditional medicines and to maintain their health practices, including the conservation of their vital medicinal plants, animals and minerals." Perhaps the most expansive references to intellectual property are set forth in Article 31(1) and 31(2):

> 1. Indigenous peoples have the right to maintain, control, protect and develop their cultural heritage, traditional knowledge and traditional cultural expressions, as well as the manifestations of their sciences, technologies and cultures, including human and genetic resources, seeds, medicines, knowledge of the properties of fauna and flora, oral traditions, literatures, designs, sports and traditional games and visual and performing arts. They also have the right to maintain, control, protect and develop their intellectual property over such cultural heritage, traditional knowledge, and traditional cultural expressions.
>
> 2. In conjunction with indigenous peoples, States shall take effective measures to recognize and protect the exercise of these rights.

Article 31(2)'s reference to "effective measures" provides a useful point of comparison with the TRIPS Agreement. One of the innovations of TRIPS

---

[83] *Id.* at paras. 46–48. A 2000 report, titled *Human Rights of Indigenous Peoples*, further developed the draft Principles and Guidelines. ESOSOC, Sub-Comm'n on Prevention of Discrimination & Prot. of Minorities, Human Rights of Indigenous Peoples: Report of the Seminar on the Draft Principles and Guidelines for the Protection of the Heritage of Indigenous People, U.N. Doc. E/CN.4/Sub.2/2000/26 (June 19, 2000). The Sub-Commission produced the report following a seminar attended by "representatives of Governments, United Nations bodies and organisations, specialised agencies, organisations of indigenous peoples and competent indigenous persons." *Id.* paras. 1, 3. Unlike the draft Principles and Guidelines, WIPO participated in the seminar. *See id.* para. 13.

was to introduce new international obligations concerning the enforcement of intellectual property rights. In particular, TRIPS obligates WTO member states to "ensure that enforcement procedures ... are available under their law so as to permit effective action against any act of infringement of intellectual property rights covered by this Agreement, including expeditious remedies to prevent infringements and remedies which constitute a deterrent to further infringements."[84] Similarly, the Declaration requires states to confirm that the intellectual property of indigenous peoples will be recognized *and* protected.

The relationship between the intellectual property provisions of the 2007 Indigenous Peoples Declaration and creators' human rights (analyzed in Chapter 3) is unclear and unexplored. Article 27(2) of the UDHR announces that "everyone has the right to the protection of the moral and material interests resulting from any scientific, literary or artistic protection of which he is the author." Similarly worded guarantees are set forth in Article 15(1)(c) of the ICESCR and Article 13 of the American Declaration on the Rights and Duties of Man. As Chapter 3 explains, this recognition of authors' moral and material interests as "human rights" challenges the conventional conceptual organization of modern intellectual property laws.[85] That challenge extends as well to the protection of traditional knowledge and cultural expressions.

Before the recent attention given to creators' human rights, some scholars reasoned that, because of the focus on *individual* human rights in these provisions, "indigenous resources and indigenous knowledge do not find protection by article 27(2) of the UDHR and article 15(1)(c) of the ICESCR."[86] However, in *General Comment No. 17*,[87] adopted in 2005, the Committee on Economic, Social and Cultural Rights interpreted Article 15(1)(c) to include the knowledge, innovations and practices of indigenous and local communities:

> The Committee considers that "any scientific, literary or artistic production", within the meaning of article 15, paragraph 1 (c), refers to creations of the

---

[84] Agreement on Trade-Related Aspects of Intellectual Property Rights, art. 41(1), Apr. 15, 1994, 1869 U.N.T.S. 299 [TRIPS Agreement].

[85] *Cf.* Lionel Bentley & Brad Sherman, The Making of Modern Intellectual Property Law (1999) (discussing the conceptual organization of intellectual property law).

[86] Peter Tobias-Stoll & Anja von Hahn, *Indigenous Peoples, Indigenous Knowledge and Indigenous Resources in International Law*, in Indigenous Heritage and Intellectual Property, *supra* note 9, at 5, 18. These authors also note, however, that a broader interpretation may be possible. *Id.*

[87] Comm. on Econ., Soc. & Cultural Rights, *General Comment No. 17: The Right of Everyone to Benefit from the Protection of the Moral and Material Interests Resulting from Any Scientific, Literary or Artistic Production of Which He or She Is the Author (Art. 15(1)(c))*, U.N. Doc. E/C.12/GC17 (Jan. 12, 2006).

human mind, that is to "scientific productions", such as scientific publications and innovations, including knowledge, innovations and practices of indigenous and local communities, and "literary and artistic productions", such as, inter alia, poems, novels, paintings, sculptures, musical compositions, theatrical and cinematographic works, performances and oral traditions.[88]

Such recognition of the (collective) rights of indigenous and local communities is in marked contrast with the Committee's view that human rights protected by Article 15(1)(c) do not extend to intellectual property owned by corporations. As we discuss in Chapter 3, *General Comment No. 17* does not explain the basis for this distinction.

Textually and, arguably, conceptually, Article 15(1)(c) is organized around the rights of the "author," a dominant notion in intellectual property laws. Commentators often highlight the "poor fit" that intellectual property laws provide for protecting traditional knowledge and cultural expressions.[89] This can be because the latter do not meet established subject-matter criteria for protection or, conversely, because the processes of their production by the relevant indigenous communities do not accommodate or endorse the private, individualist ownership concepts on which intellectual property law is often assumed to be premised. As the text of Article 15(1)(c) underscores, this problem persists whether one views indigenous peoples' creativity through either a human rights or an intellectual property lens.

Grounding Article 15(1)(c) in notions of authorship implicates a range of complex issues. According to intellectual property norms, an individual author often begins by drawing from a preexisting "intellectual commons" of public domain materials that include general knowledge, ideas, facts, and works whose term of protection has expired. He or she is then expected to create a unique "production" (in the sense that it is the author's own) that can be distinguished from the background, nonproprietary materials in the intellectual commons. In the indigenous context, this perspective creates at least three points of tension. First, indigenous groups may have different notions of what materials are in the commons free for others to use. Second, the emphasis on the individual author who creates something distinguishable from background materials in the public domain may not be so easily accommodated to group responsibility for the creation, preservation, and development of indigenous culture. Third, intellectual property laws sometimes require that a work be "fixed" in some tangible medium before it can be protected; indigenous creativity may be more fluid or ephemeral and thus less easily accommodated to a fixation requirement.

---

[88] *Id.* para. 9.
[89] *E.g.*, Moly Torsen, *Intellectual Property and Traditional Cultural Expressions: A Synopsis of Current Issues*, 3 INTERCULTURAL HUM. RTS. L. REV. 201, 201 (2008).

Many indigenous peoples have urged that their traditional knowledge and cultural productions should not be regarded as common property.[90] This perspective is grounded in a broader historical misunderstanding of – or willful blindness to – indigenous systems of property and ownership.[91] A notorious example of such willful blindness was the *terra nullius* doctrine adopted by the Crown in Australia, and, until recently, endorsed by the Australian judiciary. According to this doctrine, the continent of Australia was regarded as unoccupied and not subject to the prior rights of Aboriginal peoples who had lived there for tens of thousands of years before English colonization began in the late eighteenth century.[92] The corollary principle in the intellectual property context is the assumption that indigenous knowledge – including stories, designs, dances, ceremonies, medical techniques, knowledge of flora and fauna – is unprotected common property available for anyone to appropriate.

Those who view systems of property ownership only through Western eyes may overlook the significance – or even the existence – of indigenous systems of control and ownership over traditional knowledge.[93] Australia again provides an example. In 1966, Australia introduced a new decimal currency – a further step toward severing its colonial ties to the United Kingdom. The new one dollar note incorporated an Aboriginal theme into its design – a "line interpretation" of a bark painting by a distinguished Aboriginal artist from Arnhem Land in the far northwest of the continent. The bark paintings depicted the "mourning cycle" of the Manharingu people. It did not occur to anyone involved, even the governor of the Reserve Bank of Australia, H. C. Coombes, a known supporter of Aboriginal autonomy, to secure the artist's consent. Presumably, Aboriginal art was considered to be part of the

---

[90] *See* Graham Dutfield, *TRIPS-Related Aspects of Traditional Knowledge*, 33 CASE W. RES. J. INT'L L. 223, 238 (2001) ("TK [traditional knowledge] is often (and conveniently) assumed to be in the public domain. This is likely to encourage the presumption that nobody is harmed and no rules are broken when research institutions and corporations use it freely.").

[91] *Cf.* CAROL ROSE, PROPERTY AND PERSUASION: ESSAYS ON THE HISTORY, THEORY AND RHETORIC OF OWNERSHIP (1994). Rose's concern with the extent to which property is an expressive endeavor is particularly salient in the context of tensions that arise between different approaches to signaling appropriation that different cultures may adopt, and to explaining some of the profound and painful misunderstandings that can arise when one culture's property signals are not interpreted accurately.

[92] *See Mabo v. Queensland [No. 2]* (1992) 175 C.L.R. 1 (rejecting the notion of "terra nullius" in Australia). The International Court of Justice reached a similar result in a 1975 adivsory opinion concluding that the Western Sahara was not *terra nullius* when it was acquired by Spain in the late nineteenth century. Western Sahara, Advisory Opinion, 1975 I.C.J. 12 (Oct. 16).

[93] *See generally*, BARRY BARCLAY, MANATUTURU: MAORI TREASURES AND INTELLECTUAL PROPERTY RIGHTS (2005).

commons, free for everyone, including the Australian government, to draw upon when creating derivative works such as banknote designs. After the news media broke the story, the federal government apologized to the artist. It also gave him a gift of $1,000, a fishing kit, and a silver medal for his service to the Australian nation.[94]

As this example suggests, devising legal regimes that respond appropriately to systems of cultural production in indigenous contexts may require a conceptualization of authorship and creativity that is quite different from the individualistic focus of intellectual property systems.[95] As Graham Dutfield has explained:

> Many commentators, especially those supporting the rights of traditional peoples and communities in the developing world, emphasize the collective nature of creative processes in traditional societies, which they contrast with the individualistic view of creativity (and ownership in the end-product of that creativity) that prevails in Western societies.... The sources of much [traditional knowledge] are difficult to trace, either because two or more peoples or communities share the knowledge, or because the author is simply unknown. And for some traditional communities it would be presumptuous to attribute authorship to a human being anyway. According to the enthoecologist and indigenous rights activist Darrell Posey, ... "indigenous singers ... may attribute songs to the creator spirit."[96]

Notes and Questions

1. What, if anything, does the express recognition of indigenous intellectual property rights in the international instruments discussed previously add to the protection of creators' rights in the UDHR and the ICESCR? Consider this question in the light of *General Comment No. 17* discussed previously. In countries such as Australia and New Zealand, which opposed the adoption of the 2007 Indigenous Peoples Declaration, are the commitments to "creators' rights" set forth in the UDHR and the ICESCR likely to provide as compelling a justification for protecting indigenous intellectual property

---

[94] Justice Ronald Sackville, *Legal Protection of Indigenous Culture in Australia*, 11 Cardozo J. Int'l & Comp. L. 711, 711 (2003).

[95] *See generally*, Angela R. Riley, *Recovering Collectivity: Group Rights to Intellectual Property in Indigenous Communities*, 18 Cardozo Arts & Ent. L.J. 175 (2000).

[96] Dutfield, *supra* note 90, at 242–43 (citing Darrell Addison Posey, "Indigenous Peoples and Traditional Resource Rights: A Basis for Equitable Relationships?" 17 (June 28, 1995) (unpublished manuscript)). Dutfield also notes, however, that "for other groups this may not be true at all"; in some cases specific innovations are claimed by individuals. *Id.* at 243 (citing Anil K. Gupta, *Making Indian Agriculture More Knowledge Intensive and Competitive: The Case of Intellectual Property Rights*, 54 Indian J. Agric. Econ. 342, 346–53 [1999]).

as the Declaration? (The United States also opposed adoption of the 2007 Indigenous Peoples Declaration but has not ratified the ICESCR.)

2. Are indigenous peoples' claims regarding intellectual property appropriately characterized as human rights, or do they share greater common ground with the instrumentalist economic rights set forth in TRIPS Agreement? Does Article 31 of the 2007 Indigenous Peoples Declaration envisage a right to commercial exploitation of indigenous intellectual property? Can commercial exploitation be linked to other human rights, such as the right to development? If not, does such exploitation call into question arguments for protecting indigenous intellectual property on human rights grounds?

3. Compare the views of many indigenous peoples that the traditional knowledge used by their communities over many years is subject to their exclusive ownership and control with the intellectual property concept of the public domain, which views such knowledge as part of an intellectual commons that is freely accessible to all and that enriches future creativity. How, if at all, might these perspectives be reconciled?

4. The extensive obligations to enforce intellectual property rights were among the more controversial provisions included in TRIPS. Why might this be the case? Are the enforcement provisions in the 2007 Indigenous Peoples Declaration likely to attract similar critiques?

5. The 1992 Convention on Biological Diversity, discussed in Chapter 6, requires each member state, "subject to its national legislation, [to] respect, preserve and maintain knowledge, innovations and practices of indigenous and local communities embodying traditional lifestyles relevant for the conservation and sustainable use of biological diversity."[97] The 1992 Rio Declaration on Environment and Development similarly recognizes the "vital" role played by indigenous peoples in sustainable development "because of their knowledge and traditional practices."[98] Formally, these documents sit outside the international human rights system. How might this placement affect the scope of the obligations they articulate?

7.4. Indigenous Peoples' International Initiatives Relevant to Intellectual Property

Indigenous peoples have produced their own declarations and sets of principles relating to intellectual property. These documents include

---

[97] Convention on Biological Diversity, art. 8(j), U.N. Conference on Environment and Development, U.N. Doc. UNEP.Bio.Div./CONF.L2.1992 (1992).

[98] Rio Declaration on Environment and Development, Principle 22, U.N. Conference on Environment and Development, U.N. Doc. A/CONF.151/26 Ann.1 (1992).

statements of rights, plans of action, expressions of concern, and directives to governments, industries, and international organizations.[99] This section reviews these initiatives, many of which occurred in the lead up to, and during, the United Nations International Year for the World's Indigenous Peoples (1993) and the United Nations Decade of the World's Indigenous Peoples (1995–2004).

The Mataatua Declaration[100] was drafted at the First International Conference on the Cultural and Intellectual Property Rights of Indigenous Peoples, held at Whakatane, New Zealand, in 1993. The Conference drew together more than 150 delegates from fourteen countries and was attended by indigenous representatives from Japan, Australia, Cook Islands, Fiji, India, Panama, Peru, the Philippines, the United States, and New Zealand. The Declaration detailed provisions include recommendations directing states and national and international agencies to

2.1 Recognise that indigenous peoples are the guardians of their customary knowledge and have the right to protect and control dissemination of that knowledge.

2.2 Recognise that indigenous peoples also have the right to create new knowledge based on cultural tradition.

2.3 Note that existing protection mechanisms are insufficient for the protection of Indigenous Peoples' cultural and intellectual property rights.

2.4 Accept that the cultural and intellectual property rights of Indigenous Peoples are vested with those who created them.

2.5 Develop in full cooperation with Indigenous Peoples an additional cultural and intellectual property rights regime incorporating the following:

(a) Collective (as well as individual) ownership and origin-retroactive coverage of historical as well as contemporary works;

(b) Protection against debasement of culturally significant items;

(c) Cooperative rather than competitive framework;

(d) First beneficiaries to be the direct descendants of the traditional guardians of that knowledge; and

(e) Multi-generational coverage span.

Later the same year, at Jingarra, in the northeastern coastal region of Australia, a gathering of indigenous and nonindigenous specialists declared a further set of principles. The Julayinbul Statement on Indigenous Intellectual

---

[99] *See generally Our Culture: Our Future, supra* note 14, at 305.
[100] Mataatua Declaration, *supra* note 11.

Property Rights sets forth a number of key principles and agreed statements, including the following:

> Indigenous Peoples and Nations share a unique spiritual and cultural relationship with Mother Earth which recognises the interdependence of the total environment and is governed by the natural laws which determine our perceptions of intellectual property.
>
> Inherent in these laws and integral to that relationship is the right of Indigenous Peoples and Nations to continue to live within and protect, care for, and control the use of that environment and of their knowledge.
>
> Within the context of this Statement, Indigenous Peoples and Nations reaffirm their right to define for themselves their own intellectual property, acknowledging their own self-determination and the uniqueness of their particular heritage.
>
> Within the context of this Statement, Indigenous Peoples and Nations also declare that we are capable of managing our intellectual property ourselves, but are willing to share it with all humanity provided that our fundamental rights to define and control this property are recognised by the international community.
>
> Aboriginal Common Law and English/Australian Common Law are parallel and equal systems of law.
>
> Aboriginal intellectual property, within Aboriginal Common Law, is an inherent inalienable right which cannot be terminated, extinguished, or taken.
>
> Any use of the intellectual property of Aboriginal Nations and Peoples may only be done in accordance with Aboriginal Common Law, and any unauthorised use is strictly prohibited.
>
> Just as Aboriginal Common Law has never sought to unilaterally extinguish English/Australian Common Law, so we expect English/Australian Common Law to reciprocate.
>
> We, the delegates assembled at this conference urge Indigenous Peoples and Nations to develop processes and strategies acceptable to them to facilitate the practical application of the above principles and to ensure the dialogue and negotiation which are envisaged by the principles.
>
> We also call on governments to review legislation and non-statutory policies which currently impinge upon or do not recognise indigenous intellectual property rights. Where policies, legislation and international conventions currently recognise these rights, we require that they be implemented.[101]

In 1994, the delegates attending a meeting in Santa Cruz de la Sierra, Bolivia, promulgated an additional set of principles on this topic. The purpose of the meeting was to debate intellectual property rights and biodiversity. Among the delegates were the Coordinating Body of Indigenous Organisations

---

[101] See *Julayinbul Statement, supra* note 18.

of the Amazon Basin and a number of NGOs with an interest in intellectual property and biodiversity issues, such as the Rural Advancement Fund
International and the Working Group on Traditional Resource Rights. The
participants produced a consensus document that included recommendations for short- and long-term strategies. The document declared Western
intellectual property regimes to be instruments of domination and incompatible with indigenous cultures. The document also deemed the granting of
intellectual property rights over life forms to be unacceptable to indigenous
peoples. However, it also noted that some forms of intellectual property, specifically those that do not create true monopolies such as trademarks and
appellations of origin, were of potential use to indigenous peoples.[102]

In 2002, the International Indigenous Peoples Summit on Sustainable
Development met in the Khoi-San Territory of Kimberley, South Africa and
issued the Kimberly Statement. Focusing principally on issues relating to
environmental degradation and sustainable development, the document also
included the following provisions relating to traditional knowledge and intellectual property: "Our traditional knowledge systems must be respected, promoted
and protected; our collective intellectual property rights must be guaranteed
and ensured. Our traditional knowledge is not in the public domain; it is collective, cultural and intellectual property protected under our customary law.
Unauthorized use and misappropriation of traditional knowledge is theft."[103]

In 2008, indigenous peoples from around the world gathered together prior
to the thirty-fourth G8 Summit in Hokkaido, Japan. This was the first time
that representatives of indigenous peoples had met in conjunction with a G8
Summit. One of the outcomes of the meeting was an Official Declaration, which,
among other things, called on the G8 nations to take the following actions:

> 15. Provide support for establishing more cultural centres and museums in
> our communities, and for educational institutions and programmes promot-
> ing intercultural and bilingual education, use of Indigenous learning and
> teaching methods – including education through the traditional oral medi-
> ums of Indigenous Peoples and through honouring local ways of learning and
> knowing – as well as language courses to teach Indigenous languages.

> 16. Give effect to the protection of Indigenous Peoples' sacred sites in recog-
> nition of their human rights and intergenerational responsibilities to practice,
> teach, and maintain their spirituality and indigeneity through their traditional

---

[102] The text of the Santa Cruz Declaration is reproduced in [2001] AUSTRL. INDIGENOUS L.
REP. 11, *available at* http://www.austlii.edu.au/au/journals/AILR/2001/11.html.

[103] International Indigenous Peoples Summit on Sustainable Development, Khoi-San Territory
Kimberley, S. Afr., Aug. 20–23, 2002, *Kimberley Declaration, available at* http://www.ipcb.
org/resolutions/htmls/kim_dec.html.

languages, customs, ceremonies, and rituals to ensure the continuity of the sacred in the futures of those yet to be born.

17. Stop the theft and piracy of our traditional Indigenous knowledge, traditional cultural expressions (which include indigenous designs, arts, crafts, song and music), bio-genetic resources including our human genetic resources, by bio-technology corporations, cultural industry, and even by States and individual scientists and researchers.

18. Reform national intellectual property laws and global Intellectual Property Rights regimes including the TRIPS ... of the World Trade Organization (WTO), the Substantive Patent Law of the ... WIPO, among others, to respect and protect the collective traditional knowledge and cultural expressions of Indigenous Peoples.[104]

Notes and Questions

1. What is the legal or normative status in international law of the instruments discussed in this section? What kinds of heuristics inform them? What attention should domestic lawmakers and policymakers give to these instruments? Does the adoption of the 2007 Indigenous Peoples Declaration affect your analysis of these questions?

2. In light of the inclusion of specific provisions on intellectual property in the 2007 Indigenous Peoples Declaration, do the instruments described previously (or other instruments that indigenous peoples may promulgate in the future) continue to have any salience? If so, in what contexts?

3. Are there any relevant legal principles that limit indigenous peoples from asserting rights over traditional knowledge as set forth in these documents? As discussed in other chapters of this book, the human rights to food, health, education, and freedom of expression contain substantive values and objectives that need to be considered when analyzing the scope of intellectual property protection standards in those areas. Do any limiting principles derived from these or other human rights also apply to indigenous peoples' claims to control traditional knowledge as set forth in the declarations and statements reviewed in this section?

7.5. Intellectual Property Protections for Traditional Knowledge and Traditional Cultural Expression

Assertions of rights by indigenous peoples in the context of intellectual property encompass two distinct and opposing elements – claims *to* intellectual property protection, and claims to be protected *from* intellectual property laws and institutions.

---

[104] *Available at* http://www.kyotojournal.org/10,000things/206.html.

The right *to* intellectual property typically is premised on the idea that existing intellectual property systems provide inadequate protections for traditional knowledge.[105] Indigenous groups are doubly disadvantaged by this inadequacy. First, as we have seen, the international intellectual property system generally treats traditional knowledge and cultural expressions as unowned, enabling third parties to exploit them as upstream inputs for later downstream innovations.[106] Second, indigenous peoples seldom share in the financial and technological benefits of downstream innovations that are privatized through intellectual property vehicles such as patents, copyrights, and trademarks.[107] Recognition of these gaps in legal protection has been a catalyst for the development of new, tailored, protections for indigenous peoples' intellectual property, including the array of various options set forth in the WIPO study we extract later in this section.

Assertions of the right to be protected *from* intellectual property also reflect a view that Western legal systems are ill suited to indigenous frameworks of ownership and culture. These systems have been "accused of having an inappropriate individualist bias towards a Eurocentric model of the author, being predominantly market-oriented, and unduly emphasizing or enabling the privatization of knowledge with respect to resources."[108] Some indigenous groups view the imposition of intellectual property regimes as a modern day form of colonization that displaces and usurps indigenous worldviews, agency, and governance mechanisms.[109] In many respects, this concern is grounded in the concept of "cultural privacy,"[110] and a desire not to be required to adopt Western notions of development. This perspective is also consistent with a much more wide-ranging set of discourses on the

---

[105] *See generally* Molly Torsen, *Anonymous, Untitled, Mixed Media: Mixing Intellectual Property Law with Other Legal Philosophies to Protect Traditional Cultural Expression*, 54 Am. J. Comp. L. 173 (2006).

[106] *See* Laurence R. Helfer, *Human Rights and Intellectual Property: Conflict or Coexistence?*, 5 Minn. J. L. Sci. & Tech. 47, 52–53 (2003).

[107] *See* Special Rapporteur, *Protection of the Heritage*, *supra* note 12 (initial text draft of Principles and Guidelines); *see also*, Keith Aoki, *Neocolonialism, Anticommons Property, and Biopiracy in the (not-So-Brave) New World Order of International Intellectual Property Protection*, 6 Ind. J. Global Legal Stud. 11, 47 (1998).

[108] *See* Coombe, *supra* note 65, at 120.

[109] *See generally* Maui Solomon, *Intellectual Property Rights and Indigenous Peoples' Rights and Responsibilities*, in Mary Riley (Ed.), Indigenous Intellectual Property Rights: Legal Obstacles and Innovative Solutions 221 (2004); Graeme W. Austin, *Re-Treating Intellectual Property? The WAI 262 Proceeding and the Heuristics of Intellectual Property Law*, 11 Cardozo J. Int'l & Comp. L. 333 (2003); Rosemary J. Coombe, *The Properties of Culture and the Politics of Possessing Identity: Native Claims in the Cultural Appropriation Controversy*, 6 Can. J.L. & Jurisprudence 249, 285 (1993).

[110] *See* Peter Yu, *Cultural Relics, Intellectual Property, and Intangible Heritage*, 81 Temp. L. Rev. 433, 455–59 (2008).

imposition of external legal principles and norms – even those that offer solutions such as adapting existing intellectual property laws to "protect" traditional knowledge.[111] Among many indigenous groups, there is an acute awareness that, in the past, the overlay of Western legal forms and institutions resulted in the abrogation of ownership and control over indigenous lands and property.[112]

For some indigenous groups, the right to be protected *from* intellectual property also implicates broader questions of state sovereignty. This can be understood in the context of the internationalization of intellectual property through international agreements such as TRIPS. One of the ironies of internationalization is that it reemphasizes national borders and sovereign states, while shifting power to international institutions such as the World Trade Organization. One scholar characterizes this phenomenon as a displacement of "local ... knowledge and property ... in favor of a globalized cartography articulated upon the territorial loci of nation-states."[113]

This emphasis on the state as the principal actor risks reinstating, in the intellectual property context, the usurpation of indigenous peoples' *own* sovereignty that was achieved by colonization. For this reason, debates over intellectual property rights implicate the wider history of domination of indigenous peoples.[114] The usurpation of indigenous peoples' customary systems for managing traditional knowledge and cultural productions can thus be perceived as another affront flowing from colonization.[115]

In 1993, under the sponsorship of the U.N. Sub-commission on Promotion and Protection on Human Rights, Erica-Irene Daes authored the well-known study *Protection of the Cultural and Intellectual Property of Indigenous Peoples*.[116] The study identified widespread historical and continuing deprivation of indigenous peoples' cultural heritage. The study's findings provided

---

[111] PATRICK THORNBERRY, INDIGENOUS PEOPLES AND HUMAN RIGHTS 62–63 (2002).

[112] *See generally* Stuart Banner, *Conquest by Contract: Wealth Transfer and Land Market Structure in Colonial New Zealand*, 34 LAW & SOC'Y REV. 47 (2000); Stuart Banner, *Why Terra Nullius? Anthropology and Property Law in Early Australia*, 23 LAW & HIST. REV. 95 (2005).

[113] Johanna Gibson, *The Lay of the Land: The Geography of Cultural Expression*, in CHRISTOPH BEAT GRABER & MIRA BURRI-NENOVA (EDS.), INTELLECTUAL PROPERTY AND TRADITIONAL CULTURAL EXPRESSIONS IN A DIGITAL ENVIRONMENT 182, 185 (2008).

[114] *See* Munzer & Raustiala, *supra* note 16, at 47.

[115] *See* Moana Jackson, *The Treaty and the Word: The Colonization of Māori Philosophy*, GRAHAM ODDIE & ROY PERRET (EDS.), in JUSTICE, ETHICS & NEW ZEALAND SOCIETY 1, 2 (1992) ("The ethic of *laissez-faire* capitalism, based paradoxically on a rigid class structure and the exploitation of natural resources, could only denigrate as primitive or even dangerous an economy based on conservation and ... collective institutions.").

[116] ECOSOC, Sub-Comm'n on Prevention of Discrimination and Prot. of Minorities, *Discrimination against Indigenous Peoples: Study on the Protection of the Cultural and*

another catalyst for devising solutions to the unauthorized expropriation of indigenous cultural productions – a central concern of the right to be protected *from* intellectual property:

> 18. As industrialisation continued, European States turned to the acquisition of tribal art and the study of exotic cultures. Indigenous peoples were, in succession, despoiled of their lands, sciences, ideas, arts and cultures.
>
> 19. This process is being repeated today, in all parts of the world.... Ironically, publicity about the victimisation of indigenous peoples in these newly-exploited areas has also renewed Europeans' interest in acquiring indigenous peoples' arts, cultures and sciences. Tourism in indigenous areas is growing, along with the commercialisation of indigenous arts and the spoiling of archaeological sites and shrines.
>
> 20. At the same time, the "Green Revolution," biotechnology, and demand for new medicines to combat cancer and AIDS are resulting in a renewed and intensified interest in collecting medical, botanical and ecological knowledge of indigenous peoples.... There is an urgent need, then, for measures to enable indigenous peoples to retain control over their remaining cultural and intellectual, as well as natural, wealth, so that they have the possibility of survival and self-development.[117]

The relevant dynamics can be more complex, however, than the unidirectional assertion of legal norms over indigenous groups. As Rosemary Coombe has noted, threats of commercial exploitation of indigenous peoples' traditional knowledge in a number of Latin American countries has led indigenous communities to reassert and construct new political identities around concepts such as sustainable development.[118]

The double-sided character of the relationship between human rights and intellectual property is noted at other points in this book. For example, human rights law is frequently posited as a source of principles for curtailing the perceived excesses of intellectual property. As we explain in Chapter 3, however, the human rights protections afforded to creators reveals that instrumentalist limitations on the ability of individuals and groups to control their intellectual endeavors and output also raise human rights concerns. Similarly, in Chapter 4 we explore ways that freedom of expression is both enhanced and limited by intellectual property rights. In contrast, some indigenous peoples' assertions of rights are not necessarily derived from or accommodated within the conventional heuristics of either intellectual property law or human rights law.

Intellectual Property of Indigenous Peoples, U.N. Doc. E/CN.4/Sub.2/1993/28 (July 28, 1993) (prepared by Erica-Irene Daes).

[117] *Id.* at 7.

[118] Coombe, *supra* note 65, at 130.

Claims that several Māori *iwi* (tribes) have brought against the Crown in New Zealand illustrate the latter point. (Māori are the indigenous people of Aotearoa/New Zealand.) This litigation is known as the "indigenous flora and fauna and cultural intellectual property (Wai 262) inquiry,"[119] or, more colloquially, as the "Māori intellectual property case." The claims focus on intellectual property issues, but also cover a wider conceptual territory.[120] For example, one iwi alleged that the Crown's failure to protect "te reo o Ngati Porou" (the tribal language) led to the diminution of skills in oratory, *haka* (war dances), and *moteatea* (traditional laments). The tribe also claimed that the Crown did not adequately protect traditional *whare wānanga* (places of learning). These aspects of the case focused on the context within which traditional knowledge and cultural expressions are produced – issues not typically characterized as "intellectual property" concerns.[121] Moreover, the principal basis for these claims was not human rights law, but an 1840 treaty between the British Crown and some 500 Māori tribal chiefs, Te Tiriti o Waitangi (the Treaty of Waitangi),[122] a document whose contents, structure, and provenance are quite different from the mid-twentieth-century human rights instruments.

One of the most prominent international platforms for the discussion of claims *to* and *from* intellectual property has been the WIPO Intergovernmental Committee on Intellectual Property and Genetic Resources, Traditional Knowledge and Folklore.[123] Discussions of indigenous intellectual property issues in WIPO have taken place over many years and have generated an enormous body of reports and consultative documents, including those created under the auspices of a related initiative known as the Development Agenda. As we detail in Chapter 1, the concerns of the Development Agenda are relevant to developing *nations* as well as to specific *communities* in those and other countries. In broad terms, the agenda draws attention to the development dimensions of a diverse array of domestic and international policy initiatives. It is motivated in part by concerns about the adverse effects of expansive intellectual property protection and stricter enforcement measures

---

[119] Information about this case is provided on the official Waitangi Tribunal Web site; it is *available at* http://www.waitangi-tribunal.govt.nz (last visited Mar. 31, 2010). The numeral 262 denotes the number of the particular claim that is before the Waitangi Tribunal.

[120] *See* Austin, *supra* note 109.

[121] *Id.*

[122] *See generally* McHugh, *supra* note 60.

[123] *See* WIPO, Intergovernmental Committee on Intellectual Property and Genetic Resources, Traditional Knowledge and Folklore (IGC), *available at* http://www.wipo.int/tk/en/igc/index.html (last visited Sept. 28, 2010); *see also* Torsen, *supra* note 89, at 201.

on the most vulnerable members of the human family.[124] But the Development Agenda also reflects developing nations' search for comparative advantage – offered, for example, by some countries' abundant biodiversity – at a time when their disadvantage in the world trade regime has become increasingly apparent.[125]

Institutional dynamics within WIPO have affected the organization's conceptualization of traditional knowledge and cultural expressions. Jane Anderson has suggested that WIPO's interest in these subjects partly reflects its struggle to respond to the WTO's competence concerning international intellectual property issues following the adoption of TRIPS in 1994.[126] According to her analysis, WIPO has remained relevant by cooperating with the WTO in areas where the mandates of the two organizations intersect and, in addition, by asserting jurisdiction over intellectual property issues outside of the international trade regime. As Anderson explains:

> It is in this way that discussions regarding the possible protection of indigenous knowledge … have fallen under the auspices of WIPO. The immense litera-ture now produced by WIPO on traditional knowledge matters signals both the elevated status of the issue within the international domain as well as its discursive and political limits. One obvious limit emanates from unresolved tensions between member states and their indigenous populations. Whilst the stated ambitions of indigenous peoples in relation to intellectual property often conflict with those of member states, in the WIPO forums, they are afforded co-existence. However, any decision-making that might need to be made remains a privilege of those same member states owing to their recognition within the U.N. system. The inevitable dilemma that this creates has established a certain kind of circularity within the debate, which in turn limits the development of resolutions that might change intellectual property agendas so that they benefit indigenous peoples.[127]

WIPO's work on indigenous intellectual property issues has included a number of research projects and studies that analyze the challenges facing indigenous communities that seek to protect traditional knowledge. The following extract describes some of current legal protections that are potentially applicable to traditional knowledge and explores several proposals for reform.

---

[124] Nicole Aylwin, Rosemary J. Coombe & Anita Chan, *Intellectual Property, Cultural Heritage and Rights-Based Development: Geographical Indications as Vehicles for Sustainable Livelihood, available at* http://www.yorku.ca/rcoombe/forthcoming_articles/GI_Human_Rights_Development_Paper.pdf.

[125] *See* Susy Frankel, *Trademarks and Traditional Knowledge and Cultural Intellectual Property* 422, 433–34 in TRADEMARK LAW AND THEORY, *supra* note 64.

[126] ANDERSON, *supra* note 12, at 174.

[127] *Id.*

World Intellectual Property Organization, INTELLECTUAL PROPERTY AND TRADITIONAL KNOWLEDGE: BOOKLET NO. 2, 7–30 (2007)

What Are the Challenges Confronting Traditional Knowledge Holders?

[Traditional knowledge (TK)] holders face various difficulties. In some cases, the very survival of the knowledge is at stake, as the cultural survival of communities is under threat. External social and environmental pressures, migration, the encroachment of modern lifestyles and the disruption of traditional ways of life can all weaken the traditional means of maintaining or passing knowledge on to future generations. There may be a risk of losing the very language that gives the primary voice to a knowledge tradition and the spiritual world-view that sustains this tradition. Either through acculturation or diffusion, many traditional practices and associated beliefs and knowledge have been irretrievably lost. Thus, a primary need is to preserve the knowledge that is held by elders and communities throughout the world.

Another difficulty facing TK holders is the lack of respect and appreciation for such knowledge. For example, when a traditional healer provides a mixture of herbs to cure a sickness, the healer may not isolate and describe certain chemical compounds and describe their effect on the body in the terms of modern biochemistry, but the healer has, in effect, based this medical treatment upon generations of clinical trials undertaken by healers in the past, and on a solid empirical understanding of the interaction between the mixture and human physiology. Thus, sometimes the true understanding of the value of TK may be overlooked if its scientific and technical qualities are considered from a narrow cultural perspective. In fact, many consumers in Western countries are turning to treatments based on TK, on the understanding that such "alternative" or "complementary" systems are soundly based on empirical observation over many generations.

Yet another problem confronting TK holders is the commercial exploitation of their knowledge by others, which raises questions of legal protection of TK against misuse, the role of prior informed consent, and the need for equitable benefit-sharing. Cases involving natural products all bear evidence to the value of TK in the modern economy. A lack of experience with existing formal systems, limited economic resources, cultural factors, lack of a unified voice, and, in many cases, a lack of clear national policy concerning the utilization and protection of TK, results in these populations often being placed at a decided disadvantage in using existing IP mechanisms. At the same time, the lack of understanding and clear rules concerning the appropriate use of TK creates areas of uncertainty for those seeking to use TK in research and development of new products. There is a common need for well-established, culturally appropriate and predictable rules both for the holders and legitimate users of TK.

A further challenge is to address the international dimension of the protection of TK and benefit-sharing for associated genetic resources, while learning from existing national experiences. Only through the participation of communities and countries from all regions can this work go forward to produce effective and equitable outcomes that are acceptable to all stakeholders.

These challenges are diverse and far-reaching, and involve many areas of law and policy, reaching well beyond even the most expansive view of intellectual property. Many international agencies and processes are engaged on these and related issues. But responses to these problems should be coordinated and consistent, and need to provide mutual support for broader objectives. For instance, IP protection of TK should recognize the objectives of the Convention on Biodiversity (CBD) concerning conservation, sustainable use and equitable benefit-sharing of genetic resources. In general, the preservation and protection against loss and degradation of TK should work hand-in-hand with the protection of TK against misuse and misappropriation. So when TK is recorded or documented with a view to preserving it for future generations, care needs to be taken to ensure that this act of preservation doesn't inadvertently facilitate the misappropriation or illegitimate use of the knowledge.

What Kind of Legal Protection for TK?

The protection of TK is important for communities in all countries, particularly in developing and least developed countries. First, TK plays an important role in the economic and social life of those countries. Placing value on such knowledge helps strengthen cultural identity and the enhanced use of such knowledge to achieve social and development goals, such as sustainable agriculture, affordable and appropriate public health, and conservation of biodiversity. Second, developing and least developed countries are implementing international agreements that may affect how knowledge associated with the use of genetic resources is protected and disseminated, and thus how their national interests are safeguarded. Patterns of ownership of TK, cultural, scientific and commercial interest in TK, the possibilities for beneficial partnerships in research and development, and the risk of the misuse of TK, are not neatly confined within national boundaries, so that some degree of international coordination and cooperation is essential to achieve the goals of TK protection.

A comprehensive strategy for protecting TK should therefore consider the community, national, regional and international dimensions. The stronger the integration and coordination between each level, the more likely the overall effectiveness. Many communities, countries and regional organizations are working to address these levels respectively. National laws are currently the prime mechanism for achieving protection and practical benefits for TK holders. For instance, Brazil, Costa Rica, India, Peru, Panama, the Philippines, Portugal, Thailand and the United States of America have all adopted *sui generis* laws that protect at least some aspect of TK (*sui generis* measures are specialized measures aimed exclusively at addressing the characteristics of specific subject matter, such as TK).... In addition, a number of regional organizations, such as in the South Pacific and in Africa, have been working on defining the specific rights in TK and how to administer them. Various TK holders and other stakeholders in different countries have already found existing IP rights useful and their TK protection strategies make some use of the IP system.

While there are diverse national and regional approaches to protection, reflecting the diversity of TK itself and its social context, some common elements arise in policy debate. For instance, it is stressed that protection should reflect the aspirations and expectations of TK holders and should promote respect for indigenous and customary practices, protocols and laws as far as possible. Several *sui generis* measures, as well as conventional IP law, have recognized elements of such customary law within a broader framework of protection. Economic aspects of development need to be addressed and the effective participation by TK holders is also important, in line with the principle of prior informed consent. TK protection should also be affordable, understandable and accessible to TK holders. The view is widely voiced that holders of TK should be entitled to fair and equitable sharing of benefits arising from the use of their knowledge.

The international legal framework, within and beyond the IP system, is also an important consideration. Where TK is associated with genetic resources, the distribution of benefits should be consistent with measures established in accordance with the CBD, providing for sharing of benefits arising from the utilization of the genetic resources. Other important international instruments include the International Treaty on Plant Genetic Resources for Food and Agriculture of the Food and Agriculture Organization (FAO), the International Union for the Protection of New Varieties of Plants (UPOV), and the UN Convention to Combat Desertification (UNCCD). Other areas of international law, notably human rights and cultural policy, are also part of the context for protection of TK.

Positive Protection – Recognition of IP Rights in TK

Diversity is the very essence of TK systems, precisely because they are so closely intertwined with the cultural identity of many diverse communities. It is therefore not surprising that practical experience so far with the protection of TK has shown that no single template or comprehensive "one-size-fits-all" solution is likely to suit all the national priorities and legal environments, let alone the needs of traditional communities in all countries. Instead, effective protection may be found in a coordinated "menu" of different options for protection. This could perhaps be underpinned by an internationally agreed set of common objectives and core principles that could form part of the international legal framework. The key is to provide TK holders with an appropriate choice of forms of protection, to empower them to assess their interests and choose their own directions for the protection and use of their TK, and to ensure there is adequate capacity to carry through protection strategies.

The way in which a protection system is shaped and defined will depend to a large extent on the objectives it is intended to serve. Protection of TK, like protection of IP in general, is not undertaken as an end in itself, but as a means to broader policy goals. The kind of objectives that TK protection is intended to serve include:

- Recognition of value and promotion of respect for traditional knowledge systems
- Responsiveness to the actual needs of holders of TK
- Repression of misappropriation of TK and other unfair and inequitable uses
- Protection of tradition-based creativity and innovation
- Support of TK systems and empowerment of TK holders
- Promotion of equitable benefit-sharing from use of TK
- Promotion of the use of TK for a bottom-up approach to development.

The diversity of already existing TK protection systems and the diversity of the needs of TK holders require a degree of flexibility in how the objectives are implemented at the national level. A similar situation prevails in other branches of IP law as existing IP instruments give countries flexibility in how they make protection available.

The options for positive protection include existing IP laws and legal systems (including the law of unfair competition), extended or adapted IP rights specifically focussed on TK (*sui generis* aspects of IP laws), and new, stand-alone *sui generis* systems which give rights in TK as such. Other non-IP options can form part of the overall menu, including trade practices and labeling laws, the law of civil liability, the use of contracts, customary and indigenous laws and protocols, regulation of access to genetic resources and associated TK, and remedies based on such torts as unjust enrichment, rights of publicity, and blasphemy. Each of these has been used to some extent to protect various aspects of TK.

Use of Existing Intellectual Property Laws

The policy debate about TK and the IP system has underlined the limitations of existing IP laws in meeting all the needs and expectations of TK holders. Even so, existing IP laws have been successfully used to protect against some forms of misuse and misappropriation of TK, including through the laws of patents, trademarks, geographical indications, industrial designs, and trade secrets. However, certain adaptations or modifications to IP law may be needed to make it work better. For example, TK is often held collectively by communities, rather than by individual owners – this is often cited as a drawback in protecting TK. Yet it is possible to form associations, community corporations or similar legal bodies to act on behalf of the community. In some countries, government agencies take an active role acting in trust for the community. Some forms of protection, such as remedies against unfair competition and breach of confidence, do not require specific right holders. Communities' concerns about TK typically span generations, a much longer timeframe than the duration of most IP rights. But some IP rights, especially those that rely on a distinctive reputation, can continue indefinitely. There are also concerns that the cost of using the IP system is a particular obstacle for TK holders. This has led some to explore capacity building, evolution of legal concepts to take greater account of TK perspectives, the use of alternative dispute resolution, and a more active role for government agencies and other players.

Existing IP rights have been used in the following ways:

- Unfair competition and trade practices laws: these allow for action to be taken against false or misleading claims that a product is authentically indigenous, or has been produced or endorsed by, or otherwise associated with, a particular traditional community. For instance, a company has been legally barred from describing various handpainted products as "certified authentic" and "Aboriginal art" when they were not painted by Aboriginal people and had not undergone any certification process.
- Patents: when practitioners innovate within the traditional framework, they have been able to use the patent system to protect their innovations.

For example, in 2001 China granted 3300 patents for innovations within the field of Traditional Chinese Medicine. Equally, systems have been developed to ensure that illegitimate patent rights are not granted over TK subject matter that is not a true invention.

- Distinctive signs (trade marks, collective marks, certification marks, geographical indications): traditional signs, symbols and terms associated with TK have been protected as marks, and have been safeguarded against third parties' claims of trade mark rights. For instance, the Seri people of Mexico, faced with competition from mass production, registered the *Arte Seri* trademark to protect authentic ironwood products that are produced by traditional methods from the *Olneya tesota* tree. Conservation of this unique species of tree was also a factor in protecting the trademark. Also in Mexico, the appellations of origin *olinalá* and *tequila* are used to protect lacquered wooden products and the traditional spirit derived from the blue agave plant, both products of traditional knowledge that derive their unique characteristics also from the indigenous genetic resources of these localities.

- The law of confidentiality and trade secrets: this has been used to protect non-disclosed TK, including secret and sacred TK. Customary laws of communities often require that certain knowledge be disclosed only to certain recipients. Courts have awarded remedies for breach of confidence when such customary laws are violated. A group of North American indigenous communities, the Tulalip Tribes, have developed Storybase, a digital collection of their TK. Some of the TK may be disclosed for patent review. Community leaders identify other information as for use exclusively within the Tulalip community, according to customary law; the latter is protected as undisclosed information. Digital repatriation projects that involve the restoration of indigenous knowledge to original communities often need to apply confidentiality carefully to comply with customary law constraints on access to the knowledge.

Adaptations of Existing IP through Sui Generis Measures

A number of countries have adapted existing intellectual property systems to the needs of TK holders through *sui generis* measures for TK protection. These take different forms. A Database of Official Insignia of Native American Tribes prevents others from registering these insignia as trademarks in the United States of America. New Zealand's trade mark law has been amended to exclude trademarks that cause offence, and this applies especially to Indigenous Māori symbols. India's Patent Act has been amended to clarify the status of TK within patent law. The Chinese State Intellectual Property Office has a team of patent examiners specializing in traditional Chinese medicine.

In some communities and countries, the judgement has been made that even adaptations of existing IP rights systems are not sufficient to cater to the holistic and unique character of TK subject-matter. This has led to the decision to protect TK through *sui generis* rights.

Here are a few national experiences in using *sui generis* IP rights for protecting TK:

- The *sui generis* regime of Peru was established by Law No. 27, 811 of 2002, whose objectives are to protect TK, to promote fair and equitable distribution of benefits, to ensure that the use of the knowledge takes place with the prior informed consent of the indigenous peoples, and to prevent misappropriation. Protection is afforded to collective knowledge of indigenous peoples associated to biological resources. The law grants indigenous peoples the right to consent to the use of TK. The law also foresees the payment of equitable compensation for the use of certain types of TK into a national Fund for Indigenous Development or directly to the TK holders.

- The Biodiversity Law No. 7788 of Costa Rica aims at regulating access to TK. It provides for the equitable distribution to TK holders of the benefits arising from the use of TK. Two scopes of subject matter are defined in the Law: first, TK to which the Law regulates access, and, second, TK for which the Law provides exclusive rights. What will be the term and scope of *sui generis* community intellectual rights and who will be the title holder is determined by a participatory process with indigenous and small farmer communities to be defined by the National Commission for the Management of Biodiversity.

- The objective of Portugal's *sui generis* Decree-Law No. 118, of April 20, 2002 is the registration, conservation and legal custody of genetic resources and TK. The Law provides protection against the "commercial or industrial reproduction and/or use" of TK developed by local communities, collectively or individually.

- The Act on Protection and Promotion of Traditional Thai Medicinal Intelligence, B. E. 2542 protects "formulas" of traditional Thai drugs and "texts on traditional Thai medicine." In general, "traditional Thai medicinal intelligence" means "the basic knowledge and capability concerned with traditional Thai medicine". The Act confers the right holder – "those who have registered their intellectual property rights on traditional

Thai medical intelligence under the Act" – "the sole ownership on the production of the drug and research and development."

Other Legal Concepts for the Protection of TK

When policymakers explore suitable legal mechanisms to protect TK against misappropriation, they consider a broader range of legal concepts apart from the kind of exclusive rights used in most forms of IP law. Several of these alternative concepts are briefly described here:

Prior Informed Consent (PIC)

According to the principle of prior informed consent (PIC), TK holders should be fully consulted before their knowledge is accessed or used by third parties and an agreement should be reached on appropriate terms; they should also be fully informed about the consequences of the intended use. The agreed scope of use may be set out in contracts, licenses or agreements, which would also specify how benefits arising from the use of the TK should be shared. The principle of PIC concerning access to genetic resources is one of the cornerstones of the CBD. Given the close relationship between genetic resources and some forms of TK, this same principle is also used in a number of national laws concerning access to and use of TK.

Equitable Benefit-sharing

The idea of an equitable balancing of interests is common to many legal systems. In IP law, this is often phrased in terms of a balancing of the interests of right holders and the general public. The fair and equitable sharing of benefits from the use of genetic resources is one of the objectives of the CBD, and the CBD also encourages equitable sharing of benefits from the use of certain forms of TK. Thus the principle of equitable benefit-sharing is found in a number of national laws governing access and use of TK, especially when TK is associated with genetic resources. According to this principle, the TK holders would receive an equitable share of the benefits that arise from the use of the TK, which may be expressed in terms of a compensatory payment, or other non-monetary benefits. An entitlement to equitable benefit-sharing may be particularly appropriate in situations where exclusive property rights are considered inappropriate.

Unfair Competition

International IP standards have long required the suppression of unfair competition: this is defined as "any act of competition contrary to honest practices in industrial or commercial matters," and includes various acts that mislead the public or cause confusion. Unfair competition law has been ... discussed and used as a potential legal basis for protecting TK against various forms of unfair commercial use.

Respect for Customary Laws and Practices

Customary laws, protocols and practices often define how traditional communities develop, hold and transmit TK. For example, certain sacred or secret TK may only be permitted to be disclosed to certain initiated individuals within an Indigenous community. Customary laws and practices may define custodial rights and obligations over TK, including obligations to guard it against misuse or improper disclosure; they may determine how TK is to be used, how benefits should be shared, and how disputes are to be settled, as well as many other aspects of the preservation, use and exercise of knowledge.

For example, in North America, the inheritance and transfer of "medicine bundles" within or between families is accompanied by the transmission of traditional medical knowledge and certain rights to practice, transmit and apply that knowledge. The ownership of the physical bundle is often attached to exclusive rights to exploit the products and processes associated with the TK that the bundle signifies.

As their TK is increasingly of interest to those beyond the traditional context, TK holders have called for their customary laws, practices and beliefs to be recognized and respected by those seeking to use their TK. For many representatives of traditional communities, this is a cornerstone of appropriate forms of protection. This has led to consideration of a range of ways of respecting customary laws and practices within other legal mechanisms, including within conventional IP systems.

Defensive Protection – Safeguarding against Illegitimate IP Rights over TK

TK is protected "defensively" by steps that prevent third parties from obtaining or exercising invalid IP rights over the TK. Defensive protection can be valuable and effective in blocking illegitimate IP rights, but it does not stop others from actively using or exploiting TK. Some form of positive protection is needed to prevent unauthorized use. This is why a comprehensive approach to protection needs to consider positive and defensive protection as two sides of the same coin. For instance, publishing TK as a defensive measure may block others from patenting that TK, but it can also make the knowledge more accessible and put it in the public domain – this can, ironically, make it easier for third parties to use the knowledge against the wishes of the TK holders.

The main focus of defensive protection measures has been in the patent system. Defensive protection aims at ensuring that existing TK is not patented by third parties – ideally, by ensuring that relevant TK is taken fully into account when a patent is examined for its novelty and inventiveness.

Normally, a claimed invention in a patent application is assessed against the so-called "prior art" – the defined body of knowledge that is considered relevant to the validity of a patent. For example, if TK has been published in a journal before the applicable date of a patent application, it is part of the relevant prior art, and the application cannot validly claim that TK as an invention – the invention would not be considered novel. In recent years, concern has been expressed that TK should be given greater attention as relevant prior art, so that patents are less likely to cover existing publicly disclosed TK.

Defensive protection of TK has two aspects:

- a legal aspect: how to ensure that the criteria defining relevant prior art apply to the TK – for example, this could mean ensuring that orally disclosed information must be taken into account (since many important bodies of TK are normally transmitted and disseminated by oral means)
- a practical aspect: how to ensure that the TK is actually available to search authorities and patent examiners, and is readily accessible – for example, this can ensure that it is indexed or classified, so that it is likely to be found in a search for relevant prior art.

The broad development underlying this issue is that, as the reach of the intellectual property system in the global information society extends to new stakeholders, such as indigenous and local communities, their knowledge base, including in particular their TK, constitutes an increasingly relevant body of prior art the effective identification of which is of increasing importance for the functioning of the IP system.

Another widely-discussed approach to defensive protection is the idea that patent applicants should in some way have to disclose TK (and genetic resources) used in the claimed invention, or that are otherwise related to it. Existing patent law already requires some of this information to be disclosed by the applicant, but there are several proposals to extend and focus these requirements, and to create specific disclosure obligations for TK and genetic resources.

Amendment of Existing WIPO Administered Patent Systems

A range of practical mechanisms for the defensive protection of TK have been developed and implemented within countries and international organizations. WIPO's work on defensive protection has included amendment of WIPO-administered systems, and the development of practical capacity-building tools.

For instance, the principal tool for locating technical information for patent purposes, the International Patent Classification (IPC), has been expanded to take better account of TK subject matter, in particular concerning medicinal products based on plants extracts. This increases the likelihood that patent examiners locate already published TK that is relevant to claimed inventions in patent application, without adversely affecting the legal status of TK from the point of view of TK holders....

The Patent Cooperation Treaty (PCT) ... provides for an international search and examination. This helps clarify the possible validity of a patent application before specific national processes begin. This is significant for applicants and for defensive protection strategies alike. The minimum documentation that should be taken into account during an international search was recently expanded to include eleven TK-related information resources, thus increasing the likelihood that relevant TK will be located at an early stage in the life of a patent.

Practical Capacity-building Tools

WIPO is also developing a package of practical tools and products for the protection of TK and genetic resources. These include a Toolkit for IP Management, an Online Portal of Registries and Databases of TK and Genetic Resources, including a sample database of Ayurvedic traditional medicine from South Asia, and an agreed data standard for databases and registries of TK and associated biological resources.

A "Toolkit for IP Management When Documenting TK and Genetic Resources" is under collaborative development to provide practical assistance to TK holders and custodians of genetic resources in managing the IP-implications of their documentation work. The toolkit is intended to describe legal tools that are available, to discuss how they can be successfully used and thereby to enable informed choices by TK holders themselves. The aim is to allow stakeholders to determine whether, and in what cases, IP rights are the appropriate legal and practical mechanisms to achieve their objectives concerning their TK and genetic resources.

TK holders are involved in a wide range of TK collections, databases, registries and other forms of documenting and recording their TK. Great care needs to be taken to avoid unintended disclosure of TK, for example by making it available to the general public in violation of customary laws and practices. The toolkit illustrates how any documentation or database initiative needs to be preceded by full consideration of possible IP implications, including inadvertently placing TK in the public domain, or publishing it inappropriately. WIPO does not advise TK holders on compiling databases of TK and does not compile such databases itself.

The work on defensive approaches is being undertaken within the context of a comprehensive approach to the protection of TK, which takes account of the need, widely expressed, for more effective positive protection and for any holders or custodians of TK to be fully informed of the consequences of making any disclosure of their TK, especially when disclosure leads to publication of the TK or its more ready access by members of the public.

The activities of the WIPO Intergovernmental Committee on Intellectual Property and Genetic Resources, Traditional Knowledge and Folklore (IGC) provoked little controversy when the IGC focused on research projects and studies of legal and policy issues relevant to indigenous intellectual property. Discussions became more contentious, however, over whether the IGC should prepare the text of a legally binding agreement to protect traditional knowledge.[128] Disputes initially focused on procedural matters,[129] chief among them the inability of indigenous groups to be heard. The Chair of the Indigenous Peoples Caucus presented a formal statement to the IGC complaining that indigenous groups were classified as nongovernmental observers and therefore excluded from the negotiations.[130]

---

[128] Kaitlin Mara, *Perpetual Protection of Traditional Knowledge "Not on Table" at WIPO*, INTELLECTUAL PROPERTY WATCH, Oct. 22, 2009, *available at* http://www.ip-watch.org/weblog/2009/10/22/perpetual-protection-of-traditional-knowledge-%E2%80%9Cnot-on-table%E2%80%9D-at-wipo/.

[129] The African Group proposal called for expert-only working groups to meet intersessionally. *Recommendations of the African Group on WIPO IGC Intersessional Work, in* IGC, *Intersessional Procedures: Proposed Modalities and Terms of Reference*, WIPO/GRTKF/IC/13/10 (Oct. 11, 2008), *available at* http://www.wipo.int/meetings/en/doc_details.jsp?doc_id=109774.

[130] IGC, *Thirteenth Session Report*, para. 163–64, WIPO/GRTKF/IC/13/11 (Apr. 30, 2009), *available at* http://www.wipo.int/meetings/en/doc_details.jsp?doc_id=129092 [*Thirteenth*

Divisions between developed and developing member nations intensified at the June 2009 IGC meeting when the Committee failed to reach agreement on the renewal of its two-year mandate, set to expire by the end of 2009.[131] The dispute centered on whether a renewed mandate should include the negotiation of a *binding* legal instrument to protect traditional knowledge and cultural expressions.[132] Many developed nations opposed a binding agreement[133]; developing states generally supported the African Group's proposal to add the drafting of an "internationally legally binding instrument" to the IGC's mandate.[134] Despite an EU compromise proposal – "No outcome of the Committee's work is excluded, including the possible development of a legally-binding international instrument or instruments"[135] – the debate ended in an impasse.[136]

After nearly a year without an agreement on the IGC's future work, some governments appeared to be losing faith in WIPO as a forum for developing international legal norms relating to traditional knowledge and folklore.[137] On the last day of the 2009 General Assemblies meeting, however, the IGC recommended a compromise mandate that was promptly approved by the

---

Session Report]. Indigenous representatives were given a chance to speak at the first meeting of the IGC after the renewal of its mandate but are still classified as observers, unauthorized to participate in policy negotiations. *See* Kaitlin Mara, *Mismatch on Traditional Knowledge Treaty Text, Negotiating Sessions at WIPO*, INTELLECTUAL PROPERTY WATCH, Dec. 8, 2009, *available at* http://www.ip-watch.org/weblog/2009/12/08/mismatch-on-traditional-knowledge-treaty-text-negotiating-sessions-at-wipo/.

[131] IGC, *Fourteenth Session Report*, WIPO/GRTKF/IC/14/12 (Oct. 1 2009), *available at* http://www.wipo.int/meetings/en/doc_details.jsp?doc_id=129634 [*Fourteenth Session Report*].

[132] *See Fourteenth Session Report, supra* note 131, paras. 67–285. Compare the African Group's proposed mandate (contemplating creation of an "internationally legally binding instrument") with Australia's amendment to the proposed mandate (striking the term "legally binding"), the U.S. amendment (suggesting "recommendations" rather than the text of an international instrument), and Switzerland's amendment ("No outcome of the Committee's work is excluded, including the possible development of a legally-binding international instrument or instruments."). *Id.* para. 102.

[133] *See, e.g., id.* paras. 148, 155–156 (expressions by Germany, Canada, and France lamenting the African Group's unwillingness to remove the "legally binding" language).

[134] *See, e.g., id.* paras. 110–116, 118–124, 128–133 (expressions of support for a binding agreement from Senegal, Pakistan, Sri Lanka, Venezuela, Iran, Bolivia, Philippines, Thailand, Cuba, Yemen, India, Ecuador, Fiji, Brazil, Peru, Guatemala, Sudan, Indonesia, and China).

[135] IGC, *Elements for the New Mandate – Proposal by the European Community and Its Member States*, WIPO/GRTKF/IC/14/11 (July 3, 2009), *available at* http://www.wipo.int/meetings/en/doc_details.jsp?doc_id=127012.

[136] *Fourteenth Session Report, supra* note 131, para. 285.

[137] Indonesia delegation to WIPO, Prepared Statement, in Kaitlin Mara, *Role of WIPO on Traditional Knowledge In Question*, INTELLECTUAL PROPERTY WATCH, Sept. 30, 2009, *available at* http://www.ip-watch.org/weblog/2009/09/30/role-of-wipo-in-question/.

WIPO membership.[138] The new mandate directed the IGC to "continue its work and undertake text-based negotiations with the objective of reaching agreement on a text of an international legal instrument (or instruments) which will ensure the effective protection of [Genetic Resources, Traditional Knowledge and Traditional Cultural Expressions]."[139] Although the mandate preserves the potential of the IGC – and WIPO – to be a key venue for indigenous intellectual property issues, the divisions that plagued the IGC have not been fully resolved.[140] It thus remains to be seen whether the compromise mandate is a harbinger of greater cooperation within the IGC. As of late 2010, however, there were encouraging signs of progress.[141]

Notes and Questions

1. The 2007 WIPO report, excerpted previously, analyzes a number of international instruments and agencies, such as the Convention on Biodiversity and the Food and Agriculture Organization. The report then states: "*Other* areas of international law, notably human rights and cultural policy, are also part of the context for the protection of TK" (emphasis added). However, the report neither acknowledges nor analyzes any tensions or points of intersection between human rights and other approaches to the protection of traditional knowledge. Such an analysis was not, of course, the purpose of the report. Even so, the omission underscores one of the key points developed in Chapter 1 – the separate-track development of human rights and intellectual property approaches to many socioeconomic issues to which both legal regimes are relevant. In the indigenous peoples' context, this development is particularly striking, inasmuch as indigenous intellectual property issues have been a catalyst for U.N. human rights bodies to review intellectual property issues over the past decade. Do you detect

---

[138] WIPO G.A., *Decision on Agenda Item 28*, WIPO/GRTKF/IC/15/REF DECISION 28 (Oct. 1, 2009), *available at* http://www.wipo.int/meetings/en/doc_details.jsp?doc_id=129913.

[139] *Id.* para. (a).

[140] Already the existing divisions are apparent in different member interpretations of the "legal instrument" provision. *See* Kaitlin Mara, *"Turning Point" at WIPO Pulls Traditional Knowledge Debate out at Eleventh Hour*, INTELLECTUAL PROPERTY WATCH, Oct. 3, 2009, *available at* http://www.ip-watch.org/weblog/2009/10/03/%E2%80%9Cturning-point%E2%80%9D-at-wipo-pulls-traditional-knowledge-debate-out-at-eleventh-hour/ ("Opinions differed on whether the 'instrument' negotiations will result in a treaty, with governments wanting strong protection saying the language indicates a treaty, and a developed country delegate saying a treaty was one of several possible outcomes.").

[141] ITCSD, *WIPO Folklore Discussions Get New Energy after Years of Stalemate*, BRIDGES WEEKLY TRADE NEWS DIGEST, vol. 14, No. 28 (July 28, 2010), *available at* http://ictsd.org/i/news/bridgesweekly/81827/.

any further influence of human rights law or discourse in the 2007 WIPO report?

2. Scrutinize the WIPO report's list of "objectives that TK protection is intended to serve." Which of these objectives have more in common with the general concerns of intellectual property, and which have more in common with the general concerns of human rights?

3. Review the different legal protections that the 2007 WIPO report indicates might apply to traditional knowledge. Do these protections raise human rights issues? Put another way, if a state did *not* protect traditional knowledge using one or more of these mechanisms, would that amount to a breach of the human rights guarantees analyzed in Sections 7.2 and 7.3 of this chapter? What does the WIPO report suggest about the processes by which legal solutions to the "problem" of underprotection of traditional knowledge might be developed?

4. In a leading study of the misappropriation of "native culture,"[142] Michael Brown advances a framework of respect for indigenous cultures rather than the imposition of property regimes.[143] Can arguments grounded in human rights be marshaled in support of Brown's approach? Consider in this context the case of *Yumbulul v. Reserve Bank of Australia*,[144] in which the Galpu people of Australia initiated court proceedings to prevent reproduction of a design of a "morning star pole." Sacred ceremonies and initiation rites were among the sources for the design, which the Galpu people viewed "not so much as 'property' in the Western sense, but rather as a significant expression of culture for which clan members are temporary stewards."[145] Is "property" itself so fixed or immutable a concept that it cannot adapt to avoid the problem of "owning culture"? Might the inherent flexibility in the notion of property provide answers to criticisms of the potentially deleterious effects of the imposition of property-based principles on indigenous cultures?[146] Does intellectual property law itself provide salient examples of such adaptation?

5. As the WIPO report discusses, a number of countries permit challenges to trademark registrations on the ground that a mark is offensive or disparaging. *Pro Football, Inc. v. Harjo*, a famous U.S. case, involved objections of this

---

[142] MICHAEL F. BROWN, WHO OWNS NATIVE CULTURE? (2003).

[143] *See also* Carpenter, Katyal, & Riley, *supra* note 8.

[144] *Yumbulul v. Reserve Bank of Australia* (1991) 2 I.P.R. 481.

[145] *See* Torsen, *supra* note 89, at 178. For a recent exposition of the notion of stewardship in the context of cultural property, *see* Carpenter, Katyal, & Riley, *supra* note 8.

[146] *See* Carol M. Rose, *Property in All the Wrong Places?* 114 YALE L.J. 991 (2005) [(reviewing MICHAEL F. BROWN, WHO OWNS NATIVE CULTURE? (2003), and KAREN R. MERRILL, PUBLIC LANDS AND POLITICAL MEANING: RANCHERS, THE GOVERNMENT, AND THE PROPERTY BETWEEN THEM (2002)].

kind. In 1992, seven Native Americans filed an action before the U.S. Patent and Trademark Office seeking cancellation of six "Redskins" trademarks registered by a professional football team. They argued that the marks were impermissibly disparaging toward Native Americans. Finding that the marks were indeed disparaging, the Trademark Trial and Appeal Board cancelled the registrations. The U.S. Court of Appeals for the District of Columbia reversed, holding that the marks were to remain on the trademark register because of the delay in initiating the cancellation proceedings.[147] Which human rights issues, if any, are raised by the subsistence of the trademark registration for "Redskins"?[148]

6. Several developing countries have proposed an amendment to the TRIPS Agreement to include a new Article 29*bis* on Disclosure of Origin of Biological Resources and/or Associated Traditional Knowledge. The article would require patent applicants to (1) reveal the origin of biological resources and/or associated traditional knowledge on which an application is based, (2) obtain prior informed consent for access to those resources and/ or associated knowledge, and (3) provide fair and equitable sharing of the benefits from commercial or other utilization of the resulting innovation.[149] Other countries have sought to amend the Patent Cooperation Treaty (PCT) to authorize national patent laws to require applicants to disclose the source of genetic resources and traditional knowledge if a claimed invention is based directly on such resources or knowledge.[150]

What are the advantages and disadvantages of protecting traditional knowledge by means of an amendment to TRIPS as compared to a freestanding international instrument negotiated under the auspices of WIPO or an amendment to the PCT? One difference relates to the procedures by which states are bound to the treaty's terms. For example, an amendment to TRIPS would likely be included as part of a comprehensive package of revisions that would apply to all WTO member states. An amendment to the PCT,

[147] 565 F.3d 880 (D.C. Cir. 2009).
[148] *See generally,* Gavin Clarkson, *Racial Imagery and Native Americans: A First Look at the Empirical Evidence behind the Indian Mascot Controversy,* 11 CARDOZO J. INT'L & COMP. L. 393 (2003).
[149] WTO, Proposal of Brazil et al., *Doha Work Programme – the Outstanding Implementation Issue on the Relationship between the TRIPS Agreement and the Convention on Biological Diversity,* WTO Doc. IP/C/W/474 (July 5, 2006), *available at* http://docsonline.wto.org/imrd/directdoc.asp?DDFDocuments/t/ip/c/w474.doc.
[150] WIPO, Working Group on Reform of the Patent Cooperation Treaty, Proposals of Switzerland, *Declaration of the Source of Genetic Resources and Traditional Knowledge in Patent Applications,* WIPO Doc. PCT/R/WG/9/5 (Mar. 7, 2007), *available at* http://www.wipo.int/edocs/mdocs/pct/en/pct_r_wg_9/pct_r_wg_9_5.pdf.

by contrast, requires approval and acceptance by three-fourths of the states parties but is thereafter binding on all PCT members.[151] A new treaty on traditional knowledge would be ratified on a state by state basis.

7.6. Individual and Collective Interests in Indigenous Cultural Productions

In this section, we provide extracts from an important Australian decision involving allegations of copyright infringement made by Aboriginal artists against an unlicensed reproduction of their artwork on printed clothing fabric. The case is significant in that it explores the tensions between individual authorship, an important premise upon which Australian copyright law is based, and collective responsibility for the development of art forms within indigenous communities. Justice von Doussa attempted to resolve these tensions by invoking Australian common law concepts, principally fiduciary obligations, which, in turn, are derived from English law imported into Australia during colonization. One important legal innovation in the case is the court's willingness to view the laws and customs of the Ganalbingu people when determining the scope of the fiduciary obligations that an individual artist owes to his or her community. As you read the decision, consider whether this is the correct lens through which to view these issues.

John Bulun Bulun & Anor v. R. & T. Textiles Pty Ltd. **[1998] FCA 1082, Federal Court of Australia (Sept. 3, 1998)**

VON DOUSSA J.: These proceedings arise out of the importation and sale in Australia of printed clothing fabric which infringed the copyright of the first applicant Mr Bulun Bulun, in the artistic work known as "Magpie Geese and Water Lilies at the Waterhole" ("the artistic work").

The proceedings were commenced on 27 February 1996 by Mr Bulun Bulun and the second applicant, Mr George Milpurrurru. Both applicants are leading Aboriginal artists. The respondents were at that time, R & T Textiles Pty Ltd ("the respondent") and its three directors. Mr Bulun Bulun sued as the legal owner of the copyright pursuant to the *Copyright Act 1968* (Cth) for remedies for the infringement.... Mr Milpurrurru brought the proceedings in his own right and as a representative of the traditional Aboriginal owners of Ganalbingu country which is situated in Arnhem Land, in the Northern Territory of Australia. He claims that the traditional Aboriginal owners of

---

[151] PCT, art. 61.3.

Ganalbingu country are the equitable owners of the copyright subsisting in the artistic work.

These proceedings represent another step by Aboriginal people to have communal title in their traditional ritual knowledge, and in particular in their artwork, recognised and protected by the Australian legal system. The inadequacies of statutory remedies under the *Copyright Act 1976* as a means of protecting communal ownership have been noted in earlier decisions of this Court.

As soon as the proceedings were served the respondent admitted infringement of Mr Bulun Bulun's copyright in the artistic work, and pleaded that the infringement had occurred in ignorance of the copyright. The respondent immediately withdrew the offending fabric from sale. The respondent then consented to final declarations and orders on the claim by Mr Bulun Bulun. These included a declaration that the respondent had infringed Mr Bulun Bulun's legal title to the copyright in the artistic work, and comprehensive permanent injunctions against future infringement.

The amended application and amended statement of claim continued to plead a claim by George Milpurrurru on his own behalf and in a representative capacity for the Ganalbingu people in respect of equitable ownership of the copyright in the artistic work. The respondent did not admit the allegations concerning equitable ownership of the copyright.

Counsel for the applicants informed the Court that the artistic work incorporates within its subject matter much that is sacred and important to the Ganalbingu people about their heritage. Counsel emphasised that copyright infringements of artworks such as the artistic work affect interests beyond those of the copyright owner, and that the Ganalbingu people considered it to be of great importance that the Court recognise the rights of the Ganalbingu people and the injury caused to them by the respondent's infringement. Counsel said that Mr Milpurrurru therefore proposed to continue with his claim notwithstanding the consent orders in favour of Mr Bulun Bulun.

Evidence in Mr Milpurrurru's Claim

It ... is convenient first to record the nature of the case and the evidence which Mr Milpurrurru filed in support of the claim that he and the Ganalbingu people are equitable owners of the copyright in the artistic work.

Much of the evidence in these proceedings relates to customary rights and obligations recognised and observed by the individual members of the Ganalbingu people and the group as a whole. The High Court's decision in *Mabo v. The State of Queensland [No.2]* (1992) 175 CLR 1 shows that customary indigenous law has a role to play within the Australian legal system. Indeed the conclusion that native title survived the Crown's acquisition of sovereignty was dependent upon the Court's acceptance of antecedent traditional laws and customs acknowledged and observed by the indigenous inhabitants of the land claimed. Evidence of customary law may be used as a basis for the foundation of rights recognised within the Australian legal system.... In my opinion the evidence about Ganalbingu law and customs is admissible.

The amended application in this case alleges that the Ganalbingu people are the traditional Aboriginal owners of Ganalbingu country who have the right to permit and control the production and reproduction of the artistic work under the law and custom of the Ganalbingu people.

The amended statement of claim pleads that the Ganalbingu people are the traditional Aboriginal owners of the corpus of ritual knowledge from which the artistic work is derived, including the subject matter of the artistic work and the artistic work itself.

Mr Milpurrurru is the most senior person of all the Ganalbingu people. The Ganalbingu people are divided into "top" and "bottom" people as is the Ganalbingu country. Mr Milpurrurru is a "top" Ganalbingu. Mr Bulun Bulun is the most senior person of the "bottom" Ganalbingu and is second in line to Mr Milpurrurru of the Ganalbingu people generally.

Djulibinyamurr is the site of a waterhole complex situated close to the eastern side of the Arafura Swamp between the Glyde and Goyder river systems and the Woolen River. Djulibinyamurr, along with another waterhole site, Ngalyindi, are the two most important sites on Ganalbingu country for the Ganalbingu people. Mr Bulun Bulun describes Djulibinyamurr as the ral'kal for the lineage of the bottom Ganalbingu people. In his affidavit evidence Mr Bulun Bulun says:

> Ral'kal translates to mean the principal totemic or clan well for my lineage. Ral'kal is the well spring, life force and spiritual and totemic repository for my lineage of the Ganalbingu people. It is the place from where my lineage of the Ganalbingu people are created and emerge. It is the equivalent of my "warro" or soul.

> Djulibinyamurr is the place where not only my human ancestors were created but according to our custom and law emerged, it is also the place from which our creator ancestor emerged. Barnda, or Gumang (long neck tortoise) first emerged from inside the earth at Djulibinyamurr and came out to walk across the earth from there. It was Barnda that caused the natural features at Djulibinyamurr to be shaped into the form that they are now.

> Barnda not only created the place we call Djulibinyamurr but it populated the country as well. Barnda gave the place its name, created the people who follow him and named those people. Barnda gave us our language and law. Barnda

gave to my ancestors the country and the ceremony and paintings associated with the country. My ancestors had a responsibility given to them by Barnda to perform the ceremony and to do the paintings which were granted to them. This is a part of the continuing responsibility of the traditional Aboriginal owners handed down from generation to generation. Djulibinyamurr is then our life source and the source of our continuing totemic or sacred responsibility. The continuity of our traditions and ways including our traditional Aboriginal ownership depends upon us respecting and honouring the things entrusted to us by Barnda.

Djulibinyamurr is my ral'kal, it is the hole or well from which I derive my life and power. It is the place from which my people and my creator emerged. Damage to Djulibinyamurr will cause injury and death to the people who are its owners. Damage to a ral'kal is the worst thing that could happen to a Yolngu person. It is the ultimate act of destruction under our law and custom – it upsets the whole religious, political and legal balance underpinning Yolngu society. It destroy the relationship and the maintenance of the trust established between the creator ancestor and their human descendants and also between traditional Aboriginal owners. This relationship controls all aspects of society and life, for example ownership of country, relations with other clans, marriage and ceremonial life and its attributes. If the life source is damaged or interfered with in any way the power and stability derived from it and the power and stability which has continued from the time of creation is diminished and may collapse.

In the same way my creator ancestor formed the natural landscape and granted it to my human ancestors who in turn handed it to me. My creator ancestor passed on to me the elements for the artworks I produce for sale and ceremony. Barnda not only creates the people and landscape, but our designs and artworks originate from the creative acts of Barnda. They honour and deliberate the deeds of Barnda. This way the spirit and rule of Barnda is kept alive in the land. The land and the legacy of Barnda go hand in hand. Land is given to Yolngu people along with responsibility for all of the Madayin (corpus of ritual knowledge) associated with the land. In fact for Yolngu, the ownership of land has with it the corresponding obligations to create and foster the artworks, designs, songs and other aspects of ritual and ceremony that go with the land. If the rituals and ceremonies attached to land ownership are not fulfilled, that is if responsibilities in respect of Madayin are not maintained then traditional Aboriginal ownership rights lapse. Paintings, for example, are a manifestation of our ancestral past. They were first made, in my case by Barnda. Barnda handed the painting to my human ancestors. They have been handed from generation to generation ever since.

The creation of artworks such as "At the Waterhole" is part of my responsibility in fulfilling the obligations I have as a traditional Aboriginal owner of Djulibinyamurr. I am permitted by my law to create this artwork, but it is also my duty and responsibility to create such works, as part of my traditional Aboriginal land ownership obligation. A painting such as this is not separate from my rights in my land. It is a part of my bundle of rights in the land and must be produced in accordance with Ganalbingu custom and law.

Interference with the painting or another aspect of the Madayin associated with Djulibinyamurr is tantamount to interference with the land itself as it is an essential part of the legacy of the land, it is like causing harm to the spirit found in the land, and causes us sorrow and hardship. The land is the life force of our people. It sustains and nurtures us, as it has done for countless generations. We are very troubled by harm caused to the carrying out of the rituals which are such essential part of the management of our land, like the making of paintings or performances of ceremony. It is very important that ceremonies are carried out precisely as directed by Barnda, and that the ceremonies are respected.

"At the Waterhole" is the number one item of Madayin for Djulibinyamurr – it is the number one Madayin for Ganalbingu – Gurrumba Gurrumba people. It has all the inside meaning of our ceremony, law and custom encoded in it. "At the Waterhole" has inside meaning encoded in it. Only an initiate knows that meaning and how to produce the artwork. It is produced in an outside form with encoded meaning inside. It must be produced according to specific laws of the Ganalbingu people, our ritual, ceremony and our law. These things are not separate from the manner in which this painting is produced. To produce "at the Waterhole" without strict observance of the law governing its production diminishes its importance and interferes adversely with the relationship and trust established between myself, my ancestors and Barnda. Production without observance of our law is a breach of that relationship and trust. The continuance of that relationship depends upon the continuance and observance of our customs and law, it keeps the people and land healthy and strong. This work has within it much that is sacred and important to our people about heritage and right to claim Djulibinyamurr as our land. It is like the title of our people to his land.

Unauthorised reproduction of "at the Waterhole" threatens the whole system and ways that underpin the stability and continuance of Yolngu society. It interferes with the relationship between people, their creator ancestors and the land given to the people by their creator ancestor. It interferes with our custom and ritual, and threaten our rights as traditional Aboriginal owners of the land and impedes in the carrying out of the obligations that go with this ownership and which require us to tell and remember the story of Barnda, as it has been passed down and respected over countless generations.

The correctness of this evidence is confirmed by Mr Milpurrurru, and by Mr Djardie Ashley, himself a noted artist, who is married to Mr Milpurrurru's sister, Mrs Dorothy Djukulul, another noted artist. Mr Ashley through clan relationships to the Ganalbingu people and his marriage to Mr Milpurrurru's sister stands him in the position of Waku or Djungayi to Mr Bulun Bulun. Mr Ashley describes this role as follows:

Sometimes Balanda (non Yolngu people) refer to Djungayi as meaning manager. Other times Balanda (non Yolngu people) refer to a Djungayi as a policeman. This is because amongst a Djungayi's responsibilities is the obligation to ensure that the owners of certain land and Madayin associated with that land are dealt with in accordance to Yolngu custom, law and tradition. A Djungayi sometimes might have to issue a warning or advice to a traditional Aboriginal owner about the way certain land or the Madayin associated with that land is used. A Djungayi has an important role to play in maintaining the integrity of the land and Madayin.

Djungayi learn the paintings of the land that they manage. They produce paintings and other aspects of the Madayin for ceremony and for sale where appropriate. Some Djungayi may take a leading role in performing and/or producing aspects of Madayin. More senior Djungayi should be consulted about important decisions concerning their mothers' country, and its Madayin. For example during the preparation of this case I needed to be consulted and be present when Bulun Bulun gave statements to our lawyer. I did most of the talking as it is more appropriate for the Djungayi to speak openly about land and Madayin. I also had to be consulted when Bulun Bulun wished to take our lawyer to Djulibinyamurr.

… My rights as Djungayi of Djulibinyamurr include the right to produce paintings related to that place, and the right to be consulted by Bulun Bulun about the use of Djulibinyamurr and the Madayin related to it. I am able to speak about the law and custom of the Ganalbingu people, in particular that associated with Djulibinyamurr because of my position as Bulun Bulun's Djungayi.

Mr Bulun Bulun explained that the classes of people, described earlier in these reasons, who comprise the traditional Aboriginal owners of Ganalbingu country have interests in Djulibinyamurr and also in the Madayin including paintings such as the artistic work. Many of these people would need to be consulted on any matter that concerned Djulibinyamurr. He went on to say:

In … cases where it has been agreed in principle that the types of uses in question are allowable direct consultation and approval may not be necessary. If Bulun Bulun wanted to licence "at the Waterhole" so that somebody could mass produce it in the way that the Respondents have he would need to consult widely. If he wanted to licence "at the Waterhole" to a publisher to reproduce the painting in an art book he probably would not need to consult the other traditional Aboriginal owners at all.

The question in each case depends on the use and the manner or mode of production. But in the case of a use which is one that requires direct consultation, rather than one for which approval has been already given for a class of uses, all of the traditional Aboriginal owners must agree. There must be total consensus. Bulun Bulun could not act alone to permit the reproduction of "at the Waterhole" in the manner as was done.

The artistic work was painted by Mr Bulun Bulun in 1978 with permission of senior members of the Ganalbingu people. He sold it to the Maningrida Arts and Crafts Centre. It was [subsequently] reproduced with Mr Bulun Bulun's consent in the book *Arts of the Dreaming: Australia's Living Heritage* by Jennifer Isaacs. In the present case, the artistic work has not been exactly reproduced on the infringing fabric, but the design of the fabric obviously reproduces substantial aspects of the artwork, and constitutes a substantial reproduction of it. So much was acknowledged by the respondent as soon as the copyright was brought to its attention.

The applicants brought the proceedings to the notice of the Minister for Aboriginal and Torres Strait Islander Affairs ("the Minister"). When the matter was called on for trial, the Minister appeared by counsel and sought leave to intervene for the purpose of making submissions on legal issues, and in particular the construction and operation of the *Native Title Act* (Cth) ("the NTA"), the *Aboriginal Land Rights (Northern Territory) Act 1978* (Cth) and the *Copyright Act*, and on the claim for recognition of an equitable interest in the copyright. The claim raises important and difficult issues regarding the protection of the interests of indigenous peoples in their cultural heritage. Further, the pleadings ... appear to assert that intellectual property rights of the kind claimed by the applicants were an incident of native title in land. As there would otherwise be no contradictor, the application to intervene by the Minister was welcomed, and leave was granted.... The Attorney-General for the Northern Territory of Australia also appeared at the trial and sought leave to make a submission, as amicus curiae, on the power of the Court to make a determination as to the existence of native title rights. The Court granted leave. [The court noted that both the Minister and the Attorney-General were concerned that the pleadings claimed that (1) the intellectual property rights in the artistic work were an incident of native title; (2) being an incident of native title the intellectual property rights constituted an interest in land; and (3) the Ganalbingu people were entitled to a determination in these proceedings that they were the native title holders of the Ganalbingu country. The court held that it lacked jurisdiction to determine the questions raised by this interpretation of the pleadings in the case, and noted that "in their final form, the applicants' submissions did not seek to have the Court declare by some indirect route that the Ganalbingu people were the holders of native title in the Ganalbingu country."]

Why the Claim Is Confined to One for Recognition
of an Equitable Interest

The submissions of counsel for the applicants reflected a wide ranging search for a way in which the communal interests of the traditional Aboriginal owners in cultural artworks might be recognised under Australian law. That the claim was ultimately confined to one for recognition of an equitable interest in the legal copyright of Mr Bulun Bulun is an acknowledgment that no other possible avenue had emerged from the researches of counsel.

Whilst it is superficially attractive to postulate that the common law should recognise communal title, it would be contrary to established legal principle for the common law to do so. There seems no reason to doubt that customary Aboriginal laws relating to the ownership of artistic works survived the introduction of the common law of England in 1788. The Aboriginal peoples did not cease to observe their *sui generis* system of rights and obligations upon the acquisition of sovereignty of Australia by the Crown. The question however is whether those Aboriginal laws can create binding obligations on persons outside the relevant Aboriginal community, either through recognition of those laws by the common law, or by their capacity to found equitable rights in rem.

In 1788 there may have been scope for the continued operation of a system of indigenous collective ownership in artistic works. At that time the common law of England gave the author of an artistic work property in unpublished compositions which lasted in perpetuity. However, the common law has since been subsumed by statute. The common law right until first publication was abolished when the law of copyright was codified by the Copyright Act of 1911 in the United Kingdom. That Act, subject to some modifications, became the law in Australia.

[The] Copyright Act 1968 provides that the author of an artistic work is the owner of the copyright which subsists by virtue of the Act [which] effectively precludes any notion of group ownership in an artistic work, unless the artistic work is a "work of joint ownership." ... A "work of joint authorship" means a work that has been produced by the collaboration of two or more authors and in which the contribution of each author is not separate from the contribution of the other author or the contributions of the other authors. In this case no evidence was led to suggest that anyone other than Mr Bulun Bulun was the creative author of the artistic work. A person who supplies an artistic idea to an artist who then executes the work is not, on that ground alone, a joint author with the artist....

[Referring to High Court precedent, the court reasoned: "To conclude that the Ganalbingu people were communal owners of the copyright in the existing work would ignore the provisions of s 8 of the Copyright Act, and involve the creation of rights in indigenous peoples which are not otherwise recognised by the legal system of Australia."]

Do the Circumstances in which the Artistic Work was Created Give Rise to Equitable Interests in the Ganalbingu People?

The statement of claim alleges "on the reduction to material form of a part of the ritual knowledge of the Ganalbingu people associated with Djulibinyamurr by the creation of the artistic work, the First Applicant held the copyright subsisting in the artistic work as a fiduciary and/or alternatively on trust, for the second applicant and the people he represents." The foundation for this contention is expanded in written submissions made on Mr Milpurrurru's behalf. It is contended that these rights arise because Mr Milpurrurru and those he represents have the power under customary law to regulate and control the production and reproduction of the corpus of ritual knowledge. It is contended that the customs and traditions regulating this use of the corpus of ritual knowledge places Mr Bulun Bulun as the author of the artistic work in the position of a fiduciary, and, moreover, make Mr Bulun Bulun a trustee for the artwork, either pursuant to some form of express trust, or pursuant to a constructive trust in favour of the Ganalbingu people. The right to control the production and reproduction of the corpus of ritual knowledge relating to Djulibinyamurr is said to arise by virtue of the strong ties which continue to exist between the Ganalbingu people and their land. [The court declined to find an express trust under these circumstances.]

Did Mr Bulun Bulun Hold the Copyright as a Fiduciary?

[T]he essential characteristics of fiduciary relationships were referred to by Mason J in *Hospital Products* [*v United States Surgical Corporation* (1984) 156 CLR 41, at 96–97]: "The critical feature of [fiduciary] relationships is that the fiduciary undertakes or agrees to act for or on behalf of or in the interests of another person in the exercise of a power or discretion which will affect the interests of that other person in a legal or practical sense. The relationship between the parties is therefore one which gives the fiduciary a special opportunity to exercise the power or discretion to the detriment of that other person who is accordingly vulnerable to abuse by the fiduciary of his position.... It is partly because the fiduciary's exercise of the power or discretion can adversely affect the interests of the person to whom the duty is owed and because the latter is at the mercy of the former that the fiduciary comes under a duty to exercise his power or discretion in the interests of the person to whom it is owed."

The Court was not referred to any authority in support of the imposition of equitable principles to govern relations amongst members of a tribal group. However, the application of the principles of equity in this situation is not unknown to the common law as it has been applied outside of this country....

The relationship between Mr Bulun Bulun as the author and legal title holder of the artistic work and the Ganalbingu people is unique. The "transaction" between them out of which fiduciary relationship is said to arise is the use with permission by Mr Bulun Bulun of ritual knowledge of the Ganalbingu people, and the embodiment of that knowledge within the artistic work. That use has been permitted in accordance with the law and customs of the Ganalbingu people.

The grant of permission by the djungayi and other appropriate representatives of the Ganalbingu people for the creation of the artistic work is predicated on the trust and confidence which those granting permission have in the artist. The evidence indicates that if those who must give permission do not have trust and confidence in someone seeking permission, permission will not be granted.

The law and customs of the Banalbingu people require that the use of the ritual knowledge and the artistic work be in accordance with the requirements of law and custom, and that the author of the artistic work do whatever is necessary to prevent any misuse. The artist is required to act in relation to the artwork in the interests of the Ganalbingu people to preserve the integrity of their culture, and ritual knowledge.

This is not to say that the artist must act entirely in the interests of the Ganalbingu people. The evidence shows that an artist is entitled to consider and pursue his own interests, for example by selling the artwork, but the artist is not permitted to shed the overriding obligation to act to preserve the integrity of the Ganalbingu culture where action for that purpose is required.

In my opinion, the nature of the relationship between Mr Bulun Bulun and the Ganalbingu people was a fiduciary one which gives rise to fiduciary obligations owed by Mr Bulun Bulun.

The conclusion that in all the circumstances Mr Bulun Bulun owes fiduciary obligations to the Ganalbingu people does not treat the law and custom of the Ganalbingu people as part of the Australian legal system. Rather, it treats the law and custom of the Ganalbingu people as part of the factual matrix which characterises the relationship as one of mutual trust and confidence. It is that relationship which the Australian legal system recognises as giving rise to the fiduciary relationship, and to the obligations which arise out of it.

The Fiduciary Obligation

Central to the fiduciary concept is the protection of interests that can be regarded as worthy of judicial protection. The evidence is all one way. The ritual knowledge relating to Djulibinyamurr embodied within the artistic work is of great importance to members of the Ganalbingu people. I have no hesitation in holding that the interest of Ganalbingu people in the protection of that ritual knowledge from exploitation which is contrary to their law and custom is deserving of the protection of the Australian legal system.

Under the Copyright Act, the owner of the copyright has the exclusive right to reproduce the work in a material form, and to publish the work. The copyright owner is entitled to enforce copyright against the world at large. In the event of infringement, the copyright owner is entitled to sue and to obtain remedies of the kind actually obtained by Mr Bulun Bulun in this case.

Having regard to the evidence of the law and customs of the Ganalbingu people under which Mr Bulun Bulun was permitted to create the artistic work, I consider that equity imposes on him obligations as a fiduciary not to exploit the artistic work in a way that is contrary to the laws and custom of the Ganalbingu people, and, in the event of infringement by a third party, to take reasonable and appropriate action to restrain and remedy infringement of the copyright in the artistic work.

Whilst the nature of the relationship between Mr Bulun Bulun and the Ganalbingi people is such that Mr Bulun Bulun falls under fiduciary obligations to protect the ritual knowledge which he has been permitted to use, the existence of those obligations does not, without more, vest an equitable interest in the ownership of the copyright in the Ganalbingu people. Their primary right, in the event of a breach of obligation by the fiduciary is a right in personam to bring action against the fiduciary to enforce the obligation.

In the present case Mr Bulun Bulun has successfully taken action against the respondent to obtain remedies in respect of the infringement. There is no suggestion by Mr Milpurrurru and those whom he seeks to represent that Mr Bulun Bulun should have done anything more. In these circumstances there is no occasion for the intervention of equity to provide any additional remedy to the beneficiaries of the fiduciary relationship.

However, had the position been otherwise equitable remedies could have been available. The extent of those remedies would depend on all the circumstances, and in an extreme case could involve the intervention of equity to impose a constructive trust on the legal owner of the copyright in the artistic work in favour of the beneficiaries. Equity will not automatically impose a constructive trust merely upon the identification of a fiduciary obligation. Equity will impose a constructive trust on property held by a fiduciary where it is necessary to do so to achieve a just remedy and to prevent the beneficiary from retaining an unconscionable benefit. By way of example, had Mr Bulun Bulun merely failed to take action to enforce his copyright, an adequate remedy might be extended in equity to the beneficiaries by allowing them to bring action in their own names against the infringer and the copyright owner, claiming against the former, in the first instance, interlocutory relief to restrain the infringement, and against the latter orders necessary to ensure that the copyright owner enforces the copyright. Probably there would be no occasion for equity in these circumstances to impose a constructive trust.

On the other hand, were Mr Bulun Bulun to deny the existence of fiduciary obligations and the interests of the parties asserting them, and refuse to protect the copyright from infringement, then the occasion might exist for equity to impose a remedial constructive trust upon the copyright owner to strengthen the standing of the beneficiaries to bring proceedings to enforce the copyright. This may be necessary if the copyright owner cannot be identified or found and the beneficiaries are unable to join the legal owner of the copyright.

It is well recognised that interlocutory injunctive relief can be claimed by a party having an equitable interest in copyright. [However], I do not consider Mr Milpurrurru and those he seeks to represent have established an equitable interest in the copyright in the artistic work. In my opinion they have established that fiduciary obligations are owed to them by Mr Bulun Bulun, but as Mr Bulun Bulun has taken appropriate action to enforce the copyright, he has fulfilled those obligations and there is no occasion to grant any additional remedy in favour of the Ganalbingu people. However, in other circumstances if the copyright owner of an artistic work which embodies ritual knowledge of an Aboriginal clan is being used inappropriately, and the copyright owner fails or refuses to take appropriate action to enforce the copyright, the Australian legal system will permit remedial action through the courts by the clan. For these reasons, the proceedings by Mr Milpurrurru must be dismissed.

Notes and Questions

1. Justice von Doussa did not refer to international human rights law. Should he have done so? Would it have made any difference to his analysis or the outcome of the case? What concepts or norms does international human rights law offer that are relevant to the relationship between the individual artist and the indigenous group of which he or she is a member?

2. How should the judge have decided the case if the individual artist had been missing or uninterested in seeking copyright protection? How would international human rights law answer this question? Would domestic copyright law provide the same answer?

3. The evidence in the *Bulun Bulun* case included a creation story that recounts the shaping of the landscape by an ancestor known as "Barnda." Under copyright law concepts, indigenous creation stories, or aspects of them, may be in the public domain. The story itself may have been developed too long ago to attract copyright protection or, even if the story has evolved over time, with retellings and reinterpretation by members of the indigenous group (the more recent of which might be protected by copyright law), key aspects of the story may be unprotected under the "idea/expression" dichotomy. Assume that a recounting of the story by individuals outside the indigenous group would cause deep offense to the group's member. Is cultural offense a sufficient basis for prohibiting such a recounting?[152] Rebecca Tsosie writes: "Native people assert a right to control who can tell their stories and who can use their designs and symbols" as a means to "ensure cultural survival."[153] Does the link to cultural survival make a difference to the analysis? How should a court respond if there are divisions between members of the group as to the appropriateness of economic exploitation?

4. How do moral rights, as protected by treaties such as the Berne Convention for the Protection of Literary and Artistic Works, inform the issues raised in the previous Note? If national governments are willing to protect moral rights, should they not also be willing to protect against other forms of cultural affronts?

5. Recently, three U.S. scholars have advocated for the adoption of a principle of "stewardship" to accommodate the various interests at stake in cultural property debates,[154] arguing that "the exercise of rights and obligations independent of title ... lies at the heart of cultural stewardship."[155] Explaining this concept in more detail, they write:

> Classic ownership theory tends to overlook the possibility of nonowners exercising custodial duties over tangible and intangible goods in the absence of title or possession. Yet indigenous peoples have historically exercised such custodial duties, both as a matter of internal community values that emphasize collective obligations to land and resources, and as a matter of practical necessity following the widespread divestiture of title and possession. Indigenous cultural claims, and programs meant to effectuate them, thus reflect a fiduciary approach to cultural property that takes into account indigenous peoples' collective obligations toward land and resources. A wealth of literature has analysed the notion

---

[152] For an examination of these issues in the New Zealand context, *see* BARRY BARCLAY, MANA TUTURU: MĀORI TREASURES AND INTELLECTUAL PROPERTY RIGHTS (2005).

[153] Rebecca Tsosie, *Reclaiming Native Stories: An Essay on Cultural Appropriation and Cultural Rights*, 34 ARIZ. ST. L.J. 299, 310 (2002).

[154] Carpenter, Katyal & Riley, *supra* note 8.

[155] *Id.* at 1067.

of fiduciary duties, existing in either the presence or absence of title, indigenous, corporate, and environmental theories of "stewardship." Drawing on this literature, we identify a similar fiduciary paradigm in the context of cultural property. To the extent that indigenous cultural property claims are premised on custodial duties toward specific properties, we argue that such claims are more appropriately characterized through the paradigm of stewardship rather than ownership. Because they often act in the absence of title, such accommodations tend to fall outside the paradigms of individuality and alienability upon which classic property law is premised. Thus, without rejecting the force or utility of ownership, we propose that cultural property claims are better explained and justified through a stewardship that effectuates the dynamic pluralism of group-oriented interests.[156]

How, if at all, does this analysis differ from Justice von Doussa's exposition of the equitable interests of the Ganalbingu people?

7.7. Intersections between Indigenous Human Rights and Intellectual Property Issues

This chapter has drawn on both human rights and intellectual property to explore the conceptual and legal justifications for protecting indigenous traditional knowledge and cultural productions. We conclude with a brief discussion of how both bodies of law can contribute to debates over the appropriate scope of such protections.

Consider the following example from New Zealand. "TOI IHO Māori made" is a registered trademark that is used to promote and sell authentic high-quality arts and crafts made by Māori. The mark was originally sponsored by Te Waka Toi, the Māori arts board of Creative New Zealand, a government arts-funding authority, in consultation with Māori artists. The TOI IHO mark was principally used to authenticate artworks and performances by Māori artists. The mark was restricted to Māori artists; individuals who were licensed to use the mark were required to verify their Māori descent and satisfy the licensing authority that they were capable of creating high-quality artwork. The official web site for the initiative explained that "when people purchase a Māori artwork labelled with TOI IHO, they are guaranteed the product was made by a person of Māori descent and is of quality."[157] The TOI IHO Māori made mark was accompanied by two companion marks, the "mainly Māori" mark and the "Māori co-production mark." The TOI IHO mainly Māori mark was for groups of artists, most of whom are of Māori descent, who work together to produce, present, or perform a variety of art

[156] *Id.* at 1028–29.
[157] *See* TOI IHO: Māori made, *available at* www.toiiho.com (last visited Mar. 31, 2010).

forms. The TOI IHO Māori coproduction mark acknowledges the growth of innovative, collaborative ventures between Māori and non-Māori. This companion mark was "for Māori artists who create works with persons of non-Māori descent to produce, present or perform works across art forms." The official web site explained: "Cultural heritage and the ongoing development of creative and interpretative expression and innovation are of paramount importance to Māori. [The 'TOI IHO' mark] was created to assist Māori to retain control over their cultural heritage and maintain the integrity of their art culture in an increasingly commercialised world."[158]

In 2009, Creative New Zealand decided to stop managing and promoting the TOI IHO mark. Explaining its decision, the agency said:

> Creative New Zealand has become increasingly aware, through reviews, market research and artist feedback, that although there are artists who actively use TOI IHO to leverage their work, many more Māori artists are making successful careers without the need for the TOI IHO trademark. For many Māori artists, the quality of their work speaks for itself and this is reflected in a growth of opportunities for consumers to buy Māori art from specialist Māori art and general galleries, the Internet and Māori arts markets. Creative New Zealand has conducted several reviews of TOI IHO since its inception and a consistent theme was that while the ideas underpinning the brand have considerable merit, it has failed to deliver on its promise in terms of increasing sales of Māori art by licensed artists and stockists (retailers). The funds that supported its operation will be reallocated to other Creative New Zealand Māori arts development initiatives. Creative New Zealand is currently advising licensed TOI IHO artists [and firms that stock products on which the TOI IHO mark has been affixed] of the process to wind-down their use of the trademark.[159]

The TOI IHO initiative reveals at least two ways in which trademark law interacts with traditional knowledge and cultural expressions.[160] First, trademarks can incorporate indigenous imagery in marks owned by nonindigenous individuals and firms. New Zealand has enacted procedures to prevent this from occurring, establishing a Māori advisory board to instruct the Trademark Office whether a particular mark might cause cultural offense.[161] In other nations, indigenous groups may be able to invoke more general prohibitions against the registration of marks likely to offend any class of persons, as exemplified by the Redskins controversy discussed in the Notes and Questions to Section 7.5 of this chapter.[162]

---

[158] *Id.*

[159] *Id.*

[160] *See* Visser, *supra* note 64, at 470–71.

[161] *See* Frankel, *supra* note 125.

[162] *See* Visser, *supra* note 64, at 472 (referring to the trademark laws of South Africa and Brazil).

The TOI IHO experiment also illustrates a second level of interaction between indigenous groups and trademark law: the use of trademarks to enhance the economic exploitation of traditional cultural expressions. In New Zealand, the original reasons for the TOI IHO initiative had been overtaken by the success of individual Māori artists, many of whom apparently did not need the added benefits of an authenticating mark. In other countries, certification marks for indigenous products confer similar benefits.[163]

To the extent that trademarks such as these assist in the promotion of goods and services that are sold under the mark, they are broadly consistent with conventional rationales for trademark rights. Protecting trademarks enhances the efficiency of information available to consumers about the origin of goods and services. A trademark such as TOI IHO would, for example, inform consumers that an artwork originated from an "authentic" Māori artist. Providing reliable information about the authenticity of goods and services may, in some cases, enhance the price of products bearing the mark. Trademark law assumes that consumers consider the premium they pay for goods and services bearing accurate trademarks to be good value for money.[164]

One objection to this analysis is that initiatives such TOI IHO simply produce and protect more intellectual property, increasing the costs of goods and inhibiting competition. In some contexts, indigenous groups' control over traditional knowledge does appear to be animated by commercial imperatives that are broadly in line with other types of intellectual property. Yet it is arguably in these situations that the rationales for protection may be weakest. Two U.S. scholars, Steven Munzer and Kal Raustiala, have asserted that the case for intellectual property protection of traditional knowledge is "uneasy" at best.[165] They base their argument on a general skepticism about the expansion of intellectual property rights and the "enclosure of the intellectual commons ... [which] is increasingly the practice in both international and national law."[166] In addition, Munzer and Raustiala argue that, "[w]hether looked at individually or collectively, the chief arguments employed in the moral, political, and legal philosophies of property do not

---

[163] *See* Maureen Liebl & Roy Tirthankar, *Handmade in India: Traditional Craft Skills in a Changing World*, in J. Michael Finger & Philip Schuler (Eds.), Poor People's Knowledge: Promoting Intellectual Property in Developing Countries 53 (2004).

[164] Graeme W. Austin, *Tolerating Confusion about Confusion: Trademark Policies and Fair Use*, 50 Ariz. L. Rev. 157, 162 (2008).

[165] Munzer & Raustiala, *supra* note 16; *see generally* Reto Hilty, *Rationales for the Legal Protection of Intangible Goods and Cultural Heritage* (Max Planck Inst. for Intellectual Prop., Competition & Tax Law, Research Paper No. 09–10, 2009).

[166] *Id.* at 41.

justify a robust package of rights in [traditional knowledge]."[167] For example, justifications for property rights grounded in labor-based entitlements are difficult to apply where the descendants of the original creators (i.e., the original laborers) assert those rights.[168] Critiques such as these echo concerns about the extension of intellectual property protection more generally – that is, whether protection of traditional knowledge causes yet another unwarranted contraction of the intellectual commons.

More intellectual property, whoever owns it, also risks inhibiting speech. A passage in the 1995 Report of the Sub-commission on Prevention of Discrimination and Protection of Minorities provides a good illustration of how perspectives on this issue have changed over time. The report reviews objections to expanding intellectual property rights for traditional knowledge, in particular the claim that enhanced protections can limit speech. The report then notes:

> The Special Rapporteur … fails to understand how the right to freedom of expression includes the right to obtain commercial or other benefits from the repetition of the ideas or creative works of others. The measures she has recommended pose no more of a conflict with free expression than patent and copyright legislation, which secure to the creators of useful knowledge and artistic works the right to control, and to benefit from, what they have created.[169]

Today, many commentators would object that copyrights and patents *do* conflict with freedom of expression.[170] Drawing an analogy between intellectual property rights and traditional knowledge merely restates the problem in a new context. Indeed, the problem may be exacerbated because *limits* on intellectual property, such as copyright's fair use defense, may be difficult to transpose to traditional knowledge and cultural expressions. Many indigenous peoples assert the right to define for themselves the nature and scope of protection for such works. These assertions understandably deemphasize defenses or exceptions that further expressive freedoms, such as permitting others to parody what is sacred to indigenous communities.

These examples reveal the broader tensions that accompany analyzing traditional knowledge and cultural expressions from a human rights perspective.

---

[167] *Id.* at 40. Munzer and Raustiala acknowledge that indigenous intellectual property might be justified on grounds other than property theory, including distributive justice and human rights. Munzer & Raustiala, *supra* note 16, at 41–42.

[168] *Id.* at 59. Other scholars question the salience of "cultural property" as a distinct category of property. *See* Eric A. Posner, *The International Protection of Cultural Property: Some Skeptical Observations*, 8 CHI. J. INT'L L. 213 (2007).

[169] Special Rapporteur, *Protection of the Heritage, supra* note 12, para. 25.

[170] Chapter 4 provides additional discussion of these conflicts.

As we observe throughout this book, and as more fully developed in Chapter 8, there are protective and restrictive dimensions of human rights in the intellectual property context. In particular, human rights both protect creators and limit expansive intellectual property protection rules. This dual perspective applies no less to the creativity of indigenous communities.

With regard to the protective dimension of human rights, there are a number of bases for protecting traditional knowledge and cultural expressions. For example, a government initiative such as the TOI IHO trademark might be justified as helping indigenous groups find or expand markets for their productions and thus improve their economic circumstances (even if Māori did not ultimately need them). As discussed in Chapter 3, the Committee on Economic, Social and Cultural Rights, in *General Comment No. 17*, has interpreted the human rights of creators in Article 15(1)(c) of the ICESCR as vehicles for providing an adequate standard of living. The Committee expressly included the collective creativity of indigenous communities in the *General Comment*, thus emphasizing that the traditional knowledge and cultural expressions of those communities are protected under the rubric of creators' human rights.

The restrictive dimension, in contrast, foregrounds the potential conflicts between indigenous creativity and other human rights, such as non-discrimination, expressive freedoms, and health. As a first principle for reconciling these conflicts, we believe that if indigenous peoples assert a human rights basis for protecting traditional knowledge and cultural expressions, they must also accept the limits that international human rights law imposes on such protections. James Anaya has endorsed this approach in the context of indigenous peoples' cultural integrity claims: "The affirmation of cultural integrity as a norm within the framework of human rights establishes a strong foundation of the norm within international law. However, it also necessarily means that the exercise of culture is limited by that very human rights framework."[171] Anaya provides an example of cultural practices that discriminate against or harm women. He concludes that such practices "cannot be sustained as part of a right to cultural integrity because [they are] contrary to human rights."[172]

A similar approach can be applied to protections of traditional knowledge and cultural expressions. For example, a human rights focus calls attention to the race- or status-based restrictions that accompanied the TOI IHO initiative, most notably that non-Māori artists did not have equivalent rights to

---

[171] Anaya, *Multicultural State, supra* note 5, at 25.
[172] *Id.*

use the TOI IHO mark. Yet these restrictions may themselves have human rights justifications – as partial remedies for the history of subjugation and continuing inequality of particular indigenous groups,[173] and as a means to facilitate the economic and cultural survival of indigenous peoples.[174]

We urge lawmakers carefully to consider the empirical particularities of each case when attempting to reconcile potential conflicts between the protective and restrictive dimensions of human rights as applied to indigenous intellectual property. As the TOI IHO trademark initiative reveals, the rationales in favor of special legal protections for indigenous cultural expressions may be unfounded or may diminish over time. In the first case, legislators can refrain from enacting special protections and avoid the conflict altogether. In the second, they can minimize the clash by narrowing or phasing out those protections as circumstances change. Human rights impact assessments – a measurement tool that we discuss in Chapter 8 – can help to evaluate whether a particular proposal helps or hinders the realization of specific rights and freedoms.

Careful empirical assessments are also required in situations where conflicts appear to be unavoidable. Consider as a hypothetical example traditional knowledge that reveals the medicinal and psychotropic properties of a plant that grows on the ancestral lands of an indigenous community. Assume further that the knowledge associated with the use of the plant is sacred to the community and that its disclosure would cause acute spiritual harm.[175] If the chemical composition of the plant contains the cure for a global pandemic, should human rights law's protection of the identities, cultures, and social structures of indigenous peoples – here manifested in the community's demand for secrecy – prevail over the human right to health

---

[173] For example, Article 1 of the International Convention on the Elimination of All Forms of Racial Discrimination excludes from the treaty's prohibition of discrimination "[s]pecial measures taken for the sole purpose of securing adequate advancement of certain racial or ethnic groups or individuals requiring such protection," if such measures are "necessary in order to ensure such groups or individuals equal enjoyment or exercise of human rights and fundamental freedoms." CERD, art. 1(4). This authorization for race-conscious measures to promote substantive equality cannot, however, "lead to the maintenance of separate rights for different racial groups," nor can they "be continued after the objectives for which they were taken have been achieved." Id.

[174] Tsosie, *supra* note 153.

[175] *See* TERRI JANKE, OUR CULTURE, OUR FUTURE: REPORT ON AUSTRALIAN INDIGENOUS CULTURAL AND INTELLECTUAL PROPERTY RIGHTS 19 (1998) (describing various deculturizing uses of sacred works); *see also* Doris Estelle Long, *Traditional Knowledge and the Fight for the Public Domain*, 5 J. MARSHALL REV. INTELL. PROP. L. 317, 327 (2006) (cautioning that a workable system for traditional knowledge protection may not be possible if indigenous communities deem everything to be sacred or otherwise incapable of commercialization).

that international law obligates states to respect, protect, and fulfil for all individuals within their borders?

Framed in this way, the conflict appears irreconcilable and the outcome – disclosure – foreordained. In reality, however, the competing rights claims are rarely so stark. Although hopes were initially high for bioprospecting in regions of abundant biodiversity, predictions of a "green gold" rush have turned out to be vastly overstated. Scientists underestimated the difficulty of identifying new and useful chemical compounds from among the world's flaura and fauna.[176] As a result, the likelihood that protecting traditional knowledge will deny the world lifesaving medicines is far lower than the previous hypothetical suggests.

Equally as important, the rights and interests of many indigenous communities can be satisfied by mechanisms other than secrecy, such as consultations, prior informed consent, benefit sharing, and restricting subsequent uses to those that maintain a work's cultural integrity.[177] These mechanisms, which are likely to vary from community to community, can be accommodated in a variety of ways, including by incorporating them in bioprospecting agreements to which indigenous communities are parties. We do not suggest that such accommodations and agreements will be easy to negotiate; in fact, the empirical evidence is to the contrary.[178] Rather, we suggest that lawmakers and policymakers who consider both the protective and restrictive dimensions of a human rights approach to indigenous intellectual property and who pay careful attention to the factual particularities may identify a range of possibilities to help reconcile apparent conflicts.

---

[176] Colin Macilwain, *When Rhetoric Hits Reality in Debates on Bioprospecting*, 392 NATURE 535 (1998).

[177] *See, e.g.*, Gurdial Singh Nijar, *Incorporating Traditional Knowledge in an International Regime on Access to Genetic Resources and Benefit Sharing: Problems and Prospects*, 21 EUR. J. INT'L L. 457 (2010) (reviewing issues relating to inclusion of traditional knowledge in future international legal regimes on access and benefit sharing); Greg Young-Ing, Intellectual Property Rights, Legislated Protection, Sui Generis Models and Ethical Access in the Transformation of Indigenous Traditional Knowledge (Oct. 2006) (unpublished Ph.D. thesis, University of British Columbia), *available at* http://eprints.rclis.org/9591/ (analyzing domestic regimes that require benefit sharing with indigenous communities); Doris Estelle Long, *Crossing the Innovation Divide*, 81 TEMPLE L. REV. 507, 535 (2008) (discussing restrictions on commercial exploitation of traditional knowledge to preserve cultural integrity).

[178] *See* Sabrina Safrin, *Hyperownership in a Time of Biotechnological Promise: The International Conflict to Control the Building Blocks of Life*, 98 AM. J. INT'L L. 641, 657 (2004) ("For every bioprospecting success story, there are dozens of cases where the projects never got off the ground.").

Chapter 8

Conclusion

This book analyzes the interface of human rights and intellectual property from multiple perspectives. Chapter 1 introduces the major legal, institutional, and political aspects of each regime, explains how they came into increasing contact over the past decade, and explores alternative frameworks for conceptualizing their relationship. Each of the remaining chapters adopts a predominantly substantive orientation that examines in depth specific intersections between certain human rights and intellectual property protection rules. In this concluding chapter, we shift focus to elaborate the major transsubstantive themes that are interwoven through the preceding materials. Our aim is twofold. First, and more modestly, we seek to illuminate connections that transcend specific "hot button" controversies and to offer deeper insights about the interconnections between the two legal regimes. Second, and more ambitiously, we offer our own analytical framework to assist scholars, policymakers, civil society groups, and students in conceptualizing the relationship between human rights and intellectual property.

We begin in Section 8.1 by reiterating the inevitability of the human rights–intellectual property interface and by rejecting – both as a matter of principle and as a matter of practical politics – arguments for maintaining a firewall between the two regimes and avoiding the difficult work of normative engagement. Section 8.2 evaluates three proposals to demarcate the boundary lines between human rights and intellectual property, proposals whose particularities we describe in greater detail in previous chapters. Section 8.3 offers our own conception of the human rights–intellectual property interface, synthesizing and expanding upon the ideas developed in previous chapters. We distinguish between the *protective* and *restrictive* functions of international human rights law in the intellectual property context and propose a framework that identifies when human rights concerns favor revising

503

existing intellectual property protection rules or otherwise restructuring the incentives for human creativity and innovation.

8.1. The Unavoidable Intersection of Human Rights and Intellectual Property

The previous chapters of this book describe the growing network of international organizations, government agencies, civil society groups, attorneys, commentators, and journalists whose work focuses on both human rights and intellectual property issues. Many of the individuals who participate in this network view the increasing intersections between the two regimes as beneficial. Some, however, are suspicious of these developments, preferring instead to maintain or even fortify the boundary between the regimes. Others take aim at specific points of intersection, claiming that the overlap of previously unrelated rules and institutions will result in deleterious legal or policy outcomes.

This opposition is partly engendered by a resistance to change among actors who are habituated to the discourse of one complex legal and political system but not the other. But this resistance is animated by more than a reflexive fear of the unfamiliar. The two communities speak very different languages. Intellectual property commentators, especially those working in the Anglo-American tradition, employ the analytical tools of utilitarianism and welfare economics to evaluate the trade-offs between incentives and access and the consequences for the individuals and firms that create, own, and consume intellectual property products. The international human rights movement, by contrast, engages in a discourse of absolutes that seeks to delineate the negative and positive duties of states to respect and promote inalienable individual freedoms. As a result, to label something as a "human right" often invokes – in rhetoric if not always in reality – a language of trumps and unconditional demands. This emphasis on categorical rights and responsibilities appears ill suited to the rapidly changing technological and economic environment in which intellectual property rules operate, an environment that often engenders calls for incremental recalibrations of the balance between incentives and access.

A second basis for resistance to the intersection of human rights and intellectual property stems not from concerns about each regime as it actually exists, but rather from opposition to actors who make rhetorical and, we believe, inflated claims grounded in one regime to support arguments for changing the other. Commentators on both sides have expressed concerns about such overclaiming. Some in the human rights community, for example, fear that intellectual property owners – in particular, multinational corporations – will invoke the creators' rights and property rights provisions of international instruments to lock in maximalist intellectual property rules that will further concentrate wealth in the hands of a few at the expense of the many. Parts of the intellectual property community, by contrast, have expressed the concern that seemingly vague calls for states to "respect, protect, ensure, and fulfill" economic and social rights are code words for more radical campaigns to promote government intervention in private innovation markets and radically scale back or even abolish intellectual property protection. A common factor that unites both sets of fears is the focus on extremist arguments that ignore the actual structure and content of each legal regime.

A third explanation for resistance to the human rights–intellectual property interface stems from a concern with fragmentation of international regimes, overlapping competencies of international institutions, and conflicts among legal obligations. Worries that the international legal system is becoming overly fragmented are widespread. That system, unlike its national counterparts, lacks a single legislative, executive, or judicial body with mandatory, universal powers. It is composed of disaggregated and decentralized rules and institutions that include thousands of multilateral, regional, and bilateral treaties and customary laws; myriad nonbinding declarations and resolutions and other "soft law" norms; intergovernmental organizations with diverse memberships and subject matter competencies; international tribunals, review bodies, and arbitral panels with different jurisdictional mandates; and formal and informal networks of government, private, and hybrid regulators.

Anxieties relating to the fragmentation of international legal regimes are exacerbated by institutional competence concerns. Since the adoption of the TRIPS Agreement in the mid-1990s, many important intellectual property controversies have been litigated within the World Trade Organization (WTO). The merger of trade and intellectual property has provoked a wealth of scholarly debate, much of it unflattering. But calls for the international trading system to give greater consideration to human rights concerns – both those related specifically to intellectual property and more generally – raise difficult issues as to whether WTO decision makers are adequately equipped to mediate these competing values.

At the level of rule conflict, fragmentation concerns run especially high where human rights, intellectual property, and trade intersect. The applicable rules often pull in opposite directions, suggesting to some observers that their interaction is a zero sum game in which the only legal and policy choice is between wider access in the present or more innovation in the future, never both. These concerns have motivated international review bodies and commentators to propose normative hierarchies that privilege one regime over the other where relevant rules conflict. As the analysis of these hierarchies in Chapter 1 reveals, however, these efforts are insufficiently theorized and highly contested. Government officials, adjudicators, nonstate actors, and scholars are unlikely to accept any wholesale normative prioritization of the two regimes, and they will continue to advance competing claims in the many diverse venues made possible by the international legal system's disaggregated structure. Continued engagement of the two regimes is therefore inevitable. Providing a constructive framework for analyzing and facilitating that engagement is one of the principal motivations for writing this book.

8.2. Assessing Existing Proposals to Reconcile Human Rights and Intellectual Property

The analyses in this book and in our previously published articles and essays on which it is based are by no means the only attempts to analyze the relationship between the human rights and intellectual property regimes. A number of scholars and international expert bodies have made thoughtful interventions on these issues over the past decade, and their arguments and proposals have enriched our own ideas about the subject. In previous chapters of this book, we give these commentators and experts pride of place by reproducing and engaging with key extracts of their writings. Here, we paint with a broader brush. We group these contributions into three broad and admittedly simplified categories, highlighting common themes, strengths, and weaknesses and laying the groundwork for our own analysis.

The first group of scholars emphasizes the importance of rediscovering the historical record.[1] For these commentators, resolving the normative tensions engendered by the intersection of human rights and intellectual property requires unearthing the original understanding of the long-forgotten creators' rights and cultural benefit clauses in UDHR Article 27 and

---

[1] *See, e.g.,* Audrey Chapman, *Approaching Intellectual Property as a Human Right: Obligations Relating to Article 15(1)(c),* 35 COPYRIGHT BULL. 4 (2001); ECOSOC, Comm. on Econ., Soc. and Cultural Rights, *Drafting History of the Article 15(1)(c) of the International Covenant on Economic, Social and Cultural Rights,* E/C.12/2000/15 (Oct. 9, 2000) (*prepared by* Maria Green); Lea Shaver, *The Right to Science and Culture,* 2010 WISC. L. REV. 121 (2010); Lea Shaver & Caterina Sganga, *The Right to Take Part in Cultural Life: On Copyright and Human Rights,* 27 WISC. INT'L L. REV. 637 (2009); Peter K. Yu, *Reconceptualizing Intellectual Property Interests in a Human Rights Framework,* 40 U.C. DAVIS L. REV. 1039 (2007); Paul Torremans, *Copyright as a Human Right,* in PAUL L. C. TORREMANS (ED.), COPYRIGHT AND HUMAN RIGHTS: FREEDOM OF EXPRESSION – INTELLECTUAL PROPERTY – PRIVACY 1 (2004).

ICESCR Article 15. As we explain in greater detail in Chapter 3, these clauses set forth legal obligations and policy objectives closely analogous to those embodied in intellectual property systems. Like the latter systems, the texts of Article 27 and of Article 15, when read together, obligate governments to recognize and reward human creativity and innovation and, at the same time, to ensure public access to the fruits of those endeavors. Striking the appropriate balance between these two goals is the central challenge that both regimes share.

One of the aims of this historical research is to rediscover how the women and men who wrote Articles 27 and 15 understood that this crucial balance would be struck. By carefully parsing the negotiating histories and the wider political and social contexts that gave birth to these clauses, commentators hope to explain why the drafters included the moral and material interests of creators and the public's right to enjoy the benefits of that creativity in universal human rights instruments. For some scholars, however, this enterprise is also a precursor to a second, more ambitious goal: to provide a historical justification for giving greater weight to the public side of the balance between access and innovation and concomitantly reduced protections for the creators and owners of intellectual property products.

We fully support the first objective but are more skeptical of the second. Shedding light on this obscure corner of the human rights regime is undoubtedly a worthy endeavor. However, the historical record provides only limited and ultimately inconclusive guidance. It demonstrates that the drafters strongly endorsed the right to participate in culture and to enjoy the benefits of scientific progress and its applications, rejected proposals to include copyright protection in the UDHR and ICESCR, and divided over the decision to recognize creators' rights as human rights. In the absence of greater specificity, however, the drafting history is too slender a reed on which to ground an alternative framework for how states should balance these competing goals.

This use of history is misguided in another respect. Human rights law and intellectual property law are both famously dynamic, readily adapting to changing circumstances through new rounds of treaty making, interpretations by international tribunals, and revisions of national laws. A framework that privileges the original understanding of Articles 27 and 15 fails to engage with this dynamism and with the evolutions in law, politics, social values, and technology that engendered these adaptations.

A second group of scholars views the increasing attention to intellectual property issues in the human rights regime as an opportunity to reexamine tools that already exist in national intellectual property laws and treaties that help government decision makers to strike a socially optimal balance between incentivizing private innovation and enriching the cultural, scientific, and information commons.[2] For these commentators, gazing at intellectual property through a human rights lens illuminates the fact that governments have rarely used many of these policy levers or have allowed them to fall into desuetude. Once revived or expanded, this argument continues, these tools – which include subject matter exclusions, exceptions and limitations, compulsory licenses, and special and differential treatment of developing countries – can fully achieve the goals that the intellectual property system shares with the human rights regime while avoiding the risks of importing rights claims that are less susceptible to utilitarian balancing.

We endorse calls to revive and expand policy levers that have long been part of the intellectual property regime as a formal matter but that are infrequently utilized in practice, whether because of lack of familiarity or pressure from international organizations, developed countries, or intellectual property industries. And we agree with the conclusions of international expert bodies that the "flexibilities" in intellectual property treaties and statutes are salutary on their own terms as well as essential to maintain compatibility with international human rights law. We part company with these scholars and experts, however, to the extent they assert that bolstering these policy tools is not only necessary but also sufficient to reconcile the human rights and intellectual property regimes.

We reject this conclusion as a matter of both principle and practical politics. As a matter of principle, flexibility mechanisms provide breathing space for governments to promote a wide range of objectives that conflict or are in tension with expansive intellectual property protection rules. Commentators have offered numerous suggestions for manipulating these policy levers to enhance economic development, foster local innovation, and increase technology transfers from developed to developing countries. These are salutary goals, to be sure. But they are insufficiently connected to the protection of fundamental rights and freedoms. Stated another way, intellectual property

---

[2] *See, e.g.,* P. B. Hugenholtz, *Copyright and Freedom of Expression in Europe,* in ROCHELLE COOPER DREYFUSS, HARRY FIRST, & DIANE LEHEER ZIMMERMAN (EDS.), INNOVATION POLICY IN AN INFORMATION AGE (2000); P. Bernt Hugenholtz & Ruth L. Okediji, *Conceiving an International Instrument on Limitations and Exceptions to Copyright: Final Report* (Mar. 2008), *available at* http://www.ivir.nl/publicaties/hugenholtz/finalreport2008.pdf; Ruth Okediji, *Securing Intellectual Property Objectives: New Approaches to Human Rights Considerations,* in MARGOT E. SALOMON ET AL. (EDS.), CASTING THE NET WIDER: HUMAN RIGHTS, DEVELOPMENT AND NEW DUTY-BEARERS 211 (2007); A. Strowel & F. Tulkens, *Freedom of Expression and Copyright under Civil Law: Of Balance, Adaptation, and Access,* in J. GRIFFITHS & U. SUTHERSANEN (EDS.), COPYRIGHT AND FREE SPEECH, COMPARATIVE AND INTERNATIONAL ANALYSES (2005).

flexibility mechanisms expand the regulatory space available to governments. Yet they offer at best only limited guidance for restructuring creativity and innovation policies to promote human rights, including the treaty obligations and customary rules that the vast majority of states have ratified and recognized as legally binding.

As a matter of practical politics, calls to revivify intellectual property flexibility mechanisms face a major structural challenge, one that engagement with the international human rights regime can help to overcome. In the existing intellectual property system, the producers and owners of intellectual property products are the only "rights" holders. All other actors – consumers, future creators, and the public generally – are relegated to an implicitly inferior status. Recognizing this imbalance, commentators have recently introduced proposals for "users' rights," "maximum standards" of intellectual property protection, and new international instruments that make exceptions and limitations mandatory rather than permissive.

We believe that many of these initiatives, although beneficial, are misguided in a number of respects. First, the proposals are at odds with more than a century of international intellectual property lawmaking in which treaties establish only basic ground rules (such as national treatment) and minimum standards of protection (such as subject matter eligibility rules and exclusive rights). Expanding this settled approach to embrace user rights and mandatory exceptions and limitations is a challenging and contested enterprise, as demonstrated by recent debates in WIPO on proposals for a treaty on access for the visually impaired.[3] In contrast, arguments grounded in human rights reframe the demands of consumers, future creators, and the public as internationally guaranteed entitlements that are conceptually equivalent to those of intellectual property owners and producers.

This linguistic shift is not a semantic trick; nor is it merely a rhetorical move. It also reshapes normative agendas and negotiating strategies. From a normative perspective, such a reframing directs intellectual property reform advocates to work within international human rights venues – in particular the treaty bodies and the special rapporteurs and independent experts of the Human Rights Council whose activities we examine in previous chapters – to clarify ambiguous legal norms and evaluate the human rights consequences of existing intellectual property laws and policies. It would be myopic for

---

[3]   *See, e.g.*, James Boyle, *Obama's Mixed Record on Tech Policy*, FIN. TIMES (Jan. 25, 2010); Manon Ress, *Six Myths about the Treaty for People with Disabilities That Should Be Debunked Next Week?*, Knowledge Ecology International (Mar. 5, 2010), *available at* http://keionline. org/node/795.

these reform advocates to refrain from influencing these human rights actors and, where appropriate, from forging alliances with them, especially now that these actors have devoted significant attention to national and international intellectual property protection rules.

From a negotiating perspective, reform arguments that draw upon the output of these human rights venues have a distinct strategic advantage. They invoke legal rules and norms adopted by institutions whose provenance and legitimacy are well established and that have received the imprimatur of many governments in other international fora. By drawing upon these sources, reform advocates can more credibly claim that a rebalancing of intellectual property protection rules is necessary to harmonize two parallel regimes of internationally recognized "rights." And they can more easily deflect claims that such rebalancing efforts are merely fig leaves for self-serving legislation by well-resourced user industries or disguised attempts to distort free trade rules or free ride on foreign creators and inventors.

A third approach to reconciling human rights and intellectual property employs the rules of the former regime to bolster arguments for expanding or diminishing the rules of the latter.[4] Expansionist arguments are often raised by industries that view their business models and financial viability as tied to the exclusive exploitation rights that intellectual property protection confers. Seizing upon (and often misreading) the creators' rights and property rights clauses of international instruments, these industries seek to lock in maximalist intellectual property protection by invoking the rhetoric of human rights as trumps. A fear of such expansionist claims – and the perceived difficulty of refuting them – explains why some commentators are skeptical of attempts to analyze intellectual property issues in human rights terms.

---

[4]   *See, e.g.,* Audrey R. Chapman, *Towards an Understanding of the Right to Enjoy the Benefits of Scientific Progress and Its Applications,* 8 J. Hum. Rts. 1 (2009); Christophe Geiger, *"Constitutionalising" Intellectual Property Law? The Influence of Fundamental Rights on Intellectual Property in the European Union,* 37 Int'l Rev. Intell. Prop. & Competition L. 371 (2006); Christophe Geiger, *Fundamental Rights, a Safeguard for the Coherence of Intellectual Property Law?,* 35 Int'l Rev. Intell. Prop. & Competition L. 268 (2004); Tom Giovanetti & Merrill Matthews, Institute for Policy Innovation, *Intellectual Property Rights and Human Rights,* IDEAS, Sept. 2005, *available at* http://www.ipi.org; Burkhart Goebel, *Geographical Indications and Trademarks in Europe,* 95 Trademark Rep. 1165 (2005); *see also* Kal Raustiala, *Density and Conflict in International Intellectual Property Law,* 40 U.C. Davis L. Rev. 1021, 1032 (2007) (stating that "the embrace of [intellectual property] by human rights advocates and entities … is likely to further entrench some dangerous ideas about property: in particular, that property rights as human rights ought to be inviolable and ought to receive extremely solicitous attention from the international community").

These fears are not entirely unfounded, especially in Europe. The recently adopted Charter of Fundamental Rights of the European Union (EU) subsumes intellectual property under the rubric of property, and provides in Article 17(2) that "Intellectual property shall be protected." References to fundamental rights appear in the recitals of several EU directives on intellectual property. A few national courts in Europe have relied on property guarantees in their respective constitutions when adjudicating intellectual property disputes. And, as discussed in Chapter 3, the European Court of Human Rights has extended the right of property in Protocol No. 1 to the European Convention on Human Rights to copyrights, patents, and trademarks owned by both corporations and individuals.

Viewed in isolation, these trends appear ominous. But they are counterbalanced by a large and growing number of international and domestic decisions, in Europe and elsewhere, that invoke civil and political rights (in particular freedom of expression) and economic and social rights (in particular the right to health) to limit or cabin expansive interpretations of intellectual property protection rules. Commentators and public interest NGOs have endorsed these developments, urging decision makers to reach outside intellectual property's own flexibility mechanisms and safety valves to impose external limits, or maximum standards of protection, upon intellectual property owners.

These two opposing frameworks share a common methodology. Each begins with the existing baseline of intellectual property protection and then invokes selective provisions of international human rights law to bolster arguments for moving that baseline in one direction or the other. The frameworks also share a common flaw. They encourage uncoordinated interventions at the upper and lower boundaries of intellectual property protection, interventions that, over time, would establish both a floor and a ceiling on intellectual property.

This selective use of human rights law to impose upper and lower limits on intellectual property protection standards is worrisome. These efforts have mostly ignored the creators' rights and cultural rights provisions of UDHR Article 27 and ICESCR Article 15. They have instead invoked human rights that are unconcerned with balancing the protection of creators and innovators against the public's right to benefit from the scientific and cultural advances. Lacking a coherent blueprint to undertake the sensitive and policy-laden analysis that such balancing requires, human rights interventions at the upper and lower boundaries of intellectual property law will inevitably be ad hoc. They may also create cycles of underprotection and overprotection, depending on the vagaries of which issues are raised, in which venues, and in what order.

8.3. Toward a Human Rights Framework for Intellectual Property

In this section, we offer our own framework for understanding the interface between human rights and intellectual property. As we explain in greater detail below, our framework differs from the approaches reviewed previously in several important respects. First, it is capacious, encompassing the full panoply of human rights and freedoms whose realization is affected by intellectual property protection rules. Second, our framework rejects arguments that invoke human rights to leverage across-the-board expansions or rollbacks of intellectual property protection. Third, our framework is empirically grounded. It urges governments, before revising the status quo, first to determine whether and to what extent intellectual property – as opposed to other factors – impedes or enhances the attainment of desired human rights outcomes. Fourth, our framework is dynamic. It draws inspiration from the drafting history of the creators' rights and cultural benefit clauses, but recognizes that the human rights and intellectual property regimes are continually evolving in response to changing conceptions of legal entitlements and technological progress.

As an initial matter, we distinguish between the *protective* and *restrictive* dimensions of human rights in the intellectual property context. The protective dimension requires states (1) to recognize and respect the rights of individuals and groups to enjoy a modicum of economic and moral benefit from their creative and innovative activities and (2) to refrain from bad faith and arbitrary interferences with intellectual property rights that the state itself has previously granted or recognized. In contrast, the restrictive dimension, which includes both a process component and a substantive standard, identifies the conditions under which the realization of a specific right or freedom requires (1) a diminution of intellectual property protection standards and enforcement measures, (2) a restructuring of incentives for private creativity and innovation, or (3) both.

Our framework also stresses the importance of the process, transparency, and predictability values that are hallmarks of the rule of law.[5] The founding documents of the international human rights movement did not emphasize

---

[5] There are many different conceptions of the rule of law. *See* Note, Thom Ringer, *Development, Reform, and the Rule of Law: Some Prescriptions for a Common Understanding of the "Rule of Law" and Its Place in Development Theory and Practice*, 10 YALE HUM. RTS. & DEVELOP. L.J. 178 (2007). For a recent application to international intellectual property, *see* Laurence R. Helfer, Karen J. Alter, & M. Florencia Guerzovich, *Islands of Effective International Adjudication: Constructing an Intellectual Property Rule of Law in the Andean Community*, 103 AM. J. INT'L L. 1 (2009).

the rule of law. Today, however, the connection between human rights and the rule of law is well established[6] and provides additional arguments for contesting intellectual property initiatives that conflict with rule of law values.

A salient recent example is the Anti-Counterfeiting Trade Agreement (ACTA), a proposed multilateral treaty that would establish more robust obligations to suppress unauthorized uses of intellectual property. For two years, ACTA negotiations occurred in secret and governments refused to disclose a draft text of the treaty. Only after a French civil rights NGO leaked a document revealing "contradictions between the text and public comments by negotiators"[7] did governments release an official text.[8] Such lack of transparency involving potentially far-reaching changes to intellectual property laws and enforcement mechanisms is disturbing, as is the inability of interested constituencies, in the words of the Committee on Economic, Social and Cultural Rights, to "take part in … any significant decision making processes that have an impact on their rights and legitimate interests."[9]

A. The Protective Dimension of the Framework

The protective dimension of the human rights framework for intellectual property is grounded in state obligations to respect, protect, and fulfill creators' rights and the right of property found in several international instruments, most notably UDHR Article 27, ICESCR Article 15(1)(c), and Article 1 of the European Convention's First Protocol.

Obligations with regard to creators' rights encompass modest economic exploitation and personality guarantees that, taken together, are more circumscribed than those imposed by intellectual property treaties. The limited scope of these guarantees can be deduced from the two principal objectives of recognizing the moral and material interests of creators as human rights.

---

[6] *See generally* Randall Peerenboom, *Human Rights and Rule of Law: What's the Relationship?*, 36 GEO. INT'L L.J. 809 (2005).

[7] Monika Ermert, *Leaked ACTA Text Shows Possible Contradictions with National Laws*, Intellectual Property Watch (Mar. 29, 2010), *available at* http://www.ip-watch.org/weblog/2010/03/29/leaked-acta-text-shows-possible-contradictions-with-national-laws/.

[8] The Office of the U.S. Trade Representative Releases Statement of ACTA Negotiating Partners on Recent ACTA Negotiations (Apr. 16, 2010), *available at* http://www.ustr.gov/about-us/press-office/press-releases/2010/april/office-us-trade-representative-releases-statement-ac. The U.S. Trade Representative stressed that "ACTA will not interfere with a signatory's ability to respect its citizens' fundamental rights and liberties, and will be consistent with the … TRIPS Agreement and will respect the Declaration on TRIPS and Public Health." *Id.*

[9] Comm. Econ., Soc. & Cultural Rights, *General Comment No. 17: The Right of Everyone to Benefit from the Protection of the Moral and Material Interests Resulting from Any Scientific, Literary or Artistic Production of Which He Is the Author*, art. 15(1)(c), U.N. Doc. E/C.12/GC17, para. 34 (Jan. 12, 2006).

According to the *General Comment 17* of the Committee on Economic, Social and Cultural Rights, analyzed in depth in Chapter 3, such rights "safeguard the personal link between authors and their creations and between people or other groups and their collective cultural heritage," and they protect the "basic material interests which are necessary to enable authors to enjoy an adequate standard of living."

We interpret these two statements, which recur throughout the *General Comment*, to imply the existence of a zone of personal autonomy in which individuals can achieve their creative potential, control their productive output, and lead the independent intellectual lives that are essential requisites of any free society. The legal protections required to establish this zone are, however, significantly narrower than those mandated by intellectual property treaties and statutes. As an initial matter, these protections do not apply to corporations or other business entities. But even as to individuals and groups, a state can satisfy its obligation to protect creators' rights in myriad and diverse ways. It may, for example, recognize the same exclusive rights as are found in intellectual property treaties and statutes, but radically reduce terms of protection, expand exceptions and limitations, or both. Alternatively, a state could eschew exclusive rights altogether (except for minimal attribution and integrity guarantees) and substitute a system of liability rules, levies, or government subsidies.[10] Under either approach, governments could also designate certain socially valuable uses of knowledge goods as not requiring any remuneration to creators.

The protective dimension of the human rights framework is *more* expansive than existing intellectual property protection rules in only two respects. First, it encompasses all individuals and groups; the categorical exclusion of a class of creators would be inconsistent with the framework. The absence of protection in some countries for the traditional knowledge of indigenous communities is one example, although, as we discuss at the end of Chapter 7, the potential conflicts between the recognition and assertion of rights in indigenous creativity and other human rights must also be considered.

Second, the protective dimension of the framework imposes a more stringent test for evaluating restrictions *within* the irreducible core of rights that establishes the zone of autonomy described earlier. Such restrictions must, among other requirements, be "strictly necessary for the promotion of the general welfare in a democratic society" and must employ "the least

---

[10] For a thoughtful discussion of liability rules, *see* Arti K. Rai, Jerome H. Reichman, Paul F. Uhlir, & Colin Crossman, *Pathways across the Valley of Death: Novel Intellectual Property Strategies for Accelerated Drug Discovery*, 8 YALE JOURNAL OF HEALTH LAW, POLICY & ETHICS 53, 78–80 (2008).

restrictive measures … when several types of limitations may be imposed."
This standard is substantially more constraining than the now ubiquitous
"three-step test" used to assess the TRIPS-compatibility of exceptions and
limitations in national intellectual property laws.[11] For this reason, the rights
included in the core must be concomitantly narrow.

We emphasize, however, the limited practical consequences of these
additional obligations. For traditional knowledge, for example, a state
could eschew exclusive rights altogether in favor of government assistance
programs that seek to preserve the creative works of indigenous communities consistently with their religious beliefs and cultural traditions. As for
restrictions on creators' human rights, these must be interpreted in light of
the narrowness of the zone of autonomy itself and the many permissible
approaches to establishing that zone.

The protective dimension of the human rights framework for intellectual
property may also justify more expansive legal protections for individuals and
groups vis-à-vis other actors involved in the production and distribution of
knowledge goods. For example, the framework's emphasis on human creativity rather than economic exploitation may support a more circumscribed
approach to work for hire rules that grant authorship and control of copyrighted works to corporate employers at the expense of those who work for
them. But nothing requires that any revisions of domestic intellectual property
laws adhere to any particular template. To the contrary, the protective dimension of the framework preserves wide latitude for states to regulate innovation
and creativity to achieve socially beneficial ends and to tailor regulations to
political, economic, and cultural conditions within their borders.

The property rights component of the protective dimension is similarly
modest. Government officials included the right of property in the UDHR
and in the three regional civil and political rights conventions but excluded
it from the ICCPR and the ICESCR. This omission reveals that many countries have no treaty-based obligation to protect private property as a human
right, although they may protect property on other legal grounds. And for
states that do have such an international obligation, the treaties' drafting
histories evidence a clear intent to preserve latitude for governments to
adopt economic and social policies that adversely affect property owners
while, at the same time, condemning arbitrary deprivations of property by
state actors.

---

[11] For example, Article 13 of the TRIPS Agreement provides that "members shall confine limitations or exceptions to exclusive rights to certain special cases which do not conflict with a
normal exploitation of the work and do not unreasonably prejudice the legitimate interests
of the right holder."

Among the three regional treaties that include a property rights clause, only the European system has considered whether that provision encompasses ownership of intangible knowledge goods. In Chapter 3, we analyze recent rulings of the European Court of Human Rights that answer this question in the affirmative and also emphasize the limited protection that the Court's case law provides. Here we offer more general guidance to decision makers as to how to interpret the human right of property as applied to intellectual property.

Consistent with the rule of law values that these treaty clauses embody, decision makers should find fault only with arbitrary or *ultra vires* exercises of state power and bad faith refusals to follow intellectual property protection rules that the state itself has previously recognized as valid. Such actions include, for example, a government ministry that installs copyrighted software on its desktop computers without providing statutorily mandated remuneration to the software's owner, a state-run enterprise that refuses to pay royalties to an inventor whose locally patented process it had previously licensed, and judicial or administrative rules that eschew minimum procedural guarantees such as the ability to present evidence or legal arguments.

As these examples illustrate, the restrictions imposed by treaty-based property rights clauses are minimal and unobtrusive. They allow governments unfettered discretion to fashion their domestic innovation and creativity policies as they see fit, provided only that they adhere to the previously established rules that embody those policies. This narrow focus also justifies the application of these principles to intellectual property owned by corporations and other business entities, since arbitrary and bad faith deprivations of property are not confined to natural persons.

B. The Restrictive Dimension of the Framework

The restrictive dimension of the framework comes into play where a state expands legal protections for creativity and innovation beyond those required to establish the zone of personal autonomy described in the previous subsection. There are longstanding debates over whether capacious intellectual property protection helps or hinders economic growth, especially in least-developed and developing countries. But even assuming for purposes of argument that advocates for strong intellectual property protection have the better of this debate, they must still contend with the obligations that international human rights law imposes, obligations that may provide an independent legal basis for cabining strong intellectual property protection rules *even if* they enhance economic development. We part company, however, with commentators who invoke human rights to support an across-the-board rollback of intellectual property without regard to context or to the ways in which it can be harnessed to promote the realization of human rights. We advance instead an approach that is both faithful to the diversity of individual rights and freedoms and grounded in empirical reality.

We begin from the uncontroversial premise that the ends of international human rights law – including noninterference with civil and political rights and guaranteeing minimum levels of economic and social well-being in areas such as health, food, and education – can be achieved in a wide variety of ways. Intellectual property protection can help or hinder the attainment of these ends, or it may be entirely irrelevant to their realization. The first component of the framework's restrictive dimension, therefore, is a process inquiry that seeks to determine what role, if any, intellectual property protection actually plays in this regard.

If the institutions, resources, personnel, and other inputs necessary to achieve desired human rights outcomes do not exist or are inadequate, the issue of whether intellectual property also impedes those outcomes may be entirely irrelevant. Stated differently, the barriers to realizing human rights are often overdetermined, with intellectual property functioning as only one among a multiplicity of barriers, and not necessarily the most important one. This analysis harkens back to debates in the early 2000s, discussed in Chapter 2, as to whether pharmaceutical patents hindered access to HIV/AIDS medications in sub-Saharan Africa. Even if antiretroviral drugs were given to these countries free of charge, proponents of strong patent protection claimed, the public health infrastructure needed to distribute them was inadequate and the individuals who received the medicines were incapable of following directions for their ingestion without the assistance of medical professionals.

Nearly a decade later, these arguments have proven to be mostly groundless. But the basic insight underlying these claims – that multiple factors unrelated to intellectual property often act as barriers to human rights outcomes – remains valid. It is difficult to contend, for example, that copyright in educational materials impedes the right to education if there are no school buildings and no teachers. This illustration is, admittedly, an oversimplification. As the discussion in Chapter 5 reveals, however, even in countries with more fully functional educational systems, the adverse consequences of copyright protection are often minimal in comparison to factors such as language barriers, small domestic publishing industries, and tariffs on paper imports. Another relevant variable is the extent to which educational materials are available online without charge. Empirical analyses that consider such availability should not, however, presume that such materials are uniformly available; nor should they ignore the many economic and technological barriers to online access.

For other human rights, by contrast, the concern is not with structural factors that impede access to goods protected by intellectual property but, to the contrary, with the qualities or attributes of goods that are often widely distributed. As explained in Chapter 6 on the right to food, opposition to intellectual property protection for new plant varieties is often bound up with fears about the health and environmental consequences of genetically modified crops or opposition to the marketing practices of agrobiotechnology firms. These are legitimate concerns. But the proper response to them is not – or at least not necessarily – a diminution of intellectual property protection. Rather, what is first required is a careful evaluation of the human rights implications of these claims and the role that intellectual property does or does not play in exacerbating them. If further studies reveal, for example, that certain genetically modified crops are harmful to human health or to farmers who grow traditional plant varieties, an appropriate response by health, environment, or agriculture ministries would be to regulate or prohibit the distribution and sale of such crops. Similarly, if the consolidation of the commercial seed industry enables a few firms with excessive market power to demand artificially high prices for seeds, the remedy lies in national competition laws rather than in restricting intellectual property rules that create incentives for new plant varieties with desirable characteristics. In addition, it may be useful to distinguish between problems caused by the subsistence of intellectual property rights in genetically modified plant varieties as such, and problems engendered by the decisions of public and private actors to adopt, promote, or subsidize such varieties.

The determination of whether and to what extent intellectual property, as opposed to other factors, impedes the attainment of desired human rights outcomes requires careful, objective, and context-specific empirical assessments. Over the last several years, a growing array of international bodies, NGOs, and scholars have turned their attention to the previously understudied issue of how to measure the enjoyment of human rights. The result has been an outpouring of indicators, metrics, benchmarks, impact statements, and other measurement tools that seek to identify with greater precision the levels of rights protections in individual countries and the factors that contribute to or retard their achievement. Most of these tools focus on economic and social rights, whose realization requires identifying aggregate outcomes at the societal as well as the individual level. These quantitative and qualitative indicators and benchmarks have become key elements of the iterative process by which treaty bodies, special rapporteurs, and national courts monitor the progressive realization of rights that the ICESCR protects.[12]

---

[12] *See, e.g.,* Alana Klein, *Judging as Nudging: New Governance Approaches for the Enforcement of Constitutional Social and Economic Rights,* 39 COLUM. HUM. RTS. L. REV. 351 (2008); Office of

These measurement tools do not, as far as we are aware, systematically assess the positive and negative consequences of intellectual property protection on human rights in general or on economic and social rights in particular. But they could easily be revised to include such an evaluative component. A harbinger of this approach is a 2006 report of the National Human Rights Commission of Thailand, which reviewed a draft Thailand–United States Free Trade Agreement.[13] Among other issues, the Commission analyzed the treaty's inclusion of TRIPS Plus provisions from the perspective of the right to health and farmers' rights. It recommended, *inter alia*, that the Thai government remove from the negotiations stronger intellectual property protection for pharmaceuticals.[14] As other commentators have observed, however, the report also used "emotive language and strong claims about the effects of the FTA without recourse to empirical evidence to support those claims."[15]

The political contestations surrounding the Thai Commission's report highlight the need to develop, in advance of any particular controversy, measurement tools that have been accepted by stakeholders with divergent viewpoints, or at least that reflect their input. These measurement tools should include at least the following components: (1) an evaluation of whether existing or proposed intellectual property protection rules and policies help or hinder the realization of specific human rights outcomes; (2) an assessment, to the greatest extent possible, of the relative causal contributions of intellectual property rules and policies in comparison to other factors; and (3) an identification of the legal and policy measures, whether or not consistent with the existing intellectual property regime, that will facilitate these human rights outcomes.

If the assessment of these issues reveals that non-intellectual property factors are responsible for the lack of progress in realizing human rights ends,

the High Commissioner for Human Rights, *Report on Indicators for Monitoring Compliance with Human Rights Instruments*, U.N. Doc. HRI/MC/2006/7 (2006); AnnJanette Rosga & Margaret L. Satterthwaite, *Trust in Indicators: Measuring Human Rights*, 27 BERKELEY J. INT'L L. 254 (2009); Lea Shaver, *Defining and Measuring Access to Knowledge: Towards an A2K Index*, Yale Law School Student Scholarship Papers, *available at* http://digitalcommons.law.yale.edu/fss_papers/22/ (2007); Sally Engle Merry, *Measuring the World: Indicators, Human Rights, and Global Governance* (May 2009), *available at* http://www.iilj.org/research/documents/I.Merry.MeasuringtheworldASIL.pdf.

[13] *See* National Human Rights Institutions Forum, *Human Rights Impact Assessment of the US–Thai Free Trade Agreement* (Jan. 22, 2007), *available at* http://www.nhri.net/news.asp?ID=1115.

[14] *See* James Harrison & Alessa Goller, *Trade and Human Rights: What Does "Impact Assessment" Have to Offer?*, 8 HUM. RTS. L. REV. 587, 604 (2008).

[15] *Id.* at 608 (quoting inflamatory statements in the commission's report, including that the treaty will "pave the way for [transnational corporations] to seize power" and "US demands on patents … clearly reflect greed on [the] part of US pharmaceutical corporations").

as may be the case for the example of genetically modified crops discussed earlier, state and nonstate actors should focus their lawmaking and advocacy strategies on those factors and should not treat intellectual property issues as a proxy for them. Such categorical outcomes are likely to be rare, however. A more frequent result of the assessment process will be a finding that the specific intellectual property rule or policy under scrutiny is one among many factors responsible for deleterious human rights conditions. Such a conclusion implicates policy responses that address both the share of the problem attributable to intellectual property and the type and extent of the harm that it engenders. The structure of domestic institutions, the extent of available resources and their reallocation, the sequencing of policy prescriptions, and the interrelationship among government programs will be important issues in this regard. We hope that the analysis set forth in previous chapters of this book will assist all stakeholders in addressing these issues.

In the final analysis, however, national decision makers will need to decide whether to revise existing intellectual property protection rules and how best to do so. It is here that the second, substantive stage of the framework's restrictive dimension comes into play. In deciding what measures to take, we urge decision makers to begin from the premise that the human rights and intellectual property regimes share the same core objective – to encourage creativity and innovation that benefits society as a whole. It is the different ways that each regime achieves this objective, which create the potential for conflicts between them.

In the intellectual property system, most societal benefits accrue far in the future when knowledge goods enter the public domain and may be freely used by all. Flexibility mechanisms such as exceptions to exclusive rights and compulsory licenses mitigate the costs of this delay. But they can only do so much without harming the incentives to create and innovate in the first instance. In contrast, the human rights regime has much shorter time horizons. The legal entitlements it enshrines are both immediate and urgent. The regime has little tolerance for states that lack the present ability to meet their negative obligation to refrain from repression or their positive commitment to protect and fulfill the minimum essential needs of individuals and groups.

Intellectual property-protected knowledge goods help to satisfy these immediate demands when the owners of these goods sell or license them to consumers. But the monopoly power that accompanies intellectual property rights enables owners to maximize profits by offering knowledge goods at supracompetitive prices that exclude consumers who would have purchased or licensed the goods had they been offered in a competitive market. The result is that individuals with greater financial means can afford knowledge goods whereas those with fewer economic resources cannot.

These disparities in affordability apply to intellectual property-protected goods currently being offered for sale or license. But the disparities are exacerbated when incentives to create and innovate are considered from a dynamic perspective. Intellectual property industries respond to existing market signals by fashioning research and development strategies to satisfy the anticipated demands of consumers with financial means. The pernicious consequences of these dynamic innovation incentives are illustrated most starkly in the area of patented medicines. As we analyze in Chapter 2, pharmaceutical companies devote the bulk of their research efforts to identifying new drugs for ailments common in wealthy industrialized nations while eschewing research on diseases that afflict the world's poor, who cannot afford any treatments the companies might have developed.

The intellectual property system is generally agnostic about both the static and the dynamic distributional consequences of monopoly pricing structures. But these distributional consequences are a central concern of human rights law in general and economic and social rights in particular, which prioritize the needs of the most marginalized and disadvantaged individuals and groups above the needs of those with greater financial means. Stated more pointedly, intellectual property protection may help states to satisfy their obligations to protect and fulfill economic and social rights. But its effect is greatest where it is needed least.

There are short-term and long-term responses to this troubling state of affairs. Both responses depend upon the findings of the indicators and impact statements described previously. If these measurement tools reveal that specific intellectual property protection rules are (or, in the case of proposed rules, would be) an immediate obstacle to the realization of specific human rights, governments should revise those rules or, in the case of new rules, reject proposals to adopt them. Impact statements structured according to our recommendations should also indicate which legal and policy measures would help to achieve this result. All other things equal, we think that governments should favor measures compatible with the existing intellectual property regime over measures that are inconsistent with it. But we also believe that governments should be free to choose intellectual property-inconsistent measures where the indicators and impact statements contain credible evidence that such measures are likely to achieve more extensive human rights benefits. Where the evidence is equivocal or uncertain, measures should be temporary and include sunset clauses to force a revaluation of their merits an appropriate interval after their adoption.

With regard to long-term responses, indicators and impact statements should provide a roadmap for governments to restructure innovation incentives to further human rights ends. Strategies to encourage research relating to neglected diseases have advanced further in this regard than initiatives in other areas. As described in Chapter 2 on the right to health and pharmaceutical patents, these strategies work *with* intellectual property rather than *against* it. They redirect incentives and channel market forces to achieve socially valuable ends. Thomas Pogge's research program on human rights and global health is perhaps the most advanced proposal in this regard. We urge states, public interest NGOs, and the staff of international organizations to develop similar proposals for other intersections between the human rights and intellectual property regimes and to tailor incentive structures to the diverse economic and political realities that we describe in previous chapters.

In developing these proposals, actors should also consider whether nonproprietary innovation schemes can help to achieve salutary human rights outcomes. For example, open source systems that require follow-on innovators to share their contribution to collectively produced knowledge goods should be encouraged, provided that the system's policies are fully disclosed to participants. Private contracting and delegation mechanisms, such as Creative Commons, that permit creators to disclaim intellectual property protection in whole or in part deserve similar solicitude. But as with online access to educational materials, the widespread accessibility of nonproprietary alternatives should not be assumed. Where access disparities exist, an overemphasis on nonproprietary mechanisms may have the perverse if unintended effect of disfavoring the less technologically adept or those burdened by economic barriers to online access. Inattention to access disparities thus creates a risk that nonproprietary alternatives will be least available to those who require them most.

Even assuming widespread and equitable access, nonproprietary alternatives may appear contrary to the protective dimension of the human rights framework for intellectual property, which, as described previously, protects a zone of personal autonomy for all creators. In practice, there may be no incompatibility if individuals retain the right to be acknowledged as creators and to receive remuneration for at least some uses. The more fundamental point, however, is that although creators and innovators do indeed possess a narrow class of inalienable economic and personality rights, they can choose how best to exercise those rights so as to construct a zone of personal autonomy that is both self-empowering and conducive to the broader public values that the human rights framework for intellectual property seeks to achieve.

References

SELECTED BOOKS

ABBOTT, FREDERICK M., WTO TRIPS AGREEMENT AND ITS IMPLICATIONS FOR ACCESS TO MEDICINES IN DEVELOPING COUNTRIES (Commission on Intellectual Property Rights 2002)

AMANI, BITA, STATE AGENCY AND THE PATENTING OF LIFE IN INTERNATIONAL LAW: MERCHANTS AND MISSIONARIES IN A GLOBAL SOCIETY (Ashgate 2009)

AOKI, KEITH, SEED WARS: CASES AND MATERIALS ON INTELLECTUAL PROPERTY AND PLANT GENETIC RESOURCES (Carolina Academic Press 2007)

BERNIER, LOUISE, JUSTICE IN GENETICS: INTELLECTUAL PROPERTY AND HUMAN RIGHTS FROM A COSMOPOLITAN LIBERAL PERSPECTIVE (Edward Elgar 2010)

BURRI-NENOVA, MIRA & GRABER, CHRISTOPH, INTELLECTUAL PROPERTY AND TRADITIONAL CULTURAL EXPRESSIONS IN A DIGITAL ENVIRONMENT (Edward Elgar 2008)

CHANDRA, RAJSHREE, KNOWLEDGE AS PROPERTY: ISSUES IN THE MORAL GROUNDING OF INTELLECTUAL PROPERTY RIGHTS (Oxford 2010)

COLMENTER GUZMÁN, RICARDO J., IMPLICACIONES DE DERECHOS HUMANOS EN LAS DISPOSICIONES DE OBSERVANCIA CONTENIDAS EN EL ADPIC: TEMAS DE PROPIEDAD INTELECTUAL Y DERECHOS HUMANOS [HUMAN RIGHTS IMPLICATIONS IN THE TRIPS ENFORCEMENT PROVISIONS : INTELLECTUAL PROPERTY AND HUMAN RIGHTS TOPICS] (Escritorio Jurídico Johnson Cato & Asociados 2002)

CULLET, PHILIPPE, INTELLECTUAL PROPERTY PROTECTION AND SUSTAINABLE DEVELOPMENT (Lexis-Nexis & Butterworths 2005)

DRAHOS, PETER & MAYNE, RUTH (EDS.), GLOBAL INTELLECTUAL PROPERTY RIGHTS: KNOWLEDGE, ACCESS AND DEVELOPMENT (Palgrave Macmillan 2002)

FRANCIONI, FRANCESCO, ENVIRONMENT, HUMAN RIGHTS AND INTERNATIONAL TRADE (Hart 2001)

GEORGY, HANY, BRIDGING THE GAP BETWEEN ECONOMIC, SOCIAL AND CULTURAL RIGHTS AND INTELLECTUAL PROPERTY PROTECTION: A HUMAN RIGHTS APPROACH TO THE TRIPS AGREEMENT (2003)

GIBSON, JOHANNA, COMMUNITY RESOURCES: INTELLECTUAL PROPERTY, INTERNATIONAL TRADE, AND PROTECTION OF TRADITIONAL KNOWLEDGE (Ashgate 2005)

GIBSON, JOHANNA (ED.), PATENTING LIVES: LIFE PATENTS, CULTURE AND DEVELOPMENT (Ashgate 2008)

GRIFFITHS, JONATHAN & SUTHERSANEN, UMA (EDS.), COPYRIGHT AND FREE SPEECH: COMPARATIVE AND INTERNATIONAL ANALYSES (Oxford University Press 2005)

GROSHEIDE, WILLEM (ED.), INTELLECTUAL PROPERTY AND HUMAN RIGHTS (Edward Elgar 2010)

GROSSERIES, AXEL, STROWEL, ALAIN & MARCIANO, ALAIN (EDS.), INTELLECTUAL PROPERTY AND THEORIES OF JUSTICE (Palgrave Macmillan 2008)

HAUGEN, HANS MORTON, THE RIGHT TO FOOD AND THE TRIPS AGREEMENT (Brill 2007)

HERNANDEZ-TRUYOL, BERTA ESPERANZA & POWELL, STEPHEN J., JUST TRADE: A NEW COVENANT LINKING TRADE AND HUMAN RIGHTS (New York University Press 2009)

HESTERMEYER, HOLGER P., HUMAN RIGHTS AND THE WTO: THE CASE OF PATENTS AND ACCESS TO MEDICINES (Oxford University Press 2008)

———. HUMAN RIGHTS IN THE WTO: THE CASE OF TRIPS AND ACCESS TO MEDICINES (Oxford University Press 2007)

HOLMES, WILLIAM C., INTELLECTUAL PROPERTY AND HUMAN RIGHTS: GENEVA, 1998 (World Intellectual Property 1999)

LUMUMBA OSEWE, PATRICK, NKRUMAH, YVONNE K. & SACKEY, EMMANUEL, IMPROVING ACCESS TO HIV/AIDS MEDICINES IN AFRICA: ASSESSMENT OF TRADE-RELATED ASPECTS OF INTELLECTUAL PROPERTY RIGHTS FLEXIBILITIES UTILIZATION (World Bank 2008)

MAHOP, MARCELIN TONYE, INTELLECTUAL PROPERTY, COMMUNITY RIGHTS AND HUMAN RIGHTS: THE BIOLOGICAL AND GENETIC RESOURCES OF DEVELOPING COUNTRIES (Routledge 2010)

MELENDEZ-ORTIZ, RICARDO & ROFFE, PEDRO, INTELLECTUAL PROPERTY AND SUSTAINABLE DEVELOPMENT: DEVELOPMENT AGENDAS IN A CHANGING WORLD (Edward Elgar 2010)

MERRYMAN, JOHN HENRY, CULTURAL PROPERTY, INTERNATIONAL TRADE, AND HUMAN RIGHTS (Benjamin N. Cardozo School of Law, Yeshiva University, Jacob Burns Institute for Advanced Legal Studies 2001)

NETANEL, NEIL WEINSTOCK (ED.), THE DEVELOPMENT AGENDA: GLOBAL INTELLECTUAL PROPERTY AND DEVELOPING COUNTRIES (Oxford University Press 2008)

OQUAMANAM, CHIDI, INTERNATIONAL LAW AND INDIGENOUS KNOWLEDGE: INTELLECTUAL PROPERTY, PLANT BIODIVERSITY, AND TRADITIONAL MEDICINE (University of Toronto Press 2006)

PATTANAIK, MANOJ KUMAR, HUMAN RIGHTS AND INTELLECTUAL PROPERTY (ICFAI University Press 2008)

PRESLAVA, STOEVA, NEW NORMS AND KNOWLEDGE IN WORLD POLITICS: PROTECTING PEOPLE, INTELLECTUAL PROPERTY AND THE ENVIRONMENT (Routledge 2010)

ROFFE, PEDRO, TANSEY, GEOFF & VIVAS-EUGI, DAVID, NEGOTIATING HEALTH: INTELLECTUAL PROPERTY AND ACCESS TO MEDICINES (Earthscan 2006)

Rott, Peter, Patentrecht und Sozialpolitik Unter dem TRIPS-Abkommen [Patent law and Social Policy under the TRIPS Agreement] (Nomos Verlagsgesellschaft 2002)

Sakboon, Mukdawan & Hayes, Mike, The impact of TRIPS on Thailand's HIV/ AIDS Drug Policies: Human Rights Concerns in the Context of Global Trade (Mahidol University 2007)

Salomon, Margot E., Tostensen, Arne & Vandenhole, Wouter (Eds.), Casting the Net Wider: Human Rights, Development and New Duty-Bearers (Intersentia 2007)

Shiva, Vandana, Protect or Plunder? Understanding Intellectual Property Rights (Zed Books 2002)

Sinjela, Mpazi, Human Rights and Intellectual Property Rights: Tensions and Convergences (Martinus Nijhoff 2007)

Torremans, Paul L. C., Copyright and Human Rights: Freedom of Expression – Intellectual Property – Privacy (Kluwer Law International 2004)

———. Intellectual Property and Human Rights: Enhanced Edition of Copyright and Human Rights (Kluwer Law International 2008)

SELECTED CHAPTERS IN BOOKS

Austin, Graeme W. & Zavidow, Amy, Copyright Law Reform through a Human Rights Lens, in Torremans, Paul L. C. (Ed.), Intellectual Property and Human Rights: Enhanced Edition of Copyright and Human Rights 257 (Kluwer Law International 2008)

Cullet, Philippe & Kameri-Mbote, Patricia, International Property Protection and Sustainable Development – Towards a Common African Institutional Framework and Strategy, in Veena, V. (Ed.), Intellectual Property Rights – An Overview (ICFAI University Press 2007)

Dreyfuss, Rochelle, Patents and Human Rights: Where Is the Paradox? in Grosheide, Willem (Ed.), Intellectual Property and Human Rights (Edward Elgar 2010)

Helfer, Laurence R., Collective Management of Copyright and Human Rights: An Uneasy Alliance, in Collective Management of Copyright and Related Rights 85 (Kluwer Law International 2006)

Moufang, Rainer, The Concept of Ordre Public and Morality in Patent Law, in Patent Law, Ethics and Biotechnology 65 (Bruylant 1998)

Oyewunmi, Adejoke, The Right to Development, African Countries and the Patenting of Living Organisms: A Human Rights Dilemma, in Patenting Lives: Life Patents, Culture and Development 53 (Ashgate 2009)

Ricketson, Sam, Intellectual Property and Human Rights, in Commercial Law and Human Rights 187 (Ashgate 2001)

Strowel, Alain & Tulkens, François, Equilibrer la liberté d'expression et le droit d'auteur: A propos des libertés de créer et d'user des oeuvres, in Droit d'Auteur et Liberté d'Expression 1 (Larcier 2006)

Suthersanen, Uma, Some Initial Thoughts on Copyright, Human Rights and Market Freedom, in Emerging Issues in Modern Intellectual Property: Trade, Technology, Market Freedom (Edward Elgar 2007)

SELECTED JOURNAL ARTICLES

Abbott, Frederick M., *The Doha Declaration on the TRIPS Agreement and Public Health: Lighting a Dark Corner at the WTO*, 5 Journal of International Economic Law 471 (2002)

Abbot, Frederick M. & Reichman, Jerome H., *The Doha Round's Public Health Legacy: Strategies for the Production and Diffusion of Patented Medicines under the Amended TRIPS Provisions*, 10 Journal of International Economic Law 921 (2007)

Afori, Orit Fischman, *Human Rights and Copyright: The Introduction of Natural Law Considerations into American Copyright Law*, 14 Fordham Intellectual Property, Media & Entertainment Law Journal 497 (2004)

Aginam, Obijiofor, *Between Life and Profit: Global Governance and the Trilogy of Human Rights, Public Health and Pharmaceutical Patents*, 31 North Carolina Journal of International Law and Commercial Regulation 901 (2005–2006)

Alford, Willian P., *Making the World Safe for What: Intellectual Property Rights, Human Rights and Foreign Economic Policy in the Post-European Cold War World*, 29 New York University Journal of International Law and Politics 135 (1996–1997)

Anderson, R. D. & Wager, H., *Human Rights, Development, and the WTO: The Cases of Intellectual Property and Competition Policy*, 9 Journal of International Economic Law 707 (2006)

Arewa, Olufunmilayo B., *TRIPS and Traditional Knowledge: Local Communities, Local Knowledge, and Global Intellectual Property Frameworks*, 10 Marquette Intellectual Property Law Review 155 (2006)

Attaran, Amir, *Assessing and Answering Paragraph 6 of the DOHA Declaration on the Trips Agreement and Public Health: The Case for Greater Flexibility and a Non-Justiciability Solution*, 17 Emory International Law Review 743 (2003)

Austin, Graeme W., *Importing Kazaa – Exporting Grokster*, 22 Santa Clara Computer & High Tech. L.J. 577 (2006)

Bachner, Bryan, *Facing the Music: Traditional Knowledge and Copyright*, 12 Human Rights Brief 9 (2005)

Balganesh, Shymkrishna, *Copyright and Free Expression: Analyzing the Convergence of Conflicting Normative Frameworks*, 4 Chicago-Kent Journal of Intellectual Property 45 (2004)

Barbosa, Denis Borges, Chon, Margaret & Hase, Andres Moncayo Von, *Symposium: The International Intellectual Property Regime Complex: Slouching towards Development in International Intellectual Property*, Michigan State Law Review 71 (2007)

Belotsky, Lydia, *Human Rights and Intellectual Property*, 13 Tel Aviv University Studies in Law 305 (1997)

Berkman, Alan, Comment, *The Global AIDS Crisis: Human Rights, International Pharmaceutical Markets and Intellectual Property*, 17 Connecticut Journal of International Law 149 (2002)

Bluemel, Erik B., *Substance without Process: Analyzing TRIPS Participatory Guarantees in Light of Protected Indigenous Rights*, 86 Journal of the Patent & Trademark Office Society 671 (2004)

Blum, John D., Comment, *Law as Development: Reshaping the Global Legal Structures of Public Health*, 12 Michigan State Journal of International Law 207 (2004)

Bodeker, Gerard, *Traditional Medical Knowledge, Intellectual Property Rights and Benefit Sharing*, 11 Cardozo Journal of International & Comparative Law 785 (2003–2004)

Branco, Sergio, *Brazilian Copyright Law and How It Restricts the Efficiency of the Human Right to Education*, 6 Sur – International Journal on Human Rights 115 (2007)

Brewster, Amanda L., Chapman, Audrey R. & Hansen, Stephen A., *Facilitating Humanitarian Access to Pharmaceutical and Agricultural Innovation*, 1 Innovation Strategy Today 203 (2005)

Bronshtein, Dina M., Comment, *Counterfeit Pharmaceuticals in China: Could Changes Bring Stronger Protections for Intellectual Property Rights and Human Rights*, 17 Pacific Rim Law & Policy Journal 439 (2008)

Brown, Abbe E. L., *Human Rights: In the Real World*, 1 Journal of Intellectual Property Law & Practice 603 (2006)

———. *Access to Essential Technologies: The Role of the Interface between Intellectual Property, Competition and Human Rights*, 24 International Review of Law, Computers & Technology 51 (2010)

Brown, Abbe E. L. & Waelde, Charlotte, *Intellectual Property, Competition and Human Rights: The Past, the Present and the Future*, 2 Script-Ed (4) 450 (2005)

Brown, Abbe E. L., *Access to Essential Technologies: The Role of the Interface between Intellectual Property, Competition and Human Rights*, 24 International Review of Law, Computers & Technology 51 (2010)

Brown, Jeffrey J., *Defending the Right of Publicity: A Natural Rights Perspective*, 10 Intellectual Property Law Bulletin 131 (2006)

Cann Jr., Wesley A., *On the Relationship between Intellectual Property Rights and the Need of Less-Developed Countries for Access to Pharmaceuticals: Creating a Legal Duty to Supply under a Theory of Progressive Global Constitutionalism*, 25 University of Pennsylvania Journal of International Economic Law 755 (2004)

Carpenter, Megan M., *Intellectual Property and Indigenous Peoples: Adapting Copyright Law to the Needs of a Global Community*, 7 Yale Human Rights & Development Law Journal 51 (2004)

———. *Trademarks and Human Rights: Oil and Water? Or Chocolate and Peanut Butter?* 99 The Trademark Reporter 892 (2009)

Chander, Anupam & Sunder, Madhavi, *Symposium: Intellectual Property and Social Justice: Foreword: Is Nozick Kicking Rawls's Ass? Intellectual Property and Social Justice*, 40 U.C. Davis Law Review 563 (2007)

Chapman, Audrey R., *The Human Rights Implications of Intellectual Property Protection*, 5 Journal of International Economic Law 861 (2002)

———. *Towards an Understanding of the Right to Enjoy the Benefits of Scientific Progress and Its Applications*, 8 Journal of Human Rights 1 (2009)

Chaves, Gabriela Costa, Vieira, Marcela Fogaça & Reis, Renata, *Access to Medicines and Intellectual Property in Brazil: Reflections and Strategies of Civil Society*, 8 Sur – International Journal on Human Rights 163 (2008)

Chon, Margaret, *Intellectual Property and the Development Divide*, 27 Cardozo Law Review 2821 (2006)

Cohn, Marjorie, *The World Trade Organization: Elevating Property Interests above Human Rights*, 29 Georgia Journal of International and Comparative Law 427 (2001)

Collins, Tracy, *The Pharmaceutical Companies versus AIDS Victims: A Classic Case of Bad versus Good – A Look at the Struggle between Intellectual Property Rights and Access to Treatment*, 29 Syracuse Journal of International Law and Commerce 159 (2001)

Conway, Danielle M., *Indigenizing Intellectual Property Law: Customary Law, Legal Pluralism, and the Protection of Indigenous Peoples' Rights, Identity and Resources*, 15 Texas Wesleyan Law Review 207 (2009)

Coombe, Rosemary J., *Intellectual Property, Human Rights and Sovereignty: New Dilemmas in International Law Posed by Recognition of Indigenous Knowledge and the Conservation of Biodiversity*, 6 Indiana Journal of Global Legal Studies 59 (1998)
———. *Protecting Traditional Environmental Knowledge and New Social Movements in the Americas: Intellectual Property, Human Right, or Claims to an Alternative Form of Sustainable Development*, 17 Florida Journal of International Law 115 (2005)

Cornides, Jakob, *Human Rights and Intellectual Property: Conflict or Convergence?* 7 Journal of World Intellectual Property 135 (2004)

Correa, Carlos M., Comment, *Trips and Access to Drugs: Toward a Solution for Developing Countries without Manufacturing Capacity*, 17 Emory International Law Review 389 (2003)
———. *TRIPS Agreement and Access to Drugs in Developing Countries*, 3 SUR – International Journal on Human Rights 25 (2005)

Crook, Jamie, *Balancing Intellectual Property Protection with the Human Right to Health*, 23 Berkeley Journal of International Law 524 (2005)

Cullet, Philippe, *Patents and Medicines: The Relationship between TRIPS and the Human Right to Health*, 79 International Affairs 139 (2003)
———. *Intellectual Property Rights and Food Security in the South*, 7 Journal of World Intellectual Property 261 (2004)
———. *Human Rights and Intellectual Property in the TRIPS Era*, 29 Human Rights Quarterly 403 (2007)

Daes, Erica-Irene, *Intellectual Property and Indigenous Peoples*, 95 American Society of International Law Proceedings 143 (2001)

DeForge, Sara, *Tough Pill to Swallow: The United States' Passive Efforts in Curtailing Intellectual Property Rights in Favor of Humanity*, 4 Loyola Law and Technology Annual 75 (2003–2004)

Dommen, Caroline, *Raising Human Rights Concerns in the World Trade Organization: Actors, Processes and Possible Strategies*, 24 Human Rights Quarterly 1 (2002)

Drahos, Peter, *Indigenous Knowledge and the Duties of Intellectual Property Owners*, 11 Intellectual Property Journal 179 (1997)
———. *Intellectual Property and Human Rights*, 3 Intellectual Property Quarterly 349 (1999)
———. *Indigenous Knowledge, Intellectual Property and Biopiracy: Is a Global Bio-Collecting Society the Answer?* 22 European Intellectual Property Review 245 (2000)

————. *Universal Access to Treatment for HIV/AIDS: Does Australia's Policy on Trade and Intellectual Property Help?* 2 HIV Matters: Discussions on the Global Pandemic 5 (2007)

Durojaye, Ebenezer, *Compulsory Licensing and Access to Medicines in Post Doha Era: What Hope for Africa?* 55 Netherlands International Law Review 33 (2008)

Dwyer, Lorna, *Patent Protection and Access to Medicine: The Colombian and Peruvian Trade Promotion Agreements*, 13 Law & Business Review of the Americas 825 (2007)

El-Said, Hamed, *TRIPS-Plus Implications for Access to Medicines in Developing Countries: Lessons from Jordan-United States Free Trade Agreement*, 10 Journal of World Intellectual Property 438 (2007)

Elliott, Richard, *Delivering on the Pledge: Global Access to Medicine, WTO Rules, and Reforming Canada's Law on Compulsory Licensing for Export*, 3 McGill International Journal of Sustainable Development Law & Policy 23 (2007)

Ellis, Gregory C., *Intellectual Property Rights and the Public Sector: Why Compulsory Licensing of Protected Technologies Critical for Food Security Might Just Work in China*, 16 Pacific Rim Law & Policy Journal 699 (2007)

Eres, Tatjana, Note, *The Limits of GATT Article XX: A Back Door for Human Rights*, 35 Georgetown Journal of International Law 597 (2004)

Ferreira, Lissett, Note, *Access to Affordable HIV/AIDS Drugs: The Human Rights Obligations of Multinational Pharmaceutical Corporations*, 71 Fordham Law Review 1133 (2002)

Forman, Lisa, *Trade Rules, Intellectual Property, and the Right to Health*, 21 Ethics & International Affairs 337 (2007)

Foster, Sharon E., *Prelude to Compatibility between Human Rights and Intellectual Property*, 9 Chicago Journal of International Law 171 (2008)

Fraser, Stephen, *The Conflict between the First Amendment and Copyright Law and its Impact on the Internet*, 16 Cardozo Arts & Entertainment Law Journal 52 (1998)

Friedgen, Kelley A., Comment, *Rethinking the Struggle between Health and Intellectual Property: A Proposed Framework for Dynamic, Rather Than Absolute, Patient Protection of Essential Medicines*, 16 Emory International Law Review 689 (2002)

Friedman, Michael A., den Besten, Henk & Attaran, Amir, *Out-Licensing: A Practical Approach for Improvement of Access to Medicines in Poor Countries*, 361 Lancet 341 (2003)

Gana, Ruth L., *The Myth of Development, the Progress of Rights: Human Rights to Intellectual Property and Development*, 18 Law & Policy 315 (1996)

Garcia-Castrillon, C. O., *An Approach to the WTO Ministerial Declaration on the TRIPS Agreement and Public Health*, 5 Journal of International Economic Law 212 (2002)

Gathii, James Thuo, *Rights, Patents, Markets and the Global AIDS Pandemic*, 14 Florida Journal of International Law 261 (2002)

Geiger, Christophe, *Fundamental Rights, a Safeguard for the Coherence of Intellectual Property Law?* 35 International Review of Intellectual Property & Competition Law 268 (2004)

————. *"Constitutionalising" Intellectual Property Law? The Influence of Fundamental Rights on Intellectual Property in the European Union*, 37 International Review of Intellectual Property & Competition Law 371 (2006)

Gibson, J., *Intellectual Property Systems, Traditional Knowledge and the Legal Authority of Community*, 26 European Intellectual Property Review 280 (2004)

Goldsmith, Harry, *Human Rights and Protection of Intellectual Property*, 12 Patent, Trademark and Copyright Journal of Research and Education 889 (1968–1969)

Gonzalez, Carmen G., *Institutionalizing Inequality: The WTO Agreement on Agriculture, Food Security, and Developing Countries*, 27 Columbia Journal of Environmental Law 433 (2002)

Gopalakrishnan, N. S., *Protection of Traditional Knowledge: The Need for a Sui Generis Law in India*, 5 Journal of World Intellectual Property 725 (2002)

Greenbaum, Jessica L., Comment, *Trips and Public Health: Solutions for Ensuring Global Access to Essential AIDS Medication in the Wake of Paragraph 6 Waiver*, 25 Journal of Contemporary Health Law & Policy 142 (2008)

Gupta, Amit, *Patent Rights on Pharmaceutical Products and Affordable Drugs: Can Trips Provide a Solution?* 2 Buffalo Intellectual Property Law Journal 127 (2004)

Guzik, Beata, *Botswana's Success in Balancing the Economics of HIV/AIDS with TRIPS Obligations and Human Rights*, 4 Loyola University Chicago International Law Review 255 (2007)

Hanefeld, Johanna, *Patent Rights vs Patient Rights: Intellectual Property, Pharmaceutical Companies and Access to Treatment for People Living with HIV/AIDS in Sub-Saharan Africa*, 72 Feminist Review 2002 84 (2002)

Haugen, Hans Morten, *General Comment No. 17 on "Authors' Rights,"* 10 Journal of World Intellectual Property 53 (2007)

———. *Traditional Knowledge and Human Rights*, 8 Journal of World Intellectual Property 663 (2005)

———. *Patent Rights and Human Rights: Exploring Their Relationships*, 10 Journal of World Intellectual Property 97 (2007)

———. *Human Rights and TRIPS Exclusion and Exception Provisions*, 11 Journal of World Intellectual Property 345 (2009)

Heins, Volker, *Human Rights, Intellectual Property, and Struggles for Recognition*, 9 Human Rights Review 213 (2008)

Helfer, Laurence R., *Adjudicating Copyright Claims under the TRIPs Agreement: The Case for a European Human Rights Analogy*, 39 Harvard International Law Journal 357 (1998)

———. *A European Human Rights Analogy for Adjudicating Copyright Claims Under TRIPs*, 21 European Intellectual Property Review 8 (1999)

———. *Human Rights and Intellectual Property: Conflict or Coexistence?* 5 Minnesota Journal of Law, Science & Technology 47 (2003)

———. *Toward a Human Rights Framework for Intellectual Property*, 40 U.C. Davis Law Review 971 (2007)

———. *The New Innovation Frontier? Intellectual Property and the European Court of Human Rights*, 49 Harvard International Law Journal 1 (2008)

Ho, Cynthia M., *Biopiracy and Beyond: A Consideration of Socio-Cultural Conflicts with Global Patent Policies*, 39 University of Michigan Journal of Law Reform 433 (2006)

———. Comment, *VII. Access to Essential Medicines: A New World Order for Addressing Patent Rights and Public Health*, 82 Chicago-Kent Law Review 1469 (2007)

———. *Patent Breaking or Balancing? Separating Strands of Fact from Fiction under Trips*, 34 North Carolina Journal of International Law & Commercial Regulation 371 (2009)

Hoen, Ellen, *TRIPS, Pharmaceutical Patents, and Access to Essential Medicines: A Long Way from Seattle*, 3 Chicago Journal of International Law 27 (2002)

Horton, Curtis M., *Protecting Biodiversity and Cultural Diversity under Intellectual Property Law: Toward a New International System*, 10 Journal of Environmental Law and Litigation (1995)

Howse, Robert, *The Canadian Generic Medicines Panel – a Dangerous Precedent in Dangerous Times*, 3 Journal of World Intellectual Property 493 (2000)

Ilg, Michael, *Market Competition in Aid of Humanitarian Concern: Reconsidering Pharmaceutical Drug Patents*, 9 Chicago-Kent Journal of Intellectual Property 149 (2010)

Isaac, Grant E. & Kerr, William A., *Bioprospecting or Biopiracy? Intellectual Property and Traditional Knowledge in Biotechnology Innovation*, 7 Journal of World Intellectual Property 35 (2004)

Joseph, Sarah, *Pharmaceutical Corporations and Access to Drugs: The "Fourth Wave" of Corporate Human Rights Scrutiny*, 25 Human Rights Quarterly 425 (2003)

Kapczynski, Amy, *Addressing Global Health Inequalities: An Open Licensing Approach for University Innovations*, 20 Berkeley Technology Law Journal 1031 (2005)

Kardigamar, L., *Interfaces between Intellectual Property, Traditional Knowledge, Genetic Resources and Folklore: Problems and Solutions*, 29 Journal of Malaysian and Comparative Law 97 (2002)

Khan, Yousef Ishaq, *Traditional Knowledge, Genetic Resources and Developing Countries in Asia: The Concerns*, 8 Wake Forest Intellectual Property Law Journal 81 (2007)

Khoury, Amir H., *The "Public Health" of the Conventional International Patent Regime and the Ethics of "Ethicals:" Access to Patented Medicines*, 26 Cardozo Arts & Entertainment Law Journal 25 (2008)

Krumenacher, Thomas J., *Protection for Indigenous Peoples and Their Traditional Knowledge: Would a Registry System Reduce the Misappropriation of Traditional Knowledge?* 8 Marquette Intellectual Property Law Review 143 (2004)

Kunimi, Mariko, *TRIPS Agreement, Is It Really Successful Achievement in the WTO: The Difficulty of Balancing between Public and Private Interests*, 3 Oregon Review of International Law 46 (2001)

Kurtz, Leslie A., *Copyright and the Human Condition*, 40 U.C. Davis Law Review 1233 (2007)

Kuruk, Paul, *Protecting Folklore under Modern Intellectual Property Regimes: A Reappraisal of the Tensions between Individual and Communal Rights in Africa and the United States*, 48 American University Law Review 769 (1999)

———. *Bridging the Gap between Traditional Knowledge and Intellectual Property Rights: Is Reciprocity an Answer?* 7 Journal of World Intellectual Property 429 (2004)

Lazzarini, Zita, Essay, *Making Access to Pharmaceuticals a Reality: Legal Options under TRIPS and the Case of Brazil*, 6 Yale Human Rights & Development Law Journal 103 (2003)

Lerner, Jack, *Intellectual Property and Development at WHO and WIPO*, 34 American Journal of Law & Medicine 257 (2008)

Long, Doris Estelle, *Traditional Knowledge and the Fight for the Public Domain*, 5 John Marshall Law School Review of Intellectual Property Law 317 (2006)

Lucyk, Scott, *Patents, Politics and Public Health: Access to Essential Medicines under the TRIPS Agreement*, 38 Ottawa Law Review 191 (2006–2007)

Maskus, Keith E. & Reichman, Jerome H., *The Globalization of Private Knowledge Goods and the Privatization of Global Public Goods*, 7 Journal of International Economic Law (2) 279 (2004)

Matthews, D., *TRIPs Flexibilities and Access to Medicines in Developing Countries: The Problem with Technical Assistance and Free Trade Agreements*, 27 European Intellectual Property Review 420 (2005)

May, Christopher, *World Intellectual Property Organization and the Development Agenda*, 13 Global Governance 161 (2007)

Mazzola, Simon, *Compulsory Licensing of Genome Biotech Patents*, 4 Intellectual Property Law Bulletin 1 (1999)

McClellan, Melissa, Note, *"Tools for Success": The TRIPS Agreement and the Human Right to Essential Medicines*, 12 Washington & Lee Race & Ethnic Ancestry Law Journal 153 (2005)

McGarry, Kevin, *U.S. Patent Reform and International Public Health: Issues of Law and Policy*, 3 Intercultural Human Rights Law Review 299 (2008)

Mercurio, Bryan C., *Trips, Patents, and Access to Life-Saving Drugs in the Developing World*, 8 Marquette Intellectual Property Law Review 211 (2004)

Meyer, Anja, *International Environmental Law and Human Rights: Towards the Explicit Recognition of Traditional Knowledge*, 10 Review of European Community & International Environmental Law 37 (2001)

Mitchell, Andrew D. & Voon, Tania, *Patents and Public Health in the WTO and Beyond: Tension and Conflict in International Law* 43 (2009)

Morgan, Maxwell R., *Medicines for the Developing World: Promoting Access and Innovation in the Post-TRIPS Environment*, 64 University of Toronto Faculty of Law Review 45 (2006)

Morin, Jean-Frederic, *The Strategic Use of Ethical Arguments in International Patent Lawmaking*, 3 Asian Journal of WTO and International Health Law & Policy 503 (2008)

Muriu, Daniel Wanjau, *Third World Resistance to International Economic and Structural Constraints: Assessing the Utility of the Right to Health in the Context of the TRIPS Agreement*, 11 International Community Law Review 409 (2009)

Muscoplat, Charles C., *Lessons from the Interaction of Biotechnology, Intellectual Property and World Needs*, 6 Minnesota Journal of Law, Science & Technology 187 (2004)

Mutter, K., *Traditional Knowledge Related to Genetic Resources and Its Intellectual Property Protection in Colombia*, 27 European Intellectual Property Review 327 (2005)

Mwakyembe, H. & Kanja, G. M., *Implications of the TRIPs Agreement on the Access to Cheaper Pharmaceutical Drugs by Developing Countries: Case Study of South Africa v. The Pharmaceutical Companies*, 34 Zambia Law Journal 2002 111 (2002)

Nagan, Winston P., *International Intellectual Property, Access to Health Care, and Human Rights: South Africa v. United States*, 14 Florida Journal of International Law 155 (2002)

Nimmer, Melville B., *Does Copyright Abridge the First Amendment Guarantees of Free Speech and Press?* 17 UCLA Law Review 1180 (1970)

Novogrodsky, Noah, *Duty of Treatment: Human Rights and the HIV/AIDS Pandemic*, 12 Yale Human Rights & Development Law Journal 1 (2009)

O'Connor, B., *Protecting Traditional Knowledge: An Overview of a Developing Area of Intellectual Property Law*, 6 Journal of World Intellectual Property 677 (2003)

Odunsi, S. B., *Pharmaceutical Industry, Patenting, Human Rights and Access to Treatment in Developing Countries: Another Look at Commercialization of Biomedical Research*, 16 Lesotho Law Journal 101 (2006)

Oguamanam, Chidi, *Intellectual Property Rights in Plant Genetic Resources: Farmers' Rights and Food Security of Indigenous and Local Communities*, 11 Drake Journal of Agricultural Law 273 (2006)

Ostergard, R. L., *Intellectual Property: A Universal Human Right?* 21 Human Rights Quarterly 156 (1999)

Outterson, Kevin, *Patent Buy-Outs for Global Disease Innovation for Low- and Middle-Income Countries*, 32 American Journal of Law & Medicine 159 (2006)

———. *Foreword – Will HPV Vaccines Prevent Cervical Cancers among Poor Women of Color? Global Health Policy at the Intersection of Human Rights and Intellectual Property*, 35 American Journal of Law & Medicine 247 (2009)

Palmer, Loretta M., *Balancing Intellectual Property Rights with Public Obligations in Developing Countries: Lessons from Africa*, 20 Critical Arts: A South-North Journal of Cultural & Media Studies 62 (2006)

Paterson, Robert K. & Karjala, Dennis S., *Looking Beyond Intellectual Property in Resolving Protection of the Intangible Cultural Heritage of Indigenous Peoples*, 11 Cardozo Journal of International & Comparative Law 633 (2003–2004)

Patterson, L. Ray & Birch Jr., Stanley F., *Copyright and Free Speech Rights*, 4 Journal of Intellectual Property Law 1 (1996)

Phan, Christine T., Note, *Can the Intellectual Property-Human Rights Framework Bridge the Gap between Vietnam's Legal Reality and Rhetoric?* 22 Columbia Journal of Asian Law 143 (2008)

Pinto, T., *The Influence of the European Convention on Human Rights on Intellectual Property Rights*, 24 European Intellectual Property Review 209 (2002)

Ram, Prabhu, *India's New "TRIPS-compliant" Patent Regime: Between Drug Patents and the Right to Health*, 5 Chicago-Kent Journal of Intellectual Property 195 (2006)

Ranjan, P., *Understanding the Conflicts between the TRIPs Agreement and the Human Right to Health*, 9 Journal of World Investment & Trade 551 (2008)

Raustiala, Kal, *Density and Conflict in International Intellectual Property Law*, 20 U.C. Davis Law Review 1021 (2007)

Reinhardt, Eric, *Intellectual Property Protection and Public Health in the Developing World*, 17 Emory International Law Review 475 (2003)

Roberts, Ian Po & Alain Li Wan Chalmers, Iain, *Intellectual Property, Drug Licensing, Freedom of Information & Human Rights*, 352 Lancet (9129) 726 (1998)

Rogers, Douglas L., *Increasing Access to Knowledge through Fair Use – Analyzing the Google Litigation to Unleash Developing Countries*, 10 Tulane Journal of Technology & Intellectual Property 1 (2007)

Ross, Lester & Zhang, Libin, *Agricultural Development and Intellectual Property Protection for Plant Varieties: China Joins the UPOV*, 17 UCLA Pacific Basin Law Journal 226 (1999–2000)

Rozek, R. P., *The Effects of Compulsory Licensing on Innovation and Access to Health Care*, 3 Journal of World Intellectual Property 889 (2000)

Rozek, R. P. & Tully, N., *The TRIPs Agreement and Access to Health Care*, 2 Journal of World Intellectual Property 813 (2000)

Ryan, C., *Human Rights and Intellectual Property*, 23 European Intellectual Property Review 521 (2001)

Sacco, Solomon Frank, *A Comparative Study of the Implementation in Zimbabwe and South Africa of the International Rules That Allow Compulsory Licensing and Parallel Importation for HIV/AIDS Drugs*, 5 African Human Rights Law Journal 105 (2005)

Sagar, R., *Intellectual Property, Benefit-Sharing and Traditional Knowledge*, 8 Journal of World Intellectual Property 383 (2005)

Santamuro, J., *Reducing the Rhetoric: Reconsidering the Relationship of the TRIPs Agreement, CBD and Proposed New Patent Disclosure Requirements Relating to Genetic Resources and Traditional Knowledge*, 29 European Intellectual Property Review 91 (2007)

Sell, Susan K., *Trips and the Access to Medicines Campaign*, 20 Wisconsin International Law Journal 481 (2001–2002)

————. *Post-Trips Developments: The Tension between Commercial and Social Agendas in the Context of Intellectual Property*, 14 Florida Journal of International Law 193 (2002)

————. *What Role for Humanitarian Intellectual Property: The Globalization of Intellectual Property Rights*, 6 Minnesota Journal of Law, Science & Technology 191 (2004–2005)

Seuba, Xavier, *A Human Rights Approach to the WHO Model List of Essential Medicines*, 84 Bulletin of the World Health Organization (5) 405 (2006)

Shadlen, Kenneth C., *Intellectual Property, Trade and Development: Can Foes Be Friends*, 13 Global Governance 171 (2007)

Shiva, Vandana. *Trips, Human Rights and the Public Domain*, 7 Journal of World Intellectual Property 665 (2004)

Shockley, Rachel Simpson, *The Digital Millennium Copyright Act and the First Amendment: Can They Co-exist?* 8 Journal of Intellectual Property Law 275 (2001)

Sinjela, Mpazi & Ramcharan, Robin, *Protecting Traditional Knowledge and Traditional Medicines of Indigenous Peoples through Intellectual Property Rights: Issues, Challenges and Strategies*, 12 International Journal on Minority & Group Rights 1 (2005)

Skees, Stephanie, *Thai-ing Up the TRIPS Agreement: Are Compulsory Licenses the Answer to Thailand's AIDS Epidemic*, 19 Pace International Law Review 233 (2007)

Stein, Haley, *Intellectual Property and Genetically Modified Seeds: The United States, Trade, and the Developing World*, 3 Northwestern Journal of Technology & Intellectual Property 160 (2005)

Straub, Peter, *Farmers in the IP Wrench – How Patents on Gene-Modified Crops Violate the Right to Food in Developing Countries*, 29 Hastings International & Comparative Law Review 187 (2006)

Strauss, Joseph, *The Impact of the New World Order on Economic Development: The Role of Intellectual Property Rights System*, 6 John Marshall Law School Review of Intellectual Property Law 171 (2008)

Sutherland, Johanna, *TRIPS, Cultural Politics and Law Reform*, 16 Prometheus 291 (1998)

Tonye, M. M., *Sui Generis Systems for the Legal Protection of Traditional Knowledge and Biogenetic Resources in Cameroon and South Africa*, 6 Journal of World Intellectual Property 763 (2003)

Torremans, Paul L. C., *Is Copyright a Human Right?* Michigan State Law Review 271 (2007)

Torsen, Mollly, *Intellectual Property and Traditional Cultural Expressions: A Synopsis of Current Issues*, 3 Intercultural Human Rights Law Review 199 (2008)

Travis, Hannibal, *Cultural and Intellectual Property Interests of the Indigenous Peoples of Turkey and Iraq*, 15 Texas Wesleyan Law Review 415 (2009)

Tustin, John, *Traditional Knowledge and Intellectual Property in Brazilian Biodiversity Law*, 14 Texas Intellectual Property Law Journal 131 (2006)

Twinomugisha, Ben K., *Implications of the TRIPs Agreement for the Protection of the Right of Access to Medicines in Uganda*, 2 Malawi Law Journal 253 (2008)

Vadi, Valentina, *Balancing the Human Rights to Health and Intellectual Property Rights after DOHA*, 14 Italian Yearbook of International Law 195 (2004)

———. *Sapere Aude! Access to Knowledge as a Human Right and Key Instrument of Development*, 2008 International Journal of Communications Law & Policy 345 (2008)

Valach Jr., Anthony P., *TRIPS: Protecting the Rights of Patent Holders and Addressing Public Health Issues in Developing Countries*, 4 Chicago-Kent Journal of Intellectual Property 156 (2005)

Van Dyck, Pooja, *Importing Western Style, Exporting Tragedy: Changes in Indian Patent Law and Their Impact on AIDS Treatment in Africa*, 6 Northwestern Journal of Technology & Intellectual Property 138 (2007)

Vawda, Yosuf A., *From Doha to Cancun: The Quest to Increase Access to Medicines under WTO Rules*, 19 South African Journal on Human Rights 679 (2003)

Wager, Hannu, *Biodiversity, Traditional Knowledge and Folklore: Work Related IP Matters in the WTO*, 3 Intercultural Human Rights Law Review 215 (2008)

Walker, Simon, *The Implications of TRIPS: Ethics, Health and Human Rights*, 2 Journal of Human Development 109 (2001)

Wanis, Hega, *Agreement on Trade-Related Aspects of Intellectual Property Rights and Access to Medication: Does Egypt Have Sufficient Safeguards against Potential Public Health Implications of the Agreement*, 13 Journal of World Intellectual Property 24 (2010)

Weissbrodt, David & Schoff, Kell, *A Human Rights Approach to Intellectual Property Protection: The Genesis and Application of Sub-Commission Resolution 2000/7*, 5 Minnesota Intellectual Property Review 1 (2003)

Willow, Dawn, *The Regulation of Biologic Medicine: Innovators' Rights and Access to Healthcare*, 6 Chicago-Kent Journal of Intellectual Property 32 (2006)

Wojahn, Patrick L., Comment, A *Conflict of Rights: Intellectual Property under Trips, the Right to Health, and Aids Drugs*, 6 UCLA Journal of International Law & Foreign Affairs 463 (2001–2002)

Wong, Mary W. S., *Toward an Alternative Normative Framework for Copyright: From Private Property to Human Rights*, 26 Cardozo Arts & Entertainment Law Journal 775 (2009)

Wu, C. F., *Raising the Right to Health Concerns Within the Framework of International Intellectual Property Law*, 5 Asian Journal of WTO & International Health Law & Policy 141 (2010)

Yamin, Alicia Ely, *Defining Questions: Situating Issues of Power in the Formulation of a Right to Health under International Law*, 18 Human Rights Quarterly 398 (1996)

——. *Not Just a Tragedy: Access to Medications as a Right under International Law*, 21 Boston University International Law Journal 325 (2003)

Yu, Peter K., *TRIPS and Its Discontents*, 10 Marquette Intellectual Property Law Review 369 (2006)

——. *Reconceptualizing Intellectual Property Interests in a Human Rights Framework*, 40 U.C. Davis Law Review 1039 (2007)

——. *Ten Common Questions about Intellectual Property and Human Rights*, 23 Georgia State University Law Review 709 (2007)

——. *Cultural Relics, Intellectual Property, and Intangible Heritage*, 81 Temple Law Review 433 (2008)

SELECTED UN REPORTS

U.N. Committee on Economic, Social and Cultural Rights, Green, Maria, Int'l Anti-Poverty L. Ctr., *Drafting History of the Article 15(1)(c) of the International Covenant* (2000), http://www.unhchr.ch/tbs/doc.nsf/0/872a8f7775c9823cc1256999005c3088?Opendocument

U.N. High Commissioner, *Report of the High Commissioner on the Impact of the Agreement on Trade-Related Aspects of Intellectual Property Rights on Human Rights* (2001)

——. *Report of the High Commissioner on Liberalization of Trade in Services and Human Rights, Executive Summary*, UN Doc E/CN.4/Sub.2/2002/9 (2002)

U.N. Secretary General, *Report of the Secretary-General on Economic, Social and Cultural Rights, Intellectual Property Rights and Human Rights* (2001)

U.N. Sub-Commission on the Promotion and Protection of Human Rights Resolution 2000/7 and 2001/21 & High Commissioner for Human Rights, *The Impact of the Agreement on Trade-Related Aspects of Intellectual Property Rights on Human Rights* (2001)

WHA, Report of the Commission on Intellectual Property Rights, Innovation and Public Health, *Public Health, Innovation and Intellectual Property Rights* (2003)

SELECTED ONLINE PUBLICATIONS

Brown, Abbe E. L., *Power, responsibility and norms: could and should human rights be used as a curb on intellectual property rights* 38 (2004) available at http://www.law.ed.ac.uk/ahrc/files/29_brownipandhumanrights.pdf

Commission on Intellectual Property Rights, Final Report, *Integrating intellectual rights and development policy* (2002) available at http://www.iprcommission.org/graphic/documents/final_report.htm

Drahos, Peter, *Access to knowledge: time for a treaty?* Bridges (ICTSD) (4) 15 (2005) available at http://www.anu.edu.au/fellows/pdrahos/articles/pdfs/2005a2ktimeforatreaty.pdf

UK Commission on Intellectual Property Rights, *Integrating intellectual property rights and development policy* (2003), available at http://www.iprcommission.org/papers/pdfs/final_report/Ch2final.pdf

SELECTED NGO REPORTS

3D 6 Trade – Human Rights – Equitable Economy, *Denmark and Italy., Trade-related intellectual property rights, access to medicines and human rights* (2004), available at http://www.3dthree.org/pdf_3D/3DCESCRDenmarkItalyBriefOct04en.pdf

3D 6 Trade – Human Rights – Equitable Economy, *The impact of international trade agreements regulating intellectual property rights on access to medicines and the fulfilment of children's rights – El Salvador* (2004), available at http://www.3dthree.org/pdf_3D/3DCRCElSalvadorBrief04en.pdf

3D 6 Trade – Human Rights – Equitable Economy, *Trade-related intellectual property rights, access to HIV/AIDS medicines and the fulfilment of civil and political rights – Uganda* (2004), available at http://www.3dthree.org/pdf_3D/3DHRCUgandaBrief04en.pdf

3D 6 Trade – Human Rights – Equitable Economy, *Trade-related intellectual property rights, access to medicines and the right to health – Ecuador* (2004), available at http://www.3dthree.org/pdf_3D/3DCESCREcuadorBrief04en.pdf

3D 6 Trade – Human Rights – Equitable Economy, *Trade-related intellectual property rights, trade in services and the fulfilment of children's rights – Botswana* (2004), available at http://www.3dthree.org/pdf_3D/3DCRCBotswanaSept04en.pdf

Berne Declaration, Reinhard, Julien, *Deprive Doha of all substance: how through bilateral agreements EFTA States impose to developing countries intellectual property rules on medicines that are beyond the WTO obligations and that restrict access to medicines* (2004) (www.evb.ch/cm_data/depriveDoha.pdf)

Canadian HIV/AIDS Network, Elliot, Richard, *TRIPS and rights: international human rights law, access to medicines and the interpretation of the WTO agreement on trade-related aspects of intellectual property* (2001)

Giovanetti, Tom & Matthews, Merrill, *Intellectual Property Rights and Human Rights*, IPI Ideas, No. 34 (2005), available at http://www.ipi.org/IPI%5CIPIPublications.nsf/PublicationLookupFullText/FF5BC1CE33A784E2862570880053B054

Joint Agency Paper: Oxfam International and Health Action International, Malpani, Rhit Bloemen, Sophie, *Trading away access to medicines: how the European Union's trade agenda has taken a wrong turn* (2009), available at http://www.oxfam.org.uk/resources/policy/health/downloads/bp_trading_away_access_to_medicines_061109.pdf

Oxfam International Briefing Paper, *Patents versus patients: five years after the Doha Declaration* (2008), available at http://www.oxfam.org.uk/resources/policy/health/downloads/bp95_patents.pdf

Acknowledgments

We are grateful for the permissions we received to reproduce extracts from the following sources. In reproducing these materials, we have omitted unnecessary footnotes and citations; footnote numbers have been changed for those footnotes that are retained.

Alliance for a Green Revolution in Africa (AGRA), *AGRA: Early Accomplishments, Foundations for Growth* (June 2009), reprinted by permission.

Julian M. Alston, *Spillovers*, 48 AUSTR. J. AG. & RESOURCE ECON. 315, 333–34 (2002), reprinted by permission.

S. James Anaya, *Report of the Special Rapporteur on the situation of human rights and fundamental freedoms of indigenous peoples*, Human Rights Council, ninth session, agenda item 3, A/HRC/9/9 (2008), reprinted by permission.

Robert Bird and Daniel R. Cahoy, *The Impact of Compulsory Licensing on Foreign Direct Investment: A Collective Bargaining Approach*, 45 AM. BUS. L.J. 283, 309–12, 315–16 (2008), reprinted by permission.

Thomas Buergenthal, *International Human Rights Law and Instructions: Accomplishments and Prospects*, 63 WASH. L. REV. 1, 2–3, 5–6 (1988), reprinted by permission.

Audrey R. Chapman, *Approaching Intellectual Property as a Human Right (obligations related to Article 15(1)(c))*, 35 COPYRIGHT BULLETIN 4, 10–13, 14–17, 28–29, 30 (2001), reprinted by permission.

Marney Cheek, *The Limits of Informal Regulatory Cooperation in International Affairs: A Review of the Global Intellectual Property Regime*, 33 GEO. WASH. INT'L L. REV. 284–86, 289–99 (2001), reprinted by permission.

Margaret Chon, *Intellectual Property "from Below": Copyright and Capability for Education*, 40 U.C. DAVIS L. REV. 803, 828–33, 834–46 (2007), reprinted by permission.

Bhagirath Choudhary & Kadambini Gaur, *The Development and Regulation of Bt Brinjal in India (Eggplant/Aubergine)*, at x–xii (Int'l Serv. for the Acquisition of Agri-biotech Applications, Brief No. 38, 2009), reprinted by permission.

Commission on Intellectual Property Rights, *Final Report of the Commission on Intellectual Property: Integrating Intellectual Property Rights and Development Policy*, 11–12, 14–15, 17–18 (2002), reprinted by permission.

Lisa Forman, *"Rights" and Wrongs: What Utility for the Right to Health in Reforming Trade Rules on Medicines?*, 10 HEALTH & HUM. RTS. 37, 39, 43–45 (2008), reprinted by permission.

Hans Morten Haugen, THE RIGHT TO FOOD AND THE TRIPS AGREEMENT: WITH A PARTICULAR EMPHASIS ON DEVELOPING COUNTRIES' MEASURES FOR FOOD PRODUCTION AND DISTRIBUTION (2007), reprinted by permission of Koninklijke BRILL NV and the author.

Cynthia M. Ho, *Patent Breaking or Balancing?: Separating Strands of Fact from Fiction under TRIPS*, 34 N.C. J. INT'L L. & COM. REG. 371, 412–19 (2009), reprinted by permission.

Ariel Katz, *Substitution and Schumpeterian Effects over the Life Cycle of Copyrighted Works*, 49 JURIMETRICS J. 113, 116 (2009), reprinted by permission.

Virginia Leary, *The Right to Health in International Human Rights Law*, 1 HEALTH & HUM. RTS. 25, 28, 35–40 (1994), reprinted by permission.

Aryeh Neier, *Social and Economic Rights: A Critique*, 13/2 HUM. RTS. BRIEF 1, 1–3 (2006), reprinted by permission.

Ruth Okediji, *Securing Intellectual Property Objectives: New Approaches to Human Rights Considerations*, in CASTING THE NET WIDER: HUMAN RIGHTS, DEVELOPMENT AND NEW DUTY-BEARERS, 211–12, 213–14, 227–29, 234 (Margot E. Salomon et al. eds., 2007), reprinted by permission.

Thomas W. Pogge, *Human Rights and Global Health: A Research Program*, 36 METAPHILOSOPHY 182, 184–94, 197 (2005), reprinted by permission of Wiley-Blackwell Publishers.

Srividhya Ragavan & Jamie Mayer O'Shields, *Has India Addressed Its Farmers' Woes? A Story of Plant Protection Issues*, 20 GEO. INT'L ENVTL. L. REV. 97, 113–21, 124–26 (2007), reprinted by permission.

Megan Richardson, *Trade Marks and Language*, 26 SYDNEY L. R. 193, 195–96, 211–13 (2004), reprinted by permission.

Amartya Sen, *The Right Not to Be Hungry*, in THE RIGHT TO FOOD 69, 69–71 (Philip Alston & Katarina Tomaševski eds., 1984), reprinted by permission.

George Tsai, Note, *Canada's Access to Medicines Regime: Lessons for Compulsory Licensing Schemes under the WTO Doha Declaration*, 49 Va. J. Int'l L. 1063, 1075–79 (2009), reprinted by permission.

UNAIDS, *2008 Report on the Global AIDS Epidemic*, 13, 15–16, 131–32, 134–38 (2008), reprinted by permission.

United Nations Educational, Scientific and Cultural Organization (UNESCO), *Textbook and Learning Materials*, 1990–99 (2000), reprinted by permission of UNESCO.

World Health Organization (WHO), *Public Health, Innovation and Intellectual Property Rights: Report of the Commission on Intellectual Property Rights, Innovation and Public Health*, 42–44, 86–90 (2006), reprinted by permission.

World Intellectual Property Organization, *Intellectual Property and Traditional Knowledge: Booklet No. 2*, 7–30 (2007), reprinted by permission.

Peter K. Yu, *Reconceptualizing Intellectual Property Interests in a Human Rights Framework*, 40 U.C. Davis L. Rev. 1039, 1077–78, 1096, 1108–09, 1113, 1114 (2007), reprinted by permission.

Vera Zolotaryova, Note, *Are We There Yet? Taking "TRIPS" to Brazil and Expanding Access to HIV/AIDS Medication*, 33 Brook. J. Int'l L. 1099, 1110–12 (2008), © 2008, Brooklyn Journal of International Law. This article was originally published in the Brooklyn Journal of International Law, Volume 33, Issue 3. Reprinted with permission.

Index

Cases Discussed (Selected)

CPSIA information can be obtained at www.ICGtesting.com
Printed in the USA
BVOW030129200312

285480BV00005B/5/P